Standards for Teachers and Students

National Educational Technology Standards for Students

The technology foundation standards for students are divided into six broad categories. Standards within each category are to be introduced, reinforced, and mastered by students. These categories provide a framework for linking performance indicators within the Profiles for Technology Literate Students to the standards. Teachers can use these standards and profiles as guidelines for planning technology-based activities in which students achieve success in learning, communication, and life skills.

Technology Foundation Standards for Students

1. **Basic operations and concepts**
   - Students demonstrate a sound understanding of the nature and operation of technology systems.
   - Students are proficient in the use of technology.

2. **Social, ethical, and human issues**
   - Students understand the ethical, cultural, and societal issues related to technology.
   - Students practice responsible use of technology systems, information, and software.
   - Students develop positive attitudes toward technology uses that support lifelong learning, collaboration, personal pursuits, and productivity.

3. **Technology productivity tools**
   - Students use technology tools to enhance learning, increase productivity, and promote creativity.
   - Students use productivity tools to collaborate in constructing technology-enhanced models, prepare publications, and produce other creative works.

4. **Technology communications tools**
   - Students use telecommunications to collaborate, publish, and interact with peers, experts, and other audiences.
   - Students use a variety of media and formats to communicate information and ideas effectively to multiple audiences.

5. **Technology research tools**
   - Students use technology to locate, evaluate, and collect information from a variety of sources.
   - Students use technology tools to process data and report results.
   - Students evaluate and select new information resources and technological innovations based on the appropriateness for specific tasks.

6. **Technology problem-solving and decision-making tools**
   - Students use technology resources for solving problems and making informed decisions.
   - Students employ technology in the development of strategies for solving problems in the real world.

Second Edition

Teaching and Learning with Technology

Judy Lever-Duffy
Miami Dade College

Jean B. McDonald
Lambuth University

Al P. Mizell
Nova Southeastern University

Boston   New York   San Francisco
Mexico City   Montreal   Toronto   London   Madrid   Munich   Paris
Hong Kong   Singapore   Tokyo   Cape Town   Sydney

Senior Editor: Arnis E. Burvikovs
Editorial Assistant: Megan Smallidge
Development Editor: Shannon Morrow
Marketing Manager: Tara Whorf
Editorial Production Administrator: Anna Socrates
Editorial Production Service: Susan McNally
Composition Buyer: Linda Cox
Manufacturing Buyer: Andrew Turso
Cover Administrator: Linda Knowles
Designer and Electronic Composition: Glenna Collett
Photo Researcher: Abigail Reip
Illustrations: Deborah Schneck

For related titles and support materials, visit our online catalog at
www.ablongman.com.

Many of the designations used by manufacturers and sellers to distinguish their products
are claimed as trademarks. Where those designations appear in this book, and Allyn and
Bacon was aware of a trademark claim, the designations have been printed in caps or initial caps. Designations within quotation marks represent hypothetical products.

Between the time Website information is gathered and then published, it is not unusual for
some sites to have closed. Also, the transcription of URLs can result in unintended typographical errors. The publisher would apprieciate notification where these errors occur so
that they may be corrected in subsequent editions.

To obtain permission(s) to use material from this work, please submit a written request to
Allyn and Bacon, Permissions Department, 75 Arlington Street, Boston, MA 02116 or fax
your request to 617-848-7320.

Library of Congress Cataloging-in-Publicaiton Data

Lever-Duffy, Judy.
    Teaching and learning with technology / Judy Lever-Duffy, Jean B.
  McDonald, Al P. Mizell.—2nd ed.
      p. cm.
    Includes bibliographical references and index.
    ISBN 0-205-43048-1
    1. Educational technology.   2. Computer-assisted instruction.
  3. Computer network resources.   4. Audio-visual materials.
  I. McDonald, Jean B.   II. Mizell, Al P.   III. Title.

  LB1028.3.L49 2004
  371.33′4—dc22   2004044429

Printed in the United States of America
10 9 8 7 6 5 4 3 2   WEB 09 08 07 06 05

Brief Contents

ontents

CHAPTER 2 Designing and Planning Technology-Enhanced Instruction 32

INTERCHAPTER 1
Special Topic: The Evolution of Educational Technology   68

PART II   Applying Technologies for Effective Instruction   71

CHAPTER **4**   **Digital Technologies in the Classroom   102**

INTERCHAPTER 2

CHAPTER 5   Administrative Software   132

CHAPTER **7** Networks and the Internet **212**

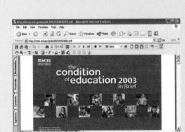

INTERCHAPTER 3
Special Topic: Designing a Classroom Web Site   **274**

CHAPTER **9**   Audio and Visual Technologies   278

CHAPTER **10**   Video Technologies   310

INTERCHAPTER 4
Special Topic: Teachers and Copyrights   338

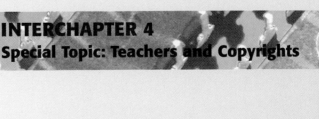

PART III **Technology in Schools: Changing Teaching and Learning   341**

CHAPTER 11   Distance Education: Using Technologies to Redefine the Classroom   342

CD and Web Resources

Chapter **3** Personal Computers in the Learning Environment

Chapter **4** Digital Technologies in the Classroom

Chapter **5** Administrative Software

Chapter 6 Academic Software

Chapter 7   Networks and the Internet

Chapter 8   Using the Web for Teaching and Learning

On CD! Software Skills Builders

Chapter **9**   Audio and Visual Technologies

ON THE WEB!

Chapter **10**   Video Technologies

ON THE WEB!

Chapter 11   Distance Education: Using Technologies to Redefine the Classroom

Chapter 12   Issues in Implementing Technology in Schools

oreword

The role of computers as instructional technology has been a topic of interest for much of the past fifty years and has been of special interest since the invention of low-cost personal computers in the late 1970s. Much of the dialog has centered around the effectiveness of these tools in the framework of an existing educational system. When viewed in this context, computers take their place alongside books and blackboards as aids for the teacher. The idea that the very structure of education needs to be reexamined in light of these tools was not a dominant theme in the field of instructional technology until recently, and even now there are many who believe that the utility (or lack thereof) of computers in the classroom must be measured against the educational paradigm inherited from a Taylorist model of schooling befitting the Industrial Era.

Against this backdrop we encounter our students—members of generation.com, who scarcely knew a world without the Internet, let alone a world without powerful computers. These students have at their fingertips power that we of another generation can hardly imagine. Rather than being dazzled by high technology, today's youth increasingly expect its tools to be available wherever they are and whenever they want them. And yet schools remain challenged to provide the access and support youngsters expect. Today's youngster is likely to find wireless Internet access at the local McDonald's, but not in her classroom.

Today's students perceive information differently from many adults as well. For them, video and images are primary, while text (still important) comes in second. Multiple, simultaneous information sources (think CNN's multiple windows for video and text) are the norm. And, most importantly, young people expect to be engaged participants, not just recipients of passive presentations.

To think intelligently about computers in education today requires that we broaden our view of learning to include self-directed activities in which students explore primary source materials on their own—tasks that are increasingly performed on networked computers found in a preponderance of America's homes. Coupled to this extension of the spaces for learning is the challenge of recognizing that computer-based instructional media (such as the web) are fundamentally different from print-based or television-based media. This insight (which can be deduced from any proper understanding of media theory) is essential, especially when educators set out to design instructional activities that make effective use of a variety of media types.

The mechanics of the machine are not nearly as important as the effect it produces in us as we use its tools to learn, to create, and to communicate our learning with others. If educators (in general) are not taking full advantage of technology in the classroom, it is not because it lacks the power to transform the practice of schooling, but because we lack the deep understanding of this expressive medium that is needed to apply its power most directly in support of our young people.

The children themselves have an intrinsic grasp of the power of technological tools to navigate informational pathways in nonlinear ways. To paraphrase Douglas Rushkoff (*Playing the Future*), many teachers prefer the linear ski slopes of a well-defined scope and sequence, while students in their classrooms skateboard with abandon across the bumpy edges of informational chaos. As Marshall McLuhan long ago observed, media are extensions of humankind. In the beginning of instructional media, books functioned as a grand extrasomatic memory of our culture. By freezing the works of masters in written form, their ideas could achieve a level of immortality impossible to imagine before. There is little question that modern instructional media have at least as much power to transform education as did the printed word. That we still don't know the scope of this power only confirms its vastness.

Technology doesn't necessarily make us think better; but it most assuredly makes us think differently. It allows us to move beyond the nouns of education (the "who, what, when, where?" of traditional history classes, for example) to focus on the verbs (the "why?"). Picasso once said computers are useless—they provide answers, never questions. In fact, he was looking through the wrong end of the telescope. Computer-based instructional technology can be of tremendous utility in support of inquiry-based learning—not because the computers ask the questions, but because they function as vehicles for the intrepid knowledge navigators who ride the waves of the web in search of answers to their own compelling questions. I believe instructional technology, properly used, can help us retain our childlike sense of wonder—a skill that will serve us masterfully in the coming years.

David Thornburg, Ph.D.,
Director, Global Operations,
The Thornburg Center

The question that emerges is deep: How do educators transform and develop their craft in light of modern technologies? This issue hasn't been raised for a long time, not since the sixteenth and seventeenth centuries, when it became apparent that the mass-produced book wasn't a fad destined for the scrap heap of history. Initially, the book was fought by educators for a variety of reasons, yet books and the ideas they conveyed spread to the masses through the force of growing literacy until, finally, educators could no longer ignore them.

With history as our guide, we can be hopeful. Education survived the widespread growth of books and extended both its reach and depth as a result. The same will be true of our modern tools. They will extend and enhance education in ways we still can hardly imagine.

And so we come to this text—a book ostensibly about instructional technology but more deeply about the nature of the educational enterprise and the role technology can play in support of learning for all. The mechanics of educational technologies pale in comparison with the effect of these tools. This book helps you understand that and provides you with more questions than it answers. If it does nothing else, it will be great reading!

David Thornburg, Ph.D.
Director, Global Operations
The Thornburg Center
http://www.tcpd.org

References

Marshall McLuhan, *Understanding Media: The Extensions of Man.* Cambridge, MA: M.I.T. Reprint Edition, 1998.

Douglas Rushkoff, *Playing the Future: What We Can Learn from Digital Kids.* New York: Riverhead Books, 1999.

Frederick W. Taylor, *The Principles of Scientific Management.* New York: Dover Reprint Edition, 1998.

Preface

Introduction

Educational technology can enrich and enhance instructional experiences for both the teacher and the learner. *Teaching and Learning with Technology* explains, on many levels, how educational technology can provide resources for teachers and students and open the door to more comprehensive learning as well as extend the learning process.

The power of the Internet can put the world body of knowledge quite literally at one's fingertips. A computer in a classroom can be an endlessly patient and positive tutor. An audio recording of a children's story can encourage the development of good listening skills and meet the needs of auditory learners, and a nature video can bring the most remote corner of the world into the classroom. These technologies, from traditional audiovisual technologies to the newest digital technologies, provide powerful tools for creative teachers and support diverse learners.

However, educational technology remains underutilized in many classrooms. Too often teachers have not learned how to work effectively with educational technologies in teaching and learning. Current and future teachers need exposure to and experience with the many and growing number of technologies that exist in schools and that schools are likely to acquire. Teachers also need a basic understanding of the technologies themselves; they need hands-on practice with them; and they need to explore how the technologies fit into the teaching and learning process.

In response to these needs, courses in educational technology are becoming a critical part of teacher preparation programs across the country. Some are computer courses adapted for educators. Others are courses in traditional media. Still others are focused on the historical and theoretical aspects of educational technology. Each approach has merit, but perhaps the most effective and pragmatic solution is a balance that includes components from all of them. To find the points at which these many approaches intersect has been challenging. This text is a result of that challenge.

Organization of This Text

Teaching and Learning with Technology was designed to combine theoretical, technical, and experiential components into a single pragmatic approach suitable for current and future teachers using educational technology in the classroom.

In creating the text, we followed three basic principles:

1. Grounding the study of educational technologies in effective teaching and learning and in the real-world classroom;
2. Exploring all technologies likely to be found in the classroom; and
3. Offering pragmatic tools and activities throughout the text that prepare students to effectively use educational technology.

We present technology throughout this text within the framework of education and from a classroom perspective. We follow our principles in three parts. **Part One** provides an overview of learning theories and instructional design, maintaining a focus on teaching and learning as the force that drives the selection and implementation of technology.

In **Part Two,** we thoroughly study the major categories of educational technologies likely to be found in schools, from traditional audiovisual technologies to the current and emerging digital technologies. These technologies are examined both as objects of instruction to be mastered by technology-literate educators and, more importantly, as tools within the broader framework of teaching and learning.

As an outgrowth of this technological exploration, we then present distance and alternative learning as an instructional model in **Part Three.** We examine these approaches both as professional development tools and as delivery systems that have the potential to redefine the classroom. The final chapter and interchapter in *Teaching and Learning with Technology* offer an in-depth consideration of the issues associated with implementing technologies in education, including the teacher's role in strategic planning for technology and the ethical, legal, and social issues resulting from its implementation. Together these topics converge to provide a powerful and complete experience for those who must soon face the challenges of the effective application of technology to their own classrooms and in their schools.

Features of the Text

In this second edition, chapter features have been enhanced, expanded, and revised. Some of our new, enhanced features reinforce and expand the content, while others offer hands-on problem solving both on a computer and in cooperative learning groups.

Real People, Real Stories, at the beginning of each chapter, initiates the discussion of the educational technology addressed in the chapter with an exemplary case, interview, or personal story by an in-service teacher. The case study is revisited at the end of the chapter to reinforce what students have read and help students connect what they have learned to the world in which they will teach.

In the Classroom stories throughout the text demonstrate real-world implementation of various technologies by highlighting particular teachers and their lessons.

Connecting Theory to Practice boxes bridge the gap between the technology addressed in the chapter and the learning theory that supports its use.

Issues in Teaching and Technology offers a deeper examination of critical issues related to using or implementing technology.

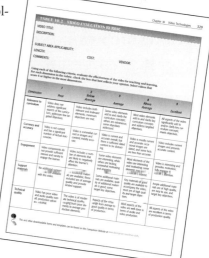

Rubrics offer students pragmatic tools and myriad opportunities to evaluate and study technologies throughout the text. They are also available for download from the web site.

Evaluation rubrics appear throughout the text and include many topics pertinent to technology use and coverage in the classroom, such as learning space, hardware, classroom equipment, productivity software, classroom management software, academic software, web sites, academic web sites, visual displays, and videos.

Topical notations in the margin, preceded by a light bulb, reference key points in adjacent paragraphs to assist students in recognizing and finding significant content.

On the Web! icons in the margin direct students to the companion web site, where text content is expanded in web activities that deepen understanding of the concepts presented through individual and group discovery and exploration of related web sites.

On CD! icons in the margin direct students to Skills Builder exercises included on their student CD. These activities include step-by-step, hands-on exercises for Microsoft Office basic skills in Word, Excel, Access, Publisher, and Explorer; for Inspiration and Kidspiration; and for HyperStudio. Many of these Software Skills Builders are offered in both PC and Macintosh versions. Additionally, On CD! icons direct students to a collection of Hardware Skills Builders. These multimedia activities teach hardware basics such as going inside a PC, using a digital camera, and using optical discs. Hardware Skills Builder activities culminate in a hardware review assessment activity.

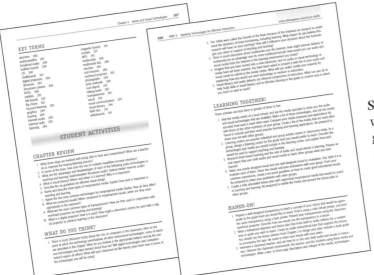

Student Activities at the end of every chapter offer various exercises, from chapter review questions to group activities, to discussion topics, to hands-on experiences.

Illustrations include screen grabs, figures, flow and process charts, and both historic and up-to-date photographs of equipment and classroom uses of technology. These illustrations present content visually to assist students in achieving competencies.

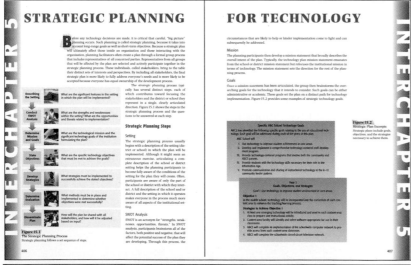

Interchapters focus on special topics in educational technology that expand on the content in the chapters they follow. Interchapters can be found following chapters 2, 4, 8, 10, and 12 and include topics such as the evolution of technology in instruction, creating a class web site, visual design basics, copyright and fair use, and strategic planning for technology.

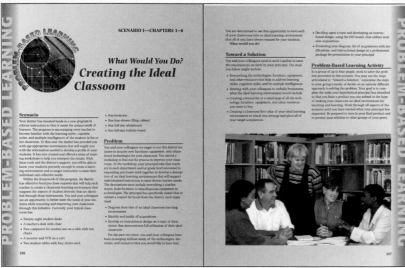

Problem-Based Scenarios, located immediately following Chapter 6, include three real-world educational technology challenges that teachers may face. Each problem is structured to include a description of the hypothetical setting, the challenge faced, and possible approaches to the challenge. A problem-based learning activity ends each scenario with a cooperative learning exercise to respond to and solve the problem presented. Scenarios include challenges related to technology acquisitions, instructional web sites, and teacher training for educational technology standards. These problem-based learning experiences give students a chance to apply what they have learned about educational technology and to build the critical-thinking skills necessary for success as educational professionals.

Presentation of the Pragmatic Approach

A constant aspect of our pragmatic approach in *Teaching and Learning with Technology* is the reader-friendly style of the text. In order to maintain interest and readability in a content area that tends toward jargon and technical detail, we deliberately engage students with a conversational tone and easy-to-use definitions and tools. Together, these elements present the complexities of educational technology in the most readable and engaging format possible.

Teaching and Learning with Technology provides current and future educators with a pragmatic survey of educational technology and an exploration of the applications and issues related to its use. This approach and style present key technological content while remaining well grounded in the theoretical foundations of teaching and learning.

Supplements

Skills Builders CD for Students

Available free with every new text is a Skills Builders CD that includes step-by-step, hands-on exercises that develop proficiency with Microsoft Office and hardware basics. Software Skills Builders are included for Word, Excel, Access, Publisher, Explorer, Inspiration and Kidspiration, and Hyperstudio in both PC and Macintosh versions. Hardware Skills Builders are multimedia activities that teach basics such as going inside a PC, using a digital camera, and using optical discs.

Companion Web Site for Students

Students using this text can take advantage of a robust, interactive companion web site that expands the learning opportunities and teaching resources beyond the printed text. In addition to On the Web! Activities, the student site includes:

- **Chapter Outliners** to help students organize their reading and aid in studying chapter content
- **Online Practice Tests** to reinforce chapter content
- **Chapter Downloads** that let students download preformatted files and all chapter rubrics to help them with lesson planning and other chapter activities
- **Power Practice Reviews,** created using Microsoft PowerPoint, to further exercise content knowledge as well as to demonstrate educational applications of the software
- **Chapter Puzzlers** including crosswords, word searches, and anagrams to help students review key terms
- **Concept Map Reviews,** created using Inspiration software that help students visually connect and review chapter concepts by filling in concept maps of content
- **Links of Interest** that provide students with suggestions for further resources and readings on chapter topics
- **Content Connections,** annotated links to articles and innovative technology integration ideas across content areas
- **Themes of the Times** educational technology articles anthology
- **Portfolio Projects** by chapter
- **Tech Tips,** technology in practice how-tos
- **Virtual Suggestion Box** to communicate your feedback on the text, resource materials, and web site so that it can be more closely adapted to your needs

For Faculty

Available with this text is a CD that includes:

- **PowerPoint Presentations** for each chapter that present key chapter points
- **Classroom Activities Ideas** for each chapter to help in presenting chapter content
- **Evaluation Suggestions** that provide alternative evaluation strategies for determining mastery of chapter concepts
- **Supplemental Readings** on content areas presented in each chapter should faculty desire to further explore in the content presented
- **Portfolio Course Materials,** which present a completely articulated portfolio-based course based on the text's chapters, including extended syllabus, projects, evaluation rubrics, and miscellaneous handouts
- **Figures and Graphics** of key illustrations in the chapter that can be downloaded and used in the preparation of custom teaching materials
- **In the Field!** activities including observation logs, reflections, and hands-on activities to be used during educational technology field experiences
- **Additional Research** in the form of annotated references presenting current research related to each chapter's content
- **Audiovisual Supports,** a list of audiovisual materials that can enhance presentation of the chapter topics, and the sources from which they can be ordered
- **Downloadable Files,** offered in Microsoft Word format, so that resources available on CD and on the student site can be downloaded and customized to your course
- **Web Sites of Interest,** annotated URLs of web sites that may be useful in teaching chapter topics

In addition to the above faculty resources, the faculty web site contains enhanced and extended faculty materials. For access to the site, contact your local sales representative. This site includes:

- A **Test Bank** with over 1,000 multiple choice, short answer, and matching questions formatted in TestGen
- **Answer Keys to Chapter Review Questions,** to assist in responding to student questions
- **Content Connections**
- **Answer Keys to Chapter Puzzlers** to assist students in solving chapter crosswords and word searches
- **PBL Scenario Solutions** which include key points for assessment and evaluation of student resolution of scenarios
- **Links to Student Resources** to facilitate exploring the components of the student web site that you may wish to include in your course
- A **Virtual Suggestion Box** to communicate your feedback on the text, resource materials, and web site so that it can be more closely adapted to your needs

Discover where the classroom comes to life! From video clips of teachers and students interacting to sample lessons, portfolio templates, and standards integration, Allyn & Bacon brings your students the tools they'll need to succeed in the classroom—with content easily integrated into your existing course. Delivered within Course Compass, Allyn & Bacon's course management system, this program gives your students powerful insights into how real classrooms work and a rich array of tools that will support them on their journey from their first class to their first classroom.

WebCT Course Content

Whether you are already using WebCT in your course or are just getting started, our rich content, student and instructor resources, and training make it even easier to integrate online course materials into your course. You no longer need to spend your free time creating all your course content from scratch—simply adopt one of our

WebCT course e-Packs and make it your own! Visit www.ablongman.com/webct for more information.

The authors of this text empathize with and understand the challenge of teaching and learning about how best to use our ever-changing technology resources to help people learn. With so many technological resources changing so quickly and so many diverse pressures affecting teachers and schools, it is difficult to determine what needs to be included in a first course in educational technology. In preparing this text for your use, we have used as our barometer the ongoing question, "What do teachers really need to know about this technology to help them use it effectively in teaching and learning?" The result of our continuous response to this question is this text, which we hope will offer you an inclusive, focused, and practical survey of educational technology.

With this second edition, we have tried to streamline content while updating the text to reflect the latest technologies currently available and on the horizon. Bundled with the support of its companion student CD and with robust faculty and student web sites, we hope we have provided both faculty and students with an abundance of useful and practical tools with which to teach and learn about technologies for education. With the electronic Instructor's Resource Manual, test-generator software, and WebCT publisher pack, we hope we have offered to our colleagues the full array of tools they might require when teaching this course. However, we know we can always do more for both the faculty and students using this text. We encourage both faculty adopting this text and students using it to share with us your thoughts about whatever further might be done to make this text, the CDs, and our web sites more useful to you. We look forward to hearing from you!

Acknowledgments

When we created the first edition of our text, we discovered how essential the help, encouragement, and support of those with whom we live and with whom we work are. It was a critical component of our very successful first edition, and we continue to be very grateful to all. As we prepared this second, greatly improved edition, we found the support of our family and colleagues to be critical once again. Indeed, this second edition could not have come into existence without their collective help. First, we would like to thank our families for thei continued encouragement and for their patience and tolerance of the time spent away from them during the creation of this edition. Special thanks to Judy's husband, Mike Duffy, son, Jonathan Lever; mom, Ena Schwartz; and sister Dori Neuwirth for the continued confidence and encouraging words that helped keep her going through another edition; to Al's wife, Mary Mizell; his children, Mike, Laurie, and Susie; their spouses; and the grandchildren for their patience and encouragement; and to Jean's children and their spouses, Mike and Mary, Tom and Jenny, Melany, and Mark and Lynn, as well as her grandchildren.

And at Allyn and Bacon, we gratefully acknowledge the patience, hard work, creativity, and support of all those known and unknown to us who made our second edition a reality. Special thanks to Arnie Burvikovs, education editor, for his tireless encouragement, support, and advice and for championing our cause time and again, which ultimately added many new features; to Shannon Morrow, development editor, who helped us put the pieces of the puzzle together as we created this second edition and who never lost patience with any of our endless questions; to our production team, with Anna Socrates, editorial production administrator, Susan McNally (production), Glenna Collett (design), Abigail Reip (photos), and Debbie Schneck (art), who together made this edition better than we had hoped, and to the Allyn and Bacon Media Production staff for their fantastic work on our CDs and web site.

We also gratefully acknowledge the many reviewers of this edition for their advice. Their suggestions and comments helped us to improve and refine this text and make it a more meaningful instructional support.

Temba Bassoppo-Moyo, Illinois State University; Tanaka Gaines, San Francisco State University; Denis Hlynka, University of Manitoba; Craig A. Kaml, Western Michigan University; Sharry A. Kimmel, Broward Community College; Donna Kitchens, University of Wisconsin at Stevens Pt.; Sandra Leslie, Belmont Abbey College; Cheryl Pritchard, West Virginia University; Cynthia Rich, Eastern Illinois University; Rick Richards, St. Petersburg College; and Locord Wilson, Jackson State University.

We would also like to thank the reviewers of the first edition:

Dara Beam, Johnson Bible College; William Beasley, Cleveland State University; Roy Bohlin, California State University; Ralph Cafolla, Florida Atlantic University; Doris Carey, formerly with University of Colorado at Colorado Springs; Marcus D. Childress, Emporia State University; Joe Codde, Michigan State University; Fred Drake, Evangel University; Angela Gerling, Westminster College; Lorana Jinkerson, Nothern Michigan University; Jerrold Kemp, San Jose State University (retired); John Kinslow, West Chester State University; Jyn-Mei Liu, Ashland University; Donald Kline, Lebanon Valley College; Dianne Kline, Miami-Dade Community College; Katie Klinger, National University; Judy Lee, University of Central Florida; Robert Lester, Faulkner University; Chris Migliaccio, Miami-Dade Community College; Jean Morrow, Emporia State University; Karen L. O'Brock, Nova Southeastern University; Teresa Orloff, Mount St. Joseph; Kay Persichitte, University of Northern Colorado; Laura Sujo de Montes, Northern Arizona University; and Lorraine G. Vitchoff, Nova Southeastern University

And finally, thanks to our many colleagues who offered up suggestions, advice, and support. At Miami-Dade College, we offer special thanks to Judy's Homestead Campus colleagues, all of whom offered continuous encouragement and support; a very special thanks to Dr. Dori Neuwirth, adjunct professor and Judy's number one sister; to Judy's master teacher and technowizard nephew, Rob Schwartz, who, together with Miami-Dade College professor Anne Nowland and Computer Courtyard manager Jeanie Canavan, made our Skills Builders CD a reality. At Nova Southeastern University, thanks go to the provost and executive dean, H. Wells Singleton and Kim Durham, as well as to Al's colleagues for their continued support. At Lambuth University, a sincere expression of gratitude to Jean's friends and colleagues: Dr. Susan Kupisch, vice president and academic dean, for her valued encouragement; assistant professor Sherry Freeman, whose insightful input reflected a through grasp of contemporary education issues and practices; Becky Sadowski, the School of Education head and department chair, who facilitated Jean's work on the second edition whenever needed; instructor Nancy Cherry, who provided Jean with extensive information on K–6 teaching; Jan Kelley, the Education Department's administrative assistant, who unfailingly stepped up to the plate with clerical advice and assistance; Laticia Hicks, student assistant and preservice teacher, Jean's right (and, sometimes, left) hand with web-based tasks; and Tina Chalk, preservice teacher, who cheerfully and promptly came to the aid of her professor as a problem solver par excellence.

Thank you all. Surely, we could not have made it through another edition without you!

Judy Lever-Duffy (judy.leverduffy@mdc.edu)
Jean B. McDonald (mcdonald@lambuth.edu)
Al P. Mizell (mizell@nova.edu)

PART 1

Technologies for Teaching and Learning

All too often, those who begin the study of educational technology expect to spend all their time learning how to use a computer and perhaps some of the other equipment available in a typical classroom. After all, isn't a course on educational technology (and its textbook) supposed to focus on the technology—the audiovisual and electronic equipment—that helps teachers teach and students learn?

The equipment is a primary concern, of course. However, equipment is simply a tool. It extends the reach of the teacher and of the learner. We can do more, and we can do it better, by using these tools—if we use them at the right time, in the right way, and for the right purpose. You can expect this text to help you explore, with great enthusiasm, the many kinds of materials and equipment that can be used to support teaching and learning. But you can also expect this text to encourage you to conduct this exploration from the perspective of, and with emphasis on, the educational processes these technologies serve.

Educators who want to understand how to use technology effectively in instruction must do so within the context of sound educational theory and practice. What is the point of knowing what a technology can do if you aren't sure where and how to use it to help teach a lesson or support a learner?

The chapters in Part One review the teaching and learning process itself, from its theory to its application. In Chapter 1, you will explore learning and the factors that help or hinder communication between teacher and learner. In Chapter 2, you will explore the process of designing effective instruction and the development and implementation of an instructional planning system that you can use when teaching. These chapters will help you build the educational framework you need as you begin your exploration of educational technologies. Without this framework, you would be learning only about how a variety of equipment works. With this framework, you will understand when, where, and why to use this equipment to help you teach and your students learn. This broader understanding is the goal of this text and the purpose for taking a course in educational technology.

CHAPTER 1

Theoretical Foundations

This chapter addresses these ISTE National Educational Technology Standards for Teachers:

II. Planning and designing learning environments and experiences

Teachers plan and design effective learning environments and experiences supported by technology. Teachers

A. design developmentally appropriate learning opportunities that apply technology-enhanced instructional strategies to support the diverse needs of learners.

B. apply current research on teaching and learning with technology when planning learning environments and experiences.

C. identify and locate technology resources and evaluate them for accuracy and suitability.

D. plan for the management of technology resources within the context of learning activities.

E. plan strategies to manage student learning in a technology-enhanced environment.

III. Teaching, learning, and the curriculum

Teachers implement curriculum plans that include methods and strategies for applying technology to maximize student learning. Teachers

A. facilitate technology-enhanced experiences that address content standards and student technology standards.

B. use technology to support learner-centered strategies that address the diverse needs of students.

C. apply technology to develop students' higher-order skills and creativity.

D. manage student learning activities in a technology-enhanced environment.

To understand the role of educational technology in the teaching and learning process, it's best to begin with a solid understanding of what teaching and learning really are. To be effectively used, educational technology should not be segregated from the teaching and learning that it supports. It is therefore critical to begin our examination of educational technology with a closer look at the teaching and learning process itself.

This chapter will help you develop the conceptual groundwork for the remaining chapters in this text. In Chapter 1, you will

- Examine differing views of educational technology
- Explore learning within the framework of communication
- Review key learning theories
- Examine the learner characteristics that affect learning
- Investigate teaching styles and their impact on learning
- Explore teaching, learning, and technology from a systems view
- Briefly review educational technology within a historical perspective
- Synthesize your own view of the relationships between teaching, learning, and technology

CHAPTER OUTLINE

Meet Sandra Burvikovs

A growing challenge in education is to find a way to meet the needs of a wide variety of youngsters in overcrowded schools with limited resources and expertise. Teachers have heard how they need to find ways to reach students with differing ways of cognitive processing including different learning styles, cognitive styles, and multiple intelligences.

We all share in this challenge in large or small ways. It is of concern to all of us. Can technology help us meet this challenge? Whereas some schools separate their exceptional students, others mainstream them. In regular classrooms, the same challenges exist—too many students with too many different learning needs for the teacher to address without help. Without help: that is the key part of the challenge. But technology can help.

The purpose of this text is to share that insight with you and to help you find ways to solve the problems you do or will face. To assist in this process, we have asked practicing educators to share some of their experiences with you. By looking first at a problem they face, as they describe it at the beginning of each chapter, you will have a focus and a problem to consider as you work through the chapter. Within the chapter, you will find hints, information, and ideas that you could use to try to solve the problem presented. At the end of the chapter, you will hear from the teacher again to see if his or her solution compares favorably with the ideas you had for solving the problem using what you learned in the chapter.

So, in this first chapter, you will examine the concept of educational technology and how it can be applied in the classroom. You will also examine three schools of thought or psychological approaches to learning to see how individual learning needs might best be met. If you agree that people learn in different ways, then you will begin to see ways to apply the use of technology to meet these needs.

Now it's time to see how one teacher of the gifted approached this problem in a crowded elementary school in Illinois. Here's Sandra Burvikovs to share the problem and challenges she faced in her school.

I teach a gifted education pilot program for grades 3–5 replacement classes. I meet with my students daily for replacement classes in reading and math; reading is a combined grades 4–5 multiage class. Last year, I taught a grades 2–5 gifted education pullout program in which I met with my students for about two hours each week.

May Whitney Elementary School is located in the center of Lake Zurich, Illinois; it is one of the oldest elementary schools in the district and has a very diverse student population. The school has approximately 500 students. Last year, the school was about 250 students over capacity. I taught my groups in the hallway for three months and then was moved to the stage in the gym because there were no other locations available. The district was in the process of building a new elementary school to accommodate the increased enrollment. About 7 percent of the students in the Lake Zurich Elementary School District take part in the district's gifted education programs.

Regardless of the overcrowding last year, the staff and administration at the school were very dedicated, innovative, and committed to providing students with a positive learning experience. A new school opened this year and I now teach gifted students in a regular classroom setting.

Last year, as the teacher of the gifted pullout program when I met with my students for two hours per week, my classes varied in size from seven to eighteen students. These students displayed a wide range of strengths, weaknesses, and individual learning styles. I met with my groups on the gym stage; my classroom consisted of two large tables, chairs, a metal storage cabinet, an old TV and VCR, and a filmstrip projector. This is not what the parents expected from the program. I knew that I had to find a way to accommodate the large variety of learning styles and still meet all of the learning objectives for these students regardless of the teaching location or the difficulties involved in finding ways to meet their unique needs.

The district had just purchased a computer cart with laptop computers and wireless Internet connections. One of the curricular goals with this group of students was for them to complete a long-term project. I knew that, regardless of where I taught, my students' parents had very high expectations about the quality of the long-term project. All of the projects were to be displayed at a districtwide fair. I knew that I had to find a way to utilize technology to change my teaching and to better meet students' individual learning needs.

SOURCE: Online interview with Sandra Burvikovs conducted by Al P. Mizell.

What Is Educational Technology?

Media refers to different means of communication.

The definition of educational technology often varies depending on whether the term is used by educators or by technologists. Many educators use the term **educational technology** very broadly. Educational technology for those educators includes any **media** that can be used in instruction. From their perspective, educational technology might include printed media, models, projected and nonprojected visuals, as well as audio, video, and digital media. Other, more computer-oriented educators take a narrower view. Those individuals confine educational technology primarily to computers, computer peripherals, and related software used in teaching and learning. For **technologists,** those whose primary responsibilities relate to the management of equipment, educational technology is often defined in terms of the hardware available that might be used in the classroom. This would include both audiovisual equipment and computers. As you can see, the body of knowledge broadly defined as educational technology is not yet exact, even in its definition.

The field, like our society in general, is in a state of rapid change under the influences of the Information Age. Therefore, to begin our exploration of educational technology, we must first define its scope. For the purposes of this text, our definition of technology is based on the definition provided by the **Association for Educational Communications and Technology (AECT).** The AECT has been prominent in the area of design and implementation of educational technology for seventy-five years. As described in its 1994 publication, *Instructional Technology: The Definition and Domains of the Field,* "Educational technology is the theory and practice of design, development, utilization, management, and evaluation of processes and resources for learning." This definition takes the broadest view possible and allows us to explore the full range of media that a teacher might use to enhance his or her instruction and augment student learning. Our definition of educational technology, then, is *any technology used by educators in support of the teaching and learning process* (see Figure 1.1 on page 6).

A technologist manages and implements materials, tools, and equipment to improve or enhance operations.

Why Study Educational Technology?

The **International Society for Technology in Education (ISTE)** has led a federally funded initiative to develop standards for technology for both teachers and students. This initiative is helping to define what you need to know about educational technology. The ISTE's project is called the National Educational Technology Standards for Teachers (NETS•T) Project. It is part of the Preparing Tomorrow's Teachers to Use Technology (PT3) grant program sponsored by the U.S. Department of Education. The NETS•T Project states, "The world is different. Kids are different . . . learning is different . . . and teaching must be different too. Today's classroom teachers must be prepared to provide technology-supported learning opportunities for their students" (NETS•T, 2002). NETS•T describes a performance profile of a technology-literate teacher and twenty-one key competencies that such a teacher should have. These competencies are listed in Figure 1.2. Clearly, the national expectation for educators is to have a sound foundation in the technologies you need to teach and your students will need to learn.

ON THE WEB! 1.1
Educational Technology
Organizations

But beyond professional standards, the need to be able to utilize educational technologies effectively is intuitive. Think about the last time you sat in a classroom taking a course. Chances are that your teacher presented information to you primarily by talking to you about the course content. This familiar teaching **method,** called lecture or presentation, is one of several that we explore more fully in Chapter 2. Like most methods of teaching, it can be enhanced through the use of educational technology. Let's consider how technology might improve this common teaching strategy.

A teaching method includes the strategy and techniques used to communicate content.

Lecture or oral presentation, when used alone, can be challenging for many students. If a teacher using this method did not occasionally stop to write a key word on the board or perhaps show a graphic using the overhead projector, most people would find it fairly difficult to follow the presentation, much less take adequate notes on what was said. We intuitively understand that common technologies, such as a whiteboard, a chalkboard, and an overhead projector, can enhance a lecture substantially and significantly improve communication. Beyond the familiar and obvious media, many dif-

Figure 1.1
Educational Technology: What Is Your Definition?
What do you think of when you think of educational technology? Check all that you think apply to educational technology in this figure.

How many did you choose? In fact, educational technology can include all of these and much more! Anything used to help you teach or your students to learn can be considered an educational technology.

ferent types of strategies and technologies can contribute substantially to the teaching and learning process. The NETS•T Project (see Figure 1.2) reminds us that educators must acquire a broad range of methods and skills to enhance teaching and support learning with technology effectively.

For those who want to teach, it is therefore essential to first have a thorough working knowledge of the many kinds of educational technologies available that might assist in teaching and in enhancing learning. Educational technologies become the tools that a teacher might use to create an effective instructional event. This text will assist you in discovering the tools that are now available and those on the technological horizon. You will learn how to use these tools and explore their application to the teaching and learning process to make it as effective and meaningful as possible.

Teaching and Learning: A Closer Look at the Instructional Event

To understand how technology fits into instruction, you must first have a very clear picture of the nature of teaching, learning, and the **instructional events** that teachers construct for transferring knowledge and skills to their students. For a teacher, this type of conceptual framework is important. A clear and precise grasp of key teaching and learning theories provides a solid knowledge base and is therefore a logical place to begin your exploration of technology in teaching and learning.

> An instructional event includes all the teaching methods and learning experiences created to support the learning process.

What Is Learning?

We teach so that our students will learn the concepts or skills we have identified as critical. Teachers want to transfer the knowledge and skills they currently possess to their students so that they too can embrace, enjoy, and use that knowledge academically, personally, and professionally. It is imperative that teachers begin the transfer process with a full understanding of learning so that they can plan and implement appropriate instruction that will result in learning success. Just as an architect must understand the properties of wood, steel, and glass and the purpose of a building before designing it, so too must a teacher understand the essential components of the teaching and learning process (see Figure 1.3 on page 10).

> Learning is a transfer of knowledge that can be ensured only when all components of the process have been incorporated into the learning event.

How Do We Learn?

The human mechanism of incorporating new knowledge, behaviors, and skills into an individual personal repertoire broadly defines learning. For a deeper understanding of how learning occurs, you must first examine the underlying psychological views of human behaviors. Psychologists are not unanimous in these views. There are, in fact, a variety of **theories** to explain how and why people do what they do. Most of these theories, however, fall within a few prevailing schools of thought. Each school has its own perspective on human behavior. To understand learning, then, you must examine the prevailing views and the learning theories that result from each.

> A theory is an idea or concept that offers an explanation for observed phenomena.

For educators, awareness of these differing views helps you understand the options you have in approaching the design of an instructional event and, indeed, the entire learning environment. Examining these sometimes opposing views of learning will help you determine the position with which you personally most agree. In turn, this will help you design instruction that is consistent with your own view of the teaching-learning process and its principles.

Understanding learning is even more critical when a teacher integrates technology into an instructional event. Technology is best viewed as a robust set of instructional tools that help you accomplish the objectives of the teaching-learning process. Technology is a means to an instructional end, not an end in itself. To use technology effectively, the teacher must have a clear understanding of learning and the teaching strategies that will result in the intended knowledge transfer. The teaching strategies you select will then determine the appropriate types of technological tools necessary to carry them out.

Profile for Technology–Literate Teachers

FIRST-YEAR TEACHING PERFORMANCE PROFILE

Upon completion of the first year of teaching, teachers

1. assess the availability of technology resources at the school site, plan activities that integrate available resources, and develop a method for obtaining the additional necessary software and hardware to support the specific learning needs of students in the classroom. (I, II, IV)

2. make appropriate choices about technology systems, resources, and services that are aligned with district and state standards. (I, II)

3. arrange equitable access to appropriate technology resources that enable students to engage successfully in learning activities across subject/content areas and grade levels. (II, III, VI)

4. engage in ongoing planning of lesson sequences that effectively integrate technology resources and are consistent with current best practices for integrating the learning of subject matter and student technology standards (as defined in the ISTE *National Educational Technology Standards for Students*). (II, III)

5. plan and implement technology-based learning activities that promote student engagement in analysis, synthesis, interpretation, and creation of original products. (II, III)

6. plan for, implement, and evaluate the management of student use of technology resources as part of classroom operations and in specialized instructional situations. (I, II, III, IV)

7. implement a variety of instructional technology strategies and grouping strategies (e.g., whole-group, collaborative, individualized, and learner-centered) that include appropriate embedded assessment for meeting the diverse needs of learners. (III, IV)

8. facilitate student access to school and community resources that provide technological and discipline-specific expertise. (III)

9. teach students methods and strategies to assess the validity and reliability of information gathered through technological means. (II, IV)

10. recognize students' talents in the use of technology and provide them with opportunities to share their expertise with their teachers, peers, and others. (II, III, V)

11. guide students in applying self- and peer-assessment tools to critique student-created technology products and the process used to create those products. (IV)

12. facilitate students' use of technology that addresses their social needs and cultural identity and promotes their interaction with the global community. (III, VI)

13. use results from assessment measures (e.g., learner profiles, computer-based testing, electronic portfolios) to improve instructional planning, management, and implementation of learning strategies. (II, IV)

14. use technology tools to collect, analyze, interpret, represent, and communicate data (student performance and other information) for the purposes of instructional planning and school improvement. (IV)

15. use technology resources to facilitate communications with parents or guardians of students. (V)

16. identify capabilities and limitations of current and emerging technology resources and assess the potential of these systems and services to address personal, lifelong learning, and workplace needs. (I, IV, V)

17. participate in technology-based collaboration as part of continual and comprehensive professional growth to stay abreast of new and emerging technology resources that support enhanced learning for PK–12 students. (V)

18. demonstrate and advocate for legal and ethical behaviors among students, colleagues, and community members regarding the use of technology and information. (V, VI)

19. enforce classroom procedures that guide students' safe and healthy use of technology and that comply with legal and professional responsibilities for students needing assistive technologies. (VI)

20. advocate for equal access to technology for all students in their schools, communities, and homes. (VI)

21. implement procedures consistent with district and school policies that protect the privacy and security of student data and information. (VI)

Figure 1.2

ISTE Professional Preparation Performance Profile

ISTE National Educational Technology Standards for Teachers (NETS•T) summarize what teachers should know about and be able to do with technology.

ISTE NATIONAL EDUCATIONAL TECHNOLOGY STANDARDS (NETS) AND PERFORMANCE INDICATORS FOR TEACHERS

All classroom teachers should be prepared to meet the following standards and performance indicators.

I. TECHNOLOGY OPERATIONS AND CONCEPTS

Teachers demonstrate a sound understanding of technology operations and concepts. Teachers

A. demonstrate introductory knowledge, skills, and understanding of concepts related to technology (as described in the ISTE National Educational Technology Standards for Students).

B. demonstrate continual growth in technology knowledge and skills to stay abreast of current and emerging technologies.

II. PLANNING AND DESIGNING LEARNING ENVIRONMENTS AND EXPERIENCES

Teachers plan and design effective learning environments and experiences supported by technology. Teachers

A. design developmentally appropriate learning opportunities that apply technology-enhanced instructional strategies to support the diverse needs of learners.

B. apply current research on teaching and learning with technology when planning learning environments and experiences.

C. identify and locate technology resources and evaluate them for accuracy and suitability.

D. plan for the management of technology resources within the context of learning activities.

E. plan strategies to manage student learning in a technology-enhanced environment.

III. TEACHING, LEARNING, AND THE CURRICULUM

Teachers implement curriculum plans that include methods and strategies for applying technology to maximize student learning. Teachers

A. facilitate technology-enhanced experiences that address content standards and student technology standards.

B. use technology to support learner-centered strategies that address the diverse needs of students.

C. apply technology to develop students' higher order skills and creativity.

D. manage student learning activities in a technology-enhanced environment.

IV. ASSESSMENT AND EVALUATION

Teachers apply technology to facilitate a variety of effective assessment and evaluation strategies. Teachers

A. apply technology in assessing student learning of subject matter using a variety of assessment techniques.

B. use technology resources to collect and analyze data, interpret results, and communicate findings to improve instructional practice and maximize student learning.

C. apply multiple methods of evaluation to determine students' appropriate use of technology resources for learning, communication, and productivity.

V. PRODUCTIVITY AND PROFESSIONAL PRACTICE

Teachers use technology to enhance their productivity and professional practice. Teachers

A. use technology resources to engage in ongoing professional development and lifelong learning.

B. continually evaluate and reflect on professional practice to make informed decisions regarding the use of technology in support of student learning.

C. use technology to communicate and collaborate with peers, parents, and the larger community in order to nurture student learning.

VI. SOCIAL, ETHICAL, LEGAL, AND HUMAN ISSUES

Teachers understand the social, ethical, legal, and human issues surrounding the use of technology in PK–12 schools and apply that understanding in practice. Teachers

A. model and teach legal and ethical practice related to technology use.

B. apply technology resources to enable and empower learners with diverse backgrounds, characteristics, and abilities.

C. identify and use technology resources that affirm diversity.

D. promote safe and healthy use of technology resources.

E. facilitate equitable access to technology resources for all students.

Figure 1.3
Building the Learning Environment
Constructing a learning environment is like constructing a building.

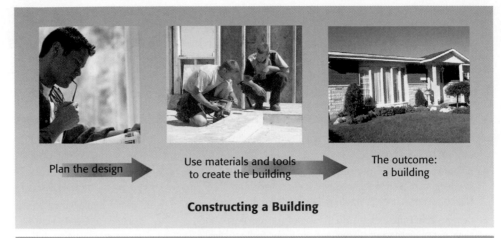

Plan the design → Use materials and tools to create the building → The outcome: a building

Constructing a Building

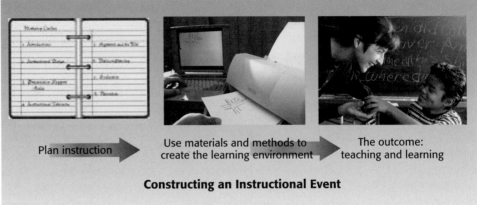

Plan instruction → Use materials and methods to create the learning environment → The outcome: teaching and learning

Constructing an Instructional Event

A decision matrix is a table or graphic that can be used to clarify and aid in making a decision.

As you review and explore the various views of learning presented in this chapter, take the time to complete the **decision matrix** in Table 1.1. It will help you identify which of the approaches is most consistent with your own view of teaching and learning.

ON THE WEB! 1.2
Focus on Communications Theory

Learning as Communication: A Framework for Exploring Teaching and Learning

One of the earliest approaches to understanding learning was to examine the phenomenon as a communication process. The teacher was the sender of a message, and the student was the receiver of the message. Within this framework, learning was considered to have occurred when the information was accurately transmitted to the receiver. To be sure that this had indeed happened, the sender checked returning messages (**feedback**) from the receiver to confirm that accurate communication had taken place. This **communications cycle** is diagrammed in Figure 1.4.

As you know from your own personal experiences, clear and precise communication does not always occur. There are three general types of variables that can interfere with the communication of ideas: (1) environmental factors, (2) psychological factors, and (3) personal filters (see Figure 1.5 on page 12). It is important for those trying to communicate to have an awareness of the nature and impact of each of these.

Environmental factors that may interfere with the communication process include environmental conditions that cause the message to be distorted or even blocked. In a classroom, as the teacher (sender) engages in the communication

TABLE 1.1   HOW DO YOU LEARN?

A DECISION MATRIX

For each statement with which you agree, place an X in the box indicated for that statement. A predominance of Xs in any column is an indicator that you tend to agree with that psychological viewpoint. A scattering of Xs across columns may indicate that you take an eclectic approach.

	Psychological Bases of Learning		
Mark the box indicated for each: Learning . . .	*B* Behaviorist	*CG* Cognitivist	*CN* Constructivist
Is based on previous experiences. *(Mark CN)*			
Results from being rewarded. *(Mark B)*			
Is influenced by one's culture. *(Mark CN)*			
Occurs to avoid punishment. *(Mark B)*			
Is a result of understanding new ideas. *(Mark CG)*			
Happens more easily if it builds on something known previously. *(Mark CN)*			
Requires a social framework. *(Mark CN)*			
Results from thinking. *(Mark CG)*			
Will be lost if not reinforced. *(Mark B)*			

Figure 1.4
The Communications Cycle
An analysis of the components of the communication process.

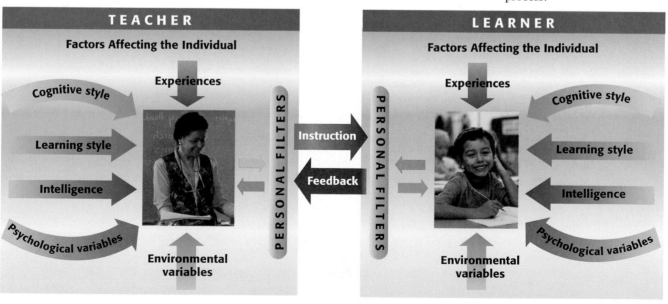

Figure 1.5
**Variables Affecting
Learning**
Environmental factors, psychological factors, and personal filters are among the many variables that affect learning.

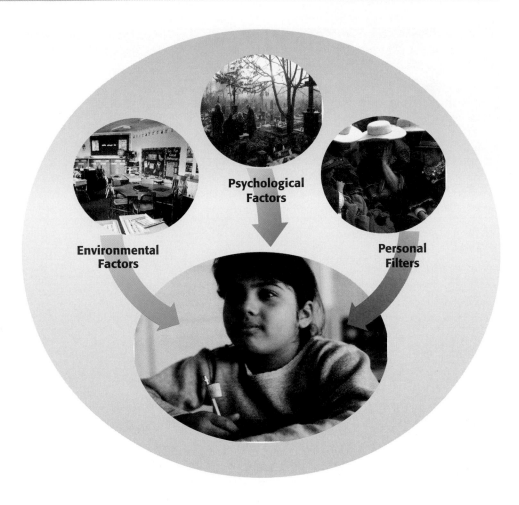

process, loud, incessant noise from outside the classroom may interrupt communication or cause environmental static that interferes with the clarity of the message the student receives. Dim lighting, excessive movement, and uncomfortable temperatures inside the classroom are among other physical distractions that can cause the participants to lose focus and thus add a different but equally disruptive static to the process. Any factors emanating from the environment that cause a learner to lose focus and disengage from active participation in the communication process may be included in

IN THE CLASSROOM
Filters Change the Message

"**S**urvival of the fittest" is the opening statement with which Mr. Tracy challenges his biology class at Johansen High School. He has begun a unit on Darwin's theory of evolution. He realizes that the course content will be filtered differently by his students. Robert Jones, a member of a church that rejects the concept that humans descended from earlier, simpler organisms and believes that God created Adam in a form identical to that of a mod-

ern man, will use a cultural filter to reject the Darwinian premise. Lucy Leakey, whose father is a physical anthropologist, will use a filter much like Mr. Tracy's own, having been raised in a home where science and religion go hand in hand with Darwin's tenet that humans have evolved, adapted, and thereby survived. What can Mr. Tracy do to teach his content in a way that will be least distorted by his students' personal filters?

environmental factors. Some environmental factors affect some learners but not others. This can be the result of those environmental factors interacting with individual psychological factors.

Psychological factors are the unique individual psychological differences that define and affect the reception of a communicated message. Psychological factors can include the receiver's emotional state at the time the message is transmitted. For a receiver who entered the communication process immediately after a highly emotional or traumatic event, internal emotional turmoil may be the source of static that distracts the individual from the message. Sometimes, it is the manner in which the message is transmitted that causes the static. Individuals all have preferences as to how they best receive information. Each of us has a preferred sensory gateway, that is, the sense that is most effective for receiving and decoding information. This collection of preferences, or **learning style,** when not addressed by the sender, can cause frustration as the learner tries to grasp the content. This frustration in turn garbles the message. If one learns best through careful examination of pictures and diagrams, then a message that is transmitted orally can be difficult and frustrating to understand and may therefore not be clearly received. If one's dominant sensory gateway is touch, then verbal or visual communication is less effective than tactile-kinesthetic experiences.

Learning styles may act as a barrier to communication when the sender does not address the receiver's preferred learning style. Thus, one's unique physiological and psychological predisposition to the way in which a message is delivered is another example of the psychological factors that may disrupt communication.

ON THE WEB! 1.3
Focus on Learning Styles

The final factor that may interfere with the communication process is the personal filters through which the message must pass. Both sender and receiver have a number of personal filters. These include the individual's personal values, cultural heritage, and social belief system. The pure message, that is, the objective set of data that is to be transferred, may be distorted by the belief system held by the sender or the receiver. For example, if the sender or the receiver comes to the process with a predisposition toward the message content, that predisposition may distort the message itself. A negative attitude toward the message or toward the participants in the communication process may cause the intended message to be distorted on delivery. This type of filter may be referred to as having a closed mind with reference to the message. Cultural beliefs can also act as filters by distorting the message content. If one holds a belief that is directly opposed to the content of the message, then the information may be distorted to be more consistent with the belief or rejected because it is in conflict with the belief. In teaching, awareness of potential filters, both your own and those of the receiver, will help you overcome the potential for distortion.

Review now the communications model diagrammed in Figure 1.4. Note each of the unique elements that affect communication, from the message itself to the filters through which it must pass. Together, these components interact to determine the success of the teaching-learning process.

Whether the message was the original content sent from sender to receiver or the feedback from receiver to sender, you can see that many factors can help or hinder communications. With an understanding of the nature of communication as a foundation, you can begin to see the complexity of successful teaching. The teaching-learning process embraces the entire component of the communication process but then continues a step further. Understanding the teaching-learning process also requires understanding what happens once the message has been correctly transmitted. Is receipt of the message learning, or is there more to it? What is the difference between hearing, understanding, and learning? To answer these questions, we must delve deeper into theories about how we learn. Thus far, we have examined teaching and learning from a macro view, that is, from the larger perspective of communication. Now it is time to consider the process from a micro view, the narrower perspective of the internal processes that determine how one learns.

Perspectives of Learning

Different schools of psychological theory interpret the process of learning differently.

Different people can look at the same thing and see it in very different ways. This describes the concept of **perspective.** Learning is a complex activity that can be explained differently depending on one's perspective on how and why people do what they do. Each of the different schools of psychology has its own view or perspective of learning.

In the next few sections, you will be introduced to differing, sometimes contrary views of learning. Each is correct from the perspective of the theorists presenting it. As you read about each of these perspectives on learning, consider which most closely coincides with your views on learning. As you consider these different viewpoints, you might find that you agree with one of the following theories part of the time and prefer a different theory at other times or for different learners. If that is the case, you have an eclectic approach that takes key ideas from multiple theories.

The Behaviorist Perspective

ON THE WEB! 1.4
Focus on Behaviorists

Behaviorism sees learning as the response to an external stimulus.

Behaviorists, that is, those who see learning from a behaviorist perspective, view all behavior as a response to external stimuli. A stimulus is the initial action directed to the organism, and a response is the organism's reaction to that action. According to behaviorists, the learner acquires behaviors, skills, and knowledge in response to the rewards, punishments, or withheld responses associated with them. A reward includes all positive, negative, or neutral reinforcement to a behavior. Rewards determine the likelihood that the behavior will be repeated. Such reinforcing responses can include rewards (positive reinforcement), punishments (negative reinforcement), or withheld responses (no reinforcement). For behaviorists, learning is essentially a passive process, that is, one learns as a response to the environment, not necessarily because of any specific mental activity. Key theorists in this perspective include **Ivan Pavlov, John Watson,** and B. F. Skinner. To learn more about these behaviorists and their theories, explore On the Web! Activity 1.4.

spotlight on

B. F. Skinner

B. F. Skinner (1904–1990) was born and raised in Susquehanna, Pennsylvania. He attended Hamilton College in Clinton, New York, intending to become a writer. However, his discovery of John B. Watson's seminal book *Behaviorism* inspired him to pursue graduate studies in psychology at Harvard University. Toward the end of 1929, he began work on the Skinner box, from which he derived his theory of operant conditioning. In 1938, he published *The Behavior of Organisms: An Experimental Analysis,* a book that would have a far-reaching effect on such diverse areas as teaching machines, programmed instruction, treatment for juvenile delinquents, industrial safety, assistive training for the disabled, and even frequent-flyer programs. To simplify child care by means of a controlled environment, Skinner invented the aircrib, or baby box. His daughter Deborah spent her first two years in this box. Skinner became chairman of the Department of Psychology at Indiana University in 1945 and in 1948 published *Walden Two,* a utopian novel, in an effort to persuade Americans to live simply by utilizing operant conditioning. He returned to Harvard in 1948 as a professor of psychology. In *The Technology of Teaching* (1968), he propounded the value of the teaching machine he had invented. His most controversial book, *Beyond Freedom and Dignity* (1972), stated his thesis that in behavioral engineering, not individual freedom, lies the key to the survival of the human race.

spotlight on

Jean Piaget

When applying his theory to teaching, **Jean Piaget** wrote, "The new methods [of teaching] are those that take account of the child's own peculiar nature and make their appeal to the laws of the individual's psychological constitution and those of his development." As a developmentalist, Piaget was interested primarily in intelligence and inferred that at specific calendar ages, a child is capable of performing specific mental functions, endeavoring to gain equilibrium with the environment through assimilation and accommodation. Piaget described four major stages of development: *sensorimotor* from birth to 18–24 months, *preoperational* from 18–24 months to 7 years, *concrete operations* from 7 years to 12 years, and *formal oper-* *ations* from 12 years on. These progressive stages allow the child to survive and prosper. Learning becomes responsive to the environment in ways that are not all measurable and observable.

As a constructivist, Piaget theorized that children build cognitive structures during all developmental stages. When children are exposed to something new that easily fits into prior experiences, they *assimilate* it. However, when children encounter new knowledge for which they do not have a previous cognitive map, they *accommodate* it. This process of assimilation and accommodation continually modifies their cognitive structures, and thus knowledge is continually under construction.

The Cognitivist Perspective

In contrast to the behaviorist view, **cognitivists** focus on learning as a mental operation that takes place when information enters through the senses, undergoes mental manipulation, is stored, and is finally used. Unlike behaviorism, with its exclusive focus on external, measurable behaviors, this theory makes mental activity (cognition) the primary source of study. Although behavior is still considered critical, it is viewed as an indicator of cognitive processes rather than just an outcome of a **stimulus-response** cycle. Cognitive theorists attempt to explain learning in terms of how one thinks. Cognitivists believe that learning is more complex than a simplistic reduction to controllable, observable responses to observable stimuli. Learning and problem solving, according to cognitivists, represent mental processes that are undetectable by mere observation. Key theorists in this perspective include **Jerome Bruner** and **David Ausubel.** The early works of constructivist Jean Piaget also significantly contributed to the cognitivist perspective. Each brings a unique perspective to the view of learning as a function of thinking. You can learn more about these theorists in On the Web! Activity 1.5.

ON THE WEB! 1.5
Focus on Cognitivists

The Constructivist Perspective

For **constructivists,** knowledge is a constructed element resulting from the learning process. Further, knowledge is unique to the individual who constructs it. Mahoney (1994) places constructivism on the cognitive family tree because it relies on the cognitive concepts of inquiry-based learning and social interaction. However, it differs from the cognitivist view in that learning is not seen as just the product of mental processes; it is an entirely unique product for each individual based on the experiences within which those mental processes occurred. Constructivism is at present the most influential force in shaping contemporary education.

Perhaps the most notable early constructivist was Jean Piaget. Piaget theorized that children construct mental maps as they encounter information. New knowledge is either assimilated (fitted into existing maps) or accommodated (existing maps are adjusted to accommodate the new information). Thus, children maintain a type of

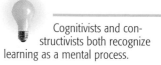

Cognitivists and constructivists both recognize learning as a mental process.

mental equilibrium (see Spotlight on Jean Piaget). In the area of educational technology, **Seymour Papert** adapted Piaget's perspective and applied it to children engaged in using technology. Papert's application of this approach resulted in the development of Logo, a graphical programming language that, when used by children, effectively transferred complex mathematical skills. Papert, a founding faculty member of MIT's Media Lab, continues to develop constructivist educational software and to research learning.

Within the constructivist school of learning, two views dominate. The first is a cognitive-constructivist view championed by **Robert Gagné.** In this perspective, learning is a result of an individual's cognitive efforts to construct his or her personal knowledge. The other view, that of social constructivism, was well articulated by **Lev Vygotsky** and **Albert Bandura.** In this view, learning is considered a result of the collaboration of a group of learners in an effort to construct a common core of knowledge. Cognitive constructivism is an outgrowth of the cognitivist view of learning. However, it differs in that the emphasis is placed on the constructs that the individual creates as a result of his or her own cognitive processes. Table 1.2 compares several important constructivists. To learn more about each of these constructivists and his theories, try On the Web! Activity 1.6.

ON THE WEB! 1.6
Focus on Constructivists

⬤—[Toward an Integrated View of Learning

All of the theoretical perspectives described in the previous section attempt to explain the complex process called learning. Depending on the psychological framework that you believe best explains why people behave the way they do, you may find one of these perspectives more attractive than the others. Still, it is best to think of all of them together as the range of possible explanations of learning and to think of each indi-

TABLE 1.2   KEY CONSTRUCTIVISTS AND THEIR DIFFERENCES

Constructivist	Defining Characteristics	Teacher Role
JEAN PIAGET (developmental theorist)	Identified key developmental stages that may affect learning; children either assimilate or accommodate knowledge based on existing schemas	Be aware of child's developmental stage when presenting content; help child construct schemas
ROBERT GAGNÉ (bridge theorist between behaviorism and cognitivism)	Controlled, external, sequential instructional events with eight conditions for learning determined by developmental stage of learner and by subject matter	Create systematic design to address student's needs; individualize instructional events
LEV VYGOTSKY (social learning theorist)	Zone of proximal development recognizes student's readiness to bond with the community; speech and language are keys to intelligence	Arrange for tutoring by skilled and learned adults as a means of student enculturation
ALBERT BANDURA (social learning theorist)	Concern with the way people acquire socially appropriate behavior; builds on Skinner to form social learning theory; agrees with Gagné that subject matter is central to learning stages	Outcome expectancies (prediction of results of a behavior) motivate students to imitate the behavior, "modeling"
SEYMOUR PAPERT (mathematician and educational technologist)	Technology should help children experience knowledge and construct meanings; developed Logo and constructivist software based on this perspective	Provide opportunities for children to develop constructs through experience; use technology to support experiences
HOWARD GARDNER (multiple-intelligences theorist)	Nine innate capabilities (with more under study): linguistic, spatial, bodily-kinesthetic, logical-mathematical, and others; every child is smart in his or her own way and possesses combined intelligences that should be encouraged to develop	Gear curricula and instructional approaches to individual intelligences and their dominant ways of knowing, for the successful pursuit of knowledge, both vocational and avocational, by all

Figure 1.6
Building Blocks of Effective Teaching
Diverse theories provide the foundation for understanding learning.

vidual approach as a unique and special addition to your collection (see Figure 1.6). Then, as an eclectic instructor, you can choose to implement those parts of the theories that best match your learners' needs and the characteristics of a particular lesson's specific objectives.

Which theory is correct? If you decided to research the answer to a question of interest to you, you would probably read a variety of resources and surf a number of web sites to get an idea of the possibilities. After reviewing these possibilities, you would ultimately form your own personal answer. Perhaps that, too, is the best approach to learning theory. To create the best possible **learning environment** for your students, you need to have an understanding of how a student learns. To do that, you need a working knowledge of learning theory. Then, once this knowledge base is in place, it is wise for you to develop your own, possibly eclectic view of learning theory. You may choose to use some parts of each theory or accept a learning theory in its entirety. At this point, you should examine all the options and let your own mental model of learning develop.

A View of the Learner

In examining the factors that can affect effective communication and theories related to the learning process, it becomes critical to carefully examine the unique nature of the learner who is participating in the process. Understanding learning itself is just the first step a teacher must take in planning effective instruction. Learning theory tells us how learning might occur. The next area for consideration is to examine characteristics that might have an impact on an individual's attempt to learn.

The learning environment refers to all the elements that make up the design and implementation of the instruction.

Cognitive style, learning style, and intelligence are key characteristics unique to each learner.

In Figure 1.5, you saw the relationship of many variables that affect learning. Each learner in a classroom is likely to have a unique cognitive style, a unique learning style, and some parameters related to intelligence. This section will help you understand how each of these relates to the teaching-learning process.

Cognitive Styles

ON THE WEB! 1.7
Bridging Theory to Practice

Cognitive style refers to how one thinks. Each person has his or her own tendencies and preferences when it comes to cognition (thinking). Such preferences can even be measured. One of the most widely used cognitive style instruments to determine one's own patterns of thinking is the Myers-Briggs Type Indicator (MBTI). The Myers-Briggs instrument is based primarily on a constructivist view of learning. In it, a learner answers a series of questions about his or her own preferences. The responses are then totaled and categorized. The clustering of responses points to one member of each of four sets of opposing cognitive preferences: extrovert (E) or introvert (I), sensing (S) or intuitive (N), thinking (T) or feeling (F), and judging (J) or perceiving (P). Everyone has a preference in each of these pairs of opposites. Thus, a person's cognitive type may turn out to be the ENFP type (Extrovert, Intuitive, Feeling, Perceiving). Such an individual would be likely to be excited by and involved in new ideas and possibilities. He or she would join in enthusiastically and energetically while maintaining a deep concern for the world and others (Martin, 2002). Everyone has preferences in each of these four pairs of opposites, and each combination of types results in noticeably different propensities in interacting with others and with the environment. These cognitive characteristics are likely also to influence how the individual might successfully learn. Awareness and understanding of students' cognitive preferences can help a teacher design instruction that is consistent with these preferences and therefore more palatable to those students. Figure 1.7 gives you a sense of the cognitive types that the MBTI identifies.

spotlight on

Myers and Briggs

Katherine Briggs wanted to become a novelist. In searching for ways to develop characterization, she explored Carl Jung's theory of personality types, from which a major field of literary criticism—archetypal criticism—is derived.

During World War II, her daughter, **Isabel Briggs Myers,** extended the use of the personality typing that her mother had studied to aid in the war effort by attempting to ascertain which workers were best suited to which wartime jobs. Decisions were based on their responses to an inventory she devised. She also added two more functions of personality: judging and perceiving.

The Myers-Briggs Type Indicator (MBTI) is a personality inventory developed by Isabel Briggs Myers and her husband, Peter B. Myers. It is widely used not only in education, but also in counseling, business, industry, and the armed forces. Unlike the personality inventories found in the popular media, the MBTI can be administered only by psychologists. Particularly important for education is an adaptation of the MBTI for children ages 6–12, the Murphy-Meisgeier Type Indicator for Children (MMTIC).

SOURCE: A. M. Fairhurst & L. L. Fairhurst. 1995. *Effective teaching, effective learning*. Palo Alto, CA: Davies-Black Publishing.

Learning Styles

Learning style is another factor influencing how an individual learns. Unlike the broader concept of cognitive style—that is, how we think—learning style refers to those conditions under which we best learn. Most learning style theorists identify three primary modalities for learning: auditory, visual, and kinesthetic. Some individuals learn best by listening; thus, they may be said to have a predominantly auditory learning style. Others may learn best by seeing, thus having a visual learning style. Yet others learn best by doing, which suggests a kinesthetic learning style. Although everyone can learn using each of these modalities, learning style theorists suggest that each person has a preference, a dominant sensory gateway. It is easiest for the individual to learn when information is presented in a manner consistent with her or his personal learning modality preference. Learning styles are therefore of considerable importance to those who are constructing the learning environment.

Learning style is consequently another individual factor that affects learning regardless of the psychological perspective with which you agree. Understanding the dominant learning styles of the people you are trying to teach and then designing the components of the instructional event to be consistent with their styles will make instruction significantly more effective for those learners.

EXTROVERT
More interested in outer world of persons and events

INTROVERT
More interested in inner world of concepts and ideas

SENSING
Perception based on real objects and solid facts

INTUITIVE
Perception based on possibilities and personal meaning

THINKING
Decides on the basis of objectively analyzing facts

FEELING
Decides on the basis of subjective values and views

JUDGING
Lives in a planned, organized way, prefers control

PERCEIVING
Prefers a more flexible and spontaneous way of life

Figure 1.7
Summary of Myers-Briggs Types
Cognitive types as measured by the MBTI.

Intelligence

A final factor affecting learning is **intelligence**, or the inherent capability of the learner to understand and learn. Intelligence quotient (**IQ**), a quantitative measure of intelligence, was once thought to be a definitive way to measure this capability within a specified range. Extensive research was done to develop an instrument that would provide a snapshot of a person's intelligence without regard to cultural or other bias. Bias is any tendency or prejudice that might distort a view. An example of cultural bias in intelligence testing would be the inclusion of questions that rely on a framework that is outside the test-taker's cultural experience, thus potentially distorting the results.

One of the most commonly used IQ tests is the Stanford-Binet. Alfred Binet, a French psychologist, initially developed the test in 1905 for the French Ministry of Education to help predict which students would succeed in school. Binet's test was later adapted for the United States by Louis Terman of Stanford University. The Stanford-Binet or a similar test is typically given to students several times during their academic careers. Teachers can easily get an idea of their students' potential by reviewing student records—or can they? Increasingly, this traditional means of measuring intelligence based on verbal and mathematical abilities has come under attack. In fact, the very definition of intelligence is being debated.

How to measure intelligence and the value system we attach to it are variables that are being given scholarly consideration. McLuhan (1998) asserts, "It is in our IQ testing that we have produced the greatest flood of misbegotten standards. Unaware of our typographic cultural bias, our testers assume that uniform and continuous habits

Learning styles are based on sensory preferences.

Intelligence is another variable in learning capability.

ON THE WEB! 1.8
Focus on IQ Tests

CHECK YOUR LEARNING STYLE

Anumber of learning style instruments are available online. The Index of Learning Styles (ILS), which assesses preferences on four dimensions, is currently under development by Richard M. Felder and Linda K. Silverman of North Carolina State University, who based it on a learning styles model they developed. Here is a sampling of the forty-four questions included in the ILS. To read more about learning styles and to try the instrument yourself, go to Dr. Felder's web site at http://www.ncsu.edu/felder-public/ILSpage.html.

ILS Sample Questions

When I start a homework problem, I am more likely to

(a) *try to fully understand the problem first.*
(b) *start working on the solution immediately.*

I understand something better after I

(a) *try it out.*
(b) *think it through.*

When I think about what I did yesterday, I am most likely to get

(a) *a picture.*
(b) *words.*

When I am learning something new, it helps me to

(a) *talk about it.*
(b) *think about it.*

I prefer to get new information in

(a) *pictures, diagrams, graphs, or maps.*
(b) *written directions or verbal information.*

Once I understand

(a) *all the parts, I understand the whole thing.*
(b) *the whole thing, I see how the parts fit.*

In a book with lots of pictures and charts, I am likely to

(a) *look over the pictures and charts carefully.*
(b) *focus on the written text.*

Learning style instruments such as this one include questions that help students identify various aspects of their personal learning styles. Try the ILS and other online instruments to determine your own learning style and to see if the results you get from various instruments provide you with a reasonably consistent and accurate description of your personal style.

SOURCE: Reprinted with permission from the Index of Learning Styles by B. A. Soloman and R. M. Felder, http://www.ncsu.edu/felder-public/ILSpage.html.

are a sign of intelligence, thus eliminating the ear man and the eye man." As a result of the inadequacies of traditional intelligence testing, extensive research is being done to develop instruments that will provide a more accurate result.

Howard Gardner provided a new view of intelligence, the **Theory of Multiple Intelligences.** He theorized that there is more to intelligence than what was historically measured by IQ tests. Gardner suggested that these objective tests did not go far enough in representing intelligence. He suggested instead that each individual has multiple types of intelligences, only a few of which can be measured by IQ tests. In Gardner's theory of multiple intelligences, he describes nine different aspects or types of intelligences that every person possesses (see Figure 1.8). These intelligences (or talents) include the following:

- Linguistic intelligence (verbal skills and talents related to sound, meanings, and rhythms)
- Logical-mathematical intelligence (conceptual and logical thinking skills)
- Musical intelligence (talents and abilities related to sound, rhythm, and pitch)
- Spatial intelligence (skill in thinking in pictures and visioning abstractly)
- Bodily-kinesthetic intelligence (skill in controlling body movements)
- Interpersonal intelligence (responsiveness to others)
- Intrapersonal intelligence (high degree of self-awareness and insight)
- Naturalist intelligence (skills in recognizing, categorizing, and interacting with the natural world)
- Existential intelligence (ability to consider and deal with questions of human existence)

According to Gardner's theory, every individual possesses some degree of each of the intelligences he details but one or more of the intelligences dominates. If any one of the intelligences is of significant capacity, the result is a prodigy in that area. Gardner's view equally recognizes the unique abilities of Mozart (musical intelligence), Frank Lloyd Wright (spatial intelligence), and Babe Ruth (bodily-kinesthetic

> Gardner theorizes that multiple intelligences exist.

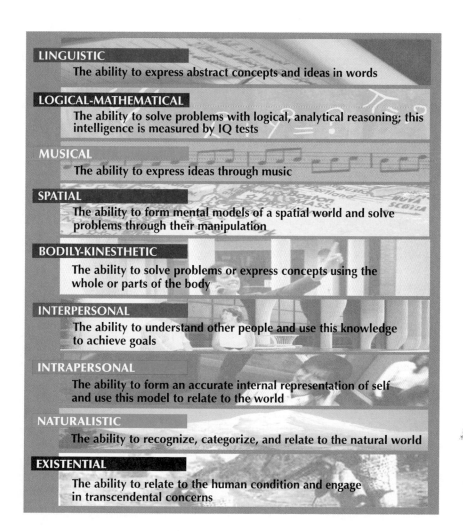

LINGUISTIC
The ability to express abstract concepts and ideas in words

LOGICAL-MATHEMATICAL
The ability to solve problems with logical, analytical reasoning; this intelligence is measured by IQ tests

MUSICAL
The ability to express ideas through music

SPATIAL
The ability to form mental models of a spatial world and solve problems through their manipulation

BODILY-KINESTHETIC
The ability to solve problems or express concepts using the whole or parts of the body

INTERPERSONAL
The ability to understand other people and use this knowledge to achieve goals

INTRAPERSONAL
The ability to form an accurate internal representation of self and use this model to relate to the world

NATURALISTIC
The ability to recognize, categorize, and relate to the natural world

EXISTENTIAL
The ability to relate to the human condition and engage in transcendental concerns

Figure 1.8
Howard Gardner's Theory of Multiple Intelligences
Multiple forms of intelligence as theorized by Howard Gardner.

spotlight on

Howard Gardner

Howard Gardner earned his undergraduate and graduate degrees from Harvard University and received a post-doctoral fellowship from the Harvard Medical School. He is now a professor of education at Harvard and directs Project Zero, a project for the study of cognition and creativity.

His own multiple intelligences are evident from his skill as a pianist, accordionist, writer, scientist, educator, philosopher, and administrator. Gardner's devotion to the arts, including a postdoctoral study of the neurological aftereffects of strokes on artists and musicians and his own performance skills, is carried on by his children: One plays the piano, another the double bass, one is a photographer, and another is an arts administrator.

Gardner's books and articles are numerous. His 1983 book *Frames of Mind: The Theory of Multiple Intelligences* is the source book for subsequent publications and studies of multiple intelligences. He has eleven other books and more than two dozen articles to his credit, as well as many coauthored writings. He has recently undertaken the study of ethics in an effort to deal with misinterpretations of his concepts. Gardner continues his ardent pursuit of diverse knowledge.

SOURCE: H. Gardner. 1999. A multiplicity of intelligences [About the author]. *Scientific American* 9(4): 23.

intelligence), whereas standard IQ tests might recognize only Albert Einstein (logical-mathematical intelligence) and William Shakespeare (linguistic intelligence). This broader view of individual capacities changes the assumptions a teacher might make about a student's potential and capacities. Such reevaluation, in turn, should change that teacher's plan for instruction. If one adopts the multiple-intelligences approach, then learning will be affected by the dominance of one or more of the intelligences in each individual student. Teaching then would have to accommodate these various propensities to maximize student learning.

A View of the Teacher

Teaching is a systematic, planned sequence of events that facilitates the communication of an idea, concept, or skill to a learner. The act of teaching requires an understanding of learning and an understanding of the individual and environmental factors that affect the learner. It also requires an understanding of yourself and the individual and environmental factors that affect you. Every teacher has his or her own learning style, cognitive style, and dominant intelligence. Given these variables, teachers also differ in their styles of teaching. **Teaching style** is typically a function of one's personal preferences. Research has shown that we teach in the way we like to learn, think, or do. Although that is unavoidable and often positive, a teacher must have an awareness of his or her own teaching strategy to be able to adjust it to meet the needs of the learners. Have you ever had instructors who were difficult to learn from? Did they lecture too much, or were they too unorganized for you? Did you notice that some of your peers did not seem to have difficulty with those instructors' teaching styles? This is the result of a conflict between how one component of the teaching-learning process prefers to interact with the other components and the environment (teaching style) and how others in the process prefer to interact (learning style).

A well-developed and well-articulated teaching style can be a positive trait that separates the master teacher from the average teacher. Yet one must always maintain awareness of how effective one's style is with reference to the goal of teaching:

Teaching styles are preferred teaching methods that mirror a teacher's learning styles.

learning. The same understanding of learning theory, cognitive styles, learning styles, and intelligence will serve you well in understanding and improving your own teaching style.

Toward a Holistic View of Teaching, Learning, and Technology

Teaching, learning, and technology work together to achieve the ultimate goal of effective knowledge transfer. When you consider the process of teaching and learning as a holistic system, you can begin to sense how all of the elements of the process, from the learning environment to teaching strategies, to learning activities, to support technologies, interact in support of the learner. (These relationships are diagrammed in Figure 1.9.) When you take the time to carefully examine each component and its interaction with other components, you are better able to design an effective process that will help you teach and help your students learn. Using such a holistic **systems approach** helps to give you the perspective needed to effectively apply each aspect of instruction to the creation of a meaningful teaching and learning process.

Once the teaching-learning process is defined, it is much simpler to see the role technology plays in it. Technology supports teaching, and it supports learning. However, educational technologies cannot be selected or implemented until the teaching and learning process they support has been planned and detailed by an educator.

At this point, you have already explored many theoretical foundations of the teaching and learning process. The next step is to consider how technology fits into the instructional system we have created.

Why Use Technology?

You have explored communication. You have examined learning theories. You have reviewed cognitive and learning styles. You have explored another way of looking at intelligence. You have been encouraged to find out how your students process information. You have applied this all to yourself to begin to understand the personal characteristics that will define your teaching style. You have viewed the whole of the teaching-learning process as a system. But what does all this have to do with the focus of this text: educational technology?

To see the relationship, it is appropriate to review the definitions and standards offered by the AECT and ISTE. The AECT definition of educational technology was offered earlier in this chapter: "Educational technology is the theory and practice of design, development, utilization, management, and evaluation of processes and resources for learning." This definition suggests that the concept of educational technology is more than a certain type of computer or a specific brand of camera. It is, instead, a wide variety of theories and practices associated with designing, developing, using, managing, and ultimately evaluating both the teaching-learning process and the technological resources used to implement that process. The ISTE NETS•T standards

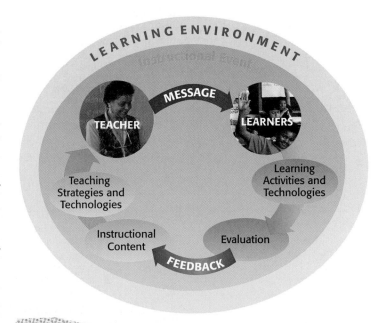

Figure 1.9

A Holistic View of Teaching, Learning, and Technology

Technology serves both learners and teachers in a variety of settings.

Technology is an Information Age teaching tool.

articulate minimum levels of technology competency and performance for teachers. Together, these two national organizations reflect the need for every teacher to have a solid command of the educational technology skills necessary for integrating appropriate and meaningful technologies into teaching and learning.

Educational technology can include any resource and any process that facilitates learning. A teacher might use educational technology to enhance the quality and clarity of communication. A teacher might employ a particular process or a specific technology to increase the likelihood that a presentation addresses a specific learning style or intelligence. Or a learner might select a process or technology because it organizes and presents content in the manner that is most comfortable for his or her personal cognitive style. Some educational technologies can be employed to ensure the rewards and feedback that are critical to a behaviorist approach. Other technologies help a learner construct and test the mental models suggested by cognitivists. Still others encourage and support social exchange to construct new knowledge through social interaction. Educational technologies can be used to enhance and support the teaching-learning process at any number of points in the process. Educational technology is a support for teaching and learning that both teacher and learner can call on to help ensure the opportunity for optimum performance.

This holistic approach to educational technology has not always been the accepted model. For many years, educational technology had a very narrow, technical definition. The evolution from an equipment-based view of educational technology to a teaching-and-learning-based view may cause confusion for those who are new to education. A brief review of this evolution may help clarify the changes (see Interchapter 1).

Educational Technology: The Past

For many, the term *educational technology* conjures up images of audiovisual equipment such as a tape recorder or videocassette player. Indeed, audiovisual equipment is so prevalent in education that it is worth exploring how this came to be and why it continues to have an impact. The audiovisual movement as we define the term today came into existence in the early 1900s with the advent of the first form of motion media: early movies. So strong was the belief in this new educational technology that Thomas Alva Edison (1913) suggested, albeit incorrectly, that "Books will soon be obsolete in schools." Although books have not become obsolete even today, motion media have indeed made their influence felt in schools, as they have in society in general. It was soon discovered that films incorporating sound and images could be used to teach as well as to entertain. Thus, the movie projector became an important addition to a teacher's arsenal of teaching tools. Thomas Edison also predicted that the movie projector would replace teachers. As far-fetched as this might sound, it was a widely believed and sometimes feared idea. By now, we have learned that predictions suggesting that any particular technology will replace professional educators or be the ultimate answer to improving teaching are not realistic.

During the 1920s and 1930s, both audio and visual educational technology evolved steadily. Technological advances in slides, radio, and sound recordings and continuing improvement in the quality of motion pictures all contributed to this evolution. With World War II and the use of audiovisual instruction by the military, a

Teachers have historically sought technology to support instruction.

surge in the development of audiovisual equipment occurred. To the array of technologies used in training and instruction, the military added the overhead projector, slide projector, simulator, and audio equipment for teaching foreign languages.

After World War II, research on the use of audiovisual tools supporting instruction was begun so that the training successes that evidently resulted from audiovisual-intensive military training could be better understood. This was followed in the 1950s by a greater articulation of the theories and models of communication and an exploration of how audiovisual technologies fit in with them.

The audiovisual movement gained further momentum with the spread of television in the 1950s. Many people assumed that instructional television would revolutionize education. Although the Federal Communications Commission (FCC) set aside television channels for educational purposes and the Ford Foundation and other organizations made serious investments in educational programming, instructional television (ITV) had slid into decline by the mid-1960s. The factors that led to this decline included teacher reluctance to use television programming in the classroom, the high cost of production of good-quality programming, and the passive nature of television viewing, which did not adequately meet student learning needs.

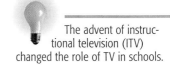

The advent of instructional television (ITV) changed the role of TV in schools.

Although not the revolutionary technology it was expected to be, broadcast television and its counterpart, videotapes, have indeed changed the face of education. Further, ITV did not disappear from the education scene. Dollars from various sources continued to flow into the Public Broadcasting System, and much fine-quality educational programming emanated from it. Much of this programming, in videotape form, is still a mainstay of school video libraries.

Educational Technology: A Modern View

The 1960s saw a change in the concept of audiovisual instruction as a model closer to our current views of educational technology began to evolve. Although audiovisual equipment remained a component of the educational technology concept, the technology was no longer limited to just equipment—audio, visual, or otherwise. By the

Instructional technology encompasses all resources that support teaching and learning.

The Skinner teaching machine was the precursor to the programmed instruction materials popular in the 1960s.

1970s, AECT's broader view dominated. Instructional technology came to be seen as all types of learning resources and the systems necessary to place them in service to teaching and learning.

The first broadly implemented educational technology appeared in the mid-1950s as an outgrowth of the popularity of B. F. Skinner's work and behaviorist views of learning. **Programmed instruction** was an instructional system in which material was presented in a series of small steps. Each step required an active learner response, to which there was immediate feedback as to the correctness of the response. Programmed instruction emphasized individualized learning materials that would require students to interact with the information presented. In keeping with Skinner's behaviorist approach, immediate feedback to student responses was a key feature. Additional features of programmed instruction included self-paced, self-selected sequencing of the materials resulting from the learner's responses. Although popular at its inception, programmed instruction faded quickly. By the late 1960s, interest in this technology had declined. Research on programmed instruction indicated that it did not significantly improve learning. This finding, combined with negative feedback from students and teachers who found the format unstimulating, moved programmed instruction to the background on the educational landscape.

However, during its short term as an educational innovation, the programmed instruction movement did manage to have a lasting impact on educational technology. It has, in fact, turned out to be the grandfather of subsequent approaches. Its methodical approach to the analysis of instruction, its rigorous statement of observable learning objectives, and its use of a systematic development process made it a forerunner to current systems approaches to designing instruction and selecting educational technologies. Programmed instruction empirically analyzed the data related to content and learner, identified strengths and weaknesses, adjusted the system accordingly, evaluated the resulting learning, and revised the system in accordance with the evaluation data. The logic and organized approach embodied in these steps ultimately gave rise to other individualized educational technology systems.

It was not until the advent of the microcomputer in the late 1970s that the concept of interactive individualized instruction introduced by programmed instruction could be fully realized. Because computers could be programmed to be interactive, to provide immediate feedback, and to allow students to navigate the material according to their own learning inclinations, educational technology entered a new era.

Computers made interactive, individualized instruction possible.

Computer-assisted instruction (CAI) broadly refers to the body of computer software that is the digital equivalent of the programmed instructional packages of the 1950s and 1960s. Early CAI was primarily text-based, drill-and-practice software; but as computing power expanded, so too did the capabilities of CAI. Today's CAI typically contains colorful graphics, easy navigation, and many instructional management features. Overall, however, the basic concepts of a systematic, organized, and responsive instructional system remain intact.

With the advent of powerful and inexpensive computers, early CAI programs have long since evolved into the powerful, multimedia programs available today that entice students to learn and support teachers' instructional efforts. Although still based on the theoretical foundations you have been introduced to in this chapter, today's educational technologies offer teachers an amazing array of teaching and learning support media from which to choose. This text is designed to introduce you to the full array of technologies you might select to help you teach and to help your students learn. How you choose to use these many and varied technologies will be your personal and professional decision.

CAI software can provide interactive learning experiences.

Teaching, Learning, and Educational Technology: A Personal Synthesis

To understand educational technology, you need to understand its role in support of the teaching-learning process. To understand the teaching-learning process, you need to understand teaching. To understand teaching, you need to understand communication and the participants in the communications cycle. To understand the participants, you need to understand the learner. To understand the learner, you need to understand learning theory and the factors that affect individual learning. This chapter has presented information related to each of these layers of understanding to help you lay a solid foundation on which to build your own personal framework for using educational technologies.

You must now synthesize the knowledge you have gained from this chapter into your own personal view of the teaching and learning process. You must decide how technology will fit into your teaching-learning model. You must consider what you have learned thus far and synthesize the following:

- Your own view of how students learn and how you should best communicate with them
- How best to assess the learning characteristics of your students
- How best to adapt your teaching style to your students' needs
- What you need to know to develop systematic and effective instruction
- How educational technology fits into your synthesized view of teaching and learning

Thinking about how you will apply these concepts is the first step toward really understanding what you need to do to be an effective educator.

Chapter 2 takes this process to its logical conclusion. Once you have developed your personal synthesized view of teaching, learning, and technology, you will be ready to explore the techniques that can make the job of designing effective instruction easier. Chapter 2 teaches you how to design effective instruction in order to focus your instructional efforts on making your teaching as meaningful as possible for your students. Further, the instructional design principles and skills that you will explore will enable you to incorporate educational technology in a manner that will be appropriate and effective for the learners you serve.

KEY TERMS

Association for Educational Communications and Technology (AECT)   5
behaviorists   14
cognitive style   18
cognitivists   15
communications cycle   10
computer-assisted instruction (CAI)   26
constructivists   15
decision matrix   10
educational technology   4
feedback   10
instructional events   7
intelligence   19
International Society for Technology in Education (ISTE)   5

IQ   19
learning environment   17
learning style   13
media   4
method   5
perspective   14
programmed instruction   26
stimulus-response   15
systems approach   23
teaching style   22
technologists   5
theories   7
Theory of Multiple Intelligences   20

KEY THEORISTS

David Ausubel   15
Albert Bandura   16
Katherine Briggs   18
Jerome Bruner   15
Robert Gagné   16
Howard Gardner   22
Isabel Briggs Myers   18

Seymour Papert   16
Ivan Pavlov   14
Jean Piaget   15
B. F. Skinner   14
Lev Vygotsky   16
John Watson   14

STUDENT ACTIVITIES

CHAPTER REVIEW

1. What is educational technology? How is it different when perceived by educators versus technologists?
2. What is the relationship between the teaching-learning process and educational technology?
3. What factors can affect effective communication? Explain how each can interfere with the sender's message.

4. Contrast the three perspectives on learning. How are they the same? How are they different? With which do you most agree?
5. Explain the difference between cognitive styles and learning styles. How might each affect learning?
6. Describe the Theory of Multiple Intelligences. How might this theory affect teaching?
7. What is a holistic approach to education? How might educational technology be viewed as a system?
8. How does the current view of educational technology differ from earlier views?
9. What is programmed instruction? What has been its impact on the current approach to educational technology?
10. Describe your synthesized view of teaching, learning, and technology.

WHAT DO YOU THINK?

1. Imagine that you are going to teach a unit on Christopher Columbus to the grade level of your choice. What immediately comes to mind as you consider how you might teach this unit? Is there any relationship between how you might want to teach this unit and your own learning or cognitive style? Describe how you think your own personal style might affect your teaching style.
2. Cultural filters can make a difference as to whether your message is communicated clearly. Considering the potential diversity of the students you will teach, imagine teaching a unit on how the U.S. president is elected. Analyze the possible cultural filters that you need to address to ensure that the lesson is communicated accurately. List these filters and suggest how you would overcome each.
3. You have learned about a variety of learning theories in this chapter. Which one of the theoretical frameworks are you most comfortable with? Explain why the theory you selected is most appealing to you.
4. For this course, the study of educational technology begins with a very close look at the teaching-learning process. Why do you think this is an important place to start?
5. In our Information Age, some educators believe that having computers in the classroom is just another educational fad, like the emphasis in the 1950s and 1960s on television in the classroom. Do you agree or disagree? Defend your answer.

LEARNING TOGETHER!

The following activities should be done in small groups.

1. Describe to your peers the teachers you have had that seem to fit into the theoretical frameworks described in this chapter. After each member of the group shares her or his experiences, select a single teacher from your collective experiences who best represents each learning theory. Summarize the teachers and the reasons they were selected. Be prepared to share your group's views with the class.
2. Select a single theorist to study in greater depth. In your group, explore the theorist's life, work, and theories. Prepare a summary of key points of interest to share in a group oral report to the rest of the class.
3. Visit a school classroom and media center to observe the technologies that are available in the spaces. Considering the historical trends in technology described in this chapter, where would you place the school in terms of its level of technological innovation? Share your observations with your group, and together build a snapshot of the state of technology in the average school today.

HANDS-ON!

1. On the Internet, visit three web sites that offer online learning styles and cognitive style instruments. Take these tests and compare the results. In a few paragraphs, summarize your own styles and describe how you think they will affect how you teach.
2. Examine software tutorials that might be considered computer-assisted instruction. Describe what you like and don't like about the software. What learning theory does the software use as its theoretical foundation? Explain your answer.
3. Using online library resources, research Howard Gardner's work on multiple intelligences. Examine information from people who agree with this theory and those who disagree. Summarize what you find on both positions. Conclude with your own position on multiple intelligences.

More from Sandra Burvikovs

Having considered the problem that Sandra Burvikovs described at the beginning of this chapter, you have had an opportunity to think of ways that she might have attempted to solve her problem of finding ways to meet the learning needs of her students. With the high expectations of the parents and the school expectations, she was able to reconsider the potential value of the technology her school had available but wasn't using. Did she take advantage of these opportunities? Did she try to solve her problem the way you would have done it? If not, was her way or your way better—or were they just different approaches? Well, let's ask her what she actually did.

As I mentioned at the beginning of this chapter, I believed that I could use technology to meet the individual learning needs of my students and thus do a better job of helping them meet the learning objectives that had been set for them. Therefore, I started inquiring about the availability of the district's laptop computers. I found that after a simple sign-up procedure, the computers were mine for a few hours each day. Unfortunately, there were only eight computers and my largest class had eighteen students. For the computers to work, I needed power connections as well as Internet connections, but I didn't have these on the gym stage. I found that if I placed the carts by the stage door, I could access the Internet connection in the gym office. Once connected, my students were able to start working on their projects. The Internet connection enabled them to search for additional information.

I know that an essential aspect of working with gifted students is to address the social and emotional needs of these children. As part of our curriculum, students work to identify their strengths and weaknesses and even address their passions. To accommodate these individual differences, the long-term project was developed with

both required elements and multiple options.

The students decided what elements they wanted to include with their technology component of the project, in addition to the computers. To accommodate different learning styles, students were given options that included videotaping their construction of models, conducting interviews, building models, designing booths in which to display their products, and recording informational audiotapes about their topics.

I developed technology goals for each grade level. Most of my second-grade students had a great deal of difficulty using a keyboard so they were only required to type part of the information that would be displayed on their posters. The third-grade students were ready to explore additional programs. These students used Inspiration, TimeLiner, and Kidspiration to help them display their information. I felt that the fourth- and fifth-grade students were capable of a more challenging project. My fourth-grade students loved seeing pictures of themselves, so I borrowed a digital camera from the Library Media Center and had the students take pictures of each other. The students then copied the images to Microsoft Word and, using Word-Art, added thought bubbles to express what the most important thing was that they had learned while researching. Given that this was one of my larger groups, the use of the digital camera allowed the class to work on different segments of the project at the same time and decreased the wait time for the computers.

I knew that my greatest challenge was going to be my fifth-grade group, because this was my largest group. I had the students work in small groups to develop PowerPoint presentations to share their research results. The final projects were well received by the parents; some were amazed at the creativity and level of proficiency that the students displayed in the projects.

Today, my students are in a regular classroom; they are taking part in a pilot program for replacement classes in math and reading. My classroom has access to two computer carts for a total of sixteen computers (all networked), a printer, and a TV and VCR; and I anticipate receiving five additional classroom computers and another printer. I also have one laptop computer connected to the Internet.

To accommodate the different skill levels, I established several stations where students can work at their own pace. They are able to access several Internet sites to review skills that are weak, use PowerPoint to share knowledge with students in their regular classroom, use Excel to create graphs and charts, and so on.

Overall, the technology that I was able to use last year and have begun using again this year has enabled my students to advance at a more appropriate level for their intellectual development and to find greater interest in their schoolwork, because the use of technology gave me a greater number of options, enabling me to match the students' learning activities with their individual learning styles.

For further information, contact Ms. Sandra Burvikovs at:
May Whitney Elementary School
120 Church Street
Lake Zurich, IL 60047
Email: sburvikovs@lz95.org

CHAPTER 2

Designing and Planning Technology-Enhanced Instruction

This chapter addresses these ISTE National Educational Technology Standards for Teachers:

II. Planning and designing learning environments and experiences

Teachers plan and design effective learning environments and experiences supported by technology. Teachers

A. design developmentally appropriate learning opportunities that apply technology-enhanced instructional strategies to support the diverse needs of learners.

B. apply current research on teaching and learning with technology when planning learning environments and experiences.

C. identify and locate technology resources and evaluate them for accuracy and suitability.

D. plan for the management of technology resources within the context of learning activities.

E. plan strategies to manage student learning in a technology-enhanced environment.

III. Teaching, learning, and the curriculum

Teachers implement curriculum plans that include methods and strategies for applying technology to maximize student learning. Teachers

A. facilitate technology-enhanced experiences that address content standards and student technology standards.

B. use technology to support learner-centered strategies that address the diverse needs of students.

C. apply technology to develop students' higher-order skills and creativity.

D. manage student learning activities in a technology-enhanced environment.

IV. Assessment and evaluation

Teachers apply technology in a variety of effective assessment and evaluation strategies. Teachers

A. apply technology in assessing student learning of subject matter using a variety of assessment techniques.

B. use technology resources to collect and analyze data, interpret results, and communicate findings to improve instructional practice and maximize student learning.

C. apply multiple methods of evaluation to determine students' appropriate use of technology resources for learning, communication, and productivity.

n Chapter 2, you will begin your exploration of the way in which effective teachers design and plan instruction enhanced and supported by technology. In Chapter 1, you learned a great deal about the teaching and learning process. Chapter 2 will help you discover how to apply what you have learned as you plan and carry out effective instruction.

In this chapter, you will examine learning environments, beginning with the physical aspects of the environment such as classroom layout and facilities. You will then have the opportunity to explore the less tangible, more critical aspects of the environment: the instructional design that drives instruction and the teaching strategies that might be incorporated in the design. You will then explore the planning of day-to-day lessons for use in your classroom. Finally, you will learn to create an instructional action plan to help ensure that your lessons are implemented just as you planned them.

In Chapter 2, you will

- Examine classroom facilities and their impact on the teaching and learning process

- Explore instructional design and how design affects instruction

- Examine performance objectives and their role in targeting learning outcomes

CHAPTER OUTLINE

- Review the instructional design process and the pedagogical cycle incorporated therein
- Examine the process of lesson planning
- Review the components of an instructional action plan and examine its role in the teaching and learning process
- Explore the role of planning in the selection and implementation of instructional technology

Meet Liz Brennan and Stacy Still

Planning may not be the most exciting part of teaching, but it is the most critical. Although the act of teaching and managing learning gives teachers the "rush" that makes teaching so rewarding, it can't happen without systematic planning. When the principal of a private elementary school recognized the difficulty teachers were experiencing as they tried to incorporate the use of technology into their lessons, she called on her technology facilitator to help solve the problem from a planning standpoint.

The principal will first describe the school and the problem one teacher faced, and then the technology facilitator will describe the challenge from the teacher's point of view. First let's hear from Liz, and then from Stacy.

OUR SETTING

University School of Nova Southeastern University is a campus-based, independent college preparatory day school located in Fort Lauderdale, Florida. The school enrolls approximately 1,600 students in prekindergarten through the twelfth grade and is situated on 17 acres of Nova Southeastern University's 250-acre main campus. The school's mission parallels that of the university, and its focus is upon educational experiences that are challenging, innovative, personalized, and technologically rich.

From the Principal's Perspective

I am Liz Brennan, associate head for academic affairs for University School of Nova Southeastern University. In my position, I am responsible for developing, monitoring, and evaluating long-range strategic school improvement plans. More specifically, as I am also the principal of the Lower School (grades prekindergarten through fifth), I am highly involved in overall divisional planning efforts as well as the more deliberate types of plans executed at the classroom level. I would estimate that at least 75 percent of the work I do each day involves curriculum design and development. Whenever we think of curriculum, we are also thinking *planning;* and one cannot think

planning without thinking *learning.* The concept of planning, for me as a professional, is paramount to the effectiveness of the school, because student learning is what it's all about. On a daily basis working with my faculty, I can see that, many times, issues with student learning can be connected to breakdowns in classroom curriculum design—in a word, planning. Starting with instructional plans at the classroom and/or lesson level and continuing on to plans for school-wide quality management, the nature of plans is the determining factor regarding how well we do what we say we will do.

From the Teacher's Perspective

My name is Stacy Still. I am the technology facilitator at the Lower School. There are many aspects to my job, but one of the most important functions involves ongoing professional development for faculty. This aspect includes technological skill training and development opportunities appropriate to teachers' individual needs and preferences. Another of the main responsibilities is to assist faculty in the planning of lessons that tie technology into the learning process. I typically try to blend staff development in two areas—computer literacy and instructional technology. So, as I work with teachers to develop their technical and operational skills, I try to focus on ways they can integrate various technologies into their daily classroom plans.

OUR CHALLENGE

University School teachers accept the premise that each child is unique in ability, talent, and learning style and recognize their responsibility in creating appropriate learning environments for all students. To that end, faculty must be responsive to planning that incorporates the school's intent to challenge students to perform, innovate the learning experiences, personalize students' instruction, and apply varied technological resources as part of "doing their jobs well." The challenge for teachers, therefore, becomes one of knowing how to create plans that do four things: reflect high standards and high expectations, activate inquiry and utilize creative procedures, originate with the needs of students, and integrate the many advances made in instructional technology—all at the same time!

From the Principal's Perspective

The problem involves a condition in which, despite her knowledge and skills in generic lesson planning, a teacher is unable to effectively or consistently "fit" appropriate uses of computer-based learning experiences into an already developed lesson plan. In addition, she may lack either the personal technical skills to feel comfortable with available hardware or an understanding of software options available either within the school or via the Internet. Whereas teachers are able to efficiently peruse and select paper and pencil materials for their lessons, the "new" time needed for planning for technology, becoming familiar with available resources, and reaching a comfort level with technological functions produces an obstacle to the design process.

From the Teacher's Perspective

I was recently approached by an elementary teacher who has been with the school for many years and has taught in many capacities. She came to me with a lesson on the rain forests of the world. Her original plan had been moderately effective in the past, but she felt that there was something missing that, if identified and included, would make the lesson even more effective. As this teacher reflected on the overall effectiveness of the original plan, she felt that a number of children had been less than successful in acquiring, retaining, and applying the concepts she hoped they would master. She believed there might be a weakness within her plan that was preventing her desired result.

Working collaboratively with teachers and with the support of the school principal, technology facilitators can offer classroom teachers valuable resources and support. But to take advantage of such resources, a teacher must have mastered the basics of planning. In this chapter you will learn planning fundamentals and the role of technology in instruction. Once you understand more about the intricacies of the instructional planning process, you will revisit Liz and Stacy to see how they accomplished their goal of helping a teacher plan for technology-rich instruction.

SOURCE: Interview with Liz Brennan and Stacy Still conducted by Al P. Mizell.

Building an Effective Learning Environment

As you learned in Chapter 1, a **learning environment** includes all conditions, circumstances, and influences that affect the learner's development. Every aspect of the milieu in which teaching and learning take place is an element in the learning environment, from the physical surroundings to the instructional events that occur within those surroundings. So let us begin our exploration of the learning environment with an examination of how physical space affects instruction.

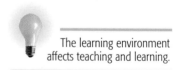

The learning environment affects teaching and learning.

The learning environment includes the space and facilities in which instruction occurs. The classroom or learning space itself, the student furniture and its arrangement in the instructional space, and the teaching facilities built into the classroom are all essential elements of the learning environment. Each can have a significant impact on the teaching-learning process. By adjusting these elements to be consistent with the students' learning styles and the educator's teaching style, the effectiveness of the instructional space can be maximized.

Rita and Kenneth Dunn have done extensive research on matching the physical environment to individual learning styles (Dunn and Dunn, 1992). Their learning styles research indicates that changes in lighting, seating, and other physical accommodations in the classroom can reduce distractions to the learning process by providing a sensory environment that accommodates individual preferences. They suggest that a teacher can readily improve the learning environment for students by making simple physical adjustments to the classroom. Such adjustments might include creating well-lit reading areas, arranging for areas of the classroom to be warmer or cooler than normal, establishing classroom sections in which students can work with a peer or a group, providing informal seating such as beanbags or a couch, and setting up

spotlight on

Dunn and Dunn

Rita Dunn, professor of administrative and instructional leadership and director of the Center for the Study of Learning and Teaching Styles at St. John's University, Jamaica, New York, has written, "Prize-winning research has made it clear that most children can master the curriculum when they're taught with strategies, methods or resources that complement how they learn" (1999). To identify students' learning style strengths, Rita and **Kenneth Dunn** created a chart to represent the five different elements that either stimulate or inhibit learning and constitute each individual's particular learning style. To capitalize on their learning styles, students must become aware of the following:

- Their reaction to the classroom environment—learning with sound or in silence, bright versus soft lighting, warm versus cool temperatures, and formal versus informal seating

- Their own emotionality—motivation, persistence and responsibility levels, and preference for structure versus options

- Their sociological preferences for learning—either alone, with peers, with a collegial or authoritative adult, and/or in a variety of ways as opposed to patterns or routines
- Their physiological characteristics—perceptual strengths (auditory, visual, tactual, and/or kinesthetic modalities), time-of-day energy highs and lows, intake (snacking or sipping while concentrating), and/or mobility needs
- Their global versus analytic processing, as determined through correlations among sound, light, design, persistence, sociological preference, and intake

---

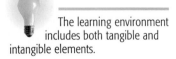

ON THE WEB! 2.1
Learning Styles and the Environment

The learning environment includes both tangible and intangible elements.

quiet or screened study areas for individuals or pairs. These adjustments can be accomplished through creative use of the floor space and traditional furniture found in most classrooms.

To adjust the physical learning space to maximize its compatibility with learners, it is important to first carefully identify the learning styles of the learners. Dunn and Dunn, among others, have a comphrehensive assessment tool for that purpose. Once learning styles have been identified, teachers should creatively rethink their instructional space, carefully plan changes, and be ready to observe the impact these changes have on student learning.

However, the learning environment also includes nonphysical components. Our definition suggests that all conditions, circumstances, and influences that affect students are also a part of the environment. How you conduct the teaching and learning process; the strategies and technologies you use to encourage learning; the plan for interaction among students and between teacher and student; your assessment techniques; and the roles you play as teacher, coach, and facilitator are all parts of the learning environment.

As an educator, you are responsible for building and maintaining the best possible learning environment for your students. To do so, it will be necessary to take the time to create a systematic plan that will ensure that each step you take, whether adjusting the physical environment or altering an instructional component, adds to the effectiveness of the learning environment. Just as a house requires a plan and specific blueprints before construction actually begins, so too must the learning environment be conceptualized and planned, and a set of instructional blueprints must be created. The processes involved in this type of systematic planning include instructional design, lesson planning, and instructional action planning. Exploration of and practice with each of these processes will provide you with the skill set that you will need to create effective learning environments.

Using an Instructional Planning System

Effective instruction is instruction that has been thoroughly thought out and articulated by a skillful and creative educator. To ensure that every moment of a learner's educational time is productive, an educator must envision a well-conceptualized learning environment in which teaching and learning will occur. The notion of a carefully planned, step-by-step process to design, create, evaluate, and revise instruction is called a **systems approach** to instruction. In the remainder of this chapter, you will explore a comprehensive three-part system that will help you maximize the quality of your teaching. The system, called the **design-plan-act! (D-P-A) system,** includes the following three planning processes (see Figure 2.1):

Design-Plan-Act! for better instruction.

1. Design: Designing the instruction
2. Plan: Articulating specific lesson plans
3. Act: Developing an instructional action plan

Together, these three system elements will help you effectively plan and implement all aspects of the learning environment and the activities that will take place within it.

The Design Phase

At this most comprehensive and strategic level of the instructional planning system, the educator envisions the delivery of the targeted curriculum in its entirety. This is the design phase of the system. All aspects of the learning environment are considered, and decisions are made with regard to each step of the teaching and learning process. Although specific details might not yet be determined, the instructional design articulates all of the broad steps that must be taken to ensure that the intended instruction occurs as conceived. Typically, an **instructional design model,** a fully articulated design template, is used to help educators in the first phase of the planning system to envision their planned instruction holistically. Using such a model as a foundation, you will ultimately be able to develop an effective daily lesson plan and a subsequent instructional action plan.

Design identifies overall goals and the steps to achieve them.

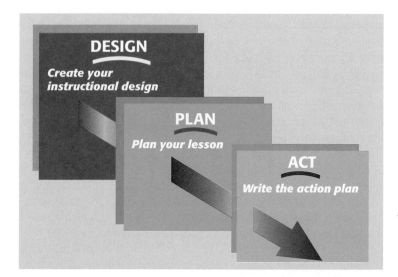

Figure 2.1
The Design-Plan-Act! (D-P-A) System
D-P-A's three system components work together to create effective instructional events.

Because this chapter specifically targets technology-enhanced instruction, the instructional design model that is used must be flexible and adaptable to accommodate the continual changes in strategies that are supported and enhanced by technology. To that end, on the following pages, the **dynamic instructional design (DID) model** is presented. It will serve as the basis for designing technology-rich instruction and as a practical guide as you conceptualize how you will create an effective learning environment for your students. The DID model will serve as the foundation for the creation of two additional tools, a lesson planner and instructional action planner, that you can use to help you plan to teach effectively and successfully in your classrooms.

The Dynamic Instructional Design Model

The Dynamic Instructional Design (DID) model is a flexible system for designing instruction.

ON THE WEB! 2.2
Spotlight on Robert Gagné

Feedback is the return of information regarding the success of each step.

The DID model includes all of the critical elements in the design of effective instruction. Every step of the model is crucial to the process and must be considered carefully. Just as the architectural process must begin with an understanding of the qualities of the land on which a building will be built and must proceed through discussions of the purpose and use of the building before any plans are made, so too must educators think broadly and strategically about their intended instruction. Although this process might initially seem somewhat laborious, effective educators eventually internalize these steps and find that they become the essence of how they approach the design of instruction.

A number of instructional design systems models are available for educators to follow. The most pervasive and influential of these is the systems model originally developed by **Robert Gagné.** Known for the application of systems thinking to instructional design, Gagné is perhaps the leading figure in instructional design systems. He was the first to promote and develop a comprehensive systems view of instructional design, that is, a system of steps that provide a logical systematic foundation for designing instruction. His definitive work is the foundation for many subsequent models.

Gagné's model and the others that were developed as a result are the foundation for today's instructional design systems. The DID model, which builds on these definitive systems models, differs primarily in its emphasis on a dynamic design, which is necessary to represent the capability for continuous adjustment and change. The instructional design must be flexible enough to embrace and use data provided by ongoing feedback from learners. The DID model is specifically designed to ensure that responsiveness while maintaining the logical sequencing of the design process.

The DID model is therefore built around a continuous internal and external feedback loop to ensure that each step of the process is functioning at its maximum effectiveness. Internal feedback loops occur within each step of the process. External loops are built between all steps of the process. Continual self-examination, feedback, and correction are built into the model to emphasize its flexibility while maintaining its system integrity. Although each step of the process includes the classic elements articulated initially by Gagné, the DID model is designed to help educators envision instruction as a changing and dynamic process.

Teachers who embrace a systems approach such as the D-P-A system better understand and are better able to envision the instructional big picture. They start with a conception of all the instructional elements necessary for effective teaching and learning and of the relationship of these elements to each other. From this strategic beginning, they can then narrow and refocus their efforts on lesson planning, through which they can specify the instructional events that fill in and flesh out their design. Finally, they reach the pragmatic stage, during which they articulate an instructional action plan or to-do list for making the instructional events flow flawlessly. The DID model is the first step in this process: the design step.

As you review the DID model illustrated in Figure 2.2, note that a formative feedback process is a component of each step. **Formative feedback** is feedback that occurs during an event or process. Formative feedback ensures a way to facilitate the continuous flow of information as a system is implemented so that corrections and adjustments can be made while the process unfolds. The DID model includes a formative **feedback loop** during every step of the process so that feedback responses can be gathered and midcourse corrections can be made. In implementation of the model, this would mean that even as the design process is under way or while instruction is being implemented, the designer would remain flexible and responsive. The ability to respond quickly to feedback reflects the necessity to be responsive to the situational or technological changes in the environment. Thus, each step is dynamic and flexible; that is, each step remains a work in process throughout and after the design phase of the plan.

Additionally, summative feedback is built into the DID model. **Summative feedback** is feedback that is returned at the end of a process. In the DID model, the summative feedback loop can return information to help revise each step of the process once the entire process is completed. Because formative feedback is continuous throughout all steps of the process, the summative feedback loop serves as a final check once all steps are completed.

The feedback loops of the DID model encourage you to create a dynamic instructional process that remains responsive even as you are actively engaged in planning and implementing the instruction. In this model, you are encouraged to think about how you intend to continuously correct and improve each step. Rather than simply completing a step and going on to the next, this model incorporates an internal process for continuous improvement. Such a continuous improvement process is at

Formative feedback occurs while the learning event is in progress.

Summative feedback occurs at the conclusion of the learning event.

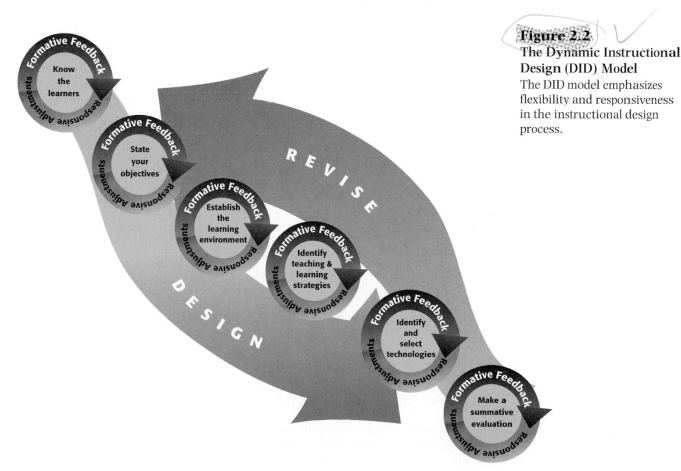

Figure 2.2
The Dynamic Instructional Design (DID) Model
The DID model emphasizes flexibility and responsiveness in the instructional design process.

TABLE 2.1   DID Formative and Summative Feedback Loops

DID Step	Formative Feedback Questions	Summative Feedback Questions
	Questions to Ask during the Design Process	Questions to Ask at the End of the Design Process
1. KNOW THE LEARNERS	• Am I responding to all learning styles? • Am I accurately depicting the students' developmental stages? • Am I correctly assessing student skill levels?	Did the design successfully meet the needs of the learners?
2. STATE YOUR OBJECTIVES	• Are my objectives targeting the performances I intended? • Are my objectives stated in a format that makes it possible to accurately measure performance? • Do my objectives include multiple levels of Bloom's taxonomy?	Did my objectives accurately capture, in performance terms, the essence of the content the students needed to learn?
3. ESTABLISH THE LEARNING ENVIRONMENT	• Does the physical space I am planning offer sufficient diversity to meet learner needs? • Is the environment nurturing and secure for all students? • Does the class management system promote positive and productive interaction? • Am I planning student and teacher exchanges that support and enhance learning?	Was the learning environment that I established effective in promoting learning?
4. IDENTIFY TEACHING AND LEARNING STRATEGIES	• Am I addressing all of the steps of the pedagogical cycle? • Does each step make sense in terms of the cycle and the student learning it is intended to promote? • Am I including sufficiently varied teaching strategies and learning activities to meet the needs of my diverse students?	Are the teaching and learning strategies sufficient for and effective in meeting the objectives I identified?
5. IDENTIFY AND SELECT TECHNOLOGIES	• Are the technologies I have selected appropriate to the content and pedagogy? • Am I selecting a variety of technologies that will meet the diversity of learning styles? • Are the technologies and support materials readily available?	Were the technologies I selected successful in supporting the targeted teaching and learning?
6. PERFORM A SUMMATIVE EVALUATION	• Am I identifying a method of assessment that will measure achievement of objectives? • Is the data to be gathered from the assessment useful to determine necessary revisions? • Are the evaluation techniques valid and reliable with reference to the design?	Does the summative evaluation provide the data I need to determine whether the objectives were achieved? Was the data sufficient for effective revision?

the core of high-quality instruction. Table 2.1 shows how formative feedback and summative feedback are used at each step in the DID model.

Let's examine how each step contributes to the design phase. Typically, these steps are initially taken in the sequence presented, but as any new information comes to light as a result of ongoing feedback, it may be necessary to step out of the sequence to respond and adjust. The DID model is designed to encourage this flexibility.

Step 1: Know the Learners

To begin the process of designing instruction, you must first have a clear picture of those for whom the instruction is being created. As much as possible, instruction must be adjusted to ensure that it is the most appropriate sequence of events for those who stand to benefit from experiencing those events. To successfully focus instruction in this way, you must begin by carefully examining the characteristics of your learners. To do so, you will need to ask yourself a number of questions about your learners. You may also have additional questions based on the instructional setting in which you are teaching. A few of the most common questions that lead to careful examination of your learners are the following:

- What are their developmental stages, both physically and cognitively?
- What are their cultural or language backgrounds that may affect how instruction is received?
- What are their incoming skills and knowledge base relative to the intended instruction?
- What are their individual characteristics, such as learning styles, cognitive styles, and types of intelligence?
- As a group, how are the learners the same and how are they different?
- How might these similarities or differences affect the design of the intended instruction?

Each of these questions must be answered to the extent possible to establish a clear picture of the learners for whom you are designing instruction. The more accurate your examination and assessment of your learners, the more likely that the instruction will be appropriate and successful. Your answers may be informal, that is, based simply on your observations of your students or discussions with them, or your answers may be formal, that is, derived from objective data. Such data may be from student records kept by your school or gathered by you using assessment tools such as the learning style inventories you learned about in Chapter 1. The more information you gather, whether formal or informal, the more likely that your instruction will be targeted correctly to meet the needs of your students. Table 2.2 shows some factors to consider in learning about your learners.

Use formal and informal methods to profile students.

Remember that at any time during or after completing this first step, you must be ready to adjust your conclusions. As the design process continues, new information may come to light, or, through feedback, you may discover that some of your conclusions about your learners need adjustment. Staying flexible and ready to alter each of the components of the process is a key element in maximizing your instruction's potential for success.

Students are diverse in many ways, including how they learn.

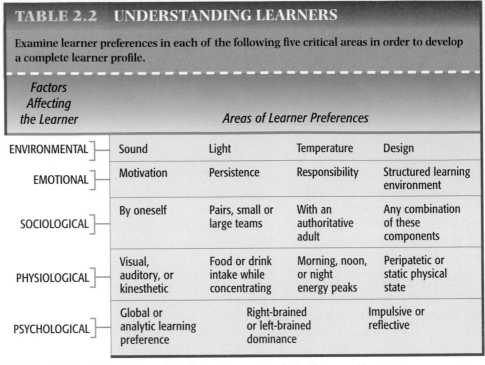

Factors Affecting the Learner	Areas of Learner Preferences			
ENVIRONMENTAL	Sound	Light	Temperature	Design
EMOTIONAL	Motivation	Persistence	Responsibility	Structured learning environment
SOCIOLOGICAL	By oneself	Pairs, small or large teams	With an authoritative adult	Any combination of these components
PHYSIOLOGICAL	Visual, auditory, or kinesthetic	Food or drink intake while concentrating	Morning, noon, or night energy peaks	Peripatetic or static physical state
PSYCHOLOGICAL	Global or analytic learning preference	Right-brained or left-brained dominance	Impulsive or reflective	

SOURCE: "How Do We Teach Them If We Don't Know How They Learn?" in *Teaching K–8, 29*(7):50–52.

Step 2: State Your Objectives

Performance objectives detail expected competencies.

Objectives are statements of what will be achieved as a result of the instruction you are designing. **Performance objectives** are objectives that specify what the learner will be able to do when the instructional event concludes. To keep your instructional design focused on helping the learner to achieve competencies or skills, it is critical that you take the time to state your instructional objectives in terms of student performance. This step will keep all subsequent steps tightly targeted on student outcomes.

Performance objectives typically include a stem plus three key components: targeted student performance, a description of the method for assessing the intended performance, and a criterion for measuring success. Let's examine a performance objective for a grammar unit in a middle school language arts class.

Objective: The student will be able to identify, with 95 percent accuracy, the subject and the verb in sentences contributed by peers and written on the board.

- *Stem:* The student will be able to
- *Target performance:* identify the subject and verb
- *Measurement conditions:* in sentences contributed by peers and written on the board
- *Criterion for success:* with 95 percent accuracy.

Notice that in this objective, the critical factor is the performance expected of the *student* as a result of the anticipated instruction, not the performance of the teacher. In our example, the student is going to be able to perform a measurable action, that is, *identify* targeted knowledge. In this case, the targeted knowledge is the concept of subject and verb. Furthermore, the objective indicates the method that will be used to assess performance. Again in our example, success in identifying the target concepts will be measured by the student's correctly identifying the subject and verb in sen-

connecting THEORY to PRACTICE

How to Know the Learner

To design a ninth-grade instructional unit on *Hamlet,* the DID model begins with an exploratory examination to ascertain the students' educational and cultural backgrounds as well as their dominant learning modalities. For example, the following steps should be taken to know the learners before designing this unit:

Assess reading levels: From in-class assessment or from guidance records, the students' reading levels need to be determined to assess how much of a stumbling block Elizabethan English will pose and what prelearning activities need to be given (plot synopsis, modern context, and anticipation questions to tap into students' experiential backgrounds).

Determine learning styles/dominant intelligences: Learning styles and intelligences should be identified through in-class

assessments or student records so that the instructional activities can be designed to enable all the students to successfully learn from the unit.

Summarize cultural backgrounds: Backgrounds are important because of the impact that the play's topics of suicide and non-traditional families have on students from different cultures. School records can provide much of this information. However, classroom observation, as well as formal or informal in-class assessments, can fill in any gaps to better construct an accurate picture of the learner. Constructivist learning theory is the primary rationale for determining learner characteristics, because of the theory's emphasis on customized instruction that builds on the knowledge and experiential backgrounds of the students.

---

tences contributed by peers and written on the board. Finally, the criterion that indicates success in achieving that objective, that is, performing the action correctly 95 percent of the time, is articulated. Thus, in our example, a student who mistakes the

subject and verb 5 percent of the time would still be considered to have sufficiently mastered the target knowledge. Objectives written in this format leave no doubt about what performance is expected of the student. This, in turn, leaves

The Components of a Performance Objective

The student will be able to identify latitude and longitude lines on a map with 100% accuracy.

STEM	TARGET PERFORMANCE	MEASUREMENT CONDITIONS	CRITERION FOR SUCCESS

no doubt about what the teacher needs to teach for the designated outcomes to occur.

This focus on student outcomes and resultant direction for the teacher is the function of fully articulated performance objectives. These objectives not only detail precisely what the student is supposed to learn and how such learning is to be measured, they also require that teachers stay centered on outcomes in their teaching. Generic objectives such as "The student will have an understanding of grammar" do little to assist the teacher in deciding what and how to teach. Furthermore, it is difficult to accurately measure something as broad as "understanding." Such overly broad objectives help neither teacher nor student to engage in a meaningful exchange. They do not assist either party in focusing on the task at hand. Indeed, they confuse what needs to happen in the learning environment and in the teaching-learning process.

Another role of performance objectives is to ensure that the teaching and learning experience includes a full range of cognitive levels, from simple recall of facts to higher-end critical thinking. Writing down performance objectives identifies exactly which skills and related cognition the teacher is targeting. If all objectives are recall objectives, that is, their outcome is the memorization of facts, it is clear before instruction begins that critical thinking and higher cognitive skills are being ignored. This is a significant loss in terms of student growth, although it is admittedly sometimes easier for a teacher to plan when the goal is to achieve lower-level objectives. Designing instruction that targets higher-order thinking skills is a much more complex task than

Use action verbs to describe expected performance.

ON THE WEB! 2.3
Examples of Performance Objectives

Bloom's taxonomy describes levels of cognition. A taxonomy is a system of levels to better organize a concept.

ON THE WEB! 2.4
Spotlight on Benjamin Bloom

asking your students to recall facts. However, the benefit to learners of engaging in such tasks far outweighs the instructional costs involved in creating them.

Several theorists have developed methods for categorizing differences in thinking skills. One of the most prominent was developed in 1956 by a group of researchers led by **Benjamin Bloom.** The categories of cognition that resulted from their efforts have come to be called **Bloom's taxonomy.** Bloom's taxonomy (Bloom, 1956) provides a very useful delineation of the levels of thinking that should be included in creating objectives. These levels do not interfere with the knowledge outcomes of the objectives. Instead, they help you identify the level of thinking desired from the learner with regard to that knowledge.

Bloom's taxonomy includes six levels of cognition ranging from recall of knowledge to evaluation of knowledge (see Figure 2.3). Each of these levels is described in the following list, along with action verbs that might be used in objectives that are aimed at that level of thinking.

- *Knowledge:* This level of cognition includes memorizing, recognizing, or recalling factual information. Objectives at the knowledge level would include verbs such as *list, identify, name, recite, state,* and *define* with reference to the material.
- *Comprehension:* At this level of cognition, the emphasis is on organizing, describing, and interpreting concepts. Verbs used in objectives at the comprehension level might include *explain, illustrate, summarize, restate, paraphrase,* and *defend* concepts or information. You can see that the thinking required at this level extends beyond rote learning.
- *Application:* The application level of cognition requires that the student apply the information presented, solve problems with it, and find new ways of using it. Objective verbs that would represent outcomes at this level of thinking would include *apply, classify, demonstrate, discover, predict, show, solve,* and *utilize.*

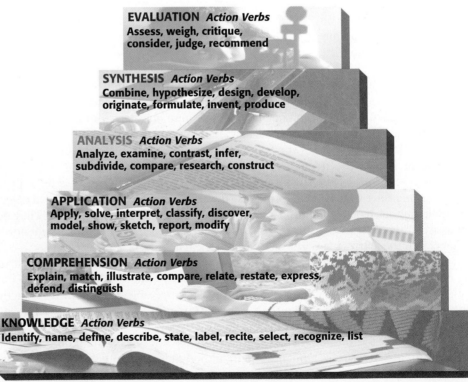

EVALUATION *Action Verbs*
Assess, weigh, critique, consider, judge, recommend

SYNTHESIS *Action Verbs*
Combine, hypothesize, design, develop, originate, formulate, invent, produce

ANALYSIS *Action Verbs*
Analyze, examine, contrast, infer, subdivide, compare, research, construct

APPLICATION *Action Verbs*
Apply, solve, interpret, classify, discover, model, show, sketch, report, modify

COMPREHENSION *Action Verbs*
Explain, match, illustrate, compare, relate, restate, express, defend, distinguish

KNOWLEDGE *Action Verbs*
Identify, name, define, describe, state, label, recite, select, recognize, list

Figure 2.3
Bloom's Taxonomy and Action Verbs
Use Bloom's taxonomy to step up to higher levels of thinking.

SOURCE: Loosely adapted from Bloom's wheel at **http://www.vacadsci.org/teaching/bwheel.htm**.

- *Analysis:* This level of the taxonomy requires higher-level thinking skills such as finding underlying structures, separating the whole into its components, identifying motives, and recognizing hidden meanings. Verbs used in objectives at this level might include *analyze, ascertain, diagram, differentiate, discriminate, examine, determine, investigate, construct,* and *contrast.*
- *Synthesis:* The synthesis level raises desired outcomes to significantly higher levels of cognition. At this level, the student is expected to create an original product based on the knowledge acquired, combine the ideas presented into a new whole, or relate knowledge from several areas into a consistent concept. Action verbs in objectives at the synthesis level would include *combine, compile, create, design, develop, expand, integrate, extend, originate, synthesize,* and *formulate.*
- *Evaluation:* The highest level of cognition in Bloom's taxonomy is the evaluation level. At this level, the learner is expected to make thoughtful value decisions with reference to the knowledge; resolve differences and controversy; and develop personal opinions, judgments, and decisions. Objective verbs at this level would include *assess, critique, judge, appraise, evaluate, weigh,* and *recommend.*

As you can see from the taxonomy, each level ratchets up the cognition required for successful achievement of the objective. Outcomes at the highest levels require significant levels of critical thinking. At the lowest level, knowledge, simple memorization is all that is required. However, after examining Table 2.3, you will see that

TABLE 2.3   BLOOM'S TAXONOMY AND PERFORMANCE OBJECTIVES

Level	Description	Performance Objective	Example Activity
KNOWLEDGE	Student recalls or recognizes information, ideas, and principles in the approximate form in which they are learned.	On an unlabeled diagram, the student will be able to label the parts of the human eye with 85 percent accuracy.	Using a model of the human eye, students attach sticky notes with the names of the parts correctly attached.
COMPREHENSION	Student translates or comprehends information based on prior learning.	In an oral presentation, the student will be able to summarize the plot of *The Lion, the Witch, and the Wardrobe,* mentioning at least five of the seven major events.	Students brainstorm a "this happened, then this happened" synopsis of the action. The teacher lists the events on the board for a discussion of plot elements.
APPLICATION	Student selects, transfers, and uses data and principles to complete a problem or task with a minimum of direction.	On a performance assessment test, the student will be able to demonstrate knowledge of graphing calculators by solving three out of five problems correctly.	A demonstration of the parts and uses of a graphing calculator is shown on an LCD panel, computer, or electronic whiteboard with interactive input from students.
ANALYSIS	Student differentiates or examines the assumptions, hypotheses, evidence, or structure of a statement or question.	In a 500-word essay, the student will be able to infer the metaphysical meaning of Byron's "Sonnet on Chillon," analyzing the connotative value of two of the four symbols.	Students are given a handout with familiar symbols on it and are asked what ideas or concepts the symbols suggest to them. A discussion follows on these associations.
SYNTHESIS	Student originates, integrates, and combines ideas into a product, plan, or proposal that is new to him or her.	For a piano performance, the student will be able to compose a concerto consisting of at least two of the traditional movements.	Students listen to Beethoven's *Emperor Concerto* and discuss the differences in the movements and how they work together to create a unified whole.
EVALUATION	Student appraises, assesses, or critiques a work or works using specific standards or other criteria.	Using a rubric created by the students, the student will be able to critique sample media on the basis of five criteria with 90 percent accuracy.	In small groups, students select five criteria they will use to decide whether recent movies, television programs, or live performances are good.

the lower levels are a necessary prerequisite as you move up the taxonomy. For example, one must know the facts to comprehend, apply, analyze, synthesize, or evaluate them. Although some performance objectives may reasonably target the lowest levels, too often a majority of objectives aim only at these levels. Awareness and application of Bloom's taxonomy in writing performance objectives will help you to create instruction that encourages and emphasizes a broad range of thinking skills for your students.

Clearly and concisely articulating the performance objectives is the second step of the DID model. Because the model emphasizes the dynamic nature of instructional design, you must remain flexible and ready to adjust your objectives if you find that they do not keep you sufficiently focused on the target skills, concepts, or levels of cognition you intended. Furthermore, if the method or criterion for measuring success that you included in an objective does not ultimately provide an accurate indicator of student success, it is crucial to alter the objective itself even while the process is continuing. Monitoring the effectiveness of the objectives you have written is an important internal feedback mechanism in the DID model. Because your objectives provide the foundation for all subsequent design decisions, their accuracy and validity are critical. As in all steps in the DID, you should be sure to establish and respond to a process for formative evaluation of the objectives themselves.

The DID's formative feedback loop ensures performance objective validity.

Step 3: Establish the Learning Environment

As was indicated earlier in this chapter, the learning environment includes all of the physical and educational components that support teaching and learning. To be effective in implementing this step, you should first take inventory of the physical space in which learning occurs. Table 2.4 provides a rubric for assessing the learning space. It is important to provide, whenever possible, alternatives in terms of learners' sensory preferences. For example, alternative seating arrangements and lighting intensities should be made available. Rigid one-size-fits-all physical facilities will not meet the needs of many learners and may impede their learning. It might not be feasible to make all the adjustments you desire, but if you make every possible effort to become aware of and adjust your teaching and learning space, you will help to optimize the conditions for your students' learning. As always, the dynamic nature of the DID model requires that you remain vigilant in assessing the effectiveness of your arrangement of the physical space. Observation of the impact of the space on students as they engage in learning activities and on student performance is an important feedback tool that will help you continually monitor and adjust the learning environment.

ON THE WEB! 2.5
Creating a Learning Environment

Nonphysical aspects of the learning environment include the general academic climate of the classroom, the dominant attitudes of learners and the instructor, and the quality of instructional organization provided by effective planning. The general climate of the classroom refers to the tone of the psychological environment in which the teaching and learning process occurs. For effective instruction, learners need a safe, nurturing environment that offers opportunities to engage in learning and to excel. Friendly competition and gentle but persistent attainable challenges are valuable motivators for learners. Too often, the classroom climate is passive and nonengaging. Some students remain unchallenged, while others may feel overwhelmed. Awareness of the nature of the classroom cli-

A classroom with diverse instructional spaces.

mate will help you continually monitor and adjust it to maximize its support of teaching and learning. Once again, use the learning environment rubric (Table 2.4) to help you focus on those components that should be observed and adjusted for.

Research has demonstrated that the attitudes of learners and of the teacher directly affect student performance (Dunn, 1999). Therefore, a component of designing instruction must be a deliberate effort to ensure that the learning environment fosters positive, confident attitudes on the part of the learner. Furthermore, it is important to ensure that the teacher's words and actions reflect a positive, caring attitude. However, with the pressures of school life, it is all too easy to shift emphasis away from this affective aspect of instruction and to focus instead on completing the planned lesson. To create an effective learning environment, it is important to stay aware of the steps you are taking to encourage attitudes that nurture learning rather than hinder it. The learning environment rubric will assist you in maintaining the level of awareness necessary to implement this step of the DID process with maximum benefit to the learner.

A rubric is a detailed rating scale that can help you make objective evaluations and assessments.

The final aspect of the nonphysical learning environment relates to the organization of the learning process itself. Well-conceived and clearly articulated instructional

TABLE 2.4   LEARNING ENVIRONMENT RUBRIC

Using the criteria below, evaluate the effectiveness of the learning environment across each dimension. Highlight the box that best reflects the learning space with reference to the evaluation dimension. Effective learning environments are those that score 4 or higher in most dimensions.

Dimension	1 Poor	2 Below Average	3 Average	4 Above Average	5 Excellent
Physical space	Space is not arranged in an orderly manner and does not promote active learning and positive interaction.	Space is arranged neatly and safely but does not address individual learner needs.	Space is adjusted to the learning style of some but not all learners. Space arrangement promotes safety and some interaction.	Space meets the needs of most learners. Arrangement clearly promotes safety and positive interaction.	Space has been maximally adjusted to meet learner diversity. Space arrangement promotes interactivity, active learning, and positive interaction.
Classroom climate	Climate is not flexible and responsive to learners. Climate promotes strong competitiveness and does not sufficiently foster cooperation or active learning.	Climate is somewhat flexible to learners. Learner is somewhat nurtured. Competitiveness exceeds cooperation. Active learning is insufficiently emphasized.	Climate is sufficiently flexible. Learner is nurtured to a moderate degree. Competitiveness is equaled by cooperation. Active learning is present.	Climate is flexible and meets most learners' needs. Minimal competitiveness is in evidence. Active learning is supported.	Classroom climate is flexible and meets diverse learners' needs. Cooperation is emphasized without loss of healthy competition. Active learning is emphasized.
Attitudes	Teacher attitude is usually cold and tends toward criticism and negativity. Learners typically demonstrate lack of self-confidence and self-criticism.	Teacher attitude is inconsistent and is often negative. Learners demonstrate inconsistency and ambivalence about their capability and self-worth.	Teacher attitude includes both positive and negative components. Learners demonstrate some confidence and self-worth.	Teacher attitude is mostly positive, friendly, and nurturing. Students appear confident and are usually risk takers.	Teacher attitude is consistently positive and encouraging. Teacher is always friendly and nurturing. Students demonstrate confidence and are clearly willing to be risk takers.

 This and other downloadable forms and templates can be found on the Companion Website at www.ablongman.com/lever-duffy.

connecting THEORY to PRACTICE

Targeting Learning with Performance-Based Objectives

For a unit on early writing systems and their significance in understanding the development of past civilizations for a middle school language arts class, performance objectives will provide the students with a clear description of the educational outcomes that are expected of them. The objectives are written in four parts: the stem, target performance, measurement conditions, and a criterion for success. Following are the theoretical bases of sample performance objectives:

* **Behaviorism:** *Knowing what* (Mergel, 1998). Knowledge competency objectives are associated primarily with behaviorism.

  (Example) On a selected response test, the students will be able to identify the areas where earliest writing developed, with 85 percent accuracy.

* **Cognitivism:** *Knowing how* (Mergel, 1998). Comprehension and application competency objectives generally reflect cognitivist theory.

  (Example) In a 500-word essay, students will be able to explain how alphabetic writing differs from hieroglyphics and cuneiform, mentioning at least four of the six points of contrast.

* **Constructivism:** *Dealing with defined problems through reflection in action* (Mergel, 1998). The competencies of synthesis and evaluation are characteristic of constructivism.

  (Example) Using presentation software, students will be able to draw conclusions about what life would be like with no writing systems, showing at least six slides.

SOURCE: B. Mergel, "Instructional Design & Learning Theory," **www.usask.ca**.

---

plans will create an organized, cohesive environment that fosters learning. Although this might seem to be common sense, all too often the pressures of time and tasks cause teachers to skip steps that are necessary for instructional success. Teachers who do not apply instructional design principles and who do not carry these through to sound lesson plans often find the learning environment turning chaotic and frustrating to both learner and teacher. Just as you would plan a house before you begin building, you must plan instruction before implementing it. Taking the time and energy to carefully plan instruction will make the teaching-learning process smooth and effective. Of course, once the instruction is planned, the DID model requires that you constantly monitor it for improvement based on the continuous feedback received. The dynamic nature of instruction makes it imperative to constantly gather data to validate what you are doing and to continually adjust all aspects of the instructional organization accordingly.

Well-designed lesson plans improve teaching and learning.

Step 4: Identify Teaching and Learning Strategies

At this point in the process, you have a high degree of awareness of your learners and their needs, your instructional objectives are clear and stated in terms of the desired student outcomes, and the learning environment has been established. Now it is time to decide on your teaching strategies. **Teaching strategies** are the methods you will use to assist your students in achieving the objectives. As you learned in Chapter 1, both teacher and learner are involved in this process, so it is important to consider both the teaching strategies and the learning strategies you intend to employ. **Learning strategies** are the techniques and activities that you will require your students to engage in to master the content.

The combination and implementation of planned teaching and learning strategies is sometimes referred to as pedagogy. **Pedagogy** is the actual function of teaching, or what teachers do when implementing their craft to assist their students' learning. A series of events that are pedagogically sound are those that are appropriate to the learning environment and that result in the students' successful achievement of the stated objectives. One way of thinking about teaching and learning strategies is to consider them components of a **pedagogical cycle** that is played out again and again as a lesson is implemented. This cycle and its eight steps are described in Figure 2.4.

The quantity of information provided in a lesson must be subdivided into manageable chunks relating to the specific performances desired before the information is introduced to students. Otherwise, the learners may be overcome by the sheer quantity of knowledge and may shut down or suffer confusion. Each information chunk may need to be handled in a unique way to be effectively communicated to students. One cycle is required for the introduction of each chunk. Once the learners have absorbed it, the next chunk is introduced. Thus the cycle is repeated again and again in the classroom. Planning what to do at each step of the cycle is the way you determine the teaching and learning strategies you intend to use. Examine carefully the pedagogical cycle illustrated in Figure 2.4 to help you complete the fourth step of the DID model.

When identifying teaching strategies, it is important to clearly understand the difference between methods and the media that support them. **Methods** are the actions and activities that a teacher uses to communicate a concept. Table 2.5 on page 51 summarizes the teaching methods that are most frequently used in the classroom.

The methods you select should address the needs and learning styles of your students. They should offer alternative ways of explaining and exploring the information presented. The methods you select should keep your learners active and engaged in learning. Concepts should be carefully matched with the most appropriate methods for communicating them. Selecting the right teaching method for the knowledge is one of the most creative activities in which a teacher engages. The right method or combination of methods is one of the keys to achieving the lesson objectives.

Figure 2.4
The Pedagogical Cycle
Each step in the cycle contributes to successful student learning.

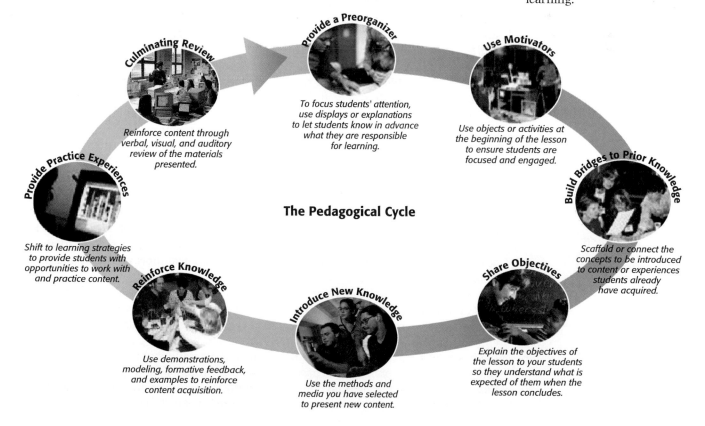

The Pedagogical Cycle

Provide a Preorganizer
To focus students' attention, use displays or explanations to let students know in advance what they are responsible for learning.

Use Motivators
Use objects or activities at the beginning of the lesson to ensure students are focused and engaged.

Build Bridges to Prior Knowledge
Scaffold or connect the concepts to be introduced to content or experiences students already have acquired.

Share Objectives
Explain the objectives of the lesson to your students so they understand what is expected of them when the lesson concludes.

Introduce New Knowledge
Use the methods and media you have selected to present new content.

Reinforce Knowledge
Use demonstrations, modeling, formative feedback, and examples to reinforce content acquisition.

Provide Practice Experiences
Shift to learning strategies to provide students with opportunities to work with and practice content.

Culminating Review
Reinforce content through verbal, visual, and auditory review of the materials presented.

connecting THEORY to PRACTICE

Environmental Factors That Nurture Learning

The psychological, or nonphysical, aspect of environmental design had as one of its first spokespersons Dr. Maria Montessori, the creator of the highly regarded Montessori educational methodology. Dr. Montessori was herself indebted to Friedrich Froebel, the founder of the kindergarten movement, who promulgated the idea that people respond actively to their environments, concluding therefore that environment can be a force for good or for bad in a learning situation. One of Dr. Montessori's students was Jean Piaget, who went on to make a great contribution to child psychology and our understanding of the role a child's developmental stage plays in determining the nature of the child's learning environment. Dr. Montessori's concept of the learning environment was that the classroom should be "a busy, happy place to be in" (American Montessori Society, n.d.). To make it so, "the threat of failure" must be removed and replaced by "a friendly, cooperative social community in which cooperation as opposed to competition" is the guiding principle.

The logical outcome of a cooperative environment as envisioned by Dr. Montessori was the advent and general acceptance of constructivism as the dominant learning theory today. "This vision [constructivism] must include [the teacher's] serving as a facilitator of learning who responds to students' needs with a flexible understanding of subject matter and a sensitivity to how the student is making sense of the world," Windschitl (1999) writes.

Not only the volumes of research supporting constructivist principles but also the behaviorists' emphasis on positive reinforcement reflect the established research findings that a nonadversarial classroom environment promotes learning. This third step in the DID process requires that you consider all aspects of the learning environment so that each factor in the environment has a similar positive impact on learning.

Media are the technologies that are used to facilitate the method (see Table 2.6). For example, lecture may be the method, but the overhead transparencies used by the teacher are the media used to support and enhance the teaching method selected. Various technologies and media are simply tools to enhance and facilitate instructional delivery. The teaching method that a creative teacher chooses is at the core of the teaching process. Instructional media and technologies play a supporting role, not a starring one. It is unfortunate that method and media are sometimes confused. This can lead to a teacher's using a technology just because it is interesting or fun to use even when it does not directly support the teaching method. This inappropriate use of technology can shift focus from the knowledge itself and the instructional task at hand. The appropriate use of technology can add excitement and interest to many methods, but the key to its use is its role as a support to teaching methodology. This differentiation is the reason that the identification of teaching and learning strategies and the selection of instructional media are two distinct steps in the DID model.

> Media must always support the delivery of instruction.

Step 5: Identify and Select Technologies

Instructional technologies are the tools used to enhance and support the teaching and learning strategies planned by the teacher. Once strategies have been mapped out, the tools needed to build the experience become evident. In this step of the instructional design process, you will identify the types of technological tools you need and select from those available to you.

> Support technologies enhance teaching and learning strategies.

As you will learn throughout this text, different technological tools have different uses, advantages, and disadvantages. Knowing what a technology can do in support of instruction, how to use it, and when it is appropriately used are the focus of this course. At this point, it is sufficient to differentiate between teaching and learning strategies and instructional technologies and to understand that technology's primary role is in support of the strategies you select for yourself and your students. The remainder of this text will familiarize you with the many technologies available to support teaching and learning, some of which are listed in Table 2.7.

ON THE WEB! 2.6

Connecting Theory to Practice

TABLE 2.5   CONTRASTING METHODS IN TODAY'S CLASSROOM

Classical Approach		Constructivist Approach	
The Teacher . . .	*Methods/Activities*	*The Teacher . . .*	*Methods/Activities*
Focuses on content.	Delivers a lecture about the Amazon.	Focuses on content and problem solving/critical thinking.	In groups, students list reasons for the decline of species in the Amazon.
Assumes students have prior knowledge of the subject.	Assigns reading from textbook.	Uses preorganizers to ensure background knowledge and interest.	Students create visual display of varied Amazonian species; teacher asks students what they already know about them.
Teaches about the Amazon as an isolated, independent unit.	Begins lecture without bridging to prior units.	Bridges to previous learning.	Teacher relates content to prior study of global geography and ecology.
Uses only objective content and skill performance guidelines.	Uses a percent grading scale on objective tests to determine competencies met.	Uses alternative assessment of performance objective competencies.	Students create a visual story of the decline of specified endangered species in the Amazon.
Allows passive learning.	Lectures on content of textbook chapters. Shows videos of Amazon without related activities.	Uses multisensory, inductive, self-managed, self-instructive learning; encourages active student participants; guides student discovery of knowledge.	Write a conservation rap, telling what was discovered in researching specific endangered animals of the Amazonian rain forest.
Believes learning is acquired by reading and listening.	Summarizes what has been read.	Encourages learning by modeling.	Teacher demonstrates a web search as a presentation process.
Emphasizes lower levels of Bloom's taxonomy.	Gives a selected-response test on chapter content.	Applies learning skills that result in higher-order thinking skills and applied levels of understanding.	Students create a map displaying results of research on the habitats of Amazonian animals; create a presentation program with script that includes a look to the future.

Step 6: Plan a Summative Evaluation

No design is ever perfect. However, a systematic process for continuous improvement will maximize quality. Therefore, it is important to end your instructional design with a plan to evaluate its effectiveness and to make appropriate revisions. The results from this summative evaluation can then be used to improve the design. Building this final evaluative step into the process ensures that a continuous improvement process will be in place and that the design will undergo positive revision with each use. Ultimately, through multiple implementations, evaluations, and revisions, your instructional design will come ever closer to your ideal.

The summative evaluation is a final review of the entire process.

Instructional design evaluation can take many forms. You can develop a success rubric (evaluation matrix) that can help you quantitatively self-evaluate the effectiveness of your lesson, or you may ask students to complete student feedback forms that you create to determine their perception of the effectiveness of the various components of the design. Regardless of the method you use for the specific evaluation of the design components, the ultimate evaluation is in the students' performance. Your instructional objectives identify very specific criteria and methods for measuring student success. Your students' achievement of your instructional objectives, then, is

IN THE CLASSROOM
Effective Learning Environments

Mr. Novum Magister, a recent graduate of Teachers R Us College, can't understand why his eighth-grade class is bored and unruly. He is striving to teach them his unit "During the Depression Era" (Morris, 1999). The classroom is meticulously arranged with six rows of desks, eight desks to a row. Mr. Magister sits behind his desk at all times. It is situated directly in front of the student desks, from which he talks and talks . . . and talks at the students. At the end of the unit, he will give a multiple-choice test, after which he will announce the results to publicize which students beat out the others for high grades. The room is harshly lit by numerous bars of neon lights. The walls are bare and painted a murky institutional brown. To keep students from gazing out the windows, he keeps the slat blinds closed. Believing warm temperatures are conducive to drowsiness, he sets the thermostat at 55°F, forcing students to fidget constantly to stave off hypothermia. The curriculum is inflexibly set. Individual interests can't be accommodated because the entire class must be on the same page at the same time. History is taught as a stand-alone subject. Because dates, names, and places are what history is all about, as Mr. Magister sees it, he expects students to memorize and take rote-recall standardized tests. He discourages any close interaction between himself and students, believing that might threaten his role as an authority figure.

Alas, some students misbehave, and others ignore everything that goes on in the class. Test results are poor, and the class attitude toward Mr. Magister is decidedly negative. Having a sincere desire to be a good teacher and realizing that he needs help, Mr. Magister turns to Mr. Al T. Lehrer, an accomplished and experienced teacher whose classes are in great demand by students and whose students consistently outdistance others in skills and content acquisition on problem-solving and critical thinking assessments. Mr. Lehrer's room is a panorama of learning resources organized to be accessible and attractive, with many books on a wide range of topics casually displayed around a quiet reading center area set off by a colorful rug and comfortable chairs. Mr. Lehrer received permission to have a workday when the students, after voting on a color scheme, painted the walls of the room. Potted plants, reading lamps, and open blinds create an aura of comfort, support, and encouragement. Because he is seldom behind the desk but circulates freely among the students, his desk is off to one side at the rear of the room. There is a computer area with six stations connected to a printer wired into a presentation platform at the front of the classroom.

After assigning *Picking Peas for a Penny* by Angela Medearis, Mr. Lehrer offers the students these choices for a unit on the Depression era: (1) viewing available documentary photos and films (visual intelligence); (2) filling penny rolls with 100 pennies donated by the students and then given to the March of Dimes and shelling peas from pods, the peas to be given to the local soup kitchen (spatial intelligence); (3) researching daily life during the Depression and preparing interview questions for an oral history to be published by the interviewers (linguistic intelligence); (4) researching popular songs of the 1930s and performing them vocally and/or instrumentally (musical intelligence); (5) figuring how to budget a given income (mathematical intelligence); (6) interviewing Depression-era survivors using the questions prepared by the linguistic learners and interview techniques learned through simulated interviews (interpersonal intelligence); (7) keeping a journal imagining what life was like for a young person in the 1930s from a background similar to the journal writer's (intrapersonal intelligence); and (8) planting a garden to grow food as a supplement to the meager food budget of a Depression-era family (naturalist intelligence) (Morris, 1999).

Contrast Magister's classroom with Lehrer's using the Learning Environment Rubric (Table 2.4). Which classroom offers a more effective learning environment?

---

the most significant evaluation of your design. Student achievement combined with results from other summative feedback efforts will give you the information you need to make future improvements to your design.

Using the DID Model to Plan Instruction

Now that you have reviewed all of the steps of the DID model, you can begin to see how they create a blueprint for the teaching-learning process. The model helps you ask yourself the critical questions that will improve the quality of the instructional experience for both you and your students. Using the model is an important first step before the instructional event and a skill that needs to be acquired through practice. Table 2.8 summarizes each step of the DID model and provides a template with a series of prompts to help you build your own design.

TABLE 2.6   METHODS VERSUS MEDIA

Methods are . . .
The strategies you use to achieve the lesson objective(s).

Methods include . . .
Teacher-Centered Strategies:

- Presentation
- Lecture
- Demonstration
- Class discussion

Student-Centered Strategies:

- Research projects
- Oral reports
- Cooperative learning groups
- Simulations
- Role playing
- Games

Media are . . .
All audio broadcasts and video or digital resources you use to carry out your methods.

Media include . . .

- Nonprojected visual media (posters, charts, bulletin boards, models, dioramas)
- Projected visuals (overhead transparencies, slides, computer displays)
- Audio media (tapes, CDs, audio broadcasts and webcasts)
- Video media (videocassettes, DVDs, broadcasts, webcasts)
- Digital media (anything generated via computer technologies)

Materials and media differ in that materials are any supplies you or your students use during a lesson.

We select media and materials that support our methods in order to achieve our objectives.

Creating Lesson Plans from the DID Model

The DID model helps you to see the instructional big picture. With it, you can build an effective instructional experience that carefully details each step of the instructional process. However, you might wonder how busy teachers manage to use instructional design models on a day-to-day basis. Essentially, even busy teachers know that, to teach effectively, they must have formulated an instructional design, either fully articulated on paper or, at the very least, jotted down in brief notes to themselves. Just as artists plan the elements of their artwork or architects create blueprints for their building, teachers use instructional design to create their personal overview of the instructional events in which they and their students will engage. Over time and with experience, such planning becomes intuitive. Very experienced teachers can create complex designs with just a few notes on each of the steps, just as an experienced and talented artist paints a

Instructional designs that include a variety of educational technologies engage students in active learning.

TABLE 2.7	SAMPLER OF SUPPORT TECHNOLOGIES	
Audio	*Visual*	*Digital*
Cassette tapes	Videotapes	Computer hardware
Radio	Video discs	Productivity software
Music CD-ROMs	Overhead projector	Educational software
Talking books	Slide projector	Presentation software
Multimedia CDs	Other projection devices	Streaming audio
Recordings: Rhymes and reading	Models, real objects	Streaming video
Recordings: Musical instruments	Boards (bulletin, white, chalk, etc.)	Webcasts
	Digital-analog converter	Internet resources
	Cartoons and drawings	Electronic whiteboards
	Document camera	

ON THE WEB! 2.7
DID designer template

powerful picture with just a few brushstrokes. Beginning teachers need to practice their instructional design technique until it becomes a skill that is second nature to them. Whether you are a new teacher who must fully articulate the design or an experienced teacher who needs only a list of summary ideas, the systematic planning of instruction remains the foundation of effective teaching and learning.

But, from a day-to-day perspective, the instructional outline provided by the design may be too broad for specific daily planning. For that activity, you must narrow the focus to more specific lesson planning. Lesson planning, although an outgrowth of the design, looks at instruction from a more concentrated perspective. It is similar to the specific punch list of tasks an architect might extrapolate from a blueprint to give to the building contractor at a complex building site. The lesson plan very specifically helps you identify what must be done each day in each class to implement the instructional activities outlined in the design. The relationship of the DID model to lesson plans is illustrated in Figure 2.5 on page 57.

Lesson Planning

The lesson plan provides a daily guide for teachers.

While the instructional design provides the overview of the planned instruction, it is the lesson plan that provides a day-to-day snapshot of what will happen in the classroom. The design is the foundation for the daily lesson plans that will emerge from it. Each component of the lesson plan grows out of the components of the design, just as a building's walls are constructed by implementing its blueprint. For that reason, the lesson plan follows the same general organization as the instructional design. Let's look now at the essential components of the lesson plan.

• Readying the Learners

In the instructional design, you have already carefully analyzed the characteristics of your learners and their specific needs. When beginning the lesson plan, you should review learner characteristics and update any information about your students that has changed. Once you feel confident that you have a clear picture of those you will teach, it is then necessary to evaluate their current level of skills, called entry skills, with respect to the targeted lesson. Such evaluation can be done formally through a

TABLE 2.8   DID Model Template with Examples for a Unit on Money and Banking

STEP 1: KNOW THE LEARNERS

Summarize the characteristics of the learners for whom you are creating the lesson.

- What are the personal demographics (ethnicity, socioeconomic level, cultural background) that might affect learning?
- What is the developmental stage of the student relative to the content?
- What is the cognitive/learning style of each student?
- What are the student's strengths in terms of multiple intelligences?
- What group dynamics might help or hinder the teaching-learning process?
- What are the student's entry skills with reference to the content?

EXAMPLE ANALYSIS OF LEARNERS

The students are seventh-grade middle-class students with an ethnic mix of 43 percent white non-Hispanic, 26 percent Hispanic, and 31 percent black. Five students are ESL students with a good command of English but who occasionally need an assist with spelling. Twenty-three students are predominantly kinesthetic learners, six show some preference for visual learning, and two show a preference for auditory learning. The two auditory learners need a quiet area in which to work. The kinesthetic learners need multiple spaces in which to move and experience the content. The visual learners need screened areas for studying. One student has strong musical intelligence, ten have strong logical intelligence, and all have good verbal intelligence. The students are generally friendly, noncompetitive, and cooperative. Working in teams is a preferred strategy for all but three students. Entry skills for this unit include only a limited understanding of money and banking.

STEP 2: ARTICULATE OBJECTIVES

State the behaviors that you expect your students to be able to demonstrate at the conclusion of the unit.

- What performance will result from the unit?
- What criteria for success are necessary to ensure mastery?
- How will you assess the performance?
- Have you included all the levels of Bloom's taxonomy that are appropriate for the content?

SAMPLE OBJECTIVES

On a written test, the student will be able to explain the difference between a checking and a savings account with 90 percent accuracy.

The student will be able to define interest with 95 percent accuracy.

Given a matching exercise, the student will be able to distinguish between credit cards, debit cards, and ATM cards with 90 percent accuracy.

The student will be able to contrast, with 85 percent accuracy, cash spending and credit spending.

In a simulated checking account, the student will be able to deposit money, write checks, and balance the account with 95 percent accuracy.

STEP 3: ESTABLISH THE LEARNING ENVIRONMENT

Clarify what you plan to do to create an environment for this unit conducive to learning.

- What changes need to be made to the classroom space?
- What reinforcers are needed for this unit to motivate and build learning success?
- How can learning be made active?
- How should students be grouped for positive interaction?

EXAMPLES

For the duration of this unit, a corner of the classroom will become a banking center in which all transactions will take place. As closely as possible, the center will be arranged to emulate the lobby of a bank. A screened quiet corner with additional lighting will be set up adjacent to the banking center.

Students will be rewarded with classroom currency for sound banking practices and for maintaining a balanced checkbook. Practices and checkbook will be evaluated weekly. Interim spot checks will be rewarded with game center time.

Audit teams will be used to check each other's progress and to assist students who need peer support to complete the unit.

STEP 4: IDENTIFY TEACHING AND LEARNING STRATEGIES

Given the objectives, describe the pedagogical cycle of teaching and learning strategies that need to be implemented to meet the objectives.

- What preorganizers are you planning?
- What prior knowledge do you need to connect to as a prerequisite for the lesson?
- How will you introduce the new information?
- What media, materials, or technologies will support the content?
- What teaching and learning strategies will support active learning?
- How will you reinforce the new knowledge?

SAMPLE PEDAGOGY FOR OBJECTIVE 1

Preorganizer: Display bank forms.

Bridge to prior knowledge: Review types of money.

Share objective: Write objective on the board and ask why it is important to know this content.

Introduce new knowledge: Share and discuss a chart of bank processes and have students act out a customer-teller interaction; invite a local banker as guest speaker; show a bank web site; add checking and savings accounts to the bank center and open each for all students.

Continued on next page

Table 2.8 continued

STEP 4: IDENTIFY TEACHING AND LEARNING STRATEGIES (cont.)	SAMPLE PEDAGOGY FOR OBJECTIVE 1 (cont.)
• What practice will be necessary to ensure mastery of the content? • How will you perform a culminating review?	*Reinforce knowledge:* Give examples and nonexamples of transactions to class and ask students to identify and/or correct them. *Provide practice:* Give students 100 hypothetical dollars to deposit in accounts at the bank center. *Culminating review:* Check students' accounts and individually reinforce or correct banking activity.
STEP 5: IDENTIFY AND SELECT TECHNOLOGIES *Given the strategies selected, identify the technologies that will be needed to support those strategies.* • What technologies and related materials are needed for this unit? • Which technologies are required for each strategy?	**EXAMPLES** *Strategies for Objective 1 of this unit will require the use of:* Scanner, printer, and copier to create bank center forms Overhead projector for guest speaker Computer connected to the web LCD display for large-group projection of computer image
STEP 6: MAKE A SUMMATIVE EVALUATION *Describe the summative feedback process you will use to evaluate the design and how the results of the evaluation will be used to revise it.* • How will you know whether the design is effective? • What assessment instruments are needed to measure effectiveness? • What is the revision process once you have the results from your evaluation?	**EXAMPLES** The design will be evaluated on the basis of student achievement of outcomes and student satisfaction. Evaluation will be completed through objective measures (tests and quizzes) and through performance assessment (observation of the performance of each student in the bank center). A summative student feedback form will assess student satisfaction with the unit and provide self-evaluation of mastery of the content.

This and other downloadable forms and templates can be found on the Companion Website at www.ablongman.com/lever-duffy.

pretest or informally through select verbal questions. The complexity of the content and the diversity of the learners will help you determine the best way to assess their entry skills. In the lesson plan, you should articulate how you plan to assess these skills.

Once you are clear on the learners' needs and on how you will determine their entry skills, you are ready to plan the lesson itself.

• Targeting Specific Objectives

Your instructional design may include multiple objectives from your DID model. Your lesson plan should identify the specific objectives the lesson is targeting. You should review the objectives in your design and then select, review, and restate one target objective within the lesson plan itself.

• Preparing the Lesson

ON THE WEB! 2.8
Lesson Planning Ideas

You are now ready to write out the lesson you plan to implement. This is the essence of the lesson itself. This component closely parallels its parent instructional design. The lesson plan should include each of the following sections, fully articulated and focused on the specific knowledge and/or performance detailed in the objective:

• *Prepare the classroom:* Describe what you need to do to create a physical environment that meets learners' needs and supports the lesson's teaching and learning strategies.

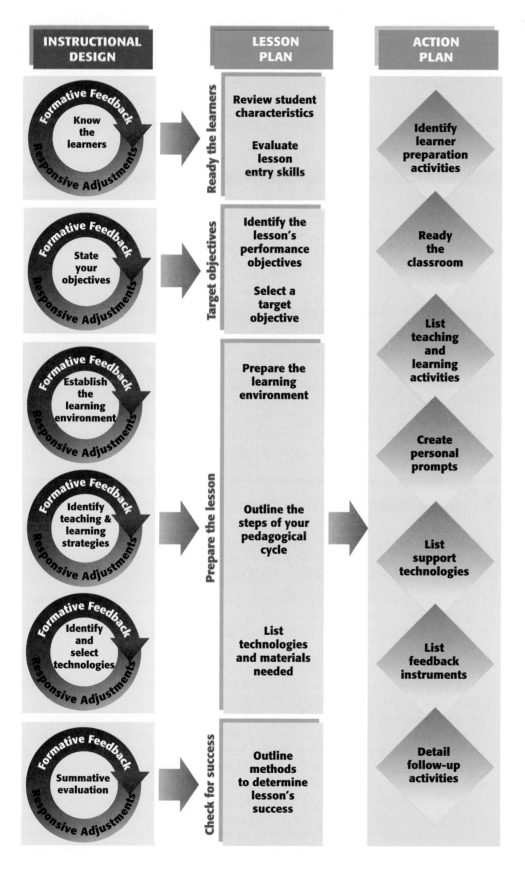

Figure 2.5
Relationship of Design-Plan-Act! Elements
All phases of the D-P-A system work together to create and implement quality instruction.

- *Summarize the steps of the planned pedagogical cycle:* Articulate exactly how you will carry out the lesson in terms of the teaching and learning strategies you intend to use. To ensure that all steps are included, use the pedagogical cycle as your guide.
- *Identify and list required technologies and materials:* Once you have planned each step in the cycle, you will need to identify and make a list of the technologies and materials you will need to carry out the strategies you have planned. This component of the lesson plan helps you organize the technologies and materials you will need.
- *Check for success:* You have your lesson ready and well planned out. The last step in the lesson planning process is the plan for summative feedback. In this section, you should identify the assessment strategies you will use to ensure that the lesson was successful. The assessment plan should provide you and your students with the feedback necessary to decide whether to go on to the next chunk of knowledge or stop and review or reinforce the current lesson.

▍The Lesson Planner: Practical Application of the DID Model

Just as the DID template provided you an assist in building an instructional design, the **lesson planner** (Table 2.9) will help you create a fully articulated lesson plan. The lesson planner is the pragmatic product of the instructional design process. With it, you will be able to narrow your focus in the planning process and create powerful and effective instructional experiences.

ON THE WEB! 2.9
Lesson Planner Template

The lesson plan itself is followed by one last step in the instructional planning process. Although less formal and complex than the previous steps in the process, this last step—action planning—is a necessary culmination to the process.

Instructional Action Planning

Instructional action planning involves articulating your lesson's to-do list. It is the detailing of all of the preparations that need to be made to successfully carry out your lesson plan. The **instructional action plan (IAP)** includes each of the following steps:

- *Identifying learner preparation activities:* This component describes the preparations that are necessary to assess and prepare the learners before the lesson. It should list the materials, props, and assessment instruments you will need.
- *Getting the classroom ready:* When action planning for the physical space, you should describe the steps you have to take in the classroom to prepare it for the lesson implementation. Be sure to list any changes to the classroom furniture or fixtures that need to be made before the lesson.
- *Listing teaching-learning activities:* In this component of the IAP, you should list the materials that need to be created, gathered, copied, or assembled for the teaching and learning strategies you have identified. Be specific about these needs so that your list can serve as a last-minute checklist before the lesson. You might also include in this section of the IAP alternative activities that could be used if unexpected circumstances interfere with the lesson plan's scheduled activities.
- *Creating personal prompts:* Personal prompts are reminders of the things you want to do and/or say as you implement the lesson. They are personal cues to remind you in case you forget to include something you had planned to do. Listing them in the IAP gives you a single point of review that you can use just before the lesson.

TABLE 2.9   THE LESSON PLANNER TEMPLATE WITH EXAMPLES FOR MONEY AND BANKING UNIT

STEP 1: READY THE LEARNERS

Describe how you will prepare the students for the lesson.

- Have any of the characteristics previously recognized changed?
- Do any assumptions about learners need to be corrected?
- What techniques will you use to gauge entry skills?

EXAMPLES

Unit on Money and Banking

Most student characteristics have not changed; however, an ESE (exceptional student education) student has now been mainstreamed into this class. This student will need additional support, so a copy of all work relating to this lesson must be given to the ESE team.

A money and banking pretest will be created and administered at the start of the lesson. The same test will be given as a posttest to measure progress.

STEP 2: TARGET SPECIFIC OBJECTIVES

State the instructional design objective that will be addressed by this lesson.

- To which of the design's objectives does this lesson relate?
- How, if at all, does this lesson relate to the other design objectives?

EXAMPLE

This lesson targets design Objective 1:

On a written test, the student will be able to explain the difference between a checking and a savings account with 90 percent accuracy.

STEP 3: PREPARE THE LESSON

Describe what you need to do to prepare for the lesson.

- What needs to be done in the classroom to get it ready?
- What must be accomplished for each step of the pedagogical cycle? How will it be accomplished?
- What materials, media, and technologies are needed and how will they be used?
- What needs to be done to implement the intended assessments?

EXAMPLES

Classroom Preparation

The banking center will consist of a refrigerator box with a cutout as the teller window and a small table behind it with a desk organizer for managing forms and transactions. The rolling bookcase will serve as a forms counter. A table on the other side of the bookcase with a study carrel next to it will provide quiet space.

Lesson Preparation

Preorganizer: Gather bank forms from a local bank, cover identifying numbers, enlarge and laminate the forms, and hang them on the front board.

Bridge to prior knowledge: Use transparencies to compare paper and coin equivalence.

Introduce new knowledge: Show students a bank process poster. Give a blank version to students to fill in as the information is presented.

1. Present and explain each banking form to students, filling out an enlarged version while they complete their paper versions.
2. Prepare a checklist of the steps in a customer-teller interaction for depositing, withdrawing, and checking balances to review with students. Give some example transactions, and have students role-play the key steps.

Reinforce knowledge: Open a class checking and savings account for the teacher, perform a series of right and wrong transactions, and let class decide whether the teacher is doing it right or wrong.

Provide practice: Have students open a checking and savings account and give them $100 in class "dollars." Have them deposit half in each of their accounts at the bank center, filling in the correct forms for the transactions. Then ask them to write a check for $10 to move this amount from checking to savings, filling in the correct forms.

Culminating review: Have each student request a bank statement at the end of the activity. Review each for accuracy. When done correctly, give each student a personal bank book to store transactions and documents.

Continued on next page

Table 2.9 continued

STEP 3: PREPARE THE LESSON (cont.)

EXAMPLES (cont.)

Technology/Media Preparation

Scan, print, and make copies of bank center forms. Enlarge one of each and laminate them.

Prepare money equivalence transparencies.

Create a chart of bank processes on a computer, print out, enlarge, and laminate.

Locate a suitable bank web site to share.

Assessment Preparation

Prepare and administer a quiz asking students to fill in each type of form and to compute their account balances.

 This and other downloadable forms and templates can be found on the Companion Website at www.ablongman.com/lever-duffy.

- *Listing support technologies:* This section of the IAP provides you with an opportunity to identify the technologies you will need and any associated materials that are required. Here you should list the technologies, what you need to do to get them into your classroom, and what preparation or practice sessions you need to successfully use the technologies you selected.
- *Listing feedback instruments:* Formative and summative feedback are a part of your lesson plan and your design. In the IAP, you should list any instruments or techniques that you need to develop or use to accomplish the feedback you have planned. You should also indicate what you need to do to utilize the feedback from the instruments. This list will serve as a feedback checklist to use before you implement your lesson.
- *Detailing follow-up activities:* Once you have collected formative and summative feedback, the data that result will prompt you to go on to the next lesson or to review and reinforce the current lesson. In this section of the IAP, you should detail what you need to do as a follow-up to a less successful lesson, what you might want to do to reinforce a successful lesson, and/or what you need to do to improve the lesson.

The Instructional Action Planner: Getting Ready to Teach

ON THE WEB! 2.10
Action Planner Template

To help you create a useful instructional action plan, a template, similar to the previously presented lesson planner, is provided in Table 2.10. The instructional action planner provides a format in which you are prompted to list your lesson requirements and to detail what you will need for successful implementation. The action planner is your last step in the planning process. With its completion, you are finally ready to teach and to help your students learn.

TABLE 2.10   THE ACTION PLANNER TEMPLATE WITH EXAMPLES FOR MONEY AND BANKING UNIT

TO-DO #1: IDENTIFY LEARNER PREPARATION ACTIVITIES

Describe what action needs to be taken to prepare the learners.

- What steps need to be taken to prepare the learners?
- What props are needed?

EXAMPLES

Learner Checklist

____ Contact ESE teacher and review unit plan for inclusion student.

____ Review prerequisite vocabulary with ESL students.

____ Obtain bank forms, bank book covers, bank signs, and customer "goodies" from local bank.

TO-DO #2: READY THE CLASSROOM

Describe what you need to do to get the classroom ready for the lesson.

- What furniture needs to be acquired or moved?
- What additional materials are needed?
- Whom do you need to contact to assist in making the intended adjustments?

EXAMPLES

Classroom Checklist

____ Stop by an appliance store for refrigerator box.

____ Borrow a rolling bookcase from the library.

____ Move the reading center temporarily to make room for the bank center.

____ Purchase or borrow three desk organizers for the teller.

TO-DO #3: LIST TEACHING AND LEARNING ACTIVITIES

List the materials you need to prepare and/or tasks that need to be done for the intended activities.

- What materials are needed by teacher and students?
- What tasks need to be completed for these activities?

EXAMPLES

Materials Checklist

____ Money equivalence transparency

____ Laminated poster

____ Deposit/withdrawal forms for checking accounts

____ Deposit/withdrawal forms for savings accounts

____ Poster-size laminates of each form

____ Blank bank statement forms for reconciliation

____ Blank bank books

Task Checklist

____ Contact a potential guest speaker to discuss lesson requirements.

____ Scan and print copies of forms if necessary.

____ Bookmark bank web sites.

Activity Back-up Plan

Locate a banking video, preview it, and prepare a related activity in case the guest speaker cancels or web access is unavailable.

TO-DO #4: CREATE PERSONAL PROMPTS

List the prompts you want to remember to use to cover all points of the lesson.

- What specifics do you want to remember to do?
- What specifics do you want to remember to say?

SAMPLE PROMPTS FOR OBJECTIVE 1

Talking Points

- Why do we save?
- What is a budget?
- Advantages and disadvantages of checks versus cash
- How banks make their money

Don't Forget To

- Close the teller window at the end of the class session
- Monitor the location of the class cash supply

Continued on next page

Table 2.10 continued

TO-DO #5: LIST SUPPORT TECHNOLOGIES	**EXAMPLE**

Describe the things you need to do to ensure that the technologies you have selected are available and working.

- What technologies and related materials need to be acquired for another source? From where?
- What hardware or software adjustments need to be made?
- Which technologies need to be checked to be sure they are functioning?

Technology Checklist

____ Make sure the scanner is working.
____ Check the printer cartridge.
____ Get colored paper from the art room.
____ Get ink-jet transparency film from the office.
____ Install a software upgrade.
____ Print the home page of web sites on which to make notes.
____ Check the LCD display for all cables and to be sure it is working.

TO-DO #6: LIST FEEDBACK INSTRUMENTS	**EXAMPLE**

Describe the feedback instruments you need to have ready for this lesson.

- What do you need for formative feedback?
- What do you need for summative feedback?

Feedback Checklist

____ Rubric for assessing performance while at the bank center
____ Quiz on filling in forms and determining balances
____ Lesson objective test on terms and concepts
____ Student satisfaction questionnaire

TO-DO #7: DETAIL FOLLOW-UP ACTIVITIES	**EXAMPLE**

Given the feedback, describe the follow-up activities.

- If the lesson was not successful, what remediation is planned?
- If the lesson was successful, what reinforcement is planned?

Remediation: PowerPoint self-paced review of key terms followed by a quiz on key points; direct tutoring or peer mentoring if mastery is not demonstrated on quiz

Reinforcement: Continued use of the bank center for a token-economy reward system

 This and other downloadable forms and templates can be found on the Companion Website at www.ablongman.com/lever-duffy.

Linking Planning, Teaching, Learning, and Technology

As you learned in Chapter 1, teaching and learning is, at its core, a process of effective and successful communication. Just as you would carefully plan and rehearse an important speech before giving it, so too must you carefully plan and rehearse the important communication process that takes place between teacher and learner. This chapter has reviewed the many components of this planning process and has provided specific planning tools for effective teaching and learning. Each step of the systematic instructional process is a critical one, and each offers a unique contribution to the process. Now that you are aware of all of the planning components, let's take a moment to see how they fit together to help you effectively plan your teaching and your students' learning experiences.

Design

Instructional design is the component of the process that helps you think strategically about the teaching and learning experience you are targeting. It offers you, through the DID model, a way to plan for and articulate every essential ingredient in the teaching-learning process. Instructional design paints the big-picture version of instruction that results in a complete and precise blueprint of what should happen and how.

Plan

The lesson plan brings the instructional design down to earth. It moves the planning process from a systems model to a mainstream, day-to-day instructional plan. While never deviating from the elements of the instructional design model, the lesson plan narrows the focus of the planning activity to a specific objective and knowledge segment. Using the lesson planner template, you are able to clarify precisely what you need to do to successfully complete each day's instructional events.

Act

Action planning is the final step in the three-part planning process. The action plan specifies everything you need to do to make learning happen in the classroom. Through the action planning step, you review the lesson plan and stop to create your lesson plan to-do list. By completing the instructional action planner, you culminate the planning phase of instruction and are ready to begin implementation.

Teachers must plan for, select, and effectively use the best technologies to support teaching and learning.

Planning for Technology in Teaching and Learning

Design-Plan-Act! completes the instructional systems cycle.

All aspects of instruction benefit from careful planning, but for using technology in instruction, planning is especially critical. Technology-enhanced teaching and learning must be well thought out, with appropriate technologies identified and justified within the framework of the instructional event. Adding a technology to your instruction just because it is available can detract from the instruction and even hamper the teaching-learning process. Technology should be employed only when instructional planning has been completed and it is clear that a technology in support of instruction is called for. A general rule of thumb suggests that a technology included in a lesson should make it possible for something that was done before to be done better or make it possible for something that couldn't have been done before to happen. A fully implemented plan, with its emphasis on carefully thought-out instructional events, helps to ensure such appropriate selection and utilization of technology.

When the instructional plan does call for technological support, the planning process helps to identify the technologies that are appropriate for a targeted instructional event. It also articulates the preparations necessary to use the technologies effectively and describes the specific activities in which they will be used. The planning process helps to ensure that identified technologies are implemented within the learning environment in a manner appropriate to stated objectives. The planning process also serves to remind you what you need to do, from acquisition to preparation, to use the technologies effectively.

As you proceed through this text, you will have the opportunity to learn about a wide variety of technologies that will assist you in effective teaching. Although each of these technologies will serve you well as a tool with which you can build a sound learning environment for your students, none should be used until you have fully planned the intended instruction. The old axiom in carpentry, "Measure twice, cut once," suggests that we should be careful to take the time to plan before taking action

A well-designed learning event ensures that the appropriate technology is used.

in order to avoid irreversible, costly mistakes. The instructional mistakes of teachers affect the students who are in our charge. No mistakes can be more costly than those that affect our students. Careful instructional planning helps us avoid instructional errors and maximize the effectiveness of our teaching time and our students' learning time. So when time pressures cause you to consider shortcutting the planning component of the teaching-learning process, remember this modified axiom: "Plan well, teach well."

KEY TERMS

Bloom's taxonomy   44
design-plan-act (D-P-A) system   37
dynamic instructional design (DID) model   38
feedback loop   39
formative feedback   39
instructional action plan (IAP)   58
instructional design model   37
learning environment   35
learning strategies   48

lesson planner   58
media   50
methods   49
pedagogical cycle   49
pedagogy   48
performance objectives   42
summative feedback   39
systems approach   37
teaching strategies   48

KEY THEORISTS

Benjamin Bloom   44
Rita and Kenneth Dunn   36
Robert Gagné   38

STUDENT ACTIVITIES

CHAPTER REVIEW

1. What components constitute a learning environment?
2. What is an instructional planning system? What are the components of the D-P-A system?
3. How can an instructional design model help you develop your instructional plan? Identify the steps of the DID model, and briefly explain each.
4. What is the difference between formative feedback and summative feedback?
5. What is a performance objective? How does it differ from more generic objectives?
6. Name and briefly describe the six levels of Bloom's taxonomy.
7. Name and briefly describe each step of the pedagogical cycle.
8. What role do educational technologies play in teaching and learning?
9. What is the difference between an instructional design and a lesson plan?
10. What is an instructional action plan? How does it help a teacher prepare for the instructional event?

WHAT DO YOU THINK?

1. Assume that you have been asked to assist a fellow teacher in writing objectives in performance terms. He shares with you the following objective for his sixth-grade science class: *"When*

I complete my instruction, my students will understand and appreciate the ecology of the rainforest." What would you say to your colleague to explain why his objective as written would not help him decide what to teach and what his students should learn? Help him rewrite this objective in performance terms.

2. Most teachers write objectives and focus their instruction at the three lowest levels of Bloom's taxonomy. Why do you think this happens? Do you believe it is an appropriate emphasis? How might it help or hurt the learners?

3. You are about to teach a lesson on the importance of the Nile in ancient Egypt at the grade level you would prefer to teach. Describe the steps you would take to effectively prepare for teaching this instructional unit.

4. Observe a teacher presenting a lesson, and note which of the steps of the pedagogical cycle he or she includes. Critique the lesson in terms of the cycle. Be sure to include how the lesson might have been improved through application of the pedagogical cycle's components.

5. Assume that the teacher in the next classroom is a computer enthusiast. He creates most of his lessons around the use of machines and software he has available in his classroom. Do you believe this is an appropriate approach to instruction? Why or why not?

LEARNING TOGETHER!

The following activities are designed for groups of three to five students:

1. Lay out an ideal classroom space that would meet the needs of a variety of learners. Include the number and placement of desks, tables, teacher's desk, file cabinets, bookcases, bulletin boards, chalkboards or whiteboards, and any less traditional fixtures and furniture you would like to include. Draw your group's ideal classroom to share with your class.

2. Select a teaching unit of your choice at the grade level you would like to teach. Together, write ten performance objectives related to the unit, with at least one at each of the levels of Bloom's taxonomy. Be prepared to share your objectives with the class.

3. Use all three components of the D-P-A system to complete a hypothetical instructional unit plan. Use as the instructional-unit content a topic appropriate to the grade level you would like to teach.

HANDS-ON!

1. Using an online library resource, research instructional design models and find at least two models that differ from the DID model. Compare the DID model with the two you find. Describe how they differ from one another and how they are the same. What features do you like best about each?

2. Search the Internet for three different lesson plans on a topic of your choice. Compare the components of each plan with the text lesson planner, and describe the components you found particularly interesting or useful. How does each lesson compare in terms of its pedagogical cycle? What aspects of the lessons you found did you like best? What did you like least? Why?

3. The Lesson Architect (**http:// www.ibinder.uwf.edu/steps/welcome.cfm**) is a useful web-based tool that helps you build an online lesson plan. Using your web browser, access that web site and use it to create a lesson plan on a concept in ecology for the grade level of your choice.

4. Visit the Dunn and Dunn web site (**http://www.learningstyles.net**) and at least one other learning styles web site for more information about creating a learning environment that is responsive to learning styles. Review the information presented, and be prepared to share at least three new discoveries or concepts that you believe will be useful to you when you teach.

More from Liz Brennan and Stacy Still

Having explored the DID planning model in this chapter, you may already have some effective ideas for ways to help our teacher in the Lower School of University School of Nova Southeastern University plan to integrate technology into her lessons. Obviously, reexamining each step in the DID model will be an integral part of the solution, but how do you get the teacher to go through this process? Using a cooperative approach, Stacy Still, the technology facilitator, will work with the teacher to help her succeed. The school principal, Liz Brennan, and Stacy will now share just how they solved the problem and also made use of the Internet to get the process started. Some of the web sites they visited should also be of value to you.

OUR SOLUTION

From the Principal's Perspective

To get the most from a planning experience, Stacy will often sit with individual teachers and plan a lesson in a collaborative mode. Stacy, with her expertise in technology, is able to guide the teachers and help them gain certain technical skills; the teachers, with their expertise in pedagogy, are able to assess the design of the plan as they study it together and make decisions as to how and where to use technology effectively. This empowers the teachers to determine whether the technological ideas that Stacy suggests, or the ones that they find together, are appropriate for the lesson, connect to the outcome objectives, address various learning styles of their students, and match the students' current performance levels. During the collaborative planning process, teachers can practice the lesson with the selected technology to simulate how it will work in their classrooms. This preinstructional step helps the teachers feel more comfortable and confident in the quality of the plan and in their use of technology.

From the Teacher's Perspective

When the teacher with a rain forest topic first approached me, we set a time to meet together to discuss her plan. My role in the meeting was one of critical friend and colleague. Through our discussion, the teacher determined that her plan was sound in most of the steps of the planning process. We identified and listed the areas of strength: clearly stated objectives, an appropriately established learning environment, and a well-targeted summative evaluation. However, given the large number of students for whom the lesson was intended, it was difficult for her not only to identify but also to manage the learning styles and specific learning needs of all of these students. We decided to strengthen several areas: knowing the learner, identifying teaching and learning strategies, and identifying and selecting technologies to be used to enhance and extend the lesson to be meaningful to more students.

Real People Real Stories

Our first step was to look at the original plan to see what types of activities the teacher had selected for the delivery of the lesson. Her first activity with the students was to locate and label all the rain forests of the world on a large classroom map. The next activity was to describe animals that inhabited each of the rain forests. Students in the primary grades would cut out pictures of animals found in each of the rain forests and then paste them onto a picture of the particular rainforest where each animal belonged. Intermediate students would categorize the animals into their proper rain forests by researching each rain forest using encyclopedias and books from the library. Then, these students would create a small rain forest book that included traced or drawn pictures of the animals. For some of the students, this plan of instruction was effective; however, there were some students who were not able to fully grasp the concepts, retain the information, or demonstrate through the application that they had mastered the content. I suggested that planning to incorporate technology into the lesson should increase the occurrence of her desired result.

Our first planning collaboration was to go online and find instructional plans that effectively integrated technology. The first time, the teacher searched while I assisted and guided her through the general search to locate the most appropriate sites for lesson plans. We started with a simple search using **www.google.com**. We found hundreds of sites that included thorough technology-enhanced lesson plans. Some plans used technology in the delivery of instruction, others used it as an assessment tool, and still others used it as an assistive-learning tool. The first web page we checked was **www.ed. sc.edu/caw/lessons/lessons.html**, titled Technology Enhanced Lesson Plans. This site was easy for the teacher to navigate, because it was nicely separated into specific topics. I told the teacher that when she does a search using a general search engine such as **www.google.com**, **www.yahoo.com**, **www.excite.com**, or **www. webcrawler.com**, many sites may surface, but she should be careful because these search engines can generate adult-oriented locations. She needed to make sure that any sites selected for use in the lesson were appropriate in content and level for her students. I suggested that we try a kid's search engine, such as **www.yahooligans.com**, **sunsite.berkeley.edu/KidsClick!**, or **www.ajkids.com**, to look for resources and lesson plan sites that would be more limited or controlled by age level and content.

Now that she had examples to follow, I instructed the teacher to go online and locate some sites and other informational resources that would be appropriate for her lesson. After a few days, she came back to me with web addresses and ideas. She had determined that using a PowerPoint presentation to deliver the instruction would be appropriate for all grade levels. Using PowerPoint would enable her to expand the amount of information she could give the students, and would enable her to use clip art to tie visual pictures to the information. She was also able to download both audio and video experiences of the rain forest using **www.rainforesteducation.com/FunNGames/canuseethem.htm**, **www.exploratorium.edu/frogs/rainforest**, and **www.christiananswers.net/kids/vidclips.html**.

The next step was to determine how to incorporate these links and the other information into a PowerPoint presentation. I encouraged the teacher to play with PowerPoint so that she would become familiar with the techniques used to create slides, change backgrounds, import pictures, import sounds, and import video clips. Having me there as a guide enabled her to learn, in a hands-on mode, how to do these things without being "afraid" of the task or the technology. Once our session was complete, I asked her to take sheets of blank white paper and create a storyboard of how she would like to lay out the information and where she felt it would be appropriate to include the web sites, sounds, and pictures.

The final step in the plan was to determine the best way to display this presentation. The Lower School is "rich" with its access to two smart boards and a multimedia screen. In this case, the teacher's classroom was already filled with living animals, interactive learning centers, and hands-on materials. For teaching the rain forest unit in her classroom to be most beneficial to the students, we decided to use the portable smart board to deliver the instruction and to present the PowerPoint project. For the first lesson, we decided to present the initial segments as a team —I would be present as she gave the lesson, as a support system in case something went wrong, and to troubleshoot any problems that might occur.

This was a tremendous experience for both of us. The teacher gained confidence in herself as a professional, and in her own ability to use the technology effectively, and I was able to see the lesson plan implemented and to use its outcome as a reference later with other teachers. A big benefit of this integration was that the teacher felt successful and, as a result, will be able to analyze other lesson plans and see where technology will be appropriate. Through the planning process, the teacher learned, too—she acquired an ability to evaluate web sites, software, and hardware. She also became more confident in using technology as an integral element in her lesson planning so that it will enable more students to master the performance objectives. Thus, her new rainforest lesson plan is not only more effective in terms of student learning, it is also more responsive to the school's mission.

For further information, you may contact the writers at these addresses:

Elizabeth C. Brennan, Ed.D.
Principal
University School of Nova Southeastern University, Lower Division
3301 College Avenue
Fort Lauderdale, FL 33314
Email: brennan@nova.edu
Phone: 954-262-4500

Stacy Still, Ed.S.
Technology Facilitator, Elementary PK–5
University School of Nova Southeastern University, Lower Division
3301 College Avenue
Fort Lauderdale, FL 33314
Email: stacy@nova.edu
Phone: 954-262-4500

SOURCE: Interview with Liz Brennan and Stacy Still conducted by Al P. Mizell.

INTERCHAPTER 1

Quill Pens and Slates
Early one-room schoolhouses in the 1700s and 1800s used these materials to teach students how to write and cipher.

1600s

Wall Charts
To save the cost of individual books, passages were sometimes printed in large letters and hung for all to see in Lancastrian schools.

1826

Manipulatives
Maria Montessori's kinesthetic approach offered a variety of manipulatives from which students could learn.

1901

Behaviorism Theory
John Watson helped establish behaviorism, which became one of the theoretical foundations for learning.

1914

1855

Models
With the introduction of kindergarten in Wisconsin, models and materials were given to students to manipulate and to learn from.

1700s

Primers
The New England Primer remained the basic school text for 100 years after its publication.

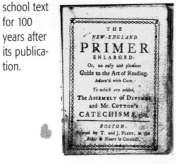

1910

Films
Edison declared after inventing motion pictures that books would soon be obsolete. Public schools in New York City implemented films for instruction for the first time.

Education as a Science
Edward Thorndike helped establish education as a science.

1904

Educational Museums
The visual-education movement resulted in educational museums with abundant visual displays.

SOURCES: A Hypertext History of Instructional Design. Retrieved October 3, 2003, from **http://www.coe.uh.edu/courses/ cuin6373/idhistory/idex.html**; P. Saettler. 1968. *A history of instructional technology.* New York: McGraw-Hill.

EDUCATIONAL TECHNOLOGY

Instructional Technologists
With the role of technology in learning increasing, the need for expertise in both education and technology grew, and professional instructional technologists emerged.

1940–1945

Objectives in Education
Ralph Tyler at Ohio State University developed and refined procedures for writing objectives.

1933

Bloom's Taxonomy
A team led by Benjamin Bloom identified and articulated levels of cognition.

1956

Radio
The Ohio "School of the Air" broadcast instruction to homes.

1929

1923

AECT
The Association for Educational Communications and Technology was created to help improve instruction through technology.

1945

Multiple Media Used by Military Armed Forces
Training used films, sound, graphics, models, and print to help prepare recruits for war.

1957

Programmed Instruction
Programmed instruction materials based on Skinner's behaviorism were used at the Mystic School in Winchester, Massachusetts.

1953

ITV
The University of Houston launches KUHT, the first noncommercial education station.

Continues on next page

Instructional Design System
Robert Gagné introduced a model for a systems approach to designing instruction.

1965

Personal Computers
The first micro-computer, the Apple, was created by Steve Wozniak and Steve Jobs.

1977

Cognitive Approach
Cognitivists including Ausubel, Bruner, Gagné, and others dominated thinking about learning.

1970

World Wide Web
The Internet became accessible to all with the creation of the web by Tim Berners-Lee.

1991

Online Life
The Internet expands to include "live" audio and video, leading to instruction anytime, anywhere.

The Grid
Using distributed computing technology, the Grid will make it possible to dynamically pool and share computer resources, making unprecedented computing power available to everyone on the Grid.

2004 and beyond

1967

PBS and NER
The Public Broadcasting Act established the Public Broadcasting Service and National Educational Radio.

PBS

1980s

CAI
Computer assisted instruction on personal computers reached its peak of popularity.

2003

Mobile Devices
Cell phones, hybrids, PDAs, and tablet PCs joined with wireless networking to make mobile computing commonplace everywhere, including in the classroom.

1990s

Constructivist Approach
The influence of Dewey, Piaget, Vygotsky, and others led to the emergence of the constructivist view of learning.

Computer-Based Technologies
Video discs, CD-ROMs, multimedia, digital presentations, interactive video, teleconferencing, compressed video, and the Internet combined to greatly increase the technologies available to enhance teaching and learning.

Virtual Reality
Digital representations of a given reality let teacher and student "experience" it, e.g., the inside of a volcano erupting.

Digital Assistants
Intelligent agents help you interact with your equipment and cyberspace.

INTERCHAPTER 1

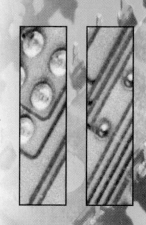

Applying Technologies for Effective Instruction

Every classroom has its own personality, which is usually defined by a teacher's teaching style. Some have desks arranged in tidy rows; others have pods of desks arranged in circles. Some classrooms have an abundance of technology to help a teacher teach and students learn; others have only a few types of technology present.

Part Two examines the many kinds of technology available, how they work, and how they might best be used to help you teach and your students learn. Chapters 3 through 7 explore the most talked-about classroom technology: the personal computer. The U.S. Census Bureau in its 2000–2001 report estimated that the total number of computers in schools has reached just over 12 million—one for every four students. This number will no doubt continue to grow. Although the distribution across classrooms nationwide may vary, most educators want to see more computers, preferably connected to the Internet, in their classrooms. Chapter 3 introduces the personal computer as a classroom tool. Chapter 4 examines how various computers and their components can support teaching and learning. Chapter 5 explores the wide variety of personal computer software tools available to help accomplish the many tasks involved in teaching and learning. Chapter 6 investigates per-

sonal computer networks as educational tools, and Chapter 7 explores the Internet and its role in education. These chapters will give you a chance to take a closer look at all aspects of the personal computer and related digital technologies as educational tools and see why so many teachers want computers in their classroom.

Chapter 8 examines audio and visual technologies. It explores the role of traditional visuals such as posters, bulletin boards, and models as well as computer software tools such as projected visuals, slides, and overhead transparencies. Chapter 9 explores digital and analog video technologies and how motion media materials and equipment can aid in instruction. Chapter 10 brings together all of the technologies in this unit in an exploration of distance learning, the technology-based alternative delivery system that is changing our definition of the classroom.

Together, these chapters will help you build the knowledge base and skills you need to evaluate and select the most appropriate technology for your instructional design. Furthermore, these chapters will help you learn how to teach with and effectively implement the technologies you will find in schools.

CHAPTER 3

Personal Computers in the Learning Environment

This chapter addresses these ISTE National Educational Technology Standards for Teachers:

I. Technology operations and concepts

Teachers demonstrate a sound understanding of technology operations and concepts. Teachers

A. demonstrate introductory knowledge, skills, and understanding of concepts related to technology (as described in the ISTE *National Education Technology Standards for Students*).

B. demonstrate continual growth in technology knowledge and skills to stay abreast of current and emerging technologies.

II. Teaching, learning, and the curriculum

Teachers implement curriculum plans that include methods and strategies for applying technology to maximize student learning. Teachers

A. facilitate technology-enhanced experiences that address content standards and student technology standards.

B. use technology to support learner-centered strategies that address the diverse needs of students.

C. apply technology to develop students' higher-order skills and creativity.

D. manage student learning activities in a technology-enhanced environment.

magine that you enter a time machine and travel back fifty years in time. When you arrive, you decide to find out how things have changed from the past to the present. You select a few places to visit. Close by, you see a hospital and decide that it would be a good place to start. You go in and are amazed at the changes. There are beds, patients, doctors, and nurses; but you wonder what happened to all of the equipment we are so used to seeing in a hospital. Where are the many monitors that keep tabs on every patient's status? Where are the many diagnostic machines that pinpoint illness? Where are the constant audio messages paging one doctor or another? Where are the sophisticated life-support systems in the operating room? It is immediately clear that the medical technologies of the twenty-first century are as abundant as they are sophisticated when compared with those available fifty years ago.

Your time-travel investigation continues as you decide to visit a school. As you walk into the school of fifty years ago, you see teachers, students, and administrators in familiar classroom and office settings. When you peek into a classroom, you see a teacher at the front of the room, chalk in hand, writing on the board while lecturing on a topic. You see maps and charts on the walls and a globe and other models around the room. Sets of books are available on classroom bookshelves. The teacher may be preparing to show a filmstrip or movie. Students are sitting in rows of desks taking notes on what the teacher is saying. Sound familiar? Unlike medicine, a field in which technology has transformed the way doctors and other medical personnel work, education has changed relatively little, despite technological advances. With the exception of the addition of a VCR and monitor and perhaps one or two personal computers in the typical classroom today, very little has really changed in the last fifty years (Adapted from the metaphor described by Seymour Papert, 1992.)

Yet the same computer revolution that dramatically altered medicine could and should have altered education. There are many reasons why this has not occurred; one of the key reasons is the fact that teachers simply don't know why and how to use much of the audio, video, and digital equipment that is available, even if it is accessible. Until only recently, courses like the one you are taking in educational technology were not emphasized in teacher preparation. Now, with the investment schools are making in technology and the need to prepare students for life in the twenty-first century, teacher technology skills have become a critical element in teacher training. This chapter introduces you to computer technologies and their role in education and helps you build the skills you need to be an effective educational user of this technology.

This chapter will help prepare you to use personal computers in your classroom for administrative tasks, classroom management, and instruction. In Chapter 3, you will

- Discover and identify the components of a computer system
- Examine the role of input devices and explore the most common types
- Explore the roles and most common types of output devices
- Investigate the relationship and functions of the central processing unit, memory, and storage
- Explore the roles and most common types of storage devices
- Relate the components and functions of a computer system to teaching and learning tasks

Meet Theodore Detjen

Many teachers find it a challenge to balance the demands of the day-to-day responsibilities as a professional educator and their roles related to the integration of personal computer technology to teaching and learning. After all, aren't teachers busy enough without having to worry about computers? Why do they need to learn so much about computers anyway? Won't there be someone at every school whose job it is to make sure the computers are working? Won't appropriate software be made available to teachers without having to bother them about it?

In most schools and districts, teachers do have to get involved in computer technology. Teachers must be able to use computers and be sufficiently computer literate to operate them. They must also be aware of when a computer problem has surpassed their knowledge and responsibility and when to call for computer support. You might find that computer-support personnel are stretched very thinly across a school and/or district. Therefore, it is important that you know enough to utilize your classroom computers with minimal assistance. Furthermore, computer-support personnel cannot be expected to know what types of equipment or software you would

find most useful in your classroom. Therefore, you need to have a sufficient working knowledge of computer hardware and related software to provide the input your school or district needs in order to acquire the computer technology that will facilitate teaching and learning in your classroom.

In this chapter, you will learn much about computers and a teacher's role relative to computers in the schools. To better understand the role of computer-support departments, let's see what a regional information-center director has to say. Theodore Detjen, now retired, was the director of the Mid-Hudson Regional Information Center in New York.

I am the retired director of one of twelve regional information centers provided by an intermediary New York State Education Department agency called the Board of Cooperative Educational Services, or BOCES. The Mid-Hudson Regional Information Center provides information services to fifty school districts in a region located sixty miles north of New York City and bordering the Hudson River. The school districts in the region vary in size from one-building districts of approximately 600 children to large urban and suburban districts with populations as large as 13,000. The majority of the districts served have student populations of approximately 3,000 to 4,000.

The fifty-five-member staff of the Mid-Hudson Regional Information Center consists of six managers, three systems programmers, two help-desk specialists, six couriers, and three administrative assistants. The remainder of the staff consists of training, application, and technical specialists.

When microcomputers began to enter school districts in the late 1970s and early 1980s, school districts struggled to bring as many of these units as possible into their buildings. Next, they searched for applications to place on these machines. During the 1990s, schools connected computers together into networks, but little had changed in applications. The applications, which were offered by a multitude of educational vendors, now were placed on file servers. In the mid-1990s, the Internet became the major application on school networks.

It continues to be a struggle to help educators understand that they must take an active role in searching for applications for computers that directly relate to the school's needs. Unless this is done, the applications can serve as distractions, and the computer systems can become ineffective devices that do not support the educational goals of the school.

Technology must be viewed as a support device; by itself, technology serves no purpose. Unfortunately, many schools view technology as a special entity with power. They create technology plans and write technology curricula. Instead, they should be concentrating on the business of schools, which is the education of youngsters and adults. As we observe the medical profession, for example, we can see a good example. Hospitals know that they are in the business of health and healing. They utilize multiple technologies to assist but give no specific attention to technology and view its role as merely supportive.

The Mid-Hudson Regional Information Center's business is to understand the needs of schools and fit specific technologies to support these needs. As we move into the twenty-first century, we will continue to urge schools to concentrate on education and not be confused by technology. They must allow technology to support them where appropriate but also to discard its use where it is a distraction.

As you can see, the role of computer support is broad and complex, and it is clear that the teacher must be an active participant in the process. It is therefore very necessary to know about personal computers and how they can best be used to fit your needs as a teacher and the needs of the learners in your charge. This chapter will help you do just that. We will check back in with Dr. Detjen at the end of the chapter.

SOURCE: Interview with Theodore Detjen conducted by Al P. Mizell. Reprinted by permission of Theodore Detjen, retired director of computer services, Mid-Hudson Regional Information Center, Board of Cooperative Educational Services–Ulster County, New York.

Computers, Teaching, and You

You might be one of the many future or current educators wondering how you are going to use computers in your classroom. Or you might wonder whether their use will undermine your role as a teacher. Or, like many educators who are happy to use a personal computer to create a test or an assignment, you might see their value in classroom management but wonder whether they are worth the expense and extra effort when it comes to teaching and learning.

Educators sometimes feel a degree of concern when they are faced with the idea of using personal computer technology in their classroom. This is not surprising, since most teachers teach in the manner they were taught. They are comfortable using the tried-and-true strategies from which they learned. There is no doubt that these strategies continue to be valuable, but new technological tools make many enhancements to these strategies possible.

To overcome any possible reluctance to using a computer, it is best to begin by becoming more familiar with computers. This process is often best begun by developing an understanding of how computers work and how they can be used for administrative and academic tasks. During this process of familiarization, it is also important to develop hands-on skills with the hardware and software that educators frequently use. Let's begin by getting to know what a computer is and how it works.

ON THE WEB! 3.1
Teachers Using Computers

How Does a Computer Work?

Computers are machines made of metal, plastic, chips, and wire. These unique machines, unlike other small appliances, have no predetermined purpose built in. Instead, they are designed to be versatile, able to do a variety of tasks depending on the instructions (programs) they are given. Understanding how this unique digital technology works will help you to judge when a computer's capabilities will be useful in your classroom and how you can use computing capability to enhance your planned instruction. It will also help you to be able to recognize and correct minor computing problems or to know when you need to call for technical support.

The computer and all its components make up a **computer system.** Regardless of the configuration of a particular system, all computers share the same basic sequence of operations: the computing cycle. Understanding what constitutes a computer system and a computer cycle is your first step in building the core computer knowledge that you need.

Computer memory is short-term storage, and storage devices offer long-term storage.

A personal computer is a device that takes in data (input) from you, processes it according to your instructions, and then sends out the finished information product (output) to you. Because the quantity of data you input might be large and the size and complexity of the processing you want done can sometimes be great, computers have both short-term memory and long-term storage capabilities. These are used to help in completing the larger and more complex processing jobs you require. Computer **memory** is a temporary electronic storage space used by the computer to do short-term tasks or to complete a task that is too complex to do all at once. Longer-term **storage** is a more permanent electronic storage space in which the computer can store instructions and data for use at a later time. The use of a combination of temporary memory and long-term storage makes it possible for the computer to work on complex jobs a little at a time until the entire task is completed.

Programs are a computer's digital instructions.

Together, these steps of taking in data, processing the data, storing it as necessary, and outputting the results to you, the end user, make up the **computing cycle.** This computing cycle and the components of a computer system are diagrammed in Figure 3.1. Regardless of the complexity of the task the computer is asked to perform, this basic computing cycle is always the same. With an understanding of this basic operational framework, you can more easily understand the interrelationship of the various components of a computer system.

The computing cycle takes place in and with the help of computer hardware and computer software. Computer **hardware** includes all of the computer components that are physical, touchable pieces or equipment. Computer **software** is the term for **programs,** or sets of computer instructions, written in special computer languages that tell a computer how to accomplish a given task. You, as the end user of the hardware and software, really need to know relatively little about the details of how the computer components work together electronically or how a program is written. What you do need to know is which pieces of hardware and software you might need to accomplish the classroom management or instructional tasks you want done and how to use these computer components effectively for teaching and learning.

On CD
Hardware Skills Builder
Setting Up a PC

What Do I Need to Know about Software?

As incredible as computers are, they lack the ability to accomplish much of anything unless someone tells them precisely what to do and how to do it. When we turn the computer's power on, the collection of metal, plastic, chips, and wires can function only because someone first created a set of instructions (program) to tell the computer

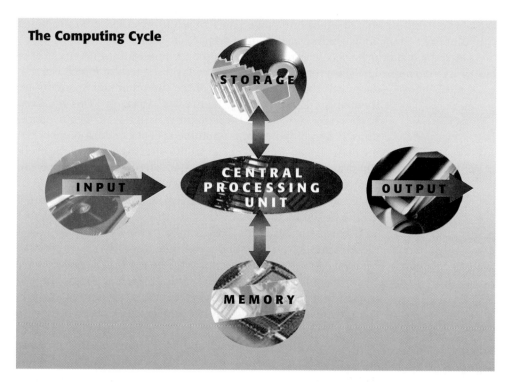

The Computing Cycle

STORAGE

INPUT

CENTRAL PROCESSING UNIT

OUTPUT

MEMORY

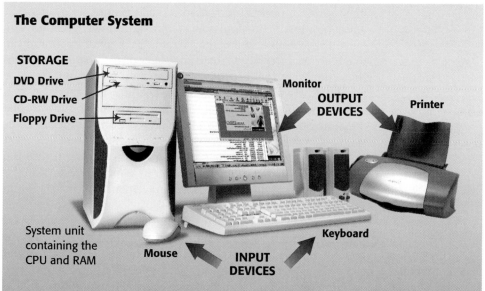

The Computer System

STORAGE
DVD Drive
CD-RW Drive
Floppy Drive

Monitor

OUTPUT DEVICES

Printer

System unit containing the CPU and RAM

Mouse

Keyboard

INPUT DEVICES

Figure 3.1
The Computing Cycle
All computers use the same computing cycle to operate.

how to start itself up. Without these instructions, it would be unable to function in any of the ways we have come to expect. These initial instructions, or Basic Input/Output System (BIOS), are stored inside the computer's hardware on special ROM **chips.** Chips are tiny silicon slices—often only $\frac{1}{4}$–$\frac{1}{2}$ inch square—which contain millions of electronic circuits. **ROM** is an acronym for "read-only memory." The computer can read the programs stored on ROM chips, but other data cannot be stored on them.

When you turn the power on, the computer reads the instructions stored in ROM that tell it how to start itself up and immediately begins to carry these instructions out. This is sometimes referred to as **booting up** the computer, a term that comes from

Booting up the computer means starting it.

the phrase "pulling oneself up by one's own bootstraps." It is in this very automated way that the system boots (starts) itself up and prepares to interact with you.

Once the machine has booted up, it runs a diagnostic program stored on another one of its internal chips. This program, called the power-on self-test, or **POST,** is a self-diagnostic that ensures that all of the computer's components are functioning as expected (see Figure 3.2). Once the POST has been successfully completed, the computer is ready to begin operations. If the computer finds an internal problem during the POST, it will display an error message on the screen describing the problem that it found and suggesting what you need to do to resolve it. The results of the POST will help you determine whether your machine needs any technical intervention before you try to use it for the task at hand.

Let's assume that the POST was completed successfully (as it most often is). Even though the computer is now ready to operate, before it can begin to function like the computing device we have become familiar with, it must first be given instructions on how to operate as a computer. It must be told how to respond to and perform the many little interactive tasks you expect, such as how to save data on a disk and what to do when you click a mouse button. The machine requires an additional program that provides specific instructions on how to act like a computer. That is done by a special program called the operating system. Every computer must have an **operating system,** a collection of programs that tells it how to function and how to manage its own operation. The operating system also creates an interface between you and the machine. An **interface** is the component of the operating system that establishes the methods of interaction (via menus, text, or graphics) between the user and the machine. The operating system is thus the first external (not built-in) piece of software the machine needs to be able to know how to run in order to communicate with you. The operating system must therefore start before you can begin your personal tasks. Learning to use the operating system on your computer is a prerequisite skill for using your computer to do the management and instructional tasks you need it to do.

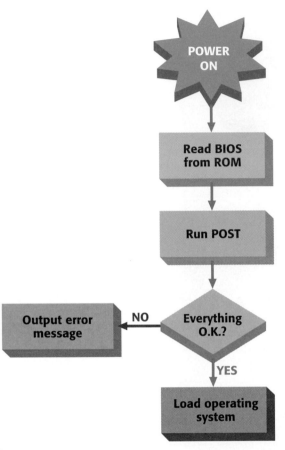

Figure 3.2
Flowchart of the Computer Startup Process
The startup process, or booting process, prepares the machine for operations.

The operating system is the program that runs the computer and provides an interface.

Today's most popular operating systems are Windows for personal computers and Macintosh OS for the Apple Macintosh computer. Both of these operating systems use an interface that is a combination of typed-in (text) commands, choices from preset menus, and selected icons that appear on the opening screen, called the desktop. A **menu** is a listing of command options that appears across the top of the program window. Usually, after the user selects one of these menu choices, additional options will appear in a submenu that drops down from it. An **icon** is a small graphic that represents one of the system's options. Typically, **commands** can be issued in multiple ways: by typing a series of keystrokes, selecting a menu option, or clicking on the appropriate icon. There is no one right way to issue most operating system commands but, instead, there are a variety of ways to use the operating system. Both **Windows** and Macintosh OS present command options to users via windows, or boxed collections of icons and text. The user can then choose commands by clicking on an icon. This style of interaction between user and machine that depends so heavily on graphics and visuals instead of text is referred to as a graphic user interface, or **GUI** (pronounced "gooey"). Every effort has been made to make it friendly and convenient for users. An example of the Windows and Macintosh interfaces appears in Figure 3.3. As a technology-

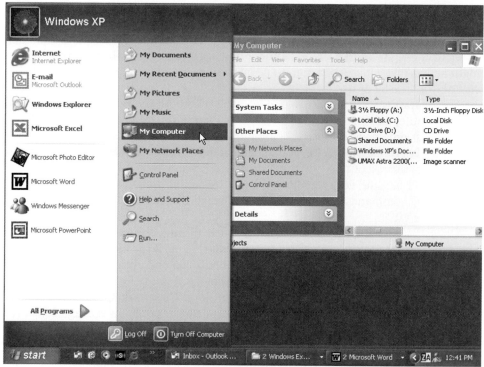

SOURCE: Windows XP® is a registered trademark of Microsoft Corporation.

GUI operating systems let users issue commands via menus and icons.

using educator, you should make it a priority to master Windows or Macintosh OS, whichever is used in the school in which you teach. Although some operating system basics are presented in this chapter, practicing with an operating system is the only way to gain the skills you need.

You can tell the machine what you want it to do by selecting a menu option, entering a text command, or pointing to an icon with an arrow that you control through manipulation of a mouse. A **mouse** is a "work-alike" pointing device that rolls about

As the mouse is moved on the real desktop, the pointer is moved on the virtual Windows desktop.

SOURCE: From http://www.apple.com/macosx.

Figure 3.3
GUI Interfaces

Windows and Macintosh OS operating systems allow users to interact by pointing and clicking.

ON THE WEB! 3.2
GUIs, Teaching, and Learning

Different software applications are needed to do specific tasks.

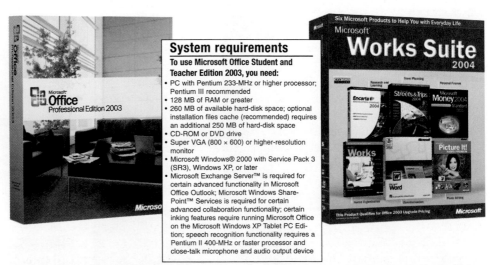

ON THE WEB! 3.3
What Software Applications Are Most Useful?

on your desk, usually on a special pad. It is called a work-alike device because it moves the pointing arrow on the computer screen in the same direction in which you move the mouse on your desk. If you roll the mouse to the right on your desk, the pointer moves to the right on the screen. Although using a mouse or other pointing device might at first take some practice, most people find it very intuitive and are comfortable with only a little bit of use.

The operating system controls and interacts with both the hardware components of the computer and any software you choose to use. It also provides common ways for you to select options and to issue commands across a wide range of programs. You control the operating system through the menu or icon choices you make, and they, in turn, control the rest of the computer's functions for you. You will find that, with practice, you will become very familiar with the operating system's menu options and icons. Giving commands will become as comfortable and familiar as using the remote control on a TV.

Once the operating system is loaded and running, the computer is ready to address your task. However, the computer still needs a more specific program to enable it to perform the particular task you have in mind. The operating system enables the computer to use software, but to understand how it must perform for you, the computer has to have instructions installed and running. These task-specific instructions are provided by an application program. An **application program** is a set of instructions that tell the computer how to complete a unique task such as word processing, database management, or drawing. Applications range from **utility programs** that improve or monitor computer operations, to administrative applications (e.g., word-processing and gradebook programs), to academic applications (e.g., tutorials and electronic encyclopedias). Every application is a specific computer program written to accomplish a single task or a group of interrelated tasks. For example, if you want to use your computer to type up a test, you need a word-processing application. If you want to use your computer to interact on the Internet, you need a telecommunications application that lets you get online. If you want to use an electronic spreadsheet to keep your grade book, you need a spreadsheet application. The advantage of this versatility is that a single bundle of hardware—the personal computer system—can do many different jobs. The disadvantage is that you need as many pieces of application software as you have tasks to perform. Table 3.1 lists some of the most frequently used types of application software.

All reputable software includes equipment specifications to help you decide whether it will work on your computer.

TABLE 3.1   POPULAR MICROCOMPUTER SOFTWARE

Common Software	Function
OPERATING SYSTEM	The operating system provides the interface for the user and controls the computer operations.
WORD PROCESSING	Word processing gives the user an environment for entering text and other data and manipulating its format prior to printing it out.
ELECTRONIC SPREADSHEETS	Spreadsheets manipulate, format, and calculate numerical data and arrange them in a display called a worksheet.
DATABASE MANAGEMENT	Database software provides an environment in which large quantities of data can be entered, stored, manipulated, queried, and reported.
PRESENTATION SOFTWARE	Presentation software enables the user to create electronic slide shows with special effects, including sound and animation.
DESKTOP PUBLISHING	Publishing software combines word-processing capability with desktop layout capability for easy-to-use layout and design of complex publication formats.
GRAPHICS PROGRAMS	Graphics programs provide an environment in which the user can draw pictures, create diagrams, or manipulate digital photos for inclusion in other programs or to print out.
COMMUNICATIONS SOFTWARE	This category of software includes the software to connect a computer to one or more other computers via phone lines and the browsers that let users examine the sites on the World Wide Web.
UTILITIES	Utilities include all of the various types of software that helps users maintain their computers in good working order.

Because software manufacturers are aware of the need for multiple types of programs to perform common tasks, they often bundle their most popular applications into a related collection (suite) of applications. One of the most popular suites available today is Microsoft's Office Suite, which includes a word processor (Word), a spreadsheet (Excel), a database management system (Access), and a presentation package (PowerPoint). Together, the programs in this suite, like those in its competitor products, can enable you to accomplish almost any administrative task.

Another approach, one that reduces the number of application programs needed, is to integrate the main features of a collection of popular applications into a single comprehensive application, called an **integrated software package.** Such a package has the capability to perform many, but not all, of the functions of the full-blown versions of the software. Microsoft Works and ClarisWorks are examples of integrated software packages. They contain most of the same types of software as does Office, but each component piece is a little less powerful than its Office counterpart, having fewer features and capabilities.

Integrated software combines popular programs into one.

Most integrated and/or bundled software products usually include the most popular types of applications—typically word processing, a graphics program, a spreadsheet program, a database management program, a communications program, and a presentation program. An advantage of both bundled and integrated packages is that all the software offered in this manner uses similar commands and looks familiar on the screen. This common "look and feel" can make it easier to learn and use each of the applications. Also, an integrated package usually takes up less space on the computer's hard disk. A disadvantage of an integrated software package is that each of its components might not contain as many functions as similar software sold in separate application packages.

It should be remembered that every piece of software is written with specific hardware in mind. Typically, software specifications identify the minimum levels of hardware necessary to use a given piece of software. It is important that you be sufficiently familiar with your hardware to be able to select appropriate software. Information about the technical aspects of hardware can be found in the documentation that accompanies the hardware when it is purchased. The hardware specifications required for determining whether software will run typically include the speed of the machine, the amount of available memory, the capability of the monitor, and the space required on the hard drive. These details are included on the side of every commercial software box. You should take a moment to jot down the specifications of the machine on which you plan to install the software and have these specifications available whenever you shop for software.

ON THE WEB! 3.4
What Do I Need to Know When Buying Software?

What Do I Need to Know about Hardware?

Although it is not necessary to understand the intricacies of how hardware works at the level of its electronics, it is important to understand what different hardware components do. This baseline knowledge will help you to identify the components you need to get the job done in your classroom. The remainder of this chapter will introduce you to these components.

Input Devices

To make the computer look for, load, and run application software, you, the user, must first tell the computer to do so. To issue this type of command and to later add your personal data, you need some way to communicate your wishes to the computer. This is done through the use of an input device. An **input device** includes any computer peripheral that you might use to enter data into the computer. A peripheral is any device that can be connected to a computer. The keyboard and the mouse are the most often used types of input devices. Let's take a closer look at each of these devices to determine its respective role in accomplishing your tasks.

The keyboard and mouse are common input devices.

The typical computer **keyboard** is laid out much like the keys on a typewriter. However, the computer keyboard has several additional keys not typically found on a typewriter, which are used to control the computer or give software commands. Typing commands or data into the machine is usually referred to as keyboarding. Because of the prevalence of computer technology in schools and in society in general, many schools now require their students to have keyboarding competencies before they leave elementary school. If you still use a personal hunt-and-peck system for keyboarding, you might want to take the time to learn a touch-typing system. Many easy-to-use and entertaining software tutorials are available for you or for your students to learn this essential computer skill.

The other most prevalent input device is the mouse. The mouse is one of several types of pointing devices that allow you to move the selection arrow on the screen. Pointing devices include any input device that enables users to point to the commands or icons they wish to use. The selection arrow, sometimes called a pointer, is an icon shaped like an arrow used to point to the command icons or menu items that you want to choose. As we noted previously, this type of device is called a work-alike device because it causes the selection arrow to work (move) in the same way the mouse moves on the desktop. Other common types of work-alike devices include a trackball, a joystick, and a touchpad. As you can see in Figure 3.4, each of these devices has a slightly different configuration, but all control the movement of the selection arrow.

The keyboard is configured like a typewriter keyboard with some additional keys. It is used primarily to enter data, but it also includes cursor keys to move the pointer.

Figure 3.4
Input Devices: The
Keyboard and Various
Pointing Devices
A variety of input devices are available for inputting data or commands.

A mouse is used to give commands, make selections, and move objects on a GUI interface. It is used by rolling it around on the desktop and clicking its buttons.

The trackball is really an upside-down mouse. It is used by rolling the ball on the top with your fingers to move the pointer on the screen. It too has buttons you can click or double click.

A touchpad is a flat, pressure-sensitive panel. To move the pointer, you just press lightly and move your fingertip around on the surface of the panel. It too has buttons for clicking.

Each of these devices also includes one, two, or, in some cases, three or more buttons. Once the pointing device is used to position the pointer arrow on the icon or menu item desired, the appropriate button is clicked to select the menu item or to execute an action represented by an icon. When a mouse has two or more buttons, the leftmost mouse button is typically preset by the software to work in a specific way, and those settings are fairly consistent across all pieces of software. For example, if you click the left mouse button once while pointing to an icon, you select that icon. However, if you rapidly double-click that same button, a different action is carried out. The other one or more mouse buttons are programmable by the software; that is, different types of software use those buttons in different ways, or you can assign special functions to them. You should read through the documentation that accompanies the software you want to use to see what convenient features may be available through the use of these other buttons.

It should also be noted that most operating systems offer you the capability to change the response of the mouse button(s). Because most people are right-handed, the left mouse button will fall under the index finger when your hand rests on the mouse. This is the most comfortable position for extended use. However, if you or any of your students are left-handed, this can be bothersome. For that reason, Windows and other operating systems provide an easy way to switch the functions of the mouse buttons to accommodate left-handed users. You should check your operating system's manual to determine how this can be done.

Although the keyboard and mouse are the two most often used input devices, there are, in fact, several others. Each of these other input devices has unique properties that make it very useful in an innovative teaching and learning environment. These other input devices are more fully described in Chapter 4, "Digital Technologies in the Classroom." For now, it is sufficient that you understand the function of input devices in general and the mouse and keyboard in particular. This will serve as a basis for contrast with the hardware necessary at the other end of the computer cycle: output devices.

▌Output Devices

Hard copy is printed output; soft copy is displayed on the monitor.

If input devices are used to put data into the computer, then **output devices** are the pieces of hardware that move information (data that has been processed) out of the computer. The two primary output devices for most computer systems are the monitor and the printer. The monitor displays information in **soft copy** (electronic form), and the printer turns that information into **hard copy** (printed form).

A **monitor** displays computer information on its screen. The screen works much like a television screen, but it typically has much higher resolution. **Resolution** refers to the clarity and crispness of the images on the monitor screen. Resolution can be measured by the number of pixels the screen displays. A **pixel,** or picture element, is a single colored dot on the monitor screen that, when combined with other pixels, forms an image. Resolution measurements are provided both vertically and horizontally (see Figure 3.5). You have probably seen this type of measurement indicated in relation to computers. A screen resolution may be 640 × 480. This measurement means the screen image is made up of 640 vertical columns of pixels in each of 480 horizontal lines of pixels. The higher the vertical number, the denser the image becomes, which in turn results in a higher-resolution image and crisper picture. Screen size may also be a factor in monitor resolution. Screen size refers to the number of inches measured diagonally across the screen. The most common monitor sizes are 14″, 15″, 17″, 19″, and 21″. Larger sizes are needed for exacting work such as digital graphics and computer-aided design. However, larger screen sizes in turn require higher resolution, or the image may appear fuzzy.

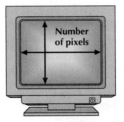

A monitor's resolution is determined by the vertical number of pixels (picture elements) and the horizontal number of pixels. Monitors also vary in terms of the number of colors they can display. The greater the resolution and the number of colors, the more realistic the picture.

16 COLORS (4-BIT COLOR)

Images will appear fuzzy.

256 COLORS (8-BIT COLOR)

Commonly used resolution in older machines and for many games. Images are adequate.

65,536 COLORS (16-BIT COLOR)

Typical resolution in current monitors. Images are crisp and clear.

16,777,216 COLORS (24-BIT COLOR)

True color images, very crisp, realistic. Used when working with photos, art, and high-end games.

Figure 3.5
Output Devices
Different monitors and screens provide different levels of display.

The viewing screen on a notebook computer is really a high-resolution color liquid crystal display (LCD) screen. It is based on the same technology that is used in digital clocks and wristwatches, only much more sophisticated. This same technology is used for flat-screen monitors.

Some monitors are adjustable, providing different resolutions to accommodate different software. Others can display in only one resolution, making it difficult to use some software. Once again, it is important to check the software's list of necessary hardware specifications to ensure that the program's output can be displayed with the monitor you are using. Generally speaking, you want to use a monitor with as high a resolution as you can afford, to minimize eyestrain and maximize the quality and naturalness of the images you and your students are viewing.

An alternative to the more traditional computer monitor is the **LCD** (liquid crystal display) screen that has been used on notebook (small portable) computers for several years. Although the LCD screens on notebooks have had some viewing limitations, new, full-size, high-resolution LCD screens do not. These LCD screens have the advantage of being much thinner than traditional monitors, making them easier to position on a desk or in the classroom. They are a newer technology, however, and are still somewhat more expensive than traditional monitors of the same screen size.

Monitors of all types display soft copy, that is, data that is still in electronic form within the computer. Soft copy is volatile (temporary). It will disappear when power to the machine is cut off. To output the same data to a more permanent form, a printer is used. There are many types of printers, each with its own advantage. The most common types of printers and their respective advantages and disadvantages are summarized in Figure 3.6.

LASER PRINTER	**INKJET PRINTERS**	**MULTIFUNCTION DEVICES**
This printer uses a laser beam, toner, and heat to transfer letters to paper, similar to copy machine technology. It offers the best resolution, fastest print speeds, and highest quality.	Ink-jet printers squirt a small puff of ink onto paper to create the image. They are available in both black/white and color. These usually inexpensive printers are slower than laser printers but offer good resolution.	These combination fax/copier/printers actually use ink-jet, thermal, or laser printing technology to print images from a fax, a computer, or another sheet of paper.

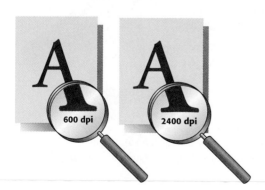

Figure 3.6
Printers and Their Print Resolutions
Printers vary in technology, speed, and quality of display.

On CD
Hardware Skills Builder
Printers

ON THE WEB! 3.5
Which Printer Is Best for
My Classroom?

Printers can create
overhead transparencies
and more.

Like monitors, printers vary in their resolution. The higher the resolution, the crisper and clearer the text and graphics that are produced. With printers, resolution is measured in **dpi** (dots per inch). Like images on a monitor, printed text and graphics are really just a series of tiny dots, in this case printed on a page. The more dots there are in an inch of print, the crisper the text or graphic appears and the more intense its color seems.

If you wish to make copies of a printout for your class, the greater the clarity of the original, the better the copies will look. For this reason, it is wise to make at least one original hard copy at the highest possible resolution. Most printers offer you the opportunity to print out in various modes, from draft to normal to high quality. Draft mode saves printer ink and usually prints more quickly. Normal is good for most documents. However, you should select high quality for your copier masters. You might need to review your printer's documentation to find out how best to adjust hard copy quality. Typically, it is done with a single click of your mouse button.

Printers not only produce their output on paper, they can also be used to produce their output on transparencies for use with an overhead projector. Specific types of transparency film must be used with different printers, however. Ink-jet printers work by squirting small bursts of ink onto the printing surface. As a printing surface, paper is absorbent enough to hold the ink. Transparency material is not absorbent unless it has been specially prepared. Ink-jet transparency material has one slick side and one side with a porous surface. This transparency material is specifically designed for use with an ink-jet printer and is distinctly labeled as such. Using a laser printer transparency film or other type of transparency material in an ink-jet printer will result in the ink running and smearing on the film.

Laser printers and copiers use heat to affix toner to the printed surface. Some transparency materials cannot withstand the heat of the laser printer's process. These transparencies will buckle and distort or possibly even melt inside the printer. It is therefore necessary to be sure to use laser or copier transparency materials in printers or copiers that use a heat process. Once again, different types of transparency materials are designed to be used in specific types of equipment. It is important to carefully read the transparency box to avoid potentially costly mistakes and wasted time.

In addition to transparency film, many other specialty papers are available for both ink-jet and laser printers. Using your classroom printer and selected specialty paper, you can print T-shirt transfers, custom stickers, CD labels, magnets, glossy digital photos, and a variety of other unique printouts. To do so, you must buy the paper

A variety of transparency film and specialty papers are available for use with ink jet and laser printers.

appropriate to your printer, whether ink-jet or laser. These specialty papers can add interest and customized activities to any classroom.

The number and variety of output devices that can be added to a computer system offer many possibilities for innovative application to teaching and learning. These devices will be explored more fully in Chapter 4.

ON THE WEB! 3.6
How Are Printers Useful in the Classroom?

The System Unit

All components of a computer system are assigned a different part of the total information-processing job. However, at the core of every computer is the system unit, the box that holds the computer's circuit board (motherboard) with the chips and circuits that make processing on the computer possible. Input, output, and storage devices enable the movement of data into and out of the system unit. But within the system unit, it is the central processing unit, or **CPU**, a powerful microprocessor chip, that is responsible for controlling all operations of the computer and processing data as instructed by the user. All computer components are ultimately interconnected through and coordinated by the CPU. Within the CPU chip, calculations are performed; flow of information between input, output, and memory is coordinated; and program instructions are transmitted at a speed measured in billionths of a second (nanoseconds). Current CPU chips, such as Intel's Pentium series, can carry out billions of instructions per second. Such speeds, typically measured in megahertz, are necessary, especially for complex software, to minimize the time the user has to wait for processing to complete. The faster the CPU, the more responsive the machine will be. For that reason, computer users want the fastest microprocessor chips with the highest number of megahertz they can acquire.

When you issue a command to begin a computing task, the CPU carries it out in two distinct steps. First, the CPU seeks out the instructions for how to do what you want done. The second step, once the CPU has found the necessary set of instructions, is to accept the data you input in order to perform the processes on it that you have requested. The CPU typically seeks its instructions in one or more of the storage devices attached to the machine and in the data it received from you via an input device.

Once the CPU has located the appropriate set of instructions or program (such as a word processor), it will load the program into the computer's memory, or random-access memory (RAM). **RAM** is the temporary memory space located on a set of chips that the CPU uses while it is carrying out its processing. The CPU reads the program from its permanent storage location (a disk) and then places a copy into RAM to make it readily accessible. Once the appropriate program is loaded into RAM, the CPU will direct RAM to store the input you enter so that it can be processed in accordance with the program's instructions. When you are finished with your processing tasks, at your command the CPU will save the processed data it has stored in RAM on a storage device so you can use it again later. Because data in RAM is volatile, it will be lost when power is lost. It is therefore critical to frequently give the Save command, which moves data in RAM to a more permanent location on a disk. When you complete your task and close the application, the CPU empties RAM of both program and data so that it is clear and available for your next task. Throughout every task you ask the computer to complete, the CPU controls the job and automatically utilizes RAM as necessary to assist in getting your processing task done.

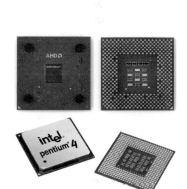

Microprocessor chips are the "brains" of a computer system.

On CD
Hardware Skills Builder
Inside the PC

Storage

Because we generally do not want to have to reenter data every time we want to use that same data, we need to store it in a more permanent location. Furthermore, we need to be able to store programs that we want available when we need to complete a specific type of job. Permanently storing data and programs is the function of the storage devices included in a computer system. All computers have a hard disk drive to store programs and data. However, there are many possible additional configurations for storage devices in a computer. You may select any combination of a floppy disk drive, one or more CD drives, and even a DVD drive. How a machine is configured in terms of storage is determined by your needs.

Hard Disks

Each type of storage device uses its own unique media. Figure 3.7 and Table 3.2 summarize and compare the most common types of disk storage media. Because of its large storage capacity, the **hard disk** drive is the most commonly used mass storage device for a computer. Inside the hard disk drive are a series of stacked metal platters (hard disks) on which data is stored. These disks comprise the storage area in which the operating system, applications programs, and most personal data are stored.

For most machines, the hard disk drive is designated with the drive letter C. The disks, or platters, built into the hard disk drive can hold **gigabytes,** or billions of bytes,

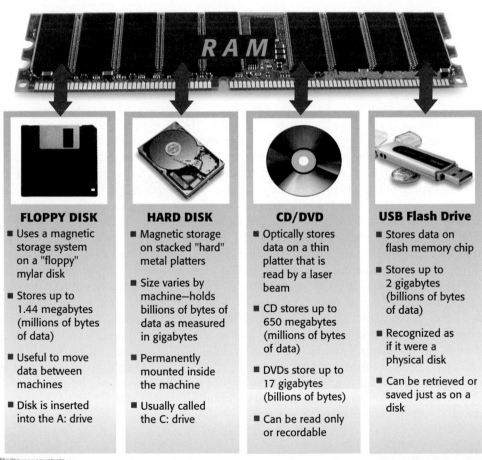

FLOPPY DISK	HARD DISK	CD/DVD	USB Flash Drive
▪ Uses a magnetic storage system on a "floppy" mylar disk	▪ Magnetic storage on stacked "hard" metal platters	▪ Optically stores data on a thin platter that is read by a laser beam	▪ Stores data on flash memory chip
▪ Stores up to 1.44 megabytes (millions of bytes of data)	▪ Size varies by machine—holds billions of bytes of data as measured in gigabytes	▪ CD stores up to 650 megabytes (millions of bytes of data)	▪ Stores up to 2 gigabytes (billions of bytes of data)
▪ Useful to move data between machines	▪ Permanently mounted inside the machine	▪ DVDs store up to 17 gigabytes (billions of bytes)	▪ Recognized as if it were a physical disk
▪ Disk is inserted into the A: drive	▪ Usually called the C: drive	▪ Can be read only or recordable	▪ Can be retrieved or saved just as on a disk

Figure 3.7
From Storage to Virtual Desktop
Data and programs are moved into RAM whenever the user needs to start an application or use information stored on one of the available storage devices. Once in RAM, the program or data is active and available to use.

of data. A **byte** of data is roughly equal to one alphabetic (A) or numeric (1) character of information (see Table 3.3). Thus, a typical hard disk can hold billions of letters or numbers (alphanumeric characters) as stored data. In the physical world, the hard disk might be analogous to a number of very large multiple-drawer file cabinets. The surfaces of hard disks are so sensitive that ordinary airborne contaminants such as dust or a strand of hair can interrupt the flow of information if it gets caught between the drive head and the disk itself. Hard disks are therefore usually fixed inside the computer's case and encased in their own protective housing. Because they are permanently fixed inside the computer, hard disks are also sometimes called fixed disks.

Permanently fixing the hard disk inside the computer does not make it immune to problems. Problems can and do affect the data you store on a disk. Because any electronic or mechan-

Today's hard disk drives offer storage space for billions of pages of text, millions of graphics, and thousands of audio and video clips.

TABLE 3.2   COMPARISON OF STORAGE MEDIA

Storage Media	Characteristics
FLOPPY DISK	• Disk of Mylar inside rigid plastic shell • Magnetic film on both sides of Mylar stores data • Up to 1,444,000 bytes (1.44 megabytes) of data can be stored on a high-density 3.5" disk • Disks must be prepared to accept data (formatted) before using • Has been the most popular portable storage medium • Some computers no longer include floppy disk drives but have replaced them with additional removable or optical media
HARD DISK	• Stack of metal platters (disks) permanently mounted inside the computer box • Platters are coated with magnetic material on both top and bottom of disk • Sensitive to contaminants, so the disk and drives are permanently encased and mounted in the system unit • Storage capacity ranges but is typically multiple gigabytes (billions of bytes) of data • Usually designated the C drive, it is the primary mass storage area for both programs and data
REMOVABLE MEDIA	• Portable hard disk and disk cartridges that can be added to a computer system • Cartridges vary in size from 250-megabyte cartridges to 1-gigabyte cartridges • Cartridges must be used with storage drives mounted in or added to the system unit • A portable hard disk is a self-contained disk and drive that plugs into one of the ports in the system unit • Portable hard disks can vary from a few to hundreds of gigabytes in capacity • Both types of removable media are convenient for transporting large multimedia files
CD-ROM, CD-R, CD-RW	• Optical discs of plastic on which microscopic holes have been burned using a laser • Holes and flat areas are read by a laser mounted in a CD drive • CD-ROMs are read-only, making them a one-way storage media, unlike disks • CD-Rs are special-purpose CDs that can be written on once and read multiple times; they require a recordable drive to create them but can be read by any CD drive • CD-RWs are specially constructed CDs that are rewritable; CD-RW drives are necessary to store and erase data on CD-RWs; CD-RWs can be read by most CD drives • CDs can store up to 650 megabytes of data • Often used for multimedia storage because of their large capacity for storing audio, video, and textual data
DVD-ROM, DVD-R, DVD-RW	• DVDs are optical media that can store up to 17 gigabytes of data depending on the format of the DVD • DVD-ROMs are read-only; after initial recording, data cannot be stored on them • DVD-Rs are recordable but require a DVD writer • Three competing formats are available: DVD-R/W and DVD-RW are competing formats with similar features; DVD-RAM offers additional features but is incompatible with some players • DVD-Rs and DVD-RWs can record approximately 2 hours of quality video

TABLE 3.3   RELATIVE SIZES OF STORED DATA

Size	Character Equivalent	Example
1 BYTE	1 alphanumeric character	The letter A or number 5
1 KILOBYTE	Approximately 1,000 characters	Slightly less than 1 page of typed, double-spaced text
1 MEGABYTE	Approximately 1 million characters	1,000 pages of typed, double-spaced, text
1 GIGABYTE	Approximately 1 billion characters	1 million pages of typed, double-spaced, text

ON THE WEB! 3.7
How Is Disk Storage
Useful?

ical device can break, it is important to remember to **back up** your data, that is, make a duplicate or backup copy of your files. Usually, when a disk crashes (loses its storage ability), all of the information that was stored on that disk is lost. If you suffer a hard or floppy disk crash, your data may be irretrievable unless you have a backup copy. For teachers with lesson plans, tests, activity sheets, and student grades stored on a hard drive, such a loss can be devastating to your work. Backup files are usually made on removable storage media (floppy disks, Zip or Jaz disks, or CD-RWs) that can be stored away from the machine. It is not necessary to back up your application programs, because they can always be reinstalled. However, it is a good idea to keep the original media and their documentation in a safe place and available for reinstallation if it becomes necessary.

Most of the time when you are working on the computer, you will be using the hard disk drive for storage. If you need to use more than one machine, perhaps one at home or in the faculty workroom as well as one in your classroom, you will need a way to move your data from one machine to the other. This is one of the reasons for the popularity of removable storage media. One of the most common types of removable storage media is the floppy disk.

Floppy Disks

On CD!
Hardware Skills Builder
Floppy Disks

The floppy disk drive is an electromechanical device that is usually mounted inside the computer. It is able to read and write magnetic pulses from and to the surface of a **floppy disk.** Although the floppy disk is encased in a hard plastic protective case, it is not considered a type of "hard" disk. Inside the floppy's hard casing, the disk itself is made of flexible (floppy) Mylar-type material coated with a magnetically sensitive coating. Like its bigger cousin, the hard drive, it is sensitive to many environmental factors. The standard floppy disk can contain 1.44 megabytes (millions of bytes) of data, compared to the gigabyte (billions of bytes) capacity of today's hard disks. A floppy disk is analogous, in the physical world, to a portable file box. It can hold many files and many folders, but it has a limited capacity when compared to a multiple-drawer file cabinet. This smaller capacity means that information is packed less densely on the floppy disk, lowering its sensitivity to contaminants. Thus, it can be removed and exposed to the environment with a significantly lower probability of data loss. The floppy disk's increased durability makes it a viable and inexpensive medium for storage and transport.

The floppy disk stores 1.44 megabytes of information.

Whether on a floppy or hard disk, the organizational units for storing data are known as files and folders, as illustrated in Figure 3.8. An electronic **file** is a collection of related data, usually a product of a single task. A file is typically created through the use of a single application program. An electronic **folder** is a digital organizer that you

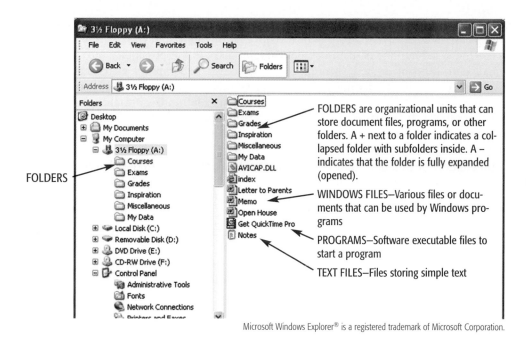

FOLDERS are organizational units that can store document files, programs, or other folders. A + next to a folder indicates a collapsed folder with subfolders inside. A – indicates that the folder is fully expanded (opened).

WINDOWS FILES—Various files or documents that can be used by Windows programs

PROGRAMS—Software executable files to start a program

TEXT FILES—Files storing simple text

Microsoft Windows Explorer® is a registered trademark of Microsoft Corporation.

Figure 3.8
Windows Explorer and Its Organizational System
Windows organizes your data using a file and folder system. When a folder is expanded, in the left pane of Explorer you will see icons representing the contents of the folder.

create to hold related files on a disk. In the physical world, a file would be equivalent to one or more printed sheets of information that resulted from the completion of a task. A folder, like its paper counterpart, the file folder, would be used to hold related documents (files).

Floppy disks are ideal for storing backup copies of files as long as the files are not very large. Since floppy disks can hold only 1.44 megabytes of data, larger files may require larger-capacity media. Most operating systems allow you to select a file icon by pointing to it and clicking on it. You can then drag the file into a folder or disk of your choice. This is a very easy method for backing up your files. To drag, after clicking on a file to select it, you depress and hold down the left mouse button. With the button held down, you move the mouse, and the selected file will move with it. As the pointer moves from one folder icon on the hard drive to another, the file is moved as well. When the mouse button is released, the file is dropped into the folder you are pointing to.

Copying files onto floppy disks also allows you to transport them from one computer to another. Just copy the file to a floppy, insert that floppy into a different computer, and copy the data from it into the new computer. Of course, it is necessary that the application software that created the file also be available in the second computer. Copying a file copies the data only; it does not copy the application program that made and initially saved the file.

Floppy disks are particularly useful in a classroom setting. Students who are creating their own personal files for an activity need a place to store them. If the files are saved on the hard disk drive, other students in the class can potentially access them. Furthermore, if you are teaching in a secondary school with a student load of more than 150 students per day, the available space on your hard drive is rapidly consumed. Instead, to ensure privacy and to save hard disk space, it is easier to give each student his or her own floppy disk(s) to use throughout the term or the project. Students can then be responsible

Although an older media, floppy disks remain one of the most versatile and popular storage formats.

For classroom use, floppy disks offer many significant advantages.

for their own data for the duration of the project. At the end of the term or year, the disks can all be erased and reused by the next group of students.

One disadvantage of using student floppy disks is the possibility of a computer virus entering your system through a student's disk. A computer **virus** is a program written specifically to disrupt computer operations and/or destroy data. Viruses are often transmitted from computer to computer by surreptitiously attaching themselves to normal files. When these carrier files are saved on a floppy disk and that disk is later used in a virus-free computer, the virus is transmitted to the "healthy" computer's hard disk drive (Figure 3.9). Once there, it executes its damaging program either immediately or at a later time. If designed to do so, the virus may infect other floppy disks used in the once-healthy computer, thus further spreading the problem.

Viruses can be a challenge for computer-using teachers. Clearly, student floppy disks are effective for ensuring student file privacy and for keeping the classroom computer's hard disk space available. However, students often exchange games and information if they have home computers, or they download files from the Internet that may be infected. Once a virus infects a student's home machine, a disk carried back and forth to school for a class assignment can result in that same virus infecting and destroying data on the classroom machine.

To protect the classroom computers, teachers and technology-support personnel often install **antivirus programs.** Antivirus programs detect and destroy computer viruses. They scan the hard drive and floppy disks used in the machine and warn if any possible virus is detected. Every classroom computer should have an antivirus program installed. It is also important to subscribe to continuous updates of the installed antivirus programs. Unfortunately, as fast as viruses are recognized and neutralized,

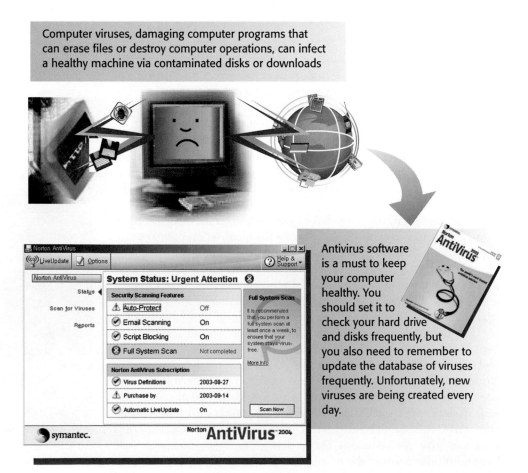

Figure 3.9
Red Alert! Computer Viruses
Schools need to be on the alert for computer viruses.

IN THE CLASSROOM
Creative Teaching with Computers

Examples of the creative use of computers to further instruction by K–12 teachers are everywhere. Many teachers have found technology to be a remarkably versatile and powerful means to the end of making learning both fun and effective in their classrooms. Here are just a few of its many innovative uses.

Having one's work published is the ultimate reward for writing. In the fourth-grade class at the Orchard School in South Burlington, Vermont, Dylan Novelli, Shannon Edmunds, and Deb Gurwicz have found a way to ensure that their students get the most visibility for their writing projects. These teachers place their students' writing on the computers' screen savers in their classroom. Mr. Novelli, Ms. Edmunds, and Ms. Gurwicz tell us, "Kids love to see their work pop up on the computer screen and enjoy reading one another's writing."

Teens' fascination with cars is the entry point that Aleta Boyce, at Tooele High School in Tooele County, Utah, uses for grabbing the attention of her high school students when she is introducing them to the uses of search engines. She has them look for prices of their favorite vehicles and narrow their searches to the most wanted car, coming up with desired colors, makes, and models. Once the car of choice is located, the students send Ms. Boyce a photo or description, along with the price, via the Internet and, finally, print out the message they have sent.

Foreign language teachers have found the computer to be an invaluable tool in teaching the language and culture of the countries under study in their classrooms. Dianne Vitaska, a French teacher at C. E. King High School in Houston, Texas, uses her web site to provide informative links for her students so that they can look up topics under discussion in the classroom. Also on the web site is a scavenger hunt that poses questions students can find answers to. In addition, she has her students prepare a PowerPoint presentation, a brochure, or a web page to demonstrate the knowledge gained from their cultural explorations.

SOURCES: D. Novelli, S. Edmunds, & D. Gurwicz. Screen-saver stories. *Instructor* (May/June 2001) 110 (8), 74; A. Boyce. 2002. Using cars to build Internet search skills. Retrieved January 10, 2002, from **http://www.nea.org/cet/wired/index.html**; D. Vitaska. 2002. The new language classroom: Bringing French to the U.S. *Media and Methods* (September/October) 39 (1), 10.

new virus programs are written by malicious programmers and let loose on unsuspecting computer users. The typical classroom computer should therefore have its antivirus program updated at least monthly. A frequent update will ensure that the antivirus program has the latest list of new viruses and virus countermeasures.

Removable Hard Disks

Some hard disk drives are designed to use removable hard disks. **Removable hard disks** offer the transportability and convenience of a floppy disk while providing much greater storage capacity and the durability of a firm, hard disk. A removable hard disk is encased in its own durable holder that can be inserted into and removed from its drive without exposing the disk surface to contaminants. Removable hard disks look similar to floppy disks but are slightly larger and thicker. The storage capacity of removable hard disks ranges from 100 megabytes to several gigabytes. The removable disk drives themselves can either be mounted in the computer or plugged into the back of the computer and run as an additional, external drive.

Removable hard disks have become very popular, now that many programs incorporate graphics, animation, and sound files. These types of **multimedia** files—files that include multiple types of media (text, graphics, sound, video, and animation)—are often too large to fit on a floppy disk. To transport them, a removable disk is ideal. However, all machines on which you want to use the disk must have the proper removable disk drive.

Removable disks are particularly useful for storing large multimedia files.

For the classroom, removable hard disks are especially useful. A single removable hard disk can serve as a backup medium for an entire class's individual personal files, or it can store all multimedia files related to a specific content area for easy access. Additionally, since removable disks offer as much storage space as you have disks, it becomes less critical to have large amounts of storage space on the internal hard drive.

connecting THEORY to PRACTICE

Hand in Hand: E-portfolios and Authentic Assessment

Authentic assessment as defined by the Pearson Education Development Group, states, "aims to evaluate students' abilities in 'real-world' contexts. In other words, students learn how to apply skills to authentic tasks and projects. . . . It focuses on students' analytical skills; ability to integrate what they learn; creativity; ability to work collaboratively; and written and oral expression skills. It values the learning process as much as the finished product."

Student portfolios fulfill this goal, because they provide a means of evaluating the steps the student has taken to complete a learning task; in other words, it is a means of making a long-term appraisal of student performance. With the electronic capabilities available for transforming the traditional portfolio into a multimedia document, a third dimension of multiple intelligences can be added to the end product. Students can work together and utilize the dominant intelligences of the group to create portfolios that call for kinesthetic, spatial, musical, verbal-linguistic, logical-mathematical, intrapersonal, and interpersonal contributions. Chris Guenter at California State University in Chico sums up this powerful integration: "The goal of this ongoing investigation and process is to construct a personal, dynamic, non-linear student teaching portfolio [relevant to all e-portfolios]

that includes text, audio, graphics, digitized photos, video, html and hypermedia presentation."

Jean Kriwox at Horizon Elementary School in Jerome, Iowa, has demonstrated how the electronic portfolio can be used to fulfill the same goals. She created a unit, "Quilting and Geometry-Patterns for Living," for which the students prepared electronic portfolios. "I required my students to keep an updated journal as we proceeded through the unit. As part of this unit and the regular curriculum, we go to the computer twice weekly. Students jotted down notes to add to their journals during the twice-weekly visits to the computer lab. For some students, this was their first experience using computer drawing tools. Most students drew and colored their quilt block with ease in their computer journals," she writes. To see the student journals, go to the Student Work hyperlink at the referenced web site below.

SOURCES: Pearson Education Development Group. (2003). Authentic assessment overview. Retrieved October 5, 2003, from **http://teachervision.fen.com/lesson-plans/lesson-4911.html**; Chris Guenter. 2003. Student teaching electronic portfolio. Retrieved October 5, 2003, from **http://www.csuchico.edu/educ/estport.htm**; J. Kriwox. 2003. Quilting and geometry-patterns for living. Retrieved October 5, 2003, from **http://ali.apple.com/ali_sites/deli/exhibits/1000077**.

This makes older machines originally designed with smaller hard drives more usable with the simple addition of a removable hard disk drive.

CD-ROMs

ON THE WEB! 3.8
CD Storage

A **CD-ROM** (compact disc–read-only memory) is also removable. However, this is a read-only medium, so you can get information from it but you cannot store any information on a typical CD-ROM. Most computers today are equipped with a drive that will read CD-ROMs. Such a drive reads the information from CD-ROMs that contain programs, files, or other data. It is also capable of reading and, given the right software and speakers, playing musical CDs as well.

Unlike magnetically recorded floppy and hard disks, CD-ROMs are recorded by a laser beam that burns pits into the tracks on the disc's surface. Then another laser reads those pits and the remaining flat surface of the disc as data. Approximately 650 megabytes of data (text, sound, graphics, animation, or video) can be stored on a single CD. This is equivalent to the storage capacity of approximately four hundred floppy disks. Because of their storage capacity, CD-ROMs are used to store and transport large programs and graphic files that should not be altered. These programs are usually full-featured applications designed to be installed on your computer. Installing a program means moving essential components of a program from a transport medium (floppy disk or CD-ROM) to the hard drive so that it can be accessed and run whenever it is requested. CDs may also store self-contained multimedia programs that are too large to install on most computer systems. These types of CD-based multimedia programs, including many academic multimedia programs, are designed to be run from the CD-ROM itself.

Other programs are designed to either install themselves on the hard drive or run from the CD drive. Typically, with this type of software, you are given the choice of whether to allow a program to be installed on your hard drive or not. Installed software can take up sizable amounts of space on the hard drive. However, programs that are run from the hard drive are quicker to access and run. If the programs are left on the CD-ROM drive, you will keep your hard drive space available for other uses, but the CD-ROM-based program may run more slowly. Furthermore, you must keep the CD available in the drive at all times to use the program. For data files (usually graphics files and clip art libraries), you must keep the CD available in the drive until you are done with the files stored on it. Many teachers prefer to install programs to classroom hard drives even though they are large programs. Doing so allows the teacher to store the original CD in a safe place and avoids costly and inconvenient loss.

On CD
Hardware Skills Builder
Optical Media

CD-Rs and CD-RWs

A **CD-R** (compact disc–recordable) is a unique type of CD-ROM on which you can record (write) data. You must have a CD-R drive, CD-R recording software, and blank CD-Rs to use for this process. Any data that you can create with any application (text, graphics, sound, video) can be stored permanently on a CD-R. Once recorded, a CD-R is not changeable. It becomes like any other CD that is read-only. However, once created, a CD-R does not need a CD-R drive to run it. Software stored on a CD-R can be accessed by any drive that will read CDs.

CD-Rs can store approximately 650 megabytes of data or 75 minutes of audio. Because of their permanence and large storage capacity, they are particularly useful for archiving information (such as student portfolios) and storing teacher- or student-created multimedia files.

A **CD-RW** (compact disc–rewritable) drive takes the concept of reusable CDs one step further. These drives and the special discs that are designed for use in them allow you not only to record but also to change stored data. Because a CD-RW holds approx-

CD-RWs can be written on repeatedly.

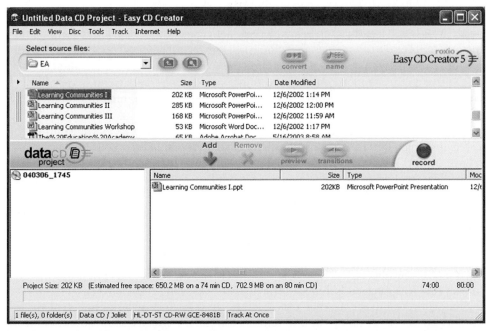

CD recording software such as Roxio's CD Creator helps you to select and organize the files you want burned on your recordable CD.

imately the same amount of data as a CD-ROM or CD-R, it offers the same advantage of large storage capacity. However, its usefulness is somewhat limited by the fact that the CD produced by a CD-RW drive might not be usable in all CD-ROM and CD-R drives; the recorded data might therefore not be readable by older machines.

The CD-RW does offer a solution to the fact that many multimedia files cannot be stored on floppy disks simply because they are too large. Instructional files you create that contain graphics, animation, video, and/or audio clips exceed the capacity of a floppy disk many times over. If you or your students will be creating and saving such larger files, a CD-RW drive might be your best solution. You might choose a removable hard disk, because these too offer additional space; however, they are not as readily transportable, because most machines are not equipped with a drive that will read them. However, many newer machines have CD drives that are capable of reading most CD-RWs. Overall, CD-RWs are proving to be the most logical and efficient choices for storing large instructional files or student information in classroom settings.

▌ DVDs

DVD-ROM (digital versatile discs) are another type of optical medium. A DVD drive will read both DVDs and CDs, thus allowing the newer DVD-equipped computers to use older CD-ROM technology as well (a phenomenon called downward compatibility). The advantage of a DVD is its ability to store considerably more data than a CD-ROM. DVDs can store data on both sides (unlike the one-sided CD-ROM) and on up to two layers per side. A DVD can store 4.7 gigabytes of data in the same physical space (one side, one layer), a great advantage compared to the 650 megabytes of data that can be stored on a CD-ROM. When both sides and both layers are used, the DVD can store up to 17 gigabytes of data, enough to hold a full-length, full-screen movie. Despite this higher storage capacity and the greater amount of information the DVD drive has to search through, the DVD drive can reach access speeds equal to the fastest CD-type drives. Consequently, there is no noticeable delay in reading DVDs.

DVD drives are able to read DVDs, CD-ROMs, CD-Rs, CD-RWs, and musical CDs, making this single drive the most versatile hardware currently available for optical (laser-technology) media. For education, DVDs also hold the promise of a high-quality, very durable video medium. Unlike videotape, which can wear out or break relatively easily, a DVD will last through years of classroom use without degrading—that is, losing any of its audio or video quality. Some DVDs even offer special options, such as displaying subtitles with the video or zooming in on an image. A DVD drive often replaces a CD drive as the standard on many of today's computers. This trend is very likely to continue, and in the near future, DVD will become the optical medium of choice for most computer users.

Additionally, recordable DVD (DVD-R) drives are emerging as an alternative storage technology. This technology allows users to record data on a DVD just as you can record on a CD-R or CD-RW. This medium will make it possible to store and update large files, teacher- or student-made videos, audios, and computer-based multimedia data all on a single disc.

Recordable DVDs are currently available in several competing formats. A DVD-R (pronounced "DVD dash R") is a nonrewritable, recordable DVD that can be played back on most DVD players. DVD-Rs can hold 4.7 gigabytes of information if recorded on a single side and 9.4 gigabytes when recorded on both sides, significantly more data than a 650-megabyte CD-R can hold. Another format, called DVD+R, is a competing format that has some additional technical features beyond those offered by the DVD-R format. However, to the average user, both of these formats will do the job of recording large amounts of data. The differences between the two are the result of competition between developers of DVDs. Similarly, competing formats exist for the rewritable versions of DVDs. DVD-RW and DVD+RW are two rewritable formats based on technology similar to that of their companion recordable discs, DVD-R and DVD+R. Most of today's compatibility problems with DVD recordable and rewritable discs will cease to exist over time. Just as early CD recordable discs had some compatibility issues, DVD standards too will ultimately combine into a single essentially universal standard.

For a teacher interested in a recordable DVD, it is important to first decide whether rewriting a DVD is necessary for the storage task at hand. If so, a DVD-rewritable device rather than a DVD-recordable device would be the better choice. Once the need for rewritability is determined, either of the competing formats will handle the typical classroom recording job. At that point, the only technical concern for the teacher is to be sure that DVD-media purchases are consistent with the type of DVD recording technology selected (– or +).

Regardless of the type of DVD player or recorder a computer is equipped with, one advantage of a DVD in a classroom computer is that it can be configured to take the place of a VCR and monitor. If the classroom is equipped with a projector capable of displaying computer images, then it can be used to display a DVD image as well. Using a computer display and the computer's DVD player, you can easily display a video recorded on DVD so that that the entire class can view it. This type of configuration thus can serve two purposes and may make a VCR and monitor combination redundant.

Educational Computing

As you have learned, computer systems offer teachers and students a unique capability. Input hardware allows you to enter vast amounts of data easily and quickly. Using a mouse, you can issue commands to a powerful machine with just the click of a button. Output hardware lets you create hard copy that once could be produced only via typesetting and printing presses. The system unit and its CPU allow you to do many complicated calculations and tasks in the time it takes to blink your eyes. But what do all these digital marvels have to do with teaching and with learning?

Like any technology, computers are a tool that can help you build the kind of learning environment you might once only have imagined. Using a computer, your students can publish their own class newsletter with digital images from their recent field trip. They can create interactive stories that their peers can explore. They can connect to online resources that place the world's knowledge base literally at their fingertips. But having such a powerful tool available means little if you don't know how to use it. Mastery of the computer basics presented in this chapter is an excellent first step.

As you increase your understanding of and skills with computers, you will find your own personal applications for this unique digital technology. Computers have changed our society and have ushered in the Information Age. There is little doubt that they will ultimately have the same impact throughout education. Your own personal mastery of this revolutionary digital tool will serve both you and your students well. And, like all educational technologies, it is important to carefully evaluate computers before selecting them for your classroom. An evaluation rubric (Table 3.4) can be a powerful tool when reviewing and evaluating computer hardware.

Of course, digital technologies include more than just a computer system. As an outgrowth of computers, a true digital revolution has begun. Many of today's cameras use digital methods of capturing and storing images instead of film. Audiotapes and vinyl records are being replaced by CDs. And you have only to visit a local video rental store to discover the ever-expanding shelves of DVDs and the shrinking shelves of videocassettes. What does all this mean to educators?

As you will see in the next four chapters, it means that more and more tools are becoming available to individualize instruction, meet unique learner needs, and help

TABLE 3.4   HARDWARE EVALUATION RUBRIC

HARDWARE:

DESCRIPTION:

VENDOR: COST:

NOTES ON USE:

Please rate the features below for each hardware component. Next to each of the items in the rubric, mark the box that best reflects your opinion.

EVALUATION CRITERIA

Hardware Feature	1 Poor	2 Below Average	3 Average	4 Above Average	5 Excellent
CPU	Speed below school standard; insufficient to run class software	Speed below standard but sufficient to run most class software	Speed at standard; will support current class software	Speed at or above standard; will support newer software	Speed above standard; likely to support next-generation software
RAM	Capacity below school standard; insufficient to run class software	Capacity below school standard but sufficient to run most class software	Capacity at standard; will support current class software	Capacity at or above standard; will support newer software	Capacity above standard; likely to support next-generation software
Input devices	Keyboard flimsy with limited features; off-brand mouse without features	Keyboard flimsy but with some extra features; off-brand mouse with some features	Keyboard includes features (wrist guard, etc..); brand-name mouse with features	Multimedia keyboard; brand-name mouse or trackball	Multimedia keyboard; brand-name optical trackball or mouse
Monitor	Low resolution; slow scan rate, minimum color depth; insufficient for newer software	Low resolution; acceptable scan rate and color depth; may be insufficient for some software	resolution, scan rate, color depth meet school standards; will display most software	Resolution, scan rate, color depth meet or exceed school standards; will display newer software	Resolution, scan rate color depth meet or exceed school standards; will display next-generation software
Hard drive	Capacity below school standard; insufficient to run class software	Capacity below school standard but sufficient to run most class software	Capacity at standard; will support current class software	Capacity at or above standard; will support newer software	Capacity above standard; likely to support next-generation software
Removable media drives	No removable media drive; no expansion capacity	Limited to 1 floppy disk drive; limited expansion capacity	1 or more floppy disk drives; expandable	Floppy disk and 1 other removable media drive; expandable	Multiple removable media drives with capacity to expand
Optical drives	No optical drive	CD-ROM only	1 optical drive (CD-R or CD-RW)	Multiple optical drives (CD-RW and CD-ROM)	Multiple optical drives (CD-RW and DVD or DVD-R)
Sound system	Minimal sound card; non-powered speakers	Minimal sound card; powered speakers	Adequate sound card; powered speakers	Upgraded sound card; amplified speakers	Upgraded sound card; amplified speakers with woofer
Ports	Minimal ports; no USB ports	Adequate ports; 1 USB port	All standard ports; 2–4 USB ports	All standard ports; 4 or more USB ports	All standard ports; 4 or more USB ports, front-accessible
Warranty support	No warranty; no free phone support	Less than 1-year warranty; no free phone support	1-year warranty; free phone support for less than 1 year	1-year warranty; free phone support for 1 year	1-year warranty; free phone support; on-site support

Total the score for each hardware component. Compare the scores. The component with the highest score is your best choice.

you teach and manage your classroom. It means that a more diverse and robust learning environment can be constructed for your students. All you need to do to use current and emerging digital innovations is, first, be aware that they exist and, second, be willing to learn to use them. Increasing your digital awareness and helping you learn to use digital technologies are the purposes of the rest of this unit.

KEY TERMS

antivirus programs   92

application program   80

back up   90

booting up   77

byte   89

CD-R   95

CD-ROM   94

CD-RW   95

chips   77

commands   78

computer system   76

computing cycle   76

CPU   87

dpi   86

DVD-ROMs   96

file   90

floppy disk   90

folder   90

gigabytes   88

GUI   78

hard copy   84

hard disk   88

hardware   76

icon   78

input device   82

integrated software package   81

interface   78

keyboard   82

LCD   85

memory   76

menu   78

monitor   84

mouse   79

multimedia   93

operating system   78

output devices   84

pixel   84

POST   78

programs   76

RAM   87

removable hard disks   93

resolution   84

ROM   77

soft copy   84

software   76

storage   76

utility programs   80

virus   92

Windows   78

STUDENT ACTIVITIES

CHAPTER REVIEW

1. Describe each of the four major components of the computing cycle.
2. What is the difference between hardware and software? Give an example of each.
3. What is the difference between memory and storage in a computer system? Why are both necessary?
4. Describe the role of the operating system. How does it help you interact with a computer?
5. What are the three different classes of application software? What different types of tasks does each perform?
6. What is the CPU, and what is its role in the computer system?
7. Describe the difference between input and output devices. Give two examples of each.

8. What do you need to know about monitor resolution before purchasing a monitor? About printer resolution before buying a printer?
9. What is a computer virus and how is it transmitted? What can you do to protect your classroom?
10. How do the following storage devices differ: hard disk, floppy disk, removable disk, CD-ROM, CD-R, CD-RW, DVD?

WHAT DO YOU THINK?

1. Interview three of your fellow students to see how they think computers affect their learning and the teaching they have been exposed to in their academic career. On the basis of the interviews and your own views, what can you conclude about the role of computers in instruction?
2. On a topic of your choice and at the grade level that you wish to teach, prepare an instructional design and/or a lesson plan that you think will benefit from the use of computer technology. In your plan, be sure to explain fully how the computer will enhance the lesson.
3. Interview one of the technical-support staff members at your school and ask what types of storage devices he or she would recommend in a computer system. Be sure to ask whether the person prefers CD-ROM, CD-R, CD-RW, or DVD drives and ask what size permanent and portable hard drives he or she recommends and why. What can you conclude about how to configure a computer for your classroom?

LEARNING TOGETHER!

The following activities are designed for learning groups of two or three students.

1. Select three different computer systems and compare them using the hardware evaluation rubric (Table 3.4). After discussing the options with your group, describe which system you would buy and explain why. Be prepared to share your preference and your reasons with the class.
2. Each member of your group should interview a teacher who uses a computer in his or her classroom. Ask the teacher how the computer is used for academic and for administrative tasks. Compare your interviews with those of the other members of your group and list the uses you discover.
3. Brainstorm how computers have changed society in general and education in particular. Identify and list all of the ways in which computers have had an impact. Then determine five ways in which they are likely to change society and education in the future. Be prepared to share your group's outcomes with your peers.

HANDS-ON!

1. Visit a computer store or surf the Internet to determine the hardware specifications for the following software packages, which are frequently used in schools: Microsoft Word, ClarisWorks, CorelDRAW, and Windows XP.
2. Use your online library resources to research recent articles about computer viruses and how to prevent the damage they can cause. Prepare a report for presentation to your class on what they should do to protect themselves.
3. Explore online lesson plans that use a computer to support the lessons. Print three that you believe are innovative. Critique them in a two- to three-page review of the plans. Include what you think are the best and least useful ideas that you might adapt when you teach.

More from Theodore Detjen

You have learned much about personal computers and how they may best support education. It is clear that teachers have a role and a responsibility related to the implementation of computer technology in their classrooms, their schools, and their districts.

Let's return now to Theodore Detjen and see the challenges a district technology-support department faces in helping teachers and schools utilize technology. As you review these challenges, consider how you might best assist computer-support personnel in meeting their goal of serving you and your students.

The Mid-Hudson Regional Information Center and the other eleven centers that serve New York State schools face several challenges as we continue to support our school districts. The first of these is technology planning. Most school districts have technology plans that are separate from the district's education plan. This can create conflict in a district's overall technology implementation. Schools' plans should be, but are not always, a subset of the district learning plan, rather than a separate entity with driving forces of its own. Then there is technology coordination. In middle- to large-size districts, we often see school buildings not communicating with each other on technology solutions. We have seen the same school district purchase two separate student information systems or use the same system in an inconsistent manner across its school buildings. For effective implementation, coordination is essential.

Meanwhile, technology continues to evolve. Hardware and software as well as their transport (telephone circuits, cable, wireless) continue to offer multiple and sometimes conflicting paths.

Furthermore, education is preoccupied with assessment. New York State and most of the other states are offering more and more standardized tests, which is leaving less time for technology to support the creative learning process. Instead, technology is being called upon to support the testing process. This direction is coming from the local states and from the current national government. Accountability is the operative word.

Schools are being asked to do more and more with less and less. Because of dwindling resources, school districts must keep class sizes high to control costs. At the same time, the number of qualified educators is decreasing. As more baby boomers, who entered teaching in the late 1960s and early 1970s, begin to retire, we discover fewer college students entering the field of education.

Because of these multiple challenges, this is an exciting time to be in the role of information support for schools. The good news is that our twelve centers are working together. I am confident that many of these challenges will diminish in size as we cooperate and discover new and creative solutions.

Contact Information: Theodore Detjen, Administrator, K–12, Mid-Hudson Regional Information Center, New Paltz, New York.

Email: tdetjen@earthlink.net

SOURCE: Interview with Theodore Detjen conducted by Al P. Mizell. Reprinted by permission of Theodore Detjen, retired director of computer services, Mid-Hudson Regional Information Center, Board of Cooperative Educational Services–Ulster County, New York.

Digital Technologies in the Classroom

This chapter addresses these ISTE National Educational Technology Standards for Teachers:

I. Technology operations and concepts

Teachers demonstrate a sound understanding of technology operations and concepts. Teachers

A. demonstrate introductory knowledge, skills, and understanding of concepts related to technology (as described in the ISTE *National Education Technology Standards for Students*).
B. demonstrate continual growth in technology knowledge and skills to stay abreast of current and emerging technologies.

II. Planning and designing learning environments and experiences

Teachers plan and design effective learning environments and experiences supported by technology. Teachers

A. design developmentally appropriate learning opportunities that apply technology-enhanced instructional strategies to support the diverse needs of learners.
B. apply current research on teaching and learning with technology when planning learning environments and experiences.
C. identify and locate technology resources and evaluate them for accuracy and suitability.
D. plan for the management of technology resources within the context of learning activities.
E. plan strategies to manage student learning in a technology-enhanced environment.

III. Teaching, learning, and the curriculum

Teachers implement curriculum plans that include methods and strategies for applying technology to maximize student learning. Teachers

A. facilitate technology-enhanced experiences that address content standards and student technology standards.
B. use technology to support learner-centered strategies that address the diverse needs of students.
C. apply technology to develop students' higher-order skills and creativity.
D. manage student learning activities in a technology-enhanced environment.

Computers have changed our world, both inside and outside the classroom. It is not just the computer itself, with all of its capabilities, that has caused this change. Indeed, the computer has proven itself to be just the forerunner of a much greater digital revolution. As a result of the advances in personal computers, many other digital devices have evolved. These devices can serve teaching and learning in dramatic and innovative ways.

Consider for a moment the process teachers once used to duplicate materials for their students. Have you ever heard the term dittos applied to teacher-prepared work sheets? Have you ever wondered where this term comes from? Before personal computers began to be mass-produced, teachers had to go through a laborious process to prepare student worksheets. Two technologies were available to them: the duplicating machine, which used blue-backed transfer paper to run a limited number of duplicate copies, and the dittograph machine, which used a waxed paper that was cut (like a stencil) by typewriter keys or by a special sharp stylus. The duplicator used an alcohol-based chemical to transfer the blue ink from the master to plain paper. The dittograph ran ink through the temporary stencil the teacher created and transferred that ink to paper. Both technologies were very messy and could reproduce a very limited number of copies before the masters deteriorated. Also, teachers had to be very careful not to make mistakes when creating those masters. No Delete keys were available on typewriters or when creating a master by hand! Mistakes were transferred along with correct content. And, of course, these types of technology could not change the size or style of the font, add graphics, or make transparencies.

With the first personal computer came the first word processor. This combination made it possible for teachers to see the finished product on the screen, correct all mistakes, adjust fonts, and even add graphics before transferring the document to paper. Furthermore, as printers became more sophisticated and cheaper, it became easy to print out high-quality transparencies and worksheets that incorporated color and graphics.

The computer was just the beginning. The tools that have resulted from it are even more amazing. The change from laborious duplication to quick word processing and printing is just one example of the digital revolution computers began. Just as this necessary teaching task was simplified and enhanced by digital technologies, so too have countless more teaching and learning tasks been improved through the application of digital equipment.

This chapter will help you explore the many digital technologies that have evolved out of the digital revolution led by the personal computer. In Chapter 4, you will

- Explore how digital input technologies can be used in teaching and learning

- Examine how digital output technologies can be used in teaching and learning

- Review the issues and concerns associated with using these diverse technologies in the classroom

- Explore emerging digital technologies that may be useful to teachers and learners in the future

Meet Mike Duffy

Teachers sometimes must take a proactive approach to technology in their classroom. You might not always have the technology you need to support your students in the way that you would like to. Mike Duffy is a special education teacher who believed that technology would help meet his students' unique needs. Consider his proactive approach as one way you might deal with the technological challenges in your classroom.

USING COMPUTERS TO INDIVIDUALIZE INSTRUCTION

I am an elementary school special education teacher. My school, Key Largo School, is a K–8 school located in the Florida Keys, an island chain at the southernmost tip of Florida. The school has approximately 700 students in the elementary school and 600 in the middle school.

Of our 1,300 students, over 100 are provided services through the Exceptional Student Education program. Our ESE students are diverse ethnically and socioeconomically. My class is a self-contained fourth- and fifth-grade ESE class. That means most of my stu-

dents are in my classes all day and some of them are mainstreamed for some of their subjects.

MY CLASSROOM CHALLENGES

As a varying exceptionalities ESE teacher, I have students in my classroom with a wide variety of learning disabilities. The students range from emotionally handicapped to mentally handicapped to language-impaired. Generally, my students are considered to have mild to moderate disabilites. It is my responsibility to make sure that all of my students, regardless of their disabilities, meet their personal goals and objectives as detailed in their Individual Education Plans (IEPs). This means that every student requires a customized approach to instruction at very different levels. My class size ranges from ten to twelve students as new students are classified into ESE and others move away from the area. I have a teacher aide to assist me, but with every student needing to be taught at his or her own personal level, at her or his own pace, and in accordance with his or her IEP, the task is always challenging. Teaching twelve ESE children in a single classroom is like teaching twelve separate classes at different grade levels simultaneously in the same room.

I decided that one of the best ways to ensure that the technology my students needed was going to be available to them was to join our school's Technology Committee and work with my colleagues and my principal to plan for our school's technology needs. We spent the next few years creating a strategic plan for technology, purchasing what we could and writing a series of grants to the district and to other agencies to fund our needs. Like many of my fellow teachers, throughout the process I was determined to continue to acquire what I could for my own classroom while my school sought the funds to change our overall level of technology.

As technology funds slowly increased as a result of our school's team effort, I was able to begin to purchase many of the components I wanted from my portion of the school technology budget, from district ESE funds, or as a reward for my participation in district technology-training programs. Once funds started to become available, my challenge was to decide what technology would best serve my students' unique needs. That took a great deal of research and creative decision making. Once spent, funds were not going to be available again. Making the most of the technology I chose became my mission.

Mr. Duffy had to become proactive and participate in his school's efforts to expand technology. He also had to learn much about the technologies he might want to use to assist his students to achieve their personal best. You have already been introduced to the hardware you may choose to use. This chapter will help you learn more about how digital technologies can be applied to a classroom setting. We will check in with this "teacher on a mission" at the end of this chapter.

SOURCE: Interview with Michael Duffy conducted by Al P. Mizell.

Digital Technologies in the Classroom

Once you have a computer system in the classroom, the possibilities for expanding its capabilities by the addition of digital peripherals are enormous. You can add input devices that let you scan photos a parent took on your field trip, that let students issue commands by simply touching the screen, or that let you dictate input via voice instead of a keyboard. Or you can add output devices that enable you to share what you see on your monitor with the whole class, that can turn segments of a videotape into digital pictures, or that can read sections of the textbook to your auditory learners. Whatever your academic or administrative needs, you can usually find and add the hardware and software you need to your typical personal computer. The subsequent sections of this chapter will examine some of the most useful and innovative digital technologies for classroom use.

What Input Devices Are Helpful to Teachers and Learners?

The keyboard and the mouse are the two most commonly used devices for inputting data into a computer. However, there are many other devices that enable you and your students to enter data as well. These include scanners, digital cameras, digital tablets, sound input, pen input, and touch screen devices, devices that let you input via voice, and electronic whiteboards. Each of these input devices is uniquely valuable in the classroom. In the following sections, you will be introduced to each.

Scanners

If you want to modify a test question or page of typed text or add notations to an image that you plan to use in teaching a lesson, you can use a scanner to easily and quickly accomplish your task. Scanners are input devices that capture and then translate printed copy or images into digital data. When you scan a page, the scanning software that is packaged with the scanner hardware turns the image or text on the page into

Scanners convert hard copy to digital data.

Figure 4.1
Scanners and Their Uses
Flat-bed scanners are the most versatile scanners, able to scan various sizes of bound or loose pages or graphics. Most flat-bed scanner software can save the scans as both graphic and OCR files.

On CD!
Hardware Skills Builder
Digital Imaging

ON THE WEB! 4.1
What Scanner Is Right for My Classroom?

its digital equivalent. The scanner is plugged into the computer; as it scans, it inputs digital images into the computer, which are then stored in RAM or on a disk. You can then use image-editing software, such as a draw, paint, or photo-styling program, to enhance or modify the image or add text to it. How this is done with each of these types of programs is explained more fully in Chapter 6. The modified image can then be printed out in black and white or in color on paper, transparency film, or even photographic paper. This same image can also be incorporated into other programs, such as a publishing program to create class newsletters or a presentation program to create effective lecture support visuals.

Scanners can also turn printed pages of text into a digital document that can be altered with word-processing software. This type of scanning requires that you use optical character recognition (OCR) software. OCR software is usually bundled with a scanner or incorporated into the scanning software. **OCR software** recognizes printed characters when they are scanned and then turns them into their electronic word-processing equivalent.

The most common type of scanner is the **flat-bed scanner** (Figure 4.1). It works something like a small personal copier with limited capabilities for printing the copy. Like a copier, a scanner makes a digital duplicate of whatever is placed face down on the bed. Once the page, photograph, or other item is scanned, the resulting digital image is saved to the computer's storage areas for further enhancement or eventually to be printed out. Through the use of OCR software, scanned text material can also be converted from the image format so that it can be modified in a word processor. Any type and most sizes of paper (and even other material, such as cloth) can be placed on the bed of a flat-bed scanner. Thickness or type of material will not interfere with the process. However, flat-bed scanners do vary in the maximum image resolution they can produce. They also vary in the way in which they connect to a computer and the resulting speed at which they send data.

In terms of resolution, it is important to note the dots per inch (dpi) the scanner is able to produce. This number is related to the number of sensors built into the scanner, which determine its ability to capture clear and crisp images. The higher the dpi, the higher the quality of the captured image. The quality of an image is important, especially when you change its size before using it. Printing out an 8 × 10 inch version of a low quality 3 × 5 inch scanned photo will result in a blurred and indistinct image. The disadvantage of a high-quality scanned image is the size of the scanned file. It can require many megabytes of file space to store a very high-resolution image. Overall, however, it is best to choose the highest-resolution scanner you can afford so that high-quality scanning will be available when you need it. High-resolution scanners can always be set to scan at lower quality (and thus lower file size) if you prefer.

Scanners also vary in the way in which they connect to a computer. Since scanned files are quite large, high-speed connections are necessary. In the past, scanners connected through the parallel port, which supports printers. **Ports** are points of connection between a computer system and its peripherals. More recently, scanners have been designed to connect through high-speed USB (universal serial bus) ports found on newer computers. Either connection will be effective; however, it is important for a teacher who wants to acquire a scanner to check which type of port is available on the computer the scanner will be connected to. If you purchase a USB scanner but your computer has no available USB ports, you will have to purchase additional hardware (e.g., a USB expansion hub) or exchange the scanner for one with another connection type.

These and the features of the software that is packaged with a flat-bed scanner cause the price differences you might find. Careful identification of your needs and

IN THE CLASSROOM

Using a Scanner—Net Worth: 1000 Words

The scanner makes it possible to insert original drawings, photographs, and hard copy into a document to enhance the presentation of computer-enriched projects of all kinds. At Alsea High School in Alsea, Oregon, the senior project under the direction of Bonnie Hill specified the use of scanners for the inclusion of photographs, slides, and X-rays in electronically written papers as one of three required components: "(1) Posting a written paper electronically for evaluation—having accessed a broad range of information; (2) Collaborating with a mentor—15-hour minimum with expert outside the school; and (3) Presenting the final results to committee." The topics for this recent senior project were orthodontia, scuba diving, and computer repair.

Elementary school projects lend themselves well to the visual interest scanners can add to the final product. *Mrs. Claus's Workshop*, prepared by Mrs. Slaven's class at Elementary West in Loo-gootee, Indiana, highlights the use of student drawings, photos, and computer graphics inserted in the unit by scanner.

Another means to an end with the scanner was undertaken by Don Prochelo and Bobbie Kmiec at Glenbard East High School in Lombard, Illinois. They were faced with combining speech and business curricula into one course, Speech with Advanced Technology. To do so, they went to "the Internet, introduced scanners, cameras, and presentation software to plan and deliver speeches to stockholders, the CEO, and other company affiliates" of the mock company they created.

SOURCES: "Senior Project," by Bonnie Hill, http://www.intel.com; "Mrs. Claus's Workshop," prepared by Mrs. Slaven's class at Elementary West in Loogootee, Indiana, http://www.siec.k12.in.us; "Speech with Advanced Technology," by Don Prochelo and Bobbie Kmiec, http://www.mcrel.org.

---

examination of the hardware and software capabilities will help you select the scanner that is best suited for your budget and purposes.

Digital Cameras

As you have learned, if you want to digitally capture a group picture of your class for use in the school newsletter, you can scan a photograph and incorporate it into your publishing program. The process requires that you first take a picture, have the film developed, and then complete the scanning process. Wouldn't it be easier just to capture the image digitally in the first place? That is exactly what can be done with a digital camera (see Figure 4.2).

Digital cameras capture pictures in digital form with varying resolutions.

A **digital camera** works like a traditional camera except that it does not use light-sensitive film. Instead, photos are stored in the camera's memory card or on CD or disks as digital data. The storage capacity of memory cards and disks varies according to the photo resolution desired. The higher the desired resolution, the more memory space needed. This reduces the total number of photos that can be stored in a digital camera's memory or recorded on a memory (or "smart") card. Typically, an 8-megabyte memory card is capable of storing approximately thirty medium-resolution images.

The memory card a camera uses varies in type as well as size. Current popular types of cards include SmartMedia, CompactFlash, and Memory Stick. Every camera manufacturer selects the type it will use for its cameras. It is therefore important to note the type of memory card used by the camera you have available. Digital camera users often keep a spare card available, like film for a photographic camera, so that a second memory card is available when the first one is full.

A final storage solution just becoming available for digital cameras is the Microdrive. This miniature hard disk drive is capable of storing multiple gigabytes of information. For digital camera users, this technology will make it possible to store hundreds of images before having to download them to a computer. To use Microdrive storage, the camera must have been designed with a storage card slot that is compatible with this technology.

When the camera's memory is full, the images must be transferred to a computer for storage. This is done by connecting the camera to the computer with a special cable

COMPARISON OF DIGITAL CAMERAS AND THEIR FEATURES

DIGITAL CAMERAS store photographs either on reusable RAM cards or on discs.

- RAM cards come in various storage sizes, and you can buy more than one if you need to be able to store large quantities of pictures. Photos from the RAM card are downloaded via cable or card reader to the computer for editing and printing.
- CD recordable disc storage uses mini compact discs for easy portability to the computer. The storage capacity is at least 156 megabytes more than RAM cards.

Figure 4.2

Comparison of Digital Cameras and Their Features

Digital cameras are made by a number of manufacturers. Each type of digital camera has features that affect its price. Most have an LCD display that lets you preview your pictures as soon as you take them.

that comes bundled with the camera or by means of a camera cradle that connects to the computer. Once copied to the computer's hard drive, the images can be enhanced with a photo-styling program or used in other software applications. Ultimately, digital photographs can be printed out on photographic or regular paper with a color printer. After transfer to the hard drive, the images can then be deleted from the camera's memory so that space is again available for new pictures.

Digital cameras allow you to input photographic images directly without having to scan them, but the scanner may be a more versatile addition because it enables you to digitize text and printed graphics as well. Compared to traditional photographic equipment, digital cameras have many unique features. In addition to letting you directly manipulate the photos with computer software, most digital cameras allow you to preview photos as you take them. Digital cameras are typically equipped with small LCD screens on the back that let you preview pictures you have taken before saving them or view the photos you have already taken and saved. This feature saves you the time and expense of taking film to a developer only to find that your photos did not turn out as you expected. It also allows you to use your available photo storage space wisely by deleting shots you don't like and retaking a photo whenever you choose.

When determining a camera's potential for high-resolution images, manufacturers specify how many megapixels the camera is capable of producing. A pixel (or picture element) is a single dot in the image captured by the camera. Millions of dots make up a single image. The higher the number of dots captured, the clearer the image will be. Thus, a digital camera's capacity is indicated by the number of megapixels (millions of dots) it can capture. Table 4.1 summarizes the relationship of a camera's megapixel capacity and the types and quality of images it can produce. When requesting or purchasing a digital camera for your classroom, its capacity for the type of image you want to create is likely to be your most important consideration.

Camera's Megapixels	Image Quality and Size
TABLE 4.1	**UNDERSTANDING DIGITAL CAMERA CAPABILITY**
1	Good screen images; prints up to 4 × 6 inches; may be capable of producing up to 5 × 7 images
2	Good, detailed screen images; excellent 4 × 6 and very good 5 × 7 prints; some cameras may produce reasonable 8 × 10 prints
3	Good quality for screen images or smaller prints; reasonably clear 8 × 10 images
4 OR MORE	Equal to 35 mm photos; able to print high-quality 8 × 10 images

Digital cameras vary in terms of many optional features as well. Some cameras record brief video and audio clips as well as still pictures. Although the digital video clip files are of relatively low resolution, if the ability to capture a brief video is important, the inclusion of this feature may be a buying consideration. Further, cameras vary in their ability to zoom in on an object. If close images of a student's work or an object of instruction is a consideration, then zoom capabilities must be taken into account. These features and others, as well as a camera's megapixel capacity, are the reasons for the dramatic variation in the prices of digital cameras. For you as a teacher, it is best to first determine what you want to use the digital camera for and then select one within your school budget that gives you the capabilities you desire.

ON THE WEB! 4.2
Which Digital Camera Should I Buy?

IN THE CLASSROOM

In the Eyes of the Beholder: Digital Cameras and Teaching

Dana Zora, a fifth-grade teacher and technology specialist in Aberdeen, Washington, has young children pose in the shapes of the uppercase letters of the alphabet and then photographs them with a digital camera. She shows them how to place the photos into electronic photo album software. The children then construct a class alphabet book. Ms. Zora places the completed book on the classroom web site. She also makes a slide show for viewing at open houses. Her project incorporates all the learning styles, with children forming the letters with their bodies (kinesthetic), making the sounds of the letter they formed (auditory), and reading the text that she has placed with the photos (visual). She suggests using butcher paper to form a neutral background for the photos.

Wearing patriotic hats, first graders at Echo Horizon School in Culver City, California, take photos of each other with a digital camera. Using electronic photo album software, they create a book with the pictures and add captions under each of the photos telling what they would do to make the country better if they were president. For children in the early grades, Elaine Wrenn, the technology coordinator, and first-grade teachers Sheryl Udell and Sally Sorensen, who devised this project, suggest that the children may need to dictate the text. The project is a culminating activity following a lesson or lessons on the presidency. The project, they note, can be modified for other grades and upon completion makes an excellent addition to e-portfolios.

Alan Landon of Redwood High School in Visalia, California, uses a digital camera as a tool to create an innovative and unique measurement system. In his activity he has students stand in a line in front of a brick wall and takes a digital photo. The image captured reveals the relative height of the students compared to the horizontal lines delineated by the bricks. Using this digital technique, he creates a "human chart" for each of his classes that can be used in a variety of mathematics lessons, including units of measure, the interpretation of charts, and ratio and proportion.

SOURCES: D. Zora. 2003. A living alphabet. Retrieved May 16, 2003, from http://www.apple.com; E. Wrenn, S. Udell, & S. Sorensen. 2003. If I were president. Retrieved May 16, 2003, from http://www.apple.com; A. Landon. 2003. How do you measure up? Retrieved October 4, 2003, from http://pegasus.cc.ucf.edu/~ucfcasio/measure.htm.

Monitor-top cameras can be used to share digital still and video images via the Web.

One other type of digital camera that is useful for the classroom is the monitor-top camera, sometimes called a webcam. This type of digital camera is mounted on the computer's monitor and connected via cable to a computer USB port. It often has a built-in microphone as well as still and video capabilities. The monitor-top camera can be used to capture still and video images for communication via the Internet. It can be used for teleconferencing across the Internet, that is, conducting a live conference via the Internet that includes still images, video, and audio as well as text communication. Or it can be used simply for sharing still or video images via the Net. This adaptation of the digital camera has some of the same resolution parameters as a still camera, but because it is attached to the computer, it does not need to have independent storage capability.

As you can see, digital cameras of all types and designed for a variety of purposes are available to classroom teachers. Applications of this technology in the classroom range from capturing a field trip to taking digital photos of children's work, to displaying work on classroom web sites, to customizing a class newsletter, to documenting a science experiment. The applications are as diverse as the talents and creativity of the teachers who use these versatile input devices.

Graphics Tablets

A **graphics tablet** lets you use a stylus with an electronic pad to draw diagrams or create artwork. A stylus is a pen-shaped device that is designed to press against the pressure-sensitive surface of a graphics tablet. Graphics tablets are also sometimes called **digitizers** or digital tablets, because they convert the lines sketched on the tablet into their digital equivalents on the screen. As the stylus presses down on the plastic-covered surface of the pad, contacts are made and electrical circuits are completed. The resulting signals are translated by the software and hardware into digital images that can be seen on the monitor, printed out, or saved for use in other documents.

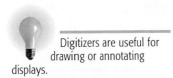

Digitizers are useful for drawing or annotating displays.

Architects, designers, and artists are the most frequent users of graphics tablets, because the stylus gives the user more precise control when drawing than a mouse or other pointing device can. However, digitizer technology can easily be adapted for educational use by teachers and learners. Using this type of tablet, teachers can place a word-processed or graphics document on the computer screen. With a digitizer, they can add their own comments to these images and mark them up as they are displayed on the computer screen. For example, when reviewing material with a small group of students, a teacher might annotate and circle key features on a computer-generated map displayed on the classroom computer's display. In combination with appropriate software, the teacher can mark up the diagram using various colors, lines of various types, and predetermined shapes. The computer image with annotation can then be saved and printed out or used in another document.

Art students can use a more typical digitizer to draw original images, enhance computer-generated images or photographs, or annotate scanned images. Digitizers that are designed primarily for this type of art function usually add color, brush, and other art command options on the tablet, making it easier for the artist to use these features. Such customized tablets are often designed to be compatible with specific art software. Once again, it is important to balance your potential uses to determine the type of equipment that will work best in your classroom. Once that decision has been made, it is important to remember to examine both software and hardware specifications to ensure compatibility.

With a digital tablet, the teacher can create complex images, emphasize points, or fully annotate graphics.

IN THE CLASSROOM

Hand in Hand: Teaching with Handheld Computers

Instant feedback, a key to the effective use of assessment instruments, is at the fingertips of teachers at Paddock Elementary School in Milan, Michigan. The school replaced its system for determining reading levels for children in first through fourth grades, the traditional paper Qualitative Reading Inventory (QRI), with a handheld computerized system. The school turned to palm computers and customized software to build a system using the QRI that allows for individual testing of the children with the results transferred automatically to the handhelds. From the handheld computers, information is downloaded for immediate viewing on a web site. This ready access to the QRI results gives teachers the opportunity to look at the rate and accuracy of the children's reading and to ascertain the kinds of mistakes that will need to be addressed to improve reading fluency.

Handheld computers adapt as easily to physical education classes as to reading. Mary Kay Roth highlights Ryan Zabawa's use of palm computers in PE. In his Goodrich Middle School PE classes, students regularly enter their fitness goals, daily progress, caloric intake, and out-of-school fitness activities into their handheld computers. They track this fitness information on their own PDAs and beam it to their teacher when completed.

The fitness information is not only organized and easily displayed for the students' review but also shared with their teacher effortlessly and without requiring multiple charts and documents.

Another innovative use of the handheld computer is in the music classroom. Bryan Bogue, a percussionist with the Spokane Symphony and an innovative music teacher in the Spokane schools for more than fifteen years, uses handheld computers and add-on music software and hardware modules to create a mini music lab at a fraction of the cost and space necessary for a traditional setup. Using these adapted devices, his fifth- and sixth-grade music students have joined with a local university to create and perform in the first palm-computer-based orchestra.

SOURCES: B. Bogue. 2003. Spokane Public Schools. Retrieved October 3, 2003, from http://www.palmone.com/us/education/studies/study53.html; C. Makled. 2002. Pilot program: Paddock project to aid in reading assessment. Retrieved May 21, 2003, from http://www.wirelessgeneration.com/web/print_milan.html (reprint from the *Milan News-Leader*, April 18, 2002); M. K. Roth. 2003. Palm pilots beaming lessons. Retrieved October 3, 2003, from http://www.pdaed.com/vertical/features/Beaming.xml.

Sound Input Devices

Computers today, especially those found in schools, are typically multimedia machines. These types of machines are equipped with the hardware and software necessary to play back and record sound and show video clips as well as display text and graphics. To play back the sound files and clips that come with multimedia software, the machines are equipped with a set of small speakers. To record audio, such machines are also usually equipped with a personal-sized microphone. Both speakers and microphone plug into ports located on the back of the machine. These ports are connected to the sound card, the computer component designed to input and output sound.

Through the microphone, music, sounds, and the spoken word can be input, digitized (turned into digital data), and stored. The digitized sound can then be played back by using a sound program, or it can be included in a multimedia program. In the classroom, the teacher might record a brief comment or an instruction to be included in a teacher-made computer tutorial, or a student might add recorded sounds from a field trip to his or her presentation of the field trip experience. Digitized sound can also be edited and enhanced by using sound-editing software. Sounds can be clarified, have special effects added to them, or be speeded up or slowed down. The edited or enhanced versions of sound recordings can be a valuable part of a computer-based lesson.

With the use of a simple, inexpensive microphone, sound can be added to round out computer-based materials and help address the needs of auditory learners. It should be noted, however, that sound files tend to be very large, requiring a lot of storage space. Therefore, classroom applications using sound need to be saved on a hard drive or a removable hard drive, or stored on a CD.

ON THE WEB! 4.3
How Can Digital Sound Capabilities Help Learners?

Pen Input Devices

Pen input devices use a stylus to input handwritten information, to select commands, and to make predetermined written symbols, called gestures, that represent computer commands. Pen input is typically used with a **personal digital assistant (PDA)** or a tablet PC. A PDA is a portable computing device that can recognize handwritten notes and translate them into a word-processed document through the use of the PDA's handwriting recognition software. These written-to-word-processed documents are then usually transferred to a desktop computer for storage or further use. PDAs also typically offer simplified office management tools, such as an appointment book, a calendar, and a phone book (see Figure 4.3). Pocket-PC types of PDAs may also include scaled-down versions of familiar computer software such as a word processor or electronic spreadsheet.

Make PDA technology considerably larger and more powerful and you have tablet PCs. A tablet PC is approximately the size of a traditional writing pad (although substantially thicker), and you use it much as you would paper. You write on the surface of the tablet with your stylus, and the software converts written text into a word-processing file or a drawing you create into a graphics file. You can also use the stylus as you would a pointer controlled by a mouse, to give commands and make selections. The tablet is essentially an LCD screen mounted over a motherboard with a hard disk drive, making this portable device a convenient and relatively lightweight pen input device. Although this device may not take the place of more versatile notebook computers in schools, it offers an excellent option for mobile computing in the classroom.

PDAs and tablet PCs can be very useful classroom management tools that allow the teacher to make notes on lessons and activities, record and annotate student behavior, and track appointments. The data written into a PDA can be stored for later use, so the information can be easily transferred into computerized gradebooks, lesson plans, and student files. Essentially, PDAs act like digital mcmo pads, the pages of which can be transferred to a computer disk for safekeeping and easy retrieval. In the

Personal digital assistants combine a handheld computer and organizer.

ON THE WEB! 4.4
Tablet Devices

Figure 4.3
Personal Digital Assistants Come to School
PDAs and Tablet PCs are versatile pen devices in the classroom. Using a stylus, these computers can be used to take notes, organize data, create drawings, and when connected to display devices, present information.

case of pocket PCs, they can also serve as very portable "palmtop" computers with many of the same capabilities of a desktop machine.

In the classroom, tablet PCs offer teachers and students some unique opportunities. Teachers can download students' word-processed essays and grade them via the tablet PC. The word processed document is displayed on the tablet screen, and the teacher can add comments via the stylus. The graded document can be saved and returned to the student electronically for review. Connected to a classroom display device, the tablet PC can also be used for sharing digital images without the physical barrier of computer and monitor between teacher and class. And, while displaying digital presentations via tablet PC, teachers can easily add annotations with the stylus to emphasize or annotate key points.

The tablet PC presents distinct options for students as well. Using this device, students can take notes and organize them into clear word-processed documents without typing. They can easily integrate multimedia and web resources into their work and create documents for activities that include a full range of resources. They can also use the tablet PC to download and read the pages of electronic books. The applications of this new pen input technology to the classroom have just begun to be fully explored.

Touch Screens

A **touch screen** is a computer monitor screen that responds to human touch. Touch screen software usually displays a series of graphics or icons. Instead of using a mouse and pointer to select an icon or command, you touch the icon itself as it is displayed on the touch screen, and the computer responds. The screen is light-sensitive,

Touch screens can be used in the classroom by pre-readers or as an assistive device for students with special needs.

and the touch screen software interprets an interruption to the light on a specific spot on the screen as a command to select the icon or option that is displayed on that spot. On computers equipped with a touch screen, a keyboard and/or mouse might not even be available.

Touch screens are quick and easy to use. If large amounts of data need to be entered or many choices need to be made from complex sets of options, touch screens are an inappropriate choice of input device. They work best with simple, straightforward displays. Touch screens are most often used in information kiosks at hotels and airports. They can also be useful in the classroom for young children who are preliterate, cannot type, or have difficulty controlling a mouse owing to physical impairment.

Touch screens receive input by being touched at relevant points on the monitor screen.

Video-to-Digital Input

Some computers are equipped with the ability to capture video images. Most computers can be enhanced for video capture through the addition of specialized expansion cards. Expansion, or add-on, cards can be plugged into special receptacles called slots on the computer's motherboard to expand its capabilities. Video capture cards are designed to enable the computer to stop motion images and capture them. The term *video capture* refers to the ability of computer hardware and software to take one or more frames of motion video and turn them into single digital image files. To do this, motion video is routed from the video device (e.g., a video camera or VCR) into the video capture card. The card and its software convert the analog video data into digital video data. Thus, single frames of a video are captured in a digital format so they can be displayed or edited. Because digital video data files are typically quite large,

Digital video offers increased editing and playback versatility.

IN THE CLASSROOM

Touch Screen Technologies

Touch screen monitors and related software that enable a traditional monitor to emulate a touch screen are powerful tools for students with disabilities. Touch screens may display graphics that the user can touch to enter commands and make software selections. Special software can display the image of a computer keyboard on the screen so that keys or commands can be pointed to and clicked on. Whether hardware- or software-based, touch screen technologies can improve the life of a student with disabilities.

The Alliance for Technology Access (**http://ataccess .org/**) is a network of resources that provides information and support services to children and adults with disabilities including information about assistive devices. Its web site includes many success stories. Two such stories demonstrate the power of touch screen technology.

United Cerebral Palsy of Idaho shared the story of Melissa. Melissa, a four-year-old with cerebral palsy, had difficulty holding her head up and moving her arms. In her school's computer lab, a TouchWindow was installed so she could play math games. In addition to practicing math concepts, Melissa was able to strengthen her right arm by reaching out to touch the screen. She was also able to strengthen her neck as she worked to keep her head up to see the monitor and work with the software. This adaptive technology not only assisted in teaching skills, it helped improve the learner's muscle tone.

Technology Assistance for Special Consumers in Huntsville, Alabama, shared the story of Steven, who had a stroke at age sixteen that left him a quadriplegic. He had partial paralysis of all extremities and was unable to speak. After the stroke, he could only move his head, but that was enough, with the help of a combination of assistive technologies that included a keyboard display on a screen. Steven learned to use a computer by scanning. Scanning is a system in which a keyboard is displayed on a screen with keys highlighted one after another. Simply by pressing a single switch button when the highlight appeared on the right key, Steven was able to communicate via computer. Today, having gained more movement in his arms, he can use a similar keyboard display that allows him to point to and click on the keys he desires with a glide pad.

SOURCE: Retrieved April 20, 2002, from **http://etacess.org/community/successes/successes.html**.

---

most video capture software also compresses the data files so that they can more easily be stored on hard and removable disks. Thus, single frames of a video are captured in a digital format so they can be displayed or edited.

As you may know, video images are composed of frame after frame of still pictures that are played back at high speed to give the impression of motion. Most analog video devices are not designed to stop and show one frame of video image at a time. In the classroom, you might want to freeze the motion of a video to study one single image that is particularly relevant to the lesson at hand. Most VCRs can pause briefly on a single image but, in doing so, sometimes distort the image. Digital video capture offers an opportunity to make video even more useful by allowing you to manipulate the digital frames one at a time or in a series, in whatever way best serves your instructional purposes.

Once video has been converted to digital data, each frame of digital video can be stored, edited, enhanced, and copied into any other computer document. Using the same type of art and graphics programs that enable the enhancement of scanned and digital camera images, you can customize digital video to suit your instructional needs. Thus, if your school had a video that included a particularly relevant underwater reef scene and you had a video capture device on your classroom computer, you could digitize frames of the video. You could then copy the frames that best demonstrate your lesson into an art program and label the instructional elements. The captured and enhanced video frames could then be saved and included in a computer presentation or printed out with a color ink-jet printer onto transparencies. The video capture capability lets you use the individual components of motion video to create, store, and produce customized teaching materials.

Electronic Whiteboards

Every classroom is equipped with display surfaces on which teachers can write and illustrate concepts as they teach. Some classrooms still have blackboards and chalk. Others use whiteboards with erasable color markers. These media offer the advantage of spontaneous explanation during the teaching and learning process. Once these display surfaces are filled with explanations, to continue, the teacher must begin to erase what has been previously written. For students who were absent on a particular day, for students who were not able to copy the information down quickly enough, or for the teacher who would like to refer back to previously erased material, the blackboard or whiteboard offers little support.

> Electronic whiteboards convert whiteboard images and text into computer files.

What if it were possible to write on a whiteboard and, just before erasing the information, print it out or save it to a computer file? That is precisely what an **electronic whiteboard** does. As you write on an electronic whiteboard, a built-in scanner records the drawings or text in the colors you are using. The recorded digital image is then displayed on a monitor. Furthermore, the recorded image can be saved, edited, or printed out. The image can then be erased from the electronic whiteboard, and a new computer file can be opened to capture and record new images. Once saved, whiteboard information can be included in other documents or placed in an electronic archive for you or your students to access for review.

If desired, some whiteboards in different locations can be connected over a phone line so that the writing in one location shows up in the other locations at the same time. This can be especially useful in bringing a distant guest speaker into your class or in delivering instruction to distant sites.

Electronic whiteboard technology is available in many different types including whiteboards that are touch-sensitive,

Electronic whiteboard technology lets teachers and students capture data and drawings for later use.

IN THE CLASSROOM

SMART Whiteboards

Electronic whiteboards add a new, interactive dimension to this traditional classroom display. Christel Smith of J. C. Charyk School in Alberta, Canada, uses the board's special features of touch sensitivity and annotation in addition to its other features. The SMART Board electronic whiteboard that she uses lets her project a computer image onto the board and then operate the software simply by touching the board at the points where buttons and menus are displayed on the board. Using the board instead of a mouse creates an interactive environment. Just as you might point to a visual image on a traditional whiteboard, pointing and pressing on the SMART Board lets you emphasize your point while you operate your software.

Using the SMART Board, Ms. Smith displays haiku she finds on the Internet. With the interactive capabilities of the board, the poems can be changed, manipulated, and annotated to demonstrate the lesson concepts. Further, she notes that with the interactive features of the board, students can use their fingers to touch the board to make changes or manipulate software. This tactile experience further helps students learn what needs to be learned.

SOURCE: Retrieved April 20, 2002, from **http://www.smarttech.com/** profiles/charyk.asp.

rear-projection whiteboards, and those designed to turn a computer plasma display into an interactive whiteboard. Each of these has its own unique features and advantages but is somewhat expensive for the average classroom. A newer technology turns your own classroom whiteboard into its electronic counterpart. This type of whiteboard technology uses a projection unit that attaches to the corner of your traditional whiteboard, and a series of electronic sleeves for your markers. Once connected to your computer, the projection device captures anything written on the whiteboard with the marker in its sleeve and saves it as a digital file. This type of system can do most of the tasks of its more expensive dedicated electronic whiteboard counterpart but typically at much less cost. Additionally, this system does not require any extra wall or floor space, since it uses your existing whiteboard. For these reasons, this input device is becoming a popular electronic whiteboard alternative for K–12 classrooms.

What Output Devices Are Helpful to Teachers and Learners?

Data Projection Units

Computer screen images can be projected using data projection units.

One of the challenges of using a computer in a classroom is that the computer's monitor is too small for display to a large group. To meet this challenge, a variety of computer data projection units are available. **Data projection units** plug into the computer's monitor port and display the signals that were to have been sent to the monitor. Data projection units are designed to display the digital data either in addition to (both monitor and unit show the image) or instead of (only the unit shows the image) the monitor. Each type of data projection unit has unique features and capabilities (see Figure 4.4) with a corresponding difference in prices.

LCD projectors are compact LCD display units with their own built-in light source. Light panels, resolution, and capability vary with price. Advantages include the typically brighter picture, enabling displays that are clear even with room and outside light, and its compact, lightweight size as compared with an overhead projector.

LCD PROJECTOR

Figure 4.4
Digital Display Technologies and Their Characteristics
Teachers have several options for displaying computer images.

Scan converters connect the computer and video monitor through a converter box that alters the computer signal so that it can be displayed on the video monitor. These very inexpensive devices are the most reasonable method for sharing and projecting computer images. The disadvantage is the reduced resolution when compared with a digital display.

SCAN CONVERTER

• LCD Projection Panels

One of the earliest projection units was the **liquid crystal display (LCD) projection panel.** Although this technology has been replaced by other types of projection units, it may still be found in some schools. The LCD panel is used with an overhead projector. The LCD panel sits on the top of the overhead projector's stage, just as a transparency would. Once the LCD panel is connected to the computer's monitor port, the computer image is routed to the panel. Because the panel has no light source of its own, the image cannot be seen until it is lit by the powerful light of the overhead projector. As the overhead projector's light shines through the panel's glass, the computer image is seen on a screen or other display surface in the classroom. Thus, the computer's image, once visible only to a small group viewing a monitor, can now be seen by everyone in the classroom.

LCD panels have a useful life that is potentially longer than that of a computer. You may therefore find LCD panels in some schools even though computers in those same schools have been replaced more frequently.

• Data Projectors

LCD panels have largely been replaced by the data projector. The **data projector** is a projection unit that combines an LCD display unit and a light source into a single, relatively lightweight box. These units can typically project both images from a computer system and video from a video source in a display that is large enough and bright enough to be seen across a classroom. For the brightest, clearest, and best results, these images should be displayed on a projection screen. Projection to a wall will not offer the same level of clarity and brightness; projection to a whiteboard will often be difficult to view, owing to the high reflectivity of the whiteboard surface.

On CD!
Hardware Skills Builder
Data Projector

Different data projectors offer different levels of resolution and brightness (measured in lumens). As the resolution and brightness of data projectors increase, there is a corresponding increase in price. It is best to purchase a projector that exceeds the capabilities of your current computer in terms of resolution. In terms of brightness, it is best to select a projector with the maximum brightness your budget will allow. If you select a less costly projector that may be of insufficient brightness, you might find that you have to turn all the lights off in the classroom and/or cover the windows to be able to see the computer display clearly.

Other features that may be available on data projectors include built-in speakers, multiple computer input capability, software storage capability, and remote control. Many projectors are designed to accept a variety of video inputs, making them an effective replacement for the large TV monitor so often seen in today's classrooms. Thus, the same projector that can display your computer image can also display a videotape, a TV program from the school's cable connection, or the images from your digital camera. Although these units cost more than large monitors, the fact that they have both computer and video capability may make them more cost-effective in the long run.

ON THE WEB! 4.5
How Can I Share My
Computer Image?

• Scan Converters

One of the most inexpensive methods for displaying a computer image to an entire class is to use a digital (computer signal) to analog (video signal) converter, or **scan converter.** This device converts a computer's image into one that can be displayed through analog (video) technology. To use it, one end of the converter's cable is plugged into the computer's monitor port and the other into the video input port on the back of a large classroom television monitor; the computer image is then visible on the monitor.

Scan converters offer low-cost classroom digital displays.

These converters are well within the budget of most schools, making it possible to share computer displays across the classroom. The disadvantage of this type of display,

IN THE CLASSROOM

The Whole Is Greater than the Parts

Louis Velez, who teaches computer classes at IS 24, an inter-mediate school on Staten Island, planned for his students a multiuse application of computer technology. The project gave the students free rein to "travel" vicariously to ideal vacation spots of their choosing. The technologies the students incorporated into carrying out the vacation of their dreams were Hyper-Studio, ClarisWorks, a digital camera, a scanner, and a printer. By searching the web for information on the travel destination they chose, the students were instructed by Mr. Velez to "create composites [on postcards] which will include a recognizable 'background' from a faraway vacation site, and a personal photograph" made with a digital camera and edited with HyperStudio for insertion onto the postcard. Turning to the word processor, the students wrote a personal postcard-type message to include on their virtual postcards before scanning and printing them.

Two middle schools in different towns in New Jersey, Emerson Junior-Senior High School and Hackensack Middle School, undertook a joint community-service and environmental-research study to seek a solution to a hypothetical problem—the existence or nonexistence of a variation in water quality in the Hackensack River. By sampling water from different locations and looking for variations in quality in the river and also in its tributaries and reservoirs, the students carried out the research using videoconferencing equipment, handheld computers, e-mail, and word-processing software. As part of the problem-solving component of the project, they formed "a mock environmental engineering company" to "develop solutions to a fictional—although realistic—environmental problem," as recounted by Ellen R. Delisio for Education World. Christopher Steil, who teaches seventh-grade science at Emerson, oversaw the project. The students had water-sampling attachments for the handhelds, which stored and sent results to computers. Instruction was disseminated through videoconferencing with professionals in the field. Students talked with each other by means of videoconferencing and by e-mail. They concluded the project by writing up their findings in what Steil described as an attempt "to create an authentic learning environment for science."

SOURCES: L. Velez. 2003. Postcards from abroad. Retrieved May 14, 2003, from http://teachersnetwork.org/teachnetnyc/lvelez/postcards.htm; E. R. Delisio. 2002. Research at the river links two schools. Retrieved April 3, 2003, from http://www.education-world.com/a_tech/tech122.shtml.

however, is in the quality and size of the image. Television monitors are not designed with the same resolution as computer monitors. Although graphics may look fine, text may appear choppy and difficult to read when displayed through a converter and on a television monitor. Additionally, even the largest television monitors can be difficult to see from the back of a large classroom. Thus, the details of the computer image may be lost to those in the back when it is displayed on the classroom television monitor.

Speakers and Headphones

Speakers and headphones help meet the needs of auditory learners.

Most computer systems today are sold with sound capabilities. **Speakers** are a common component included with every system. Some systems have built-in speakers; others have external speakers. Although sound is not critical for many administrative applications, such as word processing, it is an integral part of much of the academic software that is available today. To address multiple learning styles, most learning software is designed with a rich auditory component. To take advantage of this aspect of the software, an audio output device is necessary.

Just as is the case with home audio systems, computer speakers vary significantly in capability. Some are designed for a single user working on his or her home computer. These speakers, even at maximum volume, are often incapable of playing back sound at a level and clarity that would be useful for a small group of students. It is important to consider how audio-rich computer software will be used to determine what type of sound output hardware is necessary.

If there is a single computer in the classroom and it is used for a large-group display, good speakers are essential so that all students can hear as well as see the program. Of course, if the display unit used is multimedia-capable, that is, it includes both visual and audio capability, additional speakers might not be necessary at all. If the computer display is through a multimedia-capable data projector, the projector itself contains sufficiently large enough speakers for all to hear. Alternatively, if you use a converter, the speakers in the television monitor will carry the audio component of the software.

However, if the instructional intent is to use academic software as learning support for one student at a time, speakers might not be the preferred type of audio output. When a single student is working with software to master a targeted skill, the audio component of the software can be distracting to those around him or her. In that case, instead of speakers as audio output, you might want to select headphones. **Headphones** allow individual students to listen to audio without disturbing anyone else. Multimedia computers include headphone ports just as they do speaker ports. You might even be able to use the headphones that are available for other audio devices. Occasionally, a headphone plug may look different and will not fit into the jack (port) on the computer. It is, however, very possible that the headphones can still be used. Local electronics stores often stock a good selection of converter plugs. These are typically very inexpensive and easy to find.

Headphones can allow students to hear computer audio output without disturbing others.

IN THE CLASSROOM

The Second "R" and the Special Needs Student

Writing, the active, creative verbal skill, poses many challenges for teachers of regular classrooms and, especially, for those of inclusion classrooms where the physical act of writing creates an added hurdle to be dealt with. Assistive technology, however, provides a pathway of access to writing for the diverse range of student learning styles, intelligences, and physical limitations found in these classrooms. David Davis, a technology consultant serving nine Florida public school districts, describes four types of technologies that perform well as aids for students needing help in the physical writing process: portable writing devices, alternative keyboards, voice recognition systems, and universal access stations.

Portable writing devices assist students who can't grasp a writing instrument. This computer-writing equipment has a keyboard like a computer or laptop with alternative keyboards that accommodate the physically challenged student. These alternative keyboards work well for students with visual, physical, or cognitive limitations, making it possible for them to write by means of menu commands. The keyboards can be affixed to computers so teachers can modify the standard keyboard. Voice recognition systems are software programs that offer "speech-to-

text, document navigation and page navigation" and, with verbal commands, make any computer-based information source accessible for reading and organizing. Universal access stations comprise multimedia computers, scanners, optical character recognition (OCR) software, alternative keyboards, text-to-speech software, and other assistive devices for special populations. Mr. Davis explains the access these technologies give to students with special needs: "With the Universal Access Station available, students can scan in pages from a magazine or book, and have the computer read the text out loud. This is a great strategy for students with limited reading skills as well as students who use English as a second language. Text-to-speech software can also be used to translate web pages to spoken text. Students with limited vision can take notes using a talking word processor with the screen set to high contrast. Word prediction software provides further assistance in taking notes."

SOURCE: D. Davis. 2002. Using assistive technology to help students write. *Media & Methods* (September/October) 39 (1), 14.

Sample Assistive Devices
Many types of assistive devices, such as BrailleLite and VoicePal, have been developed to support special needs students.

Emerging Digital Technologies for the Classroom

At this point, you have learned much about computers and the peripheral digital technologies that you might use in your classroom. Computer technology, however, is in a constant state of flux, and new digital equipment is constantly emerging. As these new technologies evolve and become part of our world, many will be adapted for use in teaching and learning. Some of the most fascinating types of hardware that are likely to be adapted for use in schools are described next.

Wireless Devices

Cell phones and beepers have become commonplace. These technologies use wireless microwave communications to send voice and digital data instead of using the wires required for traditional telephony. These same wireless systems are being adapted to computers. Wireless connections for computers are quickly becoming as commonplace as cell phones and beepers are. Already, many cellular phones offer both incoming voice calls and text messages. It is clear that wireless technologies are converging.

Classroom wireless technologies can take several different forms. Unlike the cellular technology used for phones, which can use wireless modems to call in to networks, classroom wireless uses radio frequency (RF) technology to connect classroom workstations to a network server. Access points, or points at which connection is made to the wired backbone, are strategically placed throughout the school building. Adapters are used in workstations to connect to the access points. Since no wires tether computers to the wall, computers with adapters can be moved as needed, as long as they stay in range of an access point.

One of the newest and fastest-growing wireless technologies is called WiFi (wireless fidelity). It too uses radio frequency to connect WiFi-enabled computers and other digital devices to networks at very fast speeds. Base stations serve as access points, and these can be placed anywhere, inside or outside of buildings. A WiFi-enabled building, campus, or other area allows individuals to access the local network and the Internet while moving anywhere in the area. Schools use WiFi to connect buildings, auditoriums, and outside areas. Some business districts even provide WiFi capability to shops, restaurants, and offices within the WiFi zone. This technology is likely to continue to grow and to expand wireless connectivity significantly. Indeed, some metropolitan areas are already attempting to create WiFi access across their entire cities. Purchasing WiFi-enabled mobile technologies may therefore be a good investment for the future.

For educators, **wireless devices** have the potential to solve several challenges. Wireless technologies allow you to sever the wire tether necessary in the wired classroom. Using a portable wireless computer, students can research an interesting insect they discover while they are still on a field trip rather than wait until the next day when they return to their classrooms. The teachable moment when students inquire and are ready to learn does not have to be postponed until wired connections are available. Furthermore, teachers can access online resources or their stored instructional files from anywhere, whether they are in or out of the classroom. What you need to teach remains at your fingertips wherever you may be. The advent of wireless devices also means that computer-enhanced classrooms do not need to be physically arranged according to where network connections are available on walls. Instead, computers can be easily moved to locations that are best for student interaction and communication.

Wireless communications and the emerging smaller and more powerful digital devices that are supported by this type of interaction are quickly evolving and coming

Emerging hardware holds promise for teachers and learners.

into wide use. Wireless technology offers greater flexibility in terms of physical location and logistical arrangement. The devices using this technology will most likely become as commonplace as cell phones. Creative educators will no doubt develop many innovative applications for wireless devices in teaching and learning.

Handheld Computers

As computing power increases, the physical size of the systems necessary to support it continues to decrease. You were introduced to PDAs earlier in this chapter. PDAs are actually palm-size computers. PDAs represent another point of technological convergence—the digital organizer and the computer merged into a single powerful computing device that can easily be held in one hand.

On CD!
Hardware Skills Builder
Handheld Computers

Handheld computers already offer all of the capabilities of personal information management (calendar, phone list, notes, to-do list, address book, etc.) with abbreviated versions of the most popular types of software (word processing, spreadsheets, games, and music recording and playback, to name an available few). As these devices continue to evolve, their size and weight continue to decrease while their capabilities increase. Displays are improving in resolution. More and more software is being adapted for use on a handheld. Digital cameras, audio and video players, and even cell phones are now being integrated into handhelds. Add to that a browser for access to the Internet, and the handheld easily becomes a powerful, fully functional, and truly portable computer.

For teachers and students alike, handheld computing can make note taking, using educational software, or using the Internet as easy and convenient as taking out a pen and pad. Today handheld computers are used in as many diverse ways as there are student and teacher needs. For students, handhelds can be used to track and store weather information for science, word-process an essay, create diagrams while on a field trip, prepare a group presentation, conduct science experiments (by the attachment of sensors to a handheld), replace graphing calculators, create a spreadsheet, and, with appropriate software, view tutorials for many subjects. For teachers, handhelds can

PDAs let teachers move about the class while taking advantage of computer support.

be used to store grades, make impromptu annotations for a student file, connect to and display digital instructional files, organize a calendar and parent contact list, create a word document, and, in fact, do almost every task a full-size computer can do. And for handhelds connected to wireless school networks, the possibilities expand exponentially. The application of handheld technology to schools has even given rise to web sites dedicated to handheld technology in education. As this technology continues to evolve, handhelds will become even more powerful; and as prices decline, they will become more accessible to educators and their students.

E-books

Electronic books, also known as **E-books,** are electronic versions of books for PDAs. A single device can store and display many digital books along with related instructional and reference materials. E-book software typically has the capacity to allow you to take digital notes on segments as you read them, and some can play sound and audio enhancements if the text file includes them.

The educational applications for this emerging mobile technology are many. Rather than having to carry multiple textbooks and notebooks, students and teachers will need only a single, lightweight textbook-reading device, into which several texts can be downloaded. New versions of texts are quickly and easily updated without the time and expense of printing new editions. The potential of imbedding audio and visual enhancements in text makes it possible to address diverse learning styles from within the text itself. Note taking on text content is convenient and is done in a digital form that allows it to be edited and reorganized for studying. The potential for this technology is just beginning to emerge.

Voice-Activated Devices

PDAs have expanded input capabilities to include keyboard input or both keyboard and pen input. The next technology that will revolutionize how we input data into computers is voice technology. Already available for assistive devices and for business and home computing, **voice technology** enables a computer to accept voice commands and dictation of data. As voice input technology improves, more and more digital devices will be adapted to accept voice commands. Already, some cellular phones have been adapted so that callers can simply speak the name of the person to be called, and the cell phone will dial the correct number.

Voice activation makes it easier for learners who are physically disabled or who have limited keyboarding skills to fully use the capabilities of a computer. For educators, it enables you to start up and conduct an Internet-search demonstration without having to leave a part of the classroom that needs your attention. Rather than having to return to your desk to issue commands via keyboard and mouse, you can simply speak to your computer from across the room. This technology, too, has great potential for improving the convenience of using computers in the classroom.

Portable Storage

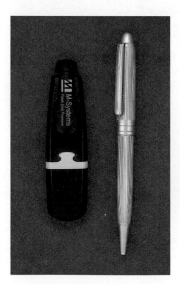

USB drives offer a way to make large files easy to move between computers equipped with a USB port.

One of the newest entries in the field of portable storage devices is the USB drive. This drive, also called a key chain drive, jump drive, or flash drive, is a portable storage device small and lightweight enough to attach to a key chain. The USB drive is approximately the size and shape of a mini highlighting pen, but it has hundreds of times the storage capacity of a floppy disk, and some exceed the storage capacity of CD-ROMs. The inner working of this drive is similar to a memory card like that found in digital cameras. Although the term *drive* is used, it is not an electromechanical device like a hard disk or floppy drive that records and plays back data from different types of disks. Instead, the USB drive is plugged into a computer's USB port, and the operating system recognizes it as an external drive, albeit based on memory-card technology. Data can be saved to the USB drive, and then the device is unplugged from the USB port. Later, the device can be plugged into a different machine's USB port, and that machine too will recognize it as an external drive. Thus, data is easily transported on a large-capacity storage device that can fit on a key chain.

For teachers and students, this inexpensive device can offer massive storage relatively inexpensively. Teachers using USB drives do not have to be concerned about finding the right disk or securing sensitive files. Data stored on the USB drive can be easily and safely carried with the teacher anywhere in the classroom, school, or even back and forth to home. Large multimedia files or presentations can be easily transported from machine to machine.

When selecting a USB drive, teachers should be aware of two possible issues. First, older machines may have few or no readily available USB ports, making the use of these devices problematic. Even if USB drives are available, they may be inconveniently located at the back of a computer in an awkward location. If that is the case, extension USB ports may be necessary to easily use this technology. Second, USB drives are still emerging and changing as their popularity rises. Newer 2.0-type USB drives may not work in older USB ports, while the original USB 1.1 type may not offer the additional features and capacity you desire. Although this is a new technology with some adjustments yet to be made as it evolves, USB drives are powerful portable storage devices that can serve a busy classroom teacher well.

Computer System Enhancements

Microprocessors

The computers that we use, whether desktop, laptop, handheld, or tablet PC versions, are all improving in the speed and power of the microprocessor. Today, a handheld's CPU chip exceeds the capabilities of the mainframes of just twenty years ago. With each microprocessor improvement, computers become more and more capable of processing at the speeds necessary to complete the most complex tasks and produce high-quality, true-to-life still and multimedia displays. The faster and more powerful the microprocessor chip, the more of your needs it can fill, from complex display and editing of digital images to graphical demonstrations of mathematical and scientific concepts. As users continue to demand more and more complex capabilities to perform a larger variety of tasks, the advances in microprocessor chips continue to keep pace. You can expect computers to continue to produce robust and sometimes amazing educational enhancements.

Storage and Memory

For storage devices and memory, as capacity increases, size decreases. Hard disks in the hundreds of gigabytes are on the horizon, while compact, portable memory cards continue to improve their capacity. For educators, this will mean that more robust multimedia software will be more easily stored and made available for students. Portable devices such as the USB drive will be able to store more software and data while being used away from the desktop computer, which itself will have increased storage space. Teachers will be able to store student work and records in digital portfolios that will provide a better profile of a student while being more readily available and accessible.

Virtual Environments

As personal computer system capacity increases, more complex programs can be created. **Virtual reality** (VR) is a combination of hardware and software that together create a digital environment with which you can interact. Using virtual reality hardware, which typically includes a headpiece and glove, you can see and interact with a three-dimensional digital world. VR environments let you take realistic virtual field trips using digital images of real and imaginary places. Some VR worlds are constructed from images of real places such as the Amazon or the Arctic. Still others are constructed from micro-worlds at a molecular or atomic level. Others are constructed from images gathered from NASA space probes. Using the headgear, you see these worlds before you. Using the special interactive glove that adjusts the VR world to the movement of your hand, you can reach out, touch, and grab a planet, a molecule, or a plant in the virtual Amazon.

Virtual reality hardware and software let you feel as if you are participating in a virtual world.

ON THE WEB! 4.6
Is Virtual Reality Worth the Visit?

Early VR worlds are already in place. As you will see in later chapters, many exist in a limited form on the Internet. Other, more complex environments exist only in research labs. Still others are beginning to appear in video arcades. These early VR environments are just a precursor to what will be possible as hardware becomes powerful enough to support the complexities of creating and displaying virtual realities. As VR evolves, it will give students unlimited opportunities to interact with places they may never visit, with environments too dangerous to visit, or with realities too small for humans to interact with directly. The potential for educational applications and experiential learning in VR environments is enormous.

From Hardware to Software

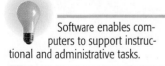

Software enables computers to support instructional and administrative tasks.

The abundant hardware resources explored in this chapter are only the beginning of the potential for computer enhancement of the teaching and learning process. A broad range of administrative and academic **software** related to almost every aspect of education is also available for you to use in your classroom. Administrative software programs support you in almost every area of classroom administration, from helping you to track and average student grades, to helping you create a class newsletter, to helping you make custom, lesson-specific crossword puzzles. Academic software packages that help you teach range from a variety of multimedia encyclopedias, to content-area drill-and-practice programs, to software that provides a simulation that promotes discovery learning. All of these programs are designed to enhance and support what you do in the classroom.

The next two chapters focus on the software resources available to you and explore how they might be effectively used to teach and to learn. Of course, hardware and software are entirely interrelated, so the understanding of hardware you have achieved in this chapter should serve you well as you select the devices you might want for your classroom and as you consider the software you might want to use. As you begin considering these various tools, it is helpful to have a way to determine the

TABLE 4.2   CLASSROOM EQUIPMENT EVALUATION RUBRIC

EQUIPMENT:

DESCRIPTION:

VENDOR: COST:

NOTES ON ITS USE:

Please rate the features below for each piece of hardware. Next to each of the items in the rubric, mark the box that best reflects your opinion.

EVALUATION CRITERIA

Hardware Feature	1 Poor	2 Below Average	3 Average	4 Above Average	5 Excellent
Ease of setup	No or minimal setup instructions; poor or missing summary list of hardware components	Instructions poorly written and somewhat difficult to follow; minimal description of equipment components	Instructions complete and adequately user-friendly; necessary equipment descriptions included	Clear and complete instructions; parts identified by letter or code to correspond to instructions	Pictorial or video guide showing step-by-step assembly with clear, easy-to-follow instructions; equipment goes together easily and smoothly
Ease of use	Equipment complex and difficult for students to use alone; time consuming and complex for teachers	Students can use with minimal support by teacher; teachers can use with some difficulty	Students can use without support after initial orientation; teachers can use with minimal practice	Students can use with brief orientation; teachers can use with little or no practice	Students can use without orientation or support, teachers can use with no practice
Space requirement	Space required may exceed maximum available	Space required somewhat large, but available room could be adjusted to accommodate equipment	Space required by equipment is appropriate to available space with current room configuration	Space requirement is appropriate and equipment will fit comfortably in the room	Space requirement is equal to or less than the space available; equipment adds to the look and usefulness of the room without crowding
Standards consistency	Little or no congruence with school standards	Matches or resembles only a few standards	Matches or resembles an adequate number of standards	Matches the majority of applicable standards	Matches all school, district, and national professional association standards
Documentation	Documentation is excessively technical and/or difficult to follow	Documentation is generally understandable but not very user-friendly	Documentation is user-friendly and is reasonably easy to follow	Clear documentation that is logical and easy to follow	Very clear, user-friendly documentation that leaves no questions
Compatibility	Excessively incompatible with existing hardware and software	Somewhat incompatible with existing equipment; may run some existing software	Adequately compatible with existing equipment and software; some modifications may be required	Mostly compatible with existing hardware and software; few modifications necessary	Fully compatible with existing hardware and software; no modifications necessary
Technical support	No local or toll-free telephone support available	No local support; phone support available for an hourly fee	Local support and phone support available for modest fees	Local tech help available for modest fee; no-charge phone support	Local help and toll-free support readily available at no charge

Continues on next page

Table 4.2, continued

	EVALUATION CRITERIA				
Hardware Feature	**1** Poor	**2** Below Average	**3** Average	**4** Above Average	**5** Excellent
Tutorials/training available	No tutorials packaged with equipment; no online or other training available	Minimal tutorials packaged with equipment; few free or inexpensive optional tutorials or training available	Brief tutorial provided on CD-ROM with equipment; some additional tutorials or training available at minimal cost	CD and online tutorials readily available for free or minimal cost; some in-house training available for a reasonable fee	CD and online tutorials and training materials available without charge; in-house training provided for free or minimal cost
Warranty	No warranty evident; no method for resolution of problems with new equipment	Warranty period is less than 6 months; complex process for resolving problems	Warranty provided for 6 months to 1 year; process for resolution of problems is reasonable	One-year warranty plus phone support provided; simple process available for resolution of new equipment problems	More than one year warranty and phone support; easy process for problem resolution
Other criteria (List your own topic and criteria)					

Total the score for each piece of hardware. Compare the scores. The piece of hardware with the highest score is your best choice.

usefulness of any particular piece of hardware. Clearly, not only do you need to be aware of many types of computer hardware and how each might be applied in your classroom, you also need to know how to evaluate it effectively. To assist you in determining the value of the hardware you are considering, a classroom equipment evaluation rubric is included in Table 4.2. Similar evaluation tools are available in Chapter 5 for software evaluations.

KEY TERMS

STUDENT ACTIVITIES

CHAPTER REVIEW

1. What is a scanner? How might it be used in the classroom?
2. How does a digital camera differ from a film camera? Which do you think would be better for you to use in teaching? Why?
3. How does a graphics tablet (digitizer) work? How might it be used to help you teach and your students learn?
4. For digitized sound to be used in your classroom, what computer input and output components must be available? Describe how you would use each to teach.
5. What is a PDA? Tablet PC? How might you find each useful in your classroom?
6. How does an electronic whiteboard differ from other whiteboards? What is the advantage of using an electronic version?
7. Why are data projection units necessary in a classroom? Describe the different choices available for data projection. Which would you purchase and why?
8. Name some emerging technologies. How might they affect teaching and learning?
9. How do increasing computer power, decreasing size, and wireless communications make technology-enhanced classrooms more flexible?
10. What is a virtual environment? What potential does it hold for education?

WHAT DO YOU THINK?

1. After considering the various types of digital technologies presented in this chapter, what three pieces of equipment do you think you would most want for your future or current classroom? Explain why you selected these three and how you would use them for teaching and learning.
2. Some teachers believe that too much emphasis is placed on computers in the classroom. Considering the computer technology you have learned about in this chapter, do you agree or disagree? Defend your view.

LEARNING TOGETHER!

The following activities are designed for learning groups of two or three students.

1. Imagine that your grade-level team or department has been given a $20,000 grant for adding technology to your classrooms. How would you spend the money to best equip your classrooms for teaching and for learning? Include a budget showing how the money would be spent.
2. Visit a technology-rich classroom and interview the teacher about how he or she uses the technology in place. Compare your interviews with those of the other members of your group, and develop your group's ideal classroom. Describe the technologies you would include and how you would plan to use them.
3. Select three different computer systems and compare them using the classroom equipment evaluation rubric in Table 4.2. After discussing the options with your group, describe which system you would buy, and explain why. Be prepared to share your preference and your reasons with the class.

HANDS-ON!

1. Visit a computer store or surf the Internet to compare makes and models of each of the following computer peripherals: *digital camera, scanner, computer display, printer.* Use the classroom equipment evaluation rubric in Table 4.2 to help you select which model you would buy.

2. Prepare a photo essay that you might use to teach the topic of your choice at the grade level you would like to teach, using either a digital camera and printer or a photographic camera, scanner, and printer. Be prepared to share your work with the class.

3. Using available technology, capture multimedia elements, including an audio clip, a video frame, a digital image, and scanned image, that you might find useful for a lesson of your choice. Share these with the class and explain how you would use each to enhance teaching or learning.

4. Using the Internet, research wireless devices that might be useful in the classroom to determine what is currently available and what types of devices are emerging. Summarize your research in a one- to two-page report to share with your peers.

More from Mike Duffy

MY TECHNOLOGY CHOICES

As I said, I was on a technology mission to select wisely and well. I took several technology training courses offered by my school so I could become familiar with new technologies and their application in the classroom. I learned about PDAs, digital still and video cameras, electronic whiteboards, and projection devices. I asked for help from our technology resource teacher and our school technician. Both of these professionals gave me valuable information on different technologies and on how I might use them in the classroom. I also contacted the school district's assistive-technology specialist to learn about the many specialized devices that can help ESE students. I volunteered to go to a variety of assistive-technology workshops to learn how these devices could be used.

I found I also needed to do a lot of research on my own. I spent many hours on the Internet looking at various technologies and reading about how other special education teachers were using these technologies to help their students. Slowly, I began to formulate my wish list of the best technologies for my classroom. Once done, whenever I was asked what I wanted for my classroom in terms of technology, I was ready with a precise technology request and rationale that resulted in my getting the top equipment on my wish list.

During my few first years of teaching, I had to make the most of an overhead projector, a few very old computers with limited software, two tape recorders for a Listening Center, and a monitor and VCR. Each year, with wish list in hand, I was able to acquire a bit more of what my students needed. Through my own research efforts and lots of training by my school, and with the help and support of my colleagues and school, I have transformed my classroom from its limited beginnings to the technology-rich classroom I have today.

MY CLASSROOM TODAY

Today my students have access in my classroom to six multimedia computers, all of them networked and able to access the Internet. Their power ranges from older Pentium II microprocessors to the newer Pentium 4s. The computers all have access to the school's office-productivity software via the network, so my students can word-process, create spreadsheets and graphs, and make presentations with PowerPoint. I have put together my own class web site using FrontPage, and this year I hope to have my students create their own pages to be added to the web site. I acquired over one hundred educational software programs; some were purchased, but many were donated, and others I acquired from bargain tables at our local office supply store. I have a full-page scanner, four color printers, two VCRs, a DVD player, four cassette-tape recorders (two with CD players), a musical keyboard with a musical instrument digital interface (MIDI), a monitor-top video camera, a digital camera, an overhead projector, and a wide variety of assistive software and devices to meet special needs. As a result of one of our school grants, I have and use a PDA regularly to schedule, to store student contact information, and to make student observational notations throughout the day. I have CD-RW drives on two of my machines, and I use them to archive my students' work and to make copies to send home to parents. I also was given and regularly use a USB drive to transport files among my classroom machines and my computer at home. My latest acquisition (and current favorite) is a digital projector and an eBeam device that turns my ordinary class whiteboard into an electronic whiteboard. I have so far used this new technology not only to display computer images while I teach but also to give my very kinesthetic students a chance to physically interact with the computer via the whiteboard technology. And because the projector happens to be connected to a computer with a DVD drive, I have also begun to use that device to show videos on DVD to my class.

After nine years of collecting, I finally feel like I have a good variety of technology to support my students' learning activities and my teaching strategies. Interestingly, though, my wish list hasn't really diminished. I continue to research and explore the new technologies coming out to see if any of them will help support my students. Mostly, I continue to regularly research via the Internet, but I also make it a point to interact with my colleagues in my school and across my district. In particular, I keep in touch with my ESE colleagues and read ESE journals to be sure I am current on the technologies and best practices that will help my students.

Even though I have acquired many incredibly useful and motivational technologies, I have discovered that just having them in the classroom isn't enough. It takes time and careful planning to select the right technology and then to use it well for the benefit of my students. I wouldn't give up a single piece of equipment, but I know it is only through good instructional strategies that each one becomes useful. As much as I appreciate the power of technological tools, they are only as good as the teacher who uses them.

For more information, to share your ideas, or to donate your technology please feel free to contact me:

Michael J. Duffy
Elementary Exceptional Student Education
Key Largo School, P.O. Box 3068, Key Largo, Florida
email: duffym@monroe.k12.fl.us

Before selecting a personal computer system and periperals for your classroom, complete the decision matrix below to help you determine whether the equipment is right for you.

Component	Questions to Ask about This Component	Place checks in the columns that match your answers.		
		Yes	No	N/A
SYSTEM UNIT				
CPU	Is the CPU chip a name brand? Is the chip speed faster than required by the majority of the software you want to use? Can the chip be upgraded if necessary?			
RAM	Does the amount of RAM exceed the requirements of the software you want to use? Can you add more RAM if needed?			
BAYS	Is there room in the system unit to add more internal drives if you want to?			
PORTS	Are there multiple USB ports available? Are some of the USB ports available on the front of the machine?			
STORAGE				
HARD DRIVE	Is this drive the largest size possible for your budget? Is this a high-speed drive?			
FLOPPY DRIVE	Is a floppy disk drive included in this machine?			
CD DRIVE(S)	Is a CD-RW drive included in this computer? Is the CD-RW drive high-speed (more than 40x)? Does CD recording software come installed? Is there more than one CD (or DVD) drive included to facilitate copying student CDs?			
DVD DRIVE	Is a DVD drive included? Is a DVD-recordable drive included?			
ZIP DRIVE	Is a Zip drive included? Is the Zip drive capable of reading 250 megabyte Zip disks?			
USB DRIVE	Does the drive provide sufficient storage space for your largest collection of files? Does the shape of the drive allow it to be easily plugged into accessible USB ports? Do any necessary software drivers come with the drive? Does the drive come with a lanyard or key chain?			
OUTPUT DEVICES				
MONITOR	Is the monitor resolution sufficient for your highest-output program? Is the monitor size appropriate to your viewing and space needs? Does the monitor have an adjustment control in front so it is easy to access?			
PRINTER	Is the page per minute (ppm) speed sufficient to print in a timely manner? If ink-jet, is each color inkwell separate so colors can be replaced independently when they run out? If laser, is the cost of replacement toner cartridges reasonably within your budget?			

INTERCHAPTER 2

CLASSROOM COMPUTERS AND PERIPHERALS

Component	Questions to Ask about This Component	Place checks in the columns that match your answers.		
		Yes	No	N/A
SPEAKERS	Is the paper tray large enough so you don't have to continuously load paper? Can the printer print two sides automtically? Are speakers included?			
	Is a headphone jack easily accessible? Are the speakers powered with a separate plug? Are the speakers and amplifier (if included) small enough for classroom space requirements?			
DIGITAL PROJECTOR	Is the brightness (in lumens) sufficient so that it will display with classroom lights on? Can the device display both video and digital data? Does it have built-in speakers? Does it have a remote control? Does it have sufficient adjustment controls (focus, align, zoom, etc.)? Are all necessary cables provided?			
INPUT DEVICES				
KEYBOARD	Are the keys sufficiently tactile (not spongy to the touch)? Does the keyboard include a wrist rest? Are there additional easy-access multimedia keys or buttons? Does the keyboard have its own port rather than using a multiuse port?			
MOUSE	Is the mouse an optical rather than a ball mouse? Is a scroll wheel included on the mouse? Is a mouse pad provided?			
MICROPHONE	Is a microphone included? Is its cord sufficiently long to be used comfortably? Is a holder provided to store the mic when not in use?			
SCANNER	Is the resolution sufficient for the type of scanning you want to do? Is the scanner software easy to use? Is the software OCR-capable? Will the scanner scan larger documents? Does the scanner have a feeder for multiple pages?			
DIGITAL CAMERA	Is this camera's image quality (in megapixels) sufficient for the types of photos you wish to take and print? Is extra storage capacity available at reasonable cost? Is the battery type rechargeable? Are extra batteries available at a reasonable cost? Can the camera zoom sufficiently for your needs? Is there an LCD display to preview pictures? Is there an easy-to-use dowload system to move images to your computer? Are the setting adjustments easy to use? Is a strap provided for easy carrying? Is a camera case provided?			
MAKE YOUR DECISION!				
TOTALS	Add the number of checks in each column. The higher the number of Yes checks, the more likely the computer system is appropriate for your classroom.			

CHAPTER 5

Administrative Software

This chapter addresses these ISTE National Educational Technology Standards for Teachers:

I. Technology operations and concepts

Teachers demonstrate a sound understanding of technology operations and concepts. Teachers

A. demonstrate introductory knowledge, skills, and understanding of concepts related to technology (as described in the ISTE *National Education Technology Standards for Students*).
B. demonstrate continual growth in technology knowledge and skills to stay abreast of current and emerging technologies.

V. Productivity and professional practice

Teachers use technology to enhance their productivity and professional practice. Teachers

A. use technology resources to engage in ongoing professional development and lifelong learning.
B. continually evaluate and reflect on professional practice to make informed decisions regarding the use of technology in support of student learning.
C. apply technology to increase productivity.
D. use technology to communicate and collaborate with peers, parents, and the larger community in order to nurture student learning.

Imagine that your school district has decided to conduct a districtwide upgrade of technology in the coming year. As a result of this initiative, you have just been given five new computer systems for use in your classroom. The computer-support department tells you that the district will make a variety of administrative software packages available to you. Will you know how to use them? Will you know how to apply them to improve the teaching and learning environment in your classroom?

As you can see, the understanding of computer hardware that you gained from Chapters 3 and 4 is only half the challenge for a computer-using educator. You must be just as competent when it comes to understanding and selecting the software programs that will run on that hardware. This chapter will lead you through an exploration of administrative software and how its types of programs can assist you in your professional responsibilities, from managing your classroom to helping your students learn. It will also help you gain the skills you need to effectively evaluate and select the software that will help you do your job and benefit your students.

In Chapter 5, you will

- Explore the differences between administrative and academic software

- Identify how various types of administrative software can help you be more effective and efficient in carrying out your professional responsibilities

- Examine how the major types of administrative software can be used to enhance the learning environment

- Explore key theoretical frameworks relating to the use of software in teaching and learning
- Investigate and use methods for reviewing and evaluating software so that your technology acquisitions will meet your needs

Meet Troy Robinson

In every school, everyone has an important job that contributes to support of the students who attend the school and to the effective operation of the school itself. Administrators, like teachers, often struggle to find the time and help that enable them to manage their critical role in school operations. Just as they can in the classroom, computers and software can lend a helping hand in the school office.

Let's take a look at how one assistant principal managed his challenges through the application of useful productivity software. You will learn much more about this type of software as you read this chapter. You too may find ways in which it will help you address your challenges as a future or current teacher.

MY SETTING

My name is Dr. J. Troy Robinson. I have been an educator for many years and have worked as an elementary school teacher, a school administrator, and a professor in higher education. Of all my experiences, one of my most challenging jobs as an educator was as an assistant principal in a K–5 elementary school. At my school, I had responsibility for many aspects of the school's daily business. Some of the more time-consuming undertakings involved keeping track of a variety of items and services, such as an inventory of textbooks and other instructional materials, records of student behavior-management activities (discipline), and the referrals and intervention strategies for at-risk students.

My school was a public elementary school in west Florida that served approximately 1,000 students. The students at my school were diverse in many ways. Academically, their test scores fell in every stanine on standardized tests.

The teaching staff consisted of thirty-nine classroom teachers, five exceptional education teachers (handling emotional handicaps, varying exceptionalities, specific learning disabilities, gifted needs, and speech), and one bilingual teacher. There were also three bilingual aides, six kindergarten aides, six custodial workers, and seven lunchroom workers. In the office, there was one principal, one assistant principal, one guidance counselor, and one media specialist. We also had an office staff that included three secretaries, one data-processing clerk, and one secretary for the media center. Together we formed the team that made our school successful.

In my role as the assistant principal, I worked with teachers in the implementation of the curriculum, maintained the school's master schedule, administered the annual standardized testing program, and coordinated the inventory and acquisition of instructional materials. I also worked with other members of the administrative staff, teachers and aides, parents and guardians, bus drivers, and lunchroom aides in the supervision of students and the administration of the schoolwide cooperative discipline plan. With so many responsibilities, I was always on the lookout for technology supports that could help me meet the challenges during our busy school days. I found that some of the basic productivity tools I had learned about in college proved to be some of my biggest helpers.

Every day I found that productivity software helped me get the job done. I used word processing for most aspects of my daily work as an assistant principal. I used PowerPoint for presentations to the faculty and parent groups. Email was a daily communication link with teachers and support staff. I learned to greatly value the computer and related technologies that were available to me in my school setting.

One of the most challenging tasks that I performed each year involved summer school. In this district, the assistant principal was responsible for the preparations prior to the end of the regular school year and the complete oversight of summer school during its operation. I accomplished this job during my first two years as an assistant principal with only the use of word processing. Form letters were used to notify parents about each student's eligibility and other important information, such as hours and days of operation, teacher and room assignments, and bus schedules. The rosters of each homeroom were used to manually notate students' eligibility criteria. Classroom teachers assisted with this process at the end of second and third quarters by providing updates with copies of the students' report cards. A count of eligible students was derived from these rosters. Preparing for summer school was a complex and time-consuming job.

I used technology regularly in performing the wide array of daily tasks in my job, including many different kinds of software in addition to word processing, so I thought that some of those same software packages might be useful to help me with summer school. I needed help with keeping track of kids who might need to go to summer school, determining eligibility by analyzing established criteria, maintaining records of communications with parents, establishing the schedule of classes and assignment of teachers, and personalizing the final notification to students and parents. There were many details throughout this five-month process that defied manual tracking in such a large school. I wanted to find a way to use technology that would make these tasks easier.

In previous years, the teachers and I had manually kept track of the at-risk students in each homeroom. We had not seen the need for a database, even though I knew the use of a database was a possibility. At that point, it seemed that learning to use a database would have simply slowed the process down. But as I faced the planning for summer school during my third year as an assistant principal, two significant changes made the task even more complicated. Grade-level expectations were introduced, and specific criteria for demonstrating mastery of the expectations were established. The school board and instructional supervisors mandated that all students who had not demonstrated mastery of the grade-level expectations would be required to attend summer school. This caused the number of

students expected to attend summer school to increase dramatically. Additionally, my school was designated as the summer school site for gifted students from three other schools in the northeast part of the district. Over 200 additional gifted students would be coming to my school.

With these changes, continuing a manual tracking process was no longer an option. It was time to turn to technology to see if there was a better way.

The application of the right software package at the right time can solve pressing challenges for both teachers and administrators. In this chapter, you will learn much about the kinds of software that are available to you to help you meet the challenges you will face as a teacher. After you know a bit more about software, we will check back in with Dr. Robinson at the end of this chapter to see how he managed his summer school challenge.

SOURCE: Interview with J. Troy Robinson conducted by Al P. Mizell. Reprinted by permission of J. Troy Robinson.

What Do Educators Need to Know about Software?

The understanding that you gained from Chapters 3 and 4 relating to the use of computer hardware in teaching and learning is the first step in a two-step process leading to the computer competencies an educator needs. The second step is to be able to identify, evaluate, and apply computer software to the direct and indirect tasks associated with teaching and learning. The use of computer hardware and software is really just making use of electronic tools to extend our capabilities. Just as a rake or a tractor can help a farmer produce crops more efficiently, the effective application of electronic tools can make us more productive educators.

Whether an educator needs to use software as a tool to create a letter to send home to parents or to turn a computer into a tireless student tutor, being able to select and use the best software package for the task is a skill every educator needs. The ability to evaluate software is especially valuable when you are selecting software specifically designed to assist educators. It is the educator's expertise in teaching and in learning that ensures that the programs acquired by a school address the specific, targeted competencies that have been articulated through the instructional design process. Educators must be sufficiently software-literate to be able to recommend software that can help their students learn and then be able to serve as guides through the software acquisition and implementation process.

Being able to select and use the best software package is a skill every educator needs.

Computer software can be divided into two major categories. The first category is **administrative software,** that is, software that assists an educator in accomplishing the administrative, professional, and management tasks associated with the profession. The second category is **academic software,** or software that assists both educators and learners in the teaching and learning process itself. Both types of software are important tools for educators in helping them work efficiently and effectively as classroom managers, educational professionals, and, ultimately, architects of the learning environment. This chapter focuses on the use of administrative software for teacher productivity and for classroom application. Chapter 6 more fully explores academic software.

The critical role of software in education is consistent with the role of software in many other aspects of contemporary life. Few businesses could do without the use of software. Word processing has become as critical a skill as typing once was. Spreadsheets are essential for accounting, budgeting, and other financial tasks. The use of the Internet and its support software for information, sales, and communication is as commonplace as the use of a library or telephone. For teachers, the role of software is no less important for their administrative and academic tasks. Standards, today's measure for effectiveness in education, have even been developed to specifically address the use of software by educators. ISTE's NETS (Appendix 1) emphasize the importance of being able to use software appropriately for teaching, learning, and productivity.

Given the recognized importance of software in education, it becomes necessary for every educator to develop sufficient software literacy, that is, the ability to effectively identify and use appropriate software. To do so, an educator must be able to locate and review software options in order to select the software package that will accomplish the desired task. Then, you must be able to objectively evaluate the software to see whether it indeed fills your need. Resources for the acquisition of educational technology are typically very limited, and careful purchases will make those limited resources go much further. Once the software has been acquired, you might even need to install it on the hardware you have available to you. Finally, so that you and your students can get the most out of the software, you will need to become familiar with how it works. If this sounds like a somewhat time-consuming process, that is because software evaluation, acquisition, installation, and training are indeed extensive tasks. The up-front investment of time and energy in this process, however, will make the difference between the acquisition of valuable educational tools and the purchase of software that looked good on first inspection but ended up gathering dust in a storage closet.

To begin the exploration of software, we will first examine administrative software, the programs you might use in accomplishing tasks associated with your teaching and professional responsibilities as well as classroom management. Administrative software can be divided into two general software types (see Table 5.1). These are productivity software and school and/or classroom management support software. **Productivity software** is typically generic business-application software that educators can use and adapt for the administrative and professional tasks they must address. Word processing, spreadsheet, and database management software are all examples of productivity software. In contrast, **classroom management support software** is usually customized software written for educators to help them manage school and classroom tasks, including the creation and maintenance of seating charts, class rolls, student records, or school budgets.

All these administrative software tools help educators do their jobs more effectively and productively. Because a fairly significant time investment is involved in finding, installing, and learning software, you should be cautious in your selections. That is the reason software evaluation skills are so important for computer-using educators. This chapter includes evaluation rubrics to assist you in this critical process.

Administrative software includes productivity and classroom management support software.

TABLE 5.1   ADMINISTRATIVE SOFTWARE FOR EDUCATORS

Software Type	Administrative Tasks	Professional Tasks	Teaching and Learning Tasks
Productivity Software	Assists educators in preparing memos, letters, reports, and budgets	Assists educators in tracking student information, computing grades, and preparing lesson plans and IEPs	Helps educators create student activity sheets, transparencies, grade reports, and parent letters
Classroom Management Support Software	**FOR DISTRICTS AND SCHOOLS**		
	Assists educators in reporting required student information	Assists educators in gathering data for student reports	Assists educators in gathering data for academic decision making
	FOR CLASSROOM		
	Helps educators prepare required reports	Assists educators in tracking and reporting grades; helps create seating charts, rolls, and other classroom tasks	Assists educators in analyzing grade and student data for better academic decision making

Administrative software can be purchased as an off-the-shelf commercial package or as a custom-made program, or it can be acquired as freeware or shareware. **Freeware** is software that is offered to users without charge; **shareware** is software that is offered to users for a small fee or for a limited time, and is sometimes paid for on the honor system after you have had a chance to try out the software and determine whether it is useful for you. Freeware and shareware present a great temptation for educators on a very constricted budget. Even though many fine administrative software tools are offered as freeware or shareware, they too must be carefully evaluated. Low-cost or no-cost software still costs you the time and effort it takes to install and learn the software. When making software decisions, it is useful to complete a rubric like those included in this chapter (Tables 5.7 and 5.8) comparing products to determine the features and value of each program you plan to purchase. Rubrics help you to objectively determine the effectiveness of the software. Freeware and shareware can be found on many education sites on the Internet, often along with some annotation or review of the software's quality.

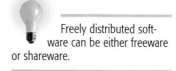

Freely distributed software can be either freeware or shareware.

Evaluating and Using Productivity Software

Much of an educator's time is consumed in completing the many administrative tasks necessary to prepare and maintain an effective learning environment and to meet the record-keeping demands of the typical school system. The office productivity software that has facilitated business operations can frequently serve educators equally well for their administrative educational tasks. Such software is typically designed for ease of

On CD!
Software Skills Builder
Office Tools and Tips

use, with each application performing a unique function for the user. And, although created for different purposes, productivity software programs are typically created with a similar look and feel so that it is easy to learn one type of software and then apply the same skills to learning another software package produced by the same vendor. On your Companion CD, you may want to try the *Office Tools and Tips* Skill Builder activity to experience the format and skills associated with one of the most common types of productivity software groups, Microsoft Office.

The four major types of productivity software found in most business environments are word processors, electronic spreadsheets, database management systems, and presentation software. These types of software can be purchased in individual packages or in application suites and are designed to run on either a PC or Macintosh platform. Often, a school system will equip the administrative component of its operation with productivity software, which teachers can adapt to address educational tasks. The district will often purchase a site license, that is, a license that allows the use of a software package on all machines at locations associated with one organization. The acquisition by district or school computing departments of a site license for productivity software for administrative purposes can benefit the educational staff as well. Although individual educators may have little choice in what productivity software is available to them, with a bit of creativity, that software can be applied to myriad teaching and professional tasks. Office productivity software, used in the classroom or other academic spaces such as the media center or faculty workroom, can be a great asset to busy educators. The computer-using educator's job is to learn to use the software and apply it to the many nonteaching tasks for which he or she is responsible. Let's look at the characteristics of the "big four" applications (word processing, spreadsheets, database management, and presentation software) that are included in office software suites and explore how educators can use each of them (see Table 5.2).

Most productivity software packages include a word processor, electronic spreadsheet, database management system, and presentation software.

TABLE 5.2 PRODUCTIVITY SOFTWARE SUMMARY

Software Type	Application to Administrative/Professional Tasks	Application to Teaching and Learning Tasks
WORD PROCESSING	Prepare letters, memos, reports, flyers, rubrics, lesson plans, forms, and newsletters	Prepare transparencies, activity sheets, posters, study guides, and class notes; help students prepare stories, essays, and group reports; use in class to dynamically illustrate writing and outlining skills
ELECTRONIC SPREADSHEETS	Prepare budgets, numeric tables and summaries, grade and attendance rosters, and compute grades; prepare visuals (charts) of numeric data	Provide students with a method for tracking and analyzing data and creating charts from it; demonstrate what-if analyses visually; support student research such as tracking stock market data
DATABASE MANAGEMENT SYSTEMS	Organize and track student and other professional data; prepare inventories, mailing lists, and reports	Organize and provide easy access to lists of academic resources; provide support for students' tracking data; extract and report targeted summaries of content or resources to address student needs
PRESENTATION SOFTWARE	Create presentations for workshops, conferences, and meetings	Create class lecture support that features text, audio, and visual elements with special effects; produce transparency masters; create student worksheets to accompany class lectures

Word Processors

Word-processing software is the most commonly used computer application. Computers loaded with word-processing software have all but replaced typewriters for text-oriented tasks, although the typewriter still has a niche in the completion of noncomputerized forms. Today's word processors, however, are capable of doing far more than even the most advanced electronic typewriter. In addition to creating, editing, and printing documents, these software packages are capable of desktop publishing, creating and editing graphics, and developing web pages. Combined with a relatively inexpensive color ink-jet printer, word-processing software packages are also powerful tools for creating full-color transparencies, classroom signs and posters, customized certificates and awards, and even personalized stickers and buttons (see Figure 5.1). Of course, they are also essential tools for creating tests, student worksheets, and memos.

Unlike most typewriters, word-processing programs maintain large amounts of data in an electronic format until it is ready to print out. This allows educators to store and easily update or modify the many documents they use in the daily administrative tasks that are a part of every educator's job. Word processing offers educators a way to easily file and access electronic documents and then to modify and update them with little effort. Furthermore, word processors typically include a built-in capacity to check grammar and spelling and an interactive thesaurus, which make this software application a valuable tool for every educator.

Most word-processing packages share several significant and useful features. These can be broadly grouped in terms of the word-processing functions they enhance. These functions include document preparation and editing, desktop publishing, and archiving and printing.

On your Companion CD, each of these functions is explored. As you try each of the word-processing exercises, you will experience and practice the unique and powerful functions built into one of today's most popular word processors, Microsoft Word.

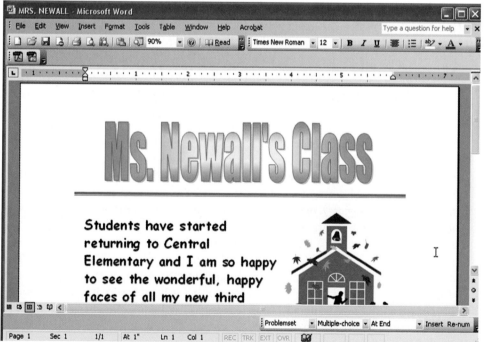

Microsoft Word® is a registered trademark of Microsoft Corporation.

Figure 5.1
Word Processing in the Classroom
Word processors can create flyers and transparency masters in addition to text documents.

• Document Preparation and Editing

Document preparation is the most common use of word-processing software. This function enables the user to type data into the software and then edit the data while it is still in the electronic format. Error correction, adjustments to the document's text, and experimentation with different fonts and formats can be completed before the document is printed on paper (i.e., in a hard copy). Editing features may vary with the complexity of the word-processing software, but all word processors include the following key features. You will practice using many of them when you try the Word Skills Builder, *Bake Sale Flyer* activity on your Companion CD.

On CD!
Software Skills Builder
Word Skills–Bake Sale Flyer

- *Insertion and Deletion of Text.* The cursor, or insertion point, that is displayed on the word-processing screen indicates the point at which text will be entered. As a document is created, the cursor typically stays at the end of the data and moves along as additional text is entered. By using the computer's mouse or arrow keys, the user can move the cursor back or forward to any point in the body of the document. By positioning the cursor at a targeted spot in the document, you can either insert additional text by typing it in at the cursor position or remove unwanted text by pressing the Backspace or Delete key on the computer keyboard.

- *Text Selection and Enhancement.* Once a document has been entered, specific letters, words, paragraphs, lines, or whole pages can be selected. Text selection is accomplished by using the mouse to point to the desired text and then dragging the cursor across it. The selected material will be highlighted in reverse color. Once text is selected, the word processor is ready to apply subsequent commands to that portion of the text only. Enhancement commands include changing the type size or font used or adding visual augmentation, such as changing normal text to bold, italics, or underlined text. After selecting text, enhancing it is typically a matter of pointing and clicking on the software button representing the enhancement desired or using a keyboard command.

- *Word Wrap and Formatting.* When you type on a traditional typewriter, it is necessary to move the paper carriage back to its start position and down one line after completing each line of type. Word processors eliminate this step with their word wrap feature. With word wrap, when the text reaches the end of the line, the software automatically moves down to the beginning of the next line in preparation for additional input. If a word does not quite fit on a line, the software will recognize this and move it down to become the first word on the next line. This feature is especially useful when you decide to insert additional text. The software makes room for the inserted text by wrapping all subsequent lines down the page. Page formatting features allow you to change the look of the page, such as changing margins, adding headers and footers, or altering line spacing on all or part of the document. Such page changes may cause the text in any given line to move. The word wrap feature will once again automatically adjust the text and line length to accommodate such formatting changes.

- *Spelling and Grammar Tools.* The most popular of the common word-processing features include built-in spell-checker, grammar checker, and thesaurus. The spell-checker will check spelling word by word against a built-in dictionary of thousands of words and suggest alternatives to words it does not recognize. This same dictionary can be used as a thesaurus to provide both synonyms and antonyms of selected words. Finally, the software is created with recognition of proper grammar and sentence construction. The software can check a document and find sentences that are questionable grammatically and make suggestions for alternative sentence construction.

- *Copy, Cut, Paste, Drag, and Undo.* Editing functions in word processors provide the user with the ability to select letters, words, or blocks of text and then remove them from the document or move them to a different location within the document. The *copy* feature creates a duplicate version of the selected text, which can be *pasted* elsewhere. The *cut* feature removes a block of text from its original location permanently. The material can then be pasted into another location. Some word processors have combined a cut-and-paste function into a single feature called *drag and drop.* This feature allows you to select text anywhere in the document and, using the mouse, drag and drop it anywhere else in the document. Finally, the *undo* feature provides a safety net against mistakes. It allows the user to back up and undo the last several actions.

Desktop Publishing

Most word processors include the ability to manipulate the look of a page. By using this feature, an attractive arrangement of graphics and text on a page can be created and manipulated with a few clicks of the mouse button. Although word processors can perform some desktop publishing tasks, they cannot perform the extensive adjustments to page displays that dedicated desktop publishing software can make. The basic desktop publishing capabilities included in most word processors are summarized here:

- *WYSIWYG Displays.* Word processors are able to display a document on the screen in a "what you see is what you get" (**WYSIWYG**) format. This feature allows the user to preview a document and see exactly what it will look like before it is printed out.
- *Graphics and Clip Art.* Most word processors today include rudimentary graphics capabilities that allow you to add and position a drawing on a document page. The creation of a complex or custom graphic is typically done with dedicated graphics programs, but most word processors include a library of clip art (ready-made artwork) that can be inserted into a document. Additional clip art can usually be added to the word-processing clip art library. The size and position of this artwork can then be changed, thus adding interest to an all-text document.
- *Tables and Columns.* Text data can easily be arranged into multiple columns of data per page or into a table or grid. These word-processing features give the user the ability to organize data, with just a few clicks of the mouse, into something other than a narrative. Once the data is in table or column form, all of the typical text enhancements can be applied.
- *Autoformats.* Tables, columns, and documents can be formatted in many different ways. Borders can be added, titles can be enhanced, and graphics can be placed in any type of document. For users who do not have the time or experience to experiment with formats, many word processors include an autoformat feature. This feature lets you preview the look of various styles that can be applied to a document and then select the one you like best to use with your document. Once selected, the format is automatically applied to the entire document under construction.
- *Word Art.* A fairly recent addition to word processors' publishing features is the ability to create fancy, colorful titles. This word art feature offers you the ability to add color, shapes, and styles to a document's title or to make sections of your document stand out.

Archiving and Printing

Once a document is completed, word processors provide the ability to save the document in numerous formats and to print it out in black and white or color, depending on the available printers. Archiving or storing a document to a floppy or hard disk

On CD!
Software Skills Builder
Word Skills—Behavior Tracker

Today's word-processing packages can create and edit documents, complete desktop publishing tasks, and develop web pages.

IN THE CLASSROOM

The Business of Writing

Word processing has proved to be a valuable tool for grammar instruction, given that students of all ages enjoy working on computers. Philip Dodge, who teaches at Elaine Wynn Elementary School in Las Vegas, Nevada, teaches grammar by showing children how to recognize grammatical errors and fix them using a word processor. Working in pairs, children are given a short story prepared by Mr. Dodge. The story contains typographical, semantic, and editorial mistakes of the kind studied in language arts class. Using Cut, Copy, and Paste, the children revise the incorrect copy. They then insert a relevant image from the File menu or Clip Art button into the revised text.

Big books and word processing form a winning combination for Susan Renner-Smith's first graders as they learn vocabulary. "I use my classroom computer monitor as a visual aid!" she writes. The children gather around the computer where Ms. Renner-Smith first shows them the pictures in a big book. She covers the words with blank sentence strips. Then, turning to the computer and a word-processing program with a font large enough to be visible to all, she lets each child in a round-robin dictate a sentence to tell the story as he or she sees it by looking only at the pictures. As they talk, she types the sentences and places their names in parentheses. The children decide on a title for their story, and their version is saved on a disk. Ms. Renner-Smith then reads the actual text of the book to the children so that they can compare their story to the original. She says, "By simply changing the color and increasing the font size of the words they use, I am increasing my first-graders' sight vocabulary and helping them to connect with a story before reading."

Not only teaching but also testing can be varied by using word-processing software. Stephanie Moore, a former instructional technologist for the Jennings, Missouri, schools, tells how interactive tests can be created with Microsoft Word. The advantages that result from word-processing quizzes and tests are time-saving templates that can be reused, accessibility to the tests on computers, printouts for grading, and, if desired, hard copies of the tests to be given in the traditional way.

SOURCES: P. Dodge. 2002. Fixing grammar with technology. Retrieved February 13, 2003, from http://www.teachers.net/lessons/posts/2584.html; S. Renner-Smith. 2002. "Fantastic" idea! *Creative Classroom* (March/April), 26; S. Moore. 2002. Creating tests with Microsoft Word. *Instructor* (September), 112 (3), 16.

stores the text you typed, along with all of its related formatting commands, in a single word-processor file. The formatting commands are called word-processing codes. These codes vary with the type of word processor used. Because there are many types of word processors, you may find that a file you create with your word processor is different in appearance or even unreadable when you open it in another type of word processor. This problem of readability or compatibility may be overcome if a word processor contains a document conversion program as a part of its program code. Even if it does not, almost every word processor provides "Save As" choices. To save a document in other formats, after selecting Save As from the File menu, you will see a dialog box that typically provides you with a choice of formats. This feature, sometimes referred to as exporting a document, lets you save the same document in multiple formats depending on the other types of word processors that read it.

The final feature shared by all word processors is the ability to print documents. One of the sets of word-processing codes saved with every document is information about the type of printer to be used to print the document out. Because a number of types of printers are available, the printer that is set up as the default printer for the word processor will be used automatically unless you instruct the program to do otherwise. Some formatting features may change when printer defaults change, thus unexpectedly changing the way your document looks. It is therefore important to save your document with the appropriate printer settings to avoid such conflicts. Of course, as you learned in Chapter 3, printers can just as easily output crisp laser copies as they can colorful transparencies, depending on the specific capabilities of the hardware.

• Ready-Made Word-Processing Tools

Because word processors are such commonly used tools in education, educators have developed many documents, templates, and macros. **Templates** are documents that are preformatted for a specific use but contain no data. An example of a template might be a meeting announcement flyer. To use it, you would open the template with your word processor to find a fully laid-out flyer. With this premade document open, you would only need to type in your organization's name and the date and time of your meeting. You can also create templates for your own future use. When you complete the Word Skills Builder, *Rubric Template* (on your Companion CD), you will be creating a template you can use in your classroom.

On CD!
Software Skills Builder
Word Skills–Rubrics

You can also modify a template further if you want to. A word-processing **macro** is a prerecorded set of commands for your word processor that automates a complex task such as formatting output to fit on labels. Macros are stored in files that can be retrieved and activated with a few keystrokes. An example of a macro might be a file that automatically sets up the official school letterhead using the school's logo and name. Very often, such predesigned templates and macros are freely shared among educators across the Internet.

issues in
teaching
and
technology

Why Can't I Use the Word Processor
I Already Know?

oftware is a medium of communication. To communicate easily and with accuracy within a designated environment, such as a school or school district, a decision must be made as to how to establish a consistent and unified system of software. Potential incompatibility exists across platforms, for example, between Apple computers and IBM-compatible PCs or between different software vendors. In fact, unless programs are designed to be totally cross-platform and totally capable of conversion between software vendors, users of one type of software will not be able to translate and/or use software created by other users within the organization. It is as if you were in a rural, isolated Chinese village and tried to communicate in English or as if you were fluent in only one of the many Chinese dialects and were able to pick out only a few words or phrases. So it is with software. All communicants need to be using the same "language."

From an economic perspective, there are additional reasons for an organization to use common software. It is clear that technology resources are scarce, so their wise use becomes an imperative. Arguments for commonality involve cost, accessibility, time, support, and training. The cost of duplicating programs and their support to cater to individual preference is prohibitive. Site licenses for basic programs represent considerable savings over single-license purchases or even purchases for small groups of users.

Support issues for multiple types of software are many. If multiple types of word processors are implemented, for example, the support staff must know how to install, use, and troubleshoot each type to support its users. They must also ensure that all the types of word processors are fully compatible with the range of equipment found at a typical work site. Multiple word processors also affect the effectiveness of network management. Maximizing the power of networking makes more software available to more people in the most cost-effective way. Time and effort can be saved by centrally managing common software rather than installing and supporting networked versions of a variety of word processors.

A final issue involved in installing multiple, platform-specific types of software is the training issue. Teachers who are new to a system must be offered adequate training opportunities to ensure that they can use the software available to them. Too great a variety of software taxes training resources beyond their capacity. Common software decisions allow training to be targeted, frequent, and at the depth the user needs.

For the classroom teacher, when software is consistent, communications and sharing are maximized. Newsletters, calendars, grade reports, and classwork can be presented and shared in a format that is consistent in content and design. For administrators, alignment of administrative and teaching tasks can be achieved only with software that is consistent. If many different programs are in use, there is not enough common ground on which to ascertain performance.

Consistency makes pragmatic sense in the quality and reliability of the services the software delivers and the ease with which these services can be rendered to the greatest number of users at the lowest cost. So although you may have learned a different word processor before coming to work at a school, it is important to be open to alternatives. As in many aspects of teaching, flexibility is an important characteristic for any teacher. This is no less true in dealing with technology.

Templates, macros, and wizards can facilitate complex word-processing tasks.

A final tool built into most word processors is a **wizard.** A wizard is a miniprogram that creates a customized template for you. It asks a series of questions about the format you desire for your document and then creates a custom template as you respond to each question. Wizards will help you create sophisticated documents without having to know how to issue complex formatting commands.

• Word Processors in the Classroom

ON THE WEB! 5.1
How Can Teachers Use Word Processing for Teaching and Learning?

Word processors offer great promise as a teaching tool as well as a productivity tool for busy educators. The same features that facilitate the creation of memos and tests can be creatively applied to teaching and learning. The application of these features to teaching and learning is summarized in Table 5.3. There are numerous examples of the creative ways in which teachers have applied the same word processing software they use for productivity tasks to teaching and learning as well. Teachers use word processors to make calendars, publish class books of poetry, create newsletters, prepare flyers, make class stationery, and even author classroom web sites. The In the Classroom feature on page 142 features just a few innovative teacher-developed applications of this common productivity software. Many more can be found in an exploration of the web and through On the Web! Activity 5.1.

▋ Electronic Spreadsheets

Electronic spreadsheet software is to numeric data what word-processing software is to text. With an **electronic spreadsheet** software package, you can organize, input, edit, and chart data, and produce accurate professional reports for any administrative task that deals extensively with numbers. Spreadsheet software not only allows you to organize numeric information, but also has built-in mathematical and statistical formulas that can be applied to the data with just a few clicks of the mouse button. Whether adding long columns of data or computing a complex weighted-averaging formula, electronic spreadsheets complete your mathematical tasks at lightning speed and with total accuracy. With a spreadsheet, budgets can be easily developed and modified, grades can be tracked and averaged, and class statistical information can be extracted. Furthermore, most spreadsheets include built-in graphing capabilities that can turn numeric data into colorful, three-dimensional pie, bar, or line charts that will visually illustrate numeric relationships.

Spreadsheets manipulate numeric data and display it in tables and charts.

One of the key advantages of electronic spreadsheets over their manual counterparts is in their accuracy. Given accurate data, a spreadsheet will always produce accurate results. A second advantage is the fact that spreadsheets can be modified easily. Consider as an example the grade-level media budget pictured in Figure 5.2. If it had been done manually and the cost of printer cartridges turned out to be $10 instead of the budgeted $8, you would have to erase and recalculate a number of different entries on the spreadsheet. With an electronic spreadsheet, however, you would only need to type in the new value, and all the other entries associated with that value would be automatically recalculated. This time-saving feature makes electronic spreadsheets easier to use, less time-consuming, and far more accurate than doing the calculations manually.

Several software vendors produce electronic spreadsheet programs. Some of these, such as Microsoft Excel or Lotus, are powerful, business-oriented software packages that have numerous features. Others are for home or general consumer use, such as the spreadsheet component of AppleWorks, ClarisWorks, or Microsoft Works. Regardless of the capabilities of any given spreadsheet package, they all have a full range of common features.

Your Companion CD demonstrates and provides you practice with Excel, one of the most common of all electronic spreadsheets. When you try the Excel Skills

TABLE 5.3   WORD PROCESSING IN TEACHING AND LEARNING

Word-Processing Feature	Application to Administrative/ Professional Tasks	Application to Teaching and Learning Tasks
DOCUMENT PREPARATION	Provides capabilities to • Enter documents • Edit documents • Format documents • Correct grammar and spelling • Enhance with graphics • Print color and black and white	Allows students to • Create organized documents • Edit errors easily • Add graphics and enhanced text elements • Print draft copies for review and proofreading • Finalize, correct, and print final copies
DESKTOP PUBLISHING	Provides or lets you create formats for • Forms • Flyers • Invitations • Newsletters	Provides students with a tool for preparing • Creative presentation of text • Alternative report formats (newsletter, comics, minibooks) • Supports for oral reports
FORMATTING	Lets you adjust documents for • Professional appearance • Emphasis on key points • Consistency of appearance • Letterhead and memo styles	Students can • Experiment with formats for best presentation Teachers can • Create appealing documents for their students • Alter documents to meet specific learning needs
GRAMMAR CHECKING	Helps to ensure that documents are grammatically correct.	Assists students in • Proofreading and correcting their work • Practicing the application of grammatical rules Assists teachers in • Demonstrating grammar corrections in real time • Helping students find and correct grammatical errors
SPELL-CHECKING	Helps to ensure that documents are free from spelling errors.	Assists students in • Proofreading and correcting their work • Practicing correct spelling Assists teachers in • Demonstrating spelling corrections in real time • Helping students find and correct spelling errors
MAIL MERGE	Provides an easy way to make form letters personal.	Can be used by teachers to individualize reports to students and letters to parents.
TABLES	Provides tools to present information professionally, concisely, and clearly in an organized format.	Assists students in • Organizing data • Presenting data clearly • Summarizing key data Assists teachers in • Creating clear summaries for study guides • Displaying organized data in support of presentation • Teaching interpretation of data
WEB FORMAT	Converts files from documents to web format so that they can be easily added to web sites.	Allows students and teachers to create documents and save them in web format for display on a class web site without knowing any HTML.
ARCHIVING	Provides an inexpensive and easy-to-access archive system for documents.	• Saved teacher data files are easy to access and update to keep lessons current and available. • Students can save files for later work or find and reprint lost hard copies. • Archived files can easily be added to electronic portfolios.

Figure 5.2
Electronic Spreadsheet Application
Spreadsheet software is a useful tool in maintaining school budgets.

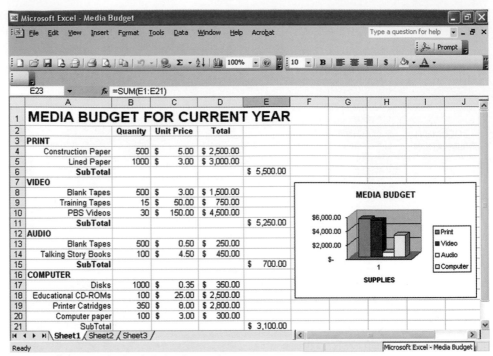

Microsoft Excel® is a registered trademark of Microsoft Corporation.

Builders, you will have an opportunity to see firsthand how the features of this useful tool can be applied in your classroom for both administrative and academic tasks.

• Spreadsheet Organization

Electronic spreadsheets, like their paper counterparts, organize data into vertical columns and horizontal rows. The user then types in alphabetic or numeric data in the appropriate locations. This organizational structure provides the framework for lining up and clearly labeling numeric information.

The intersections of spreadsheet rows and columns are called cells. It is in the nature and use of these cells that electronic spreadsheets have great advantage over their manual counterparts. Each cell of a spreadsheet can contain text, values, or a formula. This variety of cell content can be seen in Figure 5.2. The cells in column A all contain labels, and the cells in column B all contain data representing budget amounts. The cells in columns C–E contain labels, values, subtotals, or totals. Column D's cells do not contain totals calculated by hand and then typed in. Instead, they contain instructions to the spreadsheet software directing it to perform a mathematical calculation—in this case, multiplying the data entered in columns B and C.

This unique and independent data-handling capability of each spreadsheet cell makes it a quick and easy task to alter or correct the data entered. Furthermore, once a single cell's data has been changed, that change will be reflected in all cells that use that data for a calculation. Thus, if the budget amount for lined paper in Figure 5.2 is changed, the print media subtotal will also be changed, as will all other related totals. This automatic recalculation feature is one of the key reasons why spreadsheets have become as popular a tool for handling numbers as word-processing software has become for handling text.

• Formulas and Functions

As in all math, formulas are used in a spreadsheet to indicate the types of calculations that should be performed to achieve a specific outcome. The cells that contain instructions that tell the software to perform specific mathematical activities may, in fact, contain detailed formulas that the user has typed in. In addition to user-entered formulas, most spreadsheets contain hundreds of stored, premade formulas that the user can easily place into a cell. These range from formulas appropriate to finance and statistics to those necessary for trigonometry. These built-in formulas make it particularly easy to direct the spreadsheet software to perform complex mathematical tasks without the user having to remember the specific syntax of mathematical expressions. You will practice using formulas and functions in the Excel Skills Builder activity, *Club Budget* on your Companion CD. Once you are comfortable with the format, you will find electronic spreadsheets to be powerful and useful tools.

On CD!
Software Skills Builder
Excel Skills—Club Budget

• What-If Analysis

Perhaps the most intriguing feature of an electronic spreadsheet is its ability to perform **what-if analysis.** Because some cells contain outcomes that are the product of the data in other cells, changes to that data can be immediately reflected in the product. For example, if a teacher is using a spreadsheet to compute grades, the teacher will have entered not only student grade data, but also the formula needed to reflect how those grades will be averaged or weighted. So if a student wanted to know what his or her average would be if the score on the next test were 100 percent, the teacher could enter the hypothetical 100 percent into the spreadsheet, and the student could see the result in terms of a final grade computation. This is a what-if analysis; that is, what if the student gets a grade of 100 percent—how will that affect the outcome? This is a valuable tool for both business and education. Some educators have students keep a spreadsheet of their own grades to motivate their achievement and to keep in constant touch with their grade in a course.

Spreadsheets offer a what-if feature for decision making.

• Charts and Graphs

Another useful feature of almost all spreadsheet software is the ability to turn the data that has been entered into rows and columns into its graphic counterpart. The graphing (also called charting) function allows the user to select specific cells, and the software will automatically turn the data in those cells into an accurate graph in any number of formats from line, to bar, to pie charts. Some spreadsheet software even adds the ability to graph in color and three-dimensional shapes. For professional-looking displays and to assist visual learners, this spreadsheet tool is extremely useful. The *Student Measurement* Skills Builder activity on your Companion CD will demonstrate the instructional power of this feature.

Spreadsheet graphing makes it easy to visualize data.

On CD!
Software Skills Builder
Excel Skills—Student Measurement Activity

• Templates and Macros

Like word-processing software, spreadsheet software makes use of templates and macros, allowing the user to create and reuse useful spreadsheet formats and commands. Spreadsheet templates and macros can also be found as shareware or freeware at numerous educational web sites. You can also create your own spreadsheet templates. Try the Excel Skills Builder activity *Grade Keeper,* on the Companion CD, to experience this feature.

On CD!
Software Skills Builder
Excel Skills—Grade Keeper

• Electronic Spreadsheets in the Classroom

Table 5.4 shows how many of a spreadsheet's key features can be used both administratively and in teaching and learning. Just as word-processing software can be repurposed for academic projects, so too can spreadsheet software. Whether a teacher uses a spreadsheet to track grades or a student uses a spreadsheet to collect and record data from an experiment, this software provides a wealth of possibilities to the creative teacher. See the In the Classroom feature on page 148 for just a few of the many creative activities that educators around the country have developed for using this software. Many more ideas are shared on the web. Try On the Web! Activity 5.2 to discover even more creative adaptations of spreadsheet software.

ON THE WEB! 5.2
How Can Spreadsheets Enhance Teaching and Learning?

IN THE CLASSROOM

Excel-lent Teaching with Spreadsheets

Spreadsheets for teaching math to students with special needs have become an indispensable part of the repertoire for many teachers. Cindy Bush teaches math to students with a number of learning problems, and she uses spreadsheets to reach them. She starts by teaching how to use spreadsheets and follows up with problems suitable for spreadsheet application, particularly problems that call for "multiple steps . . . because they typically require students to manipulate complex data—something which computers do well and with which students with disabilities have difficulty." To begin, she has the students use grid paper that she has labeled to approximate a spreadsheet. Showing the students on an LCD panel and overhead projector and using the classroom computer, she walks them through the process of setting up a spreadsheet while they follow along on the grid paper. Moving on to formula input, she uses a similar procedure but with a transparency and provides practice time to try out the step.

In her Business Computers and Information class, Jodie Heimdal has eighth graders learn to set up and work with a personal budget using spreadsheet software. The students create a spreadsheet with personal information given them and use for-

mulas to change numbers as expenses and income fluctuate monthly. They are expected to make the spreadsheets have eye appeal as well by inserting graphics or clip art. Using the hypothetical information Ms. Heimdal has given them, students track annual and monthly income, occupation, spouse's occupation (if married), child support (if divorced), cost of living quarters (an apartment), service expenses not included in the rent, and the costs of renter's insurance, telephone, cable, automobile, entertainment, clothing (for entire family, with breakdown for each person), food, child care (including after-school care for school-aged children), household items, personal care, and holiday and birthday gifts; the remaining amount is to be deposited in a savings account. Students graph and print their spreadsheets to create visual presentations showing how they spend their income.

SOURCES: Accessing challenging math curriculum. 2003. Retrieved June 22, 2003, from http://www.ldonline.org/ld_indepthtechnology/opening_the_door_mike.html; J. Heimdal. 2001. Rates on your life insurance go up last month? Retrieved January 10, 2002, from http://www.lessonplanspage.com/printables/PCIOMDDevFamilyBudgetOnSpreadsheet812.html.

Database Management Software

Every educator's job includes the cumbersome tasks of organizing, maintaining, and retrieving many types of data. Whether it is a student's home phone number or a school district's targeted language arts objectives for the sixth grade, educators must be able to easily and quickly access and extract the information they need. The productivity software that accomplishes this type of task electronically is called a database management system.

Database management software offers educators an easy-to-use system for creating customized records to contain data, retrieving targeted records, updating and editing the information in those records, and then organizing clear and accurate reports from the data (see Figure 5.3). Furthermore, database software allows you to sort all your data automatically at the touch of a key or to query the database for a match to any single word or phrase. Considering the amount of information an educator must deal with, database management software offers many advantages over manual filing systems.

> Database management software can organize, sort, retrieve, and report data.

An electronic card catalog in a media center library is one example of the advantage of database management systems over manual systems. Consider for a moment the complexity of cataloging or locating a book using a manual system. In manual cataloging, a book must be cross-referenced on at least three different index cards under title, author, and subject. All of these must be typed out and manually sorted and filed. To find the book, the card catalog user must look through drawers full of cards until just the right card is located. For both the media specialist and the library patron, the process can be laborious. With an electronic card catalog that is a dedicated database management system of the library collections, the process is much simplified.

TABLE 5.4   ELECTRONIC SPREADSHEETS IN TEACHING AND LEARNING

Spreadsheet Feature	Application to Administrative/ Professional Tasks	Application to Teaching and Learning Tasks
SPREADSHEETS AND WORKBOOKS	Allows for the preparation and display of clearly organized numerical data on individual spreadsheets and in workbooks or related spreadsheets.	Assists students in • Organizing numerical data • Creating and testing formulas • Formatting data to produce clear and concise reports Assists teachers in • Organizing and reporting numerical data • Creating customized gradebooks • Tracking student data • Presenting clear reports
AUTO-FORMATTING	Provides premade formats to give a spreadsheet a distinct professional appearance.	Teachers and students can create appealing, professional-looking spreadsheet reports.
CHARTING	Provides easy-to-use tools for visual displays of numeric data.	Provides students with • A tool for visual presentation in student reports • A tool to view saved data visually for better understanding • A way to visually explore alterations of the numeric data stored in the spreadsheet Provides teachers with • A tool for preparing visual reports of abstract mathematical relationships • A presentation tool to demonstrate numeric data visually
FORMULAS AND FUNCTIONS	Assists in preparing accurate calculations that will automatically adjust to changes in data.	Helps students • Create and test formulas • See changes in mathematical relationships as data changes Helps teachers • Demonstrate mathematical concepts in action • Test and utilize appropriate grading formulas • Demonstrate to students how final grades are calculated
WHAT-IF ANALYSIS	Allows for the real-time demonstration of the impact of changes in data; e.g., budgeted amounts can be tested for different results.	Assists students in • Seeing how data changes impact outcomes in mathematical scenarios • Testing relationships and outcomes by manipulating data Assists teachers in • Demonstrating changes and the impact of changes in the results • Explaining how different test grades will affect a student's final grade
ARCHIVING	Provides an inexpensive and easy way to store and access worksheets for budgets and other numeric files.	Saved data files are easy to access and update to keep records current; students using spreadsheets for math practice can retrieve as needed.

Figure 5.3
Using a Database Management System for Student Data
Database management software helps teachers organize student information.

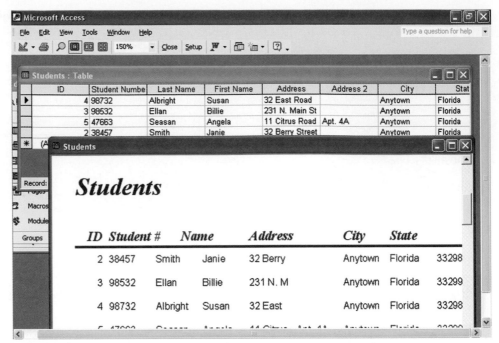

Microsoft Access® is a registered trademark of Microsoft Corporation.

All database management software contains key features to make the organization and manipulation of data easy. These key features are summarized in Table 5.5. Of course database management software packages vary significantly in the extent to which they can perform these functions, and powerful business database systems offer many additional features.

On your Companion CD, you will find activities that demonstrate and provide you practice with Access, Microsoft's popular and powerful database management software. When you try the Access Skills Builders, you will have an opportunity to experience how the features of this powerful business tool can also be creatively applied in your classroom to your administrative and academic tasks.

• Database Organization

In database management systems, a field is the electronic storage location in which a specific type of data is stored. In our library example, a field might contain an author's last name in a Last Name field. A record is a collection of all related fields, such as a record that contains all the information about a specific book. A file is a collection of all related records, such as a file containing records representing all the books in a library. This organizational structure provides the facility with the ability to organize and manipulate data at both the macro and micro levels and to easily update and accurately maintain information.

In our library example, the media specialist can simply type in the data representing a new acquisition in a new record in the media center's database file. The database software automatically stores the new record. From that point on, the user can access that new record according to the data stored in any of the information fields on the record. By typing in a key word or phrase, the user can retrieve the desired record from the database. This electronic process is a fast and accurate data input and retrieval system.

On CD!
Software Skills Builder
Access Skills–Department Inventory

TABLE 5.5   DATABASE MANAGEMENT SOFTWARE IN TEACHING AND LEARNING

Database Feature	Application to Administrative/ Professional Tasks	Application to Teaching and Learning Tasks
DATABASES	• Allows for the definition of customized database formats. • Provides for inputting and storing large amounts of complex and/or cumbersome data.	Assists students in • Thinking through and creating logical data organizations • Easily entering data for subsequent organization and reporting Assists teachers in • Creating customized data organization that suits their specific needs • Managing student and content data
FORMS	Provides a format for support staff and aides to input data.	Teachers can create easy-to-use and familiar input screens for students to use.
REPORTS	Tools and wizards create professional-looking output.	Assists students in • Presenting project data in a variety of attractive formats Assists teachers in • Customizing output for each student, class, or lesson
SORTING	Provide multiple levels of sorts to make data easy to comprehend.	Assists students in • Practicing alphabetizing skills • Thinking abstractly to determine appropriate sorts • Presenting data clearly Assists teachers in • Presenting data to students in an easy-to-use format • Demonstrating critical-thinking and alphabetizing skills • Preparing logical reports
QUERIES	Provides for customized output through the selection of specific records based on predefined criteria.	Assists students in • Practicing logical and critical-thinking skills • Finding and reporting targeted data • Identifying key criteria to look for Assists teachers in • Finding and working with only those records needed • Demonstrating concepts in equality and Boolean logic • Presenting real-time demonstrations of critical thinking
ARCHIVING	Provides an inexpensive and easy way to store and access data.	Saved database files are easy means to use to • Query data • Access data • Update information • Sort data • Make reports

• Sorting

Once entered, records can be sorted according to the data in any one or in multiple fields. Sorting arranges all records in a database into ascending or descending order based on the alphabetic or numeric characters stored in any field. In our library example, with this sort function, no matter how many additions or deletions to the library's collection of books may occur, the database of holdings is always in alphabetical order and ready to use. And because all the data are stored electronically and automatically sorted, a record cannot be as easily removed or misfiled as is possible in a manual system.

• Querying

The query feature selects and displays data that matches specific criteria.

One of the most significant features of database management is the ability to find one single item of data from the potentially thousands of items in a database. When querying a database, the user instructs the software to look for and match targeted criteria. In our library example, to find a specific author's name, you would, in a query operation, instruct the software to look in the Last Name fields of all records to find that targeted last name. Once it is found, the software returns the record in which the matching name resides. Despite the size of the database, any single item of information can be quickly and easily accessed. The *PTA Membership* Skills Builder on your Compaion CD will demonstrate an Access query and give you practice using this feature.

• Reports

On CD!

Software Skills Builder
Access Skills—PTA Membership

Whether you need to print a written summary of all of the records in the database or only those resulting from a query, most database management software packages contain report formats that ensure a professional and polished look. Reports are essentially templates built into the software to create output that is attractive and easy to read. Although it is possible to print the entire database, including all fields of all records, if the database is large, this can result in an overwhelming and difficult-to-read quantity of data. Using a report instead allows you to use the results of a database query to report only those records you want and then to identify and display only the desired fields within the records. In our library example, we can easily query the database to find any new additions to the library and then create a New Acquisitions Report that includes only the most pertinent information about each book. Your *Science Database* Skills Builder activity on your Companion CD will help you master effective reports as well as the other essential features of this versatile software.

• Database Management in the Classroom

On CD!

Software Skills Builder
Access Skills—Science Database

Like word-processing and spreadsheet software, database management software, when creatively applied by educators, can be more than a productivity tool. It can become a creative teaching and learning tool when used to categorize, store, access, and retrieve large amounts of data or to demonstrate logic when creating a query. The In the Classroom feature gives several examples of such innovation. More ideas are available in On the Web! Activity 5.3.

ON THE WEB! 5.3
Using Database Management Software to Enhance Teaching and Learning

| Presentation Software

Presentation software lets you create and show electronic slides to enhance a presentation.

Whether for teacher-led presentations or student-led class reports, presentation software can help to organize and enhance the delivery of content. **Presentation software** includes programs that are designed to create digital support materials for oral presentations. From a software perspective, presentations are a prearranged group of electronic slides that present one idea or theme after another. Completed presentations sequence and display these slides on a computer monitor, large-screen video monitor, or projection screen (see Figure 5.4). Presentations typically proceed through all slides in a linear sequence but the software has the capabilities needed for nonlinear, hyperlink-driven sequencing. These programs, originally designed for use in business as a sales and presentation tool, have been adapted by educators to assist the communication process by providing electronic visual displays that enhance verbal delivery.

Presentation software includes a wide range of capabilities in one typically very easy-to-use package. The presentation software Skills Builders on your Companion CD

IN THE CLASSROOM

Databases in Action

Database management software enables students to collect, organize, and query information. Sara Clark, a student at the University of Nevada, Las Vegas, created a lesson using these database features that combines the power of the software and students' love of cars. Students create a database of five popular cars, based on criteria supplied by the teacher. Model, color, price, year, and whether a car is used or new are some of the fields for which they have to find information. The students record the information as records and save the records in a database file. The teacher then selects a fact for one of the cars in the database. Students must search the database to match the target criterion for the right car.

A *New York Times* Lesson Plan written by Clayton DeKorne and Tanya Yasmin Chin, shows secondary school students how databases support the efforts of law-enforcement agencies to find missing persons. The students "create a database of information about themselves and detailed maps of their local community" as part of the project. Into their personal database they enter pertinent information about themselves such as full name, birth date, color and type of hair, eye color, distinguishing features, favorite clothes, food and entertainment preferences, and personal likes and dislikes. They also provide a description of the community in which they live to guide investigators to check out key locations before assuming the students have been kidnapped. In answering the questions, students input specific addresses of these places. The students "publish" all the data in personal database booklets and cover them with construction paper appropriately labeled and attractively designed. A whole-class discussion ends the project by encouraging the students to talk about how personal databases such as theirs might prove valuable in the case of missing persons and, if a personal database were a part of a national database, how parents could be persuaded to submit their children's information for it, why some parents might oppose the plan, and how else technology could help efforts to find those who are missing.

SOURCES: S. Clark. 2002. #2556. Cars. Retrieved May 20, 2003, from http://www.teachers.net/lessons/posts/2566.html; C. DeKorne, & T. Y. Chin. 2002. Links to the missing: Exploring how technology is used in locating missing persons. Retrieved May 4, 2002, from http://www.nytimes.com/learning/teachers/lessons/20020425thursday_print.html.

provide both demonstration and practice in the use of these features. The most common features of presentation software are summarized here.

On CD!
Software Skills Builder
PowerPoint Skills–Class Rules

• Multimedia Elements

The individual slides in a presentation slide show can contain a number of multimedia elements including text, graphics, animation, sound, and video clips. The software can thus create a presentation appealing to the variety of learning modalities found in a typical audience of learners. The slide show as a whole may also contain multimedia elements that tie the slides together, adding interest and excitement to the presentation. Each multimedia element included in a presentation can be constructed from scratch or copied from other sources and easily pasted into slides.

• Wizards and Templates

Although multimedia presentations of this complexity may seem difficult to create, most presentation software programs include built-in wizards that help even a novice computer user to create very professional and attractive presentations. In addition, the software includes a variety of slide templates with designer formats already created and ready to fill in. For busy teachers who use these templates, the design tasks are already done and only the content needs to be added.

• Resource Libraries

Although art, photos, and animation can be created or scanned for inclusion in a customized presentation, presentation software also offers useful libraries of multimedia from which to choose. Electronic clip art, animation, sound, and video libraries are typically included on the presentation software CD-ROM. These resources and built-in help features assist any user in creating professional-looking slides. With minimal training, educators and students alike can create and display complex and high-quality slide show presentations using just the software's library resources.

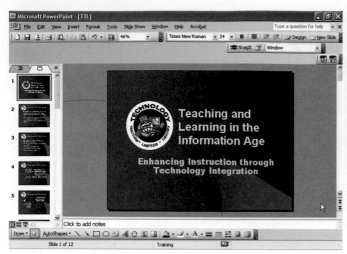

Microsoft PowerPoint® is a registered trademark of Microsoft Corporation.

Figure 5.4
Using Presentation Software
With presentation software, you can construct slides and view the results in a slide show presentation.

On CD!
Software Skills Builder
PowerPoint Skills–Creating an Outline

- Hyperlinks

Many presentation software programs include hypermedia features that make them seem more like multimedia authoring software than presentation tools adapted from business. Such programs include hyperlink capability via buttons to hyperjump (move directly to a target slide) to out-of-sequence slides, other slide shows, or even other software. Adding a hyperlink to a word, image, or button is as simple as clicking on a toolbar button and typing in the slide number or Internet address you wish to jump to.

- Animation

Many presentation software packages also come with built-in options for dramatic special effects that can be applied to the moment of transition between slides or to the way bulleted items appear on a slide. Such animation schemes add visual interest and excitement to the concepts presented in text on the screen. Sound effects may also be included with animation to add auditory interest as well.

- Printing

In addition to displaying the presentation itself, presentation software typically includes a variety of printing options for the presenter. Once the presentation is created, a hard copy can be printed and copied for distribution to the viewers. A presentation can be printed out as an outline, as a speaker's note pages, or as customized audience handouts displaying anywhere from one to six slides per page. In addition, with a color printer and transparency film, each slide of the presentation can be printed out as a transparency for use on an overhead projector.

- Display Options

In addition to a presenter-controlled display, presentation software provides alternative display options. A presentation can be set to display itself as a timed, self-playing slide show that will run without assistance by either the presenter or the viewer. This is a particularly useful feature to use for a self-guided display in a classroom center or in a library to guide students as they begin a group or individual task.

- Presentation Software in the Classroom

One of the most successful applications of presentation software takes presentation preparation beyond helping an educator prepare an effective lecture. Presentation software is especially valuable when used by students to create support materials for their own presentations. The software can help students organize their thoughts into manageable and logical chunks as a result of the automatic limitation of information displayable on any given slide. Further, discrimination and critical thinking are applied as the students review the quantity of material they have found in their research and then pare it down and identify key elements. Finally, as a by-product of using presentation software in this way, students gain valuable experience with multimedia-type software and with basic computer and software skills. Students enjoy and can be highly motivated by the software component of their report project, which in turn leads to improved retention and learning.

With the inclusion of the multimedia elements of text, sound, graphics, animation, special effects, and audio and video clips, these high-end presentation programs become essentially hybrid authoring systems. You will find that these packages are useful for anything from creating a transparency to developing multimedia tutorials.

On CD!
Software Skills Builder
PowerPoint Skills—Math Flash Cards

TABLE 5.6   PRESENTATION SOFTWARE IN TEACHING AND LEARNING

Presentation Software Feature	Application to Administrative/ Professional Tasks	Application to Teaching and Learning Tasks
SLIDES	• Allows for the creation of a sequence of screens that present content and information • Individual screens can be printed on transparency film for use with an overhead projector	Assists students in • Thinking through and organizing logical reports • Preparing support materials for oral reports Assists teachers in • Creating customized presentation of content • Creating transparencies • Presenting professional reports to colleagues
GRAPHICS	Allows for the addition of graphics, charts, and photos to illustrate content	Assists teachers and students in presenting visually rich content
MULTIMEDIA	Provides tools to include audio and video files as a component of individual slides	Assists students in • Adding multimedia to the presentation of content Assists teachers in • Adding elements to presentations to address diverse learning styles
HYPERLINKS	Provides tools for non-sequential linking of individual slides to allow for individualized exploration of content	Assists students in • Critical thinking, organizing, and planning content • Creating individualized study tools and reports • Presenting data clearly Assists teachers in • Preparing tutorials and electronic flash cards • Individualizing instruction
PRINTING OPTIONS	Provides for customized output options	Assists students in • Preparing class handouts to support oral reports Assists teachers in • Creating speaker's notes to assist in presentation • Preparing class handouts and activity worksheets • Preparing content outlines
LAYOUTS AND SPECIAL EFFECTS	Provides easy-to-use tools to add professional-looking layouts and exciting special effects to slide presentations	Assists teachers and students in presenting professional-looking and stimulating presentations and reports

IN THE CLASSROOM

Pointing the Way: Presentation Technology

Heather Tietz found a way to use PowerPoint to stimulate the interest of her fifth-grade students in the expository writing assignment given annually. The assignment was to research and write a report consisting of multiple paragraphs on a United States state. The time devoted to this project spanned three months, December to March. Ms. Tietz saw a way to transform the assignment from being boring to being fun by having her students use the computer lab and prepare PowerPoint presentations.

In their initial research, the students found material from different sources, in this case, books, web sites, and online reference sites. They used phrases in their notes—no sentences, to prevent plagiarism—which were written on index cards they would use to prepare their PowerPoint slides. The students then took the cards to the computer lab, where, after half an hour of instruction, they were ready to begin creating their presentations. The note phrases served as a starting point for the creation of the slides. With the outline created via PowerPoint, students could add visuals such as clip art and word art to make the slides attractive. The slides were then used as the basis for their written research papers. For Open House, Ms. Tietz

placed the PowerPoint presentations on the classroom computer for the students to show their parents.

In Astoria, Oregon, the students in Mike Baker's accelerated biology class at Astoria High School pursue studies of their environment near Ft. Clatsop, the site of Lewis and Clark's headquarters during the winter of 1805–1806. Mr. Baker is involved in the Lewis and Clark Rediscovery Program, which encourages combining teaching history and science in a technology-enriched curriculum. His students collect data on the water quality of the Young's River Estuary and share their findings with other students who are part of the GLOBE international environmental program (http://www.globe.gov) and with adults in the Lower Columbia Estuary Group. In collaboration with the latter group, students create electronic presentations to enhance the oral reports they deliver. Mr. Baker says his "tech-savvy kids" enjoy "making a contribution through science" to both groups.

SOURCES: H. Tietz. 2002. Savoring expository writing through PowerPoint. Retrieved June 10, 2003, from http://www.techlearning.com/db_area/archives/WCE/archives/htietz.html; Ocean in view. 2002. Retrieved May 12, 2003, from http://www97.intel.com/education/odyssey/day_289/day_289.htm.

On your Companion CD, you will be able to see and try activities that utilize the many features of presentation software. These activities feature Microsoft PowerPoint, one of the leading presentation software packages available today.

If "a picture is worth a thousand words," as the saying goes, the popularity of presentation software integrated into the curriculum is well justified. A cursory look at a few actual classroom projects in the In the Classroom feature reveals a wide range of possibilities for taking presentation software beyond its role as a productivity tool and using it as the means to an invigorating revitalization of instruction. Many more ideas can be found by completing On the Web! Activity 5.4.

ON THE WEB! 5.4
How Can Teaching and Learning Be Enhanced with Electronic Presentations?

▍Integrated Productivity Packages

As you have learned, productivity software is often packaged in application suites of programs that share a similar look and feel. Office productivity software bundles, such as Microsoft Office, are examples of this distribution format. Occasionally, however, software vendors integrate three distinct software applications (word processing, spreadsheets, and database management) into a single comprehensive blended application. These combined programs are called **integrated productivity packages.** Individual software components of integrated packages include many but not all of the capabilities of the stand-alone application packages. Typically, an integrated package contains the most popular and widely used components of each major type of productivity tool (see Figure 5.5). These are combined together in a single easy-to-use software program. Many schools opt for an integrated package for classroom use because many of the advanced features of office software are used only occasionally by educators, and combined packages are easier to learn and use than separate pro-

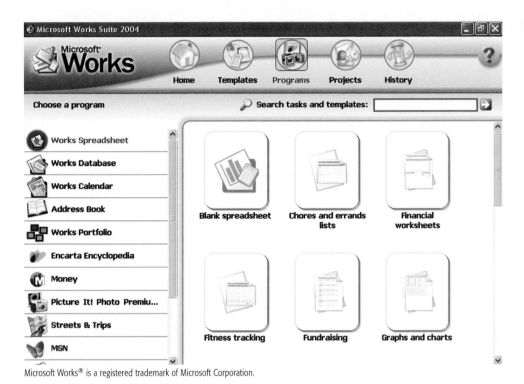

Microsoft Works® is a registered trademark of Microsoft Corporation.

Figure 5.5
Integrating Productivity Software
Several productivity applications may be merged together to form an integrated package.

grams. Typically, integrated productivity software is a more economical purchase for a school. Its reduced cost is reflected not only in the initial price of the software, but also in the time it takes to train people to use it. One of the chief advantages of an integrated productivity package is that you have to learn only one comprehensive software package rather than having to learn three individual packages. Furthermore, little of the functionality that the average educator needs is sacrificed in these streamlined applications.

Whether using a productivity suite or an integrated package, it is important to carefully review and evaluate software before purchasing it. The Productivity Software Evaluation Rubric (Table 5.7) will help you make a considered decision before selecting productivity software.

ON THE WEB! 5.5
Using Productivity Software

Evaluating and Using School and Classroom Management Support Software

The second major category of administrative software is **school and classroom management support software.** This type of software assists educators in accomplishing the many tasks associated with the day-to-day management of their classrooms or their schools. Whether the task is keeping an alphabetized grade roll, taking attendance, or creating an up-to-date seating chart, management support software is available to make the task easier.

Management support software is written for use at the district and school levels and by the individual classroom teacher (see Figure 5.6). Implemented at the district level, management software can offer many advantages. Software implemented by the district and offered to all schools and classrooms via networks can provide a standardized platform for entering and tracking student data. Furthermore, such software

Management support software helps to manage class rolls, student information, and class reporting.

TABLE 5.7   PRODUCTIVITY SOFTWARE EVALUATION RUBRIC

SOFTWARE:

DESCRIPTION:

VENDOR: COST:

NOTES ON USE:

Please rate the features below for each piece of software. Next to each of the items in the rubric, check the box that best reflects your opinion.

Software Feature	*1* *Poor*	*2* *Below Average*	*3* *Average*	*4* *Above Average*	*5* *Excellent*
Documentation	Documentation is excessively technical and/or difficult to follow	Documentation is generally understandable but not very user-friendly	Documentation is user-friendly and reasonably easy to follow	Clear documentation that is logical and easy to follow	Very clear, user-friendly documentation that leaves no questions
Technical suppport	No local or toll-free telephone support available	No local support; phone support available for an hourly fee	Local support and phone support available for modest fees	Local tech help available for modest fee; no charge phone support	Local help and toll free support readily available at no charge
Multiple users	Cannot be used by more than one user	Usable by multiple users if per-user licensing is purchased	Payment of a relatively small fee allows multiple users	No additional fee but allows addition of up to 10 users	Comes with permission for multiple users
Help features	Few or no help features available	Help limited to a Help or Read-Me file on installation CD	Clicking a Help button provides on-screen assistance with common problems	Help button is content-sensitive and provides clear help	Highlighting and clicking area of difficulty brings up a related help feature
Tutorials	No tutorials provided	Tutorials may be ordered for a fee	Limited tutorial provided on CD or may be requested without charge	Tutorials offered as an online option or on CD	Extensive online and CD-based tutorials provided

EVALUATION CRITERIA

often has the option of interfacing with the web. Web-enhanced districtwide management software can make student grades stored in a teacher's electronic gradebook accessible to the students' parents by means of a password. District-level software can also track attendance for school, districtwide, and state reporting purposes. When implemented districtwide, management software expands the capabilities of similar software used in individual classrooms.

School-level management support software typically includes customized software that helps the district track districtwide enrollment, manage finances and budgets, and report on its operations both internally and externally. For example, schools designed with a computerized attendance system may have the teacher workstation in the classroom configured so that the teacher can report attendance by entering it into the school management software on the networked computer. The attendance data is then collected with that from other schools across a district and tallied daily. This type of districtwide application allows every school to maintain and access up-to-date and accurate information on enrollment, expenditures, and attendance.

Software Feature	EVALUATION CRITERIA				
	1 *Poor*	**2** *Below Average*	**3** *Average*	**4** *Above Average*	**5** *Excellent*
Administrative features	Lacks some of the commonly included basic features	Only basic features are included	Basic features and additional features are included	Includes most of the features desired	Comprehensive features included
Multiple platforms	Works on only one operating system	Although purchased for one platform, versions for other platforms may be purchased	Program will run on multiple operating systems; features may vary with platform	May be used on multiple platforms; features similar although not identical	May be used on multiple platforms with consistent features across platforms
Conversion/ import/export features	No provision for conversion between software	Cannot be imported or exported into other programs but can be converted into a few of the more popular formats	Can be converted, imported, or exported into programs by major vendors	Easily converted into common formats; maintains most of format features	Fully compatible via conversion, import, and export with all vendors
All needed applications (if a suite or integrated software)	Missing many applications that are needed	Some needed applications missing from package	Most of the expected applications are included and compatible with each other	All basic applications included and fully integrated	Includes applications beyond those needed; full integration within suite and compatible with other vendor software
Hardware compatibility	Requires upgrades for some hardware to work on all machines	Requires limited upgrades to some machines	Will work on most machines without upgrades	Works acceptably on all machines without upgrades	Maximum performance with no hardware upgrades required on any machines
Cost	Expensive when compared to other vendors	Cost is relatively high when compared to other vendors	Average cost	Reasonably priced; includes some discounts	Special pricing for educational users

Total the score for each piece of software. Compare the scores. The piece of software with the highest score is your best choice.

At the classroom level, management support software makes managing class rolls, student information, and class reporting easier. Such software often includes a variety of tools packaged together that have the same look and feel. It is also often able to transfer data seamlessly between components. These packages contain programs that help the teacher create student rolls (often with a wide range of built-in grading functions), assist in making and maintaining seating charts, help in attendance tracking and reporting, and provide a statistical and graphing component for assessment feedback (see Figure 5.7). Teachers using one of these software tools might begin the term by entering their students' names into the class roll component of the program and then generating an alphabetical class seating chart, a daily attendance report, and summary reports of both grades and attendance whenever interim reporting is necessary. Some packages even interface with district computers so that teachers can simply download their student rolls directly from the district computers rather than having to enter the initial data by hand. Management support packages are also often customizable so that all teachers using these tools can work with a format that is comfortable for them.

ON THE WEB! 5.6
Management Software

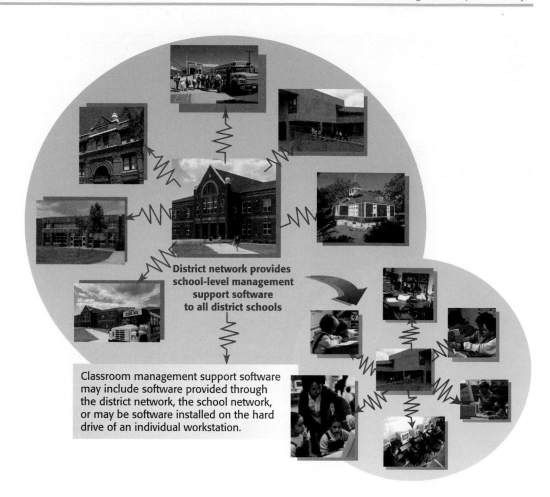

Figure 5.6
School and Classroom Management Systems

The figure contains the labels: "District network provides school-level management support software to all district schools" and "Classroom management support software may include software provided through the district network, the school network, or may be software installed on the hard drive of an individual workstation."

Portfolio Assessment Software

For teachers who regularly use portfolio assessment, an alternative type of assessment for tracking student progress, classroom management support tools provide useful assistance in the many and sometimes complex tracking tasks required. Portfolio assessment is a type of performance assessment that enables the teacher to assess competencies on the basis of a collection of student work rather than by using test scores. Portfolio assessment software provides the teacher with the tools necessary to document student achievement. Typically, these tools include portfolio formats and checklists and the ability to add comments and create custom reports. Some portfolio software tools also offer the teacher and student the option of maintaining portfolios in an electronic format with the capacity to electronically "snapshot," view, and collect student work to share with parents. For special education teachers, alternative assessment software tools include those that generate, track, and produce reports for required individual education plans (IEPs) for special needs students.

Whether portfolio software is designed for hard copy or digital output, the powerful features of this type of management software offer support for the authentic assess-

On CD!
Software Skills Builder
Using Word to Create an Electronic Portfolio

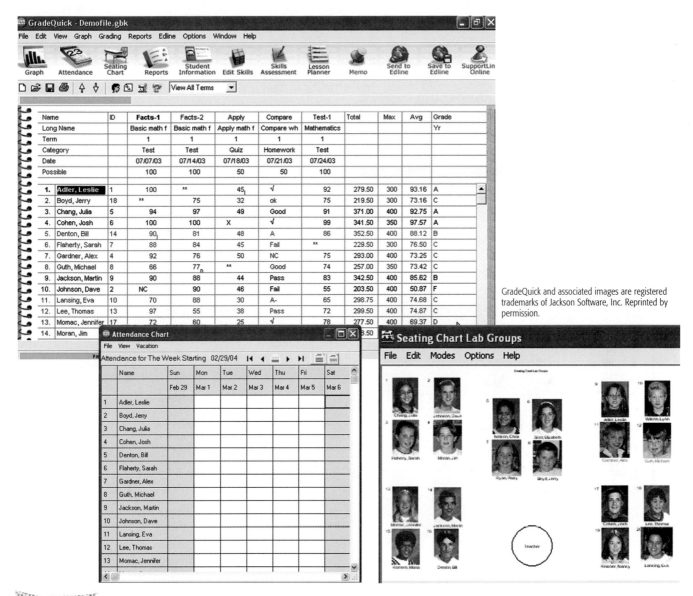

GradeQuick and associated images are registered trademarks of Jackson Software, Inc. Reprinted by permission.

Figure 5.7
Sample GradeQuick Screens
Classroom management software helps teachers maintain class grades, seating charts, and attendance.

ment of student achievement. Although each vendor adds some unique options, electronic portfolio software will typically include the following key features:

- ## Organization by Standards and Competencies

The goal of a portfolio is to create a collection of student work, teacher commentary, and other files that evidence student progress and achievement. Portfolio assessment software packages offer a variety of ways to organize and store examples of student work as well as your assessment of it. The software usually offers teachers a way to define specific content areas or other academic categories and then identify related standards and competencies. Copies of student work and its evaluation can then be organized according to the competencies it evidences. Over time, organizing and

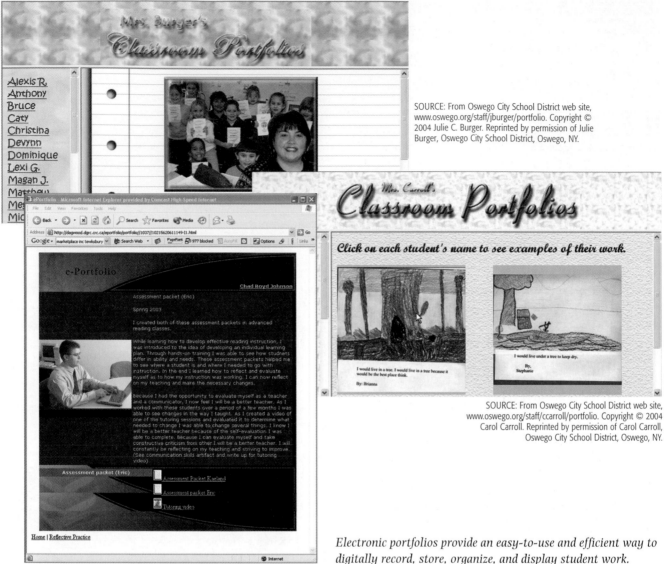

SOURCE: From Oswego City School District web site, www.oswego.org/staff/jburger/portfolio. Copyright © 2004 Julie C. Burger. Reprinted by permission of Julie Burger, Oswego City School District, Oswego, NY.

SOURCE: From Oswego City School District web site, www.oswego.org/staff/ccarroll/portfolio. Copyright © 2004 Carol Carroll. Reprinted by permission of Carol Carroll, Oswego City School District, Oswego, NY.

SOURCE: From http://www.chalkandwire.com/eportfolio/overview/Makespreso.html

Electronic portfolios provide an easy-to-use and efficient way to digitally record, store, organize, and display student work.

storing longitudinal records in this manner offers a cumulative view of student achievement over the course of an academic year or from year to year.

• Observations

Portfolio assessment software often includes a way to record observations of student behaviors and notations on academic progress. Using either standard or teacher-defined commentary, observation entries offer teachers an opportunity to record student evaluations and comments related to them.

• Multimedia Samples

Many portfolio assessment software packages include the ability to record images and audio and video samplings of student works. Audio-clip recordings of students reading standard passages or a sample of a student-created PowerPoint presentation offer multimedia evidence of current student progress.

- Customization

Since every school district has its own unique standards and assessment guidelines, most portfolio assessment software is customizable to address specific standards and to assess student work using the district's criteria. Legends identifying standards and assessment methods are often definable by teachers so that their unique grading and assessment notes match the requirements of their school or district.

- Hyperlinks

Some portfolio assessment software provides the capability of creating links that can be used to navigate the electronic portfolio of a student's work. Often related to standards, benchmarks, or competencies, these links offer an accurate and holistic picture of a student's achievement relative to target achievement. Hyperlinks also offer an intuitive and easy-to-use method for examining a portfolio's contents.

Electronic portfolio assessment software may be dedicated software designed specifically to create e-portfolios, or it may be multipurpose software adapted to creating portfolios. Several popular multimedia and authoring software packages can easily be adapted to portfolio generation. For more precise and complete e-portfolios, such as those directly related to targeted standards or those that conform to district guidelines (such as IEPs), dedicated portfolio software may be required.

ON THE WEB! 5.7
Electronic Portfolios

Evaluating and Selecting Support Software

School or districtwide management support software may be custom-tailored to meet the needs of the district. Educators' interaction with this type of districtwide software may be limited to attending the necessary training sessions to ensure that they know how to use the software effectively. Classroom management software, however, requires careful review and evaluation on the part of the teachers who will be using it. Some classroom management systems are offered via freeware or shareware from the Internet or other software sources. Others may be inexpensive packages available to educators who are using a vendor's other software titles. Still others may be substantial but expensive comprehensive classroom management solutions. Although it is tempting to decide quickly to select freeware or shareware rather than the expensive software, there is a longer-term investment that must be considered. Whichever software is selected, educators must spend precious time learning to use it and entering data into it. In addition to this initial time investment, once student records are stored in a particular software format, the format may be difficult to change. If, after the initial selection of management software, an educator decides that the program does not have all of the desired components, changing to another software package may require reentering a great deal of data. Thus, even more time is invested. As with all software acquisitions, it is important to make a careful and thoughtful selection at the onset. The Classroom Management Software Evaluation Rubric (Table 5.8) will help you evaluate and choose the most appropriate classroom management software.

Software, Teaching, and Learning: A Practical Approach

To end this discussion of administrative software, let us return to the hypothetical situation presented in the chapter preview. Imagine that your school district has decided to make a major technology initiative for the twenty-first century. As a result, you have just been given five new computer systems for use in your classroom. The computer-support department tells you that you have a software budget with which you can

TABLE 5.8   CLASSROOM MANAGEMENT SOFTWARE EVALUATION RUBRIC

SOFTWARE:

DESCRIPTION:

VENDOR: COST:

NOTES ON USE:

To help you determine the value of a piece of classroom management software that you want to evaluate, please rate the features listed below. Next to each of the items in the rubric, check the box that best reflects your opinion.

	EVALUATION CRITERIA				
Software Feature	1 Poor	2 Below Average	3 Average	4 Above Average	5 Excellent
Installation instructions	Minimal or missing installation instructions	Instructions poorly written and somewhat difficult to follow	Instructions fairly clear and complete	Clear and user-friendly written instructions	Step-by-step installation instructions appear when the CD is inserted
Site licensing provisions	No licensing available	Somewhat expensive and/or limited site licensing	Site licensing available at reasonable cost	Low licensing rates for educators	Multiple educators may use without paying a fee
Technical support	No local or toll-free telephone support available	No local support; phone support available for an hourly fee	Local support and phone support available for modest fees	Local tech help available for modest fee; no-charge phone support	Local help and toll-free support readily available at no charge
Ease of updates	No provisions for updates	Must purchase new versions; most data will transfer to new version	Updates for less than cost of new versions; data transferrable	Minimal fee for updates; data fully compatible	Free updates available online; seamless transfer of data
Tutorials	No tutorials provided	Tutorials may be ordered for a fee	Limited tutorial provided on CD or may be requested without charge	Tutorials offered as an online option or on CD	Extensive online and CD-based tutorials provided

augment the collection of district productivity software from which you can choose. Will you know what to do? Will you know which types of software will best accomplish the tasks you need to do? Will you know what to select to improve your productivity and make the administrative tasks associated with your job easier? Perhaps now you are better able to tackle these questions.

Still, even armed with an understanding of the role of administrative software in teaching and learning, with so many types of software packages available, a busy educator is faced with a significant demand of time and energy just to explore and decide on software for his or her classroom. Indeed, the tasks of researching, evaluating, and mastering the features of even the most appropriate software packages might seem daunting, but they are entirely necessary. Technology resources are limited in most school districts. Wise use of these limited funds is a skill every computer-using educator must master. This problem is no different from many others faced by educators ded-

Software Feature	EVALUATION CRITERIA				
	1 *Poor*	**2** *Below Average*	**3** *Average*	**4** *Above Average*	**5** *Excellent*
Multiple platforms	Works on only one operating system	Although purchased for one platform, versions for other platforms may be purchased	Program will run on multiple operating systems; features may vary with platform	May be used on multiple platforms; features similar although not identical	May be used on multiple platforms with consistent features across platforms
Student report capabilities	Can record and report out data only in form it was entered	Reports can be modified so only the data is reported out	Using templates, reports can be generated; minor modifications can be made	Customizable reports and forms can be easily created and printed	Data may be reported out in any format desired
Notation capabilities	No provision for notations	Can attach brief notes on problems but can't add action taken at a later time	Notes can be entered and added to later	Data entry forms include provision for unlimited comments on the problem and the actions taken	Call up record by name; click on problem type; appropriate report form appears automatically
Special needs report capabilities	No capability for notes or reports	Notes limited to 10 words; may be reported out on templates provided	Notes may be made up to 50 words and printed out; supplied templates may be modified by user	Limit of 100 words; both templates and instructor-designed forms may be used for reports	Unlimited notes may be made, and desired reports can be designed and printed out
Nonacademic information capabilities	Cannot record or report any nonacademic data	Limited provision to record and report nonacademic data in the same form it was entered	Numerical and text data, up to 50 characters, can be entered and then selectively reported out	Numerical data and text may be entered; multiple field sizes available; various templates for reporting	Unlimited data entry capabilities; customizable reports can be printed as desired

Total the score for each piece of software. Compare the scores. The piece of software with the highest score is your best choice.

icated to executing their professional responsibilities effectively and efficiently and to making the learning experiences of their students as complete and exciting as possible. From the discussion of software on the preceding pages, it is clear that administrative software can facilitate a wide variety of teaching tasks in the classroom, in your school, and across the district. It is up to you to become adequately familiar with this type of software to make the time you devote to administrative tasks as productive as possible.

In the next chapter, you will explore the other major category of software used by educators: academic software. There you will learn about the wide variety of academic software possibilities that you can integrate into teaching and into learning. For computer-using educators, knowledge of administrative and academic software packages and the hardware necessary to run them is the foundation for the effective use of computers in teaching and learning. You are well on your way toward establishing the firm foundation you will need when you teach.

KEY TERMS

STUDENT ACTIVITIES

CHAPTER REVIEW

1. How do academic and administrative software differ?
2. What is productivity software? How can it be adapted to benefit teaching and learning? Give specific examples.
3. Name three types of software that might be included in classroom management support software. Describe an application for each.
4. What is desktop publishing? How does it differ from word processing? How is it the same?
5. What are the key features of word-processing software? How might you use each in completing administrative tasks?
6. What are the advantages and features of electronic spreadsheets? How do you see them as a benefit in an educational environment?
7. Define database management software and describe how you might use it to help you in your teaching responsibilities. How might you construct a learning assignment for your students that uses this productivity tool?
8. What is presentation software?
9. Describe the difference between an integrated productivity package and a productivity suite.
10. Why is it important to take the time to fully evaluate administrative software before buying it?

WHAT DO YOU THINK?

1. List the top ten things you think you need to know about administrative software to be an effective computer-using educator. Why is each of these things critical in your technology decision making?
2. For most productivity software, many see the ability to save data in electronic format as a significant advantage over hard copy. Do you agree that this characteristic of productivity software is of value in education? Explain why or why not.
3. There is some concern over the use of database software for private student records. How might using a database management system make it easier to violate the privacy of student information? Do you think the benefits of such systems outweigh the risks? Explain your position.

4. Some educators think that it is too much trouble to learn the administrative software packages that might assist them in completing their required paperwork. Others believe that the benefits in productivity and editability of records outweigh the effort it takes to master the programs. What do you think?

LEARNING TOGETHER!

The following activities are designed for learning groups of three to five students.

1. Assume that you and your learning group make up the technology committee for your school. The committee has been assigned the task of deciding whether to upgrade or change the productivity software application suite your school has used over the past two years. Create a list of all of the issues that must be considered before making this decision. Then itemize the list and weigh each item in terms of its priority in importance to teaching and learning. Finally, describe the process you would go through to use the list and make your software decision.

2. Have each member of your learning group interview a teacher who uses any of the four major types of productivity software. Ask the teacher how he or she uses the software to help perform teacher management tasks and how he or she uses it to help children learn. Compare the interview responses with those of the other members of your group. Be prepared to share what you have learned with your peers.

3. You and your group members are team-teaching a science unit on climate to the grade level of your choice. Describe how you might integrate each of the four main types of productivity software into your unit. Create an instructional design, using the dynamic instructional design model you learned in Chapter 2, that articulates your unit.

HANDS-ON!

1. Examine the features of a productivity software suite or classroom management application. Using the evaluation rubric for the type of software you select, determine its potential for your use. Word-process a description of how you might use this type of software in teaching and learning. Be sure to add graphics and word art, if available, to help communicate your ideas. Need more practice? For word-processing Skill Builders, check the text web site: **http://www. ablongman.com/lever-duffy,** or your Companion CD.

2. Electronic portfolios enable you to capture and present student work for a more authentic and holistic assessment of progress and achievement. Visit three different electronic portfolio web sites, including an e-portfolio software vendor web site, a publication about electronic portfolios in the classroom, and a web site presenting samples of student portfolios. After visiting the sites and becoming more familiar with the use of electronic portfolios, create an e-portfolio template of your own for the presentation of your future students' work using the software of your choice. Share the portfolio template with your peers.

3. Using the productivity software of your choice, create lesson support materials that explain the steps you should take to make effective hardware or software buying decisions. You may create one of the following: a rubric or publication with a word processor; a technology budget using an electronic spreadsheet that offers what-if analysis; or a presentation that guides potential purchasers through technology decision making. Share your materials with your peers.

Return to Troy Robinson

As I pondered the mammoth summer school task before me, I realized that it was time to try out a type of productivity software I had learned about in college and used once before: database management. I decided to use my Macintosh LC II computer and Microsoft Works 3.0. Works includes several integrated programs that work together for ease of use. These programs included a word processor, a spreadsheet program, and the database program I needed.

About ten years earlier, I had used AppleWorks to track students in Chapter 1, a federally funded remedial program. The database enabled me to keep alphabetical lists of the students and their criteria and to easily sort the students by grade level and/or classroom teacher. While this was a simpler type of database, I thought I might be able to use the more powerful Works software to handle the more complicated and extensive data that I now needed to maintain and manipulate.

There were approximately 700 potential summer school students in the school population, including the additional gifted students from my school and the three neighboring schools. I had to plan for the number of classes, classroom space, instructional materials, and teachers that I would need during the summer. I needed to make the children and their parents aware of the summer school requirement for those who had not met grade-level expectations. I also needed to publicize the various enrichment classes that were available to the gifted students, and I had to keep track of the two classes that each student selected.

Staying aware of each at-risk student's status was an additional monumental problem because the checklist of indicators for mastery of the expectations was reviewed regularly throughout the period from January to May. Preparing regular reports to reveal the number of students and the required instructional area (reading, writing, and/or math) that they would need to take was just too time-consuming to do by hand. Technology had to play a role in the implementation of this year's summer school planning.

After digging out the Microsoft Works documentation and reviewing the chapter on the database application, I decided that it would be necessary to create two database files—one for the students who would be required to attend summer school to master the grade-level expectations and one for the gifted students. The types of data and the way that the data would be manipulated were totally different for the two groups of students.

In database management, one of the most important steps is defining the type of information (fields) that needs to be included. In addition to the usual fields for first and last names, teacher, and grade, I decided I would need fields for the indicators for mastery of the expectations and the various dates that had to be maintained throughout the identification process. For the gifted summer school program, I could omit the fields for eligibility criteria; but I needed to enter the school that each student attended and the first, second, and third choices for the two enrichment classes that each student wanted.

I made sure that the database template for the summer school programs was provided to each classroom teacher. A miniworkshop was provided to the teachers, so they would know how to enter their students' data. At the end of the second quarter, the teachers were able to print a full report from the database. Using that report, I was able to generate a notification letter to parents with the report cards, and the date of the letter was entered in the database. The teachers were proud of themselves for being able to use this tool, and I was happy to see how much easier the summer school preparation process was going than in previous years.

As the third quarter came to a close, district administrators requested summer school projections from the schools. This information was required to plan for bus drivers and other budget-related items such as teachers' salaries, clerical support, and lunchroom facilities. After teachers had updated the records based on third-quarter information, I asked them to send their databases to me as an email attachment. From these emails I was able to copy and paste the records from the databases into one master database file. With just a little more manipulation of the data, I was able to print the reports requested by the district administrators. As the end of the year approached, class lists were formed, names were merged into form letters, and parents were sent the final official notification about summer school.

I used the same process for the summer school gifted program. The assistant principals of the other schools sent their students' data in typed lists. I entered the data in the database and generated personalized letters to the students letting them know the classes from which they could choose for the summer program. As the students' responses were returned, I entered their choices in the database and began the process of identifying the most requested classes. When this was completed, I added two final fields in which I could enter each student's two classes. The students' names and classes were merged into form letters. These letters were sent to the students' schools for distribution.

Adapting database management software to the summer school planning process proved to be one of my best ideas yet. The process was smooth and easily managed. The data was at everyone's fingertips just when they needed it. Reports, letters, and schedules were easily generated. This one component of Works saved countless hours of work for me and for our teachers. It was the easiest summer school planning experience I ever had, and all thanks to the application of a piece of software I already had on my office computer.

As I continued in the role of assistant principal, I often marveled that many of my colleagues were not using this fabulous tool to expedite their routine tasks. I shared my success in using this tool to maintain massive amounts of important data, produce required reports for districtwide planning, and provide timely information to parents. In successive years, my basic database was adapted and shared with the assistant principals in the 100+ elementary schools across the district.

This experience taught me to always look for technology solutions, especially for those time-consuming tasks that all educators must face. Sufficient time to do all that we need to do is one of the most pressing everyday concerns for educators. Sometimes it is just a little knowledge or particular technology skill picked up in college that ends up providing some of the most useful and incredible solutions to the many challenges faced on the job.

Contact Information: J. Troy Robinson, assistant principal, Cannella Elementary School, Tampa, Florida. Email: robint@nova.edu. Web site: http://www.nova.edu/~robint.

SOURCE: Interview with J. Troy Robinson conducted by Al P. Mizell. Reprinted by permission of J. Troy Robinson.

CHAPTER 6

Academic Software

This chapter addresses these ISTE National Educational Technology Standards for Teachers:

II. Planning and designing learning environments and experiences

Teachers plan and design effective learning environments and experiences supported by technology. Teachers

A. design developmentally appropriate learning opportunities that apply technology-enhanced instructional strategies to support the diverse needs of learners.

B. apply current research on teaching and learning with technology when planning learning environments and experiences.

C. identify and locate technology resources and evaluate them for accuracy and suitability.

D. plan for the management of technology resources within the context of learning activities.

E. plan strategies to manage student learning in a technology-enhanced environment.

III. Teaching, learning, and the curriculum

Teachers implement curriculum plans that include methods and strategies for applying technology to maximize student learning. Teachers

A. facilitate technology-enhanced experiences that address content standards and student technology standards.

B. use technology to support learner-centered strategies that address the diverse needs of students.

C. apply technology to develop students' higher-order skills and creativity.

D. manage student learning activities in a technology-enhanced environment.

IV. Assessment and evaluation

Teachers apply technology in a variety of effective assessment and evaluation strategies. Teachers

A. apply technology in assessing student learning of subject matter using a variety of assessment techniques.

B. use technology resources to collect and analyze data, interpret results, and communicate findings to improve instructional practice and maximize student learning.

C. apply multiple methods of evaluation to determine students' appropriate use of technology resources for learning, communication, and productivity.

In Chapter 5, you explored the advantages of using administrative software as a tool to make you more productive as a teacher. This chapter presents the other category of software available to educators: academic software. Academic software is software that enriches the teaching and learning process. Carefully selected by the teacher, academic software can significantly enhance a lesson and address the needs of learners.

As you learned in Chapter 2, when you design instruction, you must articulate your objectives carefully and then select the appropriate methods and media to support those objectives. Even in a one-computer classroom, the many types of academic software that are available to educators today offer a broad array of new and exciting media choices. You might decide to have students research a topic using a multimedia encyclopedia that appeals to a wide variety of learning styles. Or you might have cooperative learning groups experience discovery learning through a simulation on CD-ROM. Or you might simply give a child who needs additional practice with the content an opportunity for computer center time with math practice software that lets the child shoot down aliens bearing the correct answers to math problems on their ships. The choices are broad and appealing and can add visual, auditory, and kinesthetic interest to many lessons.

To be able to select the best academic software from the thousands of such packages, you need first to be aware of the

CHAPTER OUTLINE

choices available to you. In this chapter, you will explore the principal types of academic software and review a sampling of their application in the teaching and learning process.

In Chapter 6, you will

- Explore the major categories of academic software and their application in teaching and learning

- Review a sampling of how academic software is used in different classrooms

- Investigate and use methods for reviewing and evaluating software so that your technology acquisitions will appropriately meet your needs

Meet Nancy Armstrong

Educators often fully realize that technology and educational software have the potential to enhance their teaching and their students' learning. However, too often, they do not have or know of the specific resources that are most applicable and appropriate for their situation. Here, you will meet Nancy Armstrong, a fourth-grade teacher who decided that it was time to find the technologies and software that were just right for her classes. She turned to the web to find what she needed. This is her story.

MY SETTING

I am a fourth-grade teacher in Ogallala, Nebraska, and I have held that position for the past ten years. Ogallala is situated in scenic southwestern Nebraska and is bordered by the South Platte River and Lake McConaughy, Nebraska's largest lake. My school, Progress Elementary, contains two sections each of grades 3, 4, and 5. There are approximately 140 students at Progress Elementary. I work with a team of dedicated professionals who enthusiastically practice the following mission: "The students of Progress Elementary School will be provided a safe, positive learning environment and the tools to achieve academic excellence. They will develop a respect of self and others on their journey as they become responsible citizens and lifelong learners."

MY PROBLEM

Challenged by the reality that my fourth-grade students knew more about computers than I did, I embarked on a quest into the wonders of technology. I began with many questions. Do students benefit from the use of educational technology? If so, how do they benefit from technology? What constitutes "good" software? How can I find web sites that students can use to maximize learning? Where can I find information relating to effective teaching practices using educational technology?

I searched the World Wide Web to identify current practices in the use of educational technology in the elementary classroom to help teach mathematics. I also enrolled in a master's program in elementary education with an emphasis in computer education, offered by Chadron State College. My research led me to the conclusion that educational technology is an effective way to help teach math skills to elementary students.

Harold Wenglinsky (1999), in a study conducted by the Educational Testing Service, reported that use of computers can raise student achievement. He analyzed data from the math portion of the 1996 National Assessment of Educational Progress. At the fourth-grade level, he found that when computers were used mainly for math/learning games, the students had higher math achievements compared to students who didn't use the computers for math/learning games. Wenglinsky also discovered that teachers who had received technology training used computers in more effective ways than teachers who had not received training. Supplied with the evidence that the use of educational technology increases student learning, I began searching for the best methods to use the technology.

The availability of educational software has significantly increased in recent years. After previewing several educational software programs, I decided that I really needed to establish criteria to evaluate the worth of the software. In the past, I had mainly selected software based on the manufacturers' descriptions of their products; sometimes that was enough, but at other times, the students and I were disappointed. When I attempted to find an evaluation form, the small number of forms that were available for teachers to use to evaluate educational software surprised me. I knew I had to do more to find the right software for my students.

Ms. Armstrong discovered, as many teachers do, that finding the right software tools takes considerable effort in discovering the types of software available and then evaluating it to be sure it fits your specific needs. This chapter introduces you to the many types of educational software that are available and helps you discover which will best serve the students you teach. We will return to Ms.

Armstrong's story and learn how she met her software challenges at the conclusion of this chapter.

SOURCE: Interview with Nancy Armstrong conducted by Al P. Mizell. Reprinted by permission of Nancy Armstrong.

What Is Academic Software?

Academic software includes the wide variety of software packages that can be used to enrich the teaching and learning environment for both teachers and students. Academic software may include packages that help the teacher teach and those designed to help the learner acquire targeted competencies. A teacher needs to be aware of the many common categories of academic software to be able to select the best software to achieve his or her objectives. Table 6.1 lists the most common categories of academic software and their uses. Within each of these categories, there are literally hundreds of commercial, freeware, and shareware programs available to educators. As with administrative software, although the initial costs vary, the need to invest time in mastering, using, and supporting a software program does not. Educators need to be careful in selecting the software to which they commit themselves and their students.

In the remainder of this chapter, you will be introduced to and have the opportunity to explore fully the many types of academic software that will be available to you for use in your classroom. As you can see from the list in Table 6.1, the options are many. Taking the time now to explore what each type of academic software can do to help you teach and help your students learn will save you time, effort, and your classroom budget when you teach.

Authoring Systems

As you learned in Chapter 2, the first step in effective instruction is to analyze your learners carefully so that you can adjust instruction to their needs. Although educators may teach the same grade level or the same course content, good instruction is bound to vary as the result of its responsiveness to the group of learners being addressed. Many educators are somewhat reluctant to use commercially produced instructional software simply because it does not fit well enough with their particular students or with their lesson plans and objectives. Software developers, mindful of these instructional concerns, have developed a class of academic software that allows the educator to easily create custom computer-enhanced lessons of all sorts. This category of academic software is known collectively as **authoring systems.**

Authoring systems vary greatly in their interface format, their capabilities, and the hardware requirements to run them. Some authoring systems can be used with almost any level of computer hardware and still do a very good job of helping a teacher create effective computer-based multimedia lessons. Other, more powerful authoring software packages are designed to create very high-end, commercial-looking lessons. These packages require significantly more powerful and advanced hardware platforms. Still others help educators create lessons that can be viewed with any

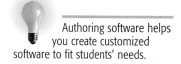

Authoring software helps you create customized software to fit students' needs.

TABLE 6.1   ACADEMIC SOFTWARE SUMMARY

Software Type	Application to Teaching and Learning
 **Authoring Systems**	Hypermedia and web authoring systems enable teachers to create their own hypermedia tutorials and web pages to support their curriculum.
 **Deskop Publishing**	Another communication tool for educators, desktop publishing software enables teachers to create professional-looking newsletters, flyers, transparencies, and other printed media.
 **Graphics**	Graphics software enables teachers and students to support teaching and learning through visuals created or enhanced electronically.
 **Reference**	Reference software, usually on CD-ROMs, includes visual- and sound-enhanced, hyperlinked electronic resources, such as dictionaries, encyclopedias, and atlases.
Tutorials and Drill-and-Practice	Tutorials and drill-and-practice software give students one-on-one, usually interactive reviews of target concepts.
Educational Games	Games present content in a format that engages the learner while providing practice.
Simulations	Simulations provide students an opportunity to interact with model environments that promote discovery learning.
Special Needs 	Software for students with special needs assists them in multiple ways, from reading screens to enlarging pointers, in order to help them function effectively in school.
 **Integrated Learning Systems**	Combining classroom management tools with tutorial software designed to reinforce target objectives, ILS software provides an integrated package of resources.

TABLE 6.2   AUTHORING SYSTEMS

Authoring System	Features	Application to Teaching and Learning Tasks
HYPERMEDIA AUTHORING SOFTWARE Examples: Macromedia Director for K–12, Asymetrix ToolBook, Apple HyperCard, Sunburst's HyperStudio	• Can include text, graphics, and audio and video elements • Screens linked by hypermedia buttons for navigation • Easy to create and/or import elements • Can be saved as "run-time" version to use on other machines • Online help available	Teachers can easily create their own multimedia tutorials to meet specific objectives within the curriculum. Students can use hypermedia authoring to create multimedia reports for class projects.
WEB AUTHORING SOFTWARE Examples: Microsoft FrontPage, Adobe GoLive, Macromedia Studio	• Automatically generates HTML documents from authored documents • Easy-to-create web pages that include text, graphics, audio, animation, and video elements • Pages automatically linked by buttons for navigation • Easy to create and/or import elements for web pages • Online help available	Teachers and students can easily create a class or personal web site accessible by parents and students from home that includes • School information • Homework and due dates • Calendar of events • Class news • Student work • Useful links

browser. Regardless of the type of authoring system, they all have in common the fact that they were written to assist teachers in creating unique, targeted lessons for their students. Table 6.2 summarizes the various types of authoring systems available and reviews their individual features. To further examine the usefulness of these programs and better understand which might fit your potential needs, let's contrast some examples of authoring systems available.

On CD!
Software Skills Builder
HyperStudio–About Me

Hypermedia Authoring Systems

Hypermedia authoring tools are available at a variety of levels of sophistication. Most include all the components necessary to create full multimedia lessons. As you recall from Chapter 3, the term *multimedia* refers to software that uses multiple types of technology that typically address different learning modalities. **Hypermedia software** is an adaptation of multimedia that not only uses multiple media, but also organizes information such that the student can make "hyperjumps," student-driven connections in either linear or nonlinear sequences, from and to different components of the instructional content, as shown in Figure 6.1. Hypermedia more closely resembles the way most people think and learn than does linear programming.

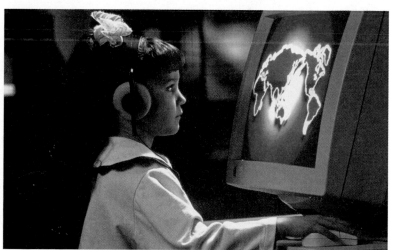

Multimedia software fully engages learners by addressing diverse learning styles while offering an interactive experience.

Available for both Macintosh computers and PCs, hypermedia authoring systems let educators or their students create a series of electronic "cards" (or frames) that can contain text, graphics, sound, animation, and/or short video clips. The cards together are ordered to create a "stack" (or file) that teaches the lesson at hand. The teacher visually plans the lesson, then uses hypermedia authoring software to turn the

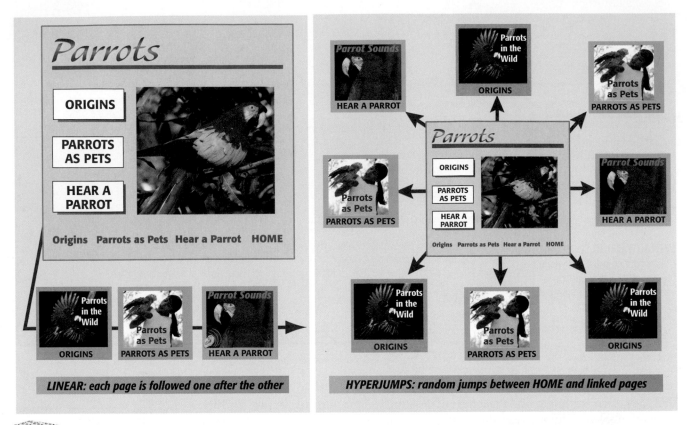

Linear versus Nonlinear Hypermedia

Hypermedia software can present information sequentially (linearly) or let students follow their own path (nonlinearly).

ON THE WEB! 6.1

Bridging Theory and Practice

ON THE WEB! 6.2

Hypermedia in Instruction

planned lesson into multimedia instructional software, such as the example shown in Figure 6.2. Teachers can then display the completed hypermedia lesson on a computer monitor, on a large-screen TV monitor, or via an LCD projector and projection screen. Students can also use the packaged lesson individually or in small groups to review the content. Because the material is presented via multiple modalities and requires active participation, it is especially effective in reaching and engaging learners.

Hypermedia software, as its name implies, gives teachers the capacity to create hyperlinks between the cards. Rather than presenting one card after another in a linear fashion, hyperlinks allow the user of the stack to jump between cards or to other stacks at the click of a button (see Figure 6.3). That way, students using the lesson stack can follow their own individual interests as they explore the content. This makes the resulting software very responsive to the students' personal learning preferences while offering the material to students via multiple media.

Web Authoring Systems

A second category of authoring tool is designed to create multimedia products specifically for use on the Internet. Internet authoring software shares many of the tools and features of other hypermedia authoring software. Programs designed for creating Internet-based displays (web pages) generate hypermedia that is saved in a format called Hypertext Markup Language (HTML). HTML is the computer language that has been agreed on for use on the Internet's World Wide Web sites. Internet browsers, that is, special programs designed to translate HTML data into computer displays, are then used to view and navigate these types of hypermedia pages.

Screen captures of HyperStudio for MultiMedia Authoring. Reprinted by permission of Vivendi Universal Games, Inc.

Figure 6.2
HyperStudio for Multimedia Authoring
HyperStudio and similar multimedia authoring software enable teachers and students to create their own tutorials.

The demand for software to assist in the creation of web pages by educators and their students has created increasing pressure on software vendors. For this reason, in addition to software that was specifically created to produce web pages, many software companies are adding an HTML conversion feature to their other types of software. Some word processors and desktop publishing software include the ability to turn a word-processed page into an HTML page with just a click on a button or a menu choice. Software that is specifically designed to create web page documents is typically much more sophisticated and full-featured than software that simply has an added

Web authoring systems translate input into HTML for presentation on the web.

IN THE CLASSROOM

Around the World in One Day! Using HyperStudio to Learn about Hispanic Countries

*H*ablamos español! Increasingly, American schools are accepting the responsibility of teaching languages other than English. Jerie Milici, a high school Spanish teacher from Greenwich, Connecticut, found a way to make not only learning the language but becoming familiar with the culture of Hispanic countries both fun and effective. Her innovative approach to this dual challenge, designing a contest for her students, employed the students' fascination with technology and their love of competition.

In this innovative activity, Ms. Milici gave students placed in groups the choice of a country in which Spanish is the native tongue. Their initial assignment was to create "a HyperStudio program on their particular country using information they downloaded from the Internet or scanned from other sources" she shared with recipients of the Etoolsweekly email list from the National Education Association. To present their programs, students were required to have "at least 5 cards plus sound and visuals" in their program and to be "responsible for submitting 10 questions that could be answered by their presentation." In addition, a different computer was designated for each country,

and the students were required to decorate the computers to be representative of the countries. For example, "Mexico wore a sombrero and Spain had a bull close by." Each group also wrote ten questions about the country that were to be answered as their presentation was viewed.

When groups had created their programs, the contest phase of the assignment began. Each group "visited" a country (computer station) they had not originally been assigned. Referring to the list of ten questions at that station, the students were challenged to come up with the right answers. Each group strove to be first to complete the hunt and receive a prize. In case students visiting the computer stations didn't know how to work the HyperStudio program, a student was placed at each of the stations to walk the contestants through the process. With this unique combination of student-made hypermedia software and kinesthetic activity, students were taught not only a language but also the culture that gave it life.

SOURCE: J. Milici. (2003). Foreign studies. Retrieved October 23, 2003, from http://www.nea.org.

Figure 6.3
Hyperlinks for Navigating Hypermedia
Hyperlinks let students jump to different cards at the click of the mouse.

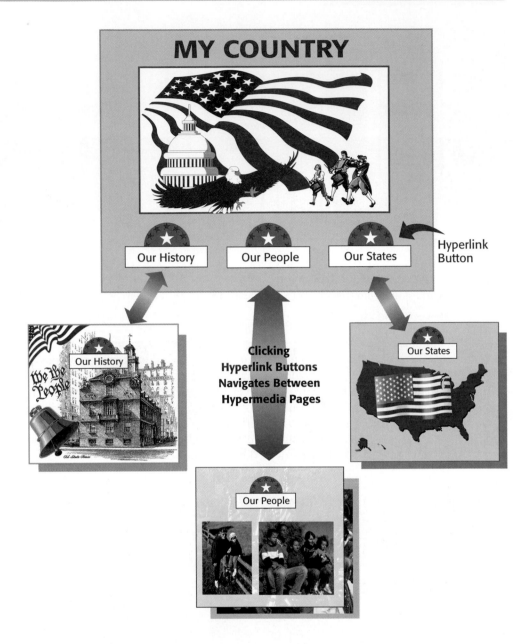

ON THE WEB! 6.3
Can You Create a Web Site?

On CD!
Software Skills Builder
Publisher Skills–Web Wizard

conversion component. Your student Companion CD includes two hands-on activities that will guide you step-by-step through the process of using Microsoft Publisher's and Microsoft Word's Web Wizard web authoring tool. You will no doubt be surprised at how simple and easy it is to create a web page—indeed an entire web site—using this web authoring tool.

Web authoring tools range from extremely sophisticated to relatively simple to use, and from very expensive to free. Indeed, some Internet hosting services that offer web space to the public also provide free and easy-to-use web authoring tools. The web pages that can be developed with this wide variety of software vary just as significantly. High-end authoring packages are used to develop very sophisticated commercial web sites; freeware or shareware authoring packages can create very attractive personal home pages or whole web sites. Educators need to carefully review and evaluate their options before investing time in learning a web authoring tool and developing a web site.

issues in
teaching
and
technology

n "The Educators' Lean and Mean No Fat Guide to Fair Use," Hall Davidson (1999), executive director of educational services and telecommunications at KOCE-TV in California, opens with the quintessential questions surrounding media and copyright:

> Is it legal for students to use copyrighted clips from videos, CDs, or the Internet to create multimedia reports? Can they save these into digital portfolios or post them on a school Web site? Does it violate copyright law for teachers to show this student work at educational conferences?

Because copyright is at heart a legal matter, Mr. Davidson's summary of copyright law is the most reliable way to inform educators succinctly about the law.

Audio: Teachers can copy portions of recordings for academic purposes other than performances and use them with students. The Conference on Fair Use (CONFU) multimedia guidelines suggest limiting the portion used to 10 percent and no more than 30 seconds. . . .

Video: You can use videotapes and movies for instruction. . . . School-made VCR recordings are more like library books that can be kept for a set time. According to widely accepted guidelines, you can show them for up to 10 days after the broadcast and keep them for an additional 45 days for evaluation purposes. If you want to keep them longer, somebody generally has to pay for them—unless the distributor has chosen to grant educators broader rights, as is often the case with educational television.

Multimedia: Authoring for curriculum-based projects may include material from CDs, books, the Internet, and other sources. The resulting projects cannot be distributed outside the classroom community, although they can be shared with family members since students' homes are considered to be part of the learning community.

Internet: Taking things off the Web and using them in projects is OK, but posting them back online is not. . . . Posting on a protected Intranet, however, is permissible since it's viewed as remaining inside the classroom community. It is generally believed that "implied public access" permits Web site builders to include links to other sites without requesting permission. Netiquette dictates removing such links, however, if the site being pointed to so requests.

Distance Learning: The Copyright Office recommends extending to teachers and students in a distance learning course the same fair use rights they would have in a regular classroom. In other words, the mere fact that the class is being taught using digital transmission should not cause it to be interpreted as a public distribution or performance.

Copyright law is a complex, frequently updated issue as technology changes. It is therefore imperative to keep abreast of changes in the law. The U.S. government maintains a web site to make it possible for you to do so: **http://www.loc.gov/copyright**. The CSU, SUNY, and CUNY university systems offer a site with guidelines at **http://www.catus.org/fairindex.html**.

Using Authoring Systems

As machine power continues to increase and more and more educators take advantage of authoring tools, more vendors are likely to offer such options. A word of caution, however, on upgrading or changing software: Once an authoring tool is acquired and learned, much time and energy go into creating customized software. It is important to ensure that any upgrade or change can accommodate and run the custom software already created by educator-authors. Careful review of upgrade and conversion specifications should precede any decision to change authoring software.

Regardless of the authoring tool that is selected, with training, both you and your students can use this software to create customized, targeted lessons. Teacher-made lessons allow you to create learning software that meets the specific lesson objectives identified in your instructional design. Such lessons can be used in large- or small-group presentations to present and demonstrate key content points. They can also be used with individual students for additional review and reinforcement of content or to study a missed lesson after an absence. Teacher-made lessons can be specifically designed to present material that is consistent with identified student learning modal-

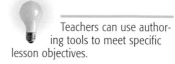

Teachers can use authoring tools to meet specific lesson objectives.

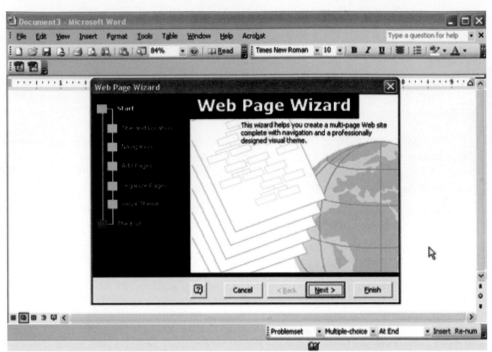

Microsoft Word® is a registered trademark of Microsoft Corporation.

Web Wizards support the creation of a web site using a familiar program such as MS Word and then converting your document.

ities and at content levels that are appropriate to those observed in any given class of students.

While authoring software will support a teacher in developing customized academic lessons, another type of software, desktop publishing software, will assist teachers who want to create customized handouts, transparencies, class newsletters, or flyers. Desktop publishing software provides tools for creating professional-looking hard copies as well as authoring web pages.

Desktop Publishing Software

Originally written to make the work of manual layout and design in the publishing business easier, **desktop publishing (DTP) software** has brought to the average computer-using educator the ability to create professional-looking printed or electronic pages. Sophisticated documents can be created that include text, graphics, digital pictures, stylized headlines, and professionally prepared design elements. These elements can then be arranged and manipulated on a page until the best possible page layout is achieved (see Figure 6.4).

Your Student Skills Builder CD contains three hands-on activities to assist you in becoming familiar with this very useful software. Trying all three activities will give you the skills you need to effectively use the software for creating handouts, flyers, transparencies, and even a classroom web site.

Desktop publishing software is an incredibly versatile tool for educators. With it, an educator can easily design and print

- Customized transparency masters to illustrate a critical concept
- Customized student worksheets with clip art or digital pictures

Desktop publishing (DTP) software produces professional-looking hard-copy output.

On CD!
Software Skills Builder
Publisher Skills—Classroom Sign

- Posters and signs for the classroom, media center, or school
- Class or school newsletters
- Customized booklets for reading, coloring, or reinforcing concepts
- Customized award certificates
- Flash cards and sight-word cards
- Custom instructional packets for review of targeted competencies

In students' hands, desktop publishing software can be used to

- Create cards and letters to give to parents
- Produce hard-copy enhancements to group projects
- Write up a field trip report
- Make classroom or school banners
- Create homework calendars and assignment tracking sheets
- Lay out school yearbooks

Many popular desktop publishing software packages also include a web site authoring component. With this feature, web pages can be laid out using the same tools and skills that it takes to create a print document. Then, with a built-in conversion component, the software automatically converts the elements of the laid-out page into one that can be viewed on the World Wide Web with any suitable browser. Thus, teachers or their students can very easily create and maintain a very sophisticated, attractive web site.

As you can see, desktop publishing software can be used to create a wide range of instructional materials, and neither teacher nor students need to be computer experts to create attractive and useful materials. To maximize effectiveness, materials created with desktop publishing software should follow some general design suggestions. Elements of effective visuals will be more extensively explored in Chapter 9, but for the purposes of desktop publishing, educators should stay mindful of the design principles demonstrated in Figure 6.5.

On CD!
Software Skills Builder
Publisher Skills—Overhead Transparency Master

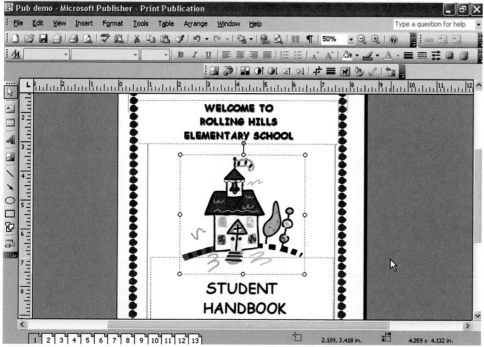

Microsoft Publisher® is a registered trademark of Microsoft Corporation.

Figure 6.4
An Example of Desktop Publishing Software
Microsoft Publisher is an easy-to-use DTP program that creates professional-looking publications.

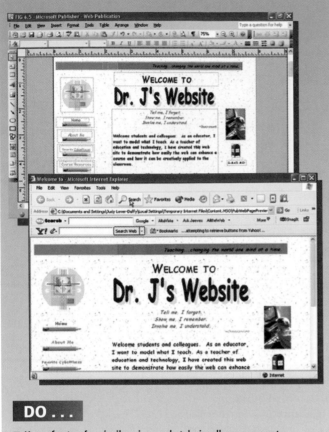

DO ...

■ Keep fonts of a similar size and style in all components
■ Be consistent in font styles throughout the document
■ Use similar style graphics and be careful of distortions when resizing
■ Strive for a consistent and balanced look for all elements of your document

DON'T ...

■ Use many different font types and enhancements
■ Mix number of columns on a single page
■ Distort graphics when sizing or use too many diverse types of graphics
■ Change line spacing or font sizes on a single page

Figure 6.5

Design Principles in Desktop Publishing

Whether publishing web pages or creating flyers, always follow the principles of good design. Contrast the balanced design of the web page on the left with the poor design of the flyer on the right. Which is more likely to effectively communicate information?

On your Student Skill Builder CD you will find hands-on Microsoft Publisher activities that demonstrate good visual design as well as the features of desktop publishing software. Try these activities to gain skill in using this useful educational software tool.

Graphics Software

Digital visual images, whether drawings, photos, or graphs, are typically referred to as graphics. **Graphics software,** then, is the broad category of software that can be used to create, edit, or enhance digital images. Different types of graphic software perform different functions and have different capabilities, as you will see next, but all help you add digital visuals to clarify and enhance instruction.

Graphics software also includes packaged collections of prepared graphics that are usually organized into libraries of images. Such collections may include drawings, photos, and even animated graphics. The images included in these graphics libraries are organized so that you can easily preview the images, copy them, and then paste them into other applications. You may choose to paste them directly into a document you create with desktop publishing software, or you can paste them into other graphics software to further edit the images before using them. In either case, these collections offer a valuable alternative to creating visual images from scratch.

Clip Art Libraries

Most software that uses graphic elements includes a library of prepared drawings and digital pictures. These libraries are called clip art libraries, a term that is carried over from the days of manual page layout when layout artists literally clipped artwork with scissors and then pasted it onto pages. **Clip art** images offer educators ready-made artwork that can easily be added to word-processed documents, presentations, or desktop-published pages. Typically, all of these types of software packages include extensive clip art libraries with thousands of prepared images. Supplemental clip art libraries are also available and may include tens of thousands of rendered or photographic images, in color or black and white. Most clip art image libraries are sold with each image preformatted in the many different digital formats that are needed for inclusion in word-processing, presentation, desktop publishing, or authoring software. Other clip art images are available via the Internet, often offered free without any copyright restrictions. For educators, this wealth of ready-made images can be used to easily enhance printed or displayed instructional materials. With just a few clicks of the mouse, visual richness can be added to text materials.

However, clip art is limited in that a ready-made image might or might not be exactly what is needed to illustrate a point. It is occasionally necessary to create or customize images to better represent a concept. For this purpose, graphics software can be used. Graphics software includes three distinct categories based on functions. The first, drawing software, gives you the electronic tools to create and edit digital images. The second, imaging software, creates images from nonelectronic sources. The third, editing software, provides the capabilities to alter, enhance, or add special effects to digital images. All of these software packages offer you the capabilities of working with graphics, but each has its own set of tools and functions to perform its unique tasks. All add to an educator's ability to add powerful visual imagery to instructional materials.

ON THE WEB! 6.4
Clip Art Online

Paint and Draw Software

Software that provides you the tools to create new images from scratch includes paint programs and draw programs. Each of these makes it possible to create new artwork or customize existing artwork. However, they operate somewhat differently, and each has a specialized set of tools.

• Paint Programs

Paint programs allow you to create and manipulate digital pictures in a manner very similar to the way one paints a picture in the real world. Like real-world painting, paint software provides electronic pen and brush tools to draw straight, curved, and freeform lines, to color in objects, or to erase them in whole or part. Paint programs also offer a variety of brush and pen sizes and shapes and even a spray-paint tool for different visual effects. Additionally, these programs provide a selection tool that lets you identify and select distinct pieces of the artwork so that specific identified components of an image can be copied into another document or printed out.

Paint programs simulate traditional painting with electronic painting tools.

Paint programs range from the extremely sophisticated software used to create the high-end digital artwork featured in magazine displays or movie backgrounds to simple-to-use software included as a free accessory program with Windows and Macintosh operating systems. Regardless of the sophistication level selected, educators and students can use paint programs to create digital images for inclusion in presentations, multimedia files, desktop-published documents, or word processing. These programs can also be used to adjust and customize existing clip art or digital photographs to better meet the objectives of an instructional event. Paint programs are powerful software tools that the teacher or students can easily use to enhance instructional materials or delivery.

• Draw Programs

Draw programs too can create and customize digital images. However, draw programs, sometimes called object-oriented or vector graphic programs, work differently from paint programs. Drawing tools do not include the familiar brushes, paint cans, pencils, or erasers you can find in paint programs. Rather than creating individual pixel elements such as lines by using an electronic pencil, draw programs create objects that can be manipulated to create images. Like paint programs, draw programs have a variety of tools to customize or create graphics. These tools are designed to define and manipulate a series of geometric objects such as squares, curves, and circles that can be arranged to create a picture. With draw programs, graphics are cre-

> Draw programs use shapes and other objects layered to create complex images.

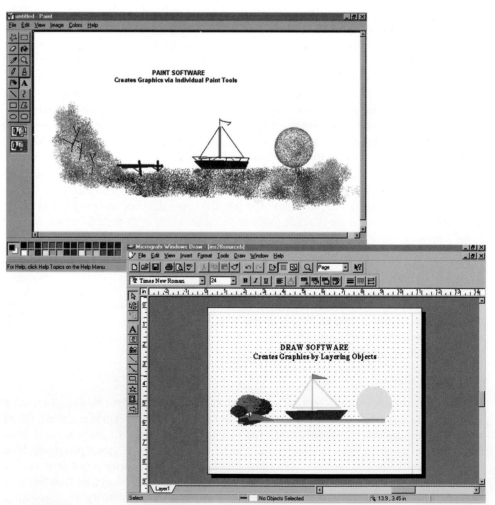

Paint® and Windows Draw® are registered trademarks of Microsoft Corporation.

Figure 6.6

A Comparison of Draw and Paint Programs

Paint programs use virtual pens, pencils, and brushes, while draw programs create images by layering shapes.

ated by layering objects on top of one another, as illustrated in Figure 6.6.

Both types of software packages are useful to teachers and their students in creating visual support for instructional content. Teachers can easily create colorful and meaningful transparencies or graphic elements for presentation with a draw program even if they do not have extensive art skills. For those who are artists, paint programs provide the electronic means to create editable artwork for inclusion in materials. For students, drawing software provides them limitless tools to create or edit just the right picture for their oral report, an electronic card to send to their parents, or a page for their class web site.

Further, both types of software are capable of editing existing clip art or graphics, although with different sets of tools. Using such software, teachers can enhance a digital image by highlighting targeted areas for emphasis or adding text annotation to a graphic's components. Students can create a collage of selected clip art to add interest and dimension to their work. Draw and paint programs can range widely in price and capabilities, but even the easiest and most inexpensive of these software packages can add significant visual enhancement to all types of instructional materials.

Imaging Software

Imaging software most often refers to the family of software packages that are used with scanners to convert hard-copy images to digital images. Typically, scanners are bundled with imaging software that is compatible with their hardware. All imaging software is capable of converting a hard-copy page of text or graphics to a digital graphic. This graphic can then be treated like any other object or clip art image. A photograph of a flower could be scanned with imaging software and saved as a digital graphic; it could then be opened in a drawing program so that arrows and text enhancements could be added to label the image. In this way you can add instructional elements to any image.

ON THE WEB! 6.5
Imaging Resources

Imaging software lets you scan, capture, and edit hard copy images including text, graphics, and photos.

Some imaging software is capable of not only converting hard copy into graphic elements, but also converting pages of text into pages of electronic text that can be manipulated by a word processor. Hard-copy versions of worksheets or tests can be digitized and saved as word-processed documents. They can then be updated, edited, or entirely repurposed for other instructional activities. This added feature found in some imaging software packages can add a valuable tool for busy educators while adding very little additional cost to the software.

Editing Software

Editing, the third category of graphics software that works with digital images, provides the tools to alter and enhance images. Whether the images are digital photographs, clip art, scanned images, or images you have created, **editing software** allows you to change the image one pixel at a time or in its entirety.

Some draw and paint software packages include an import feature that allows you to bring in an image created or saved outside of that package. The image may be a digital photo, a scanned image, clip art, or even something saved from the Internet. Once imported, the software may then let you alter the image using the same tools that are available to alter images you create. The ability to import software for further editing is a useful feature to look for when selecting draw and paint software.

Imaging software more typically offers the capability of in-depth editing of digital images, whether acquired through scanning, digital photography, or video capture. This type of imaging/editing software usually includes a variety of photo-styling and special effects software packages that range in price and capability from those used at home to the powerful packages that are used to create the dramatic digital special effects seen on television and in films. Many medium-priced programs allow you to edit images in unusual ways, ranging from blending one image into another to creat-

IN THE CLASSROOM

Synergy at Work

"Wish you were here." The postcard message almost everyone has written at some time may not be the message for Annandale Elementary School (Los Angeles, California) teacher John Rivera's "School on a Postcard" multimedia project for kindergartners, but it reveals the popularity of postcards and the recognition even the youngest schoolchildren have for this colorful, quick way of telling others about distant places. Because he knew that for many kindergarten children, various areas in and around the school would be strange, "distant" places, Mr. Rivera developed "School on a Postcard." To make sure the children understood what postcards are, he brought in postcards for the children to see before beginning the project. The project started off with a scavenger hunt to find places at the school that could be featured on postcards.

Following the choice of sites, the kindergartners used Inspiration concept-mapping software to make a web of these sites. From these they could choose the ones they wanted to make postcards for. With crayons and markers, they drew pictures of the places, which were scanned into a computer. Taking digital cameras, they then took pictures of more spots around the school and described in simple [hand]written sentences for age appropriateness both the hand-drawn and the photographed sites. The finished product was two copies of each postcard printed using Adobe Photoshop and postcard stock. Mr. Rivera put one copy of each postcard up in the classroom and mailed the second copy to a nearby school's kindergarten class. To see the postcards and the accompanying lesson plan, go to **http://media.lacoe.edu/iti/lessons/view/index.html?id=80**.

Mr. Rivera wrote of the success of the "School on a Postcard" lesson, which was accepted by the Los Angeles County Office of Education as a model lesson to feature on its web site. "More importantly," he wrote, "the students were proud of themselves and their accomplishment while gaining an appreciation for some of the great things in their school and community."

SOURCE: J. Rivera. 2002. School on a postcard. Retrieved May 29, 2003, from http://www.ciconline.com/Enrichment/Teaching/learningwithtechnology/expertadvice/default.htm.

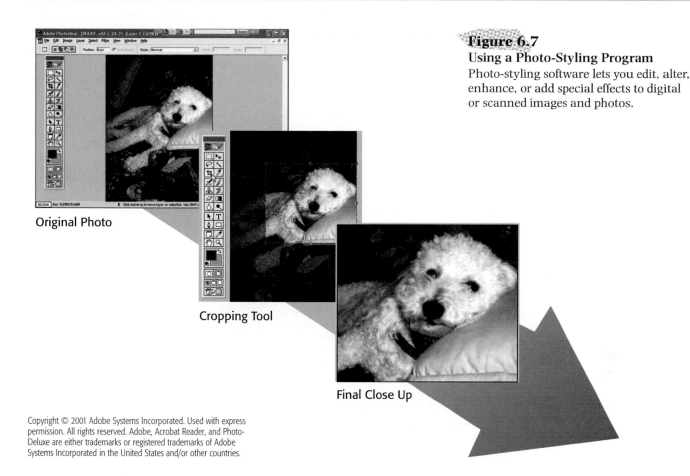

Figure 6.7
Using a Photo-Styling Program
Photo-styling software lets you edit, alter, enhance, or add special effects to digital or scanned images and photos.

Original Photo

Cropping Tool

Final Close Up

ing animations that can be included in presentation and multimedia files. These effects add significant interest and appeal but may require a substantial investment in time.

For educators, imaging and editing software adds an element of control over the quality of images produced by digital photography or via scanning. Photo-styling software can typically alter the lighting, contrast, color intensity, and cropping of a digital image. Many can also add corrections to an image, such as correcting "red-eye" in pictures of animals and people (see Figure 6.7). Still others offer some special effects capabilities such as blurring parts of the image or making it into a mosaic display.

For those who need advanced special effects features to add artistic elements, special effects software packages are available that enable all types of enhancements, from morphing, in which one image appears to melt into another, to altering images to appear as if they were created through a variety of different camera lenses. These more advanced styling features are particularly dramatic in multimedia displays, as they add interest to the multisensory elements included in that type of presentation.

Reference Software

Reference software, digital versions of volumes of reference materials, can now be easily stored on a single compact disc. This capacity has revolutionized the way in which, and speed at which, great stores of reference materials can be used. CD-ROMs typically employ a hypermedia approach to storage of reference materials. That is, although the materials are recorded in a linear fashion on the CD, the user is provided an interface that allows for hyperjumps to any points of information recorded on the

CD-ROM reference software hyperlinks multimedia data.

ON THE WEB! 6.6
Reference Software

CD. With a simple point and click on an interactive link, a student or teacher can follow an idea and questions that emerge from exploring that idea in whatever order he or she chooses. In addition, because it is just as simple to store digital images, sounds, and video as it is to store text, reference material that was once confined to text with only an occasional static illustration can become dazzling and informative multimedia information. The potential of these additional types of digital information for learners of different modalities is clear.

These types of digital enhancements, combined with the compact and easy-to-use storage media offered by CD-ROMs, have led to the creation of a variety of new educational reference software tools. These broad categories of CD-ROM-based reference programs and their applications are summarized in Table 6.3.

The wide variety of software manufacturers that produce reference CDs leads to great variability in the features in any one piece of software. Some have extensive mul-

TABLE 6.3   REFERENCE SOFTWARE SUMMARY

Software Type	Features	Application to Teaching and Learning Tasks
Encyclopedias	• Easy-to-use hypermedia connections to browse cross-referenced items • Can include text, graphics, animation, and audio and video clips to support information • Some support note taking on content	• Enables teacher and student research in all content areas • Interactive format promotes discovery learning • Presentation can help meet multiple learning styles
Atlases	• Hypermedia connections allow user to move between countries and features by pointing and clicking • Often includes satellite images from NASA to present topographical features • Can include text, graphics, animation, and audio and video clips to support information • Some support note taking on content	• Enables teacher and student examination of global geography • Interactive format promotes discovery learning • Presentation can help meet multiple learning styles
Grammar Tools	• Can include a thesaurus and grammar checker • Provides suggestions for alternative words or grammatical structures from which the writer can choose	• Provides students support for editing their work • Interactive format promotes discovery learning • Presentation can help meet multiple learning styles
Dictionaries	• Provides quick search for target words • Can include text, graphics, animation, and audio and video clips to support definitions	• Provides students support for vocabulary • Interactive format promotes discovery learning • Presentation can help meet multiple learning styles

timedia components; in others, text is dominant. Some include facilities for printing the text and graphics elements; others may not. Because of the variety in this type of software, it is important for educators to carefully review and evaluate the capabilities of this type of software before investing in it. The academic software evaluation rubric included in Table 6.4 can be a valuable tool for effective software decision making. This rubric or one like it should be used before making any academic software purchases.

Tutorials and Drill-and-Practice Software

Software designed to teach new content or reinforce a lesson can assist an educator in addressing learner needs, particularly when time demands or the teacher–student ratio limits the teacher's ability to provide sufficient one-to-one interaction. This category of academic software can offer students opportunities to learn new content or provide additional practice to reinforce concepts already presented.

Tutorials

Tutorial software presents new material, usually in a carefully orchestrated instructional sequence with frequent opportunities for practice and review. These software packages are often self-contained lessons designed and planned according to the principles of instructional design. Tutorial software programs can either be linear or use a hypermedia approach. Linear tutorials take the learner step-by-step through each phase of the instructional process for each objective. For example, a student using a linear tutorial will typically be presented with content, then evaluated to see whether the competencies have been achieved. Finally, this type of software will provide feedback to the learner as to his or her attainment of objectives along with suggestions

Tutorial software presents and pratices new concepts in a format that maintains learners' interest throughout the process.

TABLE 6.4   ACADEMIC SOFTWARE EVALUATION RUBRIC

SOFTWARE:

DESCRIPTION:

VENDOR: COST:

NOTES ON ITS USE:

Please rate the featues below for each piece of software. Next to each of the items in the rubric, check the box that best reflects your opinion.

EVALUATION CRITERIA

Software Feature	1 Poor	2 Below Average	3 Average	4 Above Average	5 Excellent
Documentation	Documentation is excessively technical and/or difficult to follow	Documentation is generally understandable but not very user-friendly	Documentation is easy to follow and understand; includes all necessary components	Clear documentation that is logical and easy to follow	Very clear, easy-to-read, logical, and complete documentation
Site license	No licensing available	Site licenses are available but limited or expensive options	Site licensing available at reasonable cost	Special, low site licensing pricing for education	Educators may use for free without a site license
Installation	Complex to install; poor installation instructions	Installation somewhat difficult; instructions minimal	Installation process typical; instructions fairly clear and complete	Easy to install; clear, easy-to-understand instructions	Self-installing; step-by-step installation included
Technical support	No toll-free telephone support available	No local support; phone support available for an hourly fee	Local support and phone support available for modest fee	Local tech help available for modest fee; no-charge phone support	Local help and toll-free support readily available at no charge

Tutorials can give the student control of the pace and, sometimes, the path of interaction.

to return to the sections that have not yet been mastered before going on to the next competency.

By contrast, tutorials that use a hypermedia approach allow students to explore more freely the various content pathways available in the program. Using hyperlinks, students can move through the materials in accordance with their personal preferences and interests. Of course, these hypermedia-style tutorials also include evaluation and feedback components.

Tutorials of both types may be primarily text or a combination of text and multimedia components, including graphics, animation, and audio and video clips. Some may have built-in classroom management support components that track, record, and report individual student progress on each included lesson. All are interactive, in that the student must respond and interact for the tutorial to progress.

Tutorials give the student control of the pace and, in the case of hypermedia tutorials, the path of instruction. Tutorials are limited by their ability to respond to students' questions or concerns outside their programming. Even the best-designed tutorial software may not be able to respond to the divergent thinking of many learners. For many users, tutorials are viewed as limiting and potentially boring because of

Software Feature	1 Poor	2 Below Average	3 Average	4 Above Average	5 Excellent
			EVALUATION CRITERIA		
Help features	No online or text-based help available	A Read-Me text file is included; no online help	Both online and text help available on CD	Online help is content-sensitive and provides clear assistance; text included	Automatic online help available for every feature; supplementary text help included
Grade level	Not suitable for intended grade level	Some features unsuitable for intended grade level	Majority of features suitable for intended grade level	Most features appropriate and suitable for intended grade level	All features both suitable and appropriate for grade level
Competencies	Does not address target competencies	Few competencies addressed; many ignored	A majority of the competencies are addressed	Most of the desired competencies are addressed	All of the target competencies and others are addressed
Active learning	Interaction is passive; no active learning encouraged	Interaction mostly passive; a few active learning opportunities included	Interaction offers average active learning opportunities; some activities too passive	Good active interaction provided through a majority of the software	Students are actively engaged during all components of software
Save features	Students cannot interrupt and save work	Student work can be saved on an external disk but it cannot be reused	Students may save their work to continue working on it in the future	Automatically saves the student's work when the program is closed	Both automatically and manually, student's work can be saved and restarted at the same point later
Hardware compatibility	Works on relatively few available computers; requires additional hardware	Works on several machines; requires upgrades to some available computers	Will work on most machines with minimal or no hardware upgrades or additions	Works on most available machines without hardware upgrades or additions	Works on all machines available without hardware upgrades or additions
Cost	High cost relative to features	Somewhat expensive relative to features	Average cost for features offered	Reasonably priced with numerous features for the cost	Special low pricing for educational users for abundant features

Total the score for each piece of software. Compare the scores. The piece of software with the highest score is your best choice.

their rigidity in the presentation of topics. Still, a well-written tutorial that is programmed with multimedia components in the presentation of materials can be very useful for support or review of material or even as an additional strategy in the communication of content.

Drill-and-Practice Software

Whereas tutorials may present new material, **drill-and-practice software** is designed to reinforce previously presented content. Drill-and-practice software is used to question learners on key content points, giving them the opportunity to practice content by responding to specific questions. This type of software provides instant feedback as to the correctness of a response. Some drill-and-practice software

Drill-and-practice software lets learners practice and review concepts as often and as long as they need in order to gain mastery.

packages track correct answers and move the level of questioning to more complex content as the students' responses indicate increased mastery.

Drill-and-practice software, like tutorials, ranges from fairly simple text-based, flash-card-type software to complex and sophisticated multimedia software. Drill-and-practice software allows the student to control the pace of the interaction, but users typically cannot alter the path of the review until they have mastered each level. Unlike answering review questions or taking a pop quiz for content practice, using drill-and-practice software provides instant feedback, and it may respond with additional drills targeting diagnosed weaknesses.

Critics of this type of software refer to it as "drill-and-kill" software, expressing the notion that it can be a boring and passive learning experience. Indeed, some drill-and-practice software lacks quality and interest. Furthermore, if used for overly long periods of time or for too many review sessions, it does not stimulate learning or promote interest in the content practiced. However, well-constructed, multimedia-rich drill-and-practice software can provide valuable supplemental experiences and targeted feedback for learners. It can also provide excellent practice before formal evaluations and can be used as a diagnostic for teachers who are fine-tuning their classroom instruction. As with all software, it is critical that educators carefully evaluate the academic value of drill-and-practice before acquiring it and using it in the classroom.

Educational Games

Educational games present and review instructional content in a game format. Content is repackaged so that it is furnished within the framework of a sequence of game rules and graphics (see Figure 6.8). Although educational games may present the same competencies that drill-and-practice or tutorial software presents, they are often better received by learners because the game component adds an element of interest and entertainment. Clearly, however, it is important to be sure the game elements do not overshadow the instructional elements.

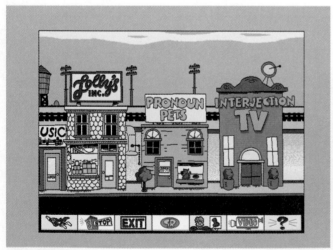

Screen capture of Reading Blaster by Knowledge Adventure, Inc. Reprinted by permission of Vivendi Universal Games, Inc.

Screen capture of Grammar Rock game by Creative Wonders. Courtesy of Riverdeep Interactive Learning.

Figure 6.8

Examples of Educational Game Software
Educational games present content in colorful and engaging formats.

IN THE CLASSROOM

Academic Software to the Rescue

Software for teaching comes in many guises, all of which present learning as fun and range from game playing to more rigorous reference and problem-solving programs. For special needs students, games software is especially valuable as they see learning can be fun even for the academically challenged. Special needs students (and mainstreamers as well) frequently find certain academic disciplines difficult to cope with. Writing is one of these. Keeping in mind that content, format, and standard English all contribute to writing, the special needs student has a particularly steep hill to climb to acquire the ability to write the basic structure of our language, the sentence. Hilary Pruett teaches in a special education resource room for third grade in an elementary school in Nevada. She knows that trying to teach these students grammar with the usual approach of drill-and-practice exercises doesn't work, at best, and, in the worst-case scenario, actually deters learning because of the negative reinforcement that arises from frequent failure. She also knows, however, that her special needs students are fascinated by computers and are comfortable working with them.

So, for her students to learn how to write a sentence, Ms. Pruett turns to Grammar Rock, a software program the children can interact with as they play games and learn grammar as they play. Drawing upon her commitment to constructivist theory, Ms. Pruett believes the children learn much more through play in an activity that is not teacher-directed than they would with an assignment that bores and frustrates them. Using what prior knowledge they have about parts of speech and sentence construction, the children pace themselves as they play games that are preceded by videos with a catchy musical background. The games are leveled from the easiest to more advanced grammatical concepts, such as locating a part of speech in a sentence. If stymied, the students can click the Help button to get a clue. Ms. Pruett advises teachers that it is important to note the limitations of their students to prevent them from trying levels that are too difficult for them.

SOURCE: H. Pruett. 2002. Having students learn basic grammar through technology. Retrieved May 23, 2003, from **http://www.techlearning.com/db_area/archives/WCE/archives/hpruett.html**.

Several broad categories of educational games are available to teachers who are interested in adding entertainment as an enhancement to the classroom, as shown in Table 6.5. Adventure games provide students the opportunity to solve mysteries and participate in educational adventures. An example of this type of game is the Carmen Sandiego adventure series. In this game series, students must have knowledge of a region or country to find the game's heroine. This educational game thus exercises social studies knowledge and critical-thinking skills while presenting the experience in an adventure game format.

A second category of educational games simulates traditional board or card games. These games typically require that the student respond with correct answers before advancing a game piece on a graphic of a board or playing a card in a virtual hand. This type of game superimposes content material on the traditional real-world game. Students must know how to play the traditional game to participate in the educational version.

Educational adaptations of television and popular video games can also add an element of "edutainment" to the classroom. Games that let students shoot down the right answer or race their virtual cars to the finish line by driving over the correct responses in the road are examples of video-game adaptations. Students enjoy the stimulating visuals and sound, practice eye–hand coordination, and review content simultaneously. Familiar and popular TV quiz shows have been adapted to software and can be used to review material preformatted into the software or added by the teacher. This category of educational games can add excitement and interest to content review.

Some controversy exists regarding the role of educational games in the classroom. Some educators see value in the excitement and active learning a gaming environment presents. Others believe that the games detract from the implicit personal excite-

TABLE 6.5   SPOTLIGHT ON ACADEMIC GAMES

Types of Games	Potential Benefits	Examples of Games	Potential Classroom Applications
Action	Exercises hand-eye coordination, reasoning, content practice	• Blaster Series (Math, Reading, etc.) *Davidson* • Jump Start Series *Vivendi*	Content practice in a shoot-em-up format
Adventure	Promotes problem-solving skills through adventure scenarios and role playing	• Carmen Sandiego Series *Broderbund* • Magic School Bus Series *Scholastic*	Geography/social studies in mystery format Math, reading, science, and art skills
Strategy/ Simulation	Exercises problem solving, decision making, critical thinking, and content	• SimCity *Maxis* • Biology Explorer *Riverdeep*	Civics/architecture/urban studies/ social studies Anatomy, science
Puzzles and Game Classic	Reinforces and builds memory, logic, verbal, and planning skills	• Scrabble *Hasbro Interactive* • Zillions of Games *Zillions Development Corp.*	English and vocabulary review General knowledge

ment and joy of learning. Still others object to educational games because they believe that students become so involved in the games themselves that they lose focus on the content that is the underlying objective of the experience. Some believe that game experiences are unnecessarily cumbersome ways to review content and that more direct instructional strategies would be less wasteful of students' time.

Whether in the use of software games or a classroom game of hangman, gaming has been a widely accepted instructional strategy that has value in a classroom. As a reward for completing class assignments or as a replacement for other review strategies, playing educational games is a popular alternative for many educators. Clearly, it is important for you to very carefully evaluate game activities in general and educational game software in particular for its suitability as a strategy to achieve your instructional objectives. Using the Academic Software Evaluation Rubric (Table 6.4) before incorporating educational game software into the classroom can help to ensure classroom time is well spent.

ON THE WEB! 6.7
Educational Games

Simulations

Simulations are software packages that present to the user a model or situation in a computerized or virtual format. When using the software, learners interact with the simulation, and it responds to their actions. For example, flight simulator software mimics the conditions of flying various types of planes. As you move the mouse or press different keys assigned to represent speed, altitude, or various other aspects of the plane's conditions in its virtual sky, the screen displays a graphic of what one would see from the plane's cockpit. Conditions are thus simulated in response to user input.

In a more educational context, simulations are available that duplicate the conditions and appearance of a chemistry lab so that students can mix and heat virtual chemicals and see the results without having to deal with the real substances. Or students can dissect a virtual frog or examine parts of the human body and be able to see how each individual component works. Social science simulations might allow students to make decisions for virtual civilizations and then watch their impact on the social order and on the individuals within that society.

Whereas tutorials and drill-and-practice software provide very structured content environments, simulations offer the student opportunities to interact with the content and to participate in discovery learning. Simulations can time-shift models by slowing processes down or by speeding up the impact of student-directed changes. They can also provide safe versions of what would be dangerous experiments in the real world.

Simulations allow students to virtually manipulate models and situations safely in the classroom.

Special Needs Software

Some educational software is specifically designed to address the requirements of learners with special needs as the result of a variety of physical or learning impairments. The category of **special needs software** includes software that reads words or letters aloud as they are displayed on the screen and software that enlarges text on the screen. These types of software address different levels of sight impairments in students. Special needs software also includes speech-synthesizing software, which converts spoken sounds and words into their graphic equivalent or into the text the sounds represent. Sounds are thus displayed on the computer screen to assist students who are hearing impaired and students who need additional perceptual feedback in reading. Specially prepared multimedia software targeting specific learning skills, such as listening skills, helps students with learning disabilities that require content presentation via additional modalities for accurate perceptual processing. Often, the assistive devices discussed in Chapter 4 are sold with customized special needs software that takes advantage of the full range of features incorporated into the device.

Assistive software and hardware can address the special needs of exceptional students not only by facilitating their interaction with computers but also by presenting content in diverse formats. Learners with special needs may require that materials be presented in unique multisensory formats in order to be understood. Assistive software provides such diverse formats and may also include features that provide note-taking support and reading support. Assistive hardware and software may also facilitate communication so that a child can participate in academic interaction and assessment.

Simulations let students take part in virtual experiences.

ON THE WEB! 6.8
Assistive Software

Special needs hardware and software assist physically challenged and special needs students to complete their academic tasks.

The software also helps the special needs child participate in social communication and recreational activities.

A new technology support for special needs children is universal design. This type of support software automatically offers materials in a format that addresses the strongest learning mode for the individual student. For example, an E-book that uses universal design may be able to read a passage aloud for a sight-impaired student and offer that same passage in large print and vibrant colors for a student with a reading disability. This new approach to special needs software holds great promise in meeting the unique and diverse needs of exceptional students.

For those interested in additional information on the implications of technology for special needs students, the web offers abundant resources. Perhaps the best place to start is at the web site of the Council for Exceptional Children (http://www.cec. sped.org). First founded in 1922 at Teachers College, Columbia University, this organization has been a significant voice in advocating for exceptional students in all areas, including assistive technologies.

Integrated Learning Systems

Integrated learning systems (ILS) are hardware–software combinations of equipment and programs designed to assist students in learning targeted objectives. Usually, an ILS is a network of computers that are all running customized software written specifically for that system. An ILS typically includes tutorial and drill-and-practice software as well as a comprehensive classroom management support system that records and can report on each student's progress after completion of every software lesson. Such systems address very detailed and specific objectives and can be used in whole or in part as reinforcement to an entire course or for a specific competency

connecting THEORY to PRACTICE

Software and Learning

Information management is acknowledged to be the definitive characteristic of the educational establishment of the future. As the saying goes, the teacher will no longer be the "sage on the stage," but the "guide on the side." The change in conceptualization of education derives from causes attributable to the ascendancy of constructivism as the academic arm of cognitive psychology and the emergence of software to support this theoretical base. Learning styles, personality types, and multiple intelligences are all interpretations of the cognitive-constructive approach to learning and teaching.

The emphasis on student involvement in actively creating the learning process is enabled by the proliferation of products and sites where information can be accessed easily and quickly. Making selections from the vast resources available on the Internet and from troves of software engages the student in making critical judgments. Higher-order thinking skills are acquired from the earliest exposure to technology-driven instruction. Constructivist teaching is notable for giving students responsibility for taking the initiative in, and responsibility for, their learning. They are expected to be able to access primary and secondary sources, a task that is made demanding by the sheer amount of material available and the lack of filtering imposed upon the sources. In contrast to source searches in libraries, where hard-copy materials such as books, journals, and magazines have been preselected by librarians and recommended by educators, online and software sources have no censors or critics. Students must learn to discern faulty logic, deceptive or unconvincing arguments, and misleading statistics; this is a critical skill they will carry with them into the arena of life for making decisions that will affect themselves, their families, their community, their nation, and the world.

The recognition of different learning styles, different personality types, and multiple intelligences has coincided with the means of implementing curriculum to address students who have these variations in cognitive profiles through the interactivity and multimodal nature of software and the Internet. For the student with auditory dominance, sound accompanies the traditional textual format. For the visually nonverbal, pictures illustrate the materials presented. For the interactive learner, dialogs with the teacher and with other students, authorities, leaders, and the software itself form part of the instructional package. For kinesthetic and tactile learners, the motor skills involved in performing the procedures to access information are routes to learning through varying neurological strengths.

Word-processing software allows students to free-write, keep journals, prepare newsletters, make signs and posters, and prepare reports and papers using visual enhancements, tables, graphs, and charts. Database and spreadsheet software provide opportunities for the analysis of surveys, inventories, and numerical information to arrive at value judgments or simply the objective exemplification of data as supportive evidence for critical-thinking tasks. Presentation software allows students to draw on their preferential learning styles, intelligences, or personality types to exhibit achievement through performance for assessment.

The synergistic and serendipitous relationship of software as a means to the end of encouraging all students to learn through experiencing successful accomplishments, the end that epitomizes learning theory, is the true measure of the bridge that software has built to enable students to cross over to cognitive development and to love making the journey—that is, to love learning!

within a course. Often, ILS software is written to cover several consecutive grade levels and can therefore be easily adapted to address the different levels of skill found in the typical classroom.

Integrated learning systems tend to be a more expensive solution to the need for technological support of instruction. They are often bundled with their own hardware as well as software and are typically set up in a centralized location that allows all grade levels in a school to share the technology. Because of the cost and the shared implementation of these systems, a typical ILS may be sold to a district as a complete solution to the need for computers in schools and may take the place of individual computers in teachers' classrooms. This has led to some controversy over how computer dollars should be spent: by individual teachers addressing their students' needs or by a school district making decisions that try to address the needs of as many students as possible. Most schools and districts continue to have limited funding for the acquisition and implementation of computers, so this controversy is very likely to persist.

ILS software includes both academic and administrative components.

Other Academic Software

Other types of software can be used for academic reinforcement, for building learning skills, and for enriching the teaching and learning environment. Some have been created with classroom use in mind; others have been creatively adapted to the classroom by innovative teachers. These software packages offer opportunities to add new dimensions to learning and to assist students in exercising critical-thinking skills.

Problem-Solving Software

Problem-solving software is written to help students acquire and practice problem-solving skills. Such skills include forming and testing a hypothesis; finding multiple-step strategies to solve problems such as math word problems; correctly applying theories, rules, and concepts to predict outcomes; and sequencing critical-thinking steps to come to targeted conclusions. Software of this type can be content oriented (e.g., math-problem-solving software) or of a more general nature to help develop problem-solving skills that can be broadly applied and transferred to other areas.

Problem-solving software gives learners a platform on which they can learn by doing. Such software is designed to allow students to try to explain why a phenomenon occurs and then to run a series of tests to find out whether they are correct. Well adapted to science experimentation, such software may let students develop an explanation of an aspect of the physical world, such as what friction is, and then test their concept to refine their assumptions. In math, the software may provide opportunities to test logical or mathematical relationships. The value for learners in using this type of software exceeds the content they experiment with. The greater value may be the refining of their ability to see and solve problems independently. The ability to transfer such problem-solving skills to other content and activities may well be the greatest benefit.

Students can use academic software to participate in problem solving, critical thinking, and creative experiences not otherwise available to them.

For teachers who are interested in developing their students' problem-solving skills, such software offers a way to enhance the learning experience via a constructivist approach and a multimedia environment. Students can extend their knowledge by extending hypotheses based on what they already know, and they can do so in an environment that offers audio, visual, and text components. Problem-solving software can add dimension and depth to content while letting students extend and refine their problem-solving skills. For many teachers, problem-solving software offers learning opportunities for their students that would be difficult to construct and present any other way.

Computer-Assisted Instruction

Computer-assisted instruction (CAI), a term originally applied to drill-and-practice software, has come to be more broadly used to describe any software that uses the computer to tutor or review content and to provide a platform for reasoning with reference to content. A similar term, **computer-managed instruction (CMI),** refers more appropriately to software that manages instruction, that is, keeps track of student

issues in
teaching
and
technology

ecisions about how to spend money for educational software are, in the best possible scenario, joint decisions of all interested parties—administrators, educators, and community representatives. However, such consensus decisions are often not what happens in the real world. Other, sometimes contradictory factors affect decision making.

Ideally, the general flow for decision making for academic software starts with teachers making their needs known to administrators, and administrators, in turn, advocating for the funds necessary to fulfill instructional software requests. There are a number of reasons why this logical flow might not occur. The first is teachers' lack of familiarity with available software, which results in missed opportunities for requesting these potentially valuable instructional aids. Courses such as this one help to remedy that lack.

Yet even if teachers are aware of useful software and do request it, other factors may affect the decision to acquire it. Many districts experience resource shortfalls each year, and "frills" such as instructional software are often placed on the acquisition back burner. This perception of software as a frill is sometimes an unfortunate product of underinformed decision making. Clearly, investment in hardware requires an equal or greater investment in software to fully utilize the hardware's capabilities. Still, real resource shortfalls can alter the software acquisition plan considerably.

Another difficulty in academic software acquisition is the diversity of software needs. Frequently, the most economical software decision for a district is site licensing, the purchase of a single software package to be used on all machines at a given site (the district's schools). Site licensing can indeed spend limited resources efficiently but tends to result in a one-size-fits-all solution that may fit no one school or classroom very well. A balance

must be sought between the economy of selecting districtwide software and the usefulness of the software in all district school settings. An ideal scenario for a district that is interested in such purchases would be to create a districtwide evaluation team representing all stakeholders in determining whether this approach is as effective as it is economically feasible.

A final factor in academic software acquisitions is the diversity of hardware that tends to build up over time in a district. Hardware ages rapidly, a reasonable useful life being three to five years. After that time, the hardware typically can no longer support the latest versions of software that are available. This in turn limits the software choices from the ideal choices to the best that can run on the older machines found in many classrooms. This particular problem is very complex; district technology specialists need to balance resources for hardware maintenance and support with those for new hardware acquisitions. Buying and supporting the many types and versions of software appropriate to the diversity of hardware found in a district can tax the capabilities of even well-funded technology-support groups.

In addition to the teacher from whom the software requests typically emanate, a key player in initiating allocations of monies for the purchase of software is the computer or technology-resource person either in the school or at the district level. This person can be a powerful ally in supporting requests for software to enhance instruction within disciplines or for a teacher or a small group of teachers. Furthermore, he or she can be very helpful in explaining the districtwide or schoolwide constraints (either technological or financial) associated with teacher requests. Every teacher who is interested in creating a technology-rich classroom should build a relationship with the technology-resource staff in the school or the district.

progress with reference to the material in addition to its tutorial features. These terms are sometimes used interchangeably, because many types of academic software incorporate elements of both.

CAI/CMI includes software that provides a platform for drill and practice of content. In this type of software, new content might not be presented. Instead, the software offers computer-based practice opportunities to improve skills already acquired (e.g., multiplication practice). In the case of CAI that is primarily tutorial in nature, the software typically presents new content with an opportunity to review and practice it. This software often also provides additional content or appropriate correction depending on student responses.

Students tend to like to use well-designed CAI/CMI software because it provides a patient, tireless tutor that offers rewards and/or help in response to every answer. It is important, however, for teachers to carefully evaluate the quality of CAI/CMI software and its appropriateness for the students who are to use it. Not all CAI/CMI software is of sufficiently good quality to keep learners actively engaged. Furthermore, the stated target age group might not be appropriate for learners in a given classroom, with their individual needs and abilities. Such software, like all computer tools, is best applied and most effective when a professional educator determines its use.

Brainstorming/Concept-Mapping Tools

On CD!
Software Skills Builder
Inspiration Skills—Lesson Brainstorming

Brainstorming tools provide a digital environment in which the learner can develop ideas and concepts and then create connections between them. Some of these software packages are primarily text based, while others allow for the creation of visual concept maps. Such **concept-mapping software** generates digital "maps" of concepts that represent a visual depiction of the brainstorming process and the interrelationships between ideas. In the classroom, this tool can be used to capture a cooperative learning group's diverse ideas and turn them into a cohesive whole; help individual learners to grasp large, complex ideas by enabling them to visualize the ideas on a computer

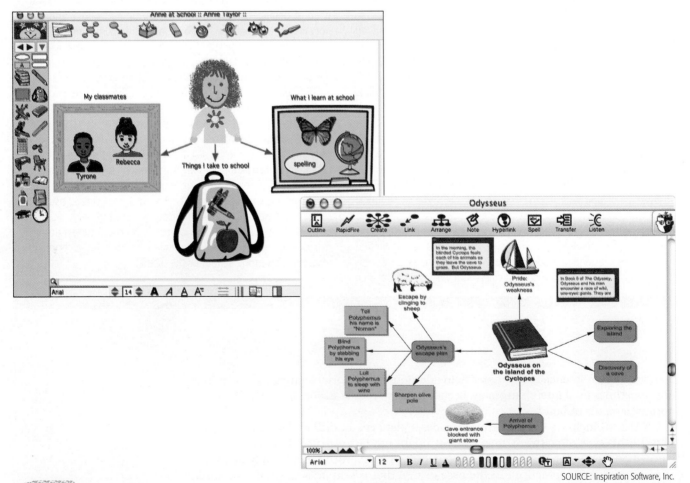

SOURCE: Inspiration Software, Inc.

Figure 6.9
Sample Diagrams Created Using Inspiration® by Inspiration Software, Inc.
Brainstorming software such as Kidspiration and Inspiration helps students to visually organize and represent ideas and their relationship to one another.

screen; or help the class as a whole to develop a joint overview of a new instructional topic that is about to be explored.

Concept-mapping tools allow students to visually organize ideas and then link them to one another to show relationships. Such maps give students an opportunity to visually represent prior knowledge and then extend that knowledge base by linking it to new ideas. This constructivist approach offers students a chance to build and then test the connections between the ideas they have already assimilated and those they are just learning. As you can see in Figure 6.9, most concept maps (also called mind maps) are not highly structured but instead allow for a free-form summary of the relationships between ideas. This type of software tool offers individual learners and cooperative learning groups an opportunity to visually plan writing projects, see relationships between concepts they have learned, and brainstorm solutions in a highly visible and flexible format.

To better understand this unique academic software tool, you may wish to experience it for yourself. Your student Skills Builder CD includes a demonstration version of Inspiration software and its companion software, Kidspiration. You may install this demonstration version on your own computer and use it for thirty days to experience concept mapping. To better help you see the instructional possibilities of this software, you may want to complete both the Inspiration and Kidspiration Skills Builders activities included on your CD.

Concept-mapping software incorporates the principles of visual learning into a single, easy-to-use software package. It offers opportunities for students to clarify thinking, understand relationships, and identify their own misconceptions. With this unique software tool, students will be encouraged toward creative thinking and deeper understanding. It can also be a powerful instructional tool for teachers wishing to visually present complex or multidimensional content to their students.

ON THE WEB! 6.9
Concept-Mapping
Software

On CD!
Software Skills Builder
Kidspiration Skills–KWL Chart

Academic Software in Teaching and Learning

As you consider the methods and media you choose to employ to achieve your instructional objectives and best address the needs of all learners, academic software can be a most valuable asset. There is indeed a wide variety of types of academic software and, within each type, hundreds of choices. With so large a selection from which to choose, it is clear that the amount of effort necessary to review, evaluate, and select academic software and integrate it into teaching and learning is indeed high. However, the benefits derived from that effort are even greater.

Whether there is only one computer in a classroom or many, carefully selected and integrated academic software can patiently and tirelessly reinforce concepts for learners who need review, offer opportunities for exploration and discovery for learners who need additional opportunity, or provide creative experiences for cooperative learning groups working together to develop a multimedia report to share with peers. The possibilities are as great as the number of academic software packages available to enrich the learning experience. It is true that exploration of academic software appropriate for your classroom does take time and effort, but for computer-using teachers and their students, inclusion of these packages in the teaching and learning environment will increasingly become a necessary and exciting part of teaching and learning in the twenty-first century.

Integrating academic software into instruction adds excitement and innovation to the teaching and learning process.

KEY TERMS

academic software   173
authoring systems   173
clip art   183
computer-assisted instruction (CAI)   198
computer-managed instruction (CMI)   198
concept-mapping software   200
desktop publishing (DTP) software   180
draw programs   184
drill-and-practice software   191
editing software   186
educational games   192

graphics software   182
hypermedia software   175
imaging software   185
integrated learning systems (ILS)   196
paint programs   183
problem-solving software   198
reference software   187
simulations   195
special needs software   195
tutorial software   189

STUDENT ACTIVITIES

CHAPTER REVIEW

1. What are authoring systems? Describe two types of authoring systems. How is each used for teaching and learning?
2. What is hypermedia software? How does it differ from presentation software?
3. Describe the differences and applications of each type of graphics software that might be used in teaching and learning.
4. What is reference software? How has it changed the research process?
5. What is the difference between drill-and-practice software and tutorial software? When is it appropriate to use each in teaching and learning?
6. How do educational games and simulations differ?
7. What is an integrated learning system? What controversies surround the implementation of such systems in schools?
8. How is special needs software effective in meeting the unique needs of special education students? Give examples.
9. What is problem-solving software? Contrast it with brainstorming tools. How does each promote critical-thinking skills?
10. How do CAI and CMI differ? Which would you prefer to use and why?

WHAT DO YOU THINK?

1. School budgets are typically limited in the amounts allocated for teachers to purchase materials and supplies for the classroom. With the additional expense of purchasing academic software packages, some teachers feel that even less money will be available for instructional basics. Do you think this may prove to be a problem as academic software continues to become a critical component in instruction? If so, how might be it be resolved?
2. If an educator is given the time and training to author pedagogically sound multimedia teaching software for use in the classroom, how might this change his or her role in the classroom, if at all? Be specific in describing what might change, how it would change, and why; or explain why it would not change.

3. Some educators fear that academic software, especially game-oriented software, shifts the focus from the content to the delivery system. Do you think the entertainment aspect of academic software interferes with and detracts from the content? Why or why not? What are the benefits and disadvantages of using such software? What are the benefits and disadvantages of using more traditional instruction?

LEARNING TOGETHER!

1. With so many types of academic software available, it seems an overwhelming task to try to examine and evaluate enough software to make an informed decision about which packages to use. In a learning group of 2–3, develop strategies for effectively selecting academic software for use in your classroom.
2. Assume that you are members of a grade or departmental team in a local school. Your grade or department has been given $2,000 to spend on educational software for this school year. Collect two to five educational software catalogs as sources, and together decide how you plan to spend your funds. Be prepared to defend your decisions.
3. With your group, examine the objectives and contents of a unit of curriculum at the grade level you would like to teach. Consider how each type of academic software might be integrated to enhance the delivery of this unit. Which type of academic software packages would you use to achieve the objectives and how might you use them? Create a group consensus lesson plan using the software and strategies you have agreed on.

HANDS-ON!

1. Examine a variety of CD-ROM-based educational software, including game, tutorial, drill-and-practice, reference, and simulation software. Use the Academic Software Evaluation Rubric (Table 6.4) to evaluate each.
2. Create a mind map using Inspiration software (a demo version on your Companion CD) that brainstorms how you might teach a social studies lesson to the grade level of your choice. After using the software and completing the mind map, create a one-page summary that you might give to your students to prepare them to use this tool.
3. Using the list of suggested web sites for Chapter 6 on the text Companion web site, download three sample programs from these sites. Use your software evaluation rubric to decide whether you would use them in your classroom.

More from Nancy Armstrong

Now that you have learned about the many types of educational software available for the classroom, let's return to see how Nancy Armstrong found the best software to meet her students' needs.

MY SEARCH AND SOLUTION

My primary sources of information on the Internet were electronic journals and professional organizations. Several electronic journals contained informative articles about using educational technology in the elementary classroom. The web site **http://www.fno.org**, authored by Jamie McKenzie, featured many articles supporting technology in the classroom. The web site **http://www.techlearning.com** covered many issues related to using educational technology in the classroom. The section I found most useful was called "Web Picks." It contained web site recommendations organized by curriculum areas. Another electronic journal that contained articles about educational technology was located at **http://www.electronic-school.com**. One of the most dynamic web sites for current information on many educational issues was located at **http://www.edweek.org**.

The most comprehensive web site that I found was the Math Forum at **http://www.forum.swarthmore.edu**. This web site was created by Swarthmore College and had clearly defined activities and resources. The web site at **http://www.nde.state.ne.us/MATH/home.html**, maintained by the Nebraska Department of Education, included pertinent information about the Mathematics and Science Frameworks and the Nebraska Mathematics & Science Coalition. Great links for math were found at the Educational Service Unit #16: **http://www.esu16.k12.ne.us/curriculum/math.html**. The National Council of Teachers of Mathematics web site at **http://www.nctm.org** included information about many aspects of math education. Topics of the web site were publications, Standards 2000, conference schedules, external links, and articles about math education. Educational Resources Information Center (ERIC), at **http://eduref.org**, contained a large, searchable database of information about educational technology and teaching math. Nebraska State Educational Association (NSEA) had a web site at **http://nsea.org/members/teaching/math.htm?** that linked to math education resources. I discovered that educators can use the aforementioned electronic resources to develop their own professional growth plans related to the use of educational technology to increase student learning.

My research focused on educational technology pertaining to the Internet (interactive web sites) and computer software. The research was also geared toward math activities relating to the Nebraska Math Standards of data analysis, probability, statistics, and algebraic concepts. Interactive web sites are sites that allow the learner to actively participate in an assignment that is located on the site. I developed a rubric, modified from a model used by John Stritt at Educational Service Unit #16, to evaluate the interactive web sites.

Categories contained in the rubric were grade-level-appropriate, clearly defined activities, standards-based, graphics/pleasing, easy to navigate, and reteaching component. I created a web site that contained the best interactive web sites relating to data analysis, probability, and algebraic concepts.

I used Microsoft Word to set up a web site named Math Counts (Math Activities with a Difference). The address is **http://toolbox.esu16.k12.ne.us/og4p/math/mathcounts.htm**, and it contains several links: The **http://www.scienceacademy.com/BI/index.html** web site offered choices of different math skills to practice, then an animated basketball shot for correct answers. Incorrect responses led to a view of the correct solution. Algebraic interactive web sites included **http://www.funbrain.com/numbers.html, http://teacher.scholastic.com/maven/index.htm**, and **http://www.dupagechildrensmuseum.org/aunty/index.html**. The activities at **http://www.funbrain.com/numbers.html** contained a variety of stimulating math games and allowed the user to set up the games in an algebraic format. The web site was designed so that the player adjusted the level of difficulty of the problems. Math mysteries involving algebraic concepts were found at **http://teacher.scholastic.com/activities/math.htm**. Problem-solving activities were discovered at **http://www.dcmrats.org/auntymath.html**. Problems required the use of higher-level thinking skills. Interactive web sites offered many opportunities for users to practice their math skills.

To help solve my problem on the selection of effective software, I found a web site, **http://www.enc.org/resources**, which had used a database format to evaluate software. I emailed the webmaster and received permission to use the original survey for educational purposes. After previewing sixteen software programs, I chose Math Arena produced by Sunburst Communications and the Graph Club by Tom Snyder Productions. Math Arena contained many activities related to patterns, algebra, data analysis, and probability. These activities included Array Reversal, Number Collider, Pattern Buster, and Predictor. One strong point of the software was the assessment of student performance. The Graph Club was a perfect match for math skills related to data analysis. I had received some grant funds to purchase math and science materials, so I purchased two copies of the Graph Club and ten copies of Math Arena for students to use to increase their math skills. Evaluation of software is a critical component in the selection of educational software. The time I invested in researching interactive web sites and computer programs ultimately benefits student learning, as the sites and programs are customized to specific math skills.

Standards-based classrooms are focused on increasing student learning. Students are more actively involved in the assessment process. I discovered a great assessment program, FunBrain Quiz

Lab, at **http://www.funbrain.com**, a web site that allowed teachers to design their own quizzes that students could take online. I created three quizzes that could be taken by any student who accessed this web site. FunBrain Quiz Lab has the students' results emailed to the teacher's electronic address. Students are actively involved in the assessment process. A student said, "These quizzes are fun. Will you make up another one tonight?"

A FINAL NOTE

I discovered the dynamic aspect of the web; it is changing all the time. One of the ways I checked for consistency and reliability was by visiting sites three different times from three different computers.

I learned that web sites change frequently and that if you find yourself faced with an outdated link, it is helpful to find the organization's main address and see whether it has restructured its web site.

Contact Information: Nancy Armstrong, fourth grade teacher, Progress Elementary School, Ogallala, Nebraska. Email: mnekarm@ megavision.com.

SOURCE: Interview with Nancy Armstrong conducted by Al P. Mizell. Reprinted by permission of Nancy Armstrong.

PROBLEM-BASED LEARNING

What Would You Do?
Creating the Ideal Classoom

Scenario

Your district has invested funds in a new program to refocus instruction so that it meets the unique needs of learners. The program is encouraging every teacher to become familiar with the learning styles, cognitive styles, and multiple intelligences of the students in his or her classroom. To that end, the district has provided you with age-appropriate instruments that will supply you with the information needed to develop a profile of your students. It has also created and offered a series of training workshops to help you interpret the results. With these tools and the district's support, you will be able to know your students precisely enough to create a learning environment and to target instruction to meet their individual and collective needs.

Within the framework of this program, the district has offered to fund purchase requests that will help each teacher to create a classroom learning environment that supports the aspects of student diversity that are identified through these instruments. You and your colleagues see an opportunity to better meet the needs of your students while renewing and improving your classrooms through this initiative. Currently, your typical classroom has

- Twenty-eight student desks
- A teacher's desk with chair
- Two computers for student use on a table with two chairs
- A monitor and VCR on a cart
- Two student tables with four chairs each

- One bookcase
- One four-drawer filing cabinet
- One full-size whiteboard
- One full-size bulletin board

Problem

You and your colleagues are eager to use this district initiative to acquire new furniture, equipment, and educational technologies for your classroom. You attend a workshop to find out the process to improve your classroom. At the workshop, your principal asks that teachers in each department and/or grade level interested in requesting purchases work together to develop a description of an ideal learning environment that will support individualized instruction to meet diverse learner needs. The descriptions must include everything a teacher wants, from furniture to miscellaneous equipment to technologies. The principal has specifically stated that to submit a request for funds from the district, each team must

- Diagram their idea of an ideal classroom learning environment
- Identify and justify *all* acquisitions
- Develop an instructional design on a topic of their choice that demonstrates full utilization of their ideal classroom

For the past two years, you and your colleagues have been managing without many of the technologies, furniture, and resources that you would like to have had.

You are determined to use this opportunity to turn each of your classrooms into an ideal learning environment that all of you have always wanted for your students.

What would you do?

Toward a Solution

You and your colleagues need to work together to meet the requirements set forth by your principal. The steps you follow might include:

- Researching the technologies, furniture, equipment, and other resources that help to address learning styles, cognitive styles, and/or multiple intelligences
- Meeting with your colleagues to verbally brainstorm what the ideal learning environment would include
- Creating a formal list or a mind map of all the technology, furniture, equipment, and other resources you want to buy
- Creating a classroom floor plan of your ideal learning environment in which you arrange and place all of your target acquisitions

- Deciding upon a topic and developing an instructional design, using the DID model, that utilizes your new acquisitions
- Presenting your diagram, list of acquisitions with justifications, and instructional design in a professional package for presentation to your principal

Problem-Based Learning Activity

In a group of up to four people, work to solve the problem presented in this scenario. You may use the steps articulated in "Toward a Solution," customize the steps to your group's needs, or decide on an entirely different approach to solving the problem. Your goal is to complete the tasks your hypothetical principal has identified so that you have a product you can submit in the hope of making your classroom an ideal environment for teaching and learning. Work through all aspects of the scenario until you have created what your principal has requested. Be prepared to turn in your final product and to present your solution to other groups of your peers.

PROBLEM-BASED LEARNING

What Would You Do?
Creating a Grade-Level Web Site

Scenario

At the urging of your school and district, your grade level (or department) has decided to enter the Information Age and create a web site. The school has provided easy-to-use web authoring tools and has offered to link your web site to the school home page. You and your fellow teachers are reasonably computer literate and should have little trouble actually creating your pages. You also have additional help from the tech support department at your school. You have decided to meet together to plan how to organize the web site. The only guidelines you have are the following district general guidelines for school web sites:

- Web sites must include the school's name and contact information.
- Web sites should introduce the teacher(s) who created the site.
- All web sites should have some academic purpose.
- To protect the safety of the students, web sites should not include individual student pictures or names.
- Web sites should provide information to encourage the participation of the community.
- Web sites should provide useful information to students and their parents.

Beyond these guidelines, you and your colleagues are free to organize and create a grade-level web site of your own choosing. You may want to have a consistent theme on a grade-level home page that is carried through to each individual classroom page. You may want to join your diverse pages together and connect them to a single

home page. You may want to have common elements that appear on all classroom pages, or you may prefer to have every page entirely unique. How you design your website and your individual classroom pages is your choice, as long as the site conforms to district guidelines.

Problem

You and your colleagues, though computer literate, have never thought about how to join your grade level together for presentation on the web. Some of your colleagues are very organized and will no doubt want a very simple, no-nonsense web site. Others are highly creative and will want to create an innovative site that stands out on the school home page.

You have all agreed that you want your web site to help your students academically. It should also help them and their parents stay involved in the activities of your school and your classrooms. You want to be able to post notices to parents about upcoming events, current homework, and important dates. You want to offer students who are absent from class a way to keep up with what they have missed. You want to highlight every student's achievement in some way. You also want to make it possible for parents to interact with you through email. You have decided to make your grade-level web site as meaningful and useful as it is attractive to view and interact with.

Your meeting with your peers is this week. You need to bring some ideas to the table so that this project can get under way. Your principal has asked that the new web sites be ready to go live in two months.
What would you do?

Toward a Solution

Before attending the first meeting, you may want to explore web sites of other schools that include links to grade-level (or departmental) sites similar to the one you are planning. When exploring those sites,

- Use your Web Site Evaluation Rubric (Table 8.1) to determine what you like best about the site
- Note any special web site features you feel are especially useful
- Examine the web sites you review in light of your district's guidelines, and note how those sites conform

You and your colleagues will then need to meet to develop your plan for your web site. The steps you follow might include:

- Verbally brainstorming what the web site home page should include and what each classroom page should include
- Deciding on any common appearance or theme for your site
- Creating a diagram or mind map showing how all pages of the site are linked

- Identifying the features to be included on the grade-level home page as well as the features that classroom pages should include
- Articulating how your site meets each of the district standards
- Preparing to orally and visually present the plan for your site to your principal

Problem-Based Learning Activity

With up to four of your peers, prepare a hypothetical grade-level (or departmental) web site that includes your own classroom pages and meets all of the district guidelines. You may use the steps articulated in "Toward a Solution" or you may decide on an entirely different approach to solving the problem. Your goal is to fully articulate and diagram your grade-level web site. Work through all aspects of the scenario until you have created and can diagram your site. Be prepared to turn in your final product and to present your solution to your class.

PROBLEM-BASED LEARNING

What Would You Do?
Training Teachers for Technology Integration

Scenario

For the current academic year, you have served on your school's Technology Committee. As a result, you have learned about the many technologies that can help you and your colleagues teach and your students learn. You

have become excited by the possibilities and have changed the way you teach to incorporate more technologies. Your have found your lessons are more exciting as a result, and your students are more engaged. You have noticed that most of your colleagues don't seem to share your enthusiasm for technology. Although you are

somewhat concerned about this, you are not surprised, since they have not had the same opportunities that you have had to become familiar with educational technology while serving on the Technology Committee. You are fairly certain that if they had, your colleagues too would embrace technology and use its potential.

Your principal has asked the Technology Committee to formulate a strategic plan for technology for next year. The plan will include all aspects of acquiring and implementing technology in your school. The committee has decided to manage the work by breaking it into tasks to be addressed by subcommittees. You have been asked to chair the subcommittee that will develop the portion of the strategic plan that will address how best to integrate technology into the curriculum and into every teacher's instruction. Your job will be to develop ideas for motivating and inspiring your colleagues as well as to develop suggestions for improving access to technology for your fellow teachers.

Problem

You and your colleagues share a belief in technology's potential in the classroom However, you are concerned about the best way to orient your peers to that potential, train them in various technologies, and encourage them to fully integrate technology into instruction.

After discussions with your principal in which you voiced your concerns about how best to encourage and motivate the other teachers in your school, your principal has offered to set aside $5,000 of the school budget for minigrants to encourage your peers in technology integration. She has also asked the school technology coordinator to work with you to develop and deliver technology training sessions as needed. You and your subcommittee colleagues need to develop a year-long plan, backed by your principal's support and funding, to help your fellow teachers embrace and use the technological resources at their disposal.

What would you do?

Toward a Solution

To approach this problem, it may be best to begin with the standards by which teacher and student technology competencies are measured. Such standards articulate the professional expectations for teachers in terms of technology. They are very often adopted by states and districts and are typically used for benchmarks in strategic plans. ISTE's NETS for teachers and students (http://cnets.iste.org) are the definitive standards, but

other organizations also provide guidelines that are useful measures for determining necessary technology competencies. You may also wish to check the technology standards provided by the National Council for Accreditation of Teacher Education (NCATE, at http://www.ncate.org); International Technology Education Association (ITEA, at http://www.iteawww.org); the Southeast Regional Education Board (SREB, at http://www.sreb.org); the North Central Regional Technology Education Consortium (NCRTEC, at http://www.ncrtec.org/pd); and the National Commission on Teaching and America's Future (NCTAF, at http://www.nctaf.org).

You may also wish to explore school strategic plans available on the web to see how other schools are addressing teacher preparation and technology integration. Further, you may wish to examine training and grant programs at various districts to see how these techniques are working to encourage teachers to use technology.

You and your colleagues will need to meet to brainstorm what your fellow teachers need to know and what is needed to encourage them to fully embrace and integrate technology. Then, you will need to develop a plan that includes initiatives that accomplish this goal.

Problem-Based Learning Activity

With up to four of your peers, review national and/or local standards and decide upon those that you feel should be met by your group's strategic planning efforts. Once you have determined this scope, prepare a plan for teacher training and technology integration that articulates

- Ideas for motivating teachers to embrace and use technology
- A method for awarding the minigrants authorized by your principal
- A training program that should be available to faculty
- Technologies that should be made available to faculty as professional resources
- Technologies that should be made available to faculty for their classrooms

You may use a plan format that is based on the suggestions in your text or one that is similar to a plan you have found on the Internet. It should, however, include goals and strategies that will achieve your technology integration goals. Be prepared to turn in your plan and to present your solution to your class.

CHAPTER 7

Networks and the Internet

This chapter addresses these ISTE National Educational Technology Standards for Teachers:

I. Technology operations and concepts

Teachers demonstrate a sound understanding of technology operations and concepts. Teachers

A. demonstrate introductory knowledge, skills, and understanding of concepts related to technology (as described in the ISTE *National Education Technology Standards for Students*).

B. demonstrate continual growth in technology knowledge and skills to stay abreast of current and emerging technologies.

II. Planning and designing learning environments and experiences

Teachers plan and design effective learning environments and experiences supported by technology. Teachers

A. design developmentally appropriate learning opportunities that apply technology-enhanced instructional strategies to support the diverse needs of learners.

B. apply current research on teaching and learning with technology when planning learning environments and experiences.

C. identify and locate technology resources and evaluate them for accuracy and suitability.

D. plan for the management of technology resources within the context of learning activities.

E. plan strategies to manage student learning in a technology-enhanced environment.

People are inherently social creatures. Being alone and without other human contact, although pleasant for a while, usually turns into a longing to interact. People like—perhaps need—to communicate with each other. It is logical, then, that computers, being a tool in the hands of such social creatures, would also be made to interact. Enabling individual, stand-alone computers and their users to interact with each other is what computer networks are all about. Enabling networks and their users across the globe to interact is what the Internet is all about.

You have learned so far that the teaching and learning process is essentially one of communication. Networked computers are an efficient and effective communication tool. It is very logical, therefore, that networking would prove to be a remarkable and useful educational resource to enable, in sometimes surprising ways, a new format for communication. Networking on a small scale, within a school, or on its largest scale, across the Internet, empowers every teacher and learner who is able to connect to the network with expanded communication capabilities. Networking and the Internet make it possible to seek, find, and communicate information that might otherwise have been impossibly out of reach. These tools make such communication as simple as pointing and clicking a mouse. Networking and the Internet make it possible for teachers and learners to interact with each other globally to discover new perspectives and broaden personal horizons. It is no wonder that so many educators are awed by the wonders and possibilities presented by Internet connections in their classroom or the media center. Most people, after their initial foray into cyberspace, are profoundly affected as they realize the significant social and educational changes heralded by this digital resource.

For educators, networks and the Internet are amazing instructional tools. They make it possible to perform essential management tasks across a school or district. They provide online facilitation and support for the many classroom tasks that are required of every teacher. Perhaps, most important, they offer the potential to add a dimension to instruction that was previously unimagined. In the hands of innovative educators, networks of all sorts, from local to worldwide, become powerful digital tools that can help them build exciting new instructional environments.

This chapter explores educational networking and telecommunication basics, the Internet, and the role of these powerful digital tools in teaching and learning. In Chapter 7, you will

- Explore how networks work

- Examine various telecommunications systems and learn how these systems support network communications

- Investigate educational applications of networking

- Review the history and current structure of the Internet

- Explore the most frequently used Internet resources

Meet Jeffrey Ross

Today's educators know that the Internet can be a valuable teaching tool. However, to use it effectively, they may find that there are obstacles that must be overcome. For some teachers, the obstacle may be their own reluctance to use the Internet because they feel underprepared to integrate it into the classroom. For others, the obstacle may not be reluctance but rather a lack of access. Here, you will meet Jeffrey Ross. He was very interested in using the Internet but first had to find ways to overcome problems of limited access. Here is his story.

MY SCHOOL SETTING

I teach Algebra 1 and Algebra 2 to students in grades 9–12 in my high school. It is an inner-city school located in the southeastern region of the United States, and it serves approximately five hundred students. The school has a magnet program that is centered on agriscience and agribusiness. Because the school is located in a metropolitan area, students from all across the city are able to attend. It turns out that approximately 95 percent of the students live in the neighborhood surrounding the school. Many of the students come from homes that are economically and socially disadvantaged. Although many of the students may be considered to be at-risk, I

have found them to be just as intelligent as the students at my previous school.

My responsibility is to instill a solid foundation of algebraic concepts in the students. In other words, I am responsible for helping my students develop a greater comprehension of and appreciation for mathematics. Our school is on a block schedule, and I normally meet with my students three times each week. Each block lasts for two hours. The good thing about being on a block schedule is that it affords me the opportunity to present my lessons in a manner that addresses all of the learning styles in my classes. The block schedule also renders me the occasion to demonstrate a wide array of examples of the different concepts that I teach. The typical class sizes that I have range from ten to twenty students. My small class size, combined with the block schedule, enables me, at times, to give my students one-on-one instruction.

MY CHALLENGES

Although I find my school a good place to work, there are some challenges that we face. For example, one is finding a way to overcome a very serious absenteeism problem. I believe that part of the reason lies in the fact that we, as educators, do not consistently take the time needed to prepare innovative lessons for our students. The second challenge is to find a way to integrate technology into the curriculum. An especially challenging and unique situation for me was to find a way to integrate the Internet into my lessons.

I spent the first three years of my teaching career at a school in central Florida, where technology was very accessible. I had a computer in my room with Internet access, and there were also four computer labs within the school. When I moved to my current high school, I never envisioned that there would be a shortage of technology. However, there was only one computer lab in the entire high school that was connected to the Internet. I believed from my prior experience that the Internet was exactly what I needed to stimulate the interest of my students.

Teachers around the country are taking courses like the one you are enrolled in to help prepare them to use the potential of the Internet

in their classrooms. However, as you can see from Mr. Ross's experiences so far, the knowledge you gain in college might not be enough when you enter the workplace. Although access to the Internet is increasing all the time, at this point, not all schools offer the level of access you might want. How then will you be able to utilize the Internet in your classroom?

This chapter will provide you with the basic knowledge of networking and the Internet. It is the first step in understanding what you can do to integrate the Internet into your classroom. After completing this chapter, we will return to Mr. Ross's story to find out how he met his challenges.

SOURCE: Interview with Jeffrey Ross conducted by Al P. Mizell. Reprinted by permission of Jeffrey Ross.

What Do I Need to Know about Computer Networks?

When you enter the teaching profession, you will most likely work at a school in which some level of networking is in place. As computers increase in number throughout our nation's schools, those who use them quickly come to realize that connecting them together through networking will make them more productive tools and greatly enhance their capabilities. Significant resources are being allocated to **retrofit** existing schools, that is, prepare them to accommodate computer networks. Given that you are likely to work in an environment that is networked, you might wonder what exactly you need to know to make use of the potential of networks for teaching and learning. The first part of this chapter will introduce computer networking and provide you with the skills you need to use this technology tool. These skills will then serve as the foundation for understanding the worldwide network of networks: the Internet.

Networking Basics

A computer **network** is a collection of computers and peripherals that are connected together so that they can communicate information and share resources. Individual computers connected to a network are usually called network **workstations.** In a network, workstations and sharable peripherals (such as printers) are connected together to a single, more powerful computer called a server. A server provides services to all the machines on the network. A network's server contains the networking software that manages networkwide communication. The server includes one or more very large hard disk drives on which it stores the network management software, common files, and programs that the workstations can share. Together, the server, the workstations and peripherals, and the wiring that connects them constitute a network.

Networks are configured, or arranged, in many different ways to suit the facilities and the number of workstations that need to connect to that particular network. Configurations vary, but all networks have some common elements and terminol-

A network connects a group of computers to a server to share resources and files.

ogy. Every workstation must connect in some way to the server. In wired networks, this is accomplished through a special piece of equipment, called a **hub,** that offers a series of centralized connections. Any workstation or peripheral that is connected to the network becomes a **node** on the network, with all nodes ultimately connected back, through one or more hubs, to their server. Individual workstations, peripherals, and hubs are connected to the server through some type of wiring or, in some cases, through a wireless communication channel. This relationship is illustrated in Figure 7.1.

In a typical school, workstations and a **server** are usually wired together by using a type of cable similar to telephone wire. The wiring is strung from the server, often above ceilings, to each classroom, where a single network wire must be dropped for every computer in the room. Each network wire, in turn, connects to a network card that must be installed in each computer that is to be connected to the network.

Often, when schools are retrofitted, because of the cost of pulling network wire through existing ceilings and walls, only one or two drops are made to a classroom. In such cases, one drop is often designed to connect a teacher workstation to the school network. A second drop in a classroom would provide for one other workstation to be connected for student use. Deciding how to use available network connections and arranging classroom space around them can be a challenge. As you learned in previous chapters, it is important to create a physical classroom environment that meets diverse learner needs. The addition of networked workstations can add further complexity to the classroom arrangement. You will need to look for the network connection point(s) in the classroom in which you will be teaching and plan your teaching and learning space accordingly.

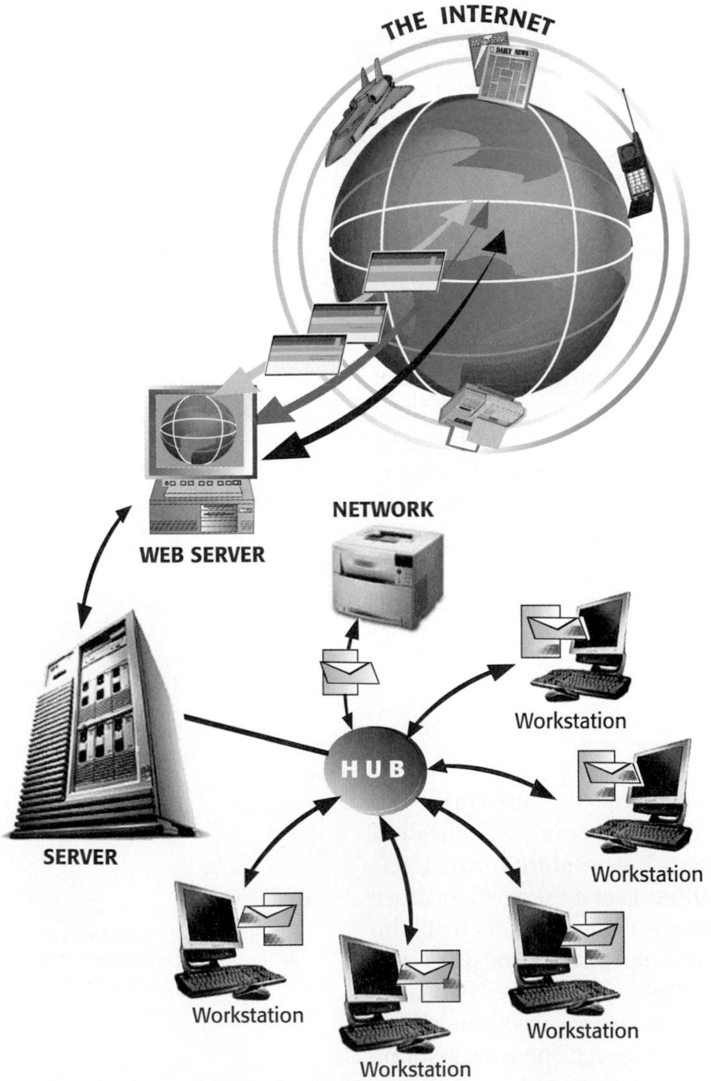

One alternative to wiring schools and classrooms that is rapidly gaining popularity is wireless networking technology. In a **wireless network,** information is transmitted via wireless technology rather than across wires. In a school, a wireless network may require that transmitters be strategically placed in rooms and across the campus to receive and transmit data from computers. This type of wireless technology may require line-of-sight transmission; that is, a computer on the wireless network and a transmitter must be able to "see" each other without walls or buildings blocking the transmissions. With radio wave wireless technology, line-of-sight issues are not relevant. The radio waves are broadcast and picked up by specialized equipment and routed to computers equipped with receiver kits. Regardless of the type of wireless technology used, this approach to networking has several advantages for schools. First, wireless networking eliminates much of the retrofitting cost. Although some retrofitting may still be required, it is less work than what is necessary for wired networks. The cost saving may enable the purchase of additional computers for classroom use. Second, a wireless network makes it easier to create a flexible learning environment that fully integrates networked resources. Classrooms no

Figure 7.1
Networks Share Hardware and Software Resources
Networks make communication and sharing resources possible.

longer have to set up workstations according to where network connections are available. Additionally, with the use of notebook and handheld computers that are equipped for wireless networking, a classroom could conceivably have a bank of computers available for students to take to their desks for individual or group research. The downside of wireless networks is the cost of the technology itself and also some security issues typical of wireless networks. As the cost falls, however, and network technology improves, wireless networking may well become the strategy of choice for more schools.

Regardless of the networking technology selected, individual classrooms with multiple computers can be networked, computer labs can be networked, schools can be networked, and entire districts can share resources across a network. Smaller networks that connect machines in local areas, such as a classroom or school, are called **local area networks (LANs).** Networks that connect machines across a wide area, such as all of the schools in a district or all of the districts in a state, are called **wide area networks (WANs).** The interconnectivity of the workstations on both types of these networks and the potential for connecting these networks to each other are what make possible our modern-day ability to communicate instantly.

ON THE WEB! 7.1
How to Optimize the Learning Environment in a Networked Classroom

Local area networks (LANs) serve local areas and wide area networks (WANs) serve large areas.

Network Connectivity, Communications, and Security

Using a workstation located in a single classroom to access or provide data to other workstations creates a potentially powerful communication scenario. Because the teaching and learning process is, at its core, a communication process, networks have promise as powerful teaching and learning tools but to communicate via networks for teaching and learning, some challenges must be addressed and overcome. Although it is usually not a teacher's responsibility to respond to these challenges alone, it is useful to understand how they affect this technology.

The first challenge in networking communications is to ensure that the computers linked via networks understand each other. Workstations on a single network and those linked to other networks all need to "speak the same language." This common, standardized communication format is called a **protocol.** Networks that use the same protocol, regardless of the type of equipment or network software they use, are able to communicate precisely with each other and share agreed-on data. Network software establishes consistent protocols among workstations on a LAN. For WAN communications and for communication across the Internet, similarly consistent protocols must be established.

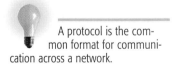

A protocol is the common format for communication across a network.

A second challenge that must be addressed is the many different sizes of the files of information being sent across a network. You learned in Chapter 3 that a single character of information is roughly equal to one byte of data. Large text files are measured in thousands of bytes or kilobytes. But other files, such as graphic, photo, video, and audio files, can be made up of multiple megabytes of data each. To better understand the impact of file sizes in networking, imagine a network wire as a roadway. On that electronic roadway, some files are of a size analogous to subcompact cars, while others are more like tractor-trailer trucks. Furthermore, some types of wiring offer a roadway the size of an alley, while others offer a roadway the size of a ten-lane superhighway. The challenge for communication occurs when you try to fit a large "tractor-trailer truck" of data through an "alley"-sized network wire. It can be done, but the going is alarmingly slow. Servers manage such feats by breaking the data into small units, or **packets,** and sending it through one packet at a time. The network software then reassembles the data at the other end into its original form. This transmission process can take considerable time with large, complex files.

Figure 7.2
Bandwidth
Different transmission media offer different speed and capacity for data transmission, just as physical highways provide different capacities for automobile traffic.

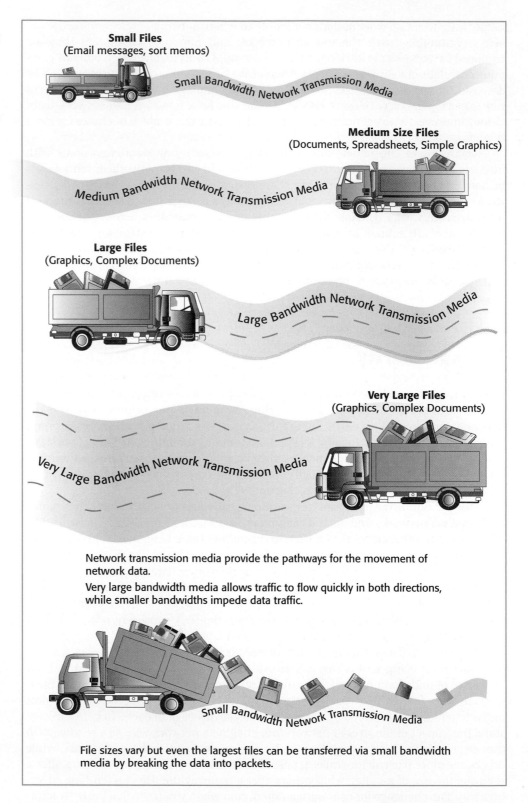

Small Files
(Email messages, sort memos)

Small Bandwidth Network Transmission Media

Medium Size Files
(Documents, Spreadsheets, Simple Graphics)

Medium Bandwidth Network Transmission Media

Large Files
(Graphics, Complex Documents)

Large Bandwidth Network Transmission Media

Very Large Files
(Graphics, Complex Documents)

Very Large Bandwidth Network Transmission Media

Network transmission media provide the pathways for the movement of network data.

Very large bandwidth media allows traffic to flow quickly in both directions, while smaller bandwidths impede data traffic.

Small Bandwidth Network Transmission Media

File sizes vary but even the largest files can be transferred via small bandwidth media by breaking the data into packets.

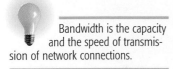

Bandwidth is the capacity and the speed of transmission of network connections.

In network terms, the carrying capacity (size of the roadway) of the transmission media for sending information is called its **bandwidth.** The speed at which the network can transmit data is measured in the number of bits that can be sent per second. The larger the bandwidth and greater the speed of the transmission media, the faster the data flows across it, even if the data includes large files. As a network-using educator, you need to be aware of the capabilities of the network you are going to use so that you can plan appropriately. If you want to share the digital or scanned photographs your class took on their last field trip with their "keypals" at another school, you need to discover how long that process will take before scheduling it into a lesson. If you want to add audio components to a PowerPoint presentation for use in all sixth-grade classes via the network, you need to be aware of a potential delay caused by the transmission of large audio files. Although you, as an educator, do not need to be able to create a network, it is important to be a well-versed consumer with regard to the network you use. Table 7.1 lists some of the key issues and how they affect teachers.

A final challenge when using a network for teaching and learning is the question of data privacy and security. For educators, ensuring that students do their own work and that their efforts are private is essential. If networks allow users to share files and resources, how can a teacher ensure the security of each student's work? Furthermore, how can a teacher's files be securely segregated from student files? This challenge is addressed by the network software and the network support staff through the use of security measures inherent in the system. User security on a network is provided through a system of user names (also called login names) and **passwords.** Even though all of the computers in any given room may be physically capable of providing access to the network, such access is granted only when the network recognizes that an authorized user is at a computer. Network software provides the capability for every individual who uses the network to have his or her own unique user or login name. Every user also selects a personal password that must be entered along with the user name. This second level of security is necessary because users may share their logins with other network users for communications. Thus, even if an individual's authorized login name is known, the network will not allow access to that person's files without the correct password as well.

Every network user is given access to some or all of the files and programs stored on the server's hard drive(s), as shown in Figure 7.3. This assigned ability to access specific files and resources is called the user's rights or privileges. When creating user accounts, the network administrator issues specific rights to every account, thus ensuring that no account has access to resources or files that are inappropriate for that user. Student network users therefore can access only files and resources for which they have been given rights. These restricted rights typically allow them only to use

Log-in names and passwords are features that help ensure network security.

TABLE 7.1   USING A NETWORK IN TEACHING AND LEARNING

To use networking in teaching and learning, you need to be aware of some networking parameters. Review this table and then ask a network administrator what he or she thinks you should know about each issue to use a network effectively.

Issue	Explanation	Teaching Responsibility
PROTOCOLS	Networks need to use a common method of communication, called a protocol, so that all network components understand each other.	Ensure that network settings on classroom machines are not changed accidentally.
BANDWIDTH	Network communications channels vary in size and speed, called bandwidth. Smaller channels take more time to communicate large files such as sound or audio files.	Be aware of the bandwidth you have available when sending and receiving network files; test real-time instructional uses of the network before using them in your class.
SECURITY	Networks limit access to only those users identified as having the right to use the network. This is accomplished through a login name and password.	Be sure to keep logins and passwords confidential; teach students about the reasons for network security and how to protect their accounts.
PRIVACY	Some areas of a network are public and accessible by all users. Data that should be confidential should not be posted in these areas.	Properly place all student data within the network; get written permission from parents before sharing student information or posting pictures.

Figure 7.3
Individual User Accounts on a Network
Every account includes a user profile that contains a login name, password, and the rights that individual user has to access files and move about the network.

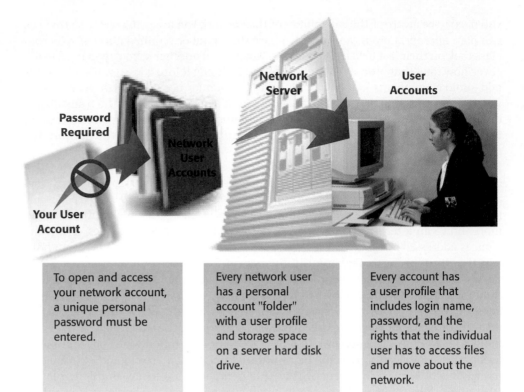

To open and access your network account, a unique personal password must be entered.

Every network user has a personal account "folder" with a user profile and storage space on a server hard disk drive.

Every account has a user profile that includes login name, password, and the rights that the individual user has to access files and move about the network.

Firewalls prevent unauthorized access to data and files from outside the network.

ON THE WEB! 7.2
What Do Schools Do to Make Their Networks Secure?

particular software and to access the files that they created themselves or that were created for them by their teacher. Teachers, with the help of the network administrator, can create and store **public files** that all students can access. This system of user names, passwords, and assigned rights ensures a high degree of security for most users. Of course, people with advanced computer skills can sometimes break through the security and hack into a network. But cautious network administrators can implement and monitor various levels of roadblocks, called **firewalls,** to keep hackers out of their networks and keep your data safe.

Sharing and Communicating via a Network

Networks enable and support communication and the sharing of resources in many ways. Communications are enhanced through a variety of tools, including the most familiar of them, electronic mail. Hardware and software resources on the server and across the network can be shared via the coordination offered by the network software. For teachers looking to maximize their computing capabilities while minimizing costs, networks offer many advantages. These are summarized in Table 7.2 and are described in more detail in the following sections.

Networked Programs

Resource sharing is one of the principal advantages of networking. Programs can be installed on the server and made available via the network to all workstations. This process can save the time and labor that would otherwise have been necessary to install identical programs on every machine. In such situations, the programs reside on the server's hard disk, and the workstations run the software from there through the network. This leaves the local workstation's drives available for file storage or for nonnetwork software. Other network scenarios use workstation hard drives to store

TABLE 7.2   NETWORK FEATURES AND APPLICATIONS

Network Feature	Use	Classroom Application
SHARED HARDWARE	Costly hardware can be shared by many workstations.	One printer, scanner, or other peripheral can be shared by all computers in the classroom.
SHARED SOFTWARE	Programs can reside on the server or be pushed to individual machines to save space, maintenance, and technical-support time.	Classroom software is simple and quick to install, upgrade, or maintain in a single process via the server.
DATA SHARING	Files and folders can be made accessible to all network users or can be tagged for use by specific users.	Class handouts and other content files can be made available to all or some students for copying or printing.
NETWORK TOOLS	**Administrative:** Groupware offers common organizing tools and calendars across the network. **Academic:** Network monitoring and tracking methods to ensure appropriate use of technology.	Class calendar and address book are simple to maintain and access from anywhere in school; teacher can monitor all students' activity while they are logged in to the network.
COMMUNICATIONS	Electronic mail provides all users the ability to communicate with each other or groups and to send attachment files along with messages.	Students can communicate with peers and their teacher; electronic pen pal (e-pal) projects can be initiated.

some or all elements of common network software. In such cases, the network can be used to "push" (copy) the software from the server to the workstations' hard drives to update or maintain it. In either scenario, sharing programs makes their update and maintenance easier and more efficient.

Another advantage of shared networked software resources is that such an arrangement may save software acquisition dollars as well as worker resources. Many software vendors provide discounts for network versions of software that can be used on all machines in the network. Such network **site licenses** allow the use of a program on any machine on the network at a defined site, usually at a substantial savings over the purchase of multiple copies of the same software for use on individual computers. When you work in a networked environment and you are considering acquisition of software that may benefit others at your school, you should explore the costs of a networked version of the program you desire. You may find that, for close to the purchase price of a few individual copies, you can buy a site license for everyone at your school.

 Site licenses offer discounts across a school.

A final advantage for sharing programs via a network relates to the support that all software eventually needs. With a network, when software upgrades become available, the support staff need only upgrade the software on the server to make the upgrade available to each workstation, rather than having to visit and upgrade every individual machine at a school. Similarly, if problems arise with any software, they are resolved at the more centralized server level, a much faster support process. For a busy teacher, waiting for a "house call" from the support staff to fix a problem with a single computer's unique software is likely to take much longer than reporting to the network administrator a network problem that can be simultaneously corrected for all workstations via the server.

Although server-based software has these support advantages, there are some disadvantages. Because workstations rely on the server's software, should any problems occur with software on the server or with the server itself, all workstations will be unable to use the programs. For that reason, many networks have redundant systems such as backup servers in place to ensure that there is no interruption of service. Other networks keep redundant backup disks of all server programs and data so that the administrator can quickly reinstall files and restore services if a problem occurs. Still other networks may store backup copies of critical software programs on the hard drives of the individual workstations as a redundancy. In a classroom that has integrated network resources into instruction, it is important to be aware of your network's backup system and to develop your own backup plan in case the network or a shared program is not accessible when you need it. Although such situations are rare, it is a good idea to anticipate them and discuss the options with the network administrator at your school.

A final concern with shared programs results from the diversity of computer equipment that is found at a typical school. All too often, a school does not have sufficient resources to replace all of its hardware and software on a regular basis. Over time, this means that a classroom may end up with a mix of both older and newer machines or even machines of different types. Such diversity can mean that some classroom or media center computers are not capable of being networked or, if networkable, of running the server's up-to-date software. As you incorporate network resources into your lesson plans, it is important that you test your classroom computers to be sure that they will work as expected. Pretesting your equipment will give you the opportunity to discuss network conflicts and possible solutions with the school's technology-support staff before you implement computer-supported lessons.

Hardware diversity on a network may conflict with some software.

Shared Data

Using programs across a network is just one of the ways networked workstations can share resources. Of equal importance is the ability to share data and other files. Network servers are usually configured with ample storage that can be used in several different ways depending on the needs of the users of that network system. Typically, each user is given a small network storage area associated with his or her user name

Figure 7.4
Classroom Shared Resources
Public storage areas offer space to make shared classroom resources available to students.

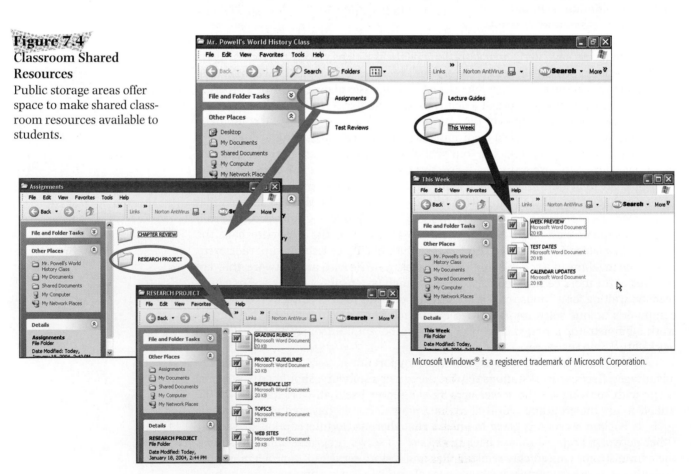

Microsoft Windows® is a registered trademark of Microsoft Corporation.

and on which he or she can store personal data. Such user storage areas are private to the extent that they can be accessed only by using both the user name and password of the individual user. The advantage of user storage areas on a network is that the user can go to any workstation, regardless of its location, and still be able to access the files in his or her user space stored on the server. For teachers, this can mean that they may access their class files from their networked classroom computer, from a workstation in a networked computer lab, or from a networked workstation in the faculty workroom. For students, this means that they can work on an interdisciplinary assignment while in the media center or in different subject-area classrooms. This ease of accessibility to files is a major advantage of user storage on a network server. The disadvantage is the quantity of hard disk storage that the network server needs to give each user. Nevertheless, the relatively low cost of expanding disk storage space and the significant benefit of easy access usually make this option worth the investment.

File sharing is a major advantage of networks.

A network can also have public storage areas from which all users or only designated users can retrieve data. Such areas are typically read-only; that is, a user can read all files in the public area but is unable to save files there. Teachers can use designated public storage areas to store presentation, text, graphic, audio, and video files for their students' use. Because students can only read data from such public spaces and not write to those spaces, the files cannot be changed. Teachers can post assignments, worksheets, presentations, or other instructional materials without concern as to loss or alteration. To complete assignments, students can access and view these files and may even save copies of the data to their own disks. This limited public access to academic files for your students makes it simple to keep homework activities continuously available for reprinting without having to handle substantial numbers of paper copies. Students who have missed a class or who need a second copy of an assignment can easily print one for themselves (see Figure 7.4).

Shared Administrative Tools

Most network software provides a series of **administrative tools** that are shared by all network users. Such **groupware,** as it is sometimes called, usually provides, at minimum, a common calendar, address book, and facilities reservation list. Using this type of shared tool, a busy educator who wishes to set up a meeting with other teachers on the network can have the server automatically poll all the teachers' electronic calendars to find a free common meeting time. If a teacher wishes to reserve a special classroom space for his or her class, the common facilities reservation list on the network can be automatically checked for open dates for that space. Although these time-saving tools vary with the network system installed, most network software provides abundant groupware options. You should explore your school's network to see which is available for your use.

ON THE WEB! 7.3
Using Groupware

Shared Academic Tools

In addition to providing the foundation technology for network-based instructional software, such as the integrated learning systems you learned about in Chapter 6, networks can offer important **academic tools.** Some network software enables the teacher to monitor activity on, and take control of, student workstations in the classroom or media center. This type of software allows the teacher to observe student progress by "tuning in" to an individual workstation and monitoring the activity on the screen. It also allows the teacher to take over one or more workstations to provide a demonstration or instruction. Finally, it allows the teacher to broadcast the images on any one workstation's monitor to all other workstations to share a student's work. Although often used in computer lab settings, this software is also useful in classrooms and media centers with multiple student workstations.

ON THE WEB! 7.4
Network Academic Tools

IN THE CLASSROOM

The More We Get Together: School Networks

Coming up with the best of both worlds, the Frederick County Public Schools in Virginia have a school network, sometimes called an intranet, that has links to the Internet. Rod Carnill points out that the two "nets" complement each other. The intranet is especially helpful to teachers because students' work and identifiable photographs, special projects, and events at school can be shown without having to obtain permission in the form of releases. The intranet, he relates, "uses a collection of HTML files in a single folder on the school's web server" and is, at the same time, "a self-created portal for Internet use." The portal provides guided access to the Internet for students to use in completing research and other coursework and also permits in-house file sharing.

Progressive schools like Tampa Catholic High School in the Diocese of St. Petersburg, Tampa, Florida, have found many ways to make their schools' intranets perform services for the teachers and administrators alike. Kevin Yarnell, the technology director, wrote in *School Executive* of some of these methods that simplify and improve the overall operating infrastructure of the school. When scheduling tests, teachers can check to see what other testing is being done on the same day. Student data—birthdays, clubs, athletics, and honors—and other information can be stored in a database on the intranet. Announcements and even personal communications to and from school personnel can be posted. School records and reports can be archived in a database for that purpose. Student work, if electronic, can also be kept on the site. The limited access to the intranet makes it invaluable to schools, whether it is a small site affecting only one or a few classrooms or a large site that connects an entire school district, for many school-related communications are confidential legally and ethically.

SOURCES: Integration via a browser-based intranet. 2002. Retrieved June 11, 2003, from http://www.nps.k12.va.us/infodiv/it/techconf/integbrw.htm; K. Yarnell. 2002. Intranets: Repositories of school data. *School Executive* (September/October), 39 (1), 28.

Shared Hardware

Networks enable sharing of hardware resources.

Software sharing is not the only type of resource sharing made possible by a network. Hardware sharing is another advantage of school networking. In a classroom or media center that is configured only with stand-alone computers, each machine needs its own printer plugged into its parallel port to be able to print. In a networked scenario, a single printer can be used by all workstations in the vicinity. This can be done either by attaching a networkable printer as an independent network node or by attaching a printer to one of the workstations on the network. In either configuration, the printer hardware is then available to be shared by all local network workstations. Using this arrangement makes it possible to maximize the use of printer resources.

Communicating via Email

Electronic mail (**email**) is the key communication tool provided in a networked environment. Email in the virtual world of networking works in a manner similar to post office boxes in the physical world. When a login name is assigned to a network user, that same login name is used to create an electronic mailbox. This is similar to assigning a post office box to an individual post office customer. Just as mail can be delivered to your post office box at any time, to be picked up by you at your convenience, so too can electronic mail be delivered to your electronic mailbox. Email addressed to your login name may be received by the server from one of the network users and then directed to your electronic mailbox, where it will be stored until you pick it up. Once you review your stored email, you can choose to delete it or save it, just as you might throw away or keep mail that has been delivered to your real-world post office box. You may even decide to forward email to other network users or to leave it in your mailbox for later disposition. Figure 7.5 summarizes some of the key features most email systems provide.

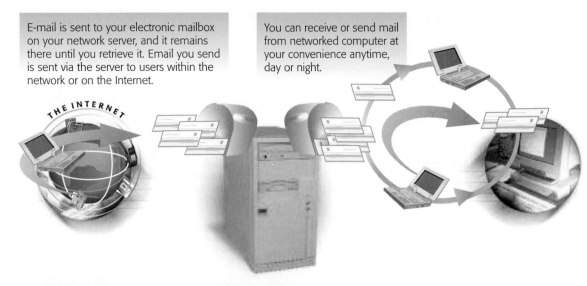

E-mail is sent to your electronic mailbox on your network server, and it remains there until you retrieve it. Email you send is sent via the server to users within the network or on the Internet.

You can receive or send mail from networked computer at your convenience anytime, day or night.

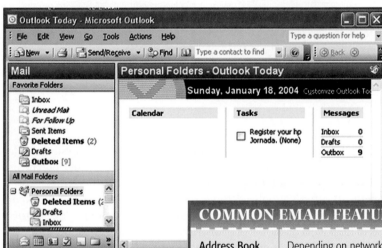

Microsoft Outlook 2000® is a registered trademark of Microsoft Corporation.

COMMON EMAIL FEATURES AND THEIR APPLICATION

Address Book	Depending on network configuration, stores frequently used email addresses and/or email addresses of all network users
To, Cc, and Bcc Options	Allow you to address your email to one or more email addresses, send a "Carbon copy" to others, and/or send a "Blind carbon copy" (send a copy without other recipients knowing)
Subject Line	Brief description of the contents of the message
Reply to Sender(s)	One-click feature that allows you to automatically address a reply email to the sender and/or to all on the sender's original recipients list
Forward to Others	One-click feature that allows you to automatically send the email message to another party or parties
Attach File	Allows you to add files to the email and send them along with the message
Save Email	Lets you save read email to a disk for later access
Print Email	Lets you print email you have received

Figure 7.5
Understanding Email
Electronic mail offers network users a powerful communication tool.

TABLE 7.3 USING ELECTRONIC MAIL IN TEACHING AND LEARNING

Application	Use	Benefits
ASSIGNMENT TRANSMISSION	Assigned activities are emailed to teacher, may be corrected and emailed back for revision.	Activities remain soft copy until final revision; absent students can keep up with assignments; copies can be sent to parents.
CLASS DISCUSSIONS	Discussion question is asked by teacher and mailed to the discussion group list; responses are sent to all group members.	Responses can be thoughtful and delivered at students' own pace; allows shy students to respond; student responses are more carefully prepared when shared; responses can be tracked for review and grading.
ELECTRONIC KEYPALS	Students are assigned pals in other classes (at the same school or other schools in the district, state, or country) to communicate with for a given assignment.	Communication with others provides for social learning opportunities and multicultural exchange; information exchanged broadens data as compared to what individuals may have gathered; student responses are more carefully prepared when shared.
COMMUNICATION: Student–Student Student–Teacher Teacher–Parent	Students can email among group members to complete group activities; teacher and students can exchange information or ask questions outside of class time; teacher and parent can communicate outside school hours about student progress.	Email participants can communicate privately or publicly with other concerned parties regarding student progress or with questions or concerns about classroom activities or homework.

Email operates like a virtual post office box.

ON THE WEB! 7.5

How to Use Email to Enhance Instruction

Schoolwide and districtwide email offers exciting communication possibilities for students and for teachers, some of which are shown in Table 7.3. Students can use email to become "keypals" or "e-buddies" with students in other classes within a school or with students at other schools within a district. Keypals can communicate socially or share written assignments for feedback. Older students can be "e-mentors" to younger students to help with grade-level transitions or to help on specific activities. Opening the lines of communication among students makes many innovative activities possible. Because email is asynchronous communication, that is, communication that can occur at different times convenient to the participants, student schedules do not impede communications.

Teacher use of email makes it possible to share ideas and lesson plans and to discuss concerns with colleagues across the school or district. Teachers often have very different schedules. If they do not have the same planning periods, it can be difficult to meet face-to-face with peers. Email provides an alternative way to interact with colleagues, share information, and get quick responses. Once accustomed to using email, few teachers would be willing to give it up.

If the school server can receive email from outside the network, such as through the Internet, your email account can also provide you with a powerful opportunity to establish links to parents. Many parents work outside the home, and communicating with them during your work hours by phone may be difficult. Printed notices carried by students might or might not make it home to parents. Even so, if you provide your email address to parents and if they too have email accounts, either personally through their Internet provider or through another source, you can establish a direct and personal communication link with them. This gives both you and your students' parents a convenient way to establish a partnership and open lines of communication for the benefit of the children in your charge. Email can be an important bridge to many homes.

Expanding Connectivity through Telecommunication

So far, you have learned about school and district networks that are wired together to share resources and enable communications. However, what about the many stand-alone computers in people's homes or businesses? Given that they do not have other computers in the immediate vicinity to connect to, how can these machines take advantage of network capabilities?

To connect stand-alone computers in one location to a network server in another location, telecommunication technologies are necessary. **Telecommunication** is essentially electronic communication between computers via telephone lines. In this type of communication scenario, computers are not directly wired together, as they are in a LAN; phone lines are used in lieu of network wiring. Because computers work with digital signals, and telephone wires were originally designed to transmit only analog (voice) signals, some adaptation is necessary. Additional equipment must be added to both ends of the communication circuit—that is, to both the home computer and the network server—to make it possible for a telecommunication connection to take place.

Telecommunication Technologies

Modems

Computers send and receive digital signals. Telephone lines transmit analog signals. For a computer to use telephone lines to send information, it must alter, or modulate, its signals into a form that is transmittable by phone lines. The computer peripheral designed to MOdulate a computer's signal so that it can be transmitted across a phone line and then to DEModulate a responding computer signal received via a phone line is called a MODEM. **Modems** are essentially translating devices. They translate computer output into a format that is transmittable via telephone lines and then translate signals that come across phone lines back into a format that the computer can understand, as illustrated in Figure 7.6.

Modems translate digital and analog signals back and forth.

Modems provide only the hardware solution that makes the communication possible. Telecommunications software is also necessary to give the hardware the instruc-

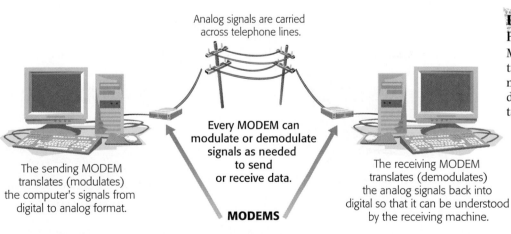

Analog signals are carried across telephone lines.

Every MODEM can modulate or demodulate signals as needed to send or receive data.

MODEMS

The sending MODEM translates (modulates) the computer's signals from digital to analog format.

The receiving MODEM translates (demodulates) the analog signals back into digital so that it can be understood by the receiving machine.

Figure 7.6
How Modems Work
Modems enable communication across phone lines. Every modem can modulate or demodulate signals as needed to send or receive data.

tions necessary to make the computer and modem work together to establish a telecommunications link. Typically, such software is packaged with the modem for which it was programmed or provided by telecommunications services you subscribe to.

When two computers at different locations each have modems that are attached and powered up and have telecommunications programs running, the two computers can communicate directly via the computer–modem–phone line connection. To accomplish this direct telecommunication link, one computer uses its telecommunications software to dial the telephone number of a phone line connected to another computer. The other computer, with modem on and its own telecommunications program running, literally answers the call and responds with a carrier signal, a high-pitched sound. The calling computer responds with a signal of its own, and the two connect. This is the process known as **handshaking.** This direct link can then be used to communicate information directly between the two participating computers.

▌ Home-to-Network Connections

If a classroom workstation can connect to other computers relatively easily via the school network, is it also possible to connect a home computer with a modem to the school network and beyond? Can you connect to your school's network to check your email from your house after school or on weekends? The answer is yes but with some limitations.

If you have a home computer, modem, phone line, and telecommunications software, your home computer can call your network modem's phone number. If your network accepts incoming calls, it will respond and establish a link to your machine. Once a connection is established, the network software will ask that you enter your login name and your password. When it is recognized as valid, you will be able to work with your network just as you would when logging in from your classroom workstation.

Even so, you might find that the network responds sluggishly and that your requests take excessive amounts of time to fulfill. This is often the case in working with a network via phone lines. Network wiring usually has sufficient bandwidth and speed to accommodate workstation requests with responsiveness. However, analog phone

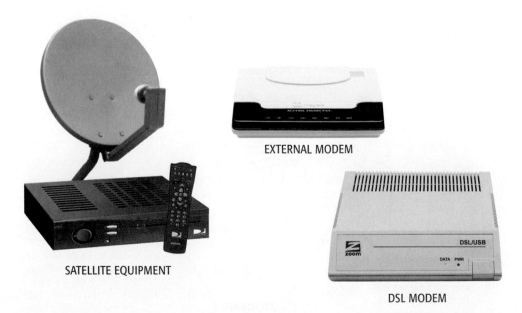

EXTERNAL MODEM

SATELLITE EQUIPMENT

DSL/USB

DSL MODEM

Modems and other connectivity hardware make it possible for computers to communicate.

lines do not have broad bandwidth, nor are they fast, so transmissions may bog down, resulting in slow responses to user requests.

Phone companies, aware of consumers' desire for better responses via phone lines, have made higher-speed digital phone lines available in many areas. **Digital Subscriber Line (DSL)** lines, a high-speed option for home users, provide speeds up to thirty times faster than a standard phone line. DSL lines offer both voice and digital communications on a single line, thus eliminating the need for two phone lines at your home, one for voice and another for data.

Another type of high-speed connection uses cable television lines. Some cable TV companies provide digital access via the lines that have already been installed for television. With the addition of a specialized modem known as a **cable modem,** home users can get access speeds potentially faster than a DSL. Although not available in all areas of the country, this alternative is fast becoming a powerful option for home users.

A final connectivity alternative that is becoming more widely available is wireless satellite access. Companies offering TV via satellite, such as Direct TV, also have the bandwidth and capability to offer access to networks that in turn connect to the Internet. Just as cable TV wiring provides faster transmission and greater capacity than phone lines, so too does the technology by which companies provide satellite television transmissions. Of course, to use this technology, you must first have the necessary dish to receive the transmission and subscribe to the service that sends the transmission via satellite.

DSL lines offer faster transmission speeds.

The Internet: Connecting Networks to Networks across the Globe

By this point, you should be beginning to see the value of connecting a stand-alone computer to the resources available through a network. Now what if you could connect that same stand-alone computer to the resources available on millions of networks across the globe? If those networks allowed you to connect to them and provided you with guest rights to all or some of their resources, you could access huge amounts of information! That is the scope of the international network of networks known collectively as the **Internet** or simply the Net (see Figure 7.7 on page 230).

The Internet is actually made up of millions of individual machines and networks that have agreed to connect, provide resources to each other, and share data. Initially, just a few select military and university networks connected, primarily for the purposes of research and national security. Since its early beginnings of just a handful of connected sites, however, the Internet has grown to an estimated 200 million host computers distributing information across the globe, and it is still growing! A common protocol called **TCP/IP** (transmission control protocol/Internet protocol) is used so that communications between these diverse computers can be understood. Internet users, whose numbers are, at the time of this writing, estimated to exceed 600 million around the world and still growing each month, can connect, via their school or business networks or from home via modem to the computers within this vast network of networks. Any single computer can, by connecting to the Internet, access an almost unimaginable wealth of information. For educators, the potential to share our world's collective knowledge base with our students is staggering.

But how does such an immense array of information become manageable and usable for a busy teacher? Even if you can access the Internet, how can you put it to work to enhance teaching and learning? How can we empower our students to use the Internet for their own academic and personal growth? To answer these questions, educators must first become familiar with the tools that the Internet and Internet applications provide to make its content accessible and responsive to users.

Millions of interconnected networks form the Internet.

ON THE WEB! 7.6
The Evolution of the Internet

Figure 7.7
The Internet
The Internet is a global network of networks connecting hundreds of millions of users to each other and to worldwide resources.

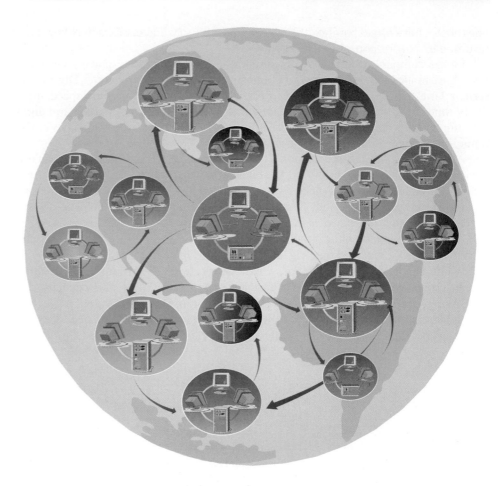

Internet Tools and Services

As the Internet has developed, a variety of tools and services have become available for our use. Some services are provided free to all Internet users. Others are offered as a part of a membership package when you subscribe to an Internet service. Still others are available for a subscription fee. To use the Internet effectively, it is important to be aware of the many types of tools and services available and how best to evaluate and select those you might want to use.

Internet Service Providers

The first step in using the Internet is accessing and connecting to it. If you are using your school network, the network itself has been connected to the Internet, and you can use that connection as an authorized network user. However, if you are connecting to the Internet from a home computer, you need first to connect your home computer to a network that is connected to the Internet to access the Net's resources. Special networks that have been created to provide home and business computers a way to connect to the Internet are called **Internet service providers,** or **ISPs.**

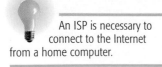 An ISP is necessary to connect to the Internet from a home computer.

ISPs are companies that provide home users with access to the Internet through their own network connections and communications software. Every ISP provides a series of phone numbers that home computers can dial via modem to attach to the ISP's computer. Most ISPs charge a service fee (typically around $20 per month) for providing Internet access, but if connecting to an ISP requires a long-distance call, those long-distance charges will cost the user extra money that is typically paid to the user's long-distance phone service provider. A few half-hour-long "surfs" on the Internet across a long-distance line can end up being an expensive experience.

For the monthly ISP service fee, some large providers include a variety of services beyond simple access (see Table 7.4). Most offer email, and some offer extensive phone support. Some of the largest providers, sometimes called online services, include exclusive member services as a part of the subscription package. Different providers vary as much in the services they provide as they do in monthly charges.

Internet-Based Communications

Email

In addition to accessing a worldwide bank of information, the Internet offers some remarkable communication tools. These tools can offer both **synchronous** (same-time) and **asynchronous** (time-shifted) **communications** over the Internet. Because of their ability to link students to other students in classrooms across the globe, most of these tools offer fascinating educational applications. By far the most popular asynchronous communication tool is electronic mail.

Email is the primary communications tool on networks and on the Internet.

TABLE 7.4   COMMON SERVICES PROVIDED BY INTERNET SERVICE PROVIDERS

ISP Service	Explanation
INTERNET ACCESS	An ISP offers you a way to connect your home or classroom computer to the Internet through its Internet server.
COMMUNICATIONS PROGRAM	ISPs provide a customized communications program that works with your modem and connects to the ISP's network. This program provides a list of local phone numbers that you can call to connect to the ISP.
BROWSER	ISP software packages may include a browser (usually Netscape Navigator or Microsoft Internet Explorer) to use on the Internet. Some ISPs (such as America Online) offer customized browsers adapted for their service.
EMAIL	Most ISPs provide email services to users. However, the size of a user's mailbox may differ from ISP to ISP. Small electronic mailboxes may fill quickly, especially when receiving attachments, and cause your email to bounce back to the sender.
TECHNICAL SUPPORT	All ISPs provide technical support when you have problems on their networks; however, you may experience long telephone wait times. User satisfaction surveys may give you an idea of the level of support from an ISP.
CHAT ROOMS	Some ISPs provide chat programs as a part of their service packages. Chats may be public or private and may include only those within the ISP network, so investigating chat options of an ISP is important if this is a critical tool.
INSTANT MESSAGING	Instant messaging services allow you to create a one-to-one chat with Internet users outside the ISP network. Nonnetwork users may need to download and install the free ISP chat software to communicate with you.
CONFERENCING	Some ISPs provide conferencing software that allows you to create and moderate an ongoing discussion group via the ISP services.
NEWSREADER	Most ISPs provide a newsreader, software that lets you read and send data to public groups dedicated to a single topic.
PERSONAL WEB SPACE	Some ISPs offer web space, web tutorials, and web authoring tools as a part of their service. As with electronic mailboxes, web space size varies with ISP; so if you plan to create a robust web site, you will want to determine if the ISP offers sufficient space.
OTHER SERVICES	ISPs offer a variety of unique services, from online malls to custom search engines to personalized, responsive home pages. It is a good idea to investigate these services to determine if they will be useful for you.

Internet email works similarly to network email, which we discussed earlier in this chapter. Like network email, Internet email provides users with a way to establish one-to-one communications; but with Internet email, electronic messages are not bound to a single network. Internet email can be sent and received across the many networks attached to the Internet. With Internet email, each Internet user is given a login name and password. That same login name is thereafter used to designate the user's email account, including the email storage space assigned to that user. You can send and receive email via your ISP or school email account. Because Internet email can be sent to any email server available on any network that is attached to the Net, you need to add some information to your assigned email name to give it more specificity. For example, if your user name is bsmith and your ISP account is with a company called bignet.com, your email address would be bsmith@bignet.com. The @ symbol that connects your user name to the name of the web server on which your email account is located enables electronic mail that is addressed to you to travel to its intended location. Similarly, to send email to colleagues via the Internet, you will need to know their full email addresses.

Some first-time users of the Internet get Internet email addresses confused with URLs. **URLs** are designations for specific locations on the World Wide Web. The World Wide Web and its relationship to the Internet are more fully discussed in Chapter 8; suffice it to say at this point that while they may have some elements in common, they are in fact very different. Email addresses designate individual users' electronic mailboxes on the Internet. Email addresses always consist of the user name, the @ symbol, and the location where the electronic mailbox is stored.

To read and send email, you will need email software, which is typically provided by your school network or ISP. Email software features typically include an address book to store frequently used email addresses and a location at the top of each email screen in which you can enter the email address of the person to whom you wish to send the email. Another area at the top of each email screen allows you to enter the email address of others to whom you wish to send a "carbon copy" of that email.

Figure 7.8
Electronic Mail Software
Most email programs share common features.

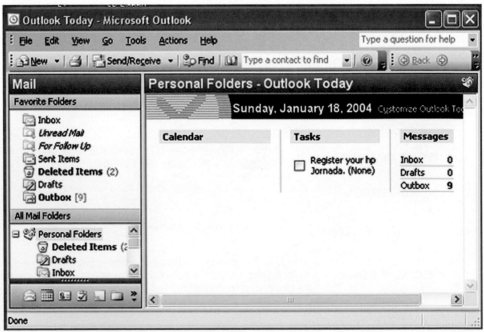

Microsoft Outlook 2000® is a registered trademark of Microsoft Corporation.

Attachments, that is, separate files or even programs, can be attached to and sent along with the message. Most email programs also provide you with some sort of filing system that allows you to systematically store incoming and read messages that you have received and messages that you have sent (see Figure 7.5).

Conferences

Another asynchronous communications tool is the computer **conference** (see Figure 7.9). Sometimes called a bulletin board, club, or forum, this tool provides users with a way to communicate one-to-many. Just as you might post a message for anyone to read on a real-world bulletin board in a public area, so too can you post a message in an Internet conference. Further, in a conference, those reading your message can post either a public or private response to your message. As various people post responses, and responses to responses, a "threaded" discussion evolves. Others accessing the conference can follow the discussion thread by reading through each original message and its responses.

Conferences can be designated either public or private. Private conferences are created by emailing an invitation to participants and then setting up the conference so that only invited members can read and respond. For teachers, conferences offer a way to open communication lines and discussions between students and among educators. Teachers can interact with colleagues across the globe to share ideas. And, their own students and students connected to the Internet anywhere in the world can join together to work collaboratively. Using a private conference, students in your class can ask a question about the culture or community of students anywhere in the nation or world. Students from multiple locations can be invited to participate and respond, resulting in a lively cultural exchange. And because conferences provide asynchronous interaction, differing time zones or constraining classroom time schedules do not interfere. Students can check the messages posted in the conference whenever class time allows.

ON THE WEB! 7.7
Building a Global Learning Community via Email

Conferences offer electronic "threaded" discussions.

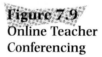

ON THE WEB! 7.8
How Conferencing Can Enhance Learning

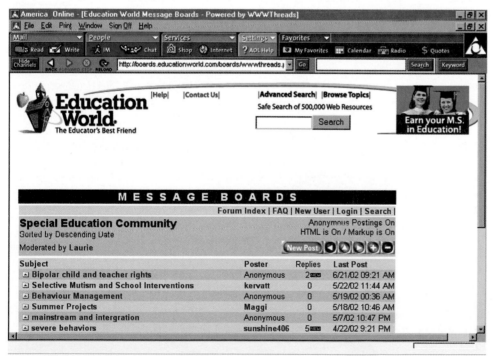

Figure 7.9
Online Teacher Conferencing
Conferencing software lets you view and participate in online discussions.

Mailing Lists

An electronic **mailing list** (sometimes known as a "Listserv") is another asynchronous communications tool. This tool automatically delivers email to those who subscribe to the list. Messages are sent to an umbrella email address of the list itself and appear in email inboxes of all subscribers; in format, they are like any other personal email message. Mailing lists can be set up so that all members can post a message that will be automatically mailed or so that only the list administrator can broadcast messages. When a list administrator monitors and broadcasts messages, the potential for junk mail is greatly reduced, and the value of the list for members is improved.

Many excellent educational lists are available for educators. Each offers teaching ideas, lesson plans, and/or links to Internet sites that are very useful. You should, however, check to see whether you are subscribing to a monitored list; even then, subscribe only to those that you find particularly useful. Subscribing to a lot of lists, especially unmonitored ones, can result in your getting many more pieces of email than you can read in a day.

ON THE WEB! 7.9
Using Educator Mailing Lists

Chats

So far we have discussed only asynchronous communication tools. These are especially useful because they can fit easily into a busy instructional schedule, but sometimes asynchronous tools simply are not the right tools for the activity you have planned. In some cases, it is important to the activity to provide real-time interaction. In that case, an Internet chat is a good option. A **chat** is a service offered by some ISPs

IN THE CLASSROOM

"You've Got Mail": Chats and Email in the Classroom

Susan Butler, a prekindergarten and kindergarten teacher at St. Simon the Apostle School in Indianapolis, Indiana, gets the children started using the Internet and email (if they haven't already done so) by joining Project Groundhog. The children work with other teams in the United States and Canada to see if, by collecting weather data for the six weeks after February 2, the groundhog really can predict more winter weather or not. In addition to sharing their weather data with children across the United States and Canada through emailing one another, these pre-K and K little ones find out about the places where their email buddies live and the schools they attend.

To review what's been studied during a week of history classes and to meet new people while reviewing are not problems for the students of a high school history teacher from Celina, Ohio, who has the students report what they've studied each week in American history class by email to students in history classes at other high schools. When the nine-week period is up, the students at all the high schools get to meet their email pen pals.

John Stetler, at Celina High School, gives the responsibility of setting up an exchange band concert to his band officers. They use email with a modifiable letter format to contact other band

directors to find the perfect match for their Internet exchange concert.

With school budgets tight and science labs big-ticket items, Stan Hughes, a biology teacher at Celina High School, has found a way to cut costs without cutting quality for his lab. By using email, students working in two labs in different schools can share their data.

Art teacher Shawn Mir has his high school general art students at Celina High School email students at another high school to share what they are doing in class. They follow up at the end of the year with a videoconference so that the students can view the work about which they have corresponded.

SOURCES: S. Butler. 2002. Project Groundhog. Retrieved January 5, 2003, from http://www.ciconline.com/Enrichment/Teaching/learningwithtechnology/expertadvice/default.htm; History pen pals. 2002. Retrieved April 10, 2003, from http://www.nea.org/helpfrom/growing/works4me/tech/techclas.html; J. Stetler. 2002. Internet exchange concert. Retrieved April 10, 2003, from http://www.nea.org/helpfrom/growing/works4me/tech/techclas.html; S. Hughes. 2002. Cutting costs. Retrieved April 10, 2003, from http://www.nea.org/helpfrom/growing/works4me/tech/technclas.html; S. Mir. 2002. Art exchange. Retrieved April 10, 2003, from http://www.nea.org/helpfrom/growing/works4me/tech/techclas.html.

and some Internet sites that set aside a space in which two or more Internet users can meet in real time. A virtual space, called a "chat room," is established, which participants can enter. Those in the chat room communicate by typing their messages and then sending them for public display in the chat room. Individuals thus respond to each other in real time in this Internet space. Internet chats require that both you and the other chat participants have the same chat software available. Chat software can be downloaded, but it is most often offered as a part of an ISP's services.

Public and private chat rooms can have multiple participants. Another form of chat, called **instant messaging (IM)**, is a one-to-one chat that can be started whenever another user is simultaneously online. With IM, you typically configure the IM software to notify you when specific individuals go online. Once you are notified that one of those people is online, you can IM that individual, that is, open a two-person temporary message room in which to communicate. Like a chat, the two parties communicate by typing messages back and forth to one another. This more informal and spontaneous communication can offer teachers and students opportunities to communicate with online peers whenever they become available.

Like conferences, chats can be public or private. Public chats are very difficult to control and monitor for content and the use of profanity. They are therefore not particularly good tools for classroom use. However, private chats allow only designated individuals to participate. Using a private chat room, you can have your students exchange data for a common science project with experts in the field or with other classes participating in the project. You can also establish national and international dialog with colleagues across the globe. A chat room can be a powerful and useful tool, one that is often a free Internet resource. Of course, because chats are synchronous, all parties must be prepared to participate at a common time. This can take a bit more advance work than emailing or conferencing, but if live interaction is desired, this is an ideal tool.

Electronic chats offer an opportunity for real-time interaction across the Internet.

Videoconferencing

If all types of files, from text to graphics to video and audio, can be transmitted over the Internet, then why not live voice and video images as well? That, too, is very doable using current Internet tools. **Videoconferencing** software allows users at either end of a synchronous connection not only to hear each other, but to see video images of each other as well. To add video to live conferencing on the Net, you must attach a video camera to your computer. Small, inexpensive monitor-top cameras are often used for this purpose. Thus, as you sit before the monitor looking at the screen, just by looking up and into the camera, you can make "eye contact" with the other participants in the video conference. Your image will display on their monitor, and theirs will display on your monitor.

In a classroom equipped with a multimedia computer, a monitor-top camera, videoconferencing software (such as the freeware program CUSeeMe), and Internet access, students can see, hear, and interact with their counterparts in similarly equipped classrooms around the world. Web sites such as the Global Schoolhouse (http://www.globalschoolnet.org/gsh) offer pages to help educators find and connect to other classrooms interested in videoconferencing. Students engaged in videoconfer-

Videoconferencing software lets you communicate via voice and visual images across a network.

encing-based interaction can participate in real-time interactive learning experiences with their peers in classrooms anywhere in the world.

Classroom-based videoconferencing might look somewhat choppy, and there may be delays in transmission, but this system does add visual images to Internet-based communications. Of course, many videoconferencing systems are much more sophisticated and provide broadcast-quality images. As Internet bandwidth and speed continue to increase, even classroom-based videoconferencing will be able to approach the quality we have all come to expect from video images.

ON THE WEB! 7.10
Exploring Videoconferencing Projects

Other Internet Services

The Internet provides a wide variety of other services that may be of interest to you as you expand your use of this network of networks. Each of the following services is described briefly so that you will be aware of its potential and use.

FTP

File transfer protocol (FTP) programs transfer files across the Internet.

File transfer protocol (FTP) is the method used for transferring files between computers on the Internet. FTP programs are usually included in your Internet software. Typically, you are using this protocol whenever you download (bring files from the Net to your computer) or upload a file (send files from your computer to the Internet), even if you are not aware that you have activated an FTP program.

There are FTP sites on the Internet, many of which are maintained by the government or a university, that contain available text, graphic, sound, and video files for your use. Although some restricted sites require a password, many are "anonymous" sites that allow you open access. Some of these require that you type in "guest" or "anonymous" at the welcome screen. Such requirements are usually clearly written on the screen.

When you upload and download files to and from FTP sites—and, indeed, most Internet sites—such files are often sent in a compressed format. Compressed files, sometimes called zipped files, have been temporarily reduced in size so that they will transfer faster and occupy less storage space on the FTP site. After they are downloaded to your computer, they must be decompressed to be usable again. Some files automatically expand after being downloaded. Others require the appropriate **unzip program.** If an unzip program is needed for an FTP site's files, it too is usually available from the FTP site and should be the first thing you download. A variety of unzip programs are also available from the Internet.

FTP sites can offer a wealth of freeware and shareware. All you need to do is know that this resource exists, visit the FTP site, and download files that are of interest to you. On many FTP sites, the files are listed by name alone, although you may find them organized by category. To be sure that you are getting the type of file you want, you should note the file's

INTERNET SERVICES FOR EDUCATORS	
✓ **Internet Service Providers (ISPs)**	Companies that provide access to the Internet and various services for a monthly fee
✓ **Electronic Mail (Email)**	Asynchronous one-to-one communications tool available to everyone on a network connected to the Internet
✓ **Conferencing**	Internet-based electronic discussion groups that allow those interested to read or post comments on a topic
✓ **Mailing Lists**	Automated lists of subscribers interested in a topic; subscribers automatically receive a copy of emails sent to the list
✓ **Chat Rooms**	Virtual spaces in which individuals can meet virtually to hold real-time conversations via text and sometimes voice
✓ **Videoconferencing**	Live video with audio across the Internet that lets individuals communicate in real time by seeing and hearing each other speak
✓ **File Transfer Protocol (FTP)**	Program that uploads and downloads files; FTP sites provide libraries of downloadable freeware and shareware software and files
✓ **Newsgroups**	Discussion groups dedicated to a specific topic and open to anyone interested in that topic

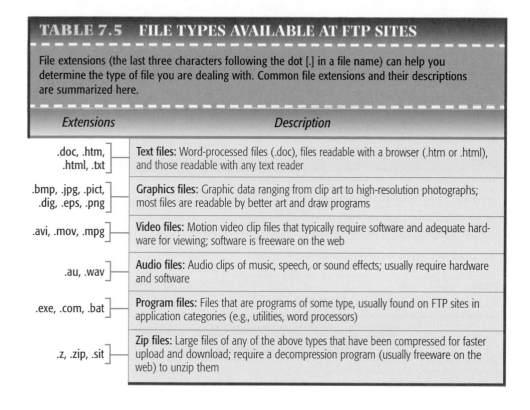

TABLE 7.5   FILE TYPES AVAILABLE AT FTP SITES

File extensions (the last three characters following the dot [.] in a file name) can help you determine the type of file you are dealing with. Common file extensions and their descriptions are summarized here.

Extensions	Description
.doc, .htm, .html, .txt	**Text files:** Word-processed files (.doc), files readable with a browser (.htm or .html), and those readable with any text reader
.bmp, .jpg, .pict, .dig, .eps, .png	**Graphics files:** Graphic data ranging from clip art to high-resolution photographs; most files are readable by better art and draw programs
.avi, .mov, .mpg	**Video files:** Motion video clip files that typically require software and adequate hardware for viewing; software is freeware on the web
.au, .wav	**Audio files:** Audio clips of music, speech, or sound effects; usually require hardware and software
.exe, .com, .bat	**Program files:** Files that are programs of some type, usually found on FTP sites in application categories (e.g., utilities, word processors)
.z, .zip, .sit	**Zip files:** Large files of any of the above types that have been compressed for faster upload and download; require a decompression program (usually freeware on the web) to unzip them

extension, the three letters following the dot in the file name. Different extensions represent different types of files. Table 7.5 summarizes the most common extensions.

Newsgroups

Using electronic conferencing, a large number of topic-oriented newsgroups are continuously running on the Internet. A **newsgroup** is a public conference dedicated to a specific topic. To participate in a newsgroup, you use a newsreader (see Figure 7.10), a program that is included with your Internet software. The newsreader lets you read all the previously posted messages and follow the threads of the discussion. You can also post your own responses or start discussion of a new topic. Most newsgroups are open discussions on specific subject areas such as education, computers, news, music, and many more. Newsgroup names often indicate their topic areas. For example, biz.jobs.computers would be a discussion group about computer employment in business, and ed.middle.science would be a discussion about teaching middle school science. A newsgroup with a name such as alt.education.disabled would be an "alternative" newsgroup for discussion of issues related to educating individuals with disabilities.

Newsgroups offer a wide variety of Internet discussion groups on every possible subject of interest.

The World Wide Web

People are often confused by the difference between the Internet and the **World Wide Web** (the web). Actually, the web is just one of the many services available on the Internet. It is not a separate network, nor is *the web* synonymous with *the Internet*. In fact, you will explore in the next chapter exactly what the World Wide Web is and how it has become an invaluable resource for educators and a powerful tool in teaching and in learning.

Figure 7.10
Using a Newsreader to Read a Usenet Group
Newsreader software lets you view and participate in newsgroup discussions.

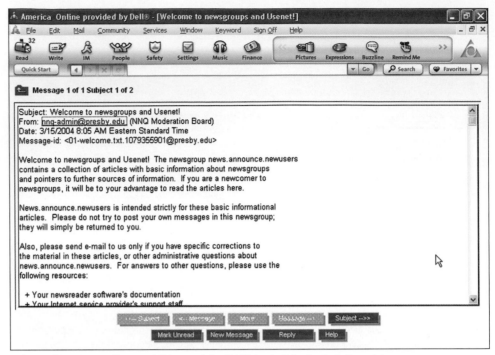

America Online provided by Dell® - [Welcome to newsgroups and Usenet!]

File   Edit   Mail   Community   Services   Window   Keyword   Sign Off   Help

Message 1 of 1 Subject 1 of 2

Subject: Welcome to newsgroups and Usenet!
From: nnq-admin@presby.edu (NNQ Moderation Board)
Date: 3/15/2004 8:05 AM Eastern Standard Time
Message-id: <01-welcome.txt.1079355901@presby.edu>

Welcome to newsgroups and Usenet! The newsgroup news.announce.newusers contains a collection of articles with basic information about newsgroups and pointers to further sources of information. If you are a newcomer to newsgroups, it will be to your advantage to read the articles here.

News.announce.newusers is intended strictly for these basic informational articles. Please do not try to post your own messages in this newsgroup; they will simply be returned to you.

Also, please send e-mail to us only if you have specific corrections to the material in these articles, or other administrative questions about news.announce.newusers. For answers to other questions, please use the following resources:

+ Your newsreader software's documentation
+ Your Internet service provider's support staff

Moderators of News.Announce.Newsusers. AOL browser window © 2002 America Online, Inc. Used with permission.

Using the Internet in Teaching and Learning

The Internet is a powerful learning tool.

The Internet has, without doubt, great potential in teaching and learning. You have learned throughout this chapter of its many tools and services, as well as some of their innovative applications to teaching and learning. This global interconnection of thousands of networks has changed the way we communicate, much as the printing press revolutionized communication hundreds of years ago. We are all just beginning to grasp the social implications of this revolution as we have moved from the Industrial to the Information Age.

In Chapter 8, we will further explore the aspect of the Internet called the World Wide Web and how it can be used in teaching and learning. We will also review some of the key issues relating to the use of the Internet about which a prudent teacher should be aware. The Internet itself and the manner in which it is used by some offer potential for abuse. Educators who use the Internet in their classrooms must be aware of these issues and see to it that their own implementation of the Internet in teaching and learning is consistent with our highest professional standards and our responsibilities to our most important charges: our students.

KEY TERMS

STUDENT ACTIVITIES

CHAPTER REVIEW

1. What is a network? What is the relationship between a server and workstations?
2. How are typical classrooms wired? What impact does this have on the learning environment?
3. How do bandwidth and transmission speed affect network communications?
4. Describe the techniques used in networking to protect the privacy of an individual's data and the security of the network.
5. Why is it advantageous for educators to share resources and programs on a network? What concerns are associated with program sharing?
6. As a teacher, how might networked administrative tools be useful for you? How might academic tools be useful?
7. What is telecommunication? What hardware and software are necessary to make it possible?
8. What is the Internet? What value does it hold for educators?
9. What is an ISP? Why is an ISP necessary for access to the Internet?
10. What is the difference between asynchronous and synchronous communication? Name and describe the Internet communication tools that fall into each category.

WHAT DO YOU THINK?

1. Interview a network administrator to discover the issues he or she is most concerned with relating to network security. Be sure to ask what other issues are of concern with regard to

helping users. Summarize the interview questions and responses. Explain how the network issues may affect the way in which you use this technology in your classroom.

2. The Internet offers an almost overwhelming wealth of information and is growing daily. It is becoming clear that it will be increasingly difficult to fully define a content area or discipline without incorporating this resource's expanding knowledge base. This may radically change the skills children will need for lifelong learning. How has the Internet changed our concept of information? What computer and Internet skills do you think children should learn so that they will be prepared for life in the Information Age?

3. Internet communication tools open broad new opportunities for interaction among students across the globe. Of the communication tools you have learned about, which do you think holds most promise? How might you use this type of tool when you teach?

4. The Internet is a public communication area that many believe is protected by the First Amendment. Others believe that the contents of the Internet ought to be moderated and the public protected from inappropriate content. What is your view on this controversial issue?

LEARNING TOGETHER!

These activities are best done in groups of three to five.

1. Each group member should interview at least three teachers who use the Internet in instruction. Be sure to ask the objectives of the Internet-based activity used in their teaching and precisely how it is carried out. Share interview findings with your peers and together develop an Internet Best Practices summary that details the best Internet activities you discovered. Be prepared to share your best practices with other groups in your class.

2. Create a private chat or conference using one of the Internet portals. Use the communication tool you have created to develop a Top Ten list of ways you might use this tool in a classroom.

3. Assume that all members of your group have decided to connect to the Internet from home. Each member should select one of the available ISPs in your area and research the features and services it provides and the costs for providing those services. Share your findings and select the best way for you to connect to the Internet from the choices your group has researched.

HANDS-ON!

1. Locate five FTP web sites that are related to education. Download one resource from each site so that you can sample its offerings. Be sure the file you copy from each site is of value. Prepare an annotated list of the FTP sites you found and be prepared to share your findings with the class.

2. Join an educational conference and an electronic mailing list. What types of information are you able to gather as a result of participation in each? What are the advantages and disadvantages of each?

3. Select a keypal in your course. Email, as an attachment, one of your course assignments to your keypal to proofread and comment on. Carbon copy (cc) your professor. Your keypal should respond via email with suggestions for improving your assignment.

More from Jeffrey Ross

MY SOLUTION

Once I identified my problems, I was better able to identify a viable solution to help my students. I brainstormed for a short while before I came to the realization that the solutions to both of my problems were intertwined. I remembered a course that I had taken at Nova Southeastern University while working on a graduate degree. The course was called Educating with the Internet. As I reflected on the course, I recalled a web site that we explored called FunBrain. I remembered how enthusiastic I was when I was first introduced to this web site. I could immediately see its usefulness to my students. The specific URL for this site is **http://www. funbrain.com**. I have found that it can be used quite effectively with high school as well as elementary students.

One feature of this site that I found attractive was the gradebook that is included on the site. The gradebook feature actually grades students' work as soon as they complete and submit it. In addition, the gradebook automatically keeps a log of the individual assessments that I prepare along with my students' performance on them. The gradebook also provides me with a detailed list of the most frequently missed questions on each of the assessments that my students take. There is also an option that allows me to select whether I want my students to receive feedback on their assessments immediately or at a later date. Finally, the gradebook gives me the option of having the students' results sent to my email address. I can have the feedback sent on a daily or weekly basis.

I use the assessment section of FunBrain for review as well as testing. I normally opt to have my students receive feedback immediately when they are reviewing concepts. This enables me to help them easily identify the area or areas where they need to improve. This feature is very beneficial because it gives my students the immediate feedback that they are often looking for.

Another feature of the site that I found helpful to my students was a section entitled Quiz Lab. This link allowed me to prepare online quizzes and tests for my students. Quiz Lab also contains a database of several thousand quizzes that were created by other educators. I believe that my implementation of the quiz lab feature is the primary reason for the significant improvement of my students' attendance and attitudes. This section has probably decreased the turnaround time on the feedback that I give to my students by tenfold.

The next feature of Funbrain that enabled me to integrate technology into my classroom is the games section. This section includes such games as Math Baseball, Math Football, Stay Afloat, and others. There are also some brainteasers included in the game section. All of the games allow the instructor to vary the level of difficulty and the style of the problems that the students have to complete to advance in the games. Many of my students find themselves attracted to the Math Baseball game. Math Football operates on similar principles as Math Baseball. I normally use the game section for practice or to further improve my students' higher-order thinking skills. I also use the games section to motivate my lessons from time to time.

I have come to the realization that if even one of my students is not overly excited about math, I can usually get her or him to give it a try simply by presenting the concept through the use of the Internet. I try to integrate use of the Internet into my curriculum at least once per week.

As I began to integrate the Internet into my curriculum, I noticed several positive changes in my students' overall demeanor. I found them to be more attentive in class, and they have also become more enthusiastic about new lessons. Attendance in my classes has improved significantly. I have a larger solid core of students who attend class regularly. These students have developed a very solid foundation of algebraic concepts as a result of my integrating FunBrain into my curriculum. They consistently show a higher level of inquisitiveness during my classroom lessons.

FunBrain has enabled me to integrate technology in my curriculum in ways that I never imagined. This web site has become an invaluable resource in my classes. My students are developing into a community of independent learners. Since the site is so user-friendly and interactive, I primarily use it as I would use an assistant. All I have to do is give my students the itinerary for the day, and they are able to navigate their way through the lesson. The only thing that I have to do is act as a resource and guide once in a while.

For additional information, to express your ideas, or to identify similar web sites, please contact me.

Contact Information: Jeffrey M. Ross, mathematics teacher. Email: rossje@yahoo.com.

SOURCE: Interview with Jeffrey Ross conducted by Al P. Mizell. Reprinted by permission of Jeffrey Ross.

CHAPTER 8

Using the Web for Teaching and Learning

This chapter addresses these ISTE National Educational Technology Standards for Teachers:

I. Technology operations and concepts

Teachers demonstrate a sound understanding of technology operations and concepts. Teachers

A. demonstrate introductory knowledge, skills, and understanding of concepts related to technology (as described in the ISTE *National Education Technology Standards for Students*).
B. demonstrate continual growth in technology knowledge and skills to stay abreast of current and emerging technologies.

III. Teaching, learning, and the curriculum

Teachers implement curriculum plans that include methods and strategies for applying technology to maximize student learning. Teachers

A. facilitate technology-enhanced experiences that address content standards and student technology standards.
B. use technology to support learner-centered strategies that address the diverse needs of students.
C. apply technology to develop students' higher-order skills and creativity.
D. manage student learning activities in a technology-enhanced environment.

V. Productivity and professional practice

Teachers use technology resources to enhance their productivity and professional practice. Teachers

A. use technology resources to engage in ongoing professional development and lifelong learning.
B. continually evaluate and reflect on professional practice to make informed decisions regarding the use of technology in support of student learning.
C. apply technology to increase productivity.
D. use technology to communicate and collaborate with peers, parents, and the larger community in order to nurture student learning.

VI. Social, ethical, legal, and human issues

Teachers understand the social, ethical, legal, and human issues surrounding the use of technology in PK–12 schools and apply that understanding in practice. Teachers

A. model and teach legal and ethical practice related to technology use.
B. apply technology resources to enable and empower learners with diverse backgrounds, characteristics, and abilities.
C. identify and use technology resources that affirm diversity.
D. promote safe and healthy use of technology resources.
E. facilitate equitable access to technology resources for all students.

Now that you have learned about network basics, the Internet, and a sampling of the services available on the Net, it is time to explore more fully its application to teaching and learning. Using the Internet, as it was configured in its earliest years, would have been a somewhat daunting task for most teachers. With complex text-based commands and no user-friendly screen displays, the early Internet challenged its most experienced users. Today much of the Net has evolved into the easy-to-use graphic format known as the World Wide Web. This new, more intuitive Internet with its simple point-and-click interface and convenient links has become a powerful tool in the hands of teachers and learners. This chapter examines the World Wide Web and the resources it makes available to teachers and learners. It explores the components of an instructional web site and reviews what such a web site should include if you decide to use or create one when you teach. The chapter concludes with a review of the steps necessary to incorporate web-based instruction in your classroom.

In Chapter 8, you will

- Survey the World Wide Web and its features

- Explore sample classroom management and academic tools available on the web

- Examine instructional support web sites and the resources they provide to you and your students

- Investigate how to use the web to enhance communication and instruction

- Explore the steps necessary to create a classroom web site and make it available on the web

Meet Rob Schwartz

Whether in a technology class or an academic subject class or any other educational setting, the instructor faces the problem of finding ways to help many different students with many different questions. Addressing and meeting diverse needs, especially within the framework of delivering complex content, challenges teachers and causes them to look for innovative solutions, often involving technology. One secondary school teacher, Rob Schwartz, faced this challenge and found a unique way to approach a solution by rethinking his conception of "the classroom" and by using the Internet as a major tool. Let's let Mr. Schwartz describe his classroom and its unique circumstances in his own words.

MY SETTING

If you're not familiar with technology education (TE), I'd like to give you a quick summary of some of the challenges faced by TE teachers. Generally speaking, the course is in the old "shop" classroom, but the woodworking tools have been moved out and the computers have been moved in. Most labs have a modular setup, meaning that there are workstations where two students work together on a particular project to learn a specific technological concept. In the same lab, students work on programming, robotics, biotechnology, desktop publishing, video editing, manufacturing, aerospace and rocketry, research and design, and a myriad of other topics—usually ten to fifteen different modules.

MY PROBLEMS

The first problem is that the students are learning all of these concepts at once. Joe and Suzy are learning robotics while Jim and Carol are working on a computer-controlled lathe. At the same time, Bob and Nancy can't figure out how to edit a video, and Lou and Gina are stuck trying to figure out how to edit a hyperlink in web design. The problem is obvious. There are fifteen different lessons all going on at the same time in the same room, but I'm only one teacher. When I stop to answer a question for a student, it doesn't benefit any other student, and I'll probably encounter the same question next week when the students rotate modules. And who is a master of *every* technology known to humankind? Even if such a person existed, tomorrow he or she would be obsolete, given all the discoveries and enhancements being made to technology today. I don't have all the answers, and I can't be in fifteen places at once answering fifteen different questions about fifteen completely unrelated topics.

The other problem is that many labs use a "canned" curriculum approach that uses videos to instruct the students. This is a fine way

to begin, but it's very expensive and also goes obsolete as soon as the software is updated. If I am using Photoshop 7.0 and Photoshop CS comes out, I not only need to pay hundreds of dollars for the new software, but I need to pay *thousands* of dollars to get the new curriculum. Of course there's no money for that, so I end up using the same outdated software and hardware for years until a grant comes along to update my lab. The instructions in the videos or books are so specific that many of the projects cannot be done on new software using the old curriculum.

My solution to the problem was simple, but it has its own set of challenges. I decided not to use "curriculum" at all. I made the decision early on to treat my classroom like the workplace. "On-the-job-learning" is the way that most of us learn the skills we use every day. The boss does not hand us a big book with instructions for each day so we know what to do. We're supposed to solve problems and develop creative solutions to the challenges we face. If we want to prepare students for real life, why should we teach them to learn in a way that's completely different from the way they will have to learn for the rest of their lives? Likewise, we need to learn to find resources to answer our questions; then we have to find the answers in those resources. We need to teach our students to learn on their own. But how will we ever find enough resources with broad enough coverage and enough depth to learn a new skill that doesn't get outdated with the technology we are currently using? Even if I found a library of books to buy, when the new software comes out my library is as obsolete as my software.

If there were only a magic box with access to a global library that was updated millions of times every single day, was easily searched, and instantly delivered all materials to my classroom on demand . . .

And one more little thing . . . make it *free*.

Enter the Internet.

Rob's instructional setting is complex, and his content problem required an innovative solution. As a technology-using educator well aware of the potential that technology has to assist him, he chose to use the Internet to solve his classroom challenge. We will revisit him at the end of this chapter once you have had the opportunity to fully explore the technologies he ultimately selected to help him meet his teaching and learning needs.

What Is the World Wide Web?

In its early days, the Internet was not particularly easy to use. Typically, commands to move about on or retrieve something from the Internet were text commands that required very exact syntax. To use Internet resources, you had to know the precise sequence of commands and be able to use them in a very specific order. The complexity involved in using and navigating the Internet and the increasing demands by non-technical users for access led to the creation of a user-friendly, graphics interface in 1991. Tim Berners-Lee, working at the European particle physics lab (CERN) in Geneva, Switzerland, wrote a program for use on the Internet that fundamentally changed how users and the Net interacted. His program allowed users to move between linked web pages located on the Internet. Simply by clicking on a link, Internet surfers could jump from one document on the Net to another, without knowing a single complex command. These links, called **hyperlinks,** made Internet navigation as easy as pointing and clicking. The vast collection of hyperlink documents available on the Internet is known as the **World Wide Web,** or W3, or simply the web.

The World Wide Web is the user-friendly graphical side of the Internet that uses hyperlinks to move from one location to the next.

Web Sites: Linked Web Pages

A document that provides information and contains a series of hyperlinks to other resources is called a **web page,** and a collection of related web pages is called a **web site.** Web sites can contain multiple pages, and each page can contain text, graphics, animation, audio, and video data. Typically, web sites have a welcome or **home page** that provides basic information about the site and one or more connections to additional information pages. These connections, or links, are usually represented by colored and underlined words or **navigation button** graphics. Each of these is "hot-linked"; that is, it contains a hyperlink to another document at that web site or at another web site. Activating a link causes a jump to that connected page or web site. Almost all web pages contain links, thus allowing you to jump from that page to other web site pages, which may also contain links to still other sites. This method of Internet navigation is considerably easier than having to type a series of cryptic commands to move from one document to another. Indeed, the web and its easy navigation have changed the face of the Internet.

Web Browsers

A special program is necessary to translate the language with which a web page is written into an image on your screen. Web pages are written by using a language called **hypertext markup language (HTML).** Your web browser is actually a type of translation software that reads HTML and then displays it as the web page you are familiar with. Browser software also enables you to easily locate a web page by typing in its web address, move to and display the target web page graphically, and even move back and forward between pages you have viewed. Figure 8.1 summarizes typical browser functions. You may also wish to try the Microsoft Internet Explorer Skills Builder on your student CD to become more familiar with a browser's features.

Web browsers display HTML code as web pages.

On CD!
Software Skills Builder
Using Microsoft Internet Explorer

Locating Web Pages

Networks that are connected to the Internet usually have a dedicated server, called a web server, that stores web pages and responds to requests from web users. Each one of those web servers is given a very specific web address so that it can be located from among the millions of computers on the Internet. Web addresses can be easily recognized because they all start with a hypertext transfer protocol designation, written

Figure 8.1
Key Browser Features
Browsers offer you a variety of features and commands via menus and buttons to make it easy to access and use the web.

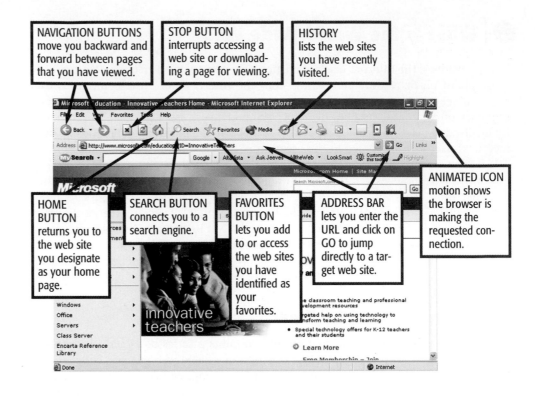

NAVIGATION BUTTONS move you backward and forward between pages that you have viewed.

STOP BUTTON interrupts accessing a web site or downloading a page for viewing.

HISTORY lists the web sites you have recently visited.

HOME BUTTON returns you to the web site you designate as your home page.

SEARCH BUTTON connects you to a search engine.

FAVORITES BUTTON lets you add to or access the web sites you have identified as your favorites.

ADDRESS BAR lets you enter the URL and click on GO to jump directly to a target web site.

ANIMATED ICON motion shows the browser is making the requested connection.

URLs identify where a web page can be found.

http://. This designation indicates that the document to be sought and transferred is using the web page protocol for transmission. A complete web address is written in a very specific format that can direct a browser to an exact location on a web server. This format is called a **uniform resource locator (URL)**. URLs include precise components indicating a web location. At minimum they include the name of a type of web server on which the home page of the web site is found. A URL may also identify the specific directory, or folder and file name for the information you are looking for. Figure 8.2 summarizes the components of a URL to help you understand how it connects you precisely to a specific document.

▌ Creating and Evaluating Web Sites

As you review various web sites, it might seem like a very complex task to create a web page. That is not necessarily the case. As you learned in Chapter 6, a wide variety of easy-to-use web page authoring software packages are available, many of which are provided as a component on common applications such as word-processing software. The fact that web page authoring can easily be accomplished is evidenced by the many teacher- and student-made web pages on the web today.

However, not all web sites created by and for educators are of equal quality. Whether you are creating your own web site or you are reviewing another educational site for use in your classroom, it is important that you carefully examine the site for quality.

A web site's design should be well organized and logical; the site should also be easy to navigate to find the information sought. Furthermore, and of critical importance for educational sites, the creator of a site should have the appropriate authority and expertise necessary to present correct and meaningful information in the area on which the site is focused. Unfortunately, many web sites can be found that should not be considered authoritative but are too often assumed to be so just because they are available on the Internet. Equally important for educators and their students, educa-

URLs start with http://
to initiate the hyper-
text transfer protocol
used by web sites.

This component of the URL
directs the browser to look
in the Resources folder on
the eric.gov web server.

http://www.eric.ed.gov/resources/index.html

The domain name tells the browser
to look on the World Wide Web for
the ERIC server on the web site of the
U.S. Department of Education.

This portion of the URL identifies
the specific document to be found
inside the Resources folder to display on the browser screen.

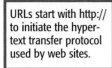

Figure 8.2
Anatomy of a URL
The uniform resource locator directs you to a very specific place on the web.

tional sites should be free of any type of bias in their presentation of information and should not be trying to sell a product or their creators' views. Finally, high-quality educational web sites should clearly cite the sources that were used in the preparation of the information presented.

Before you use a web site in your classroom, be sure to examine it carefully and evaluate it using these criteria. Although many web sites are obviously inappropriate for classroom use, others may turn out to be so only after your careful evaluation. It is the teacher's responsibility to fully preview instructional materials, whether in print or on the web, before sharing them with students. Table 8.1 provides a rubric that will help you to evaluate web site quality.

▎ Multimedia on the Web

Because educators want to appeal to a variety of learning styles, the need to make a web page more than an "electronic textbook" is critical when using it for instructional support. Fortunately, web pages support the multimedia components that are so useful in addressing diverse learning styles. Creating multimedia features for use on an educational web site is not difficult. Web page authoring programs typically enable you to include multimedia files when creating your web pages. The main disadvantage to using multimedia on a site is the fact that multimedia files can be quite large and therefore may take additional time to access and download. Furthermore, the user's browser may or may not include the program components that are needed to display multimedia. Some browsers may require an additional program, called a **plug-in,** to expand the browsers' capabilities in this area. Most plug-ins are offered free to those Internet users who wish to download them. This makes it possible for the users to easily upgrade their browser's capabilities via plug-ins so that they, too, can use web multimedia. Whenever you decide to use multimedia on a web page, you should also include the URL of the plug-in's web site. Adding this address to your web page makes it easy for those who wish to view your multimedia to upgrade their browsers if they need and want to.

ON THE WEB! 8.1
Classrooms on the Web

Plug-ins add multimedia
capabilities to browsers.

• Graphics

Graphics files are the most frequent multimedia addition to web pages. The use of pictures and visual images adds significantly to the excitement of a teaching page. To use

TABLE 8.1   WEB SITE EVALUATION RUBRIC

SITE NAME:

URL:

AREA/CONTENT OF SITE:

COMMENTS:

Using each of the criteria below, evaluate the usefulness of this web site for teaching and learning. For each dimension in the rubric, check the box that best reflects your opinion. Select web sites that score 4 or higher in the most dimensions.

EVALUATION CRITERIA

Dimension	1 Poor	2 Below Average	3 Average	4 Above Average	5 Excellent
Design	Poorly organized; contains obvious errors; loads slowly	Organization somewhat confusing; some errors; loads slowly	Organization acceptable; no obvious errors; loads adequately	Good organization; no errors; loads quickly	Excellent organization; clear and free of errors; loads quickly and completely
Navigability	Difficult to find and follow site navigation links	Navigation links visible but somewhat confusing	Navigation links clear and readily available	Navigation links clear and logical; site map included	Navigation logical and clear; site map and search engine available
Authority	Unclear who authored the site	Author name and contact information included; but credentials lacking	Author name, contact information, and some credential info included	Author name, contact information, full credentials included	Well-regarded author provides all necessary information; site is linked to by others
Bias	Site attempts to persuade or sell views	Site presents facts, but some bias is evident	Site is mostly neutral; selling pages are segregated	Site contains no attempts to sell or persuade	Site presents multiple viewpoints with no bias
Citations	No citations are evident	Citations are included on some sources but not all	All sources include brief citations, but site lacks bibliography	All sources are properly cited with site bibliography	All sources properly cited, full bibliography, with active links
Dates	No dates evident	Site contains creation date but no dates for update information	Site contains both creation and dates for update information	Site contains dates for creation and update information and some dates relating to data colllection	Site contains creation, update, and data collection dates for all key information
Content	Data quality is questionable, and quantity is limited	Data quality appears adequate, limited quantity	Data is adequate in quality and quantity	Data quality is established, and quantity is sufficient for coverage	Data quality is unquestioned, and quantity provides excellent coverage
Links	Few relevant working links included	Adequate number of links, but many no longer functional	Sufficient number of links, and all are functional	A good variety of useful, active links	Active links to wide variety of excellent sites
Handicapped access	No options available for handicapped	Some pages on site offer text-only option	Site offers text-only option on all pages	Site offers clear options for handicapped	Site includes handicapped options on all pages and links to support software
Relevance	Site does not meet instructional objectives	Site meets some aspects of instructional objectives	Instructional objectives are adequately met	Site exceeds most objectives' requirements	Site exceeds all instructional objectives

 This and other downloadable forms and templates can be found on the Companion Website at www.ablongman.com/lever-duffy.

graphics on the web, you need to be aware of the various types of graphic formats that are compatible for this purpose. Creating graphics in these formats may be done through the use of most of the popular draw or paint programs. It is simply a matter of creating the graphic and then saving it in the desired format. Art software provides the translation necessary to save from one format to another.

The most frequently used formats for web graphics are GIF and JPEG. **GIF** stands for graphic interchange format, a graphics format that is used primarily for color images, clip art, line art, and gray-scale images. Its relatively low resolution makes it a fairly quick graphic to load and display. Animated GIFs are sequences of images that, displayed in quick succession, give the appearance of movement. No doubt you have seen these popular animations on web pages. Because they are essentially low-resolution GIFs, they too are relatively quick for a browser to download and display. **JPEG** (pronounced "jay-peg") stands for Joint Photographic Expert Group, the agreed-upon standard for high-resolution images. JPEG graphics are used for photographic-quality images. This much higher-resolution image is needed to accurately reproduce scanned photos; however, JPEG files are typically large and require more time to display.

GIF and JPEG are common web graphics formats.

When displaying graphics, browsers typically load and display text first and then begin the graphics transfers. The graphics often appear to the user as partial or blurred images that gradually resolve into clear, complete, full-color images. The smaller the file and simpler the format, the faster a graphic becomes viewable.

The web contains millions of images that are available for you to use. Many of them are copyright-free; that is, you can use them without having to reimburse the owner of the image. Chapter 12 will help you better understand copyright and its impact on you as a teacher. However, at this point, it is sufficient to be aware that copyrighted images cannot be used or reproduced without the express permission of their owners. For most educators who create web sites or use images from web sites, this is not a problem, because so many free resources are available.

- Audio

Audio on a web site can add another multimedia dimension in using the web for teaching and learning. Audio files that are stored in WAV and AU formats require that you first download an entire file before playing it. Because such audio files can be quite large, long delays result from incorporating audio into web pages using these formats.

A more sophisticated audio technology for the web, called **streaming audio,** sends audio in a continuous stream or flow. Streaming audio players such as the one shown in Figure 8.3 allow you to listen to the audio as it is received by your browser. There may be some short delays, but for the most part, you are able to listen as you download. Live Internet concerts and Internet radio stations use this technology. One of the most widely used formats for this type of audio is RealOne Player, developed by Real-Networks. If you decide to listen to an audio clip that is in the RealAudio (RA) format, you may first need to download the RealPlayer or RealOne Player plug-in to enhance your browser (see Figure 8.3).

To play audio files from the web, you may need player software.

- Video

Just as audio clips can be added to a web site, so too can video clips be included. Video clips are typically brief because they take considerable amounts of time to transfer. **Streaming video** has improved that situation by allowing the user to view the video clip as it is downloaded. Given the current bandwidth and speed of most connections via modem, movement in many video images appears to be somewhat choppy and fuzzy. No doubt the constantly increasing bandwidth of available lines to homes and schools will quickly improve the quality of video on the web. For educators, being able to access and show video clips from around the world with just a click of a mouse button offers many exciting educational opportunities. Current and emerging web-based video resources will be explored in detail in Chapter 10.

Figure 8.3
Software for Playing Streaming Audio and Video
Media players (plug-ins) such as RealOne Player and Windows Media Player make listening to and viewing streaming video and audio possible.

RealOne Player, RealNetworks, Inc.

Windows Media Player® is a registered trademark of Microsoft Corporation.

Virtual reality lets viewers become participants in virtual environments.

ON THE WEB! 8.2
Virtual Worlds

• Virtual Reality

Virtual reality (VR) provides a three-dimensional graphic environment that can be accessed on the web. A web site that is a VR world is one that is rendered in three dimensions and allows the user to manipulate that 3-D environment. When you visit a VR world museum, for example, it seems on your screen as if you can move down hallways, turn corners, and go up stairs to see the museum's displays. You can even manipulate objects of interest by coming close to them, picking them up with your mouse button, and turning them around to get a view of all sides. Once again, at the moment, low bandwidth can cause such environments to move slowly and even appear choppy; however, the promise of VR worlds for education is enormous. Imagine the possibilities of a student being able to enter a VR world at the molecular level and move electrons around to alter elements, or being able to take a field trip to see the inside of the pyramids from a computer connected to the web. Clearly, firsthand experiences are the best, but for experiences that are too far away or impossible to attain, the use of VR holds great potential.

| Search Engines

If an educator is interested in using any of the web resources described so far in this chapter, how can they be located from among the millions of web sites out there? The web does not contain a central index or directory. Remember, it is, at its core, thousands of independent, interconnected networks and servers with no one single organization running it. With data spread so widely and no central index, the only way to find very specific data on the web is to use a tool that searches the web for you. This tool is called a search engine.

Search engines are programs that are designed to find web sites and pages based on key words that you enter. The key word can be a single word, a phrase, or a series of words. The search engine matches the search word against databases of web sites and

On CD!
Software Skills Builder
Using a Search Engine

IN THE CLASSROOM

A Research Tool for All Seasons: Web-Based Research

For students in the contiguous forty-eight states, Alaskan history is pretty remote. However, for the students at Port Alexander School in Port Alexander, Alaska, located on the southern tip of Baranof Island, with a population of approximately ninety people, Alaskan studies is a popular subject. Jackie Garnick taught the students at the Port Alexander school how to make a web page to display the results of their research about their home state. Students in the middle and high schools have an Alaskan history link provided by their teacher to aid in their web-based research. Alice chose her topic, Native American studies, to discover the lifestyles and history of the Native American Alaskans, noting five groups still in Alaska: the Tlingets, Haidas, Athabaskans, Eskimos, and Aleuts. Among the other students using the web to make reports about Alaskan topics, Cleve wrote on Alaskan animals, Coral on Alaskan steamboats, Brandon on the borders and boundaries of Alaska, and Sunni on ocean shipping in Alaska. Each student made a web page that featured the research he or she carried out using the web.

One of the best-known names in web research is Dr. Bernie Dodge, the originator of the WebQuest method of doing web-based research. Dr. Dodge is a professor of educational technology at San Diego State University and has been cited by *eSchool News* as one of the nation's top thirty educational technology innovators. When asked how a WebQuest differs from other web-oriented research assignments, Dr. Dodge said,

A WebQuest is built around an engaging and doable task that elicits higher order thinking of some kind. It's about *doing* some-

thing with information. The thinking can be creative or critical, and involve problem solving, judgment, analysis, and synthesis. The task has to be more than simply answering questions or regurgitating what's on the screen. Ideally the task is a scaled down version of something that adults do on the job, outside school walls.

To see some fine WebQuests that students have done, access the web addresses listed below.

WEBQUESTS

S. Post, & B. Richardson. 2002. Do you haiku? Retrieved March 20, 2003, from **http://www.teach-nology.com**; Bricker. 2002. Can you create a mutant? Retrieved March 20, 2003, from **http://www.berk.siu.k12.pa.us/webquest/index.htm**; The Odyssey. 2002. Retrieved March 25, 2003, from **http://coe.west. asu.edu/students/madams/group_1.htm**; K. Kliegman, C. Wilenski, & D. McMullan. 2002. Federal holidays webquest. Retrieved March 25, 2003, from **http//:herrickses.org/searingtown/ federalholidays**.

SOURCES: Eagle Eye News. 2002. Retrieved May 15, 2002, from http:// www.sisd.k12.ak.us/content/schools/pa/news%20letter/webmake.html; L. Starr. 2000. Meet Bernie Dodge—the Frank Lloyd Wright of learning environments! Retrieved June 1, 2003, from http://www.education-world.com/a_tech/tech020. shtml.

---

their respective key words. When a match occurs, the search engine provides you with a hyperlink to the page or site related to the search term. These matches, sometimes called hits, provide you with a direct connection to relevant web pages.

Search engines use different techniques to generate their databases. Some store and read key words that web site authors provide when they register the site. Others use automated web robot programs, sometimes called spiders, to search for new sites. Because thousands of new web sites are being added to the web daily and different engines use different techniques to build their databases, it is very possible for searches using different search engines to have very different results. You will need to experiment with different search engines to determine which ones seem to bring you the hits that are closest to what you are looking for.

When using a search engine, it is important to structure your request for information so that you do not get an unmanageable number of hits. If you were to request an engine to search on the word *education*, millions of hits would be returned to you, making it essentially impossible for you to find the few that pertain to the topic within education in which you are interested. Although there may be some variation in the techniques used by any given search engine, all provide methods to narrow the search, typically using terms such as AND, OR, or NOT to control the scope of the search. By carefully constructing your search request, you will be able to get very precise results. You should always review the search instructions provided at a search engine site

ON THE WEB! 8.3
Searching the Web

before using that search engine. Each engine differs somewhat, and a brief review will help you optimize your searches and may save you considerable time. Try the Software Skills Builder Using a Search Engine to fine-tune your search skills.

Portals

Various web sites, particularly those that began primarily as search engines, have begun to offer more and more services. Such sites, which include an assortment of services such as a search engine, news, email, conferencing, electronic shopping, and chat rooms, are called portals. A **portal** is a doorway to the Internet and its many resources. The portal provides you with access and services that facilitate your use of the Internet. Creators of sites that have become portals hope that you will set your browser to open to their sites and then proceed with your Internet activity from there. To support their services, portals sell space on their sites to advertisers that are interested in marketing to you. Some of the most popular portals include Yahoo!, Lycos, and Excite. Portals such as Education World are dedicated to educational topics and services. Exploring portals may well be worth the expenditure of a busy educator's time.

Educational Resources on the Web

On the web, educators have an almost unimaginable and continually growing electronic storehouse of tools and resources available at their fingertips. Often, the only barrier to accessing these resources is knowing that they exist and where they can be found. It is therefore useful first to become aware of the broad categories of resources available.

Online Publications

ON THE WEB! 8.4
Online Publications

Many educational journals now have an online version available via the Internet (see Figure 8.4). Most of these **online publications** include current and archived articles of interest to educators. Most also have local site-based search engines that allow you to type in key words to look for on the site. Electronic publications also typically offer a page of related links that may prove useful in your quest for information.

Once found, electronic articles can be saved or printed for your use. Many articles that you can view on the web have been converted from their original word-processed format to HTML. Your browser displays the documents you select (click on), and your browser interprets their HTML code and displays the articles on your screen. The articles can then be saved or printed from the screen using your browser's Save or Print function.

With Acrobat Reader, your PDF files will look just like the original printed page.

Other web sites may save their articles as **PDF files,** which are files that have been saved in Adobe Acrobat format. Acrobat is a conversion software package that lets the user save a publication exactly as it looked on the printed page, including custom layouts, photos, and other graphics. PDF files are frequently used to share published information since they maintain the formatting and detail that is lost when presented in HTML. To read an Acrobat file, you need Adobe Reader, a free download available from the Adobe web site. Usually, publication web sites that use Adobe Acrobat include a hot link to enable you to connect directly to Adobe's download page. Once you have downloaded and installed Reader, you are ready to use files saved in PDF format. All you will need to do is click on the files of interest to you, and your browser and Reader will then take over the process. The files will be downloaded, and Reader will be launched to display the fully formatted article (see Figure 8.5). You can then read an exact reproduction of the original published article and even print it out.

techLEARNING   http://www.techlearning.com *(Technology & Learning* magazine)
Anecdotal classroom applications supplied by teachers in the "What Works" section are creative and practical. Contributors' email addresses are given for questions and commentary.

AERA.net   http://www.aera.net *(Educational Researcher)*
ER Online from the American Educational Research Association is a downloadable publication of articles primarily on statistical research.

ASCD   http://www.ascd.org
The Association for Supervision and Curriculum Development site includes *Educational Leadership* and the *Journal of Curriculum and Supervision.* Bulletins, updates, book reviews, and software evaluations, as well as other ASCD publications, are built into this site. Articles must be purchased.

T.H.E. Journal Online   http://www.thejournal.com
Technological Horizons in Education's online version of *T.H.E. Journal* has product features, Internet information, conference listings, and suggestions.

Learning and Leading with Technology   http://www.iste.org/L&L
The International Society for Technology in Education provides *Learning and Leading with Technology* online with articles on issues and ideas encompassing all levels of instruction and all content areas.

FNO.org   http://www.fno.org
From Now On: The Educational Technology Journal is a multipurpose site with editorials by Jamie McKenzie, assessment techniques, curriculum notes, grants information, and Internet policies.

JILR   http://www.aace.org/pubs/jilr/default.htm
The *Journal of Interactive Learning Research* is a scholarly site noted for research findings on interactive learning environments focused on technology-based instruction.

Scholastic–Teachers   http://www.teacher.scholastic.com
Standards-designed, thematic lesson plans and reproducibles, web projects, research reports, and online activities from *Instructor* magazine are available here.

JIME   http://www-jime.open.ac.uk
The *Journal of Interactive Media in Education* is an online professional journal with screen and multiple-screen interfaces of articles on the latest technological developments in education.

Figure 8.4
Popular Online Publications
These publications are not rank-ordered, because their usefulness depends on the reader's purpose. The annotations list only a few of the features offered.

Whether you read and print via your browser or via Adobe Reader, be aware that many journals copyright the information presented on their web pages. You should check the specific copyright policies for the e-publications you use. Further discussion of copyright is presented later in this chapter and in Chapter 12.

Some online publications also offer a service that will automatically send email to you regarding upcoming highlights or news in brief. Most send weekly or monthly updates and may include special offers. Such emails often come with imbedded hot links to the full-text articles they summarize. This type of service is an easy and convenient way to keep up with the latest news from e-publications of interest to you. Publication mailing lists can be valuable aids, but subscribe only to those in which you have sincere interest. Subscribing to too many of these services can easily result in a great number of email messages. On some school and ISP servers, you might not have unlimited space to handle all of your email. Mailing list messages may inadvertently fill up your mailbox, causing your personal email to bounce back to the sender. Typically, should you need to discontinue receiving email from a mailing list, you need only respond with an email message that includes "unsubscribe" in either the subject line or body of the email. Details on how to unsubscribe are usually sent when you first subscribe to a mailing list, and some lists include them in every list email sent. You should save these "unsubscribe" instructions for each mailing list or newsletter that you sign up for.

Figure 8.5
Adobe Reader
With Adobe Reader, Acrobat-created files display pages just the way they look in hard-copy publications.

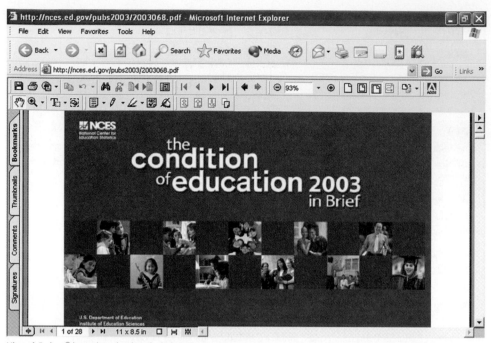

Microsoft Explorer® is a registered trademark of Microsoft Corporation.
Copyright © 2001 Adobe Systems Incorporated. Used with express permission. All rights reserved. Adobe, Acrobat Reader, and PhotoDeluxe are either trademarks or registered trademarks of Adobe Systems Incorporated in the United Stated and/or other countries.

ON THE WEB! 8.5
Online Organizations

Online Professional Organizations

Most major professional organizations now have a web presence. Teachers' unions, professional associations, content-area groups, technology groups, and many others have web sites that range from modest to robust. Organization web sites typically provide calendars of events, current and archived publications, online stores, and current news about issues critical to that organization. Some even include conferences, chats, and live audio or video Internet broadcasts featuring key people in the field.

Professional organizations offer a wide variety of services keyed to their missions. For educators, such organization web sites can offer a central repository of relevant and useful resources related to the organizational focus as well as links to other pertinent web sites. On the Web! Activity 8.5 summarizes some of the most popular organizational sites. Others, especially those related to very specific content areas, can be easily discovered by using a search engine.

Weblogs

Weblogs, or blogs, are virtual online spaces that support the posting of personal commentary on the web. Blogs provide primarily one-way communication, but with the inclusion of comments and links, blogs become powerful interactive writing tools. Bloggers post their ideas and others respond to these ideas, either in comments to the posting or in other blogs with a link back to the original posting. Bloggers can add links in their own commentaries to connect to other web resources or "backtrack" to other blogs. Since weblogs are powered by software that allows the writer and the audience to engage in an online communication cycle via the web, blogs have unique educational applications.

Unlike a structured discussion group, a blog provides each individual with his or her own web space in which to post personal views and comments on any topic rather than to comment within the confines of a discussion group topic. Whether entered daily or less frequently, blog postings can be read by anyone wishing to view them and can be responded to instantaneously. If the blogging software supports it, blog postings can be responded to with comments added to the original posting. Or, an individual can post comments about various other blogs on his or her own blog site. The ultimate effect is a lively group discussion, with readers able to jump from blog to blog via connecting links to see what others have to say. In much the same way that our attention turns from one person to another in a classroom discussion as each expresses a view, blog readers jump from one online blog to another to read comments in a posting thread. With these capabilities, educational blogging sites (edblogs) have evolved that have given online space to students from elementary age through college (see Figure 8.6). Edblogs have been successfully used to give students an opportunity to publicly post daily journal entries; to comment on peer postings; to collaborate on a group project even if participants are a world apart; to research what other bloggers have said on a topic; and to connect to resources they have found. Educational blogs have provided a unique forum for the expression of ideas and for the thoughtful consideration of other viewpoints. In the hands of a skillful technology-using educator, this tool can empower students to write and communicate and teachers to facilitate that expression. With an estimated 350,000 weblogs of all sorts on the web at this writing, this easy publish-to-the-web phenomenon is likely to become, in time, as common as the home page is today.

ON THE WEB! 8.6
Edblogs

▌ Governmental Sites

The U.S. Department of Education and most state departments of education have very comprehensive web sites with abundant resources for educators (see Figure 8.7). The U.S. Department of Education site (http://www.ed.gov) includes information about current education news, national standards, programs, grants, research, links to other federal agencies, and a wide variety of publications and reports available by mail or download. State department of education web sites offer similar services, but their emphasis is on educational issues within a given state.

Figure 8.6
Educational Weblog Web Site
Educational weblog sites offer teachers and students unique opportunity for self-expression and interaction via the web.

SOURCE: Educational Bloggers Network, Retrieved November 2003 from http://www.ebn.weblogger.com.

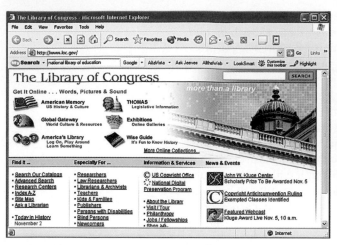

SOURCE: U.S. Library of Congress. Microsoft Internet Explorer® is a registered trademark of Microsoft Corporation.

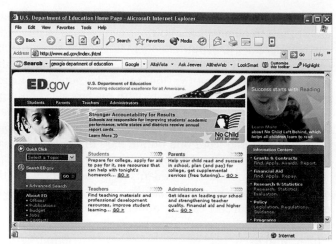

SOURCE: U.S. Department of Education. Microsoft Internet Explorer® is a registered trademark of Microsoft Corporation.

Figure 8.7
Government Web Sites
Government education sites present critical and current educational resources.

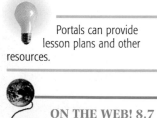

Portals can provide lesson plans and other resources.

ON THE WEB! 8.7
Accessing the Internet

The U.S. Department of Education (ed.gov) web site also provides some of the most useful and comprehensive education links available, including access to **ERIC,** the Educational Resources Information Center. ERIC is the world's largest database of education information, with more than one million abstracts of documents and journal articles, many available through the Internet.

Education Portals

A number of portals include an area focused on education. Educational resources found at portals may include teachers' guides to the Internet, lesson plans, Net events, audio and video clips, web hosting opportunities, clip art libraries, educational games, information about schools and colleges, and a variety of instructional resources accessible by grade level and content area. Each portal offers unique services, so it is valuable to investigate what specific educational resources each offers. All portals and most web sites provide you with a wide variety of current links to other resources on the Net.

ON THE WEB! 8.8
Compendiums

Favorite Links

Some of the best online resources are discovered through hot links from one site to another. Web sites often link to other sites consistent with the content of their own site. Some sites are compendiums of links created for the sole purpose of providing connections to those seeking information on a given topic. When you find a useful web site, it is a very good idea to check its links page and explore related sites.

But given that there are so many links and so many useful sites, how can a busy teacher possibly remember where they are? Browsers have a built-in function that assists you in that regard. It is a compendium of URLs called **bookmarks** or **favorites.** Bookmarking or adding to your favorites list allows you to store web site URLs that are of interest to you. When you decide to revisit a web site you have stored, you need only click on its name in your list; and the browser will immediately connect you to that site. Web sites can be added to or deleted from your list as you require. The use of book-

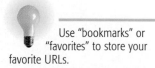

Use "bookmarks" or "favorites" to store your favorite URLs.

marks or favorites makes it easy to store and access the useful links that you discover as you search the Internet for valuable resources.

Your list is usually stored on the hard drive of the computer you are using to access the Net. If you are on a networked workstation, your list may be stored on the server hard drive or the workstation hard drive, depending on how the network administrator has configured your particular network. In any case, if you wish to remember a link but you do not happen to be at your usual computer, you can email the link to your own email account. Web browsers typically have a command that allows you to email a web site from the account you are using to other email accounts. This function lets you email an interesting link to yourself to later add to your list or to colleagues with whom you wish to share your discovery. Emailing web sites can be a very useful method of finding and storing educational Internet resources.

Classroom Management Tools

Classroom management tools on the web include downloadable or online tools that assist you in the tasks required for your classroom. Several sites offer software that creates online or paper tests and, if they are online, grades them for you and sends you the results. These **test generators** can create tests by randomly selecting questions within their databases of questions, or you can select the questions to be included. Some allow you to add your own questions to the database. Others let you create multimedia tests. Many textbooks (including this one) have added these types of resources to their companion web sites.

ON THE WEB! 8.9
Online Classroom Tools

Other Internet-based management tools include formal and informal diagnostic tests to assess learning preferences, tools that generate class rolls with seating charts, and **electronic gradebooks** that let you store and easily average student grades. Many of these tools can be used online or downloaded to your machine. If they are used online, some security and privacy issues may be involved. Student information is private and must be closely guarded. Making information accessible by using a nonsecure online resource may be an issue. A later section of this chapter will deal more fully with your responsibilities in this regard.

Academic Tools

There is an abundance of Internet tools that support instruction. Many of these can be either used online or downloaded to your computer as freeware or shareware. Some of the most popular **academic tools** include worksheet generators of many types that help you make interesting student activity sheets. These tools help you create content-specific crossword puzzles, word searches, cryptograms, math exercises, and multimedia flash cards. Most of these tools allow you to input the key content and then generate the activity sheet of your choice, which can then be either printed or saved to a file. These creative and time-saving tools help you add interest and variety to your instructional plan.

ON THE WEB! 8.10
Academic Tools Online

One of the key academic resources available on the Internet is lesson plans. Some lesson plan sites offer subject-specific plans, others offer lesson plans submitted by colleagues across the nation, and still others offer lesson plans tied to national or state standards. In addition to sites dedicated to lesson plans, links on many educational sites offer lesson plans related to the content of that site. A related resource is lesson plan software programs that generate lesson plans for you and even relate them to specific standards. The abundance of lesson plan sites and tools, from those sponsored by the U.S. Department of Education to those supported by individual teachers, is one of the most remarkable educational Internet resources available to busy educators. Browsing through these many lesson plans can offer you valuable ideas for use in your classroom.

Explore online lesson plans when developing your lesson ideas.

Reference tools and resources, including dictionaries in all languages, thesauri, grammar and spelling tools, and world atlases, are also available on the Internet. These reference tools also include translation references that translate from one language to another, specialty dictionaries and glossaries that relate to specific professions or hobbies, and other vocabulary aids to provide you with a wealth of information about acronyms, anagrams, and homonyms. These reference tools bring the reference section of a large library to every classroom via the Internet.

CD-ROM-based multimedia encyclopedias are fairly common software for school media centers. It is often too costly, however, to buy one encyclopedia for each classroom or to buy the network hardware and site licensing that allow sharing. An alternative is to access these same tools on the Internet. Many of the most popular multimedia encyclopedias and research resources are available on the Internet. These tools work similarly to those on CD-ROM, including the ability to download and save or print entries. With a classroom Internet connection, it may no longer be necessary to purchase multiple CDs or reconfigure the network. Furthermore, because students are working on the Internet, online research resources can add hot links to related information. This allows for instant hyperjumps to follow up on information, a feature that most CD-ROMs cannot offer.

In addition to the more formal academic tools and resources mentioned thus far, the Internet provides teachers with a storehouse of innovation and great teaching ideas at every grade level and for every content area. Teachers from across the globe contribute to a variety of web sites ideas that have worked well in their own classrooms. Each site then categorizes and files these innovations to make them accessible via the site's search engines. Such sites are continually being updated and contributed to by creative educators. These sites are a storehouse of best practices that can be easily accessed with a few clicks and a few keystrokes.

Connection gateways are web sites that offer users the opportunity to communicate with each other. For educators there are a number of web sites that offer conferences and chats on specific topics related to teaching, on topics related to teaching a grade level, or on content areas across all grade levels. These sites offer educators a chance to engage in an interactive exchange with colleagues across the globe. Dialog such as this expands every participant's professional perspective and is likely to be the source of many useful insights and creative ideas.

Whether Internet academic tools and resources are used by you to prepare to teach or by your students as they engage in learning, these educational resources add a dimension to your classroom that was an impossibility just a decade ago. The Internet has brought teaching and learning tools to every classroom that connects to it. But like all tools, they are only as useful as the hands that wield them. It is up to you as the leader and facilitator of the teaching and learning process to become sufficiently aware of these resources in order to make the best use of them in your instructional environment.

ON THE WEB! 8.11
Bridging Theory to Practice

Online chats and conferences can expand your professional horizons.

Web-Enhanced Instruction

Whether you choose to use the Internet in your classroom daily or only occasionally, an easy-to-use web site of your own can enhance the learning environment. The ways to integrate the Internet into instruction, particularly via your own web site, are limited only by your own imagination. This section will explore a few of the possibilities.

Enhancing Classroom Communication

As you have learned throughout this text, it is important to address the individual needs and learning styles of your students. Typically, a teacher will communicate instructional content and activities by telling students about them. However, for students who are primarily visual learners, this communication method can be difficult to follow. A classroom web site can help to support and enhance communication. For teacher-to-student communication, a classroom web site can contain daily, weekly, or unit assignments and thorough directions on how to complete them. It can also answer anticipated student questions on a linked **FAQ** (frequently asked questions) page. It can contain information about grading or tips for working on an assignment as well as links to relevant related pages such as the school's honesty or computer use policies. Finally, it can use web-based multimedia with voice, animation, or motion video to present key points in formats that address multiple learning preferences. This type of web page adds reinforcing dimensions to teacher-to-student communications as well as reiteration of key instructions.

A web site for your class can be a valuable tool for learning as well as communicating.

When teachers work cooperatively by grade level or content-area department to create a shared web site, the impact is even more pronounced. Coordinated classroom web sites provide a common ground that is familiar and therefore easy for students to use. Such sites also provide common links to school resources as well as to each other, improving communications among all of the administrators, teachers, and students involved. Teacher-to-student communication is thus clarified, consistent, and open among all those involved.

ON THE WEB! 8.12
Grade-Level Web Sites

Student-to-teacher communication can be enhanced via a classroom web site as well. Whether the student is in class but too shy to voice his or her questions or the student is at home and struggling with an assignment, email or a teacher–student electronic chat can provide an opportunity for direct, private, and meaningful communication. Additionally, for students who can't seem to carry hard copy successfully from one location to another, attaching homework to an email message can be a very effective tool for ensuring that work is turned in on time. Electronic conferencing can also support and enhance student-to-teacher communications if the teacher moderates posted public questions on activities or content. Adding some or all of these features to a classroom web site enhances student-to-teacher communications.

For student-to-student communication, a web site with email or chat options or with weblogs or electronic conferencing can encourage communication and build teamwork and communication skills. An activity in which students email the draft of a written assignment to each other for editing before completing the final version provides an opportunity for students to exercise proofreading and grammar skills. A group project that requires participation in a chat or conference helps students develop communication skills while building technology skills. For shy students who would otherwise be reluctant to contribute verbally in class, this opportunity for thoughtful communication at a pace that is comfortable for them may open new avenues of communication and build confidence in their own interaction skills. Creating such an adaptable and personal learning community within a classroom, grade level, or school is facilitated by the integration of a classroom web site.

❙ Linking Your Students to Their World

Student-to-student communication within a classroom, grade level, or school is just the beginning of what the Internet has to offer to your students. One of the most imaginative ways of utilizing your classroom web site as a communication tool is to connect your classroom to others across the globe, thereby building a **global learning community** for your students. Keypals, e-pals, and cyberpals are some of the terms used to refer to the other people with whom your students may correspond. Whatever term you prefer, the idea is to use Internet-based communications to extend interaction beyond the walls of your classroom or school.

Use the web to form a global learning community.

Keypal assignments can help students practice communication skills while enhancing cultural awareness. Whole sites are dedicated to establishing this type of learning community. Some provide teachers' guides, keypal lesson plans and projects, opportunities to request and make connections with global members, world maps, and

ON THE WEB! 8.13
Internet Pals

IN THE CLASSROOM

Keeping in Touch: The Web for Student Communicators

Dr. Barclay J. Barrios, director of instructional technology in the writing program at Rutgers, the State University of New Jersey, informs us of the value of blogs as a means of educational student communication:

> Many blog services allow multiple authors to contribute to a blog. Several students can work together on a blog centered on a single topic or assignment. Using a blog extends the collaboration space outside the classroom, allowing students to work together across time and space. At the same time, the blog records the progress of collaboration, allowing teachers to observe, comment, and intervene as needed while allowing students to reflect on the process at the end of the assignment.

Will Richardson, a teacher of journalism at Hunterdon Central Regional High School in Flemington, New Jersey, uses weblogs in his classroom and has made a web site, **http://www.weblogg-ed.com**, to encourage other teachers to jump on the bandwagon. The site is a virtual introduction to blogging. For his writing classes, he states that he "has found discussion tools the most helpful feature" of his journalism weblog, noting that the online interaction "provided students an opportunity to articulate their ideas in ways they haven't been asked to before."

But blogging is not confined to secondary levels. Anne Davis, instructional technology specialist at Georgia State College of Education, and elementary teacher Marcia Mateling successfully integrated blogging into J. H. House Elementary School in Con-

yers, Georgia. Fourth and fifth graders at first used blogs to practice writing and responding to their peers. The project, however, took on a new dimension when Will Richardson suggested the two classes collaborate via blogging. Richardson's high school students would become writing mentors for the elementary-level bloggers. This successful application of educational weblogs has the older students mentoring and supporting the younger ones as they apply their own writing skills. The elementary children in turn are motivated to write well for their high school mentors and look forward to the interaction. Davis says of her fourth and fifth graders, "My students are all reading, writing, listening, thinking, reacting." From the student mentors' perspective, Richardson points out that "The cool thing is, my students get to do a little bit of teaching. That internalizes the information for them. When they go back to doing their own writing, they see it more clearly." The integration of blogging into these two innovative classrooms has created a unique collaborative learning community that clearly benefits all.

SOURCES: B. Barrios. 2002. The subtle knife: Blog*diss: Blogs in the classroom. Retrieved May 8, 2003, from **http://www.barclaybarrios.com/tsk/blog/classroom.html**; A. Davis. 2003. Elementary writers learn to love their weblogs. Retrieved October 31, 2003, from **http://www97.intel.com/education/odyssey/day_300/day_300.htm**; W. Richardson. 2003. High school journalists use weblogs to mentor young writers. Retrieved October 31, 2003, from **http://www97.intel.com/education/odyssey/day_301/day_301.htm**.

ON THE WEB! 8.14
Getting Connected Globally

even translation services. Communicating with keypals can be an invaluable personal growth experience as well as a directed learning activity.

However you decide to develop Internet-based links between your own students and their peers across the globe, the cultural awareness, communication skills, and content-area enrichment that the web makes possible can be a significant enhancement to classroom instruction. Connecting students to other students for the purpose of learning about each other and exchanging ideas offers an opportunity for personal growth and enrichment that would not be possible otherwise.

Building Bridges to Parents and the Community

Bring parents into the classroom through the Internet.

However, communication among students locally or globally is not the only possibility provided by the integration of communication tools into the learning environment. Building bridges to parents and community is another opportunity created through implementation of the web in instruction.

Parents and teachers share the common goal of helping students meet their personal potential. By working together in partnership, you and your students' parents have the best chance of helping the children. Undeniably, life circumstances often make communications difficult. Many parents work outside the home and are available only after school hours. Time-shifted (asynchronous) interaction can help to open lines of communication that might otherwise not be possible. A classroom web page offers many opportunities for such communications.

By posting classroom rules, schedules, and homework on a classroom web page, a teacher can directly communicate expectations to the parents of all students in a class. By adding communications tools including email, chat, and conferencing, a means for private and public dialog can be established. When you are seeking parent volunteers for classroom activities, posting such requests on a classroom web site makes more partnerships and support possible.

Equally important, the ability to inform parents in a timely manner about student progress is a particularly powerful Internet-based communications tool. If you post grades via a secured web site or a secure service linked to a web site, parents can track how students are doing and even monitor their attendance. Such daily or weekly feedback to parents gives them a chance to join you in resolving performance issues before they permanently affect a student's grades. This creates a powerful home-school partnership to support learners and keep them on the right track.

Linking your classroom to the greater community is another potential opportunity provided through the Internet and a class web site. Community involvement can mean partnerships that enhance your learning environment through community members' participation as mentors or guest speakers or through community contributions to class projects. Your students might become the hub of a virtual community learning center that links generations in dialog and support. Senior citizens might share oral history with your students, or your students might mentor younger peers on a project. Parents, community members, and students can join together to explore and share views on issues of significance to the local community. In whatever way you choose to provide communications opportunities to parents and the community, the bridges you create can only enhance the learning environment you provide for your students and open doors to their world.

ON THE WEB! 8.15
Using the Web to Create a Virtual Classroom

IN THE CLASSROOM

Weaving a Web to Families and the Community

Teachers use their web sites in many innovative ways to keep their classrooms connected to their students, their students' parents, and the community. Here are some of the many creative ways to use your web site.

In an increasingly bilingual, and often with parents unilingual, nation, Doug Shivers, who teaches kindergarten in a bilingual class in Gresham, Oregon, creates his web site in both English and Spanish. Shivers knows, as do many kindergarten teachers, that children, when asked about school on any given day, will say "that they 'just played.'" He says, "The [web site] lets me explain how they're learning through play every day. I also often give [parents] ideas of how to reinforce at home what we are doing at school."

Of particular interest for teachers using their web sites to reach out to parents is the comprehensive Parent Page included on the web site of Gold Ridge Elementary School. Hyperlinks on this page cover "Ten Memos from Your Child" (such as "Don't spoil me. I know quite well that I ought not to have all that I ask for. I'm only testing you"), "Noon Supervisor Information," "Medication Forms," "Field Trip Information and Forms," "Atten-dance Note," "Parenting Help," "Gold Ridge Rules and Responsibilities," "School Calendar," and "Bell Schedule."

Mrs. Burton teaches kindergarten at Byrd Elementary School in Goochland County, Virginia. For keeping in touch with parents and with her fellow teachers, she has created a web site called KinderKonnect. It has an extensive list of links, covering rules, letters, homework, math, author studies, social studies, science, school supplies, teacher pages (where she invites early childhood teachers to contribute ideas for teaching children of this age group), schedules, awards, book orders, discussion forums, a back-to-school letter, news, article archives, and lunch menus. She says of her web site, "My mission in creating this web site is to keep parents in my classroom [and] administrators and early childhood educators in my district informed of the doings in my class and to provide tips and ideas to teachers."

SOURCES: L. Goldberg. 2002. Web pages to the rescue. *Instructor* (August), 112 (1), 27–28, 78; Gold Ridge Elementary School web site. Retrieved November 2, 2003, from http://www.sonic.net/kargo/parent.htm; Mrs. Burton. 2003. KinderKonnect web page. Retrieved November 2, 2003, from http://www.kinderkonnect.com.

Class Web Sites

As you have read through this chapter, you have discovered a wide variety of resources on the web to assist you in teaching and in helping your students to learn. Today, many teachers have created their own classroom web sites so that the resources they select are readily available from a single convenient location. A classroom web site can offer class information as well as links to any useful sites on the web, from weblog sites to e-pal sites to content-related sites that might help your students find out more about a topic under study (see Figure 8.8). Just as every teacher has his or her own teaching style, a classroom web site offers a teacher the opportunity to customize what his or her students will do and see on the web via a unique class site.

While a teacher might feel that creating a web site is too difficult, as you have learned in Chapter 6, **web authoring tools** are available to make the job easy to do. These tools range from very easy to more challenging, but for every teacher who wants a class web site, an authoring tool at his or her level of comfort and computer skills is available. The next section will review these authoring tools and help you to decide which is best for you.

Before authoring a web site, a first critical step is to design it. Designing a web site involves a series of structured and organized steps to ensure that the final product is as professional and useful as you intended. Following this chapter, you will find a special feature section (Interchapter 3) that will take you through all of the steps to design a successful class web site. Once you complete each step and have designed the web site

SITE PAGES

Classroom Connection page shares classroom information and current day's activities.

Homework Hotline page lets students and parents know what is required for homework this week.

Class Calendar tracks important due dates and holidays for students and parents.

News2View shares newsworthy events and class and student news.

Link-O-Rama offers students and parents links related to study units and school information.

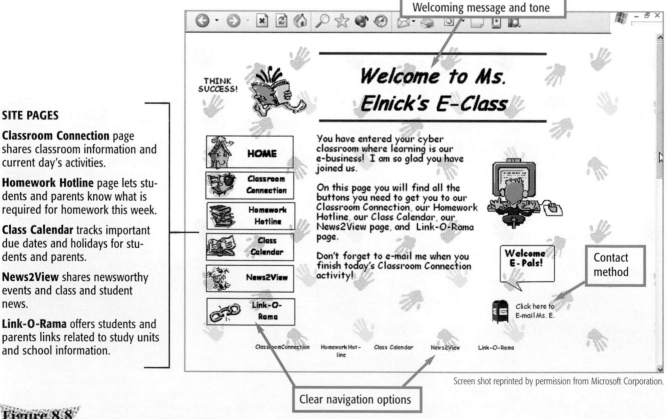

Screen shot reprinted by permission from Microsoft Corporation.

Figure 8.8

Elements of an Effective Classroom Web Site

Class web sites let teachers reflect their own style while communicating information and instructional content and while providing links to other web resources.

that best reflects your teaching style and your students' needs, then it is a simple matter to use the authoring tool to make it a reality.

Web Authoring Tools

How exactly do you go about making a class web site? Fortunately, so many web authoring tools are available today that you no longer need a working knowledge of HTML. All you need is a well-planned idea for a site, a good storyboard, and some basic computer skills. A variety of tools are available; which one you choose to use depends on your skill level and your expectations for the final product.

Authoring tools make creating your own web site something you can do.

Word Processors

One of the easiest ways to create a web page is to use a word processor with which you are already familiar. Word processors let you create files as you would any other file, laying them out with graphics and text, but then save them in HTML format for uploading to the web. Although this technique is reasonably simple to use, it creates only very straightforward and basic types of web pages.

The more sophisticated word processors also include templates and design wizards for web pages (see Figure 8.9). Templates are predefined formats, and wizards are interactive tools that not only use predesigned formats, but also ask you customization questions in the process of creating them. These tools allow you to use web pages that are already fully designed and even an entire web site with hot links between pages already in place. Using these tools, you need only enter the data you want to display, save your new web page, and upload it to a web server.

On CD!
Software Skills Builder
E-Portfolios with Word's Web Wizard

Figure 8.9
Microsoft Word Web Wizard
Wizards make creating a web site an easy process.

Microsoft Word Web Wizard® is a registered trademark of Microsoft Corporation.

The advantage of using the word-processing software with which you may already be familiar could be canceled out by its inflexibility. You might want more sophisticated layout capabilities or more features than the web component of a word processor can provide. The best way to decide is to try word-processing web authoring. Your Software Skills Builder CD includes an activity that gives you hands-on experience with Microsoft Word's Web Wizard. If Word is insufficient for your needs, there are alternative software packages to consider.

▎Desktop Publishing Software

As you learned in earlier chapters, desktop publishing software gives you much greater control of the look of a printed page than is possible with a word processor. Objects can be moved about, and new elements can be easily added and rearranged. Just as desktop publishing allows you to manipulate a printed page more easily, so too can the desktop publisher that is equipped with web production components give you more flexibility in manipulating a web site's page layouts. Additionally, like word processors, the more sophisticated desktop publishing programs include web wizards, allowing you to quickly create very dramatic web pages (see Figure 8.10). Because publishing software allows more flexibility and design features, the web pages produced by its wizards are typically a bit more sophisticated. Although this type of software will not allow you to include all of the bells and whistles you see on many commercial web sites, it will help you to create a very attractive, automatically linked web site.

Your Software Skills Builder CD includes a hands-on activity using Microsoft Publisher's Web Wizard. The Web Wizard will help you to build a colorful and powerful web site using Publisher's familiar and easy-to-use tools. It can then be easily saved in HTML format and uploaded to the web.

On CD!
Software Skills Builder
Class Web Site with Publisher's
Web Wizard

Figure 8.10
Microsoft Publisher Web Wizard
Word-processing and desktop publishing software may contain easy-to-use web authoring components.

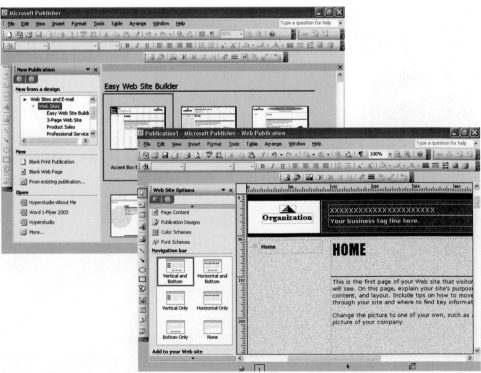

Microsoft Publisher Web Wizard® is a registered trademark of Microsoft Corporation.

▌Dedicated Web Development Software

For those who are interested in developing a more sophisticated site, web development software programs are readily available (see Figure 8.11). These programs range from fairly easy to very complex, depending on the sophistication you are trying to achieve in the finished web site. Most packages within this software category will help you author a web site that will do all of the tasks you see on commercial sites. Some will provide you with very advanced graphics and multimedia tools to add your own special effects to your site. You will have to decide what level of sophistication you want to achieve in your web site and decide for yourself how much time and how many resources you are willing to invest. Although dedicated web authoring tools are easy to use once you have mastered the skills, they are typically not as easy as using a web component of an alternative software package with which you are already familiar.

Web authoring tools can help you create web pages.

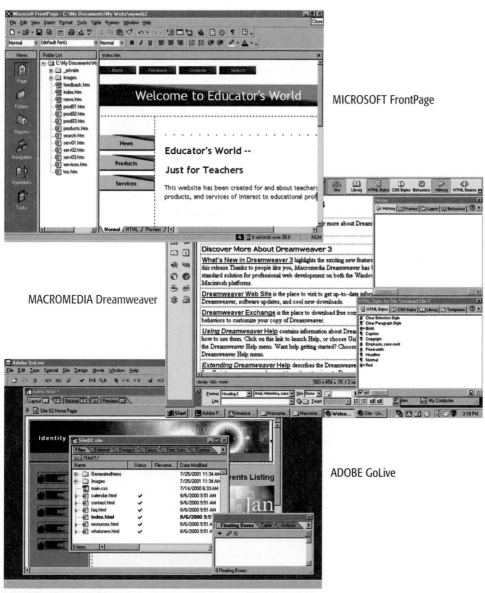

MICROSOFT FrontPage

MACROMEDIA Dreamweaver

ADOBE GoLive

Figure 8.11
Web Development Software
Web development software gives you the potential to add every level of sophistication to your site.

ON THE WEB! 8.16
Portals to the Web

A final dedicated web authoring tool may be available through the ISP or portal that you use. Some ISPs allocate web space for their customers' web pages. Typically, those that do also provide a web creation tool. Usually, such tools do not have a great number of options, but they will allow you to create a web page with relative ease. Some portals also offer web space and tools with which you can create web pages. These range from simple tools such as those provided by an ISP, to downloadable shareware or freeware web authoring programs. Different portals provide different levels of service, so it is important to shop around if you decide to use them. Remember too that most ISPs and portals that provide you with web space will also let you upload a site you have created using your own software of choice. They usually do not require you to use their specific tools.

Moving Your Site to the Internet

Adding Your Site to the School or District Site

Once you have completed your web site authoring, how do you move it to the Internet? Your web site is actually a series of HTML and multimedia files stored on your hard drive or a CD. To put them up on the web, you will need to move your collection of web site files to a web server. The web server, as you learned in Chapter 7, connects a network to the web and stores web files for others to access. So to move your site to the web, you must upload it to a web server.

Many schools and districts are now providing space on their web servers for teachers' classroom web sites. If that is the case, to add your site to the school's or district's server, you will need to give all of the related web site files, via CD or email, to the webmaster for your school. A webmaster's job is to create and maintain a site and to integrate new elements. Your school or district webmaster will take your classroom web site files and integrate them appropriately into the school or district site.

It is important to keep in mind that many webmasters have additional jobs as technical-support staff or have their hands full already maintaining complex institutional web sites. In either case, it may take a bit of time to see your web site come up on the web, a problem that may repeat itself every time you want to update the site. More importantly, if you want to use your site for posting current activities and you cannot adjust the data yourself because of your limited network rights, you might find it very difficult to alter the site daily or weekly. This may interfere with your instructional intentions for the site. For that reason, some educators choose instead to use one of the many types of web site hosting services available on the web.

Uploading to a Web Host

Free or inexpensive **web hosting** is a service offered by a number of ISPs, web sites, and portals (see Figure 8.12). To use this type of service, you need only **upload** your pages to the host, usually via an **FTP** program. The service will take care of creating the web access for you. Links to very detailed instructions on how to upload files are usually displayed prominently on the service's web development page.

Hosting services allow you a given number of megabytes of space on the service's web server; some services offer an unlimited amount of space. In exchange, those who visit your site may be asked to fill in some personal information to "join" the service in order to access your page. At the very least, they will be exposed to ads on the service's home page as they navigate to your page. Other hosting services may add a banner ad to the top of your page or require you to allow pop-up ads. Collecting data from service "members" generates a potential customer list for the service's advertisers. Getting more visitors to a web site to navigate to sites hosted there improves the salability

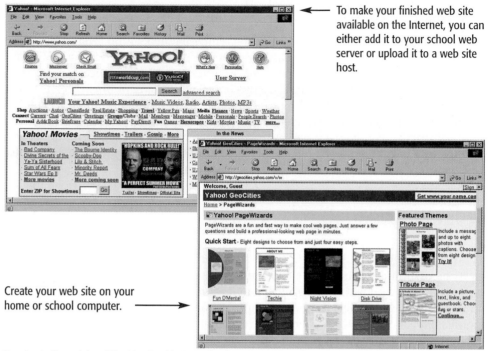

To make your finished web site available on the Internet, you can either add it to your school web server or upload it to a web site host.

Figure 8.12
Web Site Hosting
A web hosting service allows you to upload your web site to its web server to make it accessible on the web.

Create your web site on your home or school computer.

of ad space on the service's home page. This is essentially how services can offer to host your site for free or reduced cost.

You should carefully investigate sites that offer these services, including reading the fine print in the online agreements. Because you will be asking your students to use the site, if the advertisements on a service's home page or the elements added to your home page seem inappropriate or too overbearing for young visitors, you might decide that it is best not to use that service. You need to make your best professional judgment about the value of free or inexpensive web hosting service and the non-monetary costs it entails. Your first responsibility is to ensure that your students are not exposed to excessive or inappropriate advertising within the requirements of your course. Before you use a free web hosting service, you might want to check with your school or district policies and procedures to determine whether any of these issues have already been formally addressed.

Uploading to a Private Host

If you have an ISP that provides web space as well as Internet access, or if you select to subscribe to a web host, you might want to upload your classroom web site to that server instead. Private hosts do not advertise on customer web sites, and they will give you a very direct URL so that your students can bypass the host's home page. Like their public counterparts, private web hosts typically include detailed instructions on their site on how to transfer your HTML files and step-by-step procedures on how to implement the upload process.

You want to shop around when you select an ISP to see whether the available ISPs do indeed provide web hosting and how much space they will give your account. Comparison shopping is equally necessary if you are considering subscribing to a private web-hosting service. If you plan to use a number of graphics and multimedia files, web site file size can increase dramatically. You will need to compare the space you need for the type of site you want with the amount of web space various private hosts offer.

Uploading to Academic Web Services

A final type of web hosting service is one that is incorporated within broader academic services. Some private and publicly funded web sites offer schools and teachers a variety of free educational services, including web hosting. These services refrain from advertising on your web pages and strictly control advertising on their broader sites. They are designed to provide an appropriate Internet environment for your students and your site. The only disadvantage to this type of site is that it often provides only a relatively small amount of storage space, which may make it inadequate for larger web sites. On the Web! Activity 8.17 summarizes some of the most popular academic sites, and Table 8.2 provides you with a rubric for their evaluation.

ON THE WEB! 8.17
Academic Web Hosts

Internet Issues and Concerns

With any resource that is used in the learning environment, professional judgment must be used in determining the appropriateness of the resource and ensuring that the resource is used within the ethical and legal parameters of the profession. Using the Internet in your teaching and learning environment is no different. A number of significant concerns are frequently voiced relating to the use of the Internet in schools. Three of these issues—acceptable use, privacy, and filtering—are introduced in this section. An expanded discussion of these issues can be found in Chapter 12.

Acceptable Use

Like any technology, the Internet can be abused. In a school setting, it is therefore necessary to identify and enforce the acceptable use of a school's network and Internet access. This is usually done through a district's or school's acceptable use policy (AUP). This policy articulates the ways in which the Internet can be used by students. Typically, parents are asked to confirm their understanding of the policy and the consequences for violating it through a signature acknowledgment. Teachers who use the Internet and who provide links to resources via their own class web sites should be familiar with the AUP that governs their students' use of the Internet.

Privacy

When sharing your students' work or including their images or names on a web site, a teacher must be sure to carefully guard a child's privacy. To include any student's information or work, it is best to first have the parent's or guardian's permission. Further, no specific details about the child should be divulged, including his or her name. Those who might harm children might use a class web site as a way to target them. The problem has become so significant that districts and schools typically have developed very specific policies regarding the content of a class web site. It is up to each teacher to be sure his or her site is consistent with district and school guidelines.

Filtering

As you know, the Internet is not owned or controlled by any agency. Therefore, the Internet includes web sites and information inappropriate for children. A school has a responsibility to limit access to such web sites just as a parent would limit access at home. Schools use filtering software that checks the content of a site before allowing it to be displayed on the screen. Students are denied access to sites that contain or display inappropriate materials. Claims of freedom of speech are sometimes invoked

TABLE 8.2   ACADEMIC WEB SITE EVALUATION RUBRIC

DEVELOPER'S NAME:

URL:

AREA/CONTENT OF SITE:

PURPOSE:

Using each of the criteria below, evaluate the usefulness of this web site for teaching and learning. For each dimension in the rubric, check the box that best reflects your opinion. Select web sites that score 4 or higher in the most dimensions.

			EVALUATION CRITERIA		
Dimension	*1* *Poor*	*2* *Below* *Average*	*3* *Average*	*4* *Above* *Average*	*5* *Excellent*
Goal	Goal of this web site is unclear and confusing	Web site has conflicting themes, making its goal uncertain	Goal is clear, but site contains some unrelated or distracting elements	Clear purpose and goal; some elements seem unnecessary	Goal and purpose of site clear with no distracting elements
User friendliness	Site is unwelcoming to users	Site does not evoke a welcoming message	Site welcomes visitors but does not appear friendly	Site is welcoming and appears friendly	Site is exciting, welcoming, and very user-friendly
Design	Poorly organized; contains obvious errors; loads slowly; difficult to read	Organization somewhat confusing; some errors; loads slowly	Organization acceptable; no obvious errors; loads adequately; easy to read	Good organization; no errors; loads quickly; easy to read	Excellent organization; free of errors; loads quickly and clearly; all elements easy to read
Navigability	Difficult to find and follow site navigation links	Navigation links visible but somewhat confusing	Navigation links clear and readily available	Navigation links clear and logical; site map included	Navigation logical and clear; site map and search engine available
Authority	Unclear who the teacher is and what class the site relates to	Teacher name and contact included, but sufficient class information lacking	Teacher name, contact information, and some class information included	Teacher name, contact information, full class information included	Teacher provides all necessary information to student, parent, and community visitors
Dates	No dates evident	Site contains some dates	Site contains both creation and update information but no dates related to class activities	Site contains creation and update information and some dates relating to class activities	Site contains dates for creation, update, and all class activities
Content	Content limited and lacks relevance to students and parents	Content appears relevant, but quantity limited in student needs	Content is adequate in relevance and quantity to meet student needs	Content is relevant and quantity is sufficient for student needs	Content is on target and provides excellent coverage to meet student needs
Links	Few relevant working links	Adequate number of links, but many no longer functional	Sufficient number of links and all are functional	A good variety of useful, active links	Links offer connection to a wide variety of excellent sites
Handicapped access	No options available for handicapped	Some pages on site offer text-only	Site offers text-only on all pages	Site offers clear options for handicapped	Site includes handicapped options on all pages and links to support software

This and other downloadable forms and templates can be found on the Companion Website at www.ablongman.com/lever-duffy.

when filtering software is used. Such controversy is more fully addressed in Chapter 12, but most would agree that it is appropriate to keep children safe from harmful Internet content just as they are kept safe from other harm while at school.

Using the Internet in Teaching and Learning: Final Thoughts

As anyone knows who has used the Internet to discover something new or find an answer to a question, there can be little doubt that this resource holds enormous potential for education. No matter how many millions of sources are available on the Internet or how exciting the interactive multimedia sites may be, without the thoughtful integration of these marvelous resources into instruction by trained and knowledgeable teachers, learners will miss the potential of the Internet. As with all technology tools, it is not the tool itself that enhances teaching and learning, it is how the tool is used by the creative professional educator who is wielding it. The Internet is a marvel of limitless resources available at the touch of a key or click of the mouse. But your students need you, their teacher, to help make the Internet truly meaningful in their attempt to achieve their academic potential. Just as you master your content area before you teach it, so too must you master Internet skills before you can use them effectively. This chapter, along with Chapter 7, has attempted to give you a foundation for this mastery. We hope that the potential of the Internet has been made abundantly clear and your enthusiasm for using this technology amply kindled.

KEY TERMS

academic tools   257
bookmarks   256
classroom management tools   257
connection gateways   258
electronic gradebooks   257
ERIC   256
FAQ   259
favorites   256
FTP   266
GIF   249
global learning community   259
home page   245
hypertext markup language (HTML)   245
hyperlinks   245
JPEG   249
navigation button   245

online publications   252
PDF files   252
plug-in   247
portal   252
search engines   250
streaming audio   249
streaming video   249
test generator   257
uniform resource locator (URL)   246
upload   266
virtual reality (VR)   250
web authoring tools   262
web hosting   266
web page   245
web site   245
World Wide Web   245

STUDENT ACTIVITIES

CHAPTER REVIEW

1. What is a web site? What role does a browser play when you are working on the web?
2. What is HTML? Does a teacher need to know HTML to have a class web site? Why or why not?
3. What is a URL and how is it used? Why is a URL important when using the web?
4. What are streaming audio and streaming video? How have they altered the use of audio and video on the Internet?
5. How do search engines help you find specific information on the Internet?
6. What is a PDF file? What advantage does it offer over files in HTML format?
7. What is a weblog? How might it be used for teaching and learning?
8. How are government educational sites of value in terms of resources? How do they differ from commercial and organizational sites?
9. What types of classroom management and academic tools are available via the Internet? Briefly explain how each tool might help you in your classroom.
10. How can a classroom web site improve communications with students, parents, and community?

WHAT DO YOU THINK?

1. Your class has created a useful and interesting web site, but your school's technical-support staff is very overworked, so you might have to wait until the next grading period to have the site put on the web server. You decide to use a free web hosting service instead. What issues will you need to face in using a free web hosting service? How can you control unacceptable banner ads or pop-up ads that may be added to your site?
2. You have installed a filter on your stand-alone classroom computer that is connected to the Internet. You block all sites that you think might be pornographic, and then you decide to block all sites that may include what you feel might be communist propaganda. This might be a violation of your students' First Amendment rights. Why?
3. You decide that you want to create an electronic learning community for your students this semester. You would like to be sure they can converse with other students in the district, the state, and even around the globe. You have decided that you want to center the community on a multicultural theme in which they compare holiday customs and celebrations. How will you go about creating such a community? What kinds of activities will you include?

LEARNING TOGETHER!

These activities are best done in groups of three to five:

1. Search the Internet for outstanding educational sites. Each group member should find at least five sites. Prepare an annotated list of your group's top ten finds. Word process your list, and distribute it to all members of your class. You are also invited to send it to one of this textbook's authors so that it may be considered for inclusion on the web site that accompanies this text.
2. Assume that you are a grade-level team that has been asked by your school to create a grade-level web site. Storyboard the web site you want to create. You should provide enough detail so that the text to be included and the types of graphics are evident.

3. Each group member should observe a classroom in which the Internet is used. Interview the teacher to discover the successes and experiences he or she has had using the Internet in teaching and learning. Compare the information gathered through observations and interviews. Word-process a summary of your discoveries. You are also invited to email your paper to one of the text authors for inclusion on the text web site.

HANDS-ON!

1. Research a topic of your choice related to the Internet in teaching and learning. Print out at least two ERIC Digests on your topic; then word-process a summary of what you have discovered about your topic.
2. Participate in an online teachers' chat on one of the educational sites on the web. During the course of the chat, explain that you are an education major in an educational technology course. Ask what suggestions they would give you for using the Internet in the classroom.
3. Explore various projects described on the web that use the Internet in teaching and learning. Email the teacher who reported about one of these projects, and ask for an update describing the current status of the project and how it is working. Tell the teacher that this response and your reaction may be selected for inclusion on a public web page that supplements your textbook. Be sure to explain that you are an educational technology student and are working on an activity for your course. Print out the response you receive. Share the response (if you have the teacher's permission) and your brief reactions to it via email to the authors of this text so that they may consider adding it to the text web page. This is how the web page continues to grow in value.

More from Rob Schwartz

Now that you've explored the World Wide Web and have seen how you can use it in any subject area to link your students to the world, you may have developed a number of ideas for ways that Rob Schwartz could have used the Internet to help his students. No one way is the "right way," but some ways are very innovative and hold potential for technology-using educators. You may have thought to solve this problem the same way that Mr. Schwartz did, but no doubt you will appreciate his unique approach. Perhaps you will find his solution equally useful in your classroom. So, let's see how Mr. Schwartz solved his classroom challenges via the Internet.

MY TECHNOLOGY SOLUTION

Instead of spending money on expensive curriculum that spoonfed the answers to my students in step-by-step instructions, I simply wrote a set of memos that explained what the students had to do, the specifications they had to meet, and where to look for information. The memos started out as printed pages that mimicked interoffice memos for faxes from the "head office." I placed my students in a virtual workplace and gave them real-world projects to do. I didn't give them the answers ahead of time; I gave them only the problem. Finding the answers, as in the real world, was up to them.

After the first round of projects, all the students had obviously learned a few things. They typed up these tips and created "CHEAT" sheets (Concise Help, Explanations, and Tips) for the next group that would do the project. Web pages they found that were helpful were collected and placed in Favorites menus. The interoffice memos were updated and modified (with student input) and placed on the computer hard drives so they could always be easily accessed and updated. CHEAT sheets were printed out and kept near the computer used for that project. I had created a totally student-centric curriculum that the students loved, that was very challenging, that was true-to-life, and that was *free*.

Ninety percent of our information came from the Internet. Online tutorials, "how-to" web sites, and even email to industry experts were used to build our knowledge base. We had taken a lot from the Internet community, and now, like using the change dish next to the register at the gas station, we wanted to give a little back for the next guy. We decided to do this by sharing our projects on a web site.

I developed an Internet web site that was initially just Microsoft Word documents converted to HTML with a simple index page that linked to the data. Later, I used Netscape Composer (it's free!) to create a more complex web site in HTML. Eventually, I stumbled upon Macromedia Dreamweaver, began to develop the site using professional tools, and finally achieved a professional look. The site won a few awards and began to get some regular traffic. I even found that some teachers in other states were actually using my curriculum in their classrooms! The problem was that I had to keep updating the site with new information as we found it.

Recently, I discovered content management software (CMS) for developing Internet web pages. This software (usually free) allows you to update your web page from any computer in the world with Internet access! Even better, other people can register at your site and submit materials directly to your site as well! For example, students can submit web links to the site, which I check out and instantly add to my web site with a single click. Now the students enter all the data, and I just check it for acceptability and accuracy and post it live! Create downloads, post a poll that students and visitors can vote on—your site can be completely dynamic with a ton of user input. Visit **http://www.opensourcecms.com/index.php** to "test-drive" the most popular CMS programs yourself. It's a great way to go as long as your ISP supports the technology that makes CMS work.

MY CLASSROOM TODAY

Today, my program has developed into a completely web-based curriculum. The site was completely re-created over the summer after that first year using Macromedia Dreamweaver and Fireworks. Nearly all project-related resources and information are available on the web page. The curriculum has gained local, state, and even national attention. The web site is an incredible tool for increasing parent and community awareness and involvement with the curriculum. Newsletters or flyers cost money to create and send, they are easily lost, and if you need to make changes to the information, you must send out another copy at additional cost. There is also the environmental impact of using so many paper products.

Creating a web site is fun, fast, easy, and environmentally friendly. If you're just starting, look at a web site like School-Notes.com (**http://www.schoolnotes.com**). It's specifically geared toward education and provides free, easy-to-create web pages for educators. If you'd like to be a little more advanced, look into any of the multitude of free web page providers like Yahoo! (**http://www.yahoo.com**). Visit **http://www.freewebspace.net** for a comprehensive list of free web space providers.

If you really want to go all the way, download a trial version of a professional web page design tool like Macromedia Dreamweaver (**http://www.dreamweaver.com**) and create a site. The trial version of Dreamweaver is fully functional for thirty days. After that, if you're hooked, educators and students can purchase software at exceptionally low prices at educational software vendors like Journey (**http://www.journeyed.com**) or Diskovery (**http://www.diskovery.com**).

Please feel free to visit my class web site, **http://www.brainbuffet.com**. From the web site you can get more background information about the program and how the site came about, and find links related to almost every academic subject. Feel free also to email me at **rob@brainbuffet.com**.

DESIGNING A

As you explore the web, you will find that many teachers have their own class web sites. It may seem that creating a classroom or grade-level web site may be far too difficult for you. Surprising as it may seem, that is not the case. Given the abundant web authoring tools available, it is reasonably easy for any computer-using educator to create a web site. In fact, the greatest challenge for teachers wishing to create their own sites is in planning a pedagogically sound and useful educational site. This section will introduce you to the concerns you need to address to plan an educationally useful site. Once you have considered and responded to each of them, if you have not already done so, you may wish to complete the Software Skills Builder using Microsoft Publisher's Web Wizard to practice creating a site. The skills you gain from that activity will assist you in making your planned classroom web site a reality.

STEP 1: Storyboard

The first step to creating a classroom web site is to decide on the components you would like to include. Since a web site is typically intensely visual, the easiest way to plan and arrange all of the components is to storyboard it. Storyboarding is the process of sketching out each page of a web site and indicating where each textual, visual, and multimedia component will be placed. A storyboard may include a summary of the text to be included and a drawing of the intended visuals. A storyboard also indicates how each page is linked to the other pages.

Storyboarding may be done in a variety of ways. The traditional method is to write on several sheets of paper, but a more effective method is to use large index cards with each card representing a single web page. Since links can be adjusted as the web site is planned, using separate index cards allows you to rearrange your pages during the planning process. Another way to storyboard is to use your computer to help you. You may wish to use the Inspiration software included on your student CD to easily create boxes or circles as graphic representations of each of the "cards" in your storyboard. You can then add links between the pages to show relationships (see Figure I3.1).

STEP 2: Determine Your Content

As you plan the content for your classroom web site, you should have a goal in mind. Perhaps your web site is designed to showcase your students' work or to establish your class on the school's web site. However, if your goal is to use your web site instructionally to enhance teaching and learning in the classroom, there are a few key components to consider including. Each of these components emulates what you do in your classroom as you conduct your courses. Your web site is a communications support to your "live" classroom communication, so it makes sense that it should contain much of the same information.

Think of your web site visitor as a new student, and ask yourself what that new student needs to know to be comfortable and functional in your classroom. That question will give you a good idea of what a well-rounded classroom web site should include. Regardless of the goal of your site, it should include the following basic components.

• Teacher Information

The web site should clearly indicate whose classroom it relates to. Therefore, your name and the classes or grade level you teach should be prominent on the home page. Additional information about you can appear either on the home page or as an "About Me" link to another page. Such additional information might include your degree(s)

CLASSROOM WEB SITE

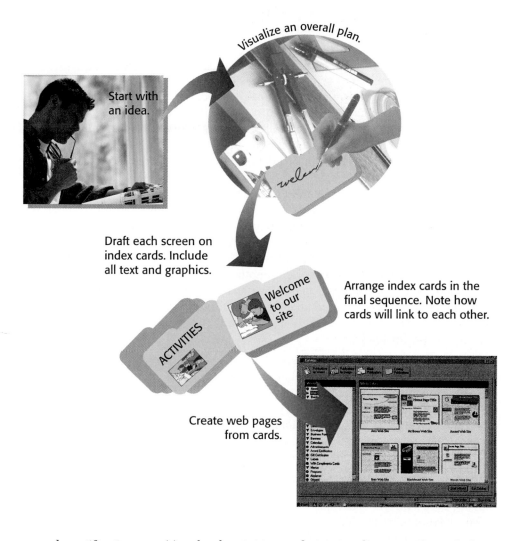

Visualize an overall plan.

Start with an idea.

Draft each screen on index cards. Include all text and graphics.

Welcome to our site

ACTIVITIES

Arrange index cards in the final sequence. Note how cards will link to each other.

Create web pages from cards.

Figure 13.1
Traditional and Digital Storyboarding
Whether using traditional pencil and paper or brainstorming software such as Inspiration, storyboarding helps you plan and design the most effective web site possible.

earned, certification area(s), school activities, and civic involvement. If you feel it is appropriate, you might also include awards earned, publications, and personal hobbies. The objective in sharing such information is to establish your credentials and to add a personal touch to the site for visitors, especially parents and community visitors.

• Class/Course Information

Your home page should clearly identify the grade level or course(s) included on the page. If you teach multiple courses, you may wish to list them as hot links with a linked page for each class or course. On the linked page relating to each class or course you teach, it is useful to give the visitor an overview of the course, your objectives, relevant standards, materials requirements, and assessment and grading criteria. For parents, this type of information provides an orientation to your course and an idea of how you will proceed instructionally.

Your course page should also list additional resources that you may be planning to use. If you have a reading or research list students are expected to use, it should be included with the course information. Your students, by accessing your course page, can then check their required resources from home, and parents can make themselves aware of the resources their children are expected to use.

Your course page should also provide an overview of the term's activities. This summary may be presented as a link on the course page with additional information on a course activity page. The overview should present the major units of study and a general timetable for their implementation.

• Daily/Weekly Information and Homework

If you intend to share homework or class activity information, it is best to use a separate page for current information, to make it easier to update. A "This Week" or "Today" link on the home page or the course page that connects to a page containing this information is your best bet. Your daily or weekly information page might include announcements, assignments, and any other information that you might have mentioned to your classes, to orient your students to the week's or day's activities.

If you decide to use web pages as the basis for activities themselves, each activity page should be linked to your daily or weekly page. Web pages with hot links can be excellent teaching and learning pages that add excitement and interest to classroom assignments. You might pose an inquiry to the students and let them discover answers on the Internet, or you might create an interactive lesson using a conference, or you might center a writing assignment around a keypad activity. Whatever the activity you select, using web activity pages adds another dimension to learning. Additionally, if a student is absent from class and has Internet access at home, posted activities allow him or her to access the current day's work so she or he does not fall behind.

• Information for Parents

Your web site opens channels of communication with parents. Although your site will contain information on every page that will probably be of interest to parents, a parents' page offers you a chance to establish an explicit communications link with them. On an "Information to Parents" page, you might include school information (or links to the appropriate location on the school's site) such as the school calendar, dress code, students' rights and responsibilities, and safety procedures. You can also include a class newsletter, announcement flyers, and requests for volunteers. In fact, any document you may have otherwise handed out in class for students to take home to their parents is a good candidate for this type of page. It is easier to update, saves paper and copying costs, and is accessible at any time. You should also include your email address so that parents who have questions can email you on the spot rather than try to remember to call you (or play telephone tag with you) during your and their busy workday. A parents' page opens almost endless opportunities to enter into an effective partnership with parents.

• Information for the Community

The addition of a community page provides you with an opportunity to build partnerships with the community your school serves. In addition to school information (or links to it), your community page can inform the community of current and upcoming projects and activities and can solicit volunteers and even donations. Many retired community members have time and valuable experience to share with your school or your class. An explanation of how to become a school volunteer or guest speaker may be just the impetus needed to establish a new and fruitful partnership. Engaging and informing the community about what you are doing in your school and in your classroom can open new doors for community members and new resources for you.

Once you have your content planned, you can use any web authoring tool to create your web pages. Microsoft Publisher and Microsoft Word both offer wizards to assist you in turning your content into HTML. Publisher offers greater flexibility in design, but both will do an adequate job in helping you create your site. More sophisticated web authoring tools, such as Microsoft Front Page and Adobe GoLive, can add more sophisticated features. Regardless of the authoring tool you select, once content is planned and web pages are created, one last step is necessary.

STEP 3: Check Guidelines

The final step to creating an effective classroom web site is to ensure that the site meets some basic guidelines for educational web sites. These are summarized in Table 13.1. As you complete each page, review it to see if it meets the criteria identified. As you review, add a check to indicate you have conformed to each guideline. When all items are checked, you can be assured your web site is ready to upload and share with your students and their parents.

TABLE 13.1 GUIDELINES FOR EDUCATIONAL WEB SITES

✓	Guideline	Explanation
	Site Consistency	• Keep each page consistent in look and feel and the entire site consistent with commonly used web conventions. • Use consistent styles and names for navigation buttons, and keep the key navigation buttons in a consistent place on every page.
	Medium vs. Message	• Do not use too many fonts and colors that might detract from the message you are trying to communicate. • Animation and graphics should add interest but not overwhelm the text messages. • High-resolution pictures should be used sparingly. • Balance should be maintained on all pages, avoiding a cluttered look and providing plenty of "white space" to separate visual displays.
	Bias-Free Content	• Information presented should be presentations of fact rather than attempts to persuade. • All aspects of the site should be free from any cultural, ethnic, or gender bias.
	Date Notifications	• Date for creation of the web site and the last update date should be included. • Time-sensitive materials should be monitored and updated as necessary.
	Site Map or Search Engine	• Either an outline of all the pages and the information located on each or a way to search the site should be provided.
	Multimedia Elements	• Include alternatives to text (audio, animation, video clips) for communicating your message to meet alternative learning styles. • As necessary, include links to plug-ins needed for the multimedia you include.
	Current Links	• Add links to other web sites to enhance a lesson or broaden its scope. • Check to be sure that links are appropriate to the content of your site and that they are current and fully functional.
	Contact Information	• Include your name, grade or department, school address, and school phone number. • Include a hot-link pop-up to your email address so that a visitor can send you an email message simply by clicking on that link.
	Copyright Information	• Clearly display copyright information throughout the site. • Provide contact information for permission to use copyrighted information, or provide permission for limited use right on your site. • Be sure you include all necessary links and citations for materials on your site.
	Student Privacy	• The site should include no student information unless expressed parental permission is obtained. • The site should ensure that shared student information does not violate a student's privacy or compromise safety.
	Disability Sensitivity	• Check your site with the Bobby online portal (http://bobby.watchfire.com/bobby/html/en/index.jsp) to test the usability of your site for those with disabilities.

CHAPTER 9

Audio and Visual Technologies

This chapter addresses these ISTE National Educational Technology Standards for Teachers:

II. Planning and designing learning environments and experiences

Teachers plan and design effective learning environments and experiences supported by technology. Teachers

A. design developmentally appropriate learning opportunities that apply technology-enhanced instructional strategies to support the diverse needs of learners.

B. apply current research on teaching and learning with technology when planning learning environments and experiences.

C. identify and locate technology resources and evaluate them for accuracy and suitability.

D. plan for the management of technology resources within the context of learning activities.

E. plan strategies to manage student learning in a technology-enhanced environment.

III. Teaching, learning, and the curriculum

Teachers implement curriculum plans that include methods and strategies for applying technology to maximize student learning. Teachers

A. facilitate technology-enhanced experiences that address content standards and student technology standards.

B. use technology to support learner-centered strategies that address the diverse needs of students.

C. apply technology to develop students' higher-order skills and creativity.

D. manage student learning activities in a technology-enhanced environment.

In the preceding chapters, you learned much about the computer technologies you are likely to find in instructional environments. However, if you were to visit any classroom today to examine the technologies in place, you would also find other types of technologies used on a daily basis. In Chapter 1, we defined educational technology in its broadest sense, that is, any technology that is used to support or enhance teaching and learning. To fully acquaint you with the types of technologies you are most likely to find in the schools you work in, it is important to become familiar with all of the types of technologies you are likely to encounter. Clearly, your classroom is likely to include a variety of computer technologies. This chapter will help you to explore some of the noncomputer technologies you will find as well.

Before the digital age, technologies that supported teaching and learning were often called audiovisual, or A/V, media. Such technologies typically included overhead projectors, slide projectors, filmstrip projectors, movie projectors, tape recorders, and televisions. Today, as you have seen in this text, digital technologies have added significantly to the instructional tools educators have available to them. In fact, the term *audiovisual/digital media*, or *A/V/D media*, is now a much more descriptive term to use when referring to educational technologies.

This chapter will introduce you to audio and visual media of all types, from the more traditional visual and audio technologies to their leading-edge digital counterparts. It will help you explore how each of these traditional and leading-edge technologies can be used to address learning styles to support the instructional event, and to help you plan how to integrate these technologies into your classroom. You will then be ready to explore how they have been used to change the face of education in many areas and the issues these changes have generated.

In Chapter 9, you will

- Examine the relationship and educational application of traditional and digital audio and visual media

- Investigate the use of audio media in support of teaching and learning

- Review the application of visual media in support of teaching and learning

- Explore the use of projected and nonprojected visual media

- Examine the role of the Internet in providing audio and visual support for teaching and learning

Meet Lucianne Sweder

This chapter introduces a variety of audiovisual (A/V) hardware, from traditional to digital. Of course, what is probably of greatest interest to you is how these media can be incorporated into your teaching. Assume that your school has directed you to enhance your instruction and to use some of the A/V media you have available in your school in new and creative ways. How will you go about it? To help you think about this, let's see the challenge facing a school district in which teachers are not taking full advantage of the A/V technologies that could be integrated into their curriculum. Meet Lucianne Sweder, who will describe how she and a group of colleagues found one way to approach this problem.

MY PROBLEM

A/V technologies have become an endangered species in many schools as a reliance on the Internet has taken center stage. Although still used in some form in today's classrooms, A/V tools aren't being used as effectively as they should be in many cases. In fact, Andrew Trotter, in "Technology in the Classroom" in *Lessons of a Century: A Nation's Schools Come of Age* (2003), explains that over the past hundred years, most technologies have "drifted into the margins of school practice . . . not disappearing, but failing to achieve the impact for which they seemed destined." As a consequence, there is a potential problem building in Illinois schools, as is true in many states, from the underutilization of A/V technologies in the curriculum.

MY PLAN

While I was the director of the Learning Technology Center Area 1 South, a group of my colleagues and I recognized this problem and wanted to do something about it. My center was one of fifteen learn-

ing technology state centers in Illinois. I also served as technology coordinator of the Professional Development Center, an intermediate service agency for Illinois.

I helped develop a team consisting of my agency plus similar agencies in Cook, Du Page, Grundy, Kane, Kendall, Lake, and Will counties in Illinois. Our goal was to find outstanding classroom teachers who had successfully integrated technology in their classrooms. We decided to form an evaluation team to select and recognize outstanding teachers with an award that was presented at a special luncheon during the annual Illinois Technology Conference for Educators.

Following the conference, I formed a small team that included Kathy Novinski, event coordinator for the Learning Technology Center Area 1 South; Jason Bross, computer network technician from the Professional Development Alliance; and me to take a road trip to visit some of the winners in the area. Kathy and Jason also took on the role of photographers during these visits so we could share some visual images from our time with these teachers.

We decided to focus on just two schools where we could observe two outstanding teachers who had integrated A/V technologies into their curriculum in different ways. Our hope was that we would be able to use their experiences as models for other teachers throughout the state so that our A/V tools would become a truly integrated and meaningful element in the curriculum, leading to improved student learning and motivation.

The two schools we selected to visit were Lockport Township High School in District 205 and Gompers Jr. High School in Joliet, in District 86. Lockport's socioeconomic base is middle- to upper-middle-class and has extensive support from the community. Gompers has about 900 students in grades 6–8 with a 90% free and reduced lunch count and 58% Hispanic, 26% black, and 16% white populations. According to the federal No Child Left Behind performance requirements, this school is in need of improvement. The principal and School Improvement Team had created a support system for the teachers to develop innovative methods to improve student achievement and create an interest for students to increase their attendance.

Our journey thus began. We were about to discover how creative and innovative teachers could be using audiovisual technologies.

We will rejoin Ms. Sweder and her team at the end of this chapter. First, let's explore the audio and visual technologies that the teachers in these districts were challenged to integrate.

What Do I Need to Know about Audio and Visual Technologies?

Teachers know instinctively that the more interactive and multisensory they make their teaching, the more likely it is that learning will occur. Common sense and instructional experiences have taught us that a lesson delivered through lecture alone is less engaging than a lesson delivered with audio and visual support. Few would disagree that giving a talk about native birds in North America becomes more meaningful when combined with presentation of the recordings of songs of such birds and either beautifully colored still images or motion images. During an instructional event, adding the appropriate audio and visual components can engage more of the learner's senses and help to build multiple cognitive connections to the content presented. And because learning styles vary, the addition of audio and visual images can make learning easier for many students by addressing their auditory or visual strength.

To be able to use all of the available technological tools at hand, educators need to be familiar with the full range of tools that will support the learner's efforts to make meaningful contact with, and build mastery of, the content presented. Audio and visual tools of all types, whether traditional technologies or those that have emerged from the digital age, can be valuable in supporting the teaching and learning process. For this reason, it is important for those who work with learners to be aware of the types of audio and visual technologies available and their application in teaching and learning.

Audio, Visual, and Digital Technologies in Instruction

In the first half of the twentieth century, education was enhanced through the introduction of sound and video technologies. The record player, tape recorder, and movie projector all came into being, became a part of society, and ultimately were introduced into the classroom. These traditional technologies have not left yet, although many have altered their form. Figure 9.1 shows a timeline of audiovisual technology use in education. Movie projectors have given way to VCRs or even DVD players; reel-to-reel tape recorders have been replaced by cassette or microcassette recorders; and the record players that were designed to play sound stored on vinyl platters have been superseded by electronic equipment designed to play sound stored on optical discs (i.e., CDs and DVDs). Although the storage and playback technology has changed, the intent remains constant. Audio and visual technologies help you teach and your students learn.

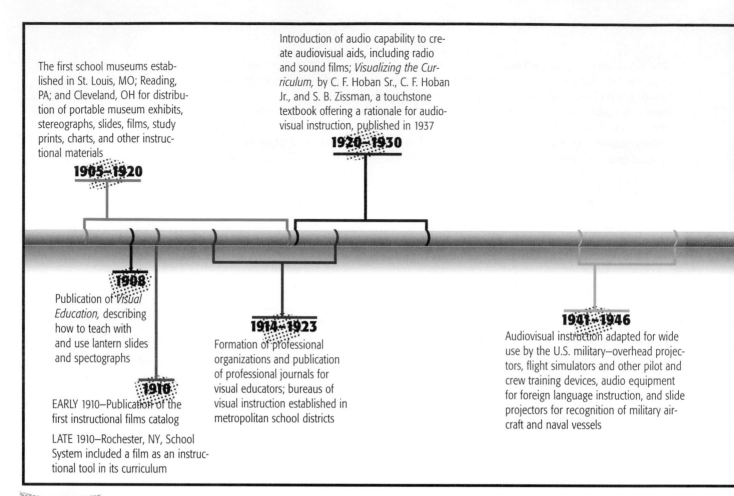

The first school museums established in St. Louis, MO; Reading, PA; and Cleveland, OH for distribution of portable museum exhibits, stereographs, slides, films, study prints, charts, and other instructional materials

1905–1920

Introduction of audio capability to create audiovisual aids, including radio and sound films; *Visualizing the Curriculum,* by C. F. Hoban Sr., C. F. Hoban Jr., and S. B. Zissman, a touchstone textbook offering a rationale for audiovisual instruction, published in 1937

1920–1930

1908

Publication of *Visual Education,* describing how to teach with and use lantern slides and spectographs

1910

EARLY 1910–Publication of the first instructional films catalog

LATE 1910–Rochester, NY, School System included a film as an instructional tool in its curriculum

1914–1923

Formation of professional organizations and publication of professional journals for visual educators; bureaus of visual instruction established in metropolitan school districts

1941–1946

Audiovisual instruction adapted for wide use by the U.S. military—overhead projectors, flight simulators and other pilot and crew training devices, audio equipment for foreign language instruction, and slide projectors for recognition of military aircraft and naval vessels

Figure 9.1
Audiovisual Technology in Education
The twentieth century was a century of dramatic technological enhancements to education.

Traditional A/V and digital technologies can help support diverse instructional designs while addressing different learning styles.

In essence, audio and visual enhancements to text and the spoken word are just as important in the digital age as they were in the beginning of the twentieth century. As technology advances, the format of audio and visual media may change, but its significance to teaching and learning will not. Given that many schools have many functional traditional audio and visual technologies still in service, it is important for educators to be aware of the potential of these traditional technologies. Digital versions of A/V technologies will no doubt continue to replace more traditional audio and visual media, but as long as these older technologies are still available, they remain useful to creative educators. And the instructional effort spent to utilize these more traditional technologies will easily transfer when they are eventually replaced by those that are emerging. The key to integrating both traditional and emerging audio and visual technologies into teaching and learning is, as with all educational technology, not a question of their technical format, but instead a question of the educator's creativity and familiarity with instructional design. Awareness of all the types of audio, visual, and digital technological tools available to you will give you more choices when you design instruction. See Table 9.1 for an overview of these technologies.

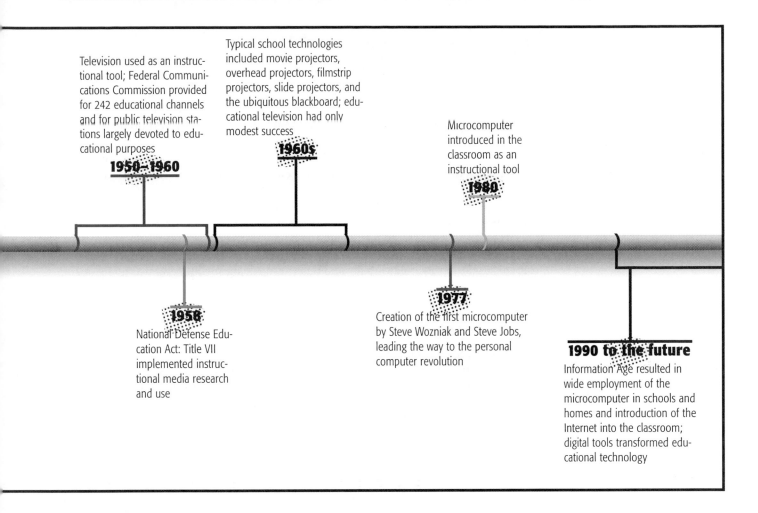

Television used as an instructional tool; Federal Communications Commission provided for 242 educational channels and for public television stations largely devoted to educational purposes
1950–1960

Typical school technologies included movie projectors, overhead projectors, filmstrip projectors, slide projectors, and the ubiquitous blackboard; educational television had only modest success
1960s

Microcomputer introduced in the classroom as an instructional tool
1980

1958
National Defense Education Act: Title VII implemented instructional media research and use

1977
Creation of the first microcomputer by Steve Wozniak and Steve Jobs, leading the way to the personal computer revolution

1990 to the future
Information Age resulted in wide employment of the microcomputer in schools and homes and introduction of the Internet into the classroom; digital tools transformed educational technology

TABLE 9.1   AUDIO/VISUAL/DIGITAL TECHNOLOGY OVERVIEW

Function	Traditional A/V Technologies	Digital and Other Emerging Technologies
DISPLAY INDIVIDUAL NONMOVING IMAGES	Overhead projector	Document camera, computer display, clip art, and photo galleries on CD or the Internet
DISPLAY PHOTOGRAPHIC IMAGES	Slide projector, bulletin board, posters	Document camera, computer display, photo galleries on CD or the Internet
DISPLAY MOVING IMAGES	Movie projector, VCR	Computer display, DVD player, computer CD-ROM, Internet video
PLAY BACK MUSIC OR SPEECH	Tape recorder, record player	CD player, MP3 player, DVD player, Internet audio
PLAY TV PROGRAMS	TV monitor	Computer display, Internet webcast
RESEARCH SUPPORT	Books	Multimedia CD-ROMs, E-books, Internet searches

Audio in Teaching and Learning

Every teacher uses auditory delivery to teach students; the source of the audio is most typically the teacher's voice. Whether the teacher is verbally introducing a concept briefly to third graders or lecturing on a complex theory to college students, audio is a dominant delivery system in every educational environment. As you no doubt know from your own learning experiences, sometimes teacher-based audio is very effective, and sometimes it is not. To discover the differences between effective and ineffective audio instruction, it is critical to first take a closer look at the audio communications process.

Audio delivery is grounded in the learner's ability to listen attentively to auditory stimulus. For an educator, understanding this basic concept is an important prerequisite to using audio effectively in teaching and learning. Have you ever been listening to a lecture and suddenly found yourself thinking about something else? Have you ever lost the train of thought presented verbally and had to quickly figure out what was going on? To understand why this occurs, you must look closely at the process of listening.

Understanding Listening and Learning

Listening skills are critical for effective learning.

ON THE WEB! 9.1
Bridging Theory to Practice

Listening—that is, being able to hear and comprehend—involves several steps. The first step in the process of listening is to actually hear the auditory stimulus. Next, the brain needs to turn that stimulus into neural pulses and process it. Finally, the appropriate cognitive connections need to be made to relate this new information to memories of real events or previously learned content. Needless to say, this entire process is as complex as it is intuitive. Listening is really a very critical prerequisite skill for effective auditory learning. For the many teachers who wish to use audio technologies for instruction, assisting learners in acquiring, improving, and applying listening skills may be a necessary first step. If you choose to use audio delivery, it is a good idea to help your students develop and practice these skills as a component of instruction.

Effective listening requires the hearing process to be accurately achieved. Consider **hearing** as the physical process that includes the generation of clear, audible sounds that are ultimately received correctly by others. In the classroom, this means that you need to ensure that the audio source is producing a clear signal and that other noises are controlled so that they do not interfere with or detract from the intended audio. This can sometimes be difficult to achieve with noise from outside the classroom intruding and perhaps even with noise generated by the school facilities, such as air conditioning, interfering. You can take some actions to mitigate intrusive noises. Physical modifications of the classroom facilities are ideal, but even the addition of simple sound-dampening materials in the classroom (e.g., drapes, area rugs, and cork materials on walls) can make a considerable difference. Before you use audio delivery, it is a good idea to be sure that all of your learners can indeed hear the signal clearly by testing it. You might record yourself speaking, using your normal-volume teach-

Steps for effective listening

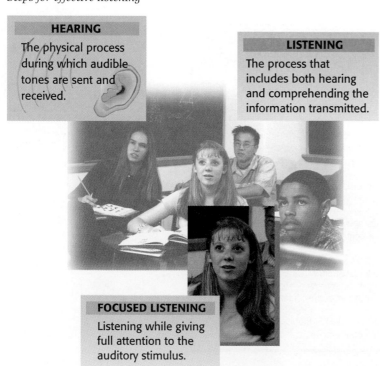

HEARING The physical process during which audible tones are sent and received.

LISTENING The process that includes both hearing and comprehending the information transmitted.

FOCUSED LISTENING Listening while giving full attention to the auditory stimulus.

ing voice, and play it back while you position yourself in various locations around the classroom. You should also test in a similar fashion any audio technologies you plan to use to be sure that the sound produced at the volume you need to use remains clear and audible. The simple addition of supplemental speakers can sometimes enhance hearing in all corners of a classroom. In any case, it is critical to ensure that the audio signal you intend to send can indeed be heard. Straining to hear will cause fatigue and frustration. Effective listening begins with being able to hear accurately.

The second step in effective listening is focused listening. To listen, you must give your full attention to the auditory stimulus. How the process we call **attention** actually happens has only recently become clearly understood through studies of the brain. Current research into how the brain works and its implication for education is called brain-based teaching. This area of educational inquiry has provided profound insights into understanding the physical process of learning. It is of particular significance in understanding how the brain gathers input from the senses and then processes it, a critical aspect of listening. Brain-based teaching suggests that it is quite normal for an individual's attention to waver. Indeed, this was an important survival skill as humans evolved.

For example, in humans' early years as hunters, it was important to scan the environment and continually shift the focus of attention among the sensory elements. Imagine for a moment that you are part of a tribe migrating through a wilderness. Moving some elements into the background of your attention (the trees, grasses swaying, rocks) and focusing your attention instead on potential danger (the pack of lions looking hungrily in your direction) are critical to your survival. This built-in capability to pay attention to multiple stimuli, with some as the focus and others just monitored, is inherent in all of us. It is what allows you to read this text while having a snack and staying aware of your surroundings. It is also what lets your students' attention wander from your instruction. Your instructional efforts may be shifted to the background of attention but still monitored by your students while they focus on

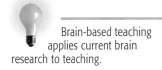

Brain-based teaching applies current brain research to teaching.

ON THE WEB! 9.2
Brain-Based Teaching

We need to teach focused listening to help our students succeed.

their neighbor's tapping of a pencil or an ant crawling along the baseboard. When they are thus distracted physically or psychologically and their attention shifts, they cease to listen momentarily.

The critical component, **focused listening,** is a skill that schools do not often teach directly as a part of curriculum. To encourage the development of focused listening in your students, you might want to structure listening games or activities into your instruction. You might also want to incorporate specific teaching techniques into your strategies that help students refocus their attention during active instruction.

The next critical component for effective listening is reinforcement of the content. Even if you do listen attentively to a new idea or concept, for it to be integrated into your knowledge base, you need to reinforce it. Research in brain-based teaching supports this as well. The brain is composed of 100 billion highly specialized cells, called **neurons,** arranged in a vast network. Learning can be traced to the activity among these neurons. You might recall from a science course that neurons have three major

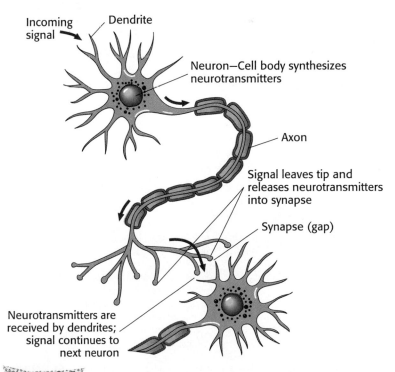

Figure 9.2
Learning via Neural Activity
Learning can be traced to the activity between neurons.

components: the cell body, the axon, and the dendrites (see Figure 9.2). Within the structure of the brain, neurons do not actually touch one another; instead, pulses are sent across a gap (synapse) between the neurons. As we learn a new concept, the chemical activity across the synapses strengthens the neurons. With sufficient stimulation, we even grow new dendrites to handle the increased activity. Learning at its most physical level includes the growth of new dendrites that results from repetitive stimulation. In addition, for each different modality that is used to convey the same information in a different way (e.g., telling a story, showing a picture of the story, or feeling a model of the story's terrain and characters), new dendrites are also grown. With these multiple connections between the neurons, it is easier for the student to recall the information because there are now multiple pathways to make the connection. From the external world, the repetitive stimulation would be the many reinforcing activities that we include in the instructional process. Effective listening happens when attention is frequently refocused on the topic and when repetition restimulates the neurons and encourages them to build new dendrites. At this point, the idea presented not only has been heard, it has also been incorporated into the brain's structure—it has been learned.

▌ Media to Enhance Listening

It is clear that to learn via auditory stimulus, then, the learner must listen effectively. During active teaching using verbal communication, as you present information, it is critical to ensure that your students are indeed listening to you. Careful observation, frequent eye contact, and asking questions that require a refocusing of attention can help you to determine whether students are engaged in active listening. However, what about the students who seem to have difficulty following your presentation or those

IN THE CLASSROOM

Little (and Big) Pitchers: Building Listening Skills with Technology

The United States Department of Education has compiled a list for teachers and child care and family providers to use to teach listening skills, because "Research shows beyond question that it is through having many opportunities to talk as well as to listen to teachers and peers that children gain language skills so valuable for their success in reading and writing." Ways to help teachers encourage good listening are shown by naming the skill and giving an example of how to teach it; for example:

Play games that will focus children's attention on the importance of listening carefully. **Teacher Talk:** Put your heads down and close your eyes. Listen very carefully. Can you hear the lawn mower outside? Can you hear water dripping in the sink? What else do you hear? [These sounds can be provided on audiotapes.] Capitalize on routine opportunities to have children follow or give directions. **Teacher Talk:** It's time for a snack. I want the boys to come to the round table and the girls to come to the square table. Kaylee, please go to the bookrack and bring me the book with the red flower on its cover. Mitch, go to the block box. Get two green blocks. Okay, please take them to Julio. Tanya, will you tell Howie to put this puzzle together?

Dr. Morton Tener, a teacher in Glassboro, New Jersey, tells how his students learn grammar, usage, and mechanics and listening skills by listening to lyrics of favorite and familiar songs he plays for them on CDs or cassettes. He plays a song such as "Home on the Range," and lets them sing along first; then, he tells them "to clap their hands when they hear a specific part of speech and verb tense or stamp their feet when they notice helping verbs, pronouns, and articles. We also use lyrics to find types of sentences or to add punctuation where needed." The students also get to choose some of the songs to listen to for the same kinds of listening and learning responses. ◆

SOURCES: Teaching our youngest: A guide for preschool teachers and child care and family providers: Developing listening and speaking skills. 2002. Retrieved January 27, 2003, from http://www.ed.gov/offices/OESE/teachingouryoungest/developing.html; M. Tener. 2002. Learning with lyrics. *Creative Classroom* (November/December), 17 (3), 27.

who have difficulty simultaneously following your presentation and taking notes? How can you assist them?

It is in such instances that audio media can help. Capturing auditory information, storing it, and playing it back can be a very useful tool to support learning. A student can listen to a presentation multiple times at the pace necessary for full comprehension. Playback can be paused or stopped while notes or questions are jotted down. Turning the synchronous experience of a classroom presentation into an asynchronous experience, the timing of which can be controlled and manipulated by the learner, can make a big difference for those who are attempting to master a concept. For students who have difficulty listening effectively, being able to manage the pace of audio communication may be enough to turn a frustrating learning scenario into one that they are able to master. Traditional and digital audio technologies offer educators the tools needed to be able to support learners in this manner.

Recorded verbal information lets students control the pace at which they listen.

Traditional Audio Media

Audiocassettes

The most commonly used traditional audio medium is the cassette tape. **Audiocassettes** are an economical, durable, and easy-to-use magnetic medium that lets you record voice, music, or other sounds. Cassette tape players are inexpensive additions to the learning environment, although some units need additional speakers so they can be heard clearly throughout the classroom. Cassette players are compact and simple to operate for even the youngest learners. As a supplement to class instruction, playing audiotapes can enrich the learning experience and add audio sensory elements such as animal sounds or music that is specific to a culture. For small-group instruction, creating and playing back an audiotape can enhance active learning. When coupled with earphones, cassette players can make a valuable addition as a classroom aid for individualized learning and review (see Table 9.2).

Cassette tapes can be a valuable supplement to classroom instruction.

One of the most popular uses of audiotapes is the **talking book.** Whether for primary students who are learning to read or high school students who enjoy the drama-

Listening centers with talking books help learners improve both listening and reading skills.

TABLE 9.2 COMPONENTS OF A LISTENING CENTER

Equipment	Purpose
 **Cassette recorder and player and CD player**	Play back student-made, teacher-made, and commercially prepared audio-tapes; record student reports, stories, read-aloud practice; record lesson instructions and reviews
 **Earphones**	Provide private listening; may require splitting device to plug in multiple sets of earphones
 **Prerecorded and blank cassettes**	Cassettes available alone, with texts, and in multimedia kits provide tutorials, music, talking books, and lessons

Variable-length, reusable blank cassettes have a wide variety of student and teacher uses |
|  **Prerecorded and blank CDs** | Audio books, music, or lessons recorded on CDs provide audio instructional support

In combination with your computer's CD recorder, blank CD-Rs can be used to create your own audio lessons for playback on your CD player |
|  **Table and chairs** | Table for listening center equipment; comfortable chairs contribute to a relaxed, nurturing learning environment |

💡 Talking books are a great way for students to practice their listening skills.

tization of a play, recorded readings of books, plays, or short stories can add an auditory dimension to such texts. Students can either read along with a talking book or listen and respond to questions as the audio book or story progresses. This type of activity provides listening skills practice while reinforcing printed material.

Another popular use of audiotapes is the creation or acquisition of multimedia kits. Whether made by the teacher or commercially produced, **multimedia kits** usually include visual elements (texts and graphics) and supplemental audio enhancements on cassette tape. Such kits also usually include student activity sheets and suggested lesson plans. Although they may also include motion video or even real objects, text, graphics, and audiotapes are most common. Commercial multimedia kits often provide high-quality graphics and difficult-to-acquire audio components such as nature sounds, speeches, or music segments. Although all of these may enhance the content under study, noncommercial multimedia kits can be equally valuable. Teacher-made kits consisting of graphics and text from your classroom lessons packaged with an audiotape of your teaching and a review activity can offer learners an opportunity to review at the pace and frequency appropriate to their needs. Student-made kits created as group or individual projects can offer opportunities to explore content in depth and to engage in active learning through cooperative groups.

Another effective classroom application of audiotapes is their use for oral history and oral journal assignments. **Oral histories** are typically interviews captured on audiotape related to a single significant event. Students might interview parents or grandparents and ask questions related to their memories of a specific historical event, such as the first moon landing. Or they might ask interview questions about a significant local event, such as a hurricane or the dedication of an important local monument. Interviews building an oral history of a significant event that have been captured on audiotape can be edited, and clips from multiple tapes can be condensed into a single audio collage of interviews. The edited oral history tape can be duplicated and distributed to all participants, creating an irreplaceable treasure that captures the voice and emotion of those who participated in history.

Likewise, oral journals provide learners with the opportunity to make unrestricted observations and reflections on their own experiences. Whether making oral notes of their observations during a field trip or reflecting on a classroom experience, oral journals give learners the chance to capture their own voices and emotions while giving them the opportunity to practice and listen to their own oral communication skills. Oral journals can later be listened to, reflected on, and synthesized by individual learners or shared with groups or the entire class.

Commercially prepared tapes or blank audiocassettes can also be valuable instructional tools. Furthermore, because both tapes and player/recorder equipment are reasonably priced, they offer an economical way to bring audio media into your classroom. Tapes can be reused or saved as desired. They can be copied quickly and in large

Oral histories and journals reinforce communication and listening skills.

ON THE WEB! 9.3
Talking Books and Other Tapes

IN THE CLASSROOM

Voices from the Past:
Oral History as a Learning Adventure

Students in Elaine Seavey's English class at Seminole High School in Seminole, Oklahoma, packed up audiotape recorders and ventured out into the community to conduct interviews of older Oklahomans. In this cross-discipline project, the students would learn about the grassroots history of the Seminole area and, in authoring an oral history for publication, would learn writing skills and publishing procedures. The purposes of the assignment, in Ms. Seavey's words, were

to involve the students actively in the pursuit of history and to develop an awareness of the interdependence of the various disciplines, Oklahoma history, and English. The skills acquired in English class can be applied in the exploration of the past. Another purpose of an oral history project is a sense of community that evolves in the students as they begin their quest of a "story." The students also develop an appreciation for the people in the community who are the "living" history.

The seven activities the teachers and students engaged in as they produced the oral history began with reviewing how to use a tape recorder, particularly during the interviews. The other six activities, in order of presentation to students, were a brainstorming session to generate topics that would encourage the interviewees to share their remembrances, such as life during the Depression, life in an oil camp, or an unsolved mystery; instruction in interviewing techniques; instruction in how to record, transcribe, and edit the interviews; word-processing the final versions; typesetting the text; and distributing the book in print to the contributors.

SOURCES: E. Seavey. 2002. A team approach to oral history. Retrieved February 14, 2003, from **http://www.col-ed.org/cur/sst/sst45.text**.

quantity by using tape-duplicating equipment. Applied creatively, cassette tapes can provide auditory enhancement, teach listening skills, and reinforce content. Because the audio experience is stored on the tape, it can be played back whenever appropriate to meet learners' needs.

Broadcast Audio

Audiocassette tapes are not the only traditional audio medium available in the learning environment. **Broadcast audio,** that is, audio received via radio, can also provide valuable enhancement to content. The popularity of radio talk shows testifies to the potential of broadcast audio. For the classroom, National Public Radio offers a variety of listening opportunities in terms of both music and discussion. For those whose geographic location allows for reception of broadcasts from other countries, radio can provide valuable social studies and language opportunities. The National Oceanic and Atmospheric Administration (NOAA) weather service broadcasts provide opportunities for real-world science and math applications. Awareness of the potential of these types of audio broadcasts for instruction will help you to stay mindful of the possibilities of incorporating radio programs into teaching and learning.

Digital Audio Media

Optical Media

Optical digital media are rapidly replacing analog audiotapes.

The more traditional analog storage media (audiotapes) are giving way to their digital counterparts, the most common of which is the **CD.** As you learned in Chapter 3, **DVDs** (digital video discs) are similar to CDs but hold significantly more information. CDs and DVDs have some distinct advantages over audiotapes. These advantages include clarity, storage format, and information access.

Digitized sound is sound recorded in distinct bits of data rather than analog waves. This results in a much crisper, clearer audio recording. Furthermore, because CDs and DVDs are highly durable media, the sounds recorded on them do not deteriorate with frequent use. Unlike magnetic tapes, which can become stretched or distorted, CDs maintain their shape and thus their clarity over time.

ON THE WEB! 9.4
CDs in the Classroom

Additionally, CDs, with their capacity of approximately 75 minutes of audio, offer a capacity roughly equal to that of cassette tapes. Their digital storage format, further, provides for random access of the data stored, which means you can directly go to and play any segment on a CD. Tapes use a process called sequential access; that is, you must move through the taped information in the sequence in which it was stored to reach the content you want. CDs save the time and effort necessary to sort through the entire sequence of stored data. This ability to access randomly is a useful advantage during instruction. Figure 9.3 summarizes the advantages of using CDs.

Internet Audio

Once digitized, audio can be delivered through the Internet as well as on digital storage media such as CDs (see Figure 9.4). The Internet lets you find and download very specific audio clips for use in your classroom. Using **Internet audio,** you can download and store only what you need rather than having to buy a full CD that may have only a few portions that are useful as supplements to your lesson. The increasing availability of Internet audio has resulted in its becoming an emerging audio technology in today's classrooms.

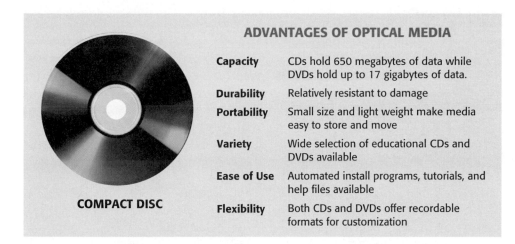

ADVANTAGES OF OPTICAL MEDIA

Capacity	CDs hold 650 megabytes of data while DVDs hold up to 17 gigabytes of data.
Durability	Relatively resistant to damage
Portability	Small size and light weight make media easy to store and move
Variety	Wide selection of educational CDs and DVDs available
Ease of Use	Automated install programs, tutorials, and help files available
Flexibility	Both CDs and DVDs offer recordable formats for customization

COMPACT DISC

Figure 9.3
Optical Media for Teaching and Learning
CDs offer unique advantages in teaching and learning.

To use Internet audio, it is necessary to be aware of its various formats and the hardware and/or software necessary for its playback. The two most common formats of audio files available on the Internet are WAV files and MP3 files. **WAV files** are the digital version of analog audio. This means that a sound or music clip has been converted directly into its digital counterpart. This can be done by recording voice or sound through a computer's microphone, converting it to its digital counterpart via the computer's sound card and software, and then storing it on disk. WAV files maintain the quality of the original sound but often result in very large digital files. A CD-quality recording in WAV format would take up approximately 2–3 megabytes of space for every minute of sound recording. Obviously, a long song or story would take an enormous amount of time to upload or download and a substantial amount of disk space for storage. For this reason, WAV files found on the Internet are often short. As a result of the size of audio files and the need for faster download times, a newer audio file format has been developed and is becoming widely used on the Internet. This format is called **MP3,** which stands for Motion Picture Experts Group, audio layer 3.

MP3 is an audio compression technology that has gained in popularity because it provides high-quality sound in one-twelfth the space required for the same clip in older audio file formats. This compression significantly reduces upload and download times as well as necessary storage space. To play MP3 files, you must have MP3 playback software installed on your computer. MP3 player programs are available for free download online, as are many MP3 audio files.

Audio recordings on the Internet are usually stored as WAV or MP3 files.

ON THE WEB! 9.5
Internet Audio

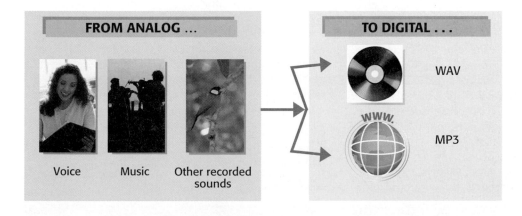

FROM ANALOG ...

Voice   Music   Other recorded sounds

TO DIGITAL ...

WAV

WWW.

MP3

Figure 9.4
Digital Audio for Teaching and Learning
Digital audio from the Internet can enhance the learning environment. Analog sound is converted to digital format for easy storage, download, playback, and ultimately integration into instructional multimedia.

Media player software makes it possible to listen to all formats of digital music and sound on your computer.

Microsoft Windows Media Player® is a registered trademark of Microsoft Corporation.

Although most MP3 files available on the web are music audio, MP3 has the capacity for other kinds of sound recordings and will no doubt experience greater applications in education. WAV files, the staple format for digital audio files used in instruction, may well be superseded by the compact MP3 format. Regardless of the

IN THE CLASSROOM

Something for Everyone and News as It Happens!
Teachers Using Digital Audio and Internet Radio

Just another day in an inclusive classroom: "The ESL kids are here. There are the kids with diagnosed disabilities, too. What's an educator to do?" asks Scott James, who already knows the answer. He uses digital audio to reach out to each one. Using MP3 players, the students press a password to hear "hooks" that engage their attention by transmitting tuneful music and some old jokes. Then they press numbers to hear the various assignments. For science, they hear "the voice of a NASA scientist explaining how stars are formed"; for reading, a section of *The Red Badge of Courage*; and, for two immigrant students, broadcasts in their first languages are available. The LD student hears the broadcast immediately because the infrared broadcast starts when he puts the headset on. "He can listen to the lesson as many times as he needs," Mr. James adds.

Current-events day in social studies class can be just plain boring for many students who are auditory learners, as well as for those who claim not to care what goes on halfway around the

world. That can all change, though, with Internet radio. News from all over the world comes through loud and clear with a click of the mouse. The prestigious BBC Online carries a sports report from Wimbledon on Venus Williams's latest victory on the tennis court; a global weather forecast; news of ongoing strife in the Middle East; what's playing at the Old Vic theater; and many more selections on Radio 1, 2, 3, 4, and 5 Live. U.S. radio stations online proliferate and can be found under their URLs or at **http://www.radio-online.com**. As Bill McKibben comments, "What makes this programming wonderful is that it's local, made for particular places—or, to put it the other way around, that it's not made for everyone, everywhere, like TV."

SOURCES S. James. 2003. One digital future. Retrieved November 9, 2003, from http://www.ldresources.com/articles/one_digital_future.html; B. McKibben. 2000. The world streaming in. *Atlantic Monthly*. (286), 78.

digital audio format you select to use, educational applications are similar to those associated with traditional audio technologies and may even exceed them. Whereas a cassette may be the storage medium of choice for analog sound, WAV and MP3 audio files can be stored on a floppy disk or network drive for playback at a computer work-station. Cassette tapes and players, although currently more portable and less expensive than some of their digital counterparts, are likely to decline as the digital technologies become more widespread.

Internet Radio

Using digital formats combined with streaming audio technology, the Internet offers a broadcast service called **Internet radio.** Internet radio uses the Internet to offer online radio stations consisting of a wide variety of programming including music, sports, science, and local, national, and world news. Live and recorded programming from around the world can enhance language, social studies, science, and current events curricula. Typically, Internet radio sites offer a brief text summary with graphics in conjunction with the audio broadcast. For educators who wish to expand their students' horizons, access to up-to-the-minute international radio broadcasts is just a mouse click away. And because visual, text, and audio information may be provided, different learning styles are addressed simultaneously. Whether used with a data projection unit for a whole class activity or with a single computer for an individual or small-group project, Internet radio broadcasts offer fascinating possibilities to creative teachers.

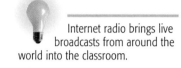

Internet radio brings live broadcasts from around the world into the classroom.

ON THE WEB! 9.6
Internet Radio

Visual Technologies in Teaching and Learning

Audio technologies directly address the needs of the auditory learner but also add dimension to instruction for all learners. Including audio in teaching and learning makes the instruction richer. However, for most learners, audio alone will not be sufficient to communicate content. Visuals are, for most learners, a necessity.

SOURCE: National Public Radio

Internet radio broadcasts like those provided by National Public Radio can offer audio resources on a wide variety of instructional content.

Whenever you visit an effective instructional environment, the most noticeable elements are the many eye-catching educational displays. Visual support for content can be seen throughout the teaching and learning space. Whether through posters, student work on bulletin boards, models, or dioramas, the content is articulated, clarified, and enhanced visually. Few educators would deny the necessity and effectiveness of visuals in teaching and learning. Learning style research, brain-based instruction, and common sense support the use of visuals in instruction. The question that remains for educators is how to determine and select the most effective and appropriate visual technologies for the content under study. To answer this question, it is important first to understand the nature of visual communication.

Visual Communication and Learning

Consider the visual displays shown in Figure 9.5. Are you able to answer the questions beneath each? No doubt you can. Because, over the years, you have developed **visual literacy** just as you are in the process of developing technological literacy through this course. The visual literacy you have acquired was developed through the many teaching and learning processes you have experienced. Some were more visually intensive than others, but by the time most people reach adulthood, they have managed to acquire the visual literacy that enables them to accurately interpret the visuals necessary for functioning effectively in our society.

Children acquire visual literacy skills throughout their educational experiences. Regardless of what you teach, you will have an impact on the visual skills your students attain. No matter the content or grade level you teach, how you design, arrange, and present visual information to learners will affect their visual literacy

Visual literacy is an important educational goal.

Figure 9.5
What Is Visual Literacy?
Visual literacy is necessary to understand and interpret displays.

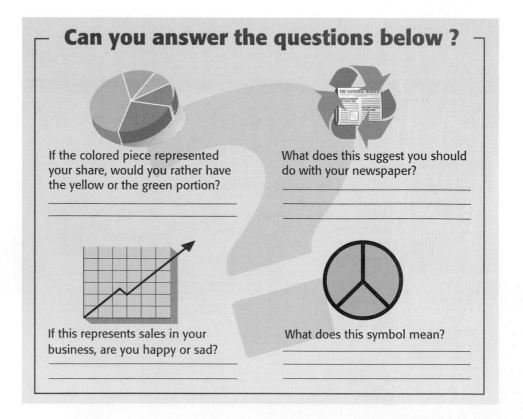

skill set, positively or negatively. Clear, consistent visual information will help them to build skills. Confusing and disconnected visual information may deter visual literacy development. For this reason, every teacher should know the basics of **visual communication** to enhance student skills.

The same oral and written communication process of encoding and decoding information that you learned about in Chapter 1 applies to visual communication as well (see Figure 9.6). Because visual information is more typically subject to the interpretation of the viewer, it is important for those who are initiating the communication to ensure that the visual message is as precise as possible. To do this, understanding the principles of effective visual design is a necessary first step.

Every **visual** consists of a number of elements presented in a deliberate arrangement. There are three primary categories of design elements: visual, text, and affective elements. Visual elements may include graphics, symbols, real objects, and organizational visuals. Text elements include all aspects of textual presentation, ranging from the words chosen to the font styles, colors, and sizes used. Affective elements are those components of a visual that can elicit a response from the viewer, such as pleasure, surprise, or humor. Selecting and arranging these elements appropriately results in effective displays. Following the guidelines summarized in Table 9.3 will assist you in creating clear and effective visuals.

The Visual Display Evaluation Rubric (Table 9.4) will help you objectively evaluate the various elements that contribute to effective visuals. Use this rubric to examine the visuals in Figure 9.7.

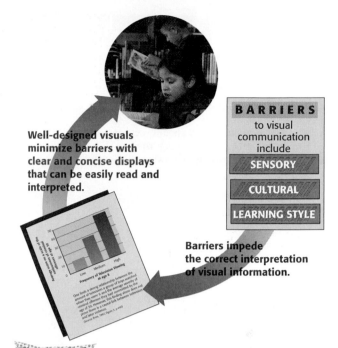

Well-designed visuals minimize barriers with clear and concise displays that can be easily read and interpreted.

BARRIERS to visual communication include

SENSORY

CULTURAL

LEARNING STYLE

Barriers impede the correct interpretation of visual information.

Figure 9.6
Factors Affecting Visual Communication
Well-designed visuals—displays that can be easily read and interpreted—can overcome communication barriers, such as sensory, cultural, and learning style barriers.

The three components of visual design are visual, text, and affective elements.

ON THE WEB! 9.7
Visual Design

TABLE 9.3	GUIDELINES FOR EFFECTIVE VISUAL DESIGN
Design Element	**Guideline**
RELEVANCE	All elements of the design add to the clarity of the overall visual; no elements detract from the message.
COHERENCE	Include only elements that support, enhance, or extend the message.
CONSISTENCY	While elements do not need to be uniform, all elements should be in harmony and work together to send a single, clear message.
PROPORTION	The relative size of all elements should be consistent with their respective importance to the visual's message.
CONTRAST	Key elements, including white space, should draw sufficient distinction between elements to emphasize key message points.
UNITY and DIRECTION	All elements should work together to focus the viewer's attention on the visual starting point of the message and then to guide the viewer through the message's visual sequence.

TABLE 9.4   VISUAL DISPLAY RUBRIC

DISPLAY DESCRIPTION:

CONTENT OF DISPLAY:

PURPOSE:

Using each of the criteria below, evaluate the effectiveness of this visual for teaching and learning. For each dimension in the rubric, check the box that best reflects your opinion. Select visual displays that score 4 or higher in the most dimensions.

EVALUATION CRITERIA

Dimension	1 Poor	2 Below Average	3 Average	4 Above Average	5 Excellent
Relevance	Visual contains a number of irrelevant elements that significantly detract from the message	Visual includes both relevant and irrelevant elements; some detract from the message	Some elements add to and clarify the message; some elements are extraneous	Most elements add to and clarify the message; all elements are relevant	All elements significantly add to and/or clarify the message; all elements are essential
Coherence	Elements of the visual are incompatible; their inclusion confuses the intended message	Elements are mixed and somewhat incompatible; message blurred by the elements	Some elements are in harmony in communicating the message; others seem misplaced	Most elements in harmony in communicating the message	All elements are in harmony and unite effectively to communicate the message
Consistency	Elements are inconsistent, resulting in a confusing visual	Elements seem minimally consistent; some detract from visual's unity	Some elements work together to communicate; others seem misplaced	Most elements work together to communicate the message	All elements work together to visually enhance and clearly communicate
Proportion	Elements are incorrectly sized and spaced, resulting in a difficult-to-understand message	Elements seem incorrectly sized and spaced in the visual, detracting from the message	Some elements are appropriately sized and spaced; others seem misplaced or mis-sized	Most elements are sized and spaced appropriately	All elements are sized and spaced to achieve message clarity
Contrast	Minimal contrast included among elements; visual seems boring	Little contrast is included, resulting in a somewhat boring visual	Contrast included is average, resulting in moderate visual interest	Some contrast is evident, resulting in visual interest and excitement	Contrast is used effectively to create visual excitement and interest
Unity and direction	Elements lack focus and direction; tend to confuse viewer's grasp of message	Elements lack focus and do not consistently guide viewer through the message	Some elements focus and guide viewer through message; others detract	Most elements work to focus and guide viewer through the message	All elements work together to focus and guide viewer through the message

   This and other downloadable forms and templates can be found on the Companion Website at www.ablongman.com/lever-duffy.

⬤—[Nonprojected Visuals in Teaching and Learning

The most common type of visuals found in today's classrooms are nonprojected visuals. These visual supports do not require projection for display and include real objects, models, exhibits, printed materials, and graphics and photographs. Although these visuals might not be high-tech, they may well be the best choice to support the con-

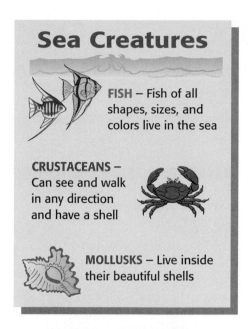

A GOOD VISUAL DESIGN

- Balanced design
- Legible text
- Minimal letter styles and sizes
- Appealing colors
- Provides unity and direction
- Consistent and cohesive
- Relevant images

A POOR VISUAL DESIGN

- Design lacks balance
- Text style difficult to read
- Too many letter styles
- Minimal color appeal
- Lacks unity and direction
- Inconsistent look
- Images disconnected

Figure 9.7
Evaluating Effective Instructional Visuals
Apply the Visual Display Evaluation Rubric (Table 9.4) to both of these visuals. What makes the left visual more effective than the one on the right?

tent under study. Table 9.5 summarizes popular nonprojected visuals and examples of how they can be used in the teaching and learning process.

Real Objects

Real objects, as the name implies, are any objects that can safely and reasonably be brought into the classroom for examination. Abstract verbal descriptions of a real object do not have the same impact as sensory input resulting from looking at, touching, and feeling the real thing. Whenever possible, it is useful to support content with real objects that learners can examine and explore.

Real objects address kinesthetic learning.

Models

Models include three-dimensional representations of concepts or real objects that cannot reasonably be brought into the classroom. Typically, models are representations that are scaled up or down to provide a three-dimensional visual, such as a scale model of a tooth (scaled up) or a globe (scaled down). Models can bring kinesthetic versions of concepts into the learning environment, and they can be manipulated and handled to provide tactile sensory support for abstract ideas.

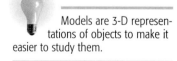

Models are 3-D representations of objects to make it easier to study them.

Exhibits

Exhibits include dioramas and classroom displays that are created and/or arranged to illustrate instructional content. **Dioramas** are usually displays that represent a scene, often created from a cut cardboard box. The diorama background is painted on the

TABLE 9.5   NONPROJECTED VISUALS AND THEIR APPLICATION

Nonprojected Visual	Examples	Applications
REAL OBJECTS	Rocks, stamps, fish, ants, plants, eggs, leaves	Scientific experiments, history projects, geology units, solar graphics, weather studies
MODELS	Globes; scale models; gear box circuit kits; timing devices; teaching clocks; teaching torsos; ear, eye, and nose models; hands-on heart models; solar system simulators	Teach and reinforce basic geographic locations; design and structure of bridges, boats, skyscrapers; human anatomy; astronomy
EXHIBITS	Dioramas, artifact collections, book displays, dinosaur mountain display, interactive dinosaur sound station, student craft projects	Show historical, geographic, or other wide-view, three-dimensional landscapes; showcase books to be read for a class or new publications; teach animal sounds through touching electronic soundspots on a vinyl play-mat; feature traveling artifact collections from local museums
PRINT MATERIALS	Books, worksheets, posters, charts, bulletin boards, games, maps, puzzles, cards, handwriting desk tapes	Required and elective books for study and recreational reading; worksheets with learning activities for all subjects; charts showing pictorial representations of a topic with activity ideas and further study suggestions; bulletin boards showing classroom rules, star students, birthdays, computer care, content-area facts and details; games to teach skills; crossword puzzles for vocabulary study; flash cards for memorization of facts; desk tapes for teaching cursive writing
GRAPHICS and PHOTOGRAPHS	Drawings, cartoons, diagrams, photographs, graphic organizers, graphing mats, graphs, Venn diagrams, glyphs	Student drawings to illustrate stories read, holidays, portraits; relevant cartoons to add humor to an assignment; photos students take of field trips, their vacations, their families and friends; graphic organizers to help students visualize and organize schoolwork; graphing mats, graphs, Venn diagrams, and glyphs to teach concepts that connect math to other subjects

back inside of the box, with objects or models situated in the foreground of the box to finish the scene. Making a diorama can be an effective activity in which students create a visual that is representative of natural habitats, geographical features, or historical events.

Classroom displays are exhibits of arranged visual objects that accentuate or enhance an instructional concept. Displays might include annotated rock collections, thematic book displays in libraries, and history displays that include antiques and photographs.

Regardless of the type of exhibit selected, such visual displays, especially if they are touchable, add both visual and concrete dimensions to concepts presented in instruction.

Print Materials

Whether created by teachers or students, **print materials** as visual displays remain a centerpiece in most learning spaces. Individual print materials may include books and worksheets, and group-oriented printed visuals may include posters and charts. Teacher-made, student-made, or commercially printed visuals, though a staple in most classrooms, vary in quality. Awareness of visual design principles and use of a design rubric will assist you in selecting high-quality print visuals for display in your classroom.

connecting THEORY to PRACTICE

Paivio's Dual Coding Theory

Most teachers understand that the use of visuals as well as text enhances student learning. Allan Paivio (2001) has developed a theory that explains this basic assumption. Paivio's dual coding theory suggests that two subsystems are at work whenever we process input. The two subsystems are a verbal subsystem to assimilate verbal input and a nonverbal subsystem to assimilate nonverbal input. Paivio further suggests that the verbal subsystem uses verbal entities that he calls "logogens," while the nonverbal system uses visual entities called "imagens." When input is presented and processed, one or both of the subsystems are engaged depending upon the type of input.

Paivio conducted a number of experiments presenting subjects with input that used one or both types of entities (logogens and/or imagens) to represent objects. He found that presenting logogens alone resulted in the lowest memory performance, and presenting imagens alone resulted in somewhat better performance. However, when he presented logogens and imagens together, memory performance improved. Using both verbal and nonverbal systems together helped the subjects more effectively interpret and remember the content.

For educators, Paivio's work provides a theoretical framework for what seems to occur in the classroom. When students are presented with both verbal and visual representations of the information being taught, they learn the information more readily. For educators, the implication is that lessons can always be enhanced with the addition of visual images, regardless of the technology that supports them.

Graphics and Photographs

A pictorial image can be created (graphics) or captured photographically (photographs). These images can be used in their original size for individual or group instruction or can be blown up for whole-class instruction. **Graphics,** including drawings, cartoons, and diagrams, can represent and clarify concepts and relationships. **Photographs** can capture real-world images and transport them into the classroom. Both graphics and photographs illustrate, clarify, and enhance abstract concepts; however, to be effective, their presentation and use in the teaching and learning environment also need to conform to the principles of effective visual design.

Display Technologies for Nonprojected Visuals

Once nonprojected visuals are planned in accordance with visual design principles, the next step is to select the appropriate technology for the creation and/or display of the visuals. Whereas real objects and models will themselves determine their display requirements, print and graphic media offer you many choices.

For creating print and graphic visuals, you might elect to use a computer and word processor or desktop publishing software to create your visuals. For graphics you might select draw or paint programs. To create charts, you might want to use spreadsheet software. For photos, both photographic equipment and digital cameras are options. Regardless of the technology you choose to use, you should stay mindful of the design principles you have learned, evaluate the product using a rubric and feedback from learners, and make revisions accordingly.

To display print or graphic visuals, most classrooms offer a variety of display surfaces. The most common is the bulletin board. **Bulletin boards** offer a flexible surface, usually cork, that provides an easy-to-change venue for a variety of print and graphic elements. A well-planned bulletin board can combine many nonprojected visual components into a single coherent instructional display.

ON THE WEB! 9.8
Bulletin Boards

Other surfaces for nonprojected visual display often found in classrooms include flip charts, magnetic boards, felt boards, and chalkboards or whiteboards. Availability varies by school and grade level, but familiarity with each will serve you well as you decide how best to share visuals with your students. Figure 9.8 shows examples of visual display surfaces.

BULLETIN BOARD

WHITEBOARD

FLIP CHART

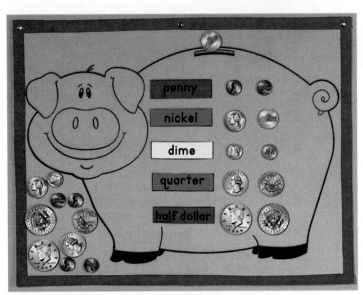

FELT BOARD

MAGNETIC BOARD

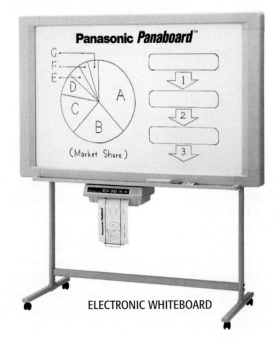

ELECTRONIC WHITEBOARD

Figure 9.8
Nonprojected Visual Display Media
Display media from traditional to high-tech can help
support instruction.

Flip charts are large (25″ × 30″) pads of paper, usually mounted on an easel. Each sheet can be used to write text or graphic messages that can be either saved on the pad or torn off and displayed around the classroom. Flip charts are useful for capturing key points of group discussion so that later they can be shared, and for creating impromptu illustrations of concepts. Thick colored markers add contrast. A recent enhancement to flip charts is the giant Post-it Note. The size of a flip chart sheet, this type of padded paper comes with its own cardboard easel and self-sticking sheets that can be hung on almost any surface without the need for tape and without damage to the surface.

Magnetic boards and felt boards are usually small surfaces that display visual elements through magnets or friction. **Magnetic boards** are usually painted metal, and small magnets are attached to the backs of the visual elements. **Felt boards** are constructed of cloth stretched over a sturdy board with visual elements cut out of flannel or felt or backed with Velcro to stick to the cloth. Both magnetic and felt boards are inexpensive and easy to manipulate by even the youngest students. For this reason, they are most frequently found in elementary classrooms.

Magnetic and felt boards are alternative display surfaces.

Black or green **chalkboards,** also called blackboards, are found in many classrooms. A variety of chalk colors can be used to create impromptu text and visual displays. Chalkboards also often include a small bulletin board surface at the top on which paper displays can be hung. Chalkboards are rapidly being replaced by whiteboards. **Whiteboards** offer a slick white surface on which a variety of specially formulated dry-erasable colored markers can be used. Whiteboards also provide a flat surface on which self-stick flip chart sheets can be hung. Additionally, some whiteboards have a metal backing that will support magnetic displays. And, as you learned in Chapter 6, when you combine the traditional whiteboard with digital technology, you get the electronic whiteboard. Whether a stand-alone version or a traditional whiteboard made electronic through the addition of an eBeam device, the whiteboard has significantly extended uses.

Electronic whiteboards expand on traditional whiteboard capabilities.

Projected Visuals in Teaching and Learning

Although the nonprojected visuals described in this chapter are indeed the most common visuals found in today's classrooms, visuals that require projection to be seen are also a critical component of many classrooms. This type of visual and the technology that supports it usually require, in addition to the visual itself, specialized equipment and a projection screen for classroom display. As a rule, the visual is enlarged from its original format so that all students can see it. For this reason, projected visuals are most commonly used for large-group instruction. Because the visual and the technology necessary to project it cannot be separated, each will be considered with its projection technologies in the following sections.

Overhead Projectors

The **overhead projector** has become an integral tool in many classrooms. Visuals are created on thin sheets of clear acetate, typically called **transparencies.** A powerful lamp inside the overhead projector shines through the plastic and then through a series of mirrors and lenses, so that the visual is magnified onto a projection screen. An enlarged image of the transparency is thereby projected for all to see.

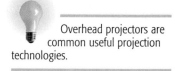
Overhead projectors are common useful projection technologies.

Visuals for overhead projection can be created by using black or color inks and can be hand drawn, printed via computer and printer, or photocopied from a printed page. To draw on a transparency, special transparency markers must be used or the ink will blotch and smear. Such markers can be either permanent or washable. Washable markers make it possible to reuse the transparency film, but because the washable marks can smear when touched, you might be wiser to create permanent transparencies, depending on the planned longevity of the content you include.

Permanent transparencies can also be created by using a color ink-jet or laser printer. To make this type of transparency, you first use a word-processing, desktop publishing, or draw program to create the visual desired. Once the visual has been created on the computer screen, you might want to print a sample hard copy before transferring it to transparency film. Once a hard copy is printed and you have verified that all the visual elements are as you desire, the next step is to print the visual on transparency film. It is important to check the type of transparency film you are selecting to make sure it is compatible with the printer you are using. Ink-jet printers, which allow you to create transparencies in black and in color inks, use a film that is porous on one side and slick on the other. As you learned in Chapter 3, ink-jet printers shoot a small bubble of ink onto the printing surface. On transparency film, the ink must be shot onto the porous side of the film for it to stick. Using the wrong type of transparency film in an ink-jet printer will result in a runny and smeared transparency that is difficult to dry. In contrast, laser printers create images by melting toner onto the surface of the media. Because heat is involved, a thicker, more heat-resistant acetate must be used. Furthermore, laser transparency film is slick on both sides, because melted toner, not ink, is used in image transfer. Because lasers and copiers use similar transfer technologies, laser and copier transparency film can be used interchangeably. It should be noted that it is very important to avoid using the thinner, porous ink-jet film in copiers or laser printers, as the film may buckle and melt under the heat of the laser printing process and leave a mess of melted plastic inside the copier or printer. Table 9.6 summarizes the variety of transparencies and their uses.

TABLE 9.6   TRANSPARENCIES AND THEIR APPLICATIONS

Type of Transparency	Features	Uses
WRITE-ON TRANSPARENCY	Clear, plastic sheet can be drawn on or written on using soft-tip pens; erasable by using a damp cloth or holding under running water if washable pens were used	Students can write short drafts and thesis statements for class feedback; teachers can write brainstormed suggestions; math problems can be demonstrated step-by-step; in-progress work can be briefly displayed for comments
COMMERCIAL TRANSPARENCY	Preprinted on clear, plastic sheet; cannot be erased; sometimes available from textbook publishers as supplementary material for instruction	Facts, graphs, tables, diagrams, outlines, rules, and other predetermined, professionally presented content can be displayed for instruction and commentary; teachers explain and amplify the content shown on the transparency as it is viewed
PHOTOCOPIED TRANSPARENCY	Teacher-selected illustrative materials can be drawn or written on; clear plastic sheets have a textured strip down one long side for controlled feed into photocopier	Graphics, cartoons, excerpts from published materials, and other printed copy can be transferred onto the transparency for sharing with an entire class or small groups
LASER-PRINTED TRANSPARENCY	Computer-prepared black-and-white and color transparencies can be printed easily according to the printer manufacturer's or transparency manufacturer's directions; a textured strip down the long side of the transparency allows the printer to grab the transparency for movement through the printer	By word processing or any other document preparation done by computer, teachers can create their own transparencies and print them out on their printers, tailoring the content to the exact purposes of the instruction, individualizing the materials by using student names, and updating activities to reflect current situations
COMPUTER-PRINTED COLOR TRANSPARENCY	An effective visual impact is disseminated by the use of color; it is usually an expensive process, involving photographic images, color photocopying, or thermal-wax color printing; on ink-jet printers, color is no longer as expensive as it once was	Circle graphs, bar graphs, reproductions of artwork, maps, and other graphic and pictorial images are more discernible when color is used to differentiate respective parts or to copy color-print originals

Commercial overhead transparencies are also very popular options for use in the classroom. These visuals are created and sold in booklets or sets and are sometimes offered as supplements to a textbook. The obvious advantage of commercial transparencies is that they are high-quality, ready-to-use visuals designed for overhead projection. A disadvantage may be that they do not fully target the instructional concepts you have selected to present.

If you use any type of presentation software on your computer, such as Power-Point but you do not have a digital projector available, you can create the visuals you want and then print them directly on the appropriate type of transparency film. These will look like commercial transparencies, but they will illustrate the topic exactly the way you want, because you created them.

Overhead projectors and the teacher-made or commercial transparencies that they project offer some unique advantages in the classroom. Perhaps the most important is that they allow the teacher to maintain eye contact with learners during group instruction. Instead of having to turn to write on a whiteboard, using an overhead allows you to face the classroom while creating impromptu visual images. Another advantage is the longevity of the visual images. Unlike the whiteboard, which must be erased as the lesson progresses, transparencies that contain previously presented information can be reprojected as needed. Transparencies also allow you to build a concept; this can be done by adding successive transparency layers, called overlays. Each overlay contains a bit of additional information that, when placed on top of the previous display, creates a more complex and detailed visual. You can also place a sheet of blank film on top of your prepared transparency and mark on it as you talk. When class is over, you can simply throw that piece of film away, and your original transparency is ready to use again.

Visuals using overhead projection technologies offer a versatile and effective support for instructional presentations. Although they require some additional hardware for display, transparencies offer an easy-to-create and easy-to-use option for educators. You should apply the same visual design principles when creating transparencies as you would when creating any other visual. Figure 9.9 offers some additional useful hints for effectively creating and using this visual technology.

ON THE WEB! 9.9
Overhead Transparencies

Transparencies should be created following standard visual design guidelines.

Learning with Visuals

• Offer visual literacy activities

• Provide practice interpreting visual messages

• Encourage students to create visuals that communicate

Use COLOR CONTRAST to add interest.

Include GRAPHICS that add interest, but keep them simple and avoid very complex diagrams.

Include MINIMAL TEXT on each transparency. A good rule is the Rule of Seven: no more than 7 lines with 7 words per line.

ELIMINATE unnecessary detail to keep the message concise and clear.

Figure 9.9
Tips for Good Transparencies
Guidelines for creating effective transparencies include limiting content, including graphics, and maintaining eye appeal through color and contrast.

ON THE WEB! 9.10
Digital or Photographic
Images

Digital Projectors

With the advent of digital imaging, **digital projectors** have taken a firm hold in schools. As you learned in Chapter 4, these computer output devices project digital images onto a projection screen, large monitor, or whiteboard so that they can be shared with a large group. (Features of digital projectors, as well as overhead projectors, are summarized in Figure 9.10.) Images can be captured with a digital still camera, with a digital video camera, from an analog videotape using a video capture card, or even from an electronic smart board.

Regardless of the method used for capturing digital images, the use of digital projectors in education will no doubt continue to expand. As teachers become more familiar with the technology and schools increase their acquisition of digital imaging hardware and software, teaching and learning will continue to be visually enhanced through their application. Digital images are already being creatively applied and incorporated into innovative instruction. Digital projectors are becoming more powerful and full-featured as their cost continues to drop. More and more educators are discovering and using this versatile technology for sharing visual images with learners.

Document Cameras

Document cameras are especially versatile projection devices.

A new projection device that combines the applications of several other types of visual projectors into one has recently begun to gain popularity. The **document camera** is actually a video camera, mounted on a stand, that captures and projects an image of whatever is placed on the stand's document table (see Figure 9.11). The camera, pointed down toward the document table, captures a live video image of the document or object placed on its table and plays that image back through a video monitor or an LCD display. By using both top and back lighting on the table and the video camera's

Figure 9.10
Comparing Projectors
Various types of projectors can be found in schools.

FEATURES
- Versatile and inexpensive
- Displays commercial or teacher-made transparencies against a screen, classroom wall, or whiteboard
- In combination with computer-generated images and a color printer, transparencies can be created that specifically target instructional objectives

OVERHEAD PROJECTOR

FEATURES
- Attached to a computer, projector displays real-time computer images
- Displays software or Internet activities for large group
- Varies from inexpensive to costly along with the quality of the display and the features available

DIGITAL PROJECTOR

Figure 9.11
Using a Document Camera in the Classroom
Document cameras provide many visual projection options.

Document cameras can

- Display real-time still images
- Display real-time 3-D objects
- Show photographic slides
- Show transparencies
- Capture video images

zoom features, overhead transparencies, slides, documents, and three-dimensional objects can all be projected to a large group.

This technology offers some unique projection advantages. Science experiments, demonstrations of small real objects, and procedural presentations can be easily shared. As the teacher proceeds with a live demonstration on the document camera table, the zoom feature built into the camera can be used to share minute detail with all students simultaneously. A teacher no longer needs to have students crowd around a demonstration to share it or walk around the classroom to show small objects. The document camera's live video makes sharing simple and readily viewable by all.

ON THE WEB! 9.11
Document Cameras

IN THE CLASSROOM

Multitasking Partnership: Projection Technology Helps Out

"If you can't beat them, join them" is a valid expression of what teachers are discovering in their classrooms. Young people are visually oriented, so why not use visual images to capture their attention and reinforce learning? Peter Gannon teaches eighth-grade social sciences at Turlock Junior High School in Turlock, California. Projection technology is the bridge he uses in moving students from pictures to print. According to Mr. Gannon, "Technology is part of their life, and when you incorporate it into a lesson, all of a sudden, the kids are riveted. Just reading from a textbook does not reel them in anymore."

By giving both pictorial and text input, Mr. Gannon sees that the double dosage is increasing retention. Going to the Internet and searching the web for information he would have had to disseminate in handouts or by lecture a few years back, he has found a way to lock in student attention on the subject at hand. He says, after finding the information he needs on the Internet, "Now, I can plug in the projector and show the kids where I got the information and how. I have kids who go home eager to get

online to continue looking for more information about subjects we covered in class."

Teachers at Washougal High School in Washougal, Washington, use projection technology for student-created visual images, photos, and graphics for a research portfolio. With projectors, they present the portfolio to a panel from the community for viewing. As a rule, the students select topics that show community interests and concerns, such as "the impact of business development on the local environment, the history of the school, or the effect of health education on reducing teen pregnancy or drug use." To create a visual statement made through projection technology, the students embellish the images with presentation software that adds color and attractive fonts for text to the overall production.

SOURCE: L. Wallace. 2002. Using projection technology to enhance teaching. *Media & Methods* (September/October), 39 (1), 6.

Multimedia in Teaching and Learning

Multimedia helps each type of learner by appealing to his or her particular learning style.

The concept of **multimedia** suggests a combination of multiple media combined into a single integrated whole. Indeed, multimedia today is synonymous with a computer-based format that combines text, graphics, audio, and even video into a single, coherent digital presentation. Furthermore, multimedia software is typically arranged in a hypermedia format that allows the learner to jump among these elements to follow his or her own learning style and personal curiosity. Multimedia is highly interactive, requiring the learner to engage in the process by selecting and navigating among screens of information and toggling between media presentations.

In this chapter, you have learned about audio media and visual media and their uses in teaching and learning. Each of these media and its supporting technologies add dimension to your instruction. When you use digital versions of audio and visual media and combine them within multimedia software, captivating opportunities for learning occur. Let's examine some examples of the effective use of multimedia in the classroom.

For elementary-age children, kinesthetic and experiential learning is very powerful learning. Field trips are therefore appropriate learning experiences. If you are teaching a unit on animals and their habitats, a field trip to the local zoo significantly reinforces what the children learn. How can you take that reinforcing experience back to the classroom with you and use it to strengthen concepts presented? Multimedia makes this possible. Capturing digital images of the animals (or photographic images that can later be scanned) lets you take the children's sensory experience back to the classroom with you. These images can be turned into classroom visuals by making posters, transparencies, a storybook, and even, with the help of draw software that creates outline images, a custom coloring book. These same images can be imported into multimedia software to which sound and text can be added. In small groups focusing on specific animals, the children can record their own versions of the sounds the animals made or comment on other sensory impressions (e.g., what the animals felt like or smelled like). After reviewing their lesson, the children can add pages of text that provide facts about each animal and its habitat as well as other graphics from clip art or their own scanned drawings. Finally, even the youngest children can add buttons and links to provide navigation paths between their pages. The children not only actively engage in formulating and arranging the concepts presented, but also reinforce their own learning pathways through both the development and use of the multimedia they have created. The field trip can be reexperienced many times.

For secondary school learners, multimedia holds great potential as well. Because the learners can handle more sophisticated digital technologies, the potential to create distinctive learning media is expanded. For example, a current theme in a number of secondary schools is that of effective conflict resolution, an important skill for these budding adults. Using multimedia authoring software, learners can work in teams to investigate and act out alternative scenarios to resolve a conflict. Students can use a digital camera to capture the setting of the conflict and the players involved, and create navigation buttons to jump to alternative resolution options. Each option screen can offer pictures, text, and student audio recordings describing the option and the possible outcome if that option is taken. Creating the multimedia program allows learners to fully explore and participate in simulated conflict resolution. Using multimedia gives learners a chance to experience alternatives and can lead to further meaningful classroom dialog.

ON THE WEB! 9.12
Multimedia in the Classroom

These are just two of the many possibilities for the creative application of multimedia. There are few limits once an innovative educator has acquired basic multimedia skills and has become aware of its potential. But whether combined into multimedia or used individually, audio and visual media and their supporting technologies can add depth to teaching and learning experiences. The only limitation will be your imagination.

KEY TERMS

STUDENT ACTIVITIES

CHAPTER REVIEW

1. What three steps are involved with being able to hear and comprehend? What can a teacher do to improve the hearing-listening process?
2. In terms of the brain, how does the use of multiple modalities increase retention?
3. What are the advantages and disadvantages of each of the following audio technologies in teaching and learning: Audiocassettes? Broadcast audio? Optical media? Internet audio?
4. What is visual literacy? Where and when is it learned? Why is it important?
5. Describe the six guidelines for effective visual design.
6. Name and describe three types of nonprojected media. Explain how each is important in teaching and learning.
7. Name the five most common technologies for nonprojected media display. How do they differ?
8. What are projected visuals? When compared to nonprojected visuals, when are they most appropriate in the classroom?
9. What are the most common types of transparencies? How are they used in conjunction with overhead projectors for teaching and learning?
10. What is a digital projector? How is it used? How might a document camera be used with a digital projector to enhance learning in the classroom?

WHAT DO YOU THINK?

1. There is much discussion today about the role of computers in the classroom, often to the point at which this technology overshadows all other instructional technologies, many of which are described in this chapter. What do you believe is the appropriate balance among the various technologies you have learned about thus far? Will digital technologies and computers indeed replace all others? What will your classroom be like twenty years from now in terms of the technologies you will be using?

2. The 1990s were called the Decade of the Brain because of the emphasis on research to understand the dynamics of brain functioning, including learning. What impact do you believe this research will have on your teaching? How will it influence your decisions about the technologies you select in support of teaching and learning?

3. There is much discussion about multimedia over the Internet. How might Internet delivery of multimedia be an advantage over its more traditional format? How would you use audio and visual media from the Internet in the learning environment you create?

4. Imagine that you have moved into a new classroom, and no audio or visual technology or media have yet been ordered. You have been asked to prepare a wish list of your audio and visual needs to submit to the media center. What will you order? Justify your requests by explaining how you would use each technology or medium in instruction.

5. Visual literacy and audio delivery are inherent components of instruction. What can you do to help build skills in visual literacy and in effective listening in the grade or content area in which you teach or wish to teach?

LEARNING TOGETHER!

These activities are best done in groups of three to five.

1. Visit the media center of a local school, and ask the media specialist to show you the audio and visual technologies that are available. Make a list of these technologies, and ask the media specialist how each is most often used. Compare your media inventory and applications list with those of the other members of your group. Create a list of the media that are most often found in schools and their most popular teaching and learning applications. Be prepared to share your list with other groups.

2. Listening centers are popular individual and group activity centers in classrooms today. As a group, design a listening center for the grade level you would prefer to teach. Describe the technologies and media you would include in the listening center, and explain how each would be used to support teaching and learning.

3. Research brain-based teaching and the role of audio and visual stimuli in learning. Prepare an oral report that uses both audio and visual media to teach other groups what you have learned.

4. Select one poorly designed visual and one well-designed visual for evaluation. Use Table 9.4 to evaluate each of them. Share the visuals and your evaluations with your group. From your common experiences, create a ten-point guideline on how to create good educational visuals. Be prepared to share your guidelines with other groups.

5. Create a fully articulated lesson plan with supporting nonprojected media that would be useful in teaching and learning. Be prepared to exhibit the media and present the lesson plan to other groups.

HANDS-ON!

1. Prepare a well-designed transparency to teach a concept of your choice that would be appropriate to the grade level you would like to teach. Print it using a color ink-jet printer, and print the same transparency using a laser printer. Present your transparencies using the classroom overhead projector. Describe how you would use the transparency in a lesson.

2. Write a behavioral objective and lesson plan that lends itself to audio delivery for a content area or grade you wish to teach. Create an audio instructional tape that supports this lesson. You should use the lesson planner from Chapter 2 to design your plan. Include a study guide to accompany the tape. Be ready to share your lesson with your peers.

3. Interview a classroom teacher, and ask how he or she uses both audio and visuals in instruction. Observe the classroom environment, the teacher, and the students using these media and technologies. Write a two- to three-page description and critique of the media, technologies,

and instruction you observed. Describe what you saw and learned that will be helpful in making you a more effective teacher.

4. Examine and evaluate a multimedia software package that is appropriate for the content area or grade level you would like to teach. Demonstrate the software for your peers, and share your evaluation of it. Describe its strengths, weaknesses, and potential for teaching and learning.

5. Research and locate five educational web sites that use audio or video effectively and that offer valuable resources that could be of use to you or your peers when you teach. Word-process an annotated list of the sites, describing their content and their URLs, that can be combined into a class directory of useful sites.

More from Lucianne Sweder

You have learned much about audio and visual technologies and about how they can be useful in teaching and learning. With that foundation in place, let's return to Lucianne Sweder and her team as they visit innovative teachers in two districts who integrate A/V into instruction.

We first went to visit Lockport Township High School, where Regina Keifer, the instructional technology specialist, met us and gave us some background about the school. The Freshman Center has been open for several years and provides a nurturing environment, ensuring a positive transition of eighth graders. This focus is carried out in all subject areas, including the freshman art course. Mary Ann Meyers and Kevin Brady both teach freshman art and they teamed together to design a technologically inclusive idea within their art program to support this nurturing concept at the school. When we entered Mary Ann's class, she explained that "many problems in our environment and society do not always receive the attention in the mass media that they really deserve. It is also well known that one of the best ways to really learn something is to have to teach it to others or present it to an audience." Mary Ann and Kevin developed a student activity called "Creating and Producing an Uncommercial" for their freshman Technology Art Survey course. Mary Ann explained: "Student teams conceive, plan, and produce Uncommercials, compelling short (30 seconds to 1 minute) desktop video movie stories that can provide inside looks [into a topic]." Mary Ann and Kevin developed the "Uncommercial" project with topics students chose from a preselected list or developed based on issues that really interested them. Some of the topics included pollution, teen drunk driving, homelessness, peer pressure, violence, stereotypes, and shoplifting. Mary Ann explained that teams used Corel Painter to create natural drawings, Adobe Photoshop to edit images and photos, MGI (now Roxio) VideoWave for capturing, editing, producing, and sharing their video on the web, and Internet resources for their research. Minisessions were given throughout the project to instruct students on the use of equipment and software, the incorporation of skills learned, and self-evaluation with editing techniques. This is a good example of "just in time learning" rather than "just in case learning." The students' process included choosing the topic; researching the history of the topic and its impact on students today; determining which segments would require "on-loca-

tion shooting" and which could be achieved through graphics; developing a storyboard to present to other teams; producing and editing the story and posting it on the web; receiving critiques from audiences; and completing production to prepare for presentation. While a due date was defined, individual adjustments were made to meet the various needs of diverse learners. Rubrics were designed and used throughout the process to help students produce high-quality audio and visual projects. Students were proud to demonstrate their work, and their desktop movie stories could be viewed by new audiences in the future.

Our road trip continued to visit Scott Paulson, an award-winning teacher for the past four years at Gompers Jr. High School. Scott has been teaching for over twenty-five years and has always been creative in developing new ideas for students to learn. His general education classes include students from the school's special education and bilingual populations. They need to learn more about themselves: where they came from, where they are, and where they are headed in life. He thought a new solution including technology might support student achievement and interest, so he created a special unit for his eighth-grade general education students that he called "All about Me."

"All about Me" included a résumé structure and narratives in essay and poem formats, created using a word processor, on the topic of possible careers. Other computer resources and applications that students used were Microsoft Excel and PowerPoint, Tom Snyder Productions TimeLiner, web page editors, Internet resources, Inspiration, and a photo program with a digital camera. Scott provided detailed instructions for this unit, which lasted over three weeks.

For example, Scott reminded his students to select audio and visuals that would add rich content to their autobiographies. The finished student products, integrated with audio and visual technologies, demonstrated students' learning throughout this unit.

Contact information: Lucianne Sweder is now a university lecturer at Governors State University in University Park, Illinois, and is completing her Ph.D. in instructional design for online learning. She can be reached at l-sweder@govst.edu.

CHAPTER 10

Video Technologies

This chapter addresses these ISTE National Educational Technology Standards for Teachers:

II. Planning and designing learning environments and experiences

Teachers plan and design effective learning environments and experiences supported by technology. Teachers

A. design developmentally appropriate learning opportunities that apply technology-enhanced instructional strategies to support the diverse needs of learners.
B. apply current research on teaching and learning with technology when planning learning environments and experiences.
C. identify and locate technology resources and evaluate them for accuracy and suitability.
D. plan for the management of technology resources within the context of learning activities.
E. plan strategies to manage student learning in a technology-enhanced environment.

III. Teaching, learning, and the curriculum

Teachers implement curriculum plans that include methods and strategies for applying technology to maximize student learning. Teachers

A. facilitate technology-enhanced experiences that address content standards and student technology standards.
B. use technology to support learner-centered strategies that address the diverse needs of students.
C. apply technology to develop students' higher-order skills and creativity.
D. manage student learning activities in a technology-enhanced environment.

Video has been a component of instruction in classrooms for almost a hundred years. Thomas Edison created the first films shown in a classroom in 1911. This initial series of films, entitled *The Minute Men*, brought key events of the American Revolution to life for the children of that day. Edison is said to have predicted that with the introduction of the movie projector, we would soon no longer need teachers to teach. However, as we have seen many times, such predictions usually fall flat on their faces. Teaching is much more than any technology or technique. Still, the tremendous impact films have had on learning experiences cannot be ignored. Today, almost a century later, via its ability to capture sight and sound, motion video still brings to life diverse instructional content. The primary aspect of video technologies that has truly changed is the kind of technology required for today's video recording and playback.

During your educational experience, you have no doubt had the opportunity to view breathtaking travelogues such as those produced by the National Geographic Society and beautiful video productions that capture the emergence, growth, and explosion of a flower into full bloom. Such video field trips to places few will actually visit and recordings of natural events that you could not otherwise witness bring home the power of motion video. Videos make impossible experiences possible for their viewers and provide stimulation through our dominant senses. Well-constructed videos help learners make sense of the abstract while providing sensory summaries of the material presented. Although videos are sometimes criticized as providing too passive a learning experience, well-planned lessons can change

CHAPTER OUTLINE

 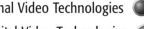

them into active learning stimuli. In addition, most educators would defend their inherent value in teaching and learning.

This chapter explores the various forms of video that are available to enrich and enhance instruction and the technologies that support them. It also explores how to implement this teaching and learning tool into the instructional event. Finally, it provides guidelines for evaluating and using motion video in instruction.

In Chapter 10, you will

● Examine the relationship and educational application of traditional and digital motion video

● Review the role of motion video in support of teaching and learning

● Explore the application of motion video in support of teaching and learning

● Examine the role of the Internet in providing motion video support for teaching and learning

● Consider the convergence of compressed video systems and video over the Internet

● Explore ways to evaluate motion video and its implementation for use in teaching and learning

Meet Denise Milam

Video remains a critical instruction resource in most schools today. This chapter looks at the broad range of video technologies, including broadcast TV, compressed video, Internet video, recorded video, and others that you will find available to you for use in your classroom. In this case study, you will meet Denise Milam, a technology teacher, who found that using video helped to motivate her students and engage them in learning.

I am the technology integration teacher and also a computer technology teacher in Williamstown Middle School, which is part of the Monroe Township Public School District, located in Gloucester County, New Jersey. The school community consists of one high school, one middle school, and four elementary schools. My middle school presently houses approximately 1,350 students and a teaching staff of over one hundred professionals.

In-class technology integration became possible during the school year of 2000–2001 with the purchase of a single cart of sixteen laptops, wireless Internet hubs throughout the building, and ten portable large-screen televisions on carts with scan converters. The middle school acquired two digital camcorders plus two new digital cameras for classroom use during the 2002–2003 school year, in addition to more laptop carts for classroom technology integration. I was transferred to the middle school at the beginning of the 2001–2002 school year. My job was to facilitate the technology inte-

gration with classroom teachers, teach a limited number of computer technology cycle classes to students, and implement the teacher laptop computer program, through which each classroom teacher would receive a laptop computer for use while teaching at the middle school, with take-home privileges during the summer.

Computer technology, especially digital video, can be an exciting yet confounding tool for teachers to incorporate and integrate in the learning environment. However, technology integration became a mandatory part of the professional goals for the teaching staff of Williamstown Middle School during the school year 2002–2003. In the state of New Jersey, teachers are required to achieve one hundred hours of professional development over a five-year period, and they track their personal professional goals through an annual personal improvement plan (PIP) they formulate. During a PIP conference, a discussion about the goals occurs between the administration and each teacher.

MY PROBLEM

My concern, as the technology integration teacher, was how I could help the classroom teachers become familiar with the technology we had available in our facility and how they could use it effectively and creatively in their classrooms. Fortunately for me, at the beginning of the 2002 school year, I was approached by a sixth-grade social studies teacher who was worried how she was going to meet the school mandate to integrate technology into her teaching. She requested assistance in the development of a project-based unit using technology as a teaching and learning tool. Although the motivation for this request came from the teacher's PIP conference and the administration's requirement to try something new using technology, I seized both the opportunity and the teacher's time.

As I met with the teacher, I learned that one of the favorite and familiar topics in sixth-grade social studies was the study of ancient civilizations, which included the study of Egypt. The classroom teacher had developed many lesson activities over the years, but she was willing to incorporate new activities to support the learning of the students and to motivate them to learn new concepts. I outlined the technologies available and offered some suggestions for ways to make effective use of them. With the technologies available, my support at hand, and an innovative and creative teacher, we went to work to enhance instruction though the application of digital video.

Ms. Milam offered the helping hand needed to begin the process of technology integration and to seed an exciting new approach to a social studies lesson. After reading this chapter and exploring the types of video technologies available to her, we will return to this project and discover how digital video was innovatively applied.

What Do I Need to Know about Video Technologies?

From the many videocassette tapes and DVDs that are available to the latest digital videos on the Internet, educators have a great wealth of motion video resources to support instruction. This instruction can be delivered in the classroom or, through technology, delivered to students at a distance. But to incorporate these many resources effectively, you will need to be familiar with the technologies required for recording and playback and be able to evaluate their appropriateness for instruction.

The learning and communications theories introduced in Chapter 1 suggest that we learn best when we experience, in a multifaceted way, the content under study. Motion video gives learners one more way to experience abstract content. Through video reenactments, learners can see and hear history. They can visit outer space or the deepest ocean. They can see inside the living body. Each of these simulated experiences, provided through motion video productions, helps to build constructs and reinforce instruction. Incorporating motion video support in your instructional design can strengthen learning and add a valuable dimension to the concepts presented.

Nevertheless, deciding how best to incorporate motion video in teaching and learning can be a challenge for educators. Too often, watching motion video becomes a passive, even boring experience for the learner. No doubt you have found yourself daydreaming during a video in one of your own courses. In those situations, you were unlikely to fully engage in the content. The medium tended to anesthetize your capacity to learn. Because the experience was limited to viewing and lacked participation, your focus was easily lost. This is the challenge of motion video. It is clearly beneficial to bring concepts to life. But how can an educator keep learners engaged? Understanding video technologies is a first step to effective use of motion video, but further steps are involved in meeting the challenge of using motion video effectively.

The challenge when using video is keeping the learner fully engaged.

Understanding Video Technologies

Video technologies have undergone a dramatic evolution from early silent movies to today's compressed video over the Internet. During each stage of this evolution, educators have utilized the most current video technology in support of teaching and learning (see Figure 10.1). As each new video technology replaced the last, over time

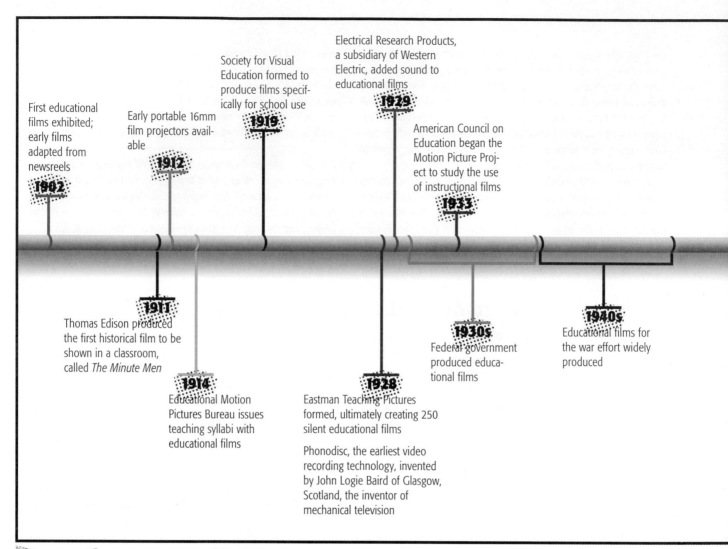

First educational films exhibited; early films adapted from newsreels
1902

Early portable 16mm film projectors available
1912

Society for Visual Education formed to produce films specifically for school use
1919

Electrical Research Products, a subsidiary of Western Electric, added sound to educational films
1929

American Council on Education began the Motion Picture Project to study the use of instructional films
1933

1911
Thomas Edison produced the first historical film to be shown in a classroom, called *The Minute Men*

1914
Educational Motion Pictures Bureau issues teaching syllabi with educational films

1928
Eastman Teaching Pictures formed, ultimately creating 250 silent educational films

Phonodisc, the earliest video recording technology, invented by John Logie Baird of Glasgow, Scotland, the inventor of mechanical television

1930s
Federal government produced educational films

1940s
Educational films for the war effort widely produced

Figure 10.1
Video Technology in the Classroom Timeline
Video has changed the nature of educational technology since the start of the twentieth century.

equipment and video media were also slowly replaced in schools. Still, because funds for technology and media are always in short supply, you will often find some older video technologies still available and still useful in educational settings.

Early movies and then television were the first major forms of motion video to affect classrooms significantly. Following these, a new method for capturing video, videotape (initially reel-to-reel, later in a cassette, and now in DVD), changed the way video was recorded and played back. Then easy-to-use and compact video cameras that stored images on videocassettes opened new opportunities to capture sound and motion. All of these traditional analog video technologies are still a part of the video resources you will find in schools. Even so, many have given way to digital video technologies that have emerged more recently.

Digital video technologies record and play back data, but the format in which the data is recorded also allows for full manipulation and editing. Because digital videos are recorded and played back using computer technology, the recorded videos can be as easily manipulated in terms of images and sound as a word-processing document can be manipulated in terms of text. This capability to record and fully manipulate

Analog video camcorders are giving way to digital video cameras.

ON THE WEB! 10.1
Discovering Digital Video

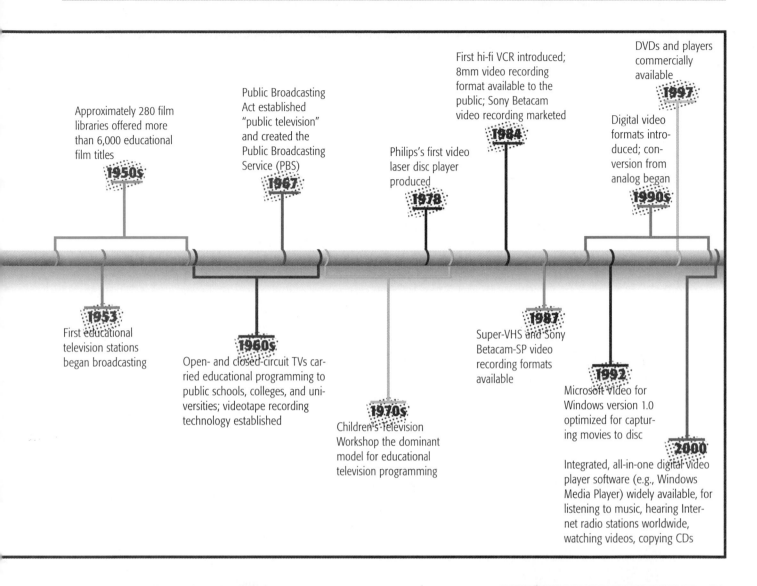

Approximately 280 film libraries offered more than 6,000 educational film titles
1950s

Public Broadcasting Act established "public television" and created the Public Broadcasting Service (PBS)
1967

Philips's first video laser disc player produced
1978

First hi-fi VCR introduced; 8mm video recording format available to the public; Sony Betacam video recording marketed
1984

DVDs and players commercially available
1997

Digital video formats introduced; conversion from analog began
1990s

1953
First educational television stations began broadcasting

1960s
Open- and closed-circuit TVs carried educational programming to public schools, colleges, and universities; videotape recording technology established

1970s
Children's Television Workshop the dominant model for educational television programming

1987
Super-VHS and Sony Betacam-SP video recording formats available

1992
Microsoft Video for Windows version 1.0 optimized for capturing movies to disc

2000
Integrated, all-in-one digital video player software (e.g., Windows Media Player) widely available, for listening to music, hearing Internet radio stations worldwide, watching videos, copying CDs

CAMCORDER

DVD PLAYER

VCR and MONITOR

Video technologies have evolved, but many older technologies can still be found in schools.

motion video opens up even more possibilities for the use of motion video in teaching and learning.

For any educator, the first step to incorporating motion video, whether traditional or digital, into instruction is to become familiar with the technology choices available and with how each can be used effectively in teaching and learning. The following sections will introduce you to your motion video options.

Traditional Video Technologies

Broadcast Video

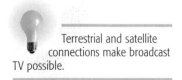
Terrestrial and satellite connections make broadcast TV possible.

Broadcast video is what is commonly thought of as television. Television images can be broadcast via **terrestrial** (land-based) equipment. The television signals are sent by TV stations and received by individual TV sets. For longer distances and to connect multiple terrestrial systems to global broadcast sources, a combination configuration of both terrestrial and satellite equipment is required. In **satellite transmission,** signals are sent to a satellite (**uplinked**) and then sent back down (**downlinked**) to a terrestrial system at another location on the globe (see Figure 10.2). The positioning of a string of such satellites around the globe allows television transmissions to be bounced via a series of uplinks and downlinks to positions anywhere on the earth.

Broadcast video can be in either a commercial format such as the programming broadcast by the major networks (such as ABC, NBC, and CBS) or an educational format such as programming on the **Public Broadcast System (PBS)** or a local learning channel. Public television, created by an act of Congress expressly to provide high-quality educational programs, includes at its core the **Corporation for Public Broadcasting (CPB).** The CPB manages the acquisition and production of educational programming, and PBS disseminates the programming through local TV channels. Local learning channels, sometimes referred to as **instructional television (ITV),** use broadcast airwaves to distribute video signals of instructional programs throughout a school district that can also be

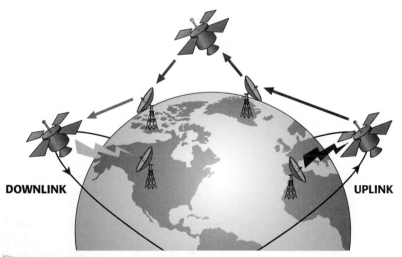

DOWNLINK   **UPLINK**

Figure 10.2
Television Uplinks and Downlinks
Television signals can be globally transmitted using terrestrial and satellite links. Signals are bounced across the globe via a system of satellites in geosynchronous orbit and dishes located strategically around the globe.

viewed by anyone who tunes in to that channel. Video images sent via broadcast can be either live or prerecorded, depending on the nature of the program. Typically, both commercial and educational broadcast television programs have high-quality production values, making them quite expensive to produce but very entertaining to watch.

For educators, broadcast video offers high-impact, high-quality video production that can dramatically demonstrate content. In particular, the educational programming offered by local PBS stations can add a wide array of video support to instruction. News commentaries, documentaries, docudramas, plays, musical productions, and educational programs such as *Sesame Street* are typically available through public television stations. However, because broadcast video is synchronous (real-time) in delivery, it is often difficult to use in a classroom setting. The time a program is broadcast might be inconsistent with scheduled lessons. Unless the teacher is willing to

IN THE CLASSROOM

It's Still a Favorite: Broadcast Video for Teaching

Daily news shows from the major networks are as typical of life in twenty-first-century America as daily radio news reports once were. Daily news shows from a middle school production facility featuring middle school students, however, are the "new kids on the block," both literally and metaphorically. Cathy Mullan, video production teacher at Landrum Middle School in Jacksonville, Florida, supervises her students as they prepare and broadcast on LNN (the Landrum News Network) every school day of the school year.

A typical newscast went like this: "Hi, I'm Ashley Hobbs with LNN sports." Ashley was "perched on a stool in front of a video camera. From her spot on the newsroom stage, she looked out at her director, at her camera reporter, at the TelePrompTer. Then she signaled she was ready, smiled, flashed a mouth full of braces—and the camera rolled."

Landrum Middle School switches on all the televisions at 9:03 every morning on Channel 3. The seven-minute broadcasts cover school news, the weather, and sports. The equipment used includes "six Sony digital video cameras, four educational iMac computers, digital editor software, studio lights and even some sound equipment."

Taking turns, the seventh and eighth graders in her classes all get a chance to work on the daily news reports. Such items as "the theme for the day, the quote for the day, news about the art club, the scheduled science fair and that drama teacher Ms. Meyers was seeking props for a future play" are typical of the content aired on a daily basis. All the jobs involved with the video broadcast production are rotated weekly among the students. Ms. Mullan affirms the inherent value of the video production class by saying, "I love teaching this, it's great. It really is a communication class on multiple levels. You have writing, you have speaking. And we're such a visual people nowadays; everybody wants to see everything."

SOURCE: M. FitzRoy. 2003, Sept. 6. Newest TV dateline: Landrum classroom. Retrieved September 8, 2003, from http://cgi.jacksonville.com.

arrange the instructional events around broadcast times, inclusion of broadcast video is difficult to implement over the school day. Of course, by using video recording technology (discussed in a later section), this disadvantage may be overcome.

Narrowcast Video

Broadcast video, as its name implies, is designed for the widest possible audience access. The video signals are broadly disseminated and can be picked up by anyone with the appropriate technology. This is fitting for transmissions that appeal to the general public. Much of broadcast video programming, however, might not be suitable for schools. The alternative to broadcast video is a video transmission format that targets educational audiences. This type of video transmission is sometimes referred to as **narrowcast video.** Types of narrowcast transmissions are summarized in Figure 10.3.

Narrowcast video includes video transmission that is targeted to a narrow audience, particularly schools. The most common system for this type of transmission is the **Instructional Television Fixed Service (ITFS).** ITFS is a terrestrial system that sends signals via microwave transmission from studios and ITFS broadcast locations to reception locations (usually schools) within a fixed area. Microwave signals require that the sender and receiver be located in a line-of-sight formation. This means that the receiving equipment must have a direct and unobstructed "view" of the microwave tower that is transmitting the signal. This can be a drawback in some physical locations, but for many school districts, ITFS is a relatively inexpensive method of setting up a broadcast system. ITFS creates a dedicated video network for instructional programs that can be offered multiple times throughout the day to accommodate school schedules. Furthermore, programming can be designed to meet specific local instructional needs. This dedicated television network, if available in your school, can provide valuable districtwide instructional video resources.

Once an ITFS signal is received by a school, it is typically distributed to all classrooms by using a **closed-circuit TV (CCTV)** system. A CCTV system is a network of

> Instructional Television Fixed Service broadcasts to a specific, limited audience.

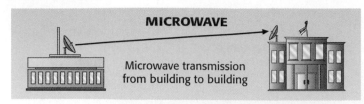

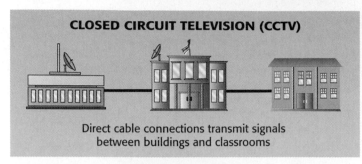

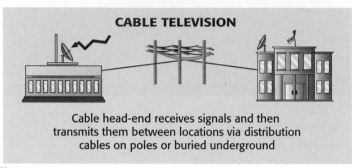

Figure 10.3
Narrowcast Systems
Narrowcast systems provide video to local areas.

television monitors connected via coaxial cables running throughout a school building that can distribute television signals to all the connected classrooms. Thus, once an ITV or ITFS transmission is received at one central point in a school, it can be distributed via CCTV to all connected classrooms within the school. As with other forms of broadcast TV, there may be some difficulty arranging instruction around transmission times; but ITFS programming is much more often arranged to accommodate school schedules. Additionally, ITFS programming can be recorded and distributed via CCTV or videocassette distribution for later replay in classrooms.

The school's CCTV system is also often used for other narrowcast transmissions. In-school TV production classes typically create video programs of daily announcements and school information. These in-school "morning shows" use the CCTV system to reach all classrooms as well.

Cablecast Video

The same coaxial cables that connect classrooms to an ITFS receiver location or a CCTV system together can also transmit cable television stations; this is often called **cablecast video.** Schools that are hooked to their local cable TV company are able to use their classroom television monitors to tune in to cable channels just as you use your home television to tune in to cable channels there. The types of programming that are available to schools through their local cable companies range from standard commercial and educational television to premium stations supplied free to schools by the cable companies. Arrangements vary widely with each local area, but if cablecast video is available at your school, you would do well to explore the instructional possibilities it presents. Many high-quality cable stations, including the Cable News Network (CNN), the Discovery Channel, and the Learning Channel, offer instructional programming that can enhance your instruction. Some programming providers, such as CNN, with its fifteen-minute daily *CNN Newsroom* program, allow schools to tape the broadcast without charge and distribute it throughout the school. Others may require copyright permission or charge fees to tape the broadcast for later distribution. In any case, if cablecast television programming is available, it might well provide an educational resource worth investigating fully.

Recorded Video Technologies

To overcome the scheduling problems inherent in broadcast, narrowcast, and cablecast systems in schools, recorded video has become the traditional video format of choice. **Videocassette recorders (VCRs)** can record video as it is transmitted, and the recording can be used for later playback, turning this otherwise synchronous technology into an asynchronous version. In the United States, VCRs use a magnetic **VHS format tape** for recording moving images. Many other countries use a different format, such as PAL; therefore, their recorded tapes will not play on U.S. machines. VHS tapes are relatively inexpensive and can contain up to 120 minutes of recording at the

IN THE CLASSROOM

"Late Breaking News!"
Video Productions Bring School News

"**G**ood morning, James B. Key Elementary School!" Each school day begins with fourth- and fifth-grade students broadcasting the news at this Columbus, Georgia, elementary school under the direction and supervision of Craig C. Harrison, who teaches math in the early intervention programs, as well as having been the computer lab manager at one time. The broadcast team shows up a half hour before school starts to get the broadcast under way. They must word-process the news in large type for the scripts to be readable in front of the cameras; then, it's rehearsal time to make sure the reading goes smoothly and correctly. Everyone moves into place five minutes before start time, and at the two-minute mark, quietness prevails.

The team members have jobs that correlate to professional newscasting assignments. Mr. Harrison's organization of their responsibilities goes like this:

Christiana serves as the director and makes sure camera operators Vicki and Bernita are ready to go. Computer operator Maria readies the script while anchors Seth and Iris and weather person Brittany take their places. Katie is ready at the video switch box.

Christiana begins her five-second countdown to broadcast time. Vicki and Bernita are moving the camera as needed, and Katie is often switching the video screen between camera and computer.

The sequence of the program is carefully laid out with the provision that newscasters must be able to make last-minute changes if necessary. There is always the chance of needing to convey unexpected and unplanned-for messages, such as "when the principal wants to add some comments, speak, or have a guest briefly address the student body," Mr. Harrison reminds his students. "At other times, the principal presents awards to members of the student body. The team must work as a unit to accommodate last-minute changes." Special features of the broadcast, such as "The Word of the Week," "Positive Action Words" (character-education vocabulary), and "This Day in History" keep an educational focus on the programming.

SOURCE: C. Harrison. 2002. The WKEY Morning News. *Learning & Leading with Technology* (October), 30 (2), 40–43.

standard playing speed or up to six or eight hours at slower speeds. Prerecorded tapes can be purchased or rented that contain movies, or you can tape a broadcast television program for later viewing. VHS tapes and their playback technology, the VCR, have replaced movie projectors in schools. They are compact, durable, inexpensive, and easy to use. Furthermore, teacher control over the screening of the video allows you to stop the tape at appropriate moments for clarification and discussion.

Videocassette recorders and monitors are available for use in most classrooms. They are usually either permanently assigned to the classroom or available on a rolling cart for checkout through the school media center. Large monitors can make it easy for a large class to view the videotape. If a larger image is desired, the VCR can be connected to a digital projector to project the image onto a large screen or light-colored wall. A broad selection of videotapes is often a part of the media center's holdings or is available through a district media distribution system. Although methods of distribution vary by locality, this video technology can usually be counted on as a useful support for your instruction. It is often wise to begin the school year by visiting the media center to review the video library. As with movies, it is important to preview any tape you might choose and to carefully plan for its use in the curriculum.

The broad availability of VCRs and monitors has made another video application readily available to most teachers. Compact **video camera/recorders,** called **camcorders,** record sound and images that can be played back by using a VCR. These relatively inexpensive and easy-to-use units make it possible to capture video images of your students, field trips, or your own instruction for later playback. You or your students can use camcorders to capture images of athletic events or debates for immediate feedback and review; to record student reports, documentaries, or dramatizations; and even to create a video historical or cultural archive of the school or community. These small recording units make it possible to produce videos economically and easily to support teaching and learning.

Your local school media center is usually your handiest source for videos.

ON THE WEB! 10.2
Educational Videocassettes

Digital Video Technologies

Traditional analog video accurately captures and displays high-quality sound and images. However, this video format is relatively inflexible. To edit or change taped analog images, cumbersome and somewhat expensive editing equipment is necessary. Additionally, to duplicate taped images, you need multiple interconnected video recorders and perhaps a signal amplifier to ensure that image quality is maintained. Clearly, for most educators, the processes and equipment necessary to edit or duplicate taped video require more time and resources than the product may be worth.

The same video images captured and stored in a digital format offer limitless editing possibilities. Video saved in a digital format, like other digital data, can be changed, edited, displayed, shared, or sent from one computer to another. Regardless of the technology used to capture and record it (including the conversion of analog video to digital), digital video provides a flexible and easy-to-alter format for video images. Educators who are familiar with digital video technologies will find it a relatively simple task to add text to video images, cut and paste video clips into multimedia presentations, or share digital video across a network. Digital video technologies offer a powerful teaching and learning resource that you can customize to support a specific lesson or to meet unique student needs.

Digital Video Basics

Traditional video captures and plays back images and sound at approximately thirty frames per second. At this playback speed, the captured video looks just like real-time motion. To turn this true-to-life image into a digital form, each frame must be converted to its digital counterpart. The sequence of digitized frames, called a digital video clip, results in a very large file. In fact, a three-minute high-quality digital video clip can require as much as a gigabyte of storage space.

Because of the large file sizes resulting from digitized video, video **compression technologies** were developed. As you may recall from Chapters 7 and 8, video compression is often used to transmit digital video across the Internet. Compression software and hardware work by capturing the initial video image in full but then ignoring the nonchanging components of the image. Rather than redigitizing and storing every bit of every image, subsequent frames store only those bits that have changed since the last frame (see Figure 10.4). Thus, the total storage requirements for the video clip are reduced.

Several popular compression formats are used for digital video. Each format requires software that can decompress and play back the compressed file, but the software is readily available. Playback software is either included with the operating system of the computer or is available for download from the Internet. The most popular digital video compression formats are Audio Video Interleaved (**AVI**), Motion Picture Experts Group (**MPEG**), and QuickTime (**MOV**). Table 10.1 lists the advantages of each.

Digital video, then, offers educators a flexible and versatile way to access, customize, and incorporate video into teaching

A *reference frame* is captured video that contains background and foreground images.

Subsequent frames omit the static, non-changing background and include only the parts of the foreground that are moving.

Video compression (smaller digital video files) is achieved because all parts of every video image are recorded only in the reference frame. Thereafter, only changed images are saved resulting in significantly less video data saved for subsequent frames. The result . . . compressed video files.

Figure 10.4
How Digital Video Compression Works
Digital video compression reduces overwhelming video file sizes.

TABLE 10.1   DIGITAL VIDEO COMPRESSION FORMATS

Format	Description	Advantages
AVI	Audio Video Interleaved	Lower resolution, smaller video files; good for animation
MPEG	Motion Pictures Experts Group	Reduces video files up to 95% yet retains near-television quality
MOV	QuickTime	Apple Computer's early nonbroadcast-quality format; easy to use and create

AVI, MPEG, and MOV digital compression formats are among the most widely used formats today.

ON THE WEB! 10.3
Digital Video Resources

and learning. As compression technologies continue to advance, the large size of digital video files will become less and less significant. Each year, digital video technologies improve geometrically in their capacity and usability. Although becoming familiar with the current digital video technologies described in the following section is a good first step, it is indeed just a beginning. Today's digital video technologies and their successors will continue to improve their usefulness to educators.

DVDs

As you have already learned, CDs offer greater storage capacity and durability than floppy disks. Still, given the current sizes of compressed video files, even CDs cannot store a full movie. To remedy this storage limitation and to provide a way to improve digital video's usefulness, a new storage technology was developed. The **digital video disc** (**DVD;** see Figure 10.5) can store 4.7 gigabytes of data on a standard disc and up to 10.5 gigabytes per side of a dual-layer DVD-ROM. This means that hours of full-motion, high-resolution video and sound can be stored in a durable and compact format. Furthermore, once stored, all of the data is directly accessible and easy to manipulate for display. For teachers, this means that you are able to access any segment of clear, high-quality video, frame by frame or in clips, simply by pressing the appropriate buttons. In the classroom, a digital video image can be instantly accessed, replayed, and discussed as a part of a lesson.

Additionally, new DVD recorders offer the opportunity to record video digitally and save to a DVD for playback at a later time. This allows teachers expanded opportunity to capture video sequences for use in subsequent lessons. DVD recorders and playback units are quickly becoming the preferred video equipment for the classroom, just as they are becoming more popular for home use.

Figure 10.5
Digital Video Discs for Teaching and Learning
Video discs offer advantages over videotape. DVDs can store video that can be directly accessed at any point in the video. Desired frames can then be played back as motion video or frame by frame.

Digital Video Capture

It is clear that digital formats can offer some distinct advantages for educators. However, over the many years of the technological dominance of traditional video technologies, countless educationally valuable programs and productions have been produced in traditional formats. How might a teacher convert valuable video resources to this newer and more flexible digital format? The technology that allows for the conversion of traditional analog video into its digital equivalent is the video capture card.

DVDs offer large storage capacity.

A **video capture card** is an expansion card that can be added to a personal computer. It plugs into one of the computer expansion slots, with the end containing video jacks extending out the back of the computer. These jacks become the video input ports. Traditional video (broadcast, narrowcast, or recorded video) can be input directly into the computer via these ports. The card and its video capture software then convert the video signal into its digital counterpart and compress it into a size that can be stored on the computer's hard disk. Once saved in a digital format, it can be edited and manipulated by using software designed to edit, enhance, and otherwise alter digital video files.

Video capture can make it possible for you to add a digital video clip from your class field trip to a presentation or to display a brief digital video clip from a television show to support your instruction. Of course, as is the case anytime you use copyrighted material when you teach, you need to stay aware of the fair use guidelines that apply to the inclusion of copyrighted video segments. Following this chapter, in the special feature on copyright in Interchapter 4, you will find an in-depth review of the copyright laws related to the use of video and the fair use guidelines associated with them. These are critical concerns to educators and should be examined carefully.

A video capture card will let you digitize analog videos.

ON THE WEB! 10.4
Video Capture Cards

ON THE WEB! 10.5
Video Camcorders

Digital Video Cameras

The most common option for creating digital video is to record it using a digital video camera (DVcam). **Digital video cameras,** like digital still cameras, capture and store the target images in a digital format that can then be downloaded to a personal computer. The resultant digital video files can then be manipulated, edited, and enhanced using **digital video editing** software.

The flexibility of digital video recording and editing has caused digital video cameras to largely replace analog camcorders. The many features included in even modest DV cams exceed the capabilities of previous camcorders, and their instant playback makes them popular favorites. These features include the ability to record digital images to mini DV tape for later transfer to a computer or for playback on a television; real-time editing and built-in special effects that can be recorded while taking the video; compatibility with popular digital video editing software; and the ability to record digital audio and still digital pictures as well as video. The compact size and ease of use have made DV cams popular, particularly as classroom tools in the hands of children. These features and many more have made digital video cameras the preferred choice for video.

You have already been introduced to one additional type of digital video camera, the monitor-top camera. Often used for videoconferencing via the Internet, this dedicated computer camera can also be configured to create instructional digital video segments. In combination with digital video production software, such as Serious Magic Visual Communicator, the monitor-top camera serves as a mainstream digital video camera when used to create professional presentation videos. The camera takes a video image of the speaker seated in front of the computer. As the speaker reads the presenta-

Apple computers equipped with iMovie and iDVD software make a digital video camera in the classroom a powerful and simple-to-use tool for instruction.

IN THE CLASSROOM

Picture This! Digital Video in the Classroom

Looking back over an entire school year and remembering all the great strides students have made in the acquisition of knowledge, skills, and maturation could be an impossible task with so many young people and so much of which to be proud. With digital video, however, it is both possible and enormously rewarding to record their remarkable accomplishments. Erin Conley, a second-grade inclusion teacher, teaches at Perry Elementary School in Perry, Ohio. She records pictures of student activities yearlong with a digital camera and photo styling software to create a video with a musical background. As the school year draws to a close, she has a movie night for the students and their parents to view the tape and see how much has been achieved by so many over the past nine months. Students were invited to bring in blank videotapes when school started, and now Ms. Conley makes copies of the master tape so that students can have their own videotaped movie to remember the year that was.

Digital video cameras can add multisensory delivery to instruction that brings subject matter to life in a way unimodal teaching can't convey. Mickey Hudson and Anthony Cooley, technology integration consultants for the Panhandle Area Educational Consortium in Chipley, Florida, share examples of how digital videos can enrich instruction in three subject areas—social studies, science, and chemistry. Historical sites in the community can be captured by digital video cameras and shown on a school's broadcast network. Mr. Hudson and Mr. Cooley describe the process beginning with the creation of a storyboard, followed by interviews recorded using the digital video cameras with people in the community who know the history associated with the sites, and then the importation of the video shots into a computer. At this point, video editing software permits the students to tweak the video. Mr. Hudson and Mr. Cooley add, "Student projects can also be converted to QuickTime movies and placed on a CD. Using a flat panel iMac with a DVD burner and iDVD software, students can also create DVDs."

SOURCES: E. Conley. 2003. Movie night. Retrieved June 2, 2003, from http://www.nea.org/helpfrom/growing/works4me/tech/equip.html; M. Hudson & A. Cooley. 2003. Digital video camera use in classrooms. *Media & Methods* (February), 39 (4), 6.

tion notes, which appear on the monitor, the computer's microphone captures the audio as well. Finally, the production software sequences and combines the recorded video with packaged special effects and transitions. The final video is a high-quality enhanced instructional digital video complete with screens and fades like those that might have been added in a studio. The result is instructional video made easily and inexpensively without significant investment in digital video editing or camera equipment. Of course, because the monitor-top camera is affixed to a computer, this type of video arrangement is primarily for videos that instruct from a single location as opposed to multiple locations. However, the software provides for the importing of other digital video as well as PowerPoint presentations to further enhance the instruction.

Software dedicated to creating digital video presentations is one type of digital editing software. There are many other video editing software packages available. These range from very high-end packages that are used with powerful dedicated video editing equipment to others that can be used on a personal computer. These software packages offer teachers yet another way to customize digital video for maximum effectiveness in teaching and learning.

SOURCE: Courtesy of Serious Magic

A monitor-top video camera, a microphone, and PC-based production software like Serious Magic Visual Communicator make it possible to create professional-looking instructional videos easily and quickly.

▌ Digital Video Editing

Once a digital video file has been recorded, it can be manipulated in an almost infinite number of ways. Its digital format makes a digital video file as easy to edit in terms of sound and image as a word-processed document is to edit in terms of text. However, just as you need word-processing software to edit a word-processed document, you need digital video software to edit video files.

iDVD courtesy of Apple Computer, Inc.

iMovie courtesy of Apple Computer, Inc.

Digital video editing software like iMovie lets you and your students create powerful instructional videos, while recording software like iDVD lets you store them in a convenient DVD format.

School TV production studios such as those that record the school's morning news might have specialized hardware for video editing. However, with the increased computing power of newer computers and the advent of desktop editing software, digital video editing is no longer confined to studios. For typical classroom or home use, video editing software that will run on a personal computer can easily be installed on the typical multimedia-capable computers that are available today. Such software allows you to select, edit, and manipulate digital video clips, add text, and even add special effects. Although not as powerful and capable as dedicated video editing hardware, this software can do a more than adequate job in customizing a digital video clip to meet your needs. For a teacher who is interested in creating and using digital video for teaching and learning, it can be a powerful software tool.

One of the most popular and easy-to-use video editing software packages is iMovie. Designed to run on an Apple Macintosh computer, iMovie offers a simple-to-use interface for creating digital videos. In addition to offering sophisticated special effects, iMovie provides options that allow you to easily integrate digital still images into the video. Advanced audio controls let you add and adjust your own or prepackaged sound tracks to the production track (the one recorded when taking the video). Particularly useful for the classroom, iMovie allows you to identify certain scenes as "chapter markers," which allow you to jump to these scenes. This feature provides instructional options in that segments of a video can be presented during lessons. And iMovie gives you full control of all these editing features so that you can arrange, enhance, and adjust your original recorded video to create the target instructional video you desire. In combination with iDVD, a digital video recording program, your final video can be stored to a recordable DVD for use in all of your classes.

Personal computers using the Windows operating system also have a variety of desktop editing systems available. These include powerful software packages such as Adobe Premier for editing, with its companion Adobe Encore for recording. But regardless of the computer you use or the digital video editing software you select to use with it, these digital tools can allow you and your students to actively engage in creating customized and exciting instructional videos. As you have already learned, engaging the learner using multiple modalities helps to ensure that more memory pathways are created in the brain and that learning is more lasting. Clearly, planning, recording, and editing instructional videos are activities likely to fully engage students and allow them to use all of their senses and creativity.

█ Compressed Video Systems

All of the digital video explored thus far has been for use in a single classroom. It would seem possible to easily transmit digitized video from one classroom to the next, just as you might send a text file to be shared between classes. Although this is indeed possible, for full-motion, broadcast-quality video, there are currently some challenges. When you consider the size of compressed video and compare it to the bandwidth that is typically available for educational use, it is clear that transmission of compressed video has some specific requirements. For this reason, schools and districts that require the capability to transmit high-quality compressed video often invest in dedicated **compressed video systems.**

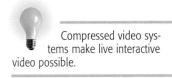

Compressed video systems make live interactive video possible.

Perhaps you have seen digital video displays that seemed choppy or fuzzy or had delayed movement. With a dedicated compressed video system, digitized video can be transmitted with image and sound as clear as broadcast video. Compressed video systems also allow you to record and display using traditional video technology.

Schools that are equipped with compressed video systems can bring live, fully interactive instruction from one location to the next or have distant guest speakers visit the classroom without having to travel (see Figure 10.6). The only requirement is to have the appropriate equipment at both locations. Such compressed video systems are particularly useful for distance learning, the subject of Chapter 11.

Although dedicated compressed video systems can provide full-motion, broadcast-quality video, what happens when digital video is transmitted over normal phone lines? As you might guess, the quality of the video image degrades, and the time it takes to transmit through lower bandwidth can be a challenge. As the availability of newer compression software and streaming technologies continues to increase, digital video is emerging and gaining popularity. For this reason, digital video via the Internet has begun to proliferate.

ON THE WEB! 10.6
Teaching with Compressed Video

Internet Video

Digital video on the Internet has taken multiple forms. As compression software reduces file sizes, bandwidth increases, and computers become more powerful, new formats will continue to arise. Already, a number of Internet video formats offer great promise to education. Keeping in mind that more will emerge rapidly and offer you even greater possibilities, the following may prove to be valuable resources for your classroom.

█ Internet Broadcasts

Many web sites are offering live **Internet broadcasts** of events and performances. These broadcasts use **streaming video** technology that compresses and plays back digital video while it is being received. Much like the streaming audio you learned about in Chapter 7, streaming video requires that a player be installed on your computer. Such video players are typically available free for download on the Internet. Web sites that are sponsoring an event may add links to their sites that allow viewers to see and hear what the live audience sees. Others broadcast via the site alone, keeping the entire audience virtual. Internet broadcasts range from musical events to scientific events and from pop entertainment talk shows to interviews with archeologists who have just made dramatic new discoveries. The capability of sharing events and interviews without having to purchase costly television time has made Internet broadcast an exciting opportunity for the education and entertainment industries.

Streaming video makes motion video over the Internet practical.

Of course, because Internet connections may be over relatively slow lines, Internet broadcasts may not have the quality of traditional video. Depending on the bandwidth, the complexity of data, and the receiving machine, the images may be degraded

ON THE WEB! 10.7
Internet Broadcasts

Monitor-Mounted Video Camera
This is a video camera mounted above the monitor which provides an "eye-to-eye" perspective as conference participants view the monitor. Autopanning cameras automatically focus on whoever is speaking.

Monitor
This is a large monitor for viewing the remote location. It may offer a picture-in-picture option for simultaneous viewing of remote and local sites.

Microphone
A directional microphone picks up sound from anywhere in the room. Additional microphones can be added as needed.

Supplemental Video Camera
Additional video cameras can be set up in strategic locations to take shots of speakers, groups, or displays.

Document Camera
A camera that captures images of documents, slides, transparencies, and models for inclusion in the video-conference.

Remote Camera
This control device lets the teacher control camera angles, zoom, microphones, monitor images, and feeds from supplemental equipment.

Computer
Connected to a videoconference system, computer displays of images such as Internet activity or PowerPoint presentations can be transmitted as a part of the conference.

VCR
Video recorder is used to capture videoconferencing activity and to play and transmit videotapes as a component of the conference.

Figure 10.6
A Compressed Video System
Compressed video systems create real-time digital communication networks.

and the sound somewhat delayed as the streaming technology completes the decompression necessary for display. However, as the technology advances and bandwidth increases, Internet broadcasts are becoming viable as a commercial alternative to traditional broadcast.

Live Cams

ON THE WEB! 10.8
Live Cams

An interesting application of Internet communication is the phenomenon of **live cams** (cameras) connected to the Internet. Live cams are cameras that are connected to a computer, which in turn is connected to the Internet. A live cam shares a digitized video image of whatever it is pointed at. For example, EarthCam (www.earthcam.com) is a gateway to a wide variety of live cams, such as the Penguin Cam at New York City's Central Park Zoo and the American Museum of Natural History's Butterfly Cam. By connecting to sites such as these, you can see live video images of whatever is in range of the camera. It is similar to setting up a blind for viewing animals in the wild, only in this case the blind is simply a video camera. Because the camera is connected to a computer that is online, you can view the digital video feed by accessing the web site that is sharing the camera's images. You and your students can monitor the live behavior of wildlife, an extraordinary virtual field trip experience made possible by this technology.

Live cams are available for viewing many geographic regions, the weather around the globe, animal habitats on the earth and in the sea, international museums and historical sites, and even other classrooms globally. The opportunities are limited only by places a camera can be carried and by Internet connectivity. Live cam sites have increased exponentially and will no doubt continue to do so. The educational possibilities for this technology will increase with their proliferation into fascinating educational locations.

SOURCE: Indianapolis Zoo

Live cams offer live streaming video feeds over the Internet so that students can view animals, science experiments, and locations from around the world.

Internet Meetings

Compressed video has produced another range of opportunities for educators and their students. **Internet meetings** are Internet-based "face-to-face" conversations with people around the world. With the addition of a monitor-top or classroom video camera and video compression software, individuals or groups can use the Internet to connect to each other and communicate live. As you learned in Chapter 7, several worldwide educational

Microsoft NetMeeting® is a registered trademark of Microsoft Corporation.

Internet meeting software like Microsoft's NetMeeting let you and your students communicate live with other classrooms anywhere in the world.

ON THE WEB! 10.9
Internet Meeting

projects use meetings across the Internet to engage in collaborative projects. Compressed video transmitted across the Internet makes it possible for students around the world to work together and share educational experiences.

A recent addition to Internet meetings is the development of dedicated Internet meeting software such as Microsoft's NetMeeting. This type of software adds more capabilities to better simulate in-person meetings. For example, such software might add a virtual whiteboard that lets all Internet meeting participants collaborate in real time on a document or graphic, and a chat feature that lets them share notes that they key in as they meet. With the expansion of the capabilities of Internet meetings software and the increased bandwidth capacities in the future, net meetings are likely to become a logical alternative for collaboration.

For educators, such Internet meeting software can let classes around the globe meet together in a single virtual classroom to share ideas, experience instruction, and communicate with each other. For teachers who are willing to work with colleagues globally to set up and implement worldwide instructional experiences, Internet meetings can offer students a chance to see and interact with their peers around the world.

Using Motion Video in Teaching and Learning

Whether you use traditional or digital video technology to support teaching and learning, the key to using motion video in instruction is to fully engage the learner in the sensory experience that motion video offers. Once you have established your instructional design and created your lesson plans, if motion video is the support technology of choice, you should carefully consider this specific medium and how it will be implemented to maximize its effectiveness. Your preview, evaluation, and appropriate implementation will help you to engage your learners in this potentially powerful technology.

An Internet meeting connects multiple sites together for a meeting or class over the Net.

Preview and Evaluation of Video Media

Video offers some exceptional qualities that make it particularly useful in education. Video can appear to alter both time and space as it captures events. Video captured in real time can be played back in slow motion so that the eye can see events that occurred too fast to register through normal vision. A slow-motion replay of the beauty and the physics of a drop of water striking a pool can initiate discussion in either art or science. Speeding up video playback (**time-lapse video**) may equally alter time for educational purposes. What might have taken days to occur can be viewed in the space of a few minutes. Events viewed through such time compression can be seen as a single, continuous, holistic experience. A time-lapse video of a seedling emerging from its shell and breaking through the soil into sunlight can offer students a science lesson that is not possible in the real world.

Slow-motion and time-lapse videos provide unique perspectives.

Of course, video has the potential to shift the viewers' location as well as the time frame they experience. Video travelogues, documentaries, and docudramas can seem to shift where viewers are located, from the classroom to the location they are viewing. Furthermore, regardless of the location, the viewing angle is always excellent and completely safe. Such location shifting is one of the key assets provided by videos in instruction.

To be sure, not all videos are of the same quality. Some offer breathtaking, well-narrated views of events, whereas others display little more than "talking heads." For this reason, before you use a video in support of your instructional design, it is critical that you preview and evaluate it. Any video that is used in support of your lesson plan should be thoroughly previewed and evaluated to be sure it is appropriate to the content and of the quality necessary to engage the learners. Table 10.2 presents a rubric that you may find helpful in previewing and evaluating video media.

TABLE 10.2   VIDEO EVALUATION RUBRIC

VIDEO TITLE:

DESCRIPTION:

SUBJECT AREA APPLICABILITY:

LENGTH: COST: VENDOR:

COMMENTS:

Using each of the following criteria, evaluate the effectiveness of the video for teaching and learning. For each dimension in the rubric, check the box that best reflects your opinion. Select videos that score 4 or higher in the most dimensions.

Dimension	*1* Poor	*2* Below Average	*3* Average	*4* Above Average	*5* Excellent
Relevance to curriculum	Video does not address significant aspects of the curriculum; addresses few targeted objectives.	Video includes both relevant and irrelevant elements; minimum objectives are met.	Some video elements add to and clarify the curriculum concepts; others are extraneous; some objectives addressed.	Most video elements add to and clarify key curriculum concepts and address targeted objectives.	All aspects of the video significantly add to and/or clarify key curriculum concepts; meets objectives.
Currency and accuracy	Video is not current and has a significant number of factual inaccuracies.	Video is somewhat current in images and content; mostly accurate.	Video is current and accurate overall, but there is sufficient dated content to be distracting.	Video is mostly current and accurate; occasional images are dated, and some facts are less than accurate.	Video includes current images and presents accurate content.
Engagement	Video components do not provide sufficient interest and variety to engage the learner.	Video includes a number of elements that are likely to negatively affect the learner's attention.	Some video elements are interesting, while others are lacking; somewhat motivating and engaging.	Most elements of the video are interesting and motivating; some elements may not keep the learner's interest.	Video is interesting and provides motivation; fully engages the learner's attention.
Support materials	No additional support materials are available with this video.	Few additional materials are available; those included are of average quality and provide limited support.	Some additional materials are available; quality of additional materials is good; some target key objectives.	Key materials of good quality are available to accompany the video; most are of high quality and target objectives.	Ample additional materials are of high quality, are easy to use, and target key objectives.
Technical quality	Video has poor video and audio quality overall; production values are minimal.	The video is of moderate technical quality, ranging from poor elements to average production elements.	Aspects of the video range from average to good quality in terms of production.	Most aspects of the video are well done in terms of audio and video production.	All aspects of the video are excellent in terms of production quality.

This and other downloadable forms and templates can be found on the Companion Website at www.ablongman.com/lever-duffy.

IN THE CLASSROOM

All the World's Their Stage: Internet Video in the Schools

VMSTV is a middle school news program produced in a state-of-the-art digital television facility at Valley Middle School in Carlsbad, California. The VMSTV web page (**http://www.vmstv.com**) proudly proclaims that it is "America's only middle school news broadcast available worldwide on the Internet." Funded by grants from the Carlsbad Education Foundation's Kids Are Worth a Million program and from Adelphia Cablevision, VMSTV is a network-quality TV news program. The biweekly live newscast features a blend of local, national, and global news with an emphasis on stories targeted to the middle school viewer. "We are a 'totally digital' broadcast facility using advanced digital video production equipment, including groundbreaking streaming media and digital virtual sets," its web site states.

VMSTV rebroadcasts "its episodes on the Internet. With cable/DSL/T1 modem speeds, the quality of the replays available on this program will be of very high quality. At regular dial-up speeds, the quality may not be as wonderful, but we think you will still enjoy our news broadcasts," the broadcast team at Valley Middle School proclaims. In fact, their broadcasts, made in conjunction with Carlsbad High School TV (CHSTV), earned two 2003 National Student Television Awards. CHSTV holds the dis-tinction of being the first daily school broadcast in this country to stream live worldwide.

VMSTV can be accessed live every other Monday afternoon at 2:05 p.m., PST or PDT. Replays for the immediate community air Wednesday nights at 6:00 on Channel 3 on Adelphia Cablevision in a time slot shared with CHSTV; worldwide reception of the replays takes place twenty-four hours a day worldwide on the VMSTV site.

An all-night party, the Big Night, with parents, teachers, and first- to fifth-grade students at Narcoossee Community School in St. Cloud, Florida, sees "more than 80 students, assisted by dozens of parents and teachers, at the school to communicate with their international peers." A crucial element of this project is contact with Internet programs that connect to worldwide class-rooms via videoconferencing, Gail McGoogan, one of the teachers, reports.

SOURCES: VMSTV 2003. Retrieved August 12, 2003, from **http://www.vmstv.com**; G. McGoogan. 2002. Around the world in 24 hours. *Educational Leadership* (October), 60 (2), 44–46.

▮ Creating Videos for Teaching and Learning

You may prefer to create your own instructional videos to precisely support the lesson you are teaching. Such teacher- or student-made videos may be necessary if appropriate support video is not commercially available or if a lesson calls for students to capture images and record them themselves.

Today's camcorders, whether traditional or digital in format, offer a relatively easy-to-use technology even for those who have never used a video camera before. In fact, creating a video is more complex in the planning stages than in the recording stage. Video production requires careful consideration of the images and sounds that will be captured. Just as it is helpful in planning a web site, storyboarding is also a powerful tool to plan a video sequence (see Figure 10.7). **Storyboarding** allows you to consider the relationships of the video images, sound, and the use and positioning of props. A well-articulated storyboard is likely to result in a well-constructed video. Of course, using technology means that you can create electronic storyboards today instead of making a physical storyboard from cards or paper.

Once you have planned your video and storyboarded its content, then you are ready to record. There are a few key considerations when recording. These are summarized in Figure 10.8. As you begin recording, you should take these into account just as you should the techniques you might like to incorporate from Table 10.3.

One note of caution should be sounded with reference to student- and teacher-made videos. Some parents prefer not to have their child videotaped. Some believe that it is a violation of their child's privacy, or they may have justifiable concerns about when and how their child's picture will be distributed. Whenever a student's image is to be captured on videotape, permission must be obtained from the student's parent or

Storyboarding is an important first step in shooting your own videos.

ON THE WEB! 10.10

Classroom Video Production

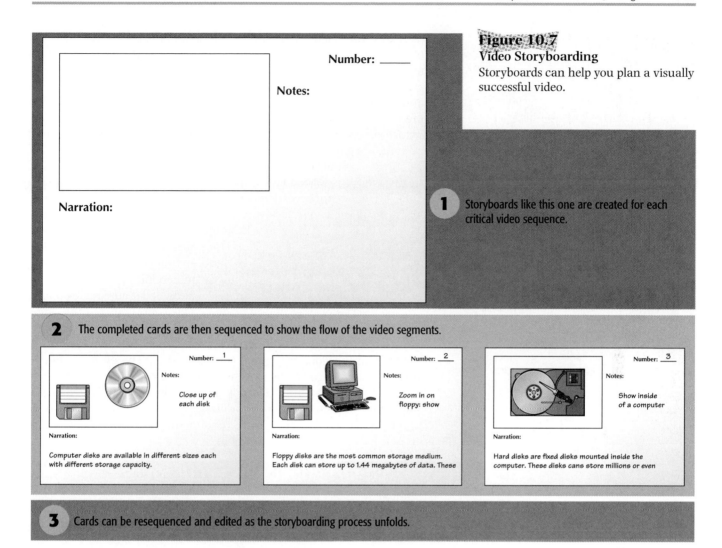

Figure 10.7
Video Storyboarding
Storyboards can help you plan a visually successful video.

1 Storyboards like this one are created for each critical video sequence.

2 The completed cards are then sequenced to show the flow of the video segments.

Number: 1 — Notes: — Close up of each disk — Narration: — Computer disks are available in different sizes each with different storage capacity.

Number: 2 — Notes: — Zoom in on floppy: show — Narration: — Floppy disks are the most common storage medium. Each disk can store up to 1.44 megabytes of data. These

Number: 3 — Notes: — Show inside of a computer — Narration: — Hard disks are fixed disks mounted inside the computer. These disks cans store millions or even

3 Cards can be resequenced and edited as the storyboarding process unfolds.

guardian before taping. When you decide to begin a video production project that contains images of students, it is best to precede it with a notification to parents of what the project entails and how the video images will be displayed. Additionally, many districts require that you obtain written permission from the parents of all the children who are participating in the taping (whether they appear in the video or not) to authorize your creating a videotape that includes the child. Taking the time to research your school's or district's requirements on videotaping students and completing the necessary paperwork before taping are vital first steps whenever you plan classroom video productions that will include your students' images.

Parental permission is required before including children in videos.

Implementing Video in Instruction

Whether you use commercial videos or those you or your students make, videos can substantially support your instructional content. It is important, therefore, to be sure that the instructional environment and your students are prepared for them. Let us assume that your instructional design and lesson plan call for video to support the content you are teaching. You have already previewed and evaluated a video and found it appropriate for the lesson. What is next?

Because video tends to be a passive experience and we know that the more engaged the learner is, the more effective learning will be, it is important to take steps

Use the potential of the medium:

1
- ✓ Capture motion to bring instruction to life.
- ✓ Use motion to add movement to the instructional sequence.

Use video to control time:

2
- ✓ Be sure video images allow enough review time.
- ✓ Record sequences that are long enough to communicate the message.
- ✓ Use slow motion and time lapse to alter time.

Add special effects and text:

3
- ✓ Add effects to emphasize the message.
- ✓ Add text elements to clarify key points.

Figure 10.8
Keys to Making a Successful Video

to ensure that viewing the video will be an engaging experience. To begin, even though it might have been previewed, the video should be tested in the environment in which it will be shown. Sound volume and quality should be tested, seating should be arranged appropriately, and lighting should be adjusted to avoid a washed-out image. Addressing these initial environmental variables before students arrive will reduce potential disruptions and distractions once the instructional event has begun.

The next, and perhaps most important, challenge is to fully engage the learner. It is a good idea to prepare your students for viewing by reviewing the concepts the video presents and discussing the objectives of the video and the key ideas it will present. Then, even though you have prepared your learners, it might be necessary to keep them engaged throughout the video screening. To create a more active video viewing experience, it is a good idea to provide a **video study guide.** Such a study guide may accompany commercial videos or could be created by you as you preview the video. A video study guide should provide a series of brief questions on key ideas presented in the same sequence as they are presented in the video. Learners should preview the study guide before the video begins so that they know what to watch for as the video progresses. Questions should be short enough to answer quickly because the video will continue running while the students are responding to their study guide. Only the most critical ideas should be questioned, and the questions should include concepts presented all the way through to the end of the video so that attention

TABLE 10.3   VIDEO PRODUCTION TECHNIQUES

Video Technique	Description and Use
CAMERA DISTANCE	Long, medium, and close-up camera positions; used to change the relative size and focus of subject and background
CAMERA ANGLE	High, eye-level, and low camera angles used to add variety and dramatic effect
OBJECTIVE/SUBJECTIVE SHOTS	Camera directly shoots subject (objective) or camera shoots over subject's shoulder (subjective); used to change audience perspective
PANNING	Moving the camera horizontally; used to capture scenes too large for a single shot
TILTING	Moving the camera vertically; used to capture sense of height
DOLLYING	Moving the camera away from or toward the subject; used to show movement
TUCKING	Moving the camera parallel to the subject; used to capture subject's movement
ZOOMING	Changing the camera's view to simulate moving away from or toward the subject
MULTICAMERA SHOTS	One close-up and one long-shot camera capture the same action; shots from each can be combined for interest and transitions
FADE IN/OUT	Visual transition fades one scene into another to separate visual segments
DISSOLVE	Transition in which one scene dissolves into the next

will be maintained throughout. Avoid asking too many questions, or the students are likely to lose their train of thought as they attempt to answer them, causing them to miss new information being presented on the video. For younger children or those with special needs, you might even choose to pause the video periodically to give learners time to respond orally or in writing. Video study guides can add significantly to the learning experience by helping to build connections to prior knowledge, focusing attention, and reinforcing learning.

A well-designed video study guide helps to engage the learner.

Video study guides are not the only method for engaging the learners in videos. You might choose, depending on your lesson plan and your students' characteristics, to structure a discussion group after the video or at key stopping points during the video, to have students complete a kinesthetic project based on the video, or to create a sequel to the video they just watched. The possibilities are limited only by your own creativity. The key is to develop, as a component of video-enhanced instruction, some way to fully engage the learners in the concepts being presented by the video they are viewing.

The indispensability of video as an instructional tool is unarguable, but it requires a committment to its responsible use. As an educator, you are responsible for ensuring that the motion video you display is as appropriate for your students as it is in direct support of your lesson. Motion video can have significant emotional as well as factual content. As an adult, as you view a video, you are able to react to content and discriminate facts from emotion because of your maturity and experience. Your learners might not be able to do this. Some video may include content that is emotionally powerful or that offers ideas that may be in conflict with the student's personal beliefs. Your responsibility when screening videos includes anticipating potential student reactions to the emotional content of a video as well as to its instructional content. After you preview a video with its emotional impact in mind, you will be able to better prepare your students for viewing the video if you conduct preliminary discussions with them to highlight the issues and ideas they are about to take in. In fact, while students are viewing the video, you might want to watch their reactions to it and take notes so that you can provide a debriefing discussion after the screening. Motion video

connecting THEORY to PRACTICE

Theory, Videos, and Study Guides

Speaking plainly and to the point about the use of video in the classroom, the National Teacher Training Institute (NTTI) reminds us that video is "a tool for teacher-to-student instruction," not for television-to-student instruction. The guidelines they establish include a "focus for media interaction," that is, "a specific task or responsibility to keep in mind while the video is on. This keeps the students on-task and directs the learning experience to the lesson's objectives." At the conclusion of video-enhanced instruction, teachers need to have planned-for activities that will tie the video into the focus of the lesson. NTTI suggests "hands-on activities, student-centered projects, and student- or teacher-designed investigations. Ideally video will be used in conjunction with field trips, guest speakers, letter-writing projects, and journal writing—the variety of activities that make up an expansive hands-on learning experience." Video, as with all media, is a means to an end, which is the lesson plan's stated objectives.

June 2001 saw the reappearance of Eyes on Art (**http://www.kn.pacbell.com/wired/art2**), a web site that uses art imagery dedicated "to continue our mission: creating models of Web-based learning that regular teachers could create (if they had the luxury we enjoy of doing this as our fulltime jobs)." This site clearly exemplifies how well-designed study guides direct instruction to the teacher's stated purposes for a given unit; that is, how a study guide becomes a road map to prevent losing sight of the instructional destination.

Strategies proposed by Eyes on Art rely on questions to direct students' attention to what is to be learned through viewing images of great art without stifling their free interpretation of the works. The questions serve as study guides, as set forth in the "Double Visions" activity: "Students choose one of nine sets of artworks to compare and contrast, then view larger versions of the artworks and answer a series of interpretive questions." These works of art may be viewed online or from video clips.

SOURCES: NTTI video utilization strategies. 2002. Retrieved November 30, 2003, from http://www.thirteen.org/edonline/ntti/resources/video2.html; T. March. 2003. Eyes on art. Retrieved May 6, 2003, from **http://www.kn.pacbell.com/wired/art2/guide/guide.html**.

can be a meaningful and positive learning tool but as with all tools, you must use it skillfully to create the educational experience you intend. Giving attention to the emotional content of videos is necessary to use this tool appropriately.

A final consideration in using videos in instruction relates to the issues of fair use of copyrighted materials. Copyright issues are more fully explored in Chapter 12, but it is important to be aware of copyrights when using video in your classroom. Commercial video, like other media, is typically copyrighted. Fair use guidelines, presented in detail in the interchapter, provide educators with a prescription for how copyrighted material may be used in an educational setting. To avoid violation of the copyright laws and possible prosecution, you should adhere to these guidelines whenever you use copyrighted motion video.

Videos for Teaching and Learning

Using videos in support of teaching and learning offers you some unique instructional features. Videos can appear to shift time and space. They can provide you with the opportunity to show your students phenomena that are either impossible or dangerous to view personally. They can dramatically demonstrate situations that can lead to complex discussions and problem solving. Video, regardless of the type of technology with which it is created, edited, and transmitted, offers a number of significant instructional advantages.

ON THE WEB! 10.11
Video in Instruction

But, like all media and technologies, video is not without its drawbacks. Video technology can be expensive and time consuming to use. Some of your instructional preparation time will be dedicated to previewing, evaluating, and preparing video activities. Creating or screening videos may also require that you check out and become familiar with the necessary equipment. This can create logistic and scheduling problems that must be contended with. Furthermore, some instructional time may need to be devoted to the learning curve that is required to create student-made videos.

Overall, the advantages of using video in teaching and learning outweigh its disadvantages. The benefits of using video in whatever format is available are more than worth the challenges involved in implementing video in the classroom. No doubt, the fact that educators see video as a positive and powerful teaching tool has resulted in its enduring place in the classroom. Regardless of how video technologies may evolve in the future, motion video will no doubt continue to be a significant tool at your disposal to help you teach and your students learn.

KEY TERMS

AVI 320
broadcast video 316
cablecast video 318
camcorders 319
closed-circuit TV (CCTV) 317
compressed video systems 325
compression technologies 320
Corporation for Public Broadcasting
 (CPB) 316
digital video disc (DVD) 321
digital video cameras 322
digital video editing 322

downlinked 316
instructional television (ITV) 316
Instructional Television Fixed Service
 (ITFS) 317
Internet broadcasts 325
Internet meetings 327
live cams 327
MOV 320
MPEG 320
narrowcast video 317
Public Broadcast System (PBS) 316
satellite transmission 316

STUDENT ACTIVITIES

CHAPTER REVIEW

1. What is broadcast video? How is it transmitted to schools? How does the fact that broadcast video is synchronous impact its usefulness in instruction?
2. What is narrowcast video? How are ITFS systems used in school districts?
3. What is the difference between cablecast video and a school CCTV system? How is each used in schools?
4. How has recorded video improved video's usefulness to education? Name and describe the media used to record video.
5. How can digital video cameras be used in classroom instruction? What technologies do you need to edit digital video?
6. What is a compressed video system? How can it assist in communications across a school district?
7. What is an Internet broadcast? What technology is necessary to view it?
8. Describe an Internet live cam and how it might be used in instruction.
9. What is an Internet meeting? How can it enhance communications?
10. Why is it important to preview and evaluate videos? What tools should you use to be sure a video is communicating the intended message to your students?

WHAT DO YOU THINK?

1. There has been much discussion about the impact of commercial television on children. How do you think the many hours children spend each day watching television have affected them? What impact might this have on the children in your classroom?
2. Computers and other digital technologies have changed our world. This change is affecting how videos are recorded and viewed. What advantages and disadvantages for education do you see in the digitization of video?
3. Student-made videos are an effective and interactive teaching and learning tool. However, there is concern over student privacy when the images of students are included on tape. Research this issue, and talk to a local teacher or administrator to gain a better understanding of the issue. Then describe the key concerns and how a teacher might best address them when filming students.
4. The great advantage of video in teaching and learning is its ability to represent a shift in time and space. Explain what this means and how you might use it in teaching a unit of your choice.
5. Videos have an emotional content as well as instructional content. Consider an educational video you recently viewed in terms of its emotional content and its effect on children for whom it was intended. How can you, as the teacher, ensure that the children to whom you show a video will get the intended message without negative emotional impact?

LEARNING TOGETHER!

These activities are best done in groups of three to five.

1. Storyboard and create a video production to teach a lesson for the grade level your group wishes to teach. Prepare a lesson plan to accompany the video, and be prepared to share both with the class.
2. Each group member should locate five Internet live cams that could be useful for educators and create an annotated list of them. Summarize your lists, eliminate duplicates, and prepare a "Top Twenty" live cam resource list to share with the class.
3. Interview five teachers who use traditional or digital video in their classrooms, and ask each for tips on using video effectively. Create a list of the helpful hints that are gathered as a result of all interviews. Share the list with your classmates.

HANDS-ON!

1. Preview an instructional video for the grade level you wish to teach. Use Table 10.2 to quantify its usefulness. Write an educational review of the video, including whether you would buy the video or not and why, to share with your peers.
2. Prepare a lesson plan that would use a teacher-made video. Then storyboard the video you might produce to teach your lesson.
3. Interview a teacher who uses compressed video, over the Internet or through a dedicated system, to support teaching and learning. Discover through the interview the advantages and disadvantages in using this technology.
4. Watch an Internet broadcast, and compare it to other forms of transmission you have experienced. Compose a critique of the broadcast, and describe how this type of technology could be used in teaching and learning. Be sure to include its strengths and weaknesses in your analysis.
5. Search the Internet for information on the fair use of video in the classroom. Summarize your research in a personal guide for video fair use that you can share with your peers.

More from Denise Milam

Having looked at various video technologies, you could probably select your favorite and come up with some unique ideas for ways to use video to motivate students and help them learn. Let's see what Denise Milam came up with to meet her colleague's needs to integrate technology into teaching and learning.

MY PROBLEM-SOLVING PROCESS

As I indicated at the beginning of this chapter, I offered several suggestions for technology integration to a sixth-grade social studies teacher who consulted me. One of the solutions I suggested was to have the students create a movie as a final project for their social studies theme, using the laptop computers, cameras, and

Apple iMovie software at their disposal. The teacher liked this idea and decided to try iMovie with one class of students. Now we had a potential solution; we just had to implement it.

The knowledge base of the classroom teacher for the laptop computer was at the beginner level, and she was completely inexperienced with the use of a digital camera, a digital camcorder, a projector, and iMovie software. Moreover, the majority of the students had not used a digital camera or camcorder, and none of them had used iMovie software. I had not facilitated an ongoing project of this scope using iMovie with laptops and sixth graders prior to this. The laptops had not been used on a regular, ongoing basis by a classroom teacher in a project-based learning environment in our school before. Also, the digital camcorders had never been used by any of our classroom teachers as a learning tool.

We had a major challenge. New hardware, new software, new students, and new concepts all had to be combined with the content and continuity of a project that was to be created in a forty-three-minute class, and we had only ten to twelve weeks to plan it. This all had to be done while I attempted to demonstrate the effectiveness of this technology as a teaching and learning tool to a beginner-level user. The classroom teacher, the students, and I needed to become partners in a heterogeneous cooperative group. Our roles would be defined during the process, and we were all in uncharted territory. This was the challenge confronting us.

I was present during the teacher's initial discussion of the project with the class. The students were very excited to realize that they were going to try using new software and new hardware. They were also excited to be able to be on camera. The class size fluctuated during the project between twenty-four and twenty-eight students. The classroom teacher grouped the students into partnerships, and our journey began.

The first step was to introduce the students and the teacher to the digital cameras. I explained that I would help one group of students practice using the digital camcorder, a Canon Mini-DV, and a digital camera, a Sony CyberShot. I have often found that students and teachers grasp a new hands-on technology with more ease when they are teaching one another, as opposed to receiving instruction from me. After showing the first group of students, I had these students show the others how to use the cameras. I observed the students instructing one another, mugging for the camera, and trying out all the options. When they had mastered the use of the digital imaging equipment, the teacher borrowed the cameras for her students whenever they needed them. To my relief, I found that my support was not needed in the classroom.

When the students were ready for the laptops, I visited the class again and we discussed some issues that might come up in their use of the laptops. The students were worried about their files, so we talked about file management. They wanted to make sure that no one dropped the laptops when they were getting them and return-

ing them, so we talked about that, and they came up with a procedure for making sure that they got the laptops that had their projects saved on the hard drives.

The students next worked on an iMovie tutorial, complete with sample files. When they were ready to work with the video and images they had created, we had a directors' meeting, and they selected film clips that would be placed on a CD for all students to use. I created a CD for each group of students with assorted film clips and digital images. The students imported the clips and images into a movie template that they had created. They cropped the clips, made still images of some film frames, added voice-overs and commentaries, sound effects, and music clips. Along the way, the students had to deal with hard drive crashes, dead batteries, missing computer files, and software glitches.

The project took more time than we anticipated, but finally the students had a finished product. Each student received a copy of the compressed QuickTime video they had created over the year. The students planned a film festival, complete with popcorn and soda. The principal of the middle school was invited to attend, along with our superintendent. Each group played their movie on a computer connected to a projector. They gave accolades to one another, described what they had learned, and grinned and moaned about each film clip. The teacher felt excited and proud. The project had been a success even though it was the first time she had tried this extensive a project incorporating the use of traditional and digital technologies.

Fast-forward to this year: this same sixth-grade teacher is working on digital pictures on her own, borrowing the camera when she needs it. The students in her class are now mixed with others to pass on the knowledge. I am still peddling technology, along with new pots and pans like PDAs and tablets. Other teachers at our school have had similar experiences. We now have a school that is making effective use of all types of technology, and the students are actively engaged in learning.

Contact Information: Denise Milam, technology integration specialist, Williamstown Middle School. Phone: 856-728-6444 ext. 3126. Email: **dmilam@monroetwp.k12.nj.us**.

TEACHERS AND

Copyright

Copyright refers to the laws that protect the interests of those who own creative works, whether text, music, artwork, software, or any other creative product. Under U.S. copyright law, the copyright owner is granted exclusive rights to the product and to the financial gain resulting from the product that he or she creates, owns, or distributes for a specified length of time. Others cannot copy the product without the copyright owner's permission. Violation of the copyright owner's rights can lead to legal action.

Whether you copy pages from a text, music from a CD, or multimedia clips from the Internet, you may be in violation of the copyright laws. Someone put time, energy, and creative talent into the product and has the complete right to decide how it is to be used and to profit from his or her work. Copying data that you did not create, or allowing your students to do so, and then using that data in your lessons or class publications may place you, your school, and your district in a position to be sued by the owner of the data. Technology makes it easy to copy from a variety of digital sources, but such action may be as illegal as it is convenient. Whether the data is text, music, art, video, or audio files, the rights of the copyright owner must be observed.

It is generally accepted that any material placed on the Internet is automatically copyrighted even if a copyright notice does not appear on the site. Most publications include clear copyright notices within them, as indicated by the inclusion of a copyright symbol (©). Even if you do not notice any copyright indicators at all, however, as a prudent educator, you must assume that unless express permission to freely use materials that you find is stated clearly on those materials, they are the property of their creator and cannot be used without permission.

Fair Use Guidelines

So how can teachers use a clever graphic, a map, or an educational photograph to enhance instruction if these elements are clearly or implicitly copyrighted? The answer is found in a special section of the copyright laws that is called "fair use." The fair use section (Section 107) of the law identifies four criteria under which you may be allowed to copy another's creative work. This section has enabled educators and students to temporarily use copy-

righted materials if they meet the stated criteria. The fair use section has been interpreted for educators through a series of guidelines that have attempted to clarify it. In 1976, the first set of guidelines, the Agreement on Guidelines for Classroom Copying in Not-For-Profit Educational Institutions With Respect to Books and Periodicals, offered educators more specific information as to making copies for class handouts and other instructional materials. For example, students may use small portions of copyrighted works in academic projects if they properly credit and cite the owner of the work. Teachers may use reproductions of a copyrighted work in face-to-face classrooms as long as such reproductions are for only one course in the school and they will not be used over a long term. It is your responsibility to be familiar with these guidelines when you select and use copyrighted materials.

The situation became even more complex as technology advanced. As educational technologies came to include not only print but also audio, film, multimedia, and digital technologies, fair use guidelines began to be developed to address these new media as well. Debate over guidelines expanded and became more intense throughout the 1990s with many efforts made to establish voluntary guidelines for fair use. These debates led to the establishment of the Conference on Fair Use (CONFU) in 1994. After four years of effort, CONFU's final report in 1998 recommended guidelines for educators in the fair use of a variety of media (http://www.uspto.gov/web/offices/dcom/olia/confu/). While not a legal document, these guidelines offered educators a consensus view of the application of fair use.

These guidelines help teachers to determine if their actions and those of their students fall within the framework of fair use. For example, you may ask your class to create a project web site. During this project your students may wish to use a popular song as background audio for their home page. Or, you may want to copy several pictures of African animals from a virtual museum you found on the web to add to a PowerPoint presentation to support your lesson. Can you and your students borrow these sound clips and images for your classroom activities? According to the guidelines, the answer is no unless the use of the audio and images falls within the guidelines limits for use of an audio and images. These limits suggest that only 10 percent of the musical composition, but not more than 30 seconds can be used. Further, once copied, the clip cannot contain any alterations

COPYRIGHTS

that change the basic melody or character of the work. As to your desire to use pictures from a virtual museum, if the museum is displaying a single artist's work, guidelines mandate that you cannot use more than five images without violating fair use. However, if the museum is displaying a collection of assorted artists, you can use no more than 10 percent of that collection or no more than fifteen images, whichever is less.

As you can see, the Fair Use Guidelines are very specific and can be somewhat complex. The Table I4.1 summarizes some of the areas of the guidelines of frequent concern to classroom teachers. It should be noted that, as copyright laws are tested in the courts and as educators and legal experts continue to explore the limits of fair use, these guidelines may change. As a professional, you have a responsibility to be aware of and adhere to the guidelines set forth by your school or district when you or your students use copyrighted works. It will be your responsi-

bility to seek out your school's or district's copyright guidelines in order to be sure you follow them. In many schools, the media specialist will be your logical first source when seeking to discover the guidelines you need to follow. Or, your school administrator may be the most knowledgeable person in that area. Regardless of whom you have to seek out to find the copyright guidelines for your school, it is your responsibility to do so before including copyrighted material in your classroom. In the area of copyrights, ignorance of the law will prove to be no excuse should your actions cause you or your school system to be sued for violation of copyright.

The TEACH Act

Before 2002, fair use guidelines applied primarily to traditional classroom instruction. Under these guidelines,

Continues on next page

TABLE I4.1 FAIR USE	
Areas of Use	*Sample Guidelines for Fair Use of Multimedia*
Students	Students can incorporate copyrighted work into their own multimedia creations when it is part of an academic assignment as long as the time, copies, and portion limitations (below) are met.
Teachers	Faculty can incorporate others' work into multimedia to create multimedia curriculum and to demonstrate that curriculum at professional symposia as long as the time, copies, and portion limitations (below) are met.
LIMITATIONS	
Time	The time limit for fair use of others' multimedia work is two years after the first instructional use.
Copies	Only a limited number of copies, including the original, may be made of an educator's educational multimedia project. There may be no more than two use copies, only one of which may be placed on reserve. An additional copy may be made for preservation purposes but may be used or copied only to replace a use copy that has been lost, stolen, or damaged.
Portion	For copyright-protected works, you can use • Up to 10% or 3 minutes whichever is less for motion media • Up to 10% or 1,000 words, whichever is less for text • Up to 10%, but in no event, more than 30 seconds for audio • No more than 5 images by an artist or photographer or, if collected works, no more than 10% or 15 images, whichever is lesser • Up to 10% or 2,500 fields or cell entries, whichever is the lesser of the numerical data sets

SOURCE: Adapted from CCMC guidelines as summarized in Georgia Harper's University of Texas System crash course in copyright retrieved from **http://www.utsystem.edu/ogc/intellectualproperty/ccmcguid.htm#3** February 2004.

These guidelines do not include adjustments for changes resulting from the TEACH Act.

INTERCHAPTER 4

educators enjoyed a fairly liberal right to use copyrighted works. However, that was not the case if the work was to be broadcast. Use of copyright-protected works was much more restricted if the work was to be shared electronically. This caused inconsistencies in the educational use of materials through traditional versus computer-mediated instruction or distance education. As a result, in 2002, the Technology, Education, and Copyright Harmonization (TEACH) Act was passed to begin to resolve these inconsistencies. The TEACH Act provides for expansion of the range of works allowed, the number of locations receiving the works, and the right to digitize works from other formats provided they meet the act's very specific requirements.

Although the terms for use of copyright-protected materials under the TEACH Act are not quite as liberal under fair use as they are for traditional instruction, this act did begin to resolve some of the issues associated with applying copyright law and fair use to education in the digital age.

Some Final Thoughts on Copyright

As you can see from the above, much controversy has surrounded fair use and many guidelines have been created to help teachers better interpret and apply its principles. While not a legal discussion or interpretation of these complex issues, this interchapter should raise your awareness of the issues and concerns associated with using copyrighted materials when you teach.

When dealing with copyright-protected works, perhaps a safer, although more time-consuming, solution is to simply ask the owner of a copyright for permission to use the image, product, or text. Very often, when the use is for educational purposes, the owner is willing to grant permission. Although it is not necessary to write for permission if the educational use clearly conforms with the guidelines provided by your school district, it may be a good idea to take steps to obtain permission if there is any doubt. Writing for permission requires that you compose a letter on school letterhead that requests permission to use the work in question. You would need to include information as to when you would use the work, how often, how you would use it, and why. It is best to include an example of how the work will be incorporated. Permission, once requested, must be received from the copyright holder before using the work. Be sure to give your school administrator a copy of the letter granting you permission as well. You should keep your permissions letter filed and available for as long as you use the copyrighted work.

As educators, it is important to model the behaviors expected of our students. Ignoring copyright laws or taking them lightly when it is convenient sets a bad example for students and suggests to them that it is acceptable to occasionally ignore or break the law. This is an unfortunate precedent to set, and it is an unprofessional and illegal activity to engage in, one for which you and your school may pay serious consequences. Teaching students about the copyright laws, on the other hand, is an opportunity to instill the values of the legal system and respect for others' property. Demonstrating adherence to and enforcement of copyright laws in your classroom can be a lasting and meaningful lesson for your students, and it remains a legal and professional responsibility for you.

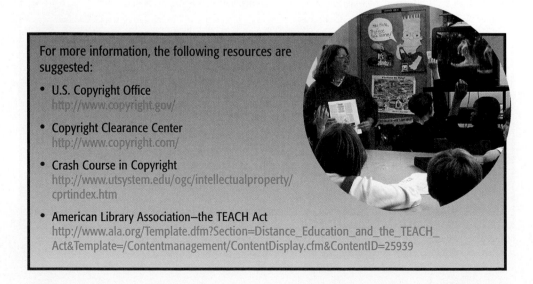

For more information, the following resources are suggested:

- U.S. Copyright Office
  http://www.copyright.gov/

- Copyright Clearance Center
  http://www.copyright.com/

- Crash Course in Copyright
  http://www.utsystem.edu/ogc/intellectualproperty/cprtindex.htm

- American Library Association—the TEACH Act
  http://www.ala.org/Template.dfm?Section=Distance_Education_and_the_TEACH_Act&Template=/Contentmanagement/ContentDisplay.cfm&ContentID=25939

Technology in Schools: Changing Teaching and Learning

Thus far, you have explored the teaching and learning process, examined how effective instruction can be designed and planned, and investigated the many technologies that can be used in support of instruction. Now it is time to take a look at how technology is changing education in today's schools and in the schools of the future.

We begin this exploration with a look at how technology helps creative teachers reinvent their classrooms. Just as you will go into your classroom at the beginning of each school year and arrange it to provide the best possible space for teaching and learning, so too you will use technology to create new spaces, even virtual ones, in which teaching and learning can occur. Some of these technology-enhanced instructional environments make it possible for the teacher and student to be at a physical distance from each other yet still allow for the teaching and learning process to occur. This type of instruction is often called distance education or distance delivery of education. Other environments add a new dimension to instruction that takes place in traditional classroom spaces. Offering such alternatives in addition to the more traditional teaching and learning methodologies is sometimes referred to as the alternative delivery of instruction.

This part begins with an exploration of what both distance and alternative learning entails and how it is implemented in today's schools. Chapter 11 will help you understand the transformations that creative application of technology in education make possible. Chapter 12 will take you further into the transformation we are experiencing as technology is implemented in schools. In this chapter, you will explore the process through which technology is implemented and then inquire into the social, ethical, and legal issues associated with the implementation of technology in our changing schools. In this chapter, you will also examine your potential role in planning for and implementing these changes. Finally, Chapter 12 will conclude with an investigation of how technology is likely to change in the next decade and how those changes will further transform the schools in which you will be teaching.

The two chapters in Part Three will help you to look ahead and to see the important role you will play as our schools continue to evolve to better serve our society. As educators, we will continue to have the goal of helping our students prepare for the world in which they will work and live. That world, rich in technology and altered integrally by its existence, will make for a fascinating and exciting environment in which we will teach and our students will learn.

OVERVIEW

11 Distance Education: Using Technology to Redefine the Classroom

This chapter addresses these ISTE National Educational Technology Standards for Teachers:

I. Technology operations and concepts

Teachers demonstrate a sound understanding of technology operations and concepts. Teachers

A. demonstrate introductory knowledge, skills, and understanding of concepts related to technology (as described in the ISTE *National Education Technology Standards for Students*).
B. demonstrate continual growth in technology knowledge and skills to stay abreast of current and emerging technologies.

II. Planning and designing learning environments and experiences

Teachers plan and design effective learning environments and experiences supported by technology. Teachers

A. design developmentally appropriate learning opportunities that apply technology-enhanced instructional strategies to support the diverse needs of learners.
B. apply current research on teaching and learning with technology when planning learning environments and experiences.
C. identify and locate technology resources and evaluate them for accuracy and suitability.
D. plan for the management of technology resources within the context of learning activities.
E. plan strategies to manage student learning in a technology-enhanced environment.

III. Teaching, learning, and the curriculum

Teachers implement curriculum plans that include methods and strategies for applying technology to maximize student learning. Teachers

A. facilitate technology-enhanced experiences that address content standards and student technology standards.
B. use technology to support learner-centered strategies that address the diverse needs of students.
C. apply technology to develop students' higher-order skills and creativity.
D. manage student learning activities in a technology-enhanced environment.

V. Productivity and professional practice

Teachers use technology resources to enhance their productivity and professional practice. Teachers

A. use technology resources to engage in ongoing professional development and lifelong learning.
B. continually evaluate and reflect on professional practice to make informed decisions regarding the use of technology in support of student learning.
C. apply technology to increase productivity.
D. use technology to communicate and collaborate with peers, parents, and the larger community in order to nurture student learning.

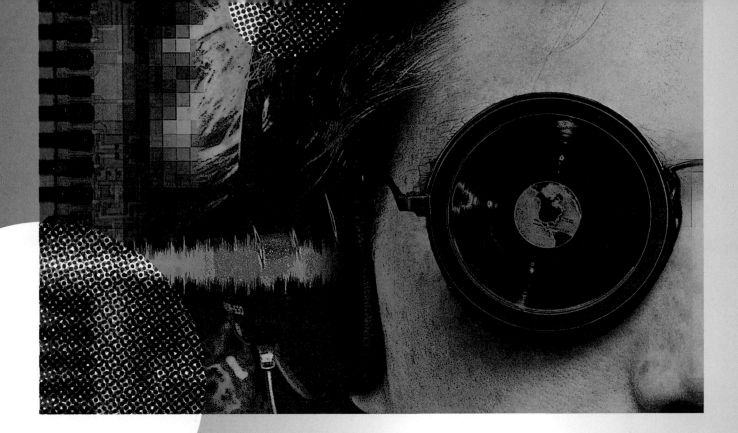

n your educational technology course, you have learned much about teaching and learning, designing instruction, and selecting the appropriate technologies to support instructional events, but all from the point of view of using technology to enhance what some refer to as traditional modes of instruction. As educators across the nation expand the use of technology in teaching and learning, it is becoming evident that technology might well end up doing more than just enhancing instruction; it might prove to be a serious force in changing the nature and form of instruction.

Consider for a moment how one technology—the cell phone—has changed the nature of personal and business communication. Being out of touch with family or business has become a thing of the past. The need for pay phones has been so significantly reduced that their numbers are steadily decreasing. Just think for a moment of the scene in one of our nation's major airports. Banks of pay phones typically line the walls in gate areas, yet these are frequently ignored by passengers, many of whom use their own cell phones to make local and long-distance calls. In this familiar scene, we can see for ourselves the decline of one technology and the rise of another.

Like this cellular technology, educational technologies are essentially communication tools. As you have learned, teaching is, at its core, communication. It may, therefore, be reasonable to anticipate that advances in educational technologies will fundamentally alter the way in which we communicate educationally, just as such advances have already fundamentally changed personal and business communications. Some say we are at the threshold of just such a change. So far, the predominant mode of educational communication has been the traditional classroom format, that is, a teacher and a given number of students working together in a predefined instructional space. But we are now beginning to see technology broaden this concept. Indeed, implementation of current and emerging technologies may well redefine the classroom itself.

Such changes are already beginning to occur. You have no doubt noticed an abundance of college courses offered as *distance education* courses. Such courses may be delivered online or through various combinations of digital and other distance-delivery technologies. But have you ever explored exactly what these courses entail? Have you considered their implications in changing the way teaching and learning are defined? Have you thought about how these new delivery systems might affect you and your students? These considerations are the topic of this chapter. And although distance education implementations are at the moment most frequently found in higher education, the instructional innovations reflected by these new delivery systems are likely to have far-reaching repercussions throughout all levels of education. It is important to be aware of their potential impact on you, on your students, and on your professional career.

In Chapter 11, you will

- Explore distance and other technology-enhanced instructional delivery systems

- Examine the relationship and educational implications of traditional and alternative delivery systems

- Review the role various technologies play in the alternative delivery of instruction

- Explore the application of and issues associated with alternative delivery systems in teaching and learning

- Examine the role of the Internet in alternative delivery

- Explore ways to evaluate distance and alternative delivery systems

Meet MaryAnn Butler-Pearson

One approach to the problems facing educators that is becoming both popular and critical for schools today is that of distance learning. When schools, for whatever reason, have been unable to offer their students what they need in a face-to-face setting, a few innovative educators have emerged who are leading the way to a new solution. By adapting higher education's approach to distance learning, K–12 schools are finding their own solutions. For example,

how does a principal offer Latin in a small school; calculus when math teachers are in scarce supply; preparation for state standardized exams when classes are full; required courses when students are involved in athletics or a TV series or travel and can't be at a school site at the time the course is offered?

Dr. MaryAnn Butler-Pearson is one of the educational leaders who has found a way to meet a growing need through distance learning. Here is her story.

MY SETTING

As a twenty-eight-year veteran high school science teacher and former Broward County (Florida) Teacher of the Year, I entered the world of distance learning rather by accident. The school district tapped one of my high school classes as the first videoconference class pilot. From the moment I saw and spoke to the teacher on the far end, I was forever hooked! The next phase of my career in education was about to begin. I was encouraged by Dr. Phyllis Schiffer-Simon to apply for the position of distance learning coordinator for Broward County Public Schools and appointed by the school board in the fall of 1997. Distance learning in Broward County schools began in the mid-1990s through a cooperative arrangement with Nova Southeastern University's Fischler Graduate School of Education to join the SAXophone videoconferencing project (**http://www.fgse.nova.edu/saxophone**) by taking Broward students to the university campus and using its equipment to interact with students around the world. Broward schools then obtained a videoconference system of its own, and distance learning was established in the county.

The Broward County School District is the fifth-largest school system in the United States; it serves over 265,000 students in more than 220 schools. Because of the sheer size and diversity within the school district, opportunities for learning were quite different from school to school before distance learning. The inequitable access to high-quality education was brought to public attention through a lawsuit brought by a group of concerned citizens. The district had already recognized this inequity, but how to resolve it was most difficult. As a start, a list of Advanced Placement (AP) courses required in all district public high schools had been developed. Unfortunately, not every high school was able to meet this requirement, either because of the inability to hire teachers with expertise in the AP coursework or because a small number of enrollments for these high-level classes made them fiscally impossible to implement. Videoconference technology was offered as a partial solution to this challenge. Needed AP courses and unique academic classes were taught by master teachers in the district to students at high schools where these courses were not available. An extra benefit from this solution was the development of new high-level academic teachers through the mentoring process. Inexperienced teachers in needed curriculum areas or experienced teachers who lacked the confidence to teach the higher-level courses were given the opportunity to facilitate in a class taught by a highly successful, advanced-level teacher through the entire course. Videoconferencing not only increased academic opportunities for students, it also helped the district build teaching capacity in needed areas.

In addition to the high school courses, many videoconferenced field trips to exotic, educational locations and interviews with important and interesting people were arranged. Students of all ages were able to see and speak with their counterparts in countries as far away as Japan, Australia, and South Africa. Students were able to interview a U.S. congressional delegate, a famous movie producer, the author of a children's book, and an aquanaut under the ocean! Using this medium, elementary and middle school children were offered the opportunity of enhancement programs to strengthen their reading, writing, math, and science skills, especially those required for success on the state of Florida's achievement test, the FCAT. To date, all of these programs are still continuing, and their success has increased multifold.

MY PROBLEM

However, one aspect of these real-time, interactive video programs was challenging and problematic. Because the district's high schools followed a variety of bell schedules and weekly calendars, organizing the videoconferenced academic classes for high school credit became a scheduling nightmare. Although videoconferencing would resolve some of the course availability challenges, it was not easy to arrange the classes because of the time and scheduling factors. When more than one facilitated school needed the same class, the district's video bridge was able to connect them, but once again, scheduling became the biggest obstacle to overcome. Schedule manipulations often depended on the teacher's schedule at the initiating school or necessitated offering the classes before or after the regular school day if the schedules of the schools involved could not be meshed at all.

The synchronicity of videoconferencing, usually an asset, turned out to be a liability when schedules could not be matched. I needed another solution.

Although videoconferencing was a powerful and useful tool, it had some drawbacks. Dr. Butler-Pearson did find an equally powerful alternative, which you will find described at the end of this chapter. But first, let's explore the delivery systems, available technologies, and issues she had to consider to find a resolution to her school system's problems.

What Do I Need to Know about Distance Education?

Few would argue that technology has had little significant impact on our society and our schools. Regardless of whether any given teacher makes use of technology in the classroom, because technology is changing our world, its impact will ultimately be felt in all social institutions, including schools. One of the most dramatic changes enabled by technology is the potential for alternative delivery of instruction that has been created through the adaptation of communications technologies to education. Businesses are already using communications technologies to conduct virtual meetings and to hold virtual training sessions for employees who are spread out across the nation or the world. Many schools and institutions of higher education have adapted this idea of moving information rather than people and have applied it to the delivery of instruction. Such technology-enhanced delivery approaches are typically referred to as **distance education.**

Technology enables us to move information instead of people.

Distance education can be broadly defined as the delivery of instruction to students who are separated from their teacher by time and/or location. The teacher may be located at a school site, but the student may be "attending" the class at home, using technology to bridge the gap. Or both teacher and student may be at either the same or different locations but available to work on the course only at differing hours. Once again, technology serves as a bridge across this time gap. In such cases, instructional events and interactions occur just as they do in traditional settings, but their form may be radically different from that found in the traditional classroom. Consider the following possibilities.

In distance education, the teacher and student may be working from different locations and/or at different times.

If you were taking a college course in a distance education format, you probably wouldn't see your teacher on a regular basis, as you would if you were taking a class that met every Monday evening. From an instructional viewpoint, how could teaching and learning occur? For example, you might have a critical question that arose while you were reviewing your text or related assignment. How would you get clarification? How is a student's interaction with an instructor and among peers possible in such a situation?

In a distance education scenario, technology is the key to providing a format for academic communication and exchange. For example, a student might choose to email a question from his or her home computer to the teacher, asking for clarification or explanation. The student and the teacher are at different locations; the student is at home, and the instructor is at school. Or a student might choose to email a question at night when doing an assignment. The instructor might not respond to that question until the next morning. Thus, student and instructor are separated by time as well as distance. The student is engaged in the learning process at night, and the teacher is engaged in the teaching process in the morning. Still, via technology, the student is able to communicate with the instructor, and the instructor with the student. An instructional event has occurred. The student has asked a question, and the teacher has clarified and expanded on the content. Without the two parties being in the same location or even working in the same time frame, teaching and learning have occurred. This type of nontraditional interaction is at the core of distance education (see Figure 11.1).

Distance education was originally developed to deliver instruction to students in remote rural locations. For many years, distance education was accomplished primarily via correspondence courses or by sending an instructor out to remote locations to deliver instruction to groups of students. With the advent of technologies that make instructional delivery possible in ways never envisioned in previous years, distance education has come to have a much broader meaning. In fact, some educators have sought to broaden the term itself to better represent these new delivery systems. Thus,

Instructor interacts with students from any place and at any time.

Distance education technologies enable interaction among all participants.

THE INTERNET

Students interact with instructors from any place and at any time.

Figure 11.1
Distance Education Technologies Enable Communication
Distance education uses technology to connect teacher and learner across time and space.

you will find terminology such as *distributed learning* or *virtual classrooms* used interchangeably with *distance education*. Regardless of the terminology, the idea behind them all is the delivery of instruction in nontraditional ways via technologies. Although the original term, *distance education*, remains dominant, it might not fully reflect the multitude of innovations and systems that make it possible for teachers and students to connect instructionally. Still, for consistency and clarity, we will use this terminology throughout this chapter but ask you to think of it in its broadest possible meaning.

Distance education is likely to have a direct impact on you on at least two significant professional levels. First, because teacher licensing requires continual renewal, you may participate as a student in a distance-delivered course to remain current professionally, to pursue an advanced degree, or to renew your professional credentials. Distance delivery of instruction to educators means that you are no longer bound by the colleges in your immediate vicinity. Through distance delivery, you have the opportunity to enroll in courses offered by any organization or institution in the nation—or indeed the world. This gives you timely access to the latest developments in the field and provides you with the widest possible professional development options.

The second impact of distance education is more subtle, though perhaps more significant. Distance-delivery systems, especially those that emphasize delivery via the

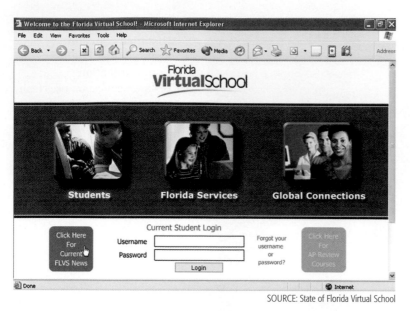

Many states have added online schools to their school systems to supplement those in traditional school districts.

SOURCE: State of Florida Virtual School

Internet, have become both more refined and more robust. Advances in communication technologies and increases in available bandwidth are driving these continual improvements in distance-delivery systems. The instructional potential offered by these systems has, in turn, caused a rethinking of the nature of instruction. Which elements of the physical instructional environment must truly be fixed? Which ones can simply be redefined by using technology? Must a teacher and student be in the same physical space for teaching and learning to occur? The answers to these types of academic questions will ultimately affect every classroom. Instruction is already being redefined in many higher education environments, and this trend is now becoming evident in state and local school systems as well.

A number of states have created virtual high school programs that offer high school credit courses statewide. These programs expand the instructional opportunities for high school students across the state. In states where such programs exist, students are no longer limited to the courses that can be offered at the local high school they are assigned to attend. In some districts that have implemented distance education, low-enrollment courses that would not be offered in a single school may be offered via a distance-delivery system that can combine students from multiple schools into a single districtwide virtual classroom. Or instruction that is not otherwise available at a school, owing to a shortage of qualified teachers in a given content area, may be offered by a districtwide master teacher to all district schools via distance delivery. These innovative programs expand the concept of the traditional classroom. Such delivery models are likely to be just a forerunner of more dramatic changes to come. As a technologically literate professional educator, you need to have an awareness of distance education and its potential application for you and your students.

Distance Education: A Brief History

As we noted earlier, the earliest distance-delivery systems were **correspondence courses,** consisting of books and assignments delivered to students via the postal system. As students did their readings and then completed assignments, they would mail their work back to the teacher. Tests were often given by local proctors, who mailed the completed exams to the teacher. Teaching was confined to the selection of books and the development of written learning activities. Learning was independent, with no interaction with peers and little interaction with the teacher. Of course, a student could mail a question to the instructor, but the time delay between question and response was critical, making meaningful exchange difficult.

As various other technologies were developed, they were added to enrich the correspondence course format (see Figure 11.2). The development of radio, and later television, resulted in instructional programming delivered via these two technologies. Distance students could listen to or watch a program featuring their teacher offering them direct instruction through audio and/or video. Distance students were also able to contact their instructor personally via telephone technology to ask a question or

Distance learning has moved from correspondence courses to a rich, immediate, interactive environment.

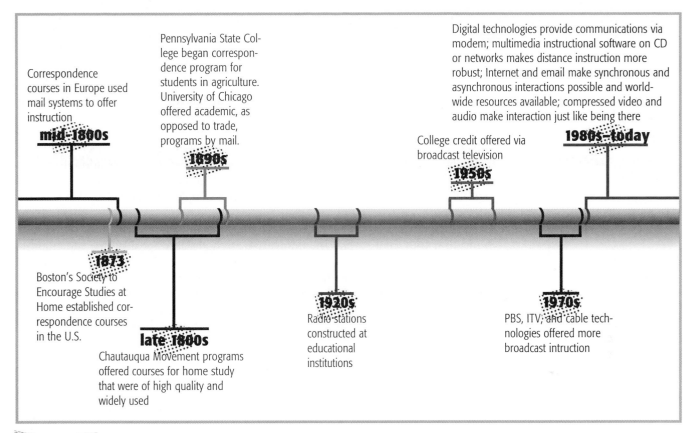

Figure 11.2
Distance Education Timeline
Distance education has evolved from correspondence courses to live interactive instruction supported by compressed video.

clarify content. Although these technologies did much to improve teacher-to-student communication when compared to a course via the postal system, they did relatively little to enable student-to-student communication. Learners who were engaged in a distance course still missed the student discussion and interaction that can lead to a broadening of ideas. Learning still took place in relative isolation.

As other technologies emerged, a solution to learner isolation became possible. Phone bridges, a sophisticated telephone conferencing system, allowed a large group of students to dial in together and connect with each other and their teacher. Students could then interact and discuss content via the phone. Then, with the advent of the personal computer and later the Internet, live and time-delayed communication via modem became possible. Today, with the addition of streaming audio and video to distance-delivery technologies, live video and audio interaction between teacher and student or among students is a viable alternative.

Each of the technologies mentioned above will be discussed in more detail later in this chapter, but it is clear that the nature of distance education is changing and is coming to emulate more closely the interaction that occurs in the traditional classroom. The impact of distance delivery may therefore have significant repercussions in education and may eventually blur the line between traditional and distance education. This potential for educational evolution offers fascinating academic possibilities, not only for distance education but also for education in traditional settings. Such alternatives to current delivery formats warrant further exploration.

ON THE WEB! 11.1
Exploring Distance Education

Distance Education and Alternative Delivery Systems

You have already learned how distance education was originally developed to deliver instruction across distances. But what if the same instructional designs, pedagogical methods, and technologies that make it possible to deliver across distance were adapted for the traditional classroom? How might these adaptations evolve into innovative classroom methodologies and alternatives? How might they affect instruction inside and outside of the classroom? How would they alter the traditional instructional delivery that is found in most classrooms? The answers to these questions are beginning to emerge as the influence of distance education techniques and technology expands.

Many educators who have taken or taught a course via distance education have found that they could adapt the innovative methods used for distance education to enrich and enhance their traditional teaching. Hybrid instructional delivery systems that use the best of both traditional and distance instruction are being adapted for and implemented in both types of programs. These **alternative delivery systems,** offered on a college campus, at a school, or across a district, may offer the first glimpse of how teaching and learning will ultimately change under the pressures of our current technological social evolution.

For schools that have begun to explore alternative delivery systems, one of the most popular formats emerging is the use of distance-delivery technology to expand school curriculum options. In such scenarios, technology-supported delivery to classrooms across a district is implemented by using some or all of the technologies and

Distance learning methods and media can enhance traditional instruction.

IN THE CLASSROOM

Time and Space Are Relative: K–12 Teachers Using Distance Education

Alaska is dotted with small, far-flung schools. To serve the students in this vast Arctic area, distance education has become the vehicle of choice. Alaska Online is a consortium that comprises nine school districts and is headed by project director Michael Opp. A July 2003 article in the *Juneau Empire* announced that the pilot program, which offered twenty-one distance education courses would be given official status in the fall of 2003. The courses have been largely designed by highly qualified Alaska teachers. For schools like the K–12 school in Tenakee Springs, which has twelve students and one teacher, the distance education offerings open up the means for these twelve students to take a full college-preparatory curriculum and to take Advanced Placement courses, options that were not feasible in their previous configuration—one by no means limited to Tenakee Springs, given the Alaskan topography and population distribution.

Connie Newman is supervisor of the four-site Cheatham School District, which extends over 32,000 square miles of the state. She says, "We really look to have some advanced-placement opportunities throughout the district and just to help us meet the standards as outlined by the state." Steve Atwater,

superintendent of the Lake and Peninsula School District, points out that his district has "a series of small high schools" staffed with teachers who are generalists. This means that the No Child Left Behind mandate for highly qualified teachers certified in the content areas they teach poses a major problem for him and other administrators in similar situations, given the fact that over two-thirds of Alaska's high schools have fewer than one hundred students.

Alaska Online will make previously unavailable courses such as advanced math and English accessible to Alaskan high schools at the click of a mouse. Each course is taught by a teacher certified in that content area, and each school district assigns a mentor to each student who takes an online course. Even for school districts with larger high schools and more comprehensive course offerings, the distance education classes can be a boon to students who can't work out a schedule with all the classes they want to take.

SOURCE: E. Fry. 2003. Rural schools look to online courses. Juneau Express (June 25). Retrieved July 1, 2003, from **http://www.juneauempire.com/stories/062503/loc_webschool.shtml**.

methodologies that are typical of a distance education program. For example, as we mentioned earlier, a master teacher may provide instruction to students located in schools across a district. Typically, each classroom to which instruction is transmitted has a facilitator present who assists with logistics and student support. Facilitators may team-teach with the distance education teacher or may simply act as aides in the distance classroom. In such scenarios, the role of the on-site classroom teacher may change dramatically during districtwide distance instruction. Do you find yourself reacting negatively to this idea? If so, be aware that this is not an unusual response. Without fully understanding how such delivery is accomplished and the critical role of all participants, classroom teachers may reject such systems out of hand. However, for those who have become more informed about distance delivery, exciting and innovative possibilities they had never before considered often emerge.

ON THE WEB! 11.2
Distance Education
in K–12

The usefulness of distance and other alternative delivery scenarios will, of course, vary with the instructional content and age of the students. To begin to grasp the inherent potential of alternative delivery systems and to be able to evaluate their effectiveness, it is first necessary to closely examine the nature of instruction in a distance education environment and see how it might be appropriately adapted to traditional settings. As is necessary whenever you take a close look at effective instruction, you must start with an examination of the intended instructional design. As you have learned, good instruction begins with a good instructional design. This is equally true for instruction that is delivered at a spatial or temporal distance. Therefore, instructional design is where we must begin our academic exploration of distance education.

Designing Instruction for Alternative Delivery

You have already learned about the importance of a well-conceived design and a carefully planned lesson to ensure the quality of your instruction. In a distance-delivery environment, planning is even more crucial. Unlike the traditional classroom, in which the teacher is present and can make adjustments to the teaching and learning process while it is being carried out, distance delivery requires that all aspects of the process be fully established before the teacher and learners engage in it. The distance education curriculum and fully articulated activities are typically prepared well in advance of the instructional event. Distance educators must anticipate learner responses and prepare a curriculum that answers questions and concerns before they are asked. Once the curriculum has been disseminated to students working in different locations or in different time frames, it can be difficult to make and disburse changes to it for other than Internet-based courses. For these reasons, every aspect of instructional planning is a critical component of distance delivery.

Detailed advance planning is even more critical in distance learning than in traditional teaching.

Beyond the Lesson Plan

The instructional design process, when applied to distance education, requires a strategic approach. The design must respond to both the instruction itself and the benefits and/or impediments of the distance-delivery technologies that will be used. Table 11.1 provides a summary of the process of preparing a distance-delivery course. Often, district or school distance education programs begin by determining which technologies are available or will be acquired to deliver instruction across spatial or temporal barriers. This may be a less-than-ideal, though necessary, approach. A better scenario would be identical to the process used for traditional instruction; that is, start with the instructional design and then determine which distance-delivery technologies are necessary and appropriate to support instruction. Unfortunately, because of the significant cost of distance delivery technologies and their integral role in the process, a district might have little choice but to begin by determining which existing

TABLE 11.1   GETTING READY FOR DISTANCE DELIVERY

Step	Process
1	Review research and similar courses for your grade level.
2	Examine existing distance learning materials and presentation ideas for your subject.
3	Analyze the available delivery technologies and consider their strengths and weaknesses relative to your students and your subject area.
4	Complete available hands-on training in the delivery technology you plan to use.
5	Discuss your needs and student needs with technical and academic support staff.
6	In your plan • Begin with instruction to students in how to use the delivery system • Plan modular instruction, with content divided into manageable units of material • Offer activities and experiences that address diverse learners to the extent the delivery system allows • Include interaction and scheduled, frequent feedback • Determine how you will assess students, both academically and logistically
7	Plan for contingencies should technologies fail.

technologies can be repurposed for distance education. These determinations will not define the instructional event, but they do place parameters around it. When preparing an instructional design for distance education, you must implement the design process with full awareness of the technologies that will be made available to you for delivery. Your design itself may suggest changes to the planned delivery technologies that will be necessary to ensure effective delivery and meaningful interaction.

The steps of the DID process you have already learned do not change in distance education. In fact, they become even more fundamental when you are conceptualizing instruction that will be difficult to alter once it has begun. The environment in which your design will be implemented is likely to be very different from the traditional classroom and therefore must be fully considered and adapted in the initial design. Because distance education teachers are not in frequent face-to-face contact with their students, impromptu changes in the instructional plan are typically not practical. Developing a fully articulated design is the only way to create an instructional sequence that is precise enough to flow unerringly without requiring it to be frequently changed and adjusted.

Although instructional design for distance education takes on a strategic and situational perspective, the most significant change to the instructional planning process occurs in the lesson plan phase. Lesson plans for the traditional classroom are typically written by the teacher for the teacher. The teacher is in the classroom throughout the lesson and can modify the lesson plan at any time. Students rarely see the lesson plan itself; they simply experience it being carried out. In distance education, however, the teacher is not present and cannot make instant modifications. It is the student who works independently through a fully articulated lesson plan that was carefully prepared by the teacher to respond to anticipated needs. The instructional support and prompting that would normally take place in the classroom are included within the plan itself, with clear and precise instructions as to how each aspect of the plan should be carried out. Table 11.2 illustrates the relationship between the steps in a traditional lesson plan and those same steps as integrated into distance education curriculum.

TABLE 11.2   COMPARING TRADITIONAL AND DISTANCE LESSON PLANNING

Traditional Class	*Distance Learning Class*
STEP 1: READY THE LEARNER	
In your classroom, you may • Ask questions to determine whether content needs to be reviewed • Review content as needed	*In your distance education materials, you should* • Prepare a pretest so students can self-assess whether they have the necessary previous content • Make review materials available
STEP 2: TARGET SPECIFIC OBJECTIVES	
In your classroom, you would • Select the target objective for the lesson • Prepare your students by explaining what they will be able to do as a result of the lesson • Respond to your students' questions about the lesson	*In your distance education materials, you should* • Post the target objective in a location students will notice • Explain the objective in detail, since there may be a time delay should students have a question • Articulate how questions should be asked and will be responded to
STEP 3: PREPARE THE LESSON	
In your classroom, you would • Decide how your classroom needs to be arranged for this particular lesson • Write notes for yourself as to how you will accomplish each step of the pedagogical cycle • Select and set up the materials, media, and technologies needed and decide how will they be used by you and your students • Decide upon assessments for the lesson, and select materials and means for implementation	*In your distance education materials, you should* • Create content modules so that students have manageable materials to work with • For each module, sequence each step of the pedagogical cycle and provide detailed explanation to the student as to how to proceed through each step • Prepare all materials with detailed instructions for their use and include them in the students' modules • Arrange for all media to be made available to students • Arrange for technologies to be available to students who do not have access • Provide students with detailed procedures for accessing and using media and technologies • Prepare assessments well in advance • Make arrangements for proctoring, and communicate procedures for assessments to students

Preparing Students

Because students must work through their lessons without benefit of the immediate presence of the teacher, they must first be prepared for the differences this type of experience will present. From the earliest grades, student behavior and expectations are shaped so that the students will be comfortable in a traditional classroom, but few learners have been similarly prepared to work in a distance environment. Therefore, in addition to preparing the learners for the content, you must prepare them to work differently than they would in a traditional classroom. Typically, that means that you must prepare them to work much more independently. This, then, is the next major consideration in designing instruction for alternative delivery.

In the traditional classroom, students listen to directions or instruction and then proceed to complete assigned work. If they have a question, they need only raise a hand, and their teacher responds to them. In a distance education environment, the process is different. Students may view, listen to, or read content and directions in the materials provided or via technology-based communications. They then begin to work

In an effort to ensure student readiness for distance education, many programs ask students to complete online self-assessments.

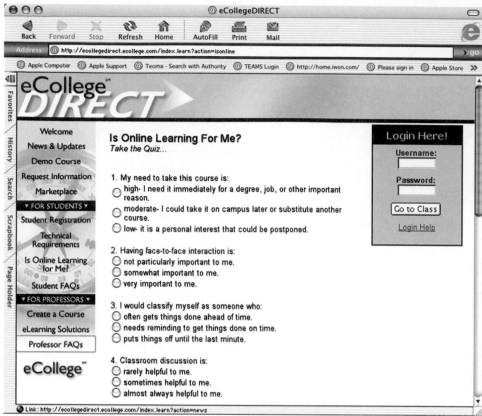

SOURCE: eCollege Direct

on their reinforcing activities. If they have a question, the teacher might not be immediately available to respond. In some distance education situations, there might not even be other students in the same location to ask a question of or to discuss a concern with. Students working in this type of environment need to be trained to find the information they need from their materials and to use the systems in place to get answers to unresolved questions. This is a more independent learning format than the one that is typical of a traditional classroom.

Many distance education programs use a combination of screening and orienting students to prepare them to be successful in a distance education environment. Screening students, that is, determining whether or not their learning styles and study habits are consistent with the distance education format, is a frequently used first step. Each distance education program uses specific technologies and methods to deliver instruction. Matching students who have the potential to work well with these methods can increase learner success and decrease frustration. A second commonly used step is to prepare students for the distance education environment by providing a very specific orientation to and training in the methods and technologies they will be expected to work with. This step helps students become as comfortable with the experiences and tools of the distance teaching and learning environment as they would be if they were participating in a traditional environment. One or both of these preparatory steps will assist learners in maximizing their potential for success.

ON THE WEB! 11.3
Getting Ready for Distance Education

Planning Ahead for Murphy's Law

Murphy's Law says that anything that can go wrong will go wrong. Admittedly, Murphy's Law is an excessively pessimistic viewpoint. It does, nevertheless, offer those engaged in distance education an important warning. In traditional environments, the teacher is present to respond to any difficulties that arise. If you are planning to show a videotape and the VCR does not work, you adjust your lesson to adapt to the circumstance with relatively little effort. But if you are teaching a distance education class to children located in neighboring schools and the communications equipment does not work, how can the lesson go on? What provision have you made for this eventuality?

Because distance delivery is heavily dependent on events and technologies outside of the teacher's immediate control, it is important to anticipate possible points of failure and to have a contingency plan. In the case of technology problems, having a redundant delivery technology available as a **backup system** can resolve crises caused by technology glitches. For example, making a speakerphone available in a compressed video classroom provides a backup communication system if the primary video system fails. Planning potential solutions for possible technological problems and communicating such backup systems with students reduces the potential for interrupted instruction. Not all failures, however, are technological. Students might not get materials on time, or books might not be available. Such events as these and other nontechnical ones are unavoidable; yet you can still plan for how such possibilities will be handled. You might want to give a fellow teacher or the students a phone number they can call or an email address where they can send mail should such problems occur. How the event will be handled will be determined by the various circumstances of the school or distance education program. But anticipating that such events may happen and articulating appropriate responses are key responsibilities for the teacher planning for distance delivery. Table 11.3 lists some areas to consider in such planning.

Like teachers, students must be prepared to function in a distance learning environment.

TABLE 11.3   CONTINGENCY PLANNING FOR DISTANCE DELIVERY

Problem	Solutions
Student Selection Is a distance education format right for the student?	Provide self-assessments of readiness for distance learning; offer online counseling and advising.
Interactivity Will interaction between student and teacher and between students be sufficient?	Establish technology and procedures for regularly scheduled electronic and/or telephone connections; train teachers to respond to students with alacrity, thoroughness, and compassion; schedule group interaction, such as group problem solving, study sessions, and online discussions; ensure that feedback is consistently and positively reinforced.
Student Support and Services Will students have available the academic advising and mentoring, as well as the on-site technological assistance, that they need?	Tutors, academic advisers, and technology paraprofessionals must be provided to allow the student to focus on the product, not the process; support staff should be available to help both synchronously and asynchronously with advising and non-subject-area matters, such as stress, time management, and study skills.
Alienation and Isolation Will social contact be sufficient?	Provide online discussions and chats, email, digitized photos, videoconferencing, and collaborative assignments to overcome isolation.
Technology Skills Will skills be sufficient to carry out the technological processes?	Prerequisite and in-progress technology training must be available; on-screen help, telephone access to technical experts, and hard-copy how-to manuals need to be easy to use.
Design of Instructional Materials Will the materials work at a distance?	Offer training sessions for teachers to help them modify materials to accommodate the delivery differences needed; include technology training and integration techniques as well as methods for interactively engaging students at a distance.

Providing Feedback

One of the greatest challenges in teaching at a distance is how to provide **feedback** to your students. In the traditional classroom, you use body language and comments as well as written feedback to provide your students with an idea of how well they are mastering the content. In a distance environment, the technology you use often determines the types of feedback formats that are available to you. If you use a speakerphone in a classroom, you can ask questions and give voice feedback to individuals or groups. If you use the Internet, email feedback may be appropriate. Regardless of the feedback mechanism you use, it is critical to plan for adequate and frequent feedback within the instructional design itself. Just as with any instruction, students need confirmation that their understanding of concepts is correct. Continual feedback, in any form, is no less valuable in distance instruction. For those who teach in a distance environment, determining how and when to provide feedback can be a challenge met through creative teaching.

Evaluating Progress

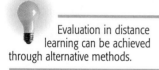

Evaluation in distance learning can be achieved through alternative methods.

ON THE WEB! 11.4

Assessing Learning at a Distance

Evaluation of students in a distance education course is one of the key issues for distance educators. How can students be fairly and accurately evaluated if they are not in a traditional testing situation? The answer to these justifiable concerns involves a creative and flexible approach to assessment. One of the most common approaches is to provide performance assessment alternatives that can be used in addition to testing. Such alternatives may be group projects conducted via Internet chat rooms, individual research projects with PowerPoint presentations that can be shared via computer, or even oral reports given via telephone. Distance educators must carefully consider the intended objectives and then creatively develop assessment alternatives that take advantage of the technologies in place. Such assessments may challenge students to demonstrate competencies even more effectively than those commonly found in traditional classrooms.

Even so, traditional tests still have a place in distance delivery. Proctored examinations remain appropriate and expected as a part of a class taught via distance education. How the proctoring takes place may vary, however. In classes that are set up with a single teacher, with facilitators at each receiving site, proctored testing is easily accomplished. The facilitators take responsibility for the testing environment, proctor the tests, and then collect and return them to the teacher for grading. Even at sites without facilitators, proctors can be arranged for and tests given in secure environments, such as media centers or administrative offices. The combination of performance assessment and testing can ultimately provide as valid an assessment of student progress in a distance instructional environment as is available in a traditional instructional environment.

Support Technologies for Distance Teaching and Learning

Once the initial planning issues have been considered, just as in traditional instructional design, the next step is to examine the supporting technologies that are available or that need to be acquired to implement the instructional design. In distance education, such technologies fall into two broad categories: technologies that support synchronous distance education and those that support asynchronous distance education. **Synchronous** distance education is instruction that occurs at the same time, although typically not in the same place. An example of synchronous instruction is a

Synchronous instruction and learning occur at the same time.

districtwide distance education foreign language class that is offered on "A" days in a block schedule, from 1:00 to 2:15. Students participating in such a class meet at the same time but at different locations across the district. In a web-based class, synchronous distance education might require that all students log on to a class chat room at the same time, although the locations from which they are working may vary. Synchronous technologies, then, are those that allow students to participate in the same time frame but in different locations. Table 11.4 lists synchronous and asynchronous technologies that can be used in distance education.

In contrast, **asynchronous** distance education is time-shifted; that is, teacher and students can participate at differing times from the same or different locations. An example of an asynchronous distance education class is one that is conducted via the Internet. In such a course, materials may be available via a web site, with students and teachers interacting via email or class conference. Students and teacher may be located at the same school, at different schools, or even at home, but they have the option of interacting at different times.

> Asynchronous learning occurs at times when the instructor is not personally present.

The nature of the distance education program that a district or school chooses to implement will depend on whether the distance-delivery approach will be synchronous, asynchronous, or a combination of both. Arguments for and against each approach can be logically made. Synchronous delivery most closely emulates traditional instruction and is the easiest for teachers and students to adjust to. However, synchronous approaches do not offer flexible time frames, a lack that can cause significant resource and scheduling problems. Asynchronous delivery is more flexible, making it easier to allocate and schedule resources while also making instruction more convenient and accessible for learners. However, asynchronous instruction is more complex to plan for and requires new teaching and learning formats that may require some accommodation for both teacher and learners. Still, both formats have their place in distance- and alternative delivery programs. Which format is best can be answered only in response to the diverse needs of the learners, the district's needs, and the content to be delivered. Whichever approach is chosen, several specific technologies can be enlisted to support instruction.

▌ Support Technologies for Synchronous Instruction

You are already familiar with a variety of technologies that can be used to support synchronous instruction. Some, like the telephone, are relatively low-tech, while others, such as Internet-based compressed videoconferencing, are emerging high-tech options. The variety of technologies that can be adapted by creative educators to assist in communicating synchronously cover the full range of technological options. The key to selecting technologies for this purpose is to look for those technologies that provide same-time communication formats and explore them for their adaptability to distance education.

• Telephone Technologies

The **telephone** and its by-product, telephone conferencing, are one of the staple technologies for synchronous delivery. Whether as a primary medium or a backup technology, the telephone offers an easy-to-use, inexpensive, and readily accessible technology for communications. Like all synchronous technologies, the phone requires that all parties participate in the same time frame. Telephone exchanges, whether direct instruction or questions and answers, can be one-to-one or, through conferencing, group communication.

The most basic type of conference system is the use of a **speakerphone** that allows participants to communicate using a single, specially equipped phone. Speakerphones offer a simple, though potentially unwieldy, conferencing system. Speakerphones are equipped with an omnidirectional microphone that is designed to pick up voices from

TABLE 11.4   DELIVERY TECHNOLOGIES SUMMARY

Synchronous Technologies		Asynchronous Technologies	
Telephone		Voice Mail/Fax	
Broadcast Video		Videocassette	
Radio Broadcast		Audiocassette	
Internet Chat		Internet Conferencing	
Videoconferencing		Email	
Net Meeting		Print Materials	

ON THE WEB! 11.5
Telephone Conferencing

anywhere in the room. They also have a speaker that is powerful enough to be heard across a room. Typically, this equipment has only a volume control to adjust sound levels. Although this makes for a very easy-to-use and economical system, the microphones and speakers imbedded in the phone might not accurately reflect voices on the other end of the line or in a larger room. Extended use of a speakerphone can be frustrating when critical content is being communicated. Furthermore, the phones pick up all sound, not just intended discussion, so extraneous room noise can be irritating.

A second audio option is the **conference call.** Conference calling can be done via personal phone services or school phone systems. Such systems typically allow three to eight participants to connect together. This type of conferencing is excellent for small-group instruction or discussion. Because all participants are speaking into their own telephone handsets, the clarity of exchange is better than that with a speakerphone. Extraneous noise is also easily filtered out. Finally, because all participants use their own phones, unlike the use of a speakerphone, which must be located in a single central place, every member of the conference can conceivably be calling from a different location. This technology bridges the location gap for every participant. Diversity of location can, however, be a disadvantage. Gathering together for a speakerphone conference offers opportunities for social learning that conference calling does not. Furthermore, the cost may be greater in these circumstances as a result of long-distance charges that may add up throughout the instructional activity.

A final and more sophisticated telephone-based method for synchronous interaction is the use of a **phone bridge.** This equipment, which is usually installed at the district level or subscribed to from phone service companies, provides the capabilities for large-group instruction via telephone. This technology allows from two to fifty callers to call a single central number and join in a conference call. The moderator or teacher has to establish ground rules so that two or more participants don't try to talk at the same time. Each speaker is also asked to identify himself or herself each time that person has something to say. The technology bridges all callers together and lets each individual caller join or leave the conference without impacting the conference itself. It is possible to arrange for a toll-free number as the bridge number, thus solving the problem of long-distance charges for participants.

Each of these telephone-based technologies adapts a common medium to distance education. Although such solutions are clever, the real challenge in using such technologies is in the design of effective instruction that takes advantage of the technology's strengths and overcomes its weaknesses. Like all instruction, effective telephone-based instruction is the result of innovative teachers being aware of this technology and able to adapt it to their purposes.

connecting THEORY to PRACTICE

Comparing Apples and Apples: Which Is More Effective— Distance Education or Face-to-Face Instruction?

Research studies report that well-designed distance education programs are highly effective. However, one caveat is that the most successful delivery systems are those focused on students who work responsibly in an online environment. Although some studies, especially early ones, report little difference in distance education versus face-to-face instruction, given similar content and strong teaching, recent research of distance learning programs shows otherwise. For programs that are media-rich and interactive, a high degree of effectiveness is evident for distance or e-learning.

A longitudinal, action research project carried out by Synnöve Kekkonen-Moneta and Giovanni B. Moneta and reported on in the August 2002 *British Journal of Educational Technology* supports the effectiveness of distance education. The purpose of the study was to evaluate "the effectiveness of Web-based, highly interactive, and multimedia-rich e-learning materials by comparing students' learning outcomes in the lecture and the online versions" of a course. In the introduction to the report, the researchers state that "e-learning tools and techniques have the potential to capture, and even enrich and individualize, the communication and interactions that normally take place in the classroom. In the wide variety of today's online courses, instructors are finding ways to supplement or replace traditional teaching methods and materials with e-learning."

The "Learning Outcomes" section of the study reports, "Students' learning outcomes were assessed in proctored midterm and final examinations." The questions were written to cover factual learning and "applied conceptual learning, that is, higher order learning defined as the capacity to understand deeply and to apply the learned concepts and skills."

A variety of statistical measures were applied to determine the conclusion: "Overall, the online course proved to be at least as effective as the lecture course in terms of students' learning outcomes," indicating "that carefully designed e-learning modules facilitate engaging interactions with the content materials and, in turn, foster higher order learning outcomes."

This study and similar research support the effectiveness of distance education as a delivery system while reinforcing the importance of meaningful and appropriate instructional planning. Like face-to-face instruction, well-conceived and well-implemented instruction supports and facilitates student learning. And, in both face-to-face and distance education, it is the teacher's planning efforts that make the difference for a successful instructional event.

SOURCE: S. Kekkonen-Moneta, & G. Moneta. 2001. E-learning in Hong Kong: Comparing learning outcomes in online multimedia and lecture versions of an introductory computing course. *British Journal of Educational Technology,* 33 (4), 2002, 423–433.

• Videoconferencing

You have already learned about the ability to communicate via computer using a compressed **videoconferencing** system. Clearly, such a system is an ideal technology for synchronous distance education. Video and audio images are compressed and transmitted in different ways. Two of the most common methods are computer-based TCP/IP systems connected over the Internet and the use of broad-bandwidth digital telephone lines. International standards have been established for the compression of these signals, making it possible for different brands of compressed video equipment to communicate with each other.

Compressed videoconferencing systems can be configured as individual systems on home or office PCs or as a classroom system. An individual system, as you will recall from previous chapters, uses the computer's speakers, a microphone, and a small monitor-top video camera for communication. Software enables the digital pictures and audio to be sent via modem to one or more similarly equipped machines on the Internet. Videoconferencing systems allow individual users to connect in a virtual meeting and exchange text, graphics, sound, and visual images. This combination of hardware and software is easily adapted for instruction at a distance. Teacher and learners connect to the Internet, create their virtual space using their meeting software, and communicate just as they would face-to-face.

This type of videoconferencing system offers individuals with the required hardware and software an excellent opportunity to participate fully in instruction. Students can be at diverse locations with the only parameter for participation being that they all go online at the same time. Students can interact in a virtual face-to-face instructional event with their teacher and/or with their peers. Despite its potential, this delivery technology does currently have some disadvantages. The typical home or school computer system might not include all of the necessary hardware. Furthermore, as you have learned, video and audio files require significant bandwidth to avoid frustrating communication delays. Many home and school systems are not connected to the Internet at the bandwidth necessary to allow this technology to offer smooth communications. Finally, for students whose learning is augmented through social interaction, this technology might not offer sufficient social contact. Unless small groups meet informally—virtually or in person—outside of the instructional time, social interaction and the broadening of learning that often results may be lacking.

Videoconferencing systems help to create interactive classrooms across a school district or a state.

Another option for configuring compressed video for distance education is to connect compressed video classrooms across a district. In this application of compressed video, the personal equipment is scaled up to create an interactive classroom that can be connected via high-speed phone service to similarly equipped classrooms at other locations. Typically, such classrooms include one or more large monitors positioned so that all participants can see them; multiple microphones in strategic locations across the room to pick up individual and multiple voices; video cameras mounted on the monitors or in positions that allow for "eye-to-eye" contact when participants are

Videoconferencing over the Internet can make distance learning come alive.

ON THE WEB! 11.6
Compressed Video
Communications

IN THE CLASSROOM

Over and Back! Compressed Video for Education

Videoconferencing serves the Plano (Texas) Independent School District well as a part of its distance education program. All middle schools, special programs, and two of the high schools have the use of two team stations, which are portable and can be connected to a network drop for Internet-transmitted interactive conferences. Elementary schools have access to smaller portable units. The role of the teacher is clearly spelled out by the school district. Facilitators are appointed to be at the remote sites, and the teacher is responsible for the students at the primary site. The first responsibility is instruction in the content area—a reminder that, after all, technology is the means, not the end product of instructional processes.

Videoconferencing, a main component of the distance education program, is intended to serve students by making it possible for them to

- Collaborate with students in other classrooms
- Learn from students, educators, and business persons anywhere in the world
- Visit faraway places without leaving [their] classrooms
- Develop communication skills
- Develop presentation skills
- Learn to use technology effectively

The benefits derived from videoconferencing are not restricted to the students. Staff also can

- collaborate with staff members across the district
- collaborate with educators worldwide
- participate in training sessions
- plan with teachers at other schools

How can this two-way conferencing be linked into distance education to improve teaching and learning conducted in this manner? The Plano Independent School District's distance education "provides a channel for communication all over the globe." On its web site, a page called "Ideas for Using Video Conferencing in the Classroom" shows teachers innovative ideas for bringing videoconferencing into the distance education classroom. One intriguing and educationally sound suggestion is for students to videoconference with students in Japan, grow a bonsai forest, develop a web site on famous Japanese, sponsor a cultural awareness week, and keep a journal of what they learn.

SOURCES: Video conferencing in Plano ISD. 2003. Retrieved June 13, 2003, from **http://k-12.pisd.edu/distance_learning/vidconf.htm**; Ideas for using video conferencing in the classroom. 2003. Retrieved June 13, 2003, from **http://k-12.pisd.edu/distance_learning/uses.htm.**

looking at the monitors; supplementary video cameras for special shots; and the hardware and software to enable communication.

The compressed video classroom most closely emulates the traditional classroom for both teachers and learners. Because students gather in each of the classrooms that are connected via compressed video, the potential for social learning is returned to the instructional environment in this configuration. Moreover, facilitators are often hired for the distant sites, so the teacher (located at the near site) has either team-teachers or aides to help meet student needs. This allows for greater flexibility and more responsiveness at each far site. For most who have participated in this type of compressed video classroom, the technology quickly seems to disappear as participants become engaged in the instructional process. The fact that most participants are comfortable in the familiar surroundings of a classroom likely contributes to their ease in using this type of distance education technology.

• Internet Chats

Another technology that is used for synchronous distance delivery is the **Internet chat.** Chat programs allow multiple Internet users to log on to and communicate within the same virtual space. This technology allows the teacher to conduct live interactive sessions or groups of students to communicate in real time with each other. Chats offer a way to hold an instructional session or a small-group discussion regardless of the participants' locations. Even though all must enter the chat room at the same time, distance barriers become irrelevant. For a large, physically spread-out

Using chats, students and the teacher can key messages to each other online in real time.

Figure 11.3
Class Discussion via an Online Chat
Online instructional chats offer students and teacher exchanges similar to those that would occur in a traditional classroom.

CHATROOM MSB01

MSB:>   Ok, class, let's see who can answer the next question. What were some of the social conditions that changed after the Civil War? *Becky, can you think of one?*-o-

BSMITH:>   Slavery was stopped.-o-

MSB:>   *Good, Becky. That is correct. Did that change the way former slaves lived? Alan, can you answer that one?*-o-

ACHAMPS:>   I'm not sure, but I don't think it made a whole lotta difference since people who were slaves didn't have anything and being free didn't give them anything but freedom. Heck, they didn't know how to not be slaves!-o-

MSB:>   *Right, Alan. It was hard for the former slaves to adjust to their new status since they had no opportunity to learn the skills they needed to function as full citizens. And, of course, the situation in the South was desperate for everyone from former plantation owners to city dwellers to former slaves. It was a very difficult time. Does anyone know what a "carpetbagger" was and what these folks did in the South after the war? Gina, do you want to take a stab at this one?*-o-

GVERRICIO:>   Sorry, Ms. B. you got me. I know they were from the North, but I don't know what they did.-o-

MSB:>   *Well, that was a good start, Gina, they were indeed from the North. Tom, can you share any type of activity a carpetbagger might have been engaged in?*-o-

school district or for a school that hires a distant expert teacher, this delivery technology provides a very effective solution to the need for interaction.

Chats can offer some marked advantages. Many who use chats for instructional interaction find that the quality of the exchange is quite high. Perhaps because participants have more time to consider and respond to questions or comments, the interaction is often more thoughtful than in the classroom. Also, unlike a classroom in which shy students may never raise their hands and contribute, chats allow the teacher to call on every student; in this way, everyone interacts. In addition, seeing that chat technology typically allows participants time to key in, reread, and correct their responses before sharing them, the delay gives reticent students a greater comfort level when participating. Figure 11.3 presents a segment of a class chat.

ON THE WEB! 11.7
Internet Chats

• Internet Classroom Sites

A final communication technology that can be used to create a virtual classroom is Internet-based meeting space. Whether in the form of software created primarily for business use (e.g., Microsoft NetMeeting) or an educational site (e.g., WebCT or Blackboard), this technology offers a variety of tools for both synchronous and asynchronous exchange. Teachers can conduct a class via the Internet in which they can engage in a group discussion in real time, show a PowerPoint presentation, or share an electronic work space. Together, these technologies, in the hands of a creative teacher, can offer a very solid learning environment.

Many sites offer authoring tools with which teachers can create and present site-based lessons. Such tools range from fill-in-the-blank virtual classroom authoring to test generators to syllabus makers. Different sites and meeting programs offer different capabilities. Some charge a school system a per-student fee to host a virtual classroom; others give the school system the software to run on its own network servers. In either case, preparing a distance education class using any of these resources requires a substantial up-front investment in a teacher's time and creativity. To be sure the invest-

ON THE WEB! 11.8
Virtual Classroom Web Sites

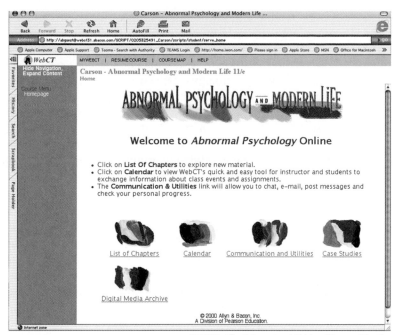

SOURCE: Allyn & Bacon, Inc. A Division of Pearson Education

Students and teachers can participate in virtual classrooms via software such as WebCT or Blackboard.

ment is well spent, it is important to try and to compare these sites or programs and their tools before committing to using them.

Support Technologies for Asynchronous Instruction

Asynchronous (time-shifted) instruction is also supported by a wide variety of analog and digital technologies. Because the term *asynchronous* suggests that teacher and students need not be connected at the same time, even the most basic classroom technologies can be considered a part of this category. Printed materials, televised broadcasts on educational channels, videotaped instruction, and audiotapes are all potentially asynchronous delivery technologies. Teacher and students do not need to be in contact at the same time or at the same place for instruction to occur. However, in using these types of technologies, interaction is typically one-way. The teacher delivers instructional content via these technologies, but there is little or no opportunity for teacher-to-student or peer-to-peer interaction. In view of the fact that most teachers build interactive experiences into their instruction, it is important for distance educators to identify and repurpose available technologies to support asynchronous interaction as well as delivery.

• Telephone Technologies

The telephone is ordinarily a synchronous technology, but when you add an answering machine or voice mail service, you also add asynchronous capability. Because these technologies allow teachers and students to leave each other **voice mail** messages, voice communication becomes possible even when none of the participants communicates via phone at the same time. For districts with more sophisticated voice mail systems, it is possible to create a virtual verbal space for a class. A phone mailbox can be created in which a teacher can request oral responses to a question. Students can then call in to the mailbox and leave their verbal answers for their teacher to listen to later. Oral responses are crucial for a foreign language class, for example, and phone mail technology can make it possible to give them asynchronously.

Voice mail can transform a telephone into an asynchronous instructional tool.

Another common telephone technology that can be adapted for asynchronous delivery is the **fax.** For instantaneous delivery of text or graphics, the fax machine provides simple yet effective communication. Teachers can fax questions, visuals, or replies to student inquiries directly to the students. Students can fax back responses, assignments, or questions. This common technology offers an instant and reasonably inexpensive communication tool yet does not require that sender and receiver be working in the same time frame. Even if you do not have a dedicated fax machine, most computer operating systems offer at least a rudimentary fax program as an accessory to the system. Thus, whoever has a PC and a modem available typically also has fax capability. This simple tool has great potential for communication in the hands of a creative teacher.

• Electronic Mail

> Email messages are a private and thoughtful form of communication.

The most significant digital asynchronous technology to support distance delivery is **electronic mail,** or email. Just as email has changed the nature of the way many individuals, businesses, and organizations communicate, so too has it revolutionized asynchronous instructional communication. This powerful tool makes possible easy yet thoughtful communications between teacher and student and among students. Unlike a voice mail message, email messages can include attachments to an original message. These attachments can even include animated graphics, audio, and compressed video clips. Messages can be very brief or long, formal or informal. Because the sender has time to carefully compose a message and proofread it before sending, email messages tend to be a more thoughtful form of communication than speech. Finally, email messages can be composed, sent, and read whenever it is most convenient for the individuals involved. Email's attributes, harnessed together in support of the distance teaching and learning process, create a powerful and elegant tool for interactivity.

Email can be used to communicate one-to-one or one-to-many. A distance education teacher can communicate privately with each student or can choose to send a group email message to all, via a group mailing option or a formal mailing list. Students can respond to progress inquiries or content questions, or they can ask further

IN THE CLASSROOM
The More We Get Together! Email in Teaching

The fascination students of all ages have with email is an undeniable plus when offering distance learning courses that call for interchanges transmitted by this means. Phuong Le has reported on the "alive and well" status of these courses and their implementation with email as a main feature in the *Indianapolis Star.* Jon Kilgore, a teacher in Chenoa, Illinois, kept in touch with one of his students, Joelle Contorno, who lives in a suburb of Chicago, as she worked on civics course assignments. "On a typical day, he pored over e-mail from students, helped one with a computer question and downloaded assignments that students e-mailed him."

Mr. Kilgore noted that practically all his communication with his distance-educated students is by email. Joelle pointed out that this form of interacting with a teacher is "good and bad. I miss that I can't talk to my friends, but I'm still learning the same material."

Susan Thetard, a teacher at University High School in Bloomington, Indiana, comments regarding her online Introduction to Theater course that she has found more widespread participation from her students taking the course than occurs when the dialogs are face-to-face. She says of shy students, "You can see them open up more."

Another service email provides for distance learners is the ability to send emailed copies of online sessions for students to refer to in the future simply to review the content of the discussions or to use as sources to continue study of the topics under consideration. W. Joy Lopez of Visions High School Academy wrote in *T.H.E. Journal,* "At the end of each session, students receive an e-mailed copy of their session so that their learning is captured for future reference."

SOURCES: P. Le. 2003, September 16. Online coursework appeals to teenagers. Retrieved September 18, 2003, from **http://www.indystar.com/print/articles/9/074716-3989-P.html**; W. J. Lopez. 2003, August. Content delivery for a virtual high school. *T.H.E. Journal,* 31 (1), 32.

questions. Additionally, because teachers can establish email processes and procedures, email interaction can be offered in private (email) or public (mailing list) formats. When private email is available to students, many feel more comfortable asking questions or requesting clarification without fear of their concerns and questions being seen as "dumb." Mailing lists, on the other hand, offer an email format in which questions and concerns can be automatically sent to all participants. Both public and private email offer channels that support the diversity of communication that might be found in a traditional classroom.

But email also offers an advantage over the typical interaction in a traditional classroom. The teacher's ability to address every student individually via email tends to increase participation. In an email-supported discussion on a topic of concern, a teacher can require that all students participate and respond via email. In this scenario, unlike the classroom, shy and thoughtful students are not overwhelmed by the enthusiastic responses of their more outgoing peers. There is also time for everyone to respond. The pressure to be the first student who has a hand up disappears. Students have enough time to respond within the framework of their own learning characteristics. Email can, in these ways, provide equity of response opportunities for all students and can fully engage everyone in an academic discussion.

In an email-supported discussion, student participation tends to be greater than in the traditional classroom setting.

ON THE WEB! 11.9
Academic Email

• Electronic Conferences

Electronic conferences, or electronic forums, offer a platform for one-to-many communications. These virtual bulletin boards let individuals post messages for all participants to read. Others can then post responses, resulting in a threaded discussion. For distance education, a class electronic conference is usually moderated by the teacher, with all students participating at a convenient time and from any location that offers access to the local network or the Internet. The teacher might post a question or an announcement and ask all students to respond. Students then post their responses or ask additional questions. All students can read all responses and can even save them

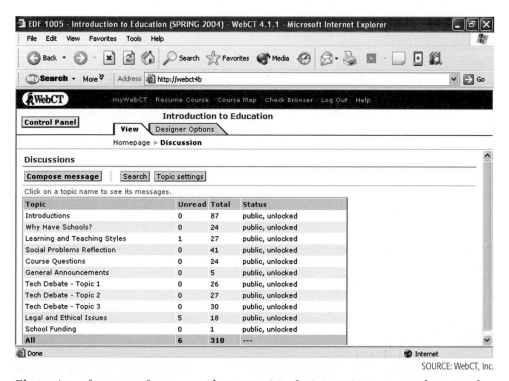

SOURCE: WebCT, Inc.

Electronic conferences or forums provide opportunities for interaction among students in a distance learning environent.

or print them out. This formalized electronic discussion provides an opportunity for thoughtful interaction and the potential for complete note taking because all discussion can be captured and reviewed.

Students can also use electronic conferencing to support distance cooperative learning groups and study groups. With one student acting as moderator, a small group of students can meet asynchronously via an electronic conference to work on a task or share content. Students can thus assemble at a time that is convenient to each of them and from any location and still participate in class activities. Electronic conferencing makes it possible for students to interact with each other on group projects even if they are located in different schools across a district or are homebound. This tool makes it possible for the distance teacher to engage students in social learning as well as with the content.

• Class Web Sites

Many asynchronous technologies and even some synchronous technologies can be combined together in a class **web site** hosted on a school or district network or an Internet hosting service. The class web site can offer a distance student a single virtual place to go, at any time and from any place, to find all of the resources and tools needed to engage in a class. For district distance education classes, the class web site can offer an easy-to-access repository of all materials, a place where all students from any location can interact, and an efficacious communication tool for the teacher. Even if students meet synchronously via compressed video, a supporting class web site can become an important resource that will help to meet both anticipated and unanticipated needs.

▌ Providing Interactivity via Distance Support Technologies

Both synchronous and asynchronous technologies support distance delivery not only by providing a channel for transmission of content, but also by providing a platform for interactivity. Unlike early distance education programs, in which instruction emanated from the teacher and learners remained essentially passive, today's technology-enhanced distance programs provide many opportunities for student-to-teacher and peer-to-peer interaction. Just as in the traditional classroom, the distance virtual learning environment can offer a variety of communication methods to meet learners' needs and preferences. A master teacher in a school district can present content to students across multiple schools or to those who are homebound via video, voice, or data. Then that same distance educator can have students engage in group activities that are not restricted by their particular location. Last, because school schedules may differ across a district, asynchronous technologies can offer a solution to scheduling problems. With these new tools at a teacher's disposal, it is no wonder that distance education programs are expanding at an amazing rate. Given its potential to emulate classroom experiences fairly accurately, distance education's early promises may soon be realized.

⬤⎡ Alternative Delivery to Enhance ⎣ Traditional Classrooms

Progress in making distance education programs more effective has benefited traditional education as well. Many of the techniques and support technologies that were originally introduced for distance education have proved to be useful in traditional classrooms. These alternative learning delivery options, when added to traditional delivery, offer more dynamic and diverse teaching and learning opportunities. Syn-

In an electronic conference, questions, answers, and announcements can be posted for all to read.

ON THE WEB! 11.10
Classrooms on the Web

Instructional techniques developed for distance education can also be used effectively in traditional classrooms.

connecting THEORY to PRACTICE

Distance Technologies and Social Learning

Older models of noninteractive distance learning were, at their core, passive and isolated experiences. Although independent writing skills inherent in older models are as important as ever, with email messages and attachments (such as written work for sharing, peer-and-teacher commentary, grading, revising, and the ensuing dialog), a real sense of community can be established. Furthermore, with the capacity to see the participants in a virtual communication, isolation can be essentially eliminated. With videoconferencing and interactive web-based communications becoming commonplace, all with audio and video enhancement, social learning opportunities can be replicated in electronic classrooms. And with the added enrichment of communication among people from every corner of the planet, social learning takes on new, expanded possibilities. Age, ethnicity, location, and nationality need erect no barriers to contact among the peoples of this world. At any time, for any length of time, from anywhere to everywhere, distance learning opens the doors to students to relate to the diverse community of humanity of which they are "a piece of the whole, a part of the main," as John Donne phrased our place in the universe. The limited, walled-in social learning opportunities of the traditional classroom can be expanded in ways that were previously never even imagined.

chronous and asynchronous technologies and methods can add a new and distinctive teaching and learning dimension to classroom instruction when implemented by creative teachers. Adapting distance education lessons to the traditional classroom creates an alternative learning format that offers teachers and learners interesting and productive new tools. These can make instruction more engaging and can better meet learners' individual needs.

ON THE WEB! 11.11
Distance Education Tools

Using Distance Education Tools for Alternative Learning

Although the typical use of textbooks for independent reading assignments is asynchronous, most classrooms are by definition synchronous. Most synchronous technologies and methods that are used in a distance education classroom would therefore be redundant in the traditional classroom. But when you begin to use asynchronous techniques from distance education in your classroom, you may find surprising results. Table 11.5 lists alternative learning strategies that can be used in traditional classrooms. These techniques are discussed in the following sections in the context of how they might enhance different aspects of the teaching and learning process.

Individualizing Instruction

The first application of asynchronous tools is in the area of **individualized instruction.** Traditional classrooms are designed to provide group instruction and to supplement that instruction with individual activities. Because children do not all learn in the same way or at the same pace, group instruction might not be as effective as intended. Distance education programs require an individualized approach because groups might or might not actually meet. Some of the techniques that are used for individualizing distance education can become important tools for traditional teachers who are seeking a supplement to group instruction. Posting classroom announcements and reminders on an electronic conference can provide students an additional resource to refer to when questions arise. Emailing class assignment calendars to parents can open lines of communication. Creating a class web site that houses content, activities, and review exercises can offer students an opportunity to revisit classroom instruction at the time and pace that works best for them. These methods and support technologies can supplement classroom group instruction and further individualize it to better meet student needs.

TABLE 11.5   DISTANCE EDUCATION TOOLS FOR ALTERNATIVE LEARNING IN TRADITIONAL CLASSES

Alternative Learning Strategy	Application in the Tradtional Setting
Online Lectures Make PowerPoint lecture or lecture notes available on network or web site.	• Provides opportunities for self-paced review of class lectures • Provides access to missed lectures for absent students • Offers review opportunities before exams
Course Calendars Post announcements and calendar on class web site or school network.	• Makes due dates available outside of class • Provides access to announcements and dates for parents • Allows for easy updating over weekends and vacations
Online Activities Post activities on class web site or school network.	• Makes activities accessible outside of class • Allows for making corrections or adjustments to activities • Provides students an opportunity to explore coming activities to better budget time

Online Interactivity
Conduct online conferences and chats; offer one-to-one interaction via email.
	• Conferences and chats provide opportunities outside of class to
	  • share concerns and exchange ideas
	  • work on group activities
	  • form study groups
	  • review materials prior to tests
	• Email provides for
	  • private teacher-to-student interaction after class hours
	  • student-to-student exchange of ideas
	  • clarification of content or procedures after class hours

Web-Based Assessments Offer online practice tests.	• Provides opportunities to practice content outside of class hours • Provides readiness feedback prior to exams

▍Promoting Interaction

The traditional classroom's large-group format might not be conducive to providing equal opportunity for **interaction.** In our often overcrowded classrooms and for students who are naturally reserved, this format is not optimal. The same distance education strategies that make it possible for all students to interact in the virtual classroom can also provide opportunity for all students to interact in a traditional classroom. An electronic conference on an important aspect of content can offer an opportunity for every student to express a view, or it can provide a place for a group's consensus opinion to be posted. Email can provide a way for students to ask private questions of their teacher or to submit homework even when they are absent. Voice mail can give parents a way to communicate with their child's teacher without having to play telephone tag. All of these communication technologies, when implemented by creative teachers, provide new avenues for interactivity between and among the teacher, students, and their parents.

Distance education can provide interaction and enhance independent learning.

▍Enhancing Independent Learning

The final area in which distance methodologies and tools can enhance and provide alternatives for traditional classrooms is in their emphasis on **independent learning.** In traditional classroom processes, students are often expected to rigorously follow specific instructions. This approach facilitates the smooth functioning of a large group, but it tends to make individuals dependent. The obvious message of this type of

IN THE CLASSROOM

The Whole Is More Than the Total of Its Parts: Enhancing Traditional Teaching

Thinkport (http://www.thinkport.org) is a program of the Maryland Digital Schools Project, whose purpose is helping teachers find ways to use distance education in their regular teaching assignments. Gail Porter Long is the project director and Christie Timms is the project manager. Thinkport offers online field trips and interactives which are total packages, ready for classroom use as extensions of in-class teaching.

Field trips available in this format include "Maryland Roots," "Pathways to Freedom," "Bay Trippers," "Picasso," "The Story of Anne Arundel County," and "Frederick County," and interactives include "Knowing Edgar Allen Poe," "Sense and Dollars," "Enviro-mysteries," and "Plastic Fork Diaries." The field trip "Picasso: The Early Years, 1892–1906" was developed with the help of a Verizon grant and begins with "First Glance—About This Site." The links "In Your Eyes" and "Take a Look" allow students to see Picasso's work during this period, as well as interviews with people from the National Gallery of Art. The link "Vantage Point" offers a video and follow-up participatory activities designed to create an interdisciplinary environment for students in math, social studies, and language arts classes. Instructional materials include "Questions to Ask of a Work of Art," addressing "Visual Inventory," "How the Parts Work Together," "Interpretation: Theme and Meaning," and "Judgment." An extensive list of resources, both online and in hard copy, is also given.

"Reflections," "Online Tours," and "Take a Look" are sections within the virtual field trips that give teachers everything they need to take their students on these trips—minus "the yellow school bus." Bill Barnes, a teacher at Ridgely Middle School in Lutherville, Maryland, is featured on Thinkport's "Spotlight on Educators" page. He says he has taken his students "on virtual journeys to places that they otherwise might never visit."

SOURCE: Maryland digital schools project: Field trips and interactives. 2003. Retrieved July 1, 2003, from http://www.thinkport.org/classroom/oftinteractive/default.tp.

---

instruction is to act only in accordance with specific instructions. The implicit message may be to not act if instructions are not specifically given—that is, to be passive in a new situation. This promotes dependency when, in fact, we actually want our learners to be self-initiating and responsible for their own learning. Because the distance environment cannot, by its very nature, provide continual instruction and redirection, its strategies must rely on a more independent and responsible approach to learning. The parameters of the virtual instructional environment thus foster independence. Using some distance education techniques as a supplement to traditional delivery can have the same effect. Placing student activities on a web page rather than handing out copies in class requires students to seek out the work they need. Emailing a class calendar of due dates or adding it to your web site helps students take responsibility for paying attention to the posted due dates. Making copies of your PowerPoint lecture available electronically offers students the chance to be responsible for content missed due to absence. These strategies, while integral to a distance education class, can become powerful tools in helping students gain independence in traditional classes as well.

Issues in Implementing Distance and Alternative Delivery Systems

Teacher and Student Readiness

Both distance and alternative learning systems require that teachers and students be ready to work within a new environment. There are two key aspects to their necessary **readiness:** readiness to accept new roles and readiness to work with new technologies. First, teachers and students must be prepared for new roles. In distance and alternative learning, teachers become guides and architects of complex learning environ-

ON THE WEB! 11.12
Are We Ready for Distance Education?

Distance education participants may need additional training.

ments. Less time is spent in direct instruction, and more is spent in creating a rich instructional environment and then guiding students through it. Students become less passive and more responsible learners. They must be ready to think through options rather than passively follow instructions. They must take more responsibility for their learning. These new roles may require some very specific orientation and training for both teacher and students for them to be ready to work in the new environments of these delivery systems.

A second type of readiness relates to being prepared to use the technologies selected to support these new environments. Both teachers and students may be expected to frequently use technologies they do not know or have not yet become comfortable with. When learners are expected to take more responsibility in these delivery formats, it can be frustrating if the technologies they need to use turn out to be a barrier to their tasks. When a teacher creates instruction to be delivered by a particular technology, it is essential for that teacher to fully understand the technology's capabilities and limitations. For teachers and students, it may be necessary to participate in very specific training sessions before being able to fully use a distance or alternative learning environment.

Preparation and Classroom Management Time

Teachers who use distance and alternative learning techniques might find themselves surprised by an increase in the demands on their time. Distance learning and alternative learning often require a greater allocation of available planning time because the learning environment must be carefully mapped out in advance of its implementation. Furthermore, because distance education methods can sharply increase interactivity and because every student may now respond, teachers might find the number of responses overwhelming. Planning for instruction and responding to students will require that you carefully think through your time management strategies. Few would disagree that comprehensive planning and full interaction are both highly desirable, but for many teachers, finding adequate time to do both may be a problem. Districts that are interested in supporting distance and alternative instruction need to consider the requirements inherent in these alternative instructional systems and make adequate arrangements to meet them.

Technical Support

Sufficient technical support is necessary for distance education to operate smoothly.

In implementing distance and alternative delivery systems that are supported by technology, it is critical to be sure that adequate **technical support** is in place. If instruction is dependent on a class web site and the district web server hosting that site goes down, how will instruction continue? If a class interacts via compressed video, what happens if one of the components does not function? Although technical problems are often unavoidable, adequate and readily available technicians, backup systems, and clear direction as to how to proceed if systems fail are critical for success. Too often, support personnel and related support costs are not fully considered in determining whether or not to engage in distance or alternative delivery systems. Even if technical support is not the central consideration, nevertheless it is one of the critical components for successful implementation.

Instructional Support

Learners in traditional classrooms have a variety of **instructional supports** readily available. In addition to the teacher being present for clarification and questions, a media center offering a wide variety of resources is also typically present. Some schools may also provide tutoring programs for students who need additional help. Together, these resources provide a comprehensive instructional support system for students. However, in a distance environment, some of these supports may be missing. In a cross-district distance course, the local media centers might not have the resources available to supplement and support the instruction. It may also be too costly to replicate resources at all participating schools. How, then, can distance learning students access the resources they need? If the students need extra help, where can they find the tutoring support they need? These questions must be addressed in determining how distance education systems will be implemented. Solutions may be as new and divergent as the programs they support. Such solutions may include providing tutor telephone hotlines and homework help chat rooms. Whatever the solutions that are finally chosen, it is important to address the issue of academic support as a critical component of a distance education program before that program is implemented.

Copyright

As you learned in Interchapter 4, respecting copyright is a critical issue for teachers. The use of copyrighted materials in distance learning and on the Internet brought concerns over fair use in the digital age to the forefront. In 1998, Congress asked the U.S. Copyright Office to address the issue. The Technology Education and Copyright Harmonization (TEACH) Act was introduced in the legislature in 2001 as a result of the report produced by the Copyright Office. With the passage of the TEACH Act in 2002, many guidelines related to fair use for distance education were clarified, yet many issues still remain. For example, the TEACH Act conditions for the use of copyrighted materials are somewhat complex and often more restrictive than the fair use guidelines operating in traditional face-to-face classrooms. Further, restrictions under the TEACH Act limit the circumstances for use, which may in turn impact the broader copyright policies adopted by the institution offering the distance education program.

Clearly, copyright will remain an issue for all teachers, but particularly those teaching in a distance environment. However, as distance education becomes even more commonplace and instructional needs become more evident, policy decisions and law will no doubt evolve to better address these concerns. Indeed, the TEACH Act is likely to be just the first step in the resolution of copyright issues in distance education.

Reinventing the Classroom: The Future of Distance and Alternative Delivery

Technology is changing our society, and that changing society is putting new demands upon our schools. In response, our schools are changing. One aspect of the change is our perception of a classroom. Must the teaching and learning environment be a physical space? Can we offer effective instruction and help our students engage in meaningful learning without time and location constraints?

Whatever your views and experiences at this point, it is clear that many schools are currently attempting to create and implement high-quality distance and alternative learning programs. The number of schools, organizations, and even businesses that offer instruction at a distance increases each year. You may be asked to participate in such programs sometime during your professional career. To adequately address such a possibility, your awareness of the methods and technologies that are currently being used and that may be used in the future to reinvent classrooms is a good start. How will classrooms evolve as the Information Age unfolds? That is difficult to predict with any precision. What is clear is that both traditional and nontraditional class-

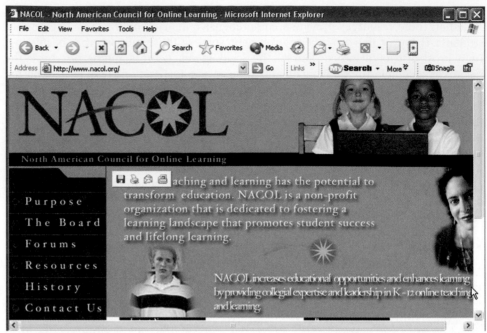

SOURCE: North American Council for Online Learning

Distance learning organizations are helping to define standards, promote quality, and support dialog among distance educators.

rooms will evolve and may be completely reinvented to better address our changing world. Eventually, perhaps, there will be no distinction between traditional education, alternative education, and distance education. Perhaps, instead, they will all be facets of the same complex and diverse educational system, offering options to meet every learner's unique situation and needs. As the future of instructional delivery unfolds, you can be sure that your classroom will be affected. Learning about and preparing for such potential change may be your best strategy for successfully changing with it.

KEY TERMS

alternative delivery systems   350
asynchronous   357
backup system   355
conference call   358
correspondence courses   348
distance education   346
electronic conferences   365
electronic mail   364
evaluation   356
fax   364
feedback   356
independent learning   368
individualized instruction   367

instructional supports   370
interaction   368
Internet chat   361
phone bridge   359
readiness   369
speakerphone   357
synchronous   356
technical support   370
telephone   357
videoconferencing   360
voice mail   363
web site   366

STUDENT ACTIVITIES

CHAPTER REVIEW

1. What is distance education? How does it overcome temporal and spatial barriers?
2. Describe the two major impacts of distance education on K–12 teachers.
3. What early technologies enhanced distance education via correspondence? How did these impact student isolation?
4. What are alternative learning systems? How might they enhance traditional education?
5. Why is planning even more critical for distance delivery than for traditional instruction? How does planning differ between traditional and distance delivery?
6. Why is giving feedback a challenge in distance environments? How can this challenge be met?
7. What issues surround student evaluation in a distance environment? How might they be resolved?
8. What is the difference between synchronous and asynchronous delivery? What technologies support synchronous delivery? What technologies support asynchronous delivery?
9. How do synchronous and asynchronous technologies support interaction?
10. What types of support are critical to the success of distance education? Why?

WHAT DO YOU THINK?

1. There has been much discussion about whether distance education can provide students with instruction that is equal in quality to what they have received from traditional education. Do you think an equivalent experience is possible via distance delivery? Why or why not?
2. Distance learning and alternative learning require a significant use of technology to support instructional delivery. How does the inclusion of the technology affect the instructional experience for better and for worse?
3. One of the primary issues associated with implementation of distance education revolves around the teacher's ability to adequately and appropriately evaluate student progress and competencies. Do you believe that this is an issue? Why or why not?
4. Synchronous and asynchronous delivery both enhance and potentially impede instruction in different ways. What are your key issues and concerns related to each of these systems?
5. What role do you think distance education will play in education as the Information Age unfolds and technologies improve? What advantages and disadvantages for teachers and students do you foresee?

LEARNING TOGETHER!

These activities are best done in groups of three to five.

1. Research and examine your state's initiatives in distance education at the K–12 and postsecondary levels. On the basis of your research, prepare a summary of the programs that are available or under way and the pros and cons of each.
2. Each group member should locate and create an annotated list of three web sites offering access to technologies appropriate for distance or alternative delivery. Compare your finds, and select your top five sites. Summarize these to share with your class.

3. Imagine that your group has been asked to develop a districtwide unit about your local ecology. You have decided to teach it by using distance delivery. Describe how you will deliver your unit across your district via synchronous and asynchronous systems.

HANDS-ON!

1. Search the Internet for a distance education primer that answers your most pressing questions about distance delivery. Download the primer or print it out, and then summarize its key points to present to your peers.

2. Interview a teacher who has taken or taught a distance education course. Discover through the interview the advantages and disadvantages of this delivery method. Summarize your interview in a word-processed document.

3. Find and try out three synchronous and asynchronous technologies that are available at a school or district or on the Internet. After using each, summarize how it would best be used and its potential strengths and weaknesses in delivering instruction.

4. Search the Internet for information on how distance education programs evaluate students. Find at least five different methods. Summarize your discoveries in a table that describes each evaluation method, explains the types of instruction it can best be used with, and indicates the issues associated with its use. Be prepared to share your table with your peers.

5. Email three distance education teachers you find on the Internet. In your email, ask what aspects of teacher readiness and student readiness need to be addressed before engaging in a distance or alternative delivery program. Create a readiness chart that includes the critical points suggested by the teachers.

More from MaryAnn Butler-Pearson

As promised, Dr. MaryAnn Butler-Pearson, a Broward County Teacher of the Year and distance learning coordinator, recognized a significant problem for her county. She then investigated how to meet the needs of what she thought were hundreds of Broward students. With her solution, she found there were actually many more students who could benefit from her approach. See how distance learning benefited this county and will serve as a model for school systems around the country.

MY SOLUTION

It was just at the time when schools in Broward County were struggling to deal with problems in scheduling videoconferenced classes that I became aware of the fledgling Florida Virtual School (FLVS; also know as Florida High School and Florida Online High School). As an academician, I had concerns about the quality of the program. What kind of curriculum could be delivered asynchro-

nously in an online format? After reviewing several of the courses, however, I became a believer. When I met with executive director Julie Young and some of her staff and learned about the student-centered, curriculum-driven philosophy of FLVS, I became an advocate. The format developed by FLVS includes the highly touted but seldom-met needs for critical-thinking skills, efficient time management, self-discipline, and accepted responsibility for learning on the part of the students.

Seeing the need for high-quality, rigorous, yet attainable virtual learning, I arranged for our school district to become an affiliate of FLVS, which allowed Broward students to take online classes from FLVS faculty. This arrangement continued for three years and met with a high degree of success. It was during the third year of our affiliation that I realized that the demand from our very large school system, the fifth-largest in the nation, would soon outdistance the ability of FLVS to provide virtual seats for our students. Time proved me correct when we had almost as many students on the waiting list as were enrolled in virtual courses. I visited Julie Young and requested that Broward County teachers have the opportunity to teach the award-winning FLVS curriculum. A few months later, she presented us with the option of being an in-state franchise of FLVS. A most supportive school board allotted initial district money to fund the pilot program, and Broward Virtual Education (BVEd) was born! During the 2001–2002 school year, six successful Broward County teachers were trained in the curriculum, pedagogy, technology skills, and philosophy of FLVS. During the first year of BVEd, we served approximately 700 students in nine courses. The passing rate was an astonishing 91 percent! Some naysayers insisted that our students were only those from higher socioeconomic families who attended the higher-achieving high schools and that most likely there were few minority students. An in-depth study was done to identify our clientele. The results proved to be most satisfying: not only was the largest number of BVEd course users from lower-achieving high schools, but also the ethnic and gender demographics were almost identical to those of the entire school district.

Because of its success, the program received district funding for a second year. The enrollments nearly doubled, as did the staff. The number of course offerings increased to thirty-five, because the schools demanded it. Students all over the district were able to accelerate their graduation, make up lost credits for failed courses, take courses not readily available to them at their high schools, and resolve the schedule conflicts that had formerly prevented them from earning credits in desired or necessary courses. Students who were hospitalized or homebound for extended periods of time were able to participate in the virtual courses. Students who traveled as performing artists or athletes could still "attend" school and earn their high school credits. The age of virtual education had arrived in Broward County, Florida.

The 2003–2004 school year marked the third and most successful year yet for virtual education in Broward County and in the state of Florida. FLVS now boasted six in-state franchises, BVEd still being the largest by far. The Florida legislature recognized virtual education as eligible for state full-time-equivalent funding, a nationwide first. The wisdom of Florida legislators and their acknowledgment that students today live in a virtual environment has advanced K–12 education in our state into the twenty-first century. The Broward Teachers Union has written into its contract with the school district specific language with respect to distance learning teachers. The school district has adopted an official policy that addresses distance learning. BVEd is prepared to serve approximately 3,000–4,000 students (full- and part-time) and has been given a Florida Department of Education school number, making it officially a high school. BVEd has applied for accreditation. Currently, there are over a dozen full-time and sixteen adjunct teachers, additional support staff in the areas of technology and clerical assistance, and one administrator. Students register 24/7 and are officially enrolled in classes twice each month. Courses run year-round so that students can use this opportunity when they find a need for it and can study their courses asynchronously, at times and places best for them. Students, their parents, school personnel, and district staff have recognized the success of the program. The district's school board has pledged continued support and has encouraged the growth of BVEd so that all students may be given the opportunity to learn in a virtual environment. BVEd has helped district schools reduce class size as mandated by the vote of the people of Florida in 2002. The Florida Department of Education selected BVEd to be the recipient of a $300,000 Enhancing Education through Technology grant. Additional grants have been solicited and awarded. The fiscal support from the 2003 state legislature assured continued money for virtual education in our state. The validation provided from these sources has given impetus to our efforts to provide our students with the best and most effective education possible and the acquisition of the skills and attitudes necessary to succeed in the twenty-first century.

Those interested in learning more about K–12 virtual education or in joining the North America Council for Online Learning (NACOL), the fastest-growing national organization for K–12 virtual schools, should visit **http://www.nacol.org**.

For more information on BVEd, go to the web site **http:// www.bved.net** *or contact MaryAnn Butler-Pearson, Ed.D., at Broward County Schools,* **mbutlerp@browardschools.com**. *For more information on the Florida Virtual School, see* **http://www. flvs.net**.

CHAPTER 12

Issues in Implementing Technology in Schools

This chapter addresses these ISTE National Educational Technology Standards for Teachers:

II. Planning and designing learning environments and experiences

Teachers plan and design effective learning environments and experiences supported by technology. Teachers

A. design developmentally appropriate learning opportunities that apply technology-enhanced instructional strategies to support the diverse needs of learners.

B. apply current research on teaching and learning with technology when planning learning environments and experiences

C. identify and locate technology resources and evaluate them for accuracy and suitability.

D. plan for the management of technology resources within the context of learning activities.

E. plan strategies to manage student learning in a technology-enhanced environment.

IV. Assessment and evaluation

Teachers apply technology in a variety of effective assessment and evaluation strategies. Teachers

A. apply technology in assessing student learning of subject matter using a variety of assessment techniques.

B. use technology resources to collect and analyze data, interpret results, and communicate findings to improve instructional practice and maximize student learning.

C. apply multiple methods of evaluation to determine students' appropriate use of technology resources for learning, communication, and productivity.

V. Productivity and professional practice

Teachers use technology resources to enhance their productivity and professional practice. Teachers

A. use technology resources to engage in ongoing professional development and lifelong learning.

B. continually evaluate and reflect on professional practice to make informed decisions regarding the use of technology in support of student learning.

C. apply technology to increase productivity.

D. use technology to communicate and collaborate with peers, parents, and the larger community in order to nurture student learning.

VI. Social, ethical, legal, and human issues

Teachers understand the social, ethical, legal, and human issues surrounding the use of technology in PK–12 schools and apply that understanding in practice. Teachers

A. model and teach legal and ethical practice related to technology use.

B. apply technology resources to enable and empower learners with diverse backgrounds, characteristics, and abilities.

C. identify and use technology resources that affirm diversity.

D. promote safe and healthy use of technology resources.

E. facilitate equitable access to technology resources for all students.

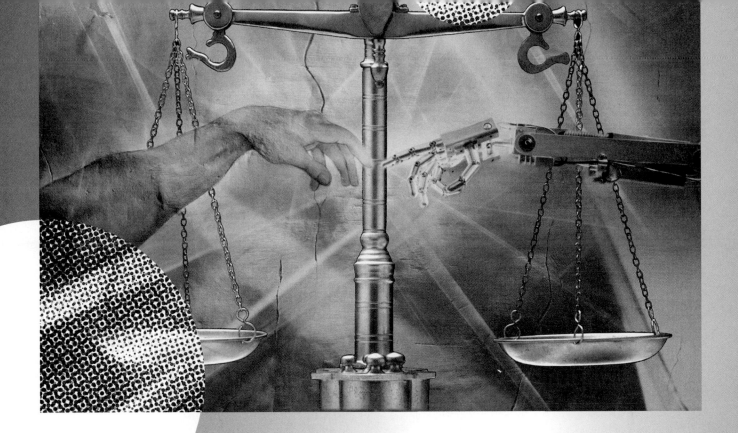

You have learned much about the many types of technologies that are available for teachers and their students. You have also learned about the theories related to teaching and learning and the process of designing effective instruction. As a result of the competencies you have gained so far in this course, you have already taken the first significant steps in using educational technology effectively in your classroom. But understanding the broader process inherent in implementing technology in schools and in districts requires that you expand your technological perspective even further. Indeed, the process of acquiring and implementing educational technologies in a school has its own set of challenges, both academic and administrative, of which you must become aware. Once a teacher has decided which technologies would be best for use in the classroom, these greater implementation issues can directly affect those initial decisions. Implementation issues, the concerns that arise in working through the details of acquiring and setting up a school's technology, may even alter the choices that have already been made. The implementation concerns that arise can be so significant that they can even change the direction and nature of a school's technology initiative. Will the preferred technology work with other types of technologies already in place? Must a school or district ensure that the technology decision making be strategic, that is, made within a larger school planning framework? Are there any legal, social, or ethical issues to attend to in implementing a technology initiative? How will technology selections fit into the future and with the technologies that are on the horizon? Will the desired technology be outdated in just a few years? Questions like these must be answered to ensure a successful technology initiative and implementation. These broad implementation issues and concerns are the focus of this chapter.

As a teacher, you might think that such concerns have little to do with you. That is not the case. You will find that teachers have a unique and significant role in addressing many of the issues associated with implementing technology in schools. You might be asked to serve on the technology strategic planning team, you might serve as the chair of your grade-level technology committee, or you might want to become your school's technology coordinator. Regardless of the role you choose, you will find that you will be more prepared to understand and successfully address technology implementation issues after you have fully examined them.

In Chapter 12, you will

- Examine legal, ethical, and social issues that arise when a school implements technology

- Explore the technological trends that affect schools

- Examine the ways in which schools are likely to change as they progress in the Digital Age

Meet David Thornburg

Dr. David Thornburg is a well-known author, futurist, technologist, humanist, musician, and popular keynote speaker all rolled into one amazing personality. His warm, friendly manner makes a room full of strangers feel at ease immediately, even when he is addressing an audience of thousands. We feel most fortunate to have met him at a Florida Educational Technology Conference many years ago when he agreed to spend some of his uncommitted evening time speaking with a group of doctoral students attending the conference.

Most important to us, Dr. Thornburg has a firm handle on the current status of technology in education and training, and he has a clairvoyant sense of where we are going and how to get there. He led you into your study of ways to teach with technology in the foreword to this book. Therefore, it is most fitting that he now lead you into the future in this final chapter.

────────────

Al P. Mizell (APM): Throughout this book, Dr. Thornburg, we've examined various technologies and ways that they might be integrated into the curriculum. As a futurist with an emphasis on the evolution of technology, would you describe what you see as some of the major social issues in the Digital Age and where you see them going in the future?

David Thornburg (DT): The growth of technology access in homes is staggering. Some research indicates that 78 percent of households with teenagers have Internet access. McDonald's restaurants are installing WiFi networks for customer use. Basically, today's youth are increasingly living in an anywhere, anytime world when it comes to access to information through the web. This does not mean that access is universal, however. High-density, upscale communities have greater access than rural areas or areas that are economically challenged. As this chapter points out, the digital divide still exists, largely on economic grounds. Although this issue has been with us since the start of the current web, it grows more essential that we address this topic with strong action. An increasing number of services provided by communities and commercial enterprises expect that clients have Internet access. Special airfares, for example, are generally offered only through the web. Government tax filings are increasingly facilitated by web access. As important as it is to celebrate the growth of access to the vast majority of our citizens, it is equally important to address the needs of those who are being left behind.

Fortunately, schools, libraries, and community centers are three places where access can be provided to the disenfranchised, so long as these places have the needed equipment in place and are accessible on evenings and weekends, as well as during normal operating hours. I think it is useful for schools to conduct informal audits of home access to measure the number of children who lack adequate access. Once the number is known, steps can be taken to address the problem.

APM: In this Digital Age, there are many ethical issues, ranging from how we use our freedom of speech to academic dishonesty. Would you identify one of these ethical issues and share your thoughts on the way you think it will be handled in the future?

DT: There are several ethical issues that need to be addressed. Some of these are explored in this chapter. For example, it is essential for students to understand the importance of citing all sources for their work. The ethics of citation actually enhances the student who shows the depth of research leading to his or her selection of material to reference. In fact, academic honesty and copyright infringement are two sides of the same coin. Even when material is incorporated under fair use, citation is essential. I am amazed to find otherwise upstanding professionals who seem to think that some resources posted electronically are fair game for appropriation, just because the capture of digital documents is so easy.

A deeper question relates to how best to address the issue of misappropriation of copyrighted material. For example, those who share music files through peer-to-peer tools are not claiming authorship of the copied materials, yet their sharing of the music may constitute violation of copyright laws. The music industry initially chose to respond in punitive ways, successfully suing, for example, a twelve-year-old girl found guilty of file sharing. In this case, the industry (in my view) failed to get an important message: customers want to get music by the song, not by the CD. Those my age recall that this is the way it used to be in the days of the 45 rpm record. We have moved from an album- to a song-centered culture once again, but the music industry ignored this desire for years, concentrating instead on suing the very people it wants as customers. However, through the efforts of Apple and others outside the music industry, it is now as easy to legally purchase songs online as it is to steal them. The rapid success of these new song-sale tools (which could have been implemented years ago) confirms that, given the chance, downloaders will pay for music by the song.

And this leads to an important point. Laws need to acknowledge shifting technologies by moving beyond the blanket application of rules for an atom-based world to a world where commerce takes place largely through the transfer of bits. Customers may want to be served differently in this new world This does not mean that theft, slander, or any of the myriad crimes found both on and off the Internet should suddenly be excused, only that some effort should be expended to look beneath the efforts of some people to circumvent the old ways of doing things.

A deeper ethical issue is that of freedom of speech combined with censorship. This topic is also explored in this chapter, so I will weigh in here with my own views.

First, Internet filters destroy the opportunity for educators to teach students ethical issues surrounding the Internet. Since these filters are either not present at home or are easily disabled by any twelve-year-old, this leaves young people with unfettered Internet access during those times when adult guidance and instruction would be most useful. That said, there is a tremendous amount of trash on the Internet. Spam clogs our mailboxes, pop-ups interfere with web browsing, and the "noise" sometimes seems to swamp the signal. Although many of us avail ourselves of software to block some of this undesired material, rudeness prevails on the Net as much as in dinnertime calls from telemarketers.

The challenge lies in responding to these problems in ways that preserve our individual freedom of access. For example, broadcast news is often tilted to reflect the point of view dominant in the country in which it is broadcast. Recent attempts by the FCC to permit further consolidation of broadcast and printed news media suggest that diversity of choice in news-related matters is in decline. But, counter to this trend, we also see the rapid and explosive growth of blogging, through which anyone with an opinion can have a web site devoted to his/her rants on any topic. And it is in the Internet that I see our greatest hope.

As broadcasting (with limited spectrum space) becomes more uniform in its presentation of news, the Internet remains a vast frontier in which each visitor can be both a receiver and a contributor of information. As long as this power remains in the hands of the people, I am hopeful that rational dialog in the world of highly managed sound-bite journalism can prevail.

Dr. Thornburg rightly perceives the many issues associated with the next evolution of technology. In this chapter, you will learn more about these issues and the emerging technology trends that cause them. We will check back with Dr. Thornburg at the end of this chapter for some parting insights.

SOURCE: Interview with Dr. David Thornburg conducted by Al P. Mizell. Reprinted by permission of David D. Thornburg, Ph.D., director, Global Operations, Thornburg Center.

Planning for Technology

Because of the cost and complexity of acquiring and implementing the many educational technologies you have explored in this text, districts and schools typically begin the process with the creation of a formal technology plan. The technology plan is strategic in nature. This means it is a long-range plan and follows a series of defined steps common to **strategic planning.** Interchapter 5, following this chapter, articulates the process of strategic planning for technology. As you review this Interchapter, you will begin to understand why school districts spend so much time and energy preparing for technology acquisition. Even though school districts often have personnel who have specific responsibility for planning and implementing the technology plan, districts recognize the importance of including all stakeholders in the process. As an educator, you are a key **stakeholder** in the plan and its outcomes. As a result, you are very likely to be asked to participate in the strategic planning for technology in your school or district. Indeed, your active participation will benefit both you and your students. If planning were completed from a technical perspective alone, many of your academic concerns and issues related to technology acquisition and implementation might not get the serious attention they deserve.

So far, you have learned a great deal about the many traditional and digital technologies that will be or could be available to you when you teach. This knowledge, along with that which you will acquire in the remainder of this chapter regarding technology issues and emerging technology, will help you to be an effective participant in the strategic planning process. Your competencies in educational technologies will make you a most valuable contributor to your school's technology plan.

Once technology is planned for and implementation has begun, many issues and concerns beyond those that are technical arise. A variety of legal, social, and ethical issues result from the use of technologies in schools. Teachers must be aware of these issues to ensure that they create a climate in their classroom that fosters respect for ethics, fairness, and the law as they relate to the implementation of technology. These issues are the subjects of the next section of this chapter.

Legal Issues in the Digital Age

Implementation of technology, whether in the classroom, school, or district, involves a number of legal issues (see Figure 12.1). Some of these issues, such as copyright violations, were of concern in education before the advent of technology. Technology implementation and the ease of accessing and incorporating digital data, including copyrighted text, graphics, video, and audio, exacerbated the problem. Other issues,

Figure 12.1
Issues in the Digital Age
The Digital Age has enhanced education while giving rise to significant issues.

- Copyright and fair use
- Privacy
- Acceptable use
- Software Piracy

The Digital Divide

- Freedom of speech
- Privacy
- Academic dishonestly

such as the inequity of access to technology, sometimes called the **digital divide,** have arisen as a result of technology. Another set of issues involves ethical questions. Each of these issues affects how technology is ultimately implemented at all levels of an educational institution, from the classroom to the entire district. As a professional, you are responsible for becoming aware of these implementation issues and acting in accordance with professional ethics.

ON THE WEB! 12.1
Legal Issues in the Digital Age

Copyright and Fair Use

You have already been introduced to many of the issues related to **copyright.** In Interchapter 4, you discovered that although materials protected by the copyright laws should generally not be used without the owner's permission, there are some occasions when such use is allowed. **Fair use** guidelines describe circumstances under which a teacher can use copyrighted materials in face-to-face instruction. The TEACH Act offers similar guidelines for the use of copyrighted materials in distance learning. Perhaps the easiest way for educators to use such materials is to ask themselves four basic questions related to the use of a copyrighted work. These questions, summarized in Table 12.1, are focused on the instructional intent of the use and the potential

Copyright protects the rights of the owner of intellectual property.

TABLE 12.1   FAIR USE GUIDELINES SELF-TEST

When concerned about whether or not to use copyrighted materials, answer this self-test to help you decide.

Fair Use Consideration	Ask Yourself:
Purpose and character of use	What is the intended use? • Are you using it for educational purposes? • Is the use noncommercial in nature?
Nature of the copyrighted work	What type of work is it? • Is the work primarily factual in nature? • Does the work contain relatively little creative or imaginative substance?
Amount and sustainability of the portion used	How much of the work do you intend to use?
Effect of the use on the work's marketability	What impact does this kind of use have on the market for the work? • Would the use substitute for purchasing the original? • Would the use negatively affect the market potential of the original?

If your intended classroom use of copyrighted materials falls within fair use, then observe the following guidelines:

⇨ Use the work only in face-to-face teaching. For distance learning, follow the guidelines in the TEACH Act.

⇨ Limit copied materials to small amounts of the copyrighted work.

⇨ Avoid making unnecessary copies.

⇨ Be sure to include copyright notice and to attribute the work.

⇨ Limit use to a single class and only one year. You need pemission to use the work repeatedly.

For more detailed information, see Circular 21, "Reproduction of Copyrighted Works by Educators and Librarians," and other related materials at **http://www.loc.gov/copyright**.

ON THE WEB! 12.2
Fair Use Guidelines

impact on the owner of the work. Asking yourself these questions before using copyrighted materials in your classroom will help you to avoid copyright infringement, an illegal act. As copyright law evolves in the Digital Age, new guidelines will emerge. The use of multimedia clips and information from the Internet has developed into an entirely new and complex area of the law. Regardless of the ultimate rulings by legislators or courts, it will continue to be an educator's professional and legal responsibility to stay aware of changes to the law and to model its application in his or her classroom.

Privacy

Every child in your charge, like every citizen in the United States, has a right to **privacy.** For minors, their parents must give permission to share any information about them to which you might be privy as a result of your position as their teacher. Technology has made the sharing of information simple and convenient. Nevertheless, this same convenience can lead to inadvertent or intentional abuse. The right to privacy is one of the most significant issues in the Digital Age, both in society and in education.

Protecting student privacy in the Digital Age is a critical technology implementation issue.

Violations of privacy via technology can take many forms. One of the most significant relates to online privacy. Internet sites that serve children have not been reluctant to gather and share personal information about these children, including their names, addresses, phone numbers, and photographs and even information about their families, all without asking parents' permission to gather the information or to share it. At one time, this was often done simply by asking children to complete a form to gain access to a tempting game or entertainment site. However, the problem became serious enough to lead to a congressional investigation that ultimately resulted in the passage of the Children's Online Privacy Protection Act (COPPA) in October 1998. Given the climate of concern and the passage of this law, how might the law affect you as you protect your students' privacy?

Although the legal landscape dealing with the Internet is continually changing, as a prudent teacher, you should be aware of the steps you should take to protect the privacy of your students. For example, if you want to show a picture of your class or a sample of your students' work on your web site, you need to be sure that you are acting within the stated policies and procedures of your school and district. Typically, schools and districts require that you get written permission from a child's parent or guardian before you post anything regarding that child that would otherwise have been private. When a child turns in work to you, there is usually an assumption that only you will read it. Although it is customary to hang children's work in a classroom, that is different in scope from posting it on the Internet. You typically do not have the right to share a child's work publicly without parental permission. Most importantly, above and beyond the legal issue, indicating on the Internet that a child is in a particular class at a particular school and perhaps even including that child's name can jeopardize the safety of that child. Unsavory individuals can use such information to stalk a child or target the child for crime. Your primary responsibility, above all else, is to protect the safety of the children in your charge. Inadvertently exposing a child to risk by posting information about him or her on the Internet is a violation of your prime responsibility. A prudent teacher will become fully aware of the school and district policies related to posting students' names, pictures, or work on the Internet. The school and/or district policy will guide you in determining how student images or work can be used, as well as when and how parental permissions must be obtained.

Another area of concern is the collection of information about students at web sites they might visit. COPPA addressed this issue as well. Beginning April 21, 2000, operators of web sites directed at children under thirteen had to conform to a series of rules and regulations regarding the request for and handling of personal information about their child visitors. One of the most significant regulations in this rigorous component of COPPA requires that these web site operators obtain verifiable parental permission before collecting personal data from children. Given that children may visit such sites in the course of a school day, what is the teacher's responsibility relative to such permission? COPPA allows teachers to act on behalf of parents during online school activities but does not require them to do so. However, district or school acceptable use policies may interpret this requirement differently. Each teacher should be fully aware of the school or district's acceptable use policy and act in accordance with it.

Because there is so much concern over children's privacy, particularly while online, the Federal Trade Commission has set up an informational web site that provides information to children, parents, and teachers (http://www.ftc.gov/bcp/conline/edcams/kidzprivacy; see Figure 12.2). This site is a source of significant information and resources and should be explored fully by every educator.

Privacy when not online must also be protected. Software that allows you to manage grades and personal data relating to your students must be protected so that no others can access information about them. If the school is networked, such grading software is installed on the network with specific rights for each account. That means that your account, as a teacher, has associated with it the rights to see and use software and data about all of your students. Student accounts have rights that may allow them to see only their own work. To protect student privacy, then, it is important for you to protect your own login and password because they allow access to private student data. Irresponsible sharing of your network account can result in a serious violation of a student's privacy. Even inattentiveness might be damaging. Leaving your computer logged in to the network when you are not using it can make the areas you are privy to available to others. On stand-alone machines that are available for student use, it is best to be sure that no files that may be considered private are stored on a drive that is available for all to use. It is your responsibility to guard the privacy of your students whether you are using the Internet, a network, or a public-access machine in your classroom.

ON THE WEB! 12.3
Online Privacy

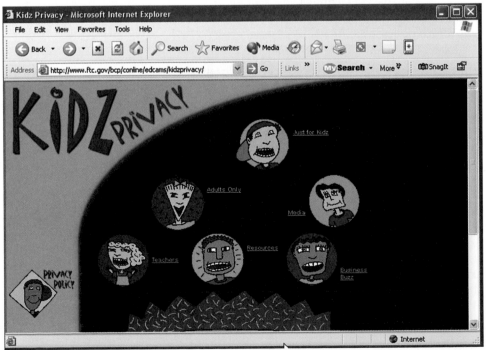

SOURCE: Federal Trade Commission

Figure 12.2
The Federal Trade Commission's Kidz Privacy Web Site
Web sites such as Kidz Privacy offer educators current and relevant information on how to protect their students' privacy.

issues in
teaching
and
technology

Protecting Privacy

ust as you wouldn't post students' grades on your classroom door or tack letters to individual parents about student performance on your bulletin board, so too you must protect privacy in the Digital Age. Review this checklist for ways in which you can protect your students' privacy.

- Don't place confidential data or commentary on any unsecured electronic equipment.

- Guard your login names and passwords.

- Secure storage devices (floppies and CD-RWs) in places where they are not obtainable by people unauthorized to view their contents.

- Don't leave hard copy of assessments, evaluations, and reports of student behavior and achievement on printer trays in common areas.

- Once used, file privileged information, whether on storage devices or on hard copy, in secured spaces or, if no longer needed, shred it (preferably with a crosscut shredder).

- Follow school district policies and procedures in place to guard students' privacy.

- Guard photographs of students as well as text.

- Become aware of classroom and district software that offers parents access to their children's progress by password in read-only format.

Acceptable Use

Teachers must take steps to ensure students' acceptable use of technology.

Once technology is made available to students, it is the obligation of educators to ensure that it is used appropriately. Just as teachers oversee how students utilize textbooks and other media, they have a responsibility, to the extent possible, to ensure that access to and use of technology are consistent with the appropriate academic behaviors expected in the classroom. Just as educators would not allow questionable or inappropriate printed materials into the classroom, so too must they ensure that such materials available via technology be kept out of the classroom. The issues surrounding the use of technology in a manner that protects students from inappropriate behaviors and information are together referred to as **acceptable use** issues.

The most frequently voiced concern involving the acceptable use of technology relates to the Internet. The Internet contains salacious and inappropriate materials that do not belong in the classroom. You can do little to change the nature of the Internet, but a prudent teacher can help to ensure that the Internet is used appropriately in the classroom. Although your actions might not be able to guarantee that your students will never access an inappropriate web site, you can take every step possible to protect them.

The first important action you should take is to be sure that your students understand what constitutes appropriate use. Just as you might begin the school year explaining your expectations of classroom behavior, so too should you explain your expectations of how the Internet should be used in your classroom. Often, this is done through a **code of ethics** for computer use, a set of written expectations and definitions of what is considered appropriate or acceptable use. Codes of ethics should be signed by both students and their parents to ensure that parents too are aware of these expectations. Signed codes should be stored for the duration of the school year. You should check with your school or district for its code of ethics or acceptable use policy. Most districts have established formal acceptable use policies, and schools within those districts are expected to follow them. After you check the details of the policy, it is wise to duplicate it and be sure to have your students and their parents sign it before your students are given Internet access or Internet assignments. If no such formal code has

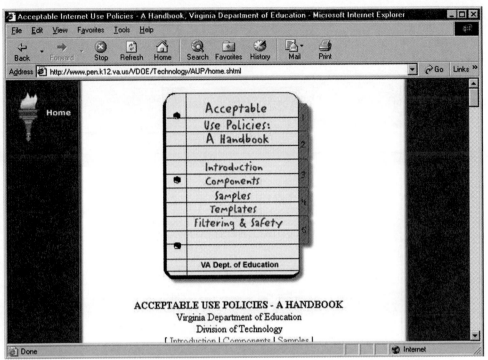

Courtesy of the Virginia Department of Education. Microsoft Internet Explorer® is a registered trademark of Microsoft Corporation.

Figure 12.3
Acceptable Use Policy Web Sites
You can learn about other organizations' acceptable use policies online.

been established in your school or district, you should discuss these concerns with your school administrator. You might also want to review examples of various codes of ethics to determine what you might expect (see Figure 12.3).

Many networked school systems have implemented **filtering software,** that is, software that filters out unacceptable Internet sites so students cannot access them (see Figure 12.4). Although not always successful in catching unacceptable sites, such filters do improve the chances of intervening if a child accidentally or deliberately attempts to access an inappropriate site.

Typically, filtering software will not allow access to off-limit sites, and many packages also gather the names of the users who are attempting to access such sites. Because users might innocently mis-key a URL or click on a link that inadvertently brings them to an unacceptable site, network administrators typically take minimal action, if any, for an occasional attempted access. However, if a user repeatedly and purposefully tries to access inappropriate sites using a school network, the administrator does typically track such activity and records it. For students and teachers alike, such activity is grounds for disciplinary action.

ON THE WEB! 12.4
Appropriate Use

Software Piracy

Copying software to share with others or installing software on multiple machines when only one copy was purchased is software **piracy.** It is a violation of copyright laws to make and distribute copies of software or to install illegal copies of software on the machines in your classroom. Just as it is a violation to make copies of a music CD or a movie on videotape, it is illegal to copy and distribute software packages. The owners of the software have invested considerable resources in creating the software, and they have the right to sell and distribute their creation. Just because you purchased one copy does not mean that you have the right to make and use multiple copies.

Teachers who pirate software by making duplicate copies of a software package or by installing one software package on multiple machines in a classroom are in viola-

Figure 12.4
Filtering Software Web Sites
Software and web sites help to prevent unwanted materials from being downloaded to your computer.

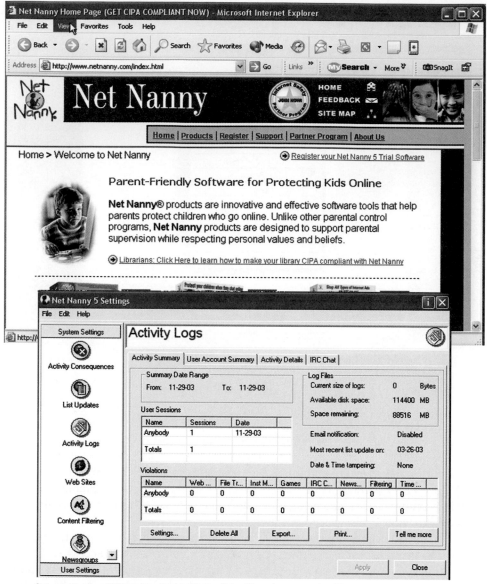

Screen capture from NetNanny.com. Reprinted by permission. Microsoft Internet Explorer® is a registered trademark of Microsoft Corporation.

tion of the copyright laws. Teachers who know of and allow students to pirate software in their classrooms are condoning and allowing illegal activities. It is important to model appropriate behavior and ethical conduct and to proactively discourage software piracy whenever it is noticed. When a student offers you a copy of the new software he or she just got from a friend, you have a chance to model the correct behavior by refusing to accept it. You also have a teachable moment in which you have the opportunity to inform your student about copyright and his or her potential violation of the law.

Network administrators are charged with ensuring that all software on a network is appropriately licensed (the legal right to use the software). Every software package on a network must either be custom-made for that network or have a site license (a purchased right to use multiple copies) associated with it. Some network administrators also monitor all software that has been installed on the hard drives of any machine that is on the network to ensure that no pirated software is present on or

ON THE WEB! 12.5
Software Piracy

attached to the network. It is therefore important for teachers to keep the software packages and documentation for any non-networked software that they install on the machines in a classroom. The network administrator who finds software on a classroom machine typically has the right and responsibility to ask to see the license. If the documentation and license are not available, the school or district network administrator may be required to erase any software that the teacher cannot prove was purchased.

Your school and/or district is likely to have very specific policies that address software piracy. A prudent teacher should research and become aware of such policies so that he or she does not personally violate them or allow students to violate them. Remember, like violating copyright laws with respect to multimedia, violating copyright with respect to software is also a violation of the law, which may result in you, your school, and your district being sued by the copyright holder. It is your responsibility as a professional and a public servant to uphold and support the laws relating to copyright.

Social Issues in the Digital Age

The Digital Age has brought up a number of new issues that have more to do with society in general than with education specifically. These societal concerns are nevertheless reflected in schools and relevant to them. Equity and accessibility of technology are the most pressing and critical of these issues. Inequities in access to technology can result in some children leaping ahead in technological skills and knowledge through their readily available technological resources and others falling behind because of their lack of access to technology. This gap between digital haves and have-nots is often referred to as the digital divide.

For households in which parents are sufficiently affluent to afford a home computer and modem, computers and Internet access are often present and readily available for the children in the home to use. A recent report by the National Telecommunications and Information Administration, *Falling through the Net* (2000), indicates that approximately 46 percent of households earning $35,000–$49,000 have Internet access, while 66 percent of households earning more than $50,000 have access. This level of accessibility gives children in wealthier households a head start in gaining computer skills and in developing the cognitive skills necessary to use hardware and software and to explore the Internet. For households that cannot afford a home computer, the child's use is limited to school time or perhaps time that is available through the local library. This type of relatively limited access may well cause such children to fall behind in the skills they need to use computers and the Internet in school. Other factors may also limit access. Not all schools and libraries are equally equipped with computers and Internet connections. The ones with less technology are often in poorer areas, causing limited access for people who cannot afford computers at home.

The digital divide does not occur along socioeconomic lines alone. Research in *Falling through the Net* shows that the divide also occurs along ethnic, gender, and education lines. Despite the increased presence of technology in our society, minorities and people with disabilities still have less access than others (see Figure 12.5). Furthermore, 60 percent of people with college degrees use the Internet, whereas Internet use is limited to only 7 percent of those whose education stopped at elementary school. Finally, gender differences exist as well. Although the numbers of men and women using the Internet are approximately equal, fewer women have computer-related degrees or work in computer-related fields. This reflects the continued math/science gender gap that has been present in schools for decades. This gap has now transferred to technology. According to many studies, boys are more encouraged

The digital divide is the separation between those who have access to technology and those who do not.

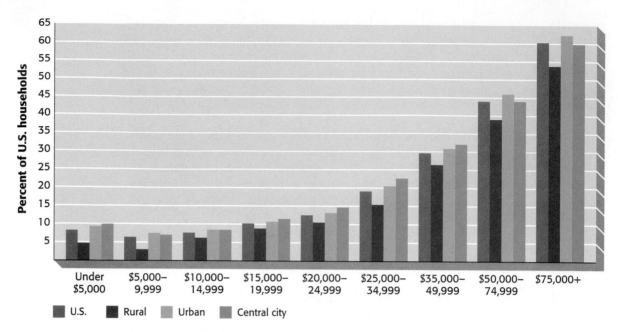

INTERNET ACCESS BY INCOME AND LOCATION

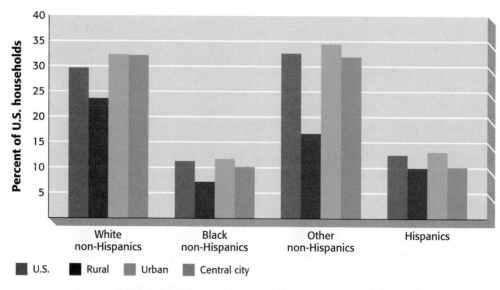

INTERNET ACCESS BY ETHNIC GROUP AND LOCATION

SOURCE: NTIA, *Falling through the Net* (2000).

Figure 12.5

The Digital Divide: A Closer Look

The digital divide separates technological haves and have-nots.

ON THE WEB! 12.6
The Digital Divide

to engage in technology-related activities than girls are, which may ultimately lead to the gender difference within the digital divide.

The digital divide cannot help affecting technology literacy at every level of education. Awareness of the gap in access and the possible inequities along ethnic, economic, gender, and education lines can help teachers to become sensitive to their students' needs (see Figure 12.6). Once aware that the digital divide does indeed exist, a

Digital Divide, PBS National Series, Studio Miramar, 415-643-6315. Reprinted by permission. Microsoft Internet Explorer® is a registered trademark of Microsoft Corporation.

Figure 12.6
Teacher Resources on the Digital Divide from the Public Broadcasting System
Teacher awareness helps to bridge the digital divide.

teacher can choose to design technology and other content-area lessons to help bridge technological inequities. You might also decide to research and share information about community resources that provide access for those who do not have computers at home. You might decide to advocate in your school and your community for more and equitable opportunities for all of your students. The issue of the digital divide is so pressing and pervasive that many others are taking steps to close the gap as well.

To make technology broadly available to all citizens, the Federal Commerce Commission has established an education rate (**e-rate**), a discounted cost for telecommunications service for community access centers (e.g., schools and libraries). The e-rate has enabled schools and libraries to connect to the Internet at a significantly accelerated pace. Private foundations, such as the Bill and Melinda Gates Foundation, have donated computers to libraries in rural areas to help make technology more available to all. Schools are testing the possibility of providing notebook computers to students to help equalize access. These and many similar initiatives are working in combination to help bridge the digital divide and ensure that all citizens have equal access to the tools of our Digital Age.

The e-rate has enabled schools and libraries to connect to the information superhighway.

Ethical Issues in the Digital Age

Freedom of Speech

In addition to social issues, the Digital Age has also engendered ethical concerns. One of the most significant of these is **freedom of speech** and the Internet. The content on the Internet is not regulated and, as a result, does contain materials that are objectionable and inappropriate for children. However, an issue that arises whenever regulation of Internet content is discussed is the constitutional right to free speech. The Internet is essentially a forum for sharing information and opinions. Some of the

IN THE CLASSROOM
Ethics and the Internet

In this Digital Age, schools, districts, and organizations are making efforts to address key ethical issues of privacy, free speech, and academic dishonesty. An abundance of resources is available to help teachers deal with these issues. The Computer Ethics Institute (**http://www.brook.edu/its/cei/cei_hp.htm**) has developed the Ten Commandments for Computer Ethics:

1. Thou shalt not use a computer to harm other people.
2. Thou shalt not interfere with other people's computer work.
3. Thou shalt not snoop around in other people's files.
4. Thou shalt not use a computer to steal.
5. Thou shalt not use a computer to bear false witness.
6. Thou shalt not use or copy software for which you have not paid.
7. Thou shalt not use other people's computer resources without authorization.
8. Thou shalt not appropriate other people's intellectual output.
9. Thou shalt think about the social consequences of the program you write.
10. Thou shalt use a computer in ways that show consideration and respect.

Sharing these commandments with your students is an excellent first step for dealing with these ethical issues.

Other resources include the U.S. Department of Justice online guide to using the Internet written exclusively for kids. This guide helps students become aware of the issues they will face when using the Internet.

Another excellent resource is the Truste organization's "Parent's and Teachers' Guide to Online Privacy," available for download at **http://www.truste.org/education/users_parents_teacher_guide.html**. This guide offers advice for dealing with privacy and other ethical issues related to student Internet use. A second valuable resource, *Technology & Learning* magazine's "The Concerned Educator's Guide to Safety and Cyber-Ethics" by Jerry Crystal, Cherie A. Geide, and Judy Salpeter (November 2000, vol. 21, no. 4), suggests a variety of strategies and resources teachers can use to address "cyber-ethics."

Although no solutions for ethical issues will fit all school or district situations, you will find that many expert online and print resources are available for your use in determining the best policies and responses to the issues facing you.

Source: The Computer Ethics Institute. The Ten Commandments for Computer Ethics. Retrieved August 27, 2002, from http://www.brook.edu/its/cei/cei_hp.htm.

ON THE WEB! 12.7
Free Speech

Free speech and privacy are two of the critical ethical issues related to Internet use.

information and opinions expressed are grounded in scientific fact and academic research. Others are simply personal viewpoints that may be offensive to some. The question then arises whether society should censor some views expressed on the Internet. Is the right to express a viewpoint digitally as protected by the Constitution as the right to free speech is? Is it the responsibility of an ISP or portal to monitor the content of the information and opinions expressed on the web sites, conferences, and emails available from its service? When do the actions of a few cross over into the legal domains that address fraud, libel, and hate crimes? The conflict between freedom on the Internet and the rights of individuals is a serious and far-reaching one that will have long-term ramifications for our society.

While this controversy continues to rage, it remains a school's responsibility to control access on its network to areas of the Internet that are inappropriate for an academic setting. Through monitoring and filtering software and through teacher observation, schools can make a reasonable effort to curb access to objectionable materials. Ultimately, society will decide whether objectionable materials are within the realm protected by free speech. Until then, teachers need to be aware of their professional responsibilities to guarantee students' "digital safety" while using technology.

Privacy

A second ethical issue arising in the Digital Age relates to privacy versus control and monitoring. Individual rights and privacy are significant values in our society. In using any network or the Internet, it is technologically possible to monitor what an individual is doing and which sites he or she is visiting while connected. The controversy arises as to the rights of any agency, whether governmental or commercial, to closely monitor and record an individual's personal information or online activities. Is that not a violation of privacy? Should the government be allowed to monitor people who engage in illegal or dangerous activities? Who is responsible if activities are not monitored and someone gets hurt?

These complex social questions and the legal issues associated with them are evolving as the Digital Age unfolds. For educators, however, the situation is a bit less murky. In schools, the primary responsibility is the safety of the children. Because schools and their technologies are public entities, usually with clearly defined acceptable use policies, monitoring activities is both appropriate and expected. Students and public employees alike agree to use the school facilities to engage in appropriate activities. It is typically understood that monitoring to assure appropriate use and the safety of students will be done. Network administrators can monitor activity, and software can track what is said and what is sent by network users. Personal activities on the Internet, though monitored, are thus no more curtailed than they would be in the classroom.

Academic Dishonesty

The ease of manipulating and sharing digital data has led to numerous problems relating to **academic dishonesty.** Some web sites offer "services" to students so that they can hire someone to write papers for them. Others let students post assignments they have written or retrieve assignments written by others. Even web sites that do not intend to encourage dishonesty may support it as students copy and paste information from such sites into their assignments without giving the true authors credit. Cheating and plagiarizing are clearly not products of the Digital Age, but technology has made them easier to do and harder to detect.

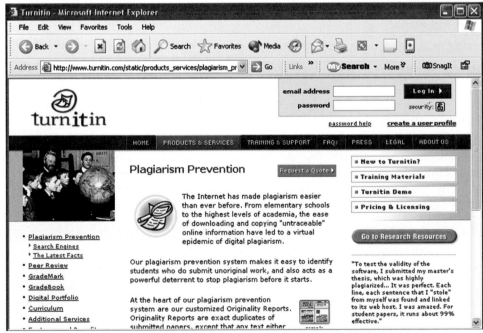

SOURCE: From http://www.turnitin.com

Software and web sites are available to educators to help reduce plagiarism.

ON THE WEB! 12.8
Academic Dishonesty

To address potential digital dishonesty, teachers and schools should have clearly stated and enforced policies to deal with digital academic dishonesty just as they do for dishonesty of the more traditional sort. If academic dishonesty is widespread, a school can even install, or use online, **antiplagiarism software** that compares student's work with well-known authors' work and with work posted on the web. Whether the approach is to enforce policy or to monitor student work via software, it is a teacher's responsibility to ensure, to the extent possible, that checks are in place to promote and enforce academic honesty.

Resources for Teachers

The legal, ethical, and social issues presented in this chapter are far-reaching and critically important. But a teacher is not alone in addressing and dealing with these issues. Typically, a school has a media specialist and/or a technology specialist available to assist teachers in addressing these issues. Both media and technology specialists have typically undergone special training sessions or have taken in-depth courses dealing with the issues related to technology implementation. A prudent teacher, when faced with questions regarding technology and its use in the classroom, would be wise first to contact the school media specialist, technology coordinator, or a school administrator for guidance. You will likely be surprised at the wealth of information and enthusiastic support you will be provided.

Emerging Technologies

New Technologies for Schools

A final consideration in implementing technology in today's schools relates to how technologies are likely to change and emerge in the coming years. Today's purchases are most wisely made when they are likely to be compatible with the technologies that will be available tomorrow. Although they are not always possible to predict, some emerging technologies are clearly on the horizon and should be considered even now in planning for and implementing technology in schools. The specifics of an emerging technology as it is finally formulated may be unclear in the present, but its potential to change education in the future must be taken into account today. Following are some of the most significant emerging trends that need to be kept in mind in considering technology in today's schools.

• Virtual Environments

As the speed and capacity of computers and communications increase, **virtual environments** will become possible. As you have learned, virtual reality (VR) refers to three-dimensional representations of real or imagined places. Virtual environments are fully rendered environments in which the user becomes immersed. Such immersion might mean that the individual participating in a virtual environment will feel, smell, taste, see, and hear aspects of the environment. VR systems today are the most rudimentary examples of the virtual environments on the horizon. Teachers and learners will someday be able to take full-immersion field trips in which they will be able to fully interact with the virtual world they are visiting. Virtual models will be able to be constructed and manipulated to determine how their real-world counterparts would work. People with physical disabilities will be free to "move" about and fully experience the virtual world without impediments.

For education, improvements to VR offer the potential for full sensory experiences in learning scenarios constructed to teach. This technology also offers the possibility

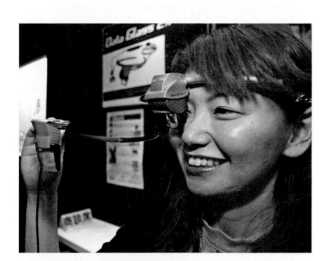

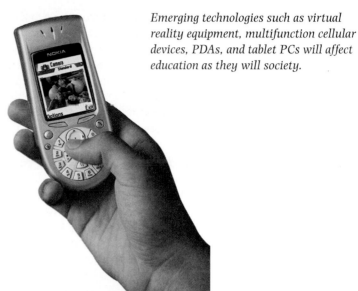

Emerging technologies such as virtual reality equipment, multifunction cellular devices, PDAs, and tablet PCs will affect education as they will society.

of altering virtual instructional environments to present and respond to unique differences in learners. Although this technology is still only on the horizon, its applications hold amazing promise for teaching and learning. For implementation of technology now, it is important simply to stay aware of the current VR resources and the emergence of VR environments and to explore how they might be used in teaching and learning. This is appropriate preparation for the next-generation VR.

• Artificial Intelligence

Artificial intelligence (**AI**) refers to programs that work in manners that are similar to the way the human brain works. In AI circles, software that learns and adjusts its responses on the basis of previous interactions is called a **neural network. Fuzzy logic software** is an AI program that resembles human decision making. **Expert systems** are AI programs that offer suggestions and advice on the basis of a database of expertise. Some AI systems use **intelligent agents** that are called on to help with specific tasks.

Artificial intelligence programs provide intelligent assistants to help with computing tasks.

Intelligent agents may ask questions, monitor work to determine patterns of action, and perform requested tasks. All of these types of AI programs are in existence now but have not yet sufficiently evolved to become significant tools in current teaching and learning environments.

Yet when applied to education, AI has the potential to improve and adapt software to a student's individual learning patterns and needs. An agent might be created for each individual student that would automatically customize learning software and instructional experiences in a manner that is responsive to the learner's learning style and needs. For education, AI holds the promise of programs that could become virtual teacher aides.

• Communications

ON THE WEB! 12.9
New Connections

At the core of communications capabilities is available bandwidth. As bandwidth increases, so does the potential of the Internet and local networks. With improved bandwidth, communications could become almost instantaneous without regard to the size or type of files. Video files would be available on demand and of the highest quality via a broad-bandwidth Internet connection. Teachers would be able to access instructional videos or live broadcasts from a source anywhere in the world at the time most appropriate to their lesson. Instruction in a single classroom could be broadcast simultaneously to homebound students or to other schools via their Internet connection. Audio conferencing and videoconferencing would link experts across the world to be available for a guest lecture in your class. Regardless of the technology used to increase bandwidth, its implementation will make the Internet, local-area networks, and wide-area networks significantly more powerful tools.

• Grid Computing

Communication via networking, whether local or across the Internet, has begun a new phase that some suggest may be as significant as the creation of the Internet itself. You will recall that the Internet began as a few networks experimentally connected together for research purposes. In a similar vein, some experimental networks, the purpose of which is to maximize computing power, are now being connected together. These computers are joined together on a "grid" to share resources and to communicate data so that the available computing power is a factor of the number of computers on the grid. The more computers connected to the grid, the more CPU power is available for the targeted task. One of the first major breakthroughs using grid computing has been the SETI@home project. In this experiment, individuals volunteer their personal computers' idle computing power to help to analyze radio telescope data for the SETI (Search for Extraterrestrial Intelligence) project. This popular and continuously growing grid uses the idle computing power of approximately 500,000 personal computers, resulting in the fastest dedicated computer in the world (Foster, 2000).

Today grid computing standards and tools are being refined, and more and more scientific computer grids are being created. Considering the cost and limited time available for the use of supercomputers, grid computing offers a viable alternative. For education, this may someday mean that everyday educators can access data and power previously reserved to only the most advanced research universities. Further, the power needed for intensive and complex multimedia instruction may become readily available to all despite any potential limitations of the computers located in any one classroom. The availability of seamless and powerful computing resources on every computer connected to the grid may revolutionize educational computing. For our society, grid computing may become a ubiquitous virtual master-computer available on demand to anyone requiring its use. Indeed, it may well be the next evolution in worldwide computing and communications.

Today, on a smaller scale, the basic operating principle of the grid, resource sharing, is already in place in the form of **peer-to-peer networking.** This type of networking differs from the more conventional networking structure in several significant ways. In a traditional network, we typically store the files we want to share on a network server's hard drive, which in turn is made accessible to others on the network or the Internet. We must go through the server to reach one another. Peer-to-peer networking offers another communication alternative. Instead of connecting via a server, in this networking structure, computers connect together directly. Each "peer" computer in the network then makes a portion of its hard drive public or shares its drives. This "public" drive acts like a type of virtual miniserver in that it allows others to use the resources we store there and gives us space to store resources we borrow from others. The need for specific services that offer server space and function and to which we must pay a fee is eliminated.

Such a technology has been used extensively on the Internet to share music (MP3) files. Unfortunately, many of the files made available through this type of peer-to-peer network have violated copyright laws. Many of the MP3 files stored on this type of private-public network were created by turning copyrighted musical CDs into digital files shared with other peers in the network without compensation to the artists and record companies that owned the music. As you know, this type of violation of copyright law is illegal. As a result, many of the music sites using this type of technology have been forced to shut down.

Although some people chose to use peer-to-peer networking in an unethical and illegal manner, the core technology of sharing resources and data directly between computers remains a great potential for education. Whether ultimately adapted to become a worldwide computing grid or simply used to share resources on a smaller scale, this new communications technology holds great promise for teachers and their students. Using a similar peer-to-peer structure, learning communities working on an international science project could share data easily. Teachers interested in teaching a common subject could share their lesson plans and research without the need of an education portal. For educators, this quiet, ongoing evolution in networking may indeed offer every teacher in every classroom all of the resources necessary to help students learn.

• Wireless Connectivity

Many schools have spent a great deal of money retrofitting buildings for network cabling or creating new facilities to be network-ready. The rapid improvement in wireless connectivity may change this scenario. **Wireless networking** connects computers to a server and to each other just as wireless cell phones are connected to a phone company network, although the technology that is used to connect them may differ. Wireless technologies are changing quickly and dramatically. The future may hold an entirely different connectivity technology than what is in place today. Wireless connectivity, however, is likely to make all aspects of computing as commonplace as making a call on a cell phone.

Several new technologies are supporting the wireless revolution. WiFi (wireless fidelity) is a wireless networking technology that is based on the common 802.11 standard, a standard set for wireless LAN technology. Using radio frequencies set aside for consumer use, WiFi technology packages wireless networking that can offer connectivity across a school campus in hardware barely larger than a text-

Notebook computers connected via a wireless network add high-tech flexibility to any classroom.

book. Then, using computers, notebooks, tablet PCs, or PDAs equipped with inexpensive WiFi networking cards, broadband Internet access is readily available everywhere within the WiFi range. Further, public WiFi networks are being created across the country in stores, airports, neighborhoods, and even city parks. Simply by being located within a public WiFi network's range, using your WiFi-equipped device, you can use free broadband access to the Internet.

For schools, WiFi offers a reasonably simple and reliable technology that can make retrofitting schools for networking a thing of the past. However, because of their open access, some security issues arise. For districts and schools that must protect the privacy of student information, these issues will need to be resolved for wide implementation. Still, WiFi has the potential to change the way we access the Internet and all digital resources at home, at work, and at school. This emerging technology is one about which every educator should stay aware.

For connectivity within a classroom among various computing devices, other standards are evolving. Bluetooth technology, named after Harald Bluetooth, a tenth-century Danish king who unified Denmark and Norway, allows diverse types of electronic equipment to communicate with each other. Using Bluetooth-compliant devices, different kinds of equipment communicate with each other, and a personal area network (PAN) is automatically created. Within the PAN, devices can share data or interconnect so that one device can be controlled by another. With Bluetooth-ready devices, when you place the devices within the range of a PAN, your computer sends data to your printer; your PDA synchronizes with your computer; the phone book in your mobile phone exchanges new data with your notebook's Microsoft Outlook address book; and your television and DVD player operate together to play your favorite movie . . . all without wires.

IN THE CLASSROOM
Going Wireless in Schools

The ever-changing world of technology is seeing the increasing popularity of wireless computing in schools. An interesting and successfully implemented example of the versatility of handheld wireless technology has taken place at New Hanover High School in Wilmington, North Carolina, where seniors are required to write senior project papers. With the help of student teachers from the University of North Carolina at Wilmington's Watson School of Education and HP Jornada Pocket PCs obtained with a Preparing Tomorrow's Teachers to Use Technology (PT3) grant, seniors in one English class did their research in a way quite remote from the usual method of searching through books and journals in the library and sitting at desks while scanning the Internet.

UNC-W's preservice teachers will be expected to use technology in their classrooms upon licensure, so the PT3 project prepares student teachers to bring the latest technological support to their internships. Amy Hawk, a student teacher, coordinated the senior project paper assignment with the requirement to use technology by giving her senior English class the pocket PCs to word-process and, with their wireless Internet capability, to compose a letter proposing the topic they wished to write on. Upon approval of the topic, the pocket PCs were used for Internet research, participation in research-related class activities, and preparation of the final copy of the reports. It became apparent that, because of the flexibility of meeting times and space needs when using the handhelds, the students could complete their senior reports much more quickly than the students in other classes who lacked the wireless technology.

Ms. Hawk's sophomore English class enjoyed other valuable uses for the handhelds. These students were not averse to availing themselves of the speed and practicality the wireless handhelds offered for Internet research. Ms. Hawk could assure her students "instant availability to search the Web during class activities and gave herself an incentive to incorporate technology into her teaching." She is convinced that "it is important that school administrators support using handheld technologies in teaching and learning and believe that students will benefit from the experience."

SOURCE: LEARN NC. 2003, March. Student teachers and high school seniors beam the Internet. Retrieved April 2, 2003, from http://www.learnnc.org/Index.nsf/printView.

In the classroom, Bluetooth technology will make it possible to arrange the learning environment without the limitations dictated by the length of cables. It will allow you to create classroom PANs so that all your classroom computers can use your single printer even if the school network is not working at the moment. Your students can gather and record data on their PDAs or take digital pictures, all of which can be transferred to the computers without need of cabling. As Bluetooth technology becomes more widespread and more and more devices are Bluetooth-enabled, this wireless technology may make setting up and using a technology-rich classroom as simple as turning the technology on.

In many schools, students can already access their school network and the Internet from any location on the campus by using one of these wireless technologies. For these students, a laptop computer or PDA connects to network resources and the Internet at the click of a button, regardless of whether the student happens to be in class, in the library, or sitting outside on the school grounds. In schools that already have wireless networking, the promise of classrooms without walls is beginning to come to fruition. As wireless connectivity emerges as a dominant technology, that same promise has the potential to expand to any location anywhere, making everyone capable of connecting whenever they wish to.

For education, these emerging trends in connectivity will bring about a significant change in the way networks are implemented. The potential for limitless connections in every classroom and the capability of arranging the instructional environment without regard for power or network nodes will be possible. Emerging connectivity capabilities combined with portable computing make computers in instruction truly powerful and flexible instructional tools.

• Displays

Another area of emerging technologies that holds significance for education is in display devices. Flat-panel LCD monitors, although an advance over bulky CRT monitors, are primitive compared to displays currently under development. The new prototypes use flexible plastic film that can be rolled up or laid flat on a desktop to display computer data. Though still in prototype stage, two of these technologies bear mentioning.

Flexible organic light-emitting devices (FOLEDs) are computer displays on flexible plastic that have the potential to be made small enough to roll up into a pen or large enough to be used as a wall-size mural and will be able to be bent or folded without harm. These capabilities give them the potential to expand well beyond the limits of current monitors and ultimately to become wearable computer displays, folded electronic newspapers, or displays that can be embedded in other devices, such as car windshields. These devices also offer better viewing, are less expensive to make, and are less power-hungry than LCD screens, in addition to being flexible. For the classroom, paper-size FOLEDs may become portable monitors that can be opened and laid flat on a student's desk or moved easily about the classroom and the school while staying connected to a CPU via wireless technology. Wall-size FOLEDs could potentially replace costly projection devices. Educational uses and applications for this emerging display technology have only begun to be projected. Clearly, as this technology evolves, educators will embrace its flexibility and potential to unclutter the technology-rich learning space.

A second, related display is electronic paper. Electronic paper is a sheet of transparent film containing millions of black-and-white beads of ink. When a current is applied, the beads rotate, showing either their black or white sides, thus creating an image on the film. The image can remain or be repeatedly refreshed with new data, depending on the current applied. The data can be text, graphics, or even video. Both writable and erasable, a single sheet of electronic paper is capable of displaying an electronic newspaper or the pages of a multimedia textbook. With information stored

*Flexible display and electronic ink proto-
types have the potential to change the way
we display and interact with computer data
in the classroom.*

on a chip or other portable device and a sheet of electronic paper powered by a battery, an entire library could be carried and viewed anywhere. Although thus far they have been marketed primarily as refreshable displays in stores, newer prototypes of electronic paper hold the promise for education of changing how and when the printed page might be used in the classroom. With the potential of providing all of a student's class textbooks while at the same time making the contents of the entire school library available to the student via a single sheet of electronic paper, the possibilities for the application of this technology to education are almost limitless.

• Convergence

Convergence refers to the blending of technologies into a single multipurpose technology. Imagine a world in which the functions of television, radio, telephone, cell phone, beeper, and computer have blended into a single pocket device. Convergence of the many technologies already available is happening now. Cell phones can send and receive email across the Internet. PDAs have calling and email capabilities. This trend is likely to continue until the lines between all these technologies have blurred to the point of invisibility.

Converging technologies
are blending into a single
multipurpose technology.

For schools, convergence will mean being able to pull limited resources away from acquiring many types of technologies and to focus instead on buying more of the multipurpose convergent technologies for teachers and learners. It will also mean less time and fewer resources spent training to use diverse equipment and more time for mastering the skills necessary to make the most of convergent equipment. As technologies continue to converge, educational planning and implementation are likely to become less complex and more coordinated in scope and purpose.

ON THE WEB! 12.10
Converging Technology

Emerging Issues: The Changing Face of Instruction in the Digital Age

With so much technological change occurring each day, the future look and feel of technology are difficult to predict. Clearly, some emerging trends, such as those we have discussed, are evident, but others have yet to become visible even to the most astute observer. In fact, the only thing that is constant about technology is that it is in a constant state of change. How do all of these changes affect education in planning for technology today, and how are they likely to affect education in looking ahead?

• Computers as Appliances

As you learned earlier in this chapter, the digital divide does exist; but as a result of many initiatives, it will ultimately close. Eventually, the computer, regardless of the shape into which it evolves, will be as commonplace in households as the television or the telephone is today. Over time, it will become an essential appliance that future generations will not be able to imagine living without. As this change occurs, schools will no longer be able to lag behind societal change. Classrooms will no longer be accept-

Tablet PCs will become as commonplace as cell phones.

Tablet or pocket PCs with portable keyboards make computing power accessible everywhere students need it.

able if they include primarily the instructional tools of fifty years ago. Instead, societal pressure will ultimately force change and demand that schools reflect the realities of the Digital Age.

In the emerging Digital Age schools, tablet PCs will be as common as backpacks, with every student responsible for bringing his or her own to every class. They may well replace books and paper and pencil. Students might simply download the text components they need to read to their tablet PCs, complete their work on their digital devices using voice or handwriting recognition software, and then send it to their teacher's email account.

In a scenario in which computers become commonplace and indispensable educational appliances, students will need training in how to use future technologies for academic pursuits. Teachers will need to learn how to design lessons using such tools, just as they now plan lessons using rulers and calculators. Privacy and security issues will continue to challenge the technical staff as these new technologies proliferate. Schools and districts will need to determine appropriate policy and add staff to support both technologies and procedures.

In such an environment, instruction will be able to be highly individualized as teachers will be able to download intelligent agents to guide students through lessons developed to meet their particular learning needs. Assessment and evaluation of student progress will be able to be gathered electronically and shared appropriately to determine performance. The teaching and learning process will be able to be customized and then evaluated for effectiveness. When computer technology reaches the societal saturation point of the telephone, teachers will have the ultimate teaching tool at their fingertips.

• Computer Literacy

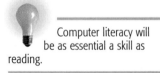

Computer literacy will be as essential a skill as reading.

Each year, more and more children become computer literate in the elementary grades. Indeed, the NETS for Students (see Appendix A) already identify levels of technology literacy expected today. For people who have already completed school, lifelong learning opportunities via higher education and community schools will make it possible for more and more adults to achieve **computer literacy.** As the Digital Age unfolds, using a computer will become as essential a skill as reading.

For educators, this change will mean that it will no longer be necessary to spend time or resources catching up those who missed learning about computers in their public school years. In years to come, teachers will be able to expect computer literacy just as they expect students to read and write. This will make it easier for teachers to more easily integrate computer-enhanced instruction into the instructional design of their courses. At the same time, it will challenge teachers to maintain and improve their own levels of educational technology literacy to effectively use these powerful tools.

Teachers will have become computer literate either through preservice training or, eventually, through their own K–12 school experience. Expanded educational technology and computer literacy will allow courses like this one and in-service workshops to focus on integration skills rather than introductory skills. With teachers working at higher levels of technology integration competencies, the quality of technology-enhanced teaching and learning will no doubt improve.

• Decentralizing Instruction

The definition of schools may change as the Digital Age unfolds.

Perhaps the greatest change that may occur will not be in the equipment or the skill level of those who use technology. The most significant change may well be in the nature of instruction itself. As you have learned, distance delivery and alternative delivery already have the potential to redefine instruction. Classrooms that are now set within the framework of a given time and located in a particular place may expand to include virtual communities of learners located anywhere in the world. Virtual learning communities and environments may take students anywhere they wish to learn and at any time they wish to learn. Master teachers may join together from anywhere in the world to team-teach in their particular areas of expertise. Powerful communities of learners may assemble anytime, anyplace, and engage learners from anywhere.

Under such altered circumstances, will schools as we know them today survive? The answer is most likely yes, although schools must be prepared to fully evolve into institutions that prepare children for lives that will be lived in the Digital Age. Classrooms may ultimately look quite different from their nineteenth-century counterparts, but they will no doubt provide enriched learning environments where children can share and grow into their potential. Schools may no longer be so isolated from one another. Like stand-alone computers that are networked together and become more powerful because of it, the term *school* may come to refer to a network of educational opportunities, both physical and virtual, for learners. And teachers, like their classrooms, will need to change to embrace the Digital Age and use its resources to help students learn.

Computers in the classroom will continue to be a ubiquitous tool for both teachers and learners.

• The Changing Role of the Teacher

Some people believe that with so many coming changes, teachers will become obsolete. That is not the case. The technologies of the Digital Age can support instruction, but teachers will continue to have the central role in designing it, just as they do today. Of course, a Digital Age instructional design with so much capacity for individualization might look quite different from contemporary curriculum, but the educator behind it will never be obsolete.

Teachers may find themselves in a new, more challenging role. Rather than directing instruction in a single classroom setting, teachers will facilitate learning by creating optimal instructional experiences and then assisting their students through these. Furthermore, the same technology that supports worldwide student interaction will support professional interaction among educators. Teachers will not be isolated in their classrooms but will instead become part of a collegial network that is focused on high-quality educational practices. With the help of virtual teaching communities and with the ever-expanding resources available through technology, students will be better served than was ever before thought possible.

Your role in teaching will most likely change over the course of your teaching career. Technology will play a large role in instigating the changes in both our society

ON THE WEB! 12.11
The Classroom of Tomorrow

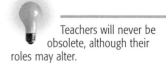

Teachers will never be obsolete, although their roles may alter.

in general and education in particular. Knowledge of educational technology will enable you to anticipate and easily adjust to the changes to come in this Digital Age. It will also help you to become an educational professional who is empowered by extraordinary technological tools that you can harness to help your students succeed. The tools are there for you, and your students are waiting. You need only pick up the tools and use them to build the powerful, technology-rich learning environments your students need and deserve.

KEY TERMS

academic dishonesty 391	filtering software 385
acceptable use 384	freedom of speech 389
antiplagiarism software 392	fuzzy logic software 393
artificial intelligence (AI) 393	intelligent agents 393
code of ethics 384	neural network 393
computer literacy 400	peer-to-peer networking 395
convergence 398	piracy 385
copyright 381	privacy 382
digital divide 381	stakeholder 380
e-rate 389	strategic planning 380
expert systems 393	virtual environments 392
fair use 381	wireless networking 395

STUDENT ACTIVITIES

CHAPTER REVIEW

1. What are the legal, social, and ethical issues arising in the Digital Age? Summarize each.
2. What four questions related to the fair use guidelines should teachers ask before using copyrighted materials?
3. What does the right to privacy entail for students in your class?
4. How do acceptable use policies help protect students and schools?
5. What is software piracy?
6. What is the e-rate? How has it helped schools and libraries connect to the Internet?
7. How might virtual environments enhance teaching and learning?
8. What is artificial intelligence? How might intelligent agents assist teachers and learners?
9. What advantages can broad bandwidth and wireless networking offer schools? Describe the current technologies available for wireless connectivity.
10. What display devices are emerging that may have significant impact on the classroom? Briefly describe each.

WHAT DO YOU THINK?

1. As emerging technologies continue to affect education, there is little question that the role of the teacher will change. Imagine yourself teaching a class in the technological future. How do you think your role is different from the typical teacher's role today?

2. There is much controversy over issues of privacy in the Digital Age. Schools have an obligation to ensure student safety, both physical and virtual. When using the Internet or the network, this requires keeping close tabs on students' activity when they are using computers. Do you think this is a violation of privacy? Justify your opinion. Include in your justification your consideration of both points of view.

3. Of the emerging technology trends presented in the chapter or those you discovered through your research on the web, which emerging technology or trend do you think will have the most significant impact on education? Be prepared to share your views with your peers.

LEARNING TOGETHER!

These activities are best done in groups of three to five.

1. Strategic planning is a complex, formal process that results in more effective and efficient technology implementation. After reviewing Interchapter 5 on strategic planning for technology, ask each member of the group to interview a teacher or administrator from a different school or district office to determine whether strategic planning for technology took place in that school or district. If strategic planning occurred, ask the interviewee to describe the process. If you discover that it did not occur, ask the interviewee how technology is acquired and implemented. Compare your interviews. Be prepared to share them with the class.

2. Examine your institution's acceptable use policy and compare it with two others you find on the web. Discuss how well the policies you reviewed address the ethical issues described in the chapter. On the basis of your discussions, together create an acceptable use policy that you agree would be useful for your own classrooms.

3. The digital divide is a serious inequity that may well affect the children whom members of your group will eventually teach. Together, review the issues of inequity and access. Then identify ten strategies that you might use to mitigate the impact of the digital divide on the children you will teach.

HANDS-ON!

1. Select an emerging technology or trend of your choice, and research it thoroughly. Create a PowerPoint presentation summarizing your research to share with your class. Be sure to include a section describing how you believe the trend or technology you researched will affect education.

2. After reviewing Interchapter 5, examine three strategic plans for technology for schools on the Internet. Using those plans and the components described in the chapter, word-process a planning template that you might use as a starting point for a strategic plan in which you might participate when you teach. Include citations to the plans you examined.

3. Join an online forum that addresses the legal, ethical, or social issues described in this chapter. After participating in the online discussions and deciding your own position on the issues, word-process a summary of the pros and cons of the issues to share with your peers.

More from David Thornburg

Now that you have learned much about emerging technologies, their implications for schools, and the issues that result from their implementation, let's return to Dr. David Thornburg and discover the changes he is anticipating.

APM: You've written about the need to change paradigms as we progress in the Digital Age. How do you think the paradigm will (or should) change in the next ten to twenty years?

DT: We are at the point where it is clear that modern information technologies have great value in education when used in appropriate ways. For this reason, I believe the greatest paradigm shift we face is one that says these tools are an expectation, not an option. Every classroom should have the same free broadband access found at my local McDonald's. Period. Every classroom should have educators for whom technology is second nature. Period. In my view, for a classroom teacher to display discomfort or a lack of understanding regarding (for example) web access today is equivalent to a teacher from the 1960s having a hard time reading. Today's youth have never known a world without the Internet. They have largely grown up with the expectation that computers, along with books and other informational tools, are just a common part of society. Unlike the fledgling computers of the late 1970s, today's systems are amazingly powerful, far easier to use, and incredibly affordable. Consider this: I can go to my local discount store and, for under $1,000, leave with an Internet-ready computer whose raw power rivals that of mainframes a decade ago. Much of this power is harnessed to run a user interface that, largely, gets out of the user's way to facilitate access to software and resources of immeasurable value. What price tag can be placed on every student's ability to gather original source documents in social studies from the Library of Congress? Or photos of the latest space telescope images from NASA? Or any of the other amazingly high-quality educational resources provided for free? The fact is that the average student has, at home, greater access to educational materials than I had at the university when I was getting my Ph.D.

But access is not enough. Educators who fully grasp the overwhelming power of these tools are needed in every classroom to guide young people as they learn to conduct research on academic topics. Research skills must be taught, and they must be taught by educators who are so comfortable with these tools that they scarcely know they are using them. That paradigm shift is one I eagerly await.

APM: As you look at the technologies in use today, what changes do you see in your crystal ball that will be coming in the near future?

DT: Many of the technologies of the future will be extensions of those mentioned in this book: PDAs, digital cameras, and so on. What is changing is the ubiquity of these tools and their capacity to share information with each other. Ever since Hedy Lamarr and

Real People
Real Stories

George Antheil copatented spread-spectrum communication in 1942, the potential for low-power interdevice communication has existed. The rapid growth of 802.11 and Bluetooth technologies are merely the most recent developments in this area. Cell phones can now share data with PDAs, and any device can communicate with almost any other device.

On the ubiquity front, personal technology is advancing by leaps and bounds. In the year 2003, for example, cell phones outnumbered wired phones worldwide for the first time. It was also the first year when digital cameras outsold film-based cameras worldwide.

The rapid growth of high tech in our personal lives has resulted in a new trend: technology as high fashion. To avoid commoditization, just about every piece of technology, from cell phones to desktop computers, is starting to sport flair. When raw specifications no longer function as product differentiators, style becomes a selling feature. Nowhere is this more evident than in the technologies being purchased by young people directly.

APM: Looking ahead twenty or thirty years, as these new technologies are incorporated into the classroom, do you think we may finally see some significant changes in the way we go about educating our youth and adults? If so, would you describe what you believe the twenty-first century classroom will look like at that point?

DT: The biggest transformation I see in the coming years is one toward inquiry-driven, project-based learning (PBL), since the strategies used in this pedagogical model continue to work seamlessly once students leave school. I anticipate that schooling and work will become better integrated as adults realize that lifelong learning is a survival skill, not an abstract desire. In fact, the technology and pedagogy needed to effect this transformation are in place today, and it scares a lot of people because it represents such a shift from the way most people my age were educated. For example, the bulk of No Child Left Behind (NCLB) is geared to create a fear of changing to new pedagogical practices. This fear is instilled through the perpetuation and growth of high-stakes testing that includes (largely) multiple-choice instruments or short essay segments to be graded in high volume by minimum-wage graders. Many teachers, fearful of the consequences to their schools if the scores are low, are hiding behind NCLB in their quest to hang on to directed instructional models. Research shows that students who have been taught in more open ways (through PBL, for example) perform on tests as well or better than those directly instructed in content. This fact is not disseminated widely.

This will change soon. First, there will be a backlash driven by parents whose children are denied a high school diploma based on a single high-stakes test result, no matter how well they performed in their classes over the four years of high school. The thousands of children denied graduation in Florida in 2003 are just the tip of the iceberg that will crash into Congress and force a major rewrite of NCLB in the coming years. I see the good parts of NCLB remaining (highly qualified teachers, research-based pedagogical models) and the bad parts removed and replaced by a more learnercentric model of education along the lines I have described. And through it all, technologies will become commonplace tools for the exploration of subjects, serving in multiple stages from research to final project, with the understanding that physical libraries, books, pens, paper, and the other traditional tools of learning will continue to be used when appropriate. In twenty years, technology will have proven its worth to such an extent that we won't be talking about it anymore.

Dr. David Thornburg is director of global operations for the Thornburg Center and senior fellow of the Congressional Institute for the Future. He writes and speaks extensively on the future of education and the role of telematic technologies as tools for learning. Dr. Thornburg has received numerous awards for his work and is a popular conference presenter throughout the United States and Brazil. He may be reached by email at dthornburg@aol.com or by phone at 847-277-7691.

David D. Thornburg, Ph.D., Director, Global Operations, The Thornburg Center, 711 Beacon Drive, Lake Barrington, IL 60010.

SOURCE: Interview with Dr. David Thornburg conducted by Al P. Mizell. Reprinted by permission of David D. Thornburg, Ph.D. Director, Global Operations, Thornburg Center.

STRATEGIC PLANNING

Before any technology decisions are made, it is critical that careful, "big picture" planning occurs. Such planning is called strategic planning, because it takes into account long-range goals as well as short-term objectives. Because a strategic plan will ultimately affect those inside an organization and those interacting with the organization, planning facilitators often create a plan through a formal group process that includes representatives of all concerned parties. Representatives from all groups that will be affected by the plan are selected and actively participate together in the strategic planning process. These individuals, called stakeholders, bring to the table their distinct sets of interests and perspectives. By including all stakeholders, the final strategic plan is more likely to fully address everyone's needs and is more likely to be accepted because everyone has equal ownership of the development process.

The strategic planning process typically has several distinct steps, each of which contributes toward focusing the stakeholders and the district or school they represent in a single, clearly articulated direction. Figure I5.1 shows the steps in the strategic planning process and the questions to be answered at each step.

Strategic Planning Steps

Setting

The strategic planning process usually begins with a description of the setting (district or school) in which the plan will be implemented. Although it might seem an extraneous exercise, articulating a complete description of the school or district setting helps the planning participants to become fully aware of the conditions of the setting for the plan they will create. Often, participants are aware of only the part of the school or district with which they interact. A full description of the school and/or district and the setting in which it operates makes everyone in the process much more aware of all aspects of the institutional setting.

SWOT Analysis

SWOT is an acronym for "strengths, weaknesses, opportunities, threats." In SWOT analysis, participants brainstorm all of the factors, both positive and negative, that will affect the potential success of the plan they are developing. Through this process, the

Describing the Setting		What are the significant features in the setting in which the plan will be implemented?
Conduct SWOT Analysis		What are the strengths and weaknesses within the setting? What are the opportunities and threats related to implementation?
Determine Mission and Goals		What are the technological mission and the significant technology goals of the institution formulating the plan?
State Objectives		What are the specific technology objectives that must be met to achieve the goals?
Develop Strategies		What strategies must be implemented to successfully achieve the stated objectives?
Determine Evaluation		What methods must be in place and implemented to determine whether objectives were met successfully?
Disseminate Plan		How will the plan be shared with all stakeholders, and how will it be adjusted based on input?

Figure I5.1
The Strategic Planning Process
Strategic planning follows a set sequence of steps.

FOR TECHNOLOGY

circumstances that are likely to help or hinder implementation come to light and can subsequently be addressed.

Mission

The planning participants then develop a mission statement that broadly describes the overall intent of the plan. Typically, the technology plan mission statement emanates from the school or district mission statement but refocuses the institutional mission in terms of technology. The mission statement sets the direction for the rest of the planning process.

Goals

Once a mission statement has been articulated, the group then brainstorms the overarching goals for the technology that it intends to consider. Such goals can be either administrative or academic. These goals set the plan on a distinct path for technology implementation. Figure 15.2 provides some examples of strategic technology goals.

Specific ABC School Technology Goals

ABCS has identified the following specific goals relating to the use of educational technology. Each goal will be addressed during each of the years of this plan.

ABC School will

I. Use technology to improve student achievement in core areas.
II. Develop and implement a comprehensive technology-centered staff development program.
III. Provide technology-centered programs that involve both the community and ABCS parents.
IV. Provide students with the technology skills necessary for their role in the Information Age.
V. Promote communication and sharing of instructional technology in the K–12 community feeder pattern.

Year 1
Goals, Objectives, and Strategies

Goal I: Use technology to improve student achievement in core areas.

Objective 1
In the middle school, technology will be incorporated into the curriculum of each content area to enhance the teaching/learning process.

Strategies to Achieve Objective 1
1. At least one emerging technology will be introduced and used in each content-area class to prepare one instructional activity.
2. Content-area faculty will identify and select software appropriate for use in their classrooms.
3. ABCS will complete its implementation of the schoolwide computer network to provide access from each content-area classroom.
4. ABCS will complete the schoolwide closed-circuit television network.

Figure 15.2
Strategic Plan Excerpts
Strategic plans include goals, objectives, and the strategies necessary to achieve them.

Objectives with Criteria

Once goals have been established, specific objectives are articulated that describe what must happen to achieve the goals. Much like lesson objectives, which focus on teaching and describe intended outcomes, strategic planning objectives focus on the implementation efforts and describe the desired outcome. Also, like lesson objectives, planning objectives describe the criteria that will be used to determine whether the objectives were successfully met. Because strategic plans often cover a period of more than one year, objectives are often organized sequentially by year. Subsequent years' objectives are typically built on the assumption that the previous years' objectives will have been met.

Strategies

Given the objectives articulated in the plan, the group then addresses precisely how the objectives can be achieved. The planning participants brainstorm possible strategies that will achieve the objectives. These strategies are often quite specific and are typically arranged by the year when they will be achieved. In this component of the process, it is particularly valuable that the planning team consists of diverse participants, each with a different perspective and expertise. The description of strategies, like a lesson plan's description of methods and media, provides the formal guidelines for implementation of technology in the school or district.

Evaluation

The final component of a strategic plan is evaluation. How will the strategies be evaluated to determine their effectiveness? Using the criteria identified in the objectives, what process will demonstrate that the objective was met? In this final section, the participants plan the process that will inform them that the plan has been successfully carried out.

Dissemination

When all steps of the planning process are completed, the planning team disseminates the plan to all stakeholders. That wider group would include not only the constituencies that the planning team represents but all others who have an interest (stake) in the technology plan. Feedback from dissemination may validate the plan as presented, or it may suggest to the planning team that modifications to the plan need to be made before implementation.

The Action Plan

Once the planning team has disseminated the strategic plan and it is approved, the final step is implementation. The actual implementation often requires that an action plan be formulated that describes how each of the strategic plan's strategies will be accomplished. An action plan might include a description of which technologies need to be acquired and in what sequence. It might also include a description of services that need to be contracted from within or outside of the school or district. The action plan summarizes, in chronological order, each point of action that needs to be carried out for the plan to be fully implemented.

The action plan thus creates a blueprint for activities to be carried out, whereas the strategic plan articulates the overall direction and the necessary strategies to achieve the objectives that will move the school or district in the desired direction (see Figure 15.3).

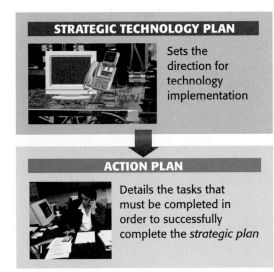

The Teacher's Role in Technology Planning

The purpose of technology in schools is to improve either the teaching and learning process or the administrative processes that support schools. Because teachers play a significant role in both academic and administrative processes, teachers are major stakeholders in strategic planning for technology. Thus, teachers play a critical role in the planning processes that ultimately result in technology implementation.

Figure 15.3
Technology Action Planning
An action plan completes the planning process.

School technology planning teams typically include a number of teachers from various departments or grade levels. District planning teams include teachers from various schools. As a professional educator, you will be asked to serve on committees that address the technology implementation issues that affect your colleagues and your students. Although some districts and schools plan less formally than the process we have just described depicts, all will expect and need your input when determining how best to acquire and implement technology.

Your role as a teacher in the school or district planning process requires that you maintain your awareness of current and emerging technologies and their usefulness in supporting teaching and learning. You do not need to be a technical expert, but you do need to be educational-technology literate to make a sound contribution to the planning process that will shape the way your school or district addresses technology.

Educational Technology Resources and Organizations

American Educational Research Association
http://www.aera.net

Apple Classrooms of Tomorrow
http://www.eworld.com/education/k12/leadership/acot

Association for Career and Technical Education
http://www.acteonline.org

Association for Educational Communications and Technology
http://www.aect.org

Association for Supervision and Curriculum Development
http://www.ascd.org

Association for the Advancement of Computing in Education
http://www.aace.org

Center for Children and Technology
http://www2.edc.org/CCT

Computer Learning Foundation
http://www.computerlearning.org

Computer-Using Educators
http://www.cue.org

Consortium for School Networking
http://www.cosn.org

Digital Divide Network
http://www.digitaldividenetwork.org

EDUCAUSE
http://www.educause.edu

Global SchoolNet Foundation
http://www.globalschoolnet.org

Intercultural E-Mail Classroom Connections
http://www.teaching.com/iecc

International Council for Educational Media
http://www.aect.org/Affiliates/National/icem.htm

International Society for Techology in Education
http://www.iste.org

International Technology Education Association
http://www.iteawww.org

National Center for Technology Planning
http://www.nctp.com

National Council for Accreditation of Teacher Education
http://www.ncate.org

National Educational Computing Conference
http://www.neccsite.org

National School Boards Association Education Technology Programs
http://www.nsba.org/itte

National Telecommunications and Information Administration
http://www.ntia.doc.gov

Regional Technology in Education Consortia
http://www.rtec.org

Society for Applied Learning Technology
http://www.salt.org

Society for Information Technology and Teacher Education
http://www.aace.org/site

Special Education Resource Center (SERC)
http://www.serc.org

TEAMS Distance Learning
http://www.teams.lacoe.edu

Technology in Education
http://www.tie-online.org

U.S. Department of Education, Office of Educational Technology
http://www.ed.gov/Technology

U.S. Department of Education, Technology State Contacts
http://www.ed.gov/about/contacts/state/technology.html

U.S. Distance Learning Association
http://www.usdla.org

www4teachers
http://www.4teachers.org

Glossary

academic dishonesty Cheating and/or plagiarizing in academic work that may be facilitated by the ease of copying and pasting information from web sites or multimedia.

academic software Software designed to assist and support both educators and learners in teaching and learning.

academic tools On a computer network, academic software that provides the teacher with tools to help in the instructional process; for example, the ability to monitor student activities on each networked computer, including the ability to take control of individual computers to demonstrate a process.

acceptable use The school or district policies to help ensure that school technology made available to students is used appropriately and for academic purposes.

action plan The plan listing the specific action steps that describe how each of the plan's strategies will be accomplished.

administrative software Software that assists an educator in accomplishing the administrative, professional, and management tasks associated with the profession.

administrative tools Software programs that are shared by all network users and usually provide, at a minimum, a common calendar, address book, and facilities reservation list. Also called groupware.

alternative delivery system A hybrid instructional delivery system that uses the best of both traditional and distance strategies for the delivery of instruction.

analog video An electronic signal that varies continuously in strength and is generated by a camera or a videotape source.

antiplagiarism software Software that compares a student's work with well-known authors' work and with work posted on the web to detect plagiarism.

antivirus program Programs that detect and destroy computer viruses.

application program A set of instructions that tell a computer how to complete a unique task such as word processing, database management, or drawing.

artificial intelligence (AI) Programs that work in manners that are similar to the way the human brain works, allowing computers to adapt and respond beyond their initial programming.

AskERIC A personalized Internet-based service that provides education information to teachers, librarians, counselors, administrators, parents, and anyone else who is interested in education.

Association for Educational Communications and Technology (AECT) A professional association of thousands of educators and others whose activities are directed toward improving instruction through technology.

asynchronous A method of instructional delivery that is time shifted; that is, teacher and students can participate at differing times from the same or different locations.

asynchronous communications Online tools that do not require real-time interaction; examples are email and electronic bulletin boards.

attention Focusing on a specific object or thought sufficiently to become fully aware of it.

audiocassette An economical, durable, and easy-to-use magnetic tape medium that lets you record voice, music, or other sounds.

authoring system A category of software that allows the educator to easily create custom computer-enhanced lessons of all types, including multimedia lessons and web-based lessons.

AVI (Audio Video Interleaved) A popular digital video format that offers low resolution and smaller file sizes compared to other formats; good for animation.

back up To create a duplicate copy on another storage medium for use in case the original copy is lost.

backup system A system of redundant processes and technologies that provide for continuity of instructional delivery even when problems occur in the primary delivery system.

bandwidth The carrying capacity (size of the "roadway") of electronic transmission media for sending and receiving information.

behaviorists Those who view all behavior as a response to external stimuli; they believe that the learner acquires behaviors, skills, and knowledge in response to the rewards, punishments, or withheld responses associated with them.

Bloom's taxonomy A method for categorizing differences in thinking skills; it includes six levels of cognition ranging from recall of knowledge to evaluation of knowledge.

bookmarks A collection of URLs that have been saved by using the bookmark function of the browser, allowing the user to go to a desired web page again without having to retype its URL; also known as favorites.

Boolean logic A type of logic that uses operators, such as AND, OR, or NOT, to limit or expand the scope of a search such as one would do on the Internet using a search engine.

booting up The process of powering on a computer during which it reads the instructions stored in ROM to tell it how to start itself up.

broadcast audio Audio that is transmitted and received via radio.

broadcast video Video that is broadcast via terrestrial equipment or by a combination of terrestrial and satellite equipment; Commonly thought of as television.

bulletin board A surface usually made of cork that provides a flexible, easy-to-change display area for a variety of print and graphic elements.

byte Eight bits (on-off pulses) of data, roughly equal to one alphabetic (A) or numeric (1) character of information.

cable modem A specialized modem that provides high-speed connections for digital access via cable lines that are already installed for cable television. Users can use get speeds up to 100 to 1,000 times faster than is possible with a standard modem and a telephone line.

cablecast video Video that is transmitted by a cable company via coaxial cable to remote locations.

camcorder A compact video device that includes a camera and recorder; used to record sound and images that can be played back by using a VCR.

CD Compact Disk, also CD-ROM. An optical media that stores digital data via tiny holes burned into the disk surface with a laser.

CD-R (compact disc-recordable) A type of compact disc on which the user can record (write) data. Once recorded, the data cannot be changed. Each disc is capable of storing approximately 600 megabytes of data (text, sound, graphics, animation, or video).

CD-ROM (compact disc read-only memory) An optical storage device on which data is stored and read via optical technology. CD-ROM disks are written on when created, can be read many time, but the original data cannot be changed.

CD-RW (compact disc/rewritable) A type of compact disc that allows the user to record many times and to change the data stored on the CD. Each disc is capable of storing approximately 600 megabytes of data (text, sound, graphics, animation, and/or video).

chalkboard A hard-surfaced board that can be written on with a variety of chalk colors to create impromptu text and visual displays.

chat A network or online service that sets aside a virtual space in which two or more users can meet in real time by typing their messages and then sending them for display in the chat room.

chip A small square of highly refined silicon on which microscopic electronic components (such as transistors and resis-

tors) have been embedded. Chips can be designed to serve many different purposes, from memory to CPU chips, such as Intel's Pentium IV microprocessor.

classroom management support software Off-the-shelf or customized software written for educators to help them manage school and classroom tasks, including the creation and maintenance of seating charts, class rolls, student records, and school budgets.

classroom management tools Downloadable or online tools such as test generators, diagnostic tests, and class roll generators that assist you in the tasks required for your classroom.

clip art A term that is carried over from the days of manual page layout but now refers to collections of prepared artwork that can be inserted into electronic documents.

closed-circuit TV (CCTV) A network of television monitors connected via coaxial cables running throughout a school building that can distribute television signals to all the connected classrooms.

code of ethics A set of written expectations and definitions of what is considered appropriate or acceptable use that is published by a school or district.

codec A compression/decompression algorithm that is used to digitize and compress video and audio signals for transmission and to reverse the process on reception.

cognitive style How one thinks. Each person has his or her own unique tendencies and preferences when it comes to cognition (thinking).

cognitivists Those who focus on learning as a mental operation that begins when information enters through the senses, undergoes mental manipulation, is stored, and finally used.

coherence An element of a good visual that suggests logical connection or integration of diverse elements, relationships, or values.

command An instruction that the user gives the computer or a program for the next operation to be performed.

communications cycle The interchange of information between two or more individuals, such as the teacher and a student. In the cycle, information is encoded by the sender and decoded by the receiver, with various filters affecting the clarity of the message.

compressed video system An integrated system that includes a video camera and microphone with a codec to compress the signals to transmit them over ISDN phone lines for two-way video and audio communication.

compression technologies Software and hardware that make video files smaller by capturing the initial video image in full but then ignoring the nonchanging components of the image in transmitting the images.

computer literacy The basic computer skills and knowledge necessary to ensure that individuals can effectively use computers.

computer system The combination of input devices, central processing unit, memory, output devices, and storage devices.

computer-assisted instruction (CAI) A term that was originally applied to drill-and-practice software but is now more broadly used to describe any software that uses the computer to tutor or review content and provide a platform for reasoning with reference to content.

computer-managed instruction (CMI)   Software that instructs as well as manages instructional lessons; in addition to reviewing content, it keeps track of student progress with reference to the material.

computing cycle   A processing cycle that includes the steps of taking data in, processing it, storing it as necessary, and outputting the finished information to the user.

concept-mapping software   Software that generates visual, digital "maps" of concepts that depict the outcome of the brainstorming process and the interrelationships between ideas.

conference call   A telephone call placed via personal phone services or the school phone system that allows three to eight participants to connect together to support small-group instruction or discussion.

conference   A tool that provides users with a way to communicate one-to-many. Participants post a message for anyone to read; those reading the message can post either a public or a private response. Sometimes called bulletin boards, clubs, or forums.

connection gateway   Node or web site that serves as an entrance point to another network.

consistency   An element of a visual that suggests that diverse elements work together and build on each other to produce a single clear message.

constructivists   Those who believe that knowledge is a constructed element resulting from the learning process and that knowledge is unique to the individual who constructs it.

contrast   The communication power of a visual as determined by the arrangement and balance of the elements.

convergence   The blending of diverse digital technologies into a single multipurpose technology such as a cell phone that can also access the Internet and provide the functions of a handheld computer.

copyright   The laws that protect the interests of those who own creative works, whether text, music, artwork, software, or any other creative product.

Corporation for Public Broadcasting (CPB)   A public corporation that manages the acquisition and production of educational programming while PBS (Public Broadcasting System) disseminates the programming via local TV channels.

correspondence course   The earliest distance delivery system, consisting of books and assignments delivered to students via the postal system.

CPU (central processing unit)   The "brain" of a computer, incorporated into a single microprocessor chip. Within it, calculations are performed; the flow of information between input, output, and memory is coordinated; and program instructions are transmitted.

data projection unit   A projection device that plugs into a computer's monitor port and displays the computer image in an enlarged, room-size format.

data projector   A computer projection unit that combines an LCD display unit and a light source in a single, relatively lightweight box.

database management software (DBMS)   A software system that can be used to easily and quickly record, organize, access, and extract information electronically from stored data.

decision matrix   A chart containing choices to help the individual determine which choice is the one that she or he believe is best.

Design-Plan-Act! (D-P-A) system   A comprehensive three-part system that is designed to help maximize the quality of teaching plans. The Design-Plan-Act! (D-P-A) system includes three planning processes: designing the instruction, articulating specific lesson plans, and developing an instructional action plan.

desktop publishing (DTP) software   Software that can not only perform typical word-processing tasks, but also make extensive and precise adjustments to page displays, such as creating an attractive arrangement of graphics and text on a page.

digital camera   A camera that takes pictures and stores them digitally rather than on photographic film. Photos are stored in the camera's memory card or on a disk inside the camera and then transferred to a computer for processing or display.

digital divide   A descriptive term referring to the gap between those who have ready access to and knowledge of digital technologies and those who do not.

digital projector   A computer output device that projects digital images onto a projection screen, large monitor, or whiteboard so that they can be seen by a large group.

Digital subscriber line (DSL)   A special phone line that provides speeds up to 25 times faster than those possible with a standard phone line. Both voice and digital communications are provided on a single line, thus eliminating the need to subscribe to two phone lines.

Digital video disc (DVD)   A type of optical storage device that uses laser technology to store data. DVD discs store considerably more data than CD-ROMs because they store data on both sides of the disc (unlike the one-sided CD-ROM) and on up to two layers per side.

digital video   Video signals that are recorded as discrete numerical values that represent the video images.

digital video camera   A video camera that captures and stores the video in a digital format that can then be directly manipulated by using a personal computer.

digital video editing   Integrated hardware and software that allow the user to edit images and audio frame by frame.

digitizer   An electronic device that converts lines drawn on a special tablet into digital data that can be manipulated on a computer. Sometimes called a graphics tablet.

diorama   A display that represents a scene with a foreground containing three-dimensional objects and a two-dimensional painted background.

direction   Arrangement of visual elements to establish the initial focus and the appropriate direction for viewers' attention to follow when looking at a visual.

dissemination   The sharing of a strategic plan with all stakeholders when all steps of the planning process have been completed.

distance education   The delivery of instruction to students who are separated from their teacher by time and/or location.

document camera   A video camera mounted on a stand that takes and projects an image of whatever is placed on the stand's document table.

downlink   A data link by which signals are transmitted from a satellite to a terrestrial system at another location on the globe.

dpi (dots per inch)   A measure of resolution in printers and some other output devices.

draw programs   Software that provides tools to create digital images; this software is known as object-oriented or vector graphic programs because the graphics are created by layering objects on top of one another.

drill-and-practice software   Software that uses a behaviorist format that offers rewards following successful completion of routine exercises.

DVD (digital video disc)   A laser disc that is similar to a CD-ROM but is designed and recorded to hold significantly more information than a CD. DVD discs can store data on both sides of the disc (unlike the one-sided CD-ROM) and on multiple layers per side.

DVD-ROM (digital video disc read-only memory)   An optical storage device that is similar to a CD-ROM disc but can store considerably more data. DVD discs can store data on both sides of the disc (unlike the one-sided CD-ROM) and on multiple layers per side.

dynamic instructional design (DID) model   An instructional design model that includes these six phases: know the learners, articulate your objectives, establish the learning environment, identify teaching and learning strategies, identify and select support technologies, and evaluate and revise the design.

e-book   Electronic book. A computing device designed to download, store, and display electronic versions of books. These devices may include multimedia features as well as access to the Internet to enhance or expand on linked text within the book.

editing software   Software that provides the user with the capabilities to alter, enhance, or add special effects to digital images.

educational games   Software that presents and reviews instructional content in a game format.

educational technology   Any technology used by educators in support of the teaching and learning process.

electronic conferences   A method of one-to-many electronic communication much like a virtual bulletin board on which individuals post messages for all participants to read and then others post responses, resulting in an online discussion.

electronic gradebooks   Grading tools that let a teacher store and easily average students' grades.

electronic mail   An asynchronous communication method in which a written message can be sent from one user to another; messages can include extended attachments enhancing the original message with animated graphics, audio, and compressed video clips in addition to text.

electronic spreadsheet   Software that enables the user to organize, input, edit, chart, and produce accurate professional reports for task dealing extensively with numbers.

electronic whiteboard   A combination of computer technology with a whiteboard display that not only displays information like any other whiteboard, but also captures the information written on it into a computer file. A digital projector can project the image on the computer screen onto the board, where it becomes a touch screen to which the computer will respond.

email   Electronic messages sent from one computer to another across the many networks attached to the Internet.

e-rate   Also called the Education Rate, a discounted cost for telecommunications service for community access centers (schools, libraries, etc.).

ERIC   A national information system that is supported by the U.S. Department of Education, the U.S. Office of Educational Research and Improvement, and the National Library of Education; the world's largest database of education information, with more than one million abstracts of documents and journal articles, many available through the Internet.

evaluation   The final component of strategic planning in which the participants plan the processes that will be used to determine whether the plan has been successfully carried out. It is also a method of assessing a student's achievement of stated objectives. In a distance environment, it may include alternative assessments and proctored testing.

exhibit   A diorama or other classroom display created and/or arranged to illustrate instructional content.

expert systems   Artificial intelligence programs that offer suggestions and advice based on a database of expertise.

fair use   A section of the copyright law that identifies the criteria under which you may be allowed to copy another's creative work.

FAQ   An abbreviation for the "frequently asked questions" that many web sites include to anticipate the questions that users will have.

favorites   A collection of URLs that have been saved by using a function of the browser, allowing the user to go to a desired web page again without having to retype its URL; also known as bookmarks.

fax   Technology that, with a combination of a scanner, a modem, and a printer, translates hard copy into digital signals, sends them across communications channels, and then prints them when they are received by another fax machine; fax technology is useful for communication of materials in a distance education environment.

feedback   Providing another person with information on how well a task was performed or how successful an experience was in order to help improve future performance.

feedback loops   Provisions within the instructional design plan to collect evaluative information for two main purposes: The information is used by the learners to see how they are doing so that they can change their approach, and the data is used so that immediate changes can be made to improve the plan.

felt board   A cloth-covered board on which visual elements cut out of flannel or felt and backed with VelcroTM can be arranged to illustrate instructional content.

file   A collection of related data, usually a product of a single task, that is saved on a storage device.

File transfer protocol (FTP)   The application protocol that is used to facilitate the transferring of files between computers on the Internet.

filtering software   Software that filters out and blocks unacceptable Internet sites so that students cannot access them.

firewall   A combination of software and hardware that provides various levels of security measures designed to keep computer hackers out of networks and to keep data safe.

flat-bed scanner   A scanner with a flat glass plate on which the original is placed (allowing the user to scan a page from a book); a cover can then be placed over the back of the original to block ambient light during the scan process.

flip chart   A large ($25'' \times 30''$) pad of paper usually mounted on an easel.

floppy disk   A nonvolatile, portable magnetic storage device. The standard floppy disk can contain 1.44 megabytes (millions of bytes) of data.

focused listening   Giving one's full attention to an auditory stimulus.

folder   A digital organizer that is created by the user to hold related files on a disk; also known as a directory in non-Windows operating systems.

formative feedback   Feedback that ensures a way to facilitate the continuous flow of information as a system is implemented so that corrections and adjustments can be made while the process unfolds.

freedom of speech   The ethical issue that arises whenever Internet content is regulated such that it restricts the constitutionally guaranteed right to free speech.

freeware   Software that is offered to users without charge.

FTP (file transfer protocol)   A protocol used on the Internet for uploading and downloading files.

fuzzy logic software   Artificial intelligence software that functions in a manner that resembles human decision making.

GIF (Graphic Interchange Format)   A graphics format that is used primarily for color images, clip art, line art, and grayscale images.

gigabyte   Approximately one billion bytes of data or characters of data.

global learning community   A community of learners built through the use of communication tools on a classroom web site to connect one classroom to others across the globe.

goals   In strategic planning, the overarching direction and purpose for technology that set the plan on a distinct path of technology implementation.

graphic   A pictorial image, such as a drawing, cartoon, or diagram, that can represent and clarify concepts and relationships.

graphics software   Software that enables the user to create images from nonelectronic sources and to create, edit, alter, enhance, and add special effects to digital images; the three categories of graphics software are drawing, imaging, and editing.

graphics tablet   An electronic device that converts lines sketched on a special tablet into their digital equivalent on the screen. Sometimes called a digitizer.

groupware   Administrative software tools that are shared by all network users and usually include, at a minimum, a common calendar, address book, and facilities reservation list.

GUI (graphical user interface)   The method of interaction in which the user enters commands by using a device such as a mouse or trackball to point to and click on icons displayed on the monitor.

H.320 Standard   International standards established for the compression of video signals across ISDN lines so that diverse brands of compressed video equipment can communicate with each other.

H.323 Standard   International standards established for the compression of video signals across networks and the Internet.

handheld computer   Also Personal Digital Assistants (PDA). Palm size computer that offers a scaled-down version of PC operating system and applications programs. Most are also internet capable and offer wireless connectivity to networks.

handshaking   The process that occurs when one computer calls another computer and the second computer answers the call and responds with a high-pitched sound known as a carrier signal.

hard copy   The printed version of material generated by a computer. It is the most common output of a computer other than what appears of the monitor screen.

hard disk   A disk storage area in which the operating system, applications programs, and most personal data are stored. The disk or platter is built into the hard disk drive and can hold gigabytes, or billions of bytes, of data.

hardware   Computer hardware includes all of the computer components that are physical, touchable pieces of equipment.

headphones   Miniature speakers that are placed directly over the ears. They allow individual students to listen to audio without disturbing anyone else.

hearing   The physical process that includes the correct receiving of clear, audible sounds.

home page   On a web site, a welcome page that orients the visitor to the site and provides a connection to additional information pages.

hub   A series of centralized connections for workstations or peripherals so that they can be connected to the network.

hypertext markup language (HTML)   The formatting language that is used to determine how the information presented on web pages will look.

hyperlink   A graphic or segment of text on a web page that contains instructions to link to another web page or a different web site.

hypermedia software   A type of multimedia software that not only uses multiple media but also organizes information such that the student can make "hyperjumps," student-driven connections in either linear or nonlinear sequences, from and to different components of the instructional content.

icon   A small graphic image that represents one of a GUI's system options.

imaging software   Software that creates a digital version or images from a nonelectronic source.

independent learning   A type of learning strategy in which students must take greater responsibility for the processes and procedures necessary to master content.

individualized instruction   An instructional approach in which the techniques used are focused more on the individual learner than on a class or larger group; often the approach used for distance learners.

input device   A computer peripheral that the user might use to enter data into a computer system.

instant messaging (IM)   A type of chat software that allows two users to spontaneously open a private two-person chat room when both are online.

instructional action plan (IAP)   A template in which the teacher is prompted to list lesson requirements and to detail what he or she will need for successful implementation.

instructional design model   A plan of instruction that results in a complete and precise blueprint of what should happen and how to arrange the key critical components necessary to designing effective instruction.

instructional event   A learning experience that has been designed by a teacher from specific learning objectives to outcomes with the use of appropriate media to enhance the learner's achievement of the objective.

instructional support   Systems to support learners, such as a teacher being present for clarification and questions or a media center or tutoring program for students who need additional help. Such systems are often absent in distance education; alternative support systems are required in their place.

instructional television (ITV)   Local learning channels that use broadcast airwaves to distribute video signals of instructional programs throughout a school and/or district.

Instructional Television Fixed Service (ITFS)   A terrestrial system that sends signals via microwave transmission from studios and ITFS broadcast locations to reception locations (usually schools) within a fixed area.

integrated learning systems (ILS)   A network of computers, all running customized software designed to assist students in learning targeted objectives.

integrated productivity package   A software package that includes the major applications (word processing, spreadsheet, database management, presentation) but not all of the features and capabilities of the stand-alone application packages.

Integrated Services Digital Network (ISDN)   High-speed digital phone lines that can provide speeds up to five times that of regular analog phone lines and can offer both voice and digital communications on a single line.

integrated software package   A collection of the main features of popular applications integrated into a single comprehensive application.

intelligence   The inherent capability of a learner to understand and learn.

intelligent agents   Subprograms used by artificial intelligence systems to help with specific tasks such as asking questions, monitoring work to determining patterns of action, and performing requested tasks.

interaction   Communications and discussion between teacher and student and among students that clarify and enhance their understanding of course content.

interface   The component of an operating system that establishes the methods of interaction (via menus, text, and/or graphics) between the user and the machine.

International Society for Technology in Education (ISTE)   A nonprofit professional organization dedicated to promoting appropriate uses of information technology to support and improve teaching and learning.

Internet   An electronic communications network of networks that connects computers and organizational computer facilities around the world with a standardized means of communication called Internet protocols (IP).

Internet audio   Audio, usually digitized as a WAV or MP3 file, that is delivered to the user over the Internet.

Internet broadcast   The broadcasting of live events and performances over the Internet, using streaming video technology that compresses digital video and plays it back while it is being received.

Internet chat   A synchronous communication in which two or more people online at the same time communicate, typically via typed messages in a virtual space.

Internet meeting   An Internet-based "face-to-face" conversation with people around the world via compressed video.

Internet radio   Online radio stations consisting of a wide variety of programming, including music, sports, science, and local, national, and world news broadcast over the Internet.

Internet service provider (ISP)   A company that provides home and business computers with a way to temporarily connect to the Internet usually for a monthly, quarterly, or annual fee.

ISDN   High-speed telephone lines that are often used to connect compressed videoconferencing systems.

JPEG (Joint Photographic Experts Group)   The agreed-upon standard for high-resolution images; pronounced "jay-peg."

keyboard   The primary input device for a computer. A typical computer keyboard is laid out much like the keys on the typewriter but with several additional keys, not typically found on a typewriter, that are used to control the computer or give software commands.

kilobyte   Approximately 1000 bytes or 1000 characters of data.

laser disc   Eight- or twelve-inch optical discs that are made and played by using laser technology similar to that used for CDs; a recording medium that was developed to provide a higher quality of image and sound than videotape provides.

LCD (liquid crystal display)   A display screen made of two sheets of a flexible polarizing material with a layer of liquid crystal solution between the two.

learning environment   The instructional climate in which the student is expected to learn. It includes all aspects of the environment from the physical to the nonphysical.

learning strategies   The way in which instruction is presented to the learner determines how the learner can process the information. Providing for active learning activities is an example of the use of an effective learning strategy.

learning style   Those conditions under which an individual best learns. The most common learning style theory identifies three primary modalities for learning: auditory, visual, and kinesthetic.

lesson planner   A detailed guide to creating a daily or weekly lesson plan. It is the pragmatic product of the instructional design process.

link   A connection to another point on the web, either on the same document, on a different page of the site, or on another web site altogether.

liquid crystal display (LCD) projection panel   A display device made up of a large glass panel in which the liquid crystals can be activated by an electrical current to form letters, numbers, and visual images. The panel is connected to the computer and placed on an overhead projector so that the projector's light shines through the panel's glass and projects the computer image onto a screen.

listening   Being able to hear and comprehend auditory stimuli; it involves several steps: (1) actually hearing the auditory stimulus, (2) the brain turning that stimulus into neural pulses and processing them, and (3) making the appropriate cognitive connections to relate this new information to memories of real events or previously learned content.

live cam   A digital video camera that is connected to a computer, which in turn is connected to the Internet so that the digital images from the camera can be seen by those connecting to the live cam web site.

local area network (LAN)   Small networks that connect machines in local areas, such as a classroom or school.

macro   A prerecorded set of commands that automates a complex task such as formatting output to fit on labels.

magnetic board   A metal display surface on which visual elements with magnets attached to them can be arranged to illustrate instructional content.

mailing list   An electronic list of email addresses for individuals and/or companies that is equivalent to a printed phone list. Email can be sent electronically to everyone on the mailing list with one command.

media   Aids to teaching that assist a teacher during instruction. They range from printed materials to audiovisual equipment to computers.

megabyte   One million bytes or 1,000,000 characters of data.

memory   A series of RAM chips that provide temporary, volatile electronic storage that is used by the CPU to store short-term data.

menu   A listing of command options. In the Windows and Mac operating systems, command menus appears across the top of open windows.

method   A technique or strategy of teaching, such as lecture, demonstration, or discussion.

mission statement   A statement that broadly describes the overall intent of a strategic plan; typically, a mission statement emanates from the school or district.

model   A three-dimensional representation of a real object or concept that cannot reasonably be brought into the classroom.

modem   A device that Modulates a computer's signal so that it can be transmitted across a phone line to a similar device that DEModulates the signal.

monitor   The primary output device of a computer, displaying computer information on its screen. Monitor screens typically have higher resolution than TV screens.

motivators   Objects or activities that get the learners' attention and encourage them to become engaged in the lesson.

mouse   A pointing device that rolls about on the user's desk. It is often called a "work-alike" device because it moves the cursor on the computer screen in the same direction that the user moves the mouse on the desk.

MOV   The file type of one of the most popular digital video formats; it is known as QuickTime, and the file type is abbreviated as MOV for "movie."

MP3 (Moving Picture Experts Group Audio Layer 3)   An audio compression technology that provides high-quality sound in one twelfth of the space that the same sound would take in previous formats of audio files.

MPEG (Moving Picture Experts Group)   A popular digital video format that reduces the size of video files up to 95 percent yet retains near-television quality.

multimedia   Multiple types of media that are combined into an integrated whole that presents instructional content. Although not only digital media may be included, the term is often used to refer to a computer-based format that combines text, graphics, audio, and even video into a single, coherent, digital presentation.

multimedia kit   An instructional kit that includes multiple media to present content; a kit may include visual elements (texts and graphics), cassette tapes, student activity sheets, suggested lesson plans, motion video, and even real objects.

multimedia software   Software that uses multiple types of technology that typically address different learning modalities.

narrowcast video   Video transmission that is targeted to a small (narrow) audience, particularly schools.

navigation button   Connections or links to other locations on the same or a different web site; they are usually colored or underlined words or graphics, and when they are passed over with a cursor, the cursor arrow turns into a pointing hand, indicating something that can be clicked on.

network   A collection of computers and peripherals that are connected together so that they can communicate information and share resources.

network interface card (NIC)   An expansion card with an electronic port with connectors that is placed in each computer that is to be connected to a computer network.

network modem   A modem that is connected to a network server, allowing computers that are connected by the network to share a single Internet connection.

neural network   Artificial intelligence software that learns and adjusts responses on the basis of previous interactions.

neuron   A nerve cell that consists of three major components—the cell body, the axon, and the dendrites—and is part of a vast neural network.

newsgroup   An electronic public discussion or conference, dedicated to a specific topic, that is continuously running on the Internet. It may be hosted privately on one server, or it may be hosted on many servers in a decentralized fashion.

node   Any workstation or peripheral that is connected to a network. All nodes are ultimately connected back, through one or more hubs, to a server.

objectives   Carefully articulated statements that describe what must happen to achieve the goals of a strategic plan; strategic planning objectives focus the implementation efforts and describe the desired outcome.

OCR (optical character recognition) software   Software that recognizes printed characters when they are scanned and then turns them into their electronic word-processing equivalent.

online publications Online, electronic versions of material that would traditionally be produced in hard copy. Also known as e-publications, these resources typically include current and archived articles of interest to educators.

operating system A program that tells the computer how to function and how to manage its own operation.

oral history Historical commentary that is made up of a series of interviews captured on audiotape.

output device The pieces of hardware that move information (data that has been processed) out of the computer.

overhead projector A projector that uses a powerful lamp and a series of mirrors and lenses to shine through a clear acetate sheet (i.e., a transparency) so that the images on the transparency can be seen by all.

packet Data that is broken into small units and sent through a network one unit or packet at a time.

paint programs Software that uses an electronic pen, brush, and other tools to create and manipulate digital pictures in a manner very similar to the way in which one paints a picture in the real world.

palmtop computer A palm-sized, hand-held computer that merges the digital organizer and the computer into a single powerful but small computing device.

password A combination of letters and numerals that a user must enter along with the login name as a second level of security.

PDF files Files that have been saved in Adobe Acrobat format so that the publication appears exactly as it would look on the printed page, including custom layouts, photos, and other graphics; these files require the use of Acrobat Reader to display them.

pedagogical cycle Teaching and learning strategies are components of a continuing cycle that is played out again and again as a lesson is implemented.

pedagogy The actual function of teaching or what teachers do when implementing their craft to assist their students' learning.

peer-to-peer networking A network configuration that allows users to share files, not by uploading them to a central site, but instead by making files available on their machine, which in turn is accessible to others on the network.

performance objectives Objectives that specify what the learner will be able to do when the instructional event concludes.

personal digital assistant (PDA) A hand-held computer that may vary in capabilities from simply functioning as a personal organizer to running scaled-down versions of productivity software.

perspective The way in which people look at things and interpret them; different people can look at the same thing and see it in their own unique ways.

phone bridge Communications technology that allows multiple users to call in to a central phone number to participate in a phone conference.

photograph A pictorial image captured via camera, film, and a photochemical development process.

piracy Illegally copying software to share with others or installing software on multiple machines when only one copy was purchased.

pixel The smallest unit of information in an image. Each pixel represents a portion of the image in a specific color. The term pixel stands for "picture element."

plug-in A program that may be downloaded from the Internet, usually free, to expand a browser's capabilities, for example, to allow multimedia to be displayed.

port A connection on a computer into which peripheral devices can be plugged.

portal A site on the Internet that offers an assortment of services, such as a search engine, news, email, conferencing, electronic shopping, and chat rooms.

POST (power-on self-test) A self-diagnostic program that ensures that all of the computer's components are functioning as expected.

preorganizer An early warning system to let the learners know what knowledge they are responsible for acquiring.

presentation software Software that includes programs designed to create digital support materials for oral presentations.

print material Hard-copy printed pages that may include books and worksheets as well as posters and charts.

print server A dedicated computer that provides printing services to all local network workstations by attaching the printer to one of the workstations on the network or by directly connecting the printer to the network.

privacy An ethical issue that arises when an individual's right to privacy conflicts with the rights of any agency, whether governmental or commercial, to closely monitor and record an individual's personal information or online activities.

problem-solving software Programs that involve the learner by focusing on creative problem-solving situations rather than on routine drill-and-practice skills.

productivity software Generic business application software that educators can use and adapt for the administrative and professional tasks they must address.

program A set of computer instructions, written in a special computer language, that tells a computer how to accomplish a given task.

programmed instruction An instructional system in which material is presented in a series of small steps. Each step requires active learner response, to which there is immediate feedback to the learner as to the correctness of the response.

proportion The relative size of elements in a visual in comparison to their importance.

protocol A common, standardized set of conventions for the format for communication that governs the formatting of data and the way it is handled.

Public Broadcast System (PBS) A local nonprofit television channel that disseminates high-quality educational programs, especially to schools but also to the general public; part of a nationwide system of public stations.

public files Public storage areas on a network where files can be stored and read by all users; the files can be read-only, or they may be designated as read/write.

RAM (random-access memory) The series of chips that make up a computer system's temporary memory area. This area empties when the application is closed and fills up again when the user opens a new application.

readiness   In distance and alternative learning, the capacity of teachers and students to work within the new environments; includes readiness to accept new roles and readiness to work with new technologies.

real object   An object that can be safely and reasonably brought into the classroom for examination or demonstration.

reference software   Digital versions of volumes of reference materials recorded in a linear fashion on a compact disc that contains an interface that enables hyperjumps to any point of information recorded on the CD.

removable hard disk   A hard drive that can be removed from the computer. It can either be mounted in the computer or plugged into the back of the computer and run as an additional, external drive.

resolution   The clarity and crispness of the images on the monitor screen or printer. Pixels are the measure of resolution in monitors; printer resolution is measured in dpi.

resource sharing   A network function that allows programs that are installed on the network server to be available to all workstations.

retrofit   To prepare and remodel existing facilities to accommodate computer networks.

ROM (read-only memory)   A chip created to hold a stored program such as the BIOS (Basic Input/Output System) that provides instructions to the computer as to how to start itself up. ROM chips are read but are typically not written on.

router   Connecting devices used to direct (route) network communications along the correct pathways to and from the appropriate network.

satellite transmission   Signals transmitted to a satellite (uplinked) and then sent back down (downlinked) to a terrestrial communication system at another location on the globe; the satellites are in orbits that allow signals to be bounced via uplinks and downlinks to positions anywhere on the globe.

scaffolding   The process of building bridges to prior knowledge at the beginning of a lesson.

scan converter   A device that converts a computer's image into one that can be displayed through analog (video) technology by converting a digital (computer) signal to an analog (video) signal.

scanner   An input device that captures and then translates printed copy or images into digital data.

school and classroom management support software   See *classroom management support software*.

search engine   A special program on the Internet that allows the user to type in keywords to look for online material that contains those words or topics.

server   A powerful computer that provides services to other computers in the network, such as email, program sharing, and printer sharing.

shareware   Software that is offered to users for a small fee, usually paid on the honor system after the user has had a chance to try out the software and determine whether it is indeed useful for the user's purposes.

sheet-fed scanner   A scanner that allows the user to feed a series of pages into the scanner one after the other. Some sheet-fed scanners include a document feeder so that the user does not have to do this manually.

simulations   Software packages that present to the user a model or situation in a computerized or virtual format.

site licenses   Purchased rights to use a single copy of a program on any machine on the network at a defined site.

site map   An outline of all the pages included on a web site, usually with a description of the type of information that can be located on each page.

slide   A small photographic transparency made from pictures taken on slide film and then permanently mounted in a cardboard holder.

slide projector   A projector that shines a bright light through a slide (usually 35mm) to display the image on a screen.

soft copy   Data that is still in an electronic form within the computer. Soft copy is volatile; it will disappear when power to the machine is cut off.

software   Computer programs created to accomplish specific tasks or perform specific functions.

speaker   An audio output device to amplify the sound generated by a computer program, a CD, or other sound device.

speakerphone   Telephone technology usually equipped with an omnidirectional microphone designed to pick up voices from anywhere in the room that allows all participants in a room to communicate using a single, specially equipped phone.

special needs software   Software specifically designed to address the needs of learners with special needs as the result of a variety of physical or learning impairments.

stakeholders   Representatives from all groups that will be affected by a strategic plan who, as a result, are selected and actively participate together in the strategic planning process.

stimulus-response   A stimulus is the initial action directed to the organism, and the response is the organism's reaction to that action.

storage   A nonvolatile, electronic space on a magnetic or optical disc that the computer can use to store instructions and data for use at a later time.

storyboarding   A technique that is used to plan a video sequence by sketching each of the main planned image ideas (and script if desired), one per card, to allow the planner to consider the relationships of the video images, sound, and use and positioning (staging) of props and to revise as desired.

strategic planning   A process that includes a series of several distinct steps, each of which helps to focus the stakeholders and institution participating in the process in a single, clearly articulated direction.

strategies   As a component of the strategic plan, statements that describe how the plan's objectives can be accomplished.

streaming audio   An audio technology for the web that sends audio in a continuous stream or flow to allow the user to listen to the audio as it is received by the browser.

streaming video   A video technology that compresses and plays back digital video that is sent in a continuous stream, allowing the user to view the video clip while it is being downloaded over the Internet.

summative feedback   Data that is returned at the end of a process.

SWOT analysis   An acronym for "strengths, weaknesses, opportunities, threats"; during this component of a strategic plan, participants brainstorm all of the factors, both positive and negative, that will affect the potential success of the plan they are developing.

synchronous   A method of instructional delivery that occurs at the same time, although typically not in the same place.

synchronous communication   A method of communicating in which the participants interact at the same (or in real) time.

systems approach   A model that specifies a methodical approach to the analysis and design of instruction, including a statement of observable learning objectives and the use of a systematic process that includes the specific evaluation techniques and instructional experiences.

talking book   A dramatization of a play or the recorded reading of a book, play, or short stories usually recorded on cassette tape or CD-ROM.

TCP/IP   The agreed-on transmission protocol that is used on the Internet and on networks so that communications between diverse computers can be understood.

teaching strategies   The techniques or methods a teacher uses to present information to students. The teaching strategies can take student learning styles into account by providing different approaches to the same topic.

teaching style   Typically, a teacher's personal preferences as to how to teach, frequently influenced by the way the teacher previously found effective for his or her own learning.

technical support   Support personnel for distance or alternative delivery systems who are available when systems fail and/or who provide technical assistance to users so that instructional delivery can continue.

technologists   Those whose primary responsibilities relate to the management of equipment, or educational technology.

telecommunication   Electronic communication between computers via telephone lines.

telephone   Traditional synchronous voice technology that allows two people to communicate orally via phone lines.

telephony   The transmission of sounds between widely removed points with or without connecting wires. Telephony with computers uses the speakers and microphone of two or more computers connected to the Internet to transmit audio conversation across the Internet.

template   A document that has been preformatted for a specific use but contains no data.

terrestrial   A land-based component of a video broadcast system.

test generator   Software that creates tests by either randomly selecting questions within the database of questions or allowing the user to select the questions to be included.

theories   Scientists' statements of their beliefs about an event or a cause usually supported by a large amount of experimental or observational evidence.

Theory of Multiple Intelligences   Howard Gardner theorized that each individual has multiple types of intelligences, only a few of which can be measured by IQ tests. These intelli-gences (or talents) include the verbal-linguistic, mathematical-logical, musical, visual-spatial, bodily-kinesthetic, interpersonal, intrapersonal, naturalistic, and existential intelligences.

time-lapse video   Video whose playback has been sped up to give the appearance of altering time so that what may have taken days to occur can be viewed in the space of a few minutes.

touch screen   A monitor that has a light-sensitive screen and software that interprets an interruption to the light on a specific spot on the screen as a command to select the icon or option that is displayed on that spot.

transparency   A visual created on a thin sheet of clear acetate for projection on an overhead projector.

tutorial software   Software that presents new content with an opportunity to review and practice it; frequently, it also provides additional content or appropriate correction depending on student responses.

twisted-pair wire   An inexpensive, flexible type of cable similar to telephone wire that is made up of a pair of copper wires twisted around each other.

uniform resource locator (URL)   The address for a web page (the designation for a specific location) on the World Wide Web; the most common type of URL typically begins with "http://www" followed by a web site's domain name.

unity   The elements of a visual in which the components work together to help focus the viewer's attention.

unzip program   A program that decompresses and makes usable files that have been compressed (or zipped).

uplink   A data link by which signals are transmitted from a terrestrial system to a satellite so that they can be bounced back down to another point on the globe.

upload   To transfer data from a microcomputer to a remote computer, typically one that is connected to the Internet.

URL (uniform resource locator)   The addresses for a web pages (designations for a specific location) on the World Wide Web. A URL typically begins with "http://www" and then a domain name.

Usenet   A collection of thousands of newsgroups.

utility program   Specialized programs that manage, improve, or oversee computer operations.

VHS tape   A relatively inexpensive type of magnetic recording tape that can contain up to 120 minutes of recording at the standard playing speed (SP) or up to six or eight hours at slower speeds.

video camera recorder   A camera that records sound and images on magnetic tape that can be played back by using a VCR. Also called a camcorder (camera and recorder).

video capture card   A component that can be added to a computer to allow for the conversion of traditional analog video into its digital equivalent.

video disc   Eight- or twelve-inch optical discs that are made and played by using laser technology similar to that used for CDs; a recording medium that was developed to provide a higher quality of image and sound than videotape provides.

video study guide   A study guide that accompanies a video and usually provides the viewer with a series of brief questions on key ideas presented in the same sequence as that in which they are presented in the video.

videocassette recorder (VCR) A type of recorder that uses a VHS magnetic tape for recording moving images and can also record video as it is being transmitted for delayed playback. Prerecorded tapes can be played in class and stopped for discussion when desired.

videoconferencing A combination of software and hardware that enables users at either end of a synchronous connection not only to hear each other, but to see video images of each other as well. The audio and video may be transmitted over the Internet via ISDN or regular phone lines by being compressed at the sending end and decompressed at the receiving end.

virtual environments Fully rendered three-dimensional representations of real or imagined environments that allow the user to become fully immersed in the system.

virtual reality (VR) A combination of hardware and/or software that together create a three-dimensional digital environment with which the user can interact.

virus A program written specifically to disrupt computer operation and/or destroy data.

visual Any combination of text or images, projected or not projected, that is used for illustration or demonstration.

visual communication Encoding and decoding information so that a message is communicated through visual elements.

visual literacy A type of literacy that enables the viewer to accurately interpret the visuals necessary for functioning effectively in our society.

voice mail Asynchronous voice recording technology that allows teachers and students to leave each other messages even when none of the participants are available to communicate via phone at the same time.

voice technology Technology that enables the computer to accept voice commands and dictation of data.

WAV file The digital version of analog audio. WAV files maintain the quality of the original sound, but the file size is often very large.

web authoring tools Software tools that automatically generate HTML code, making it reasonably easy to create a web site.

web hosting A service by which the user can upload the pages of a web site to the web host server, usually via an FTP program, which then makes the site available on the web; such services can be free or charge a monthly or annual fee.

web page A document written in HTML that displays information for use on the web and may contain a series of hyperlinks to other resources on the web.

web site A collection of related web pages.

what-if analysis A capability of spreadsheets that allows the user to ask a "what-if?" question and then change the value in one or more cells to see how those changes will affect the outcome.

whiteboard A slick, white surface on which a variety of specially formulated dry-erasable colored markers can be used. Whiteboards also provide a flat surface on which self-stick flip chart sheets can be hung. Additionally, some whiteboards have a metal backing that will support magnetic displays.

wide area network (WAN) Networks that connect machines across a wide area, such as all of the schools in a district or all of the districts in a state.

Windows The operating system software for some types of personal computers that tells the computer how to work. It is primarily a graphical user interface but also includes typed-in (text) commands, choices from preset menus, and icons.

wireless devices Devices that use wireless communications technology (e.g., microwave) to send and receive voice and digital data.

wireless network A network in which information is transmitted via infrared, radio wave, or microwave technology rather than through wires.

wireless networking Networking technologies and configurations that allow for connections between computer workstations and a server without cabling.

wizard A miniprogram that creates a customized template according to the user's instructions.

word-processing software Software that is used for text-oriented tasks such as creating, editing, and printing documents. It has all but replaced typewriters.

workstation An intelligent terminal or personal computer that is connected to a computer network.

World Wide Web The part of the Internet that uses a graphical user interface and hypertext links between different addresses to allow easier navigation from one site of interest to another.

WYSIWYG ("What You See Is What You Get") A feature of many word-processing and web-authoring programs that allows the user to preview a document and see exactly what it will look like before it is printed out or put on the web.

References

Abaya, B. 2000. Brisbane. Retrieved September 2, 2000, from www.wested.org/tie/dlrn/k12de.html.

Abdullah, M. H. 1998. Guidelines for evaluating web sites. Eric Digest. Retrieved May 12, 2002, from www.ed.gov.databases/ERIC_Digests/ed426440.html.

Acceptable Use Policies: Bangor, Michigan Public Schools/Bangor Computer Network. 2001. Retrieved July 31, 2001, from www.bangorvikings.org/BTS/aup.

Acceptable Use Policies—A handbook. 2001. Retrieved June 21, 2001, from www.pen.k12.va.us/go/VDOE/Technology/AUP/home.shtml.

Acceptable Use Policy: Bellingham, Washington Schools. 2001. Retrieved July 31, 2001, from www.rice.edu/armadillo/About/bellingham.html.

Accessing challenging math curriculum. 2003. Retrieved June 22, 2003, from http://www.ldonline.org/ld_indepthtechnology/opening_the_door_mike.html.

AECT home page. Retrieved March 22, 1999, from www.aect.org.

AECT. 1994. Instructional Technology: The Definition and Domains of the Field. Bloomington, IN: AECT.

Alliance for Technology Access. 2002. Retrieved April 20, 2002 from http://ataccess.og/community/successes/successes.html.

American Montessori Society. n.d. The Montessori method of education. Retrieved May 18, 2001, from www.amshq.org.

American Psychological Association. 1997. *Publication manual of the American Psychological Association*, 4th ed. Washington, DC: American Psychological Association.

Andrews, J. F., & Jordan, D. L. 1998. Multimedia stories for deaf children. *Teaching Exceptional Children* (May/June): 29.

Andrews, K., & Marshall, K. 2000. Making learning connections through telelearning. *Educational Leadership* 58(October): 53–56.

Archambault, R. D. ed. 1974. *John Dewey in education*. Chicago: University of Chicago.

Artificial intelligence (AI). 2001. Retrieved June 26, 2001, from www.britannica.com/original?content_id=1209.

ASPIN: Innovative K–12 Connectivity with CATV: Enhancing math and science through technology. 2001. Retrieved June 27, 2001, from http://aspin.asu.edu/projects/catv.

Association for Supervision and Curriculum Development. 1995. *Constructivism: Facilitator's guide*. Alexandria, VA: Association for Supervision and Curriculum Development.

Ausubel, D. P., J. D. Novak, & H. Hanesian. 1978. *Educational psychology: A cognitive view*. 2nd ed. New York: Holt, Rinehart & Winston.

Banathy, B. H. 1995. Developing a systems view of education. *Educational Technology* 35:55.

Bandura, A. 1971. Analysis of modeling processes. In *Psychological modeling: Conflicting theories* (pp. 1–62), edited by A. Bandura. Chicago: Aldine Atherton.

Bandura, A. 1976. *Social learning theory*. Englewood Cliffs, NJ: Prentice-Hall.

Barlow, J. A. 1963. Programmed instruction in perspective: Yesterday, today, and tomorrow. In *Prospectus in programming: Proceedings of the 1962 Center for Programmed Instruction*, edited by R. T. Filer. New York: Macmillan.

Barrios, B. 2002. The subtle knife: Blog*diss: Blogs in the classroom. Retrieved May 8, 2003, from http://www.barclaybarrios.com/tsk/blog/classroom.html.

Bates, A. W. 1995. Technology, open learning and distance education (London: Routledge). Retrieved December 27, 2000, from www.ed.gov/databases/ERIC_Digests/ed395214.html.

BBC Online. 2000. Audio/video: The best of BBC in sound and pictures. Retrieved July 6, 2000, from www.bbc.co.uk/audiovideo.

Behrmann, M. M. 1998. Assistive technology for young children in special education. In *Learning with technology: ASCD yearbook 1998* (p. 90), edited by C. Dede. Alexandria, VA: Association for Supervision and Curriculum Development.

Berlo, D. K., & Reiser, R. A. 1987. Instructional technology: A history. In *Instructional technology: Foundations* (p. 16), edited by R. M. Gagné. Hillsdale, NJ: Erlbaum.

Bernard, J. Cotter High School's virtual school. Retrieved April 15, 2000, from www.rrr.net.

Bloom, B. 1956. *Taxonomy of educational objectives: The classification of educational goals*, 1st ed. New York: David McKay.

Bloom's taxonomy. Learning Skills Program. Retrieved May 8, 1999, from www.coun.vic.ca/learn/program/hndouts/bloom.html.

Boerner, G. 1999. Videoconferencing skills to maximize student learning. *School Executive* (January/February): 6–7.

Boettcher, J.V. 2001. The spirit of invention: Edging our way to 21st century teaching. *Syllabus* (June): 14, 10–11.

Bogue, B. 2003. Spokane Public Schools. Retrieved October 3, 2003, from http://www.palmone.com/us/education/studies/study53.html.

Bolton, T. Cognitive flexibility theory. Retrieved April 21, 1999, http://alcor.concordia.ca?~tbolton/edcomp/mod10b.html.

Bolze, S. 1998. Spin city. *Instructor* 108(November/December): 20.

Boyce, A. 2002. Using cars to build Internet search skills. Retrieved January 10, 2002, from http://www.nea.org/cet/wired/index.html.

Brangwin, N. 1999. Carmen Sandiego: A fifth-grader discovers a special tutor. Retrieved December 4, 1999, from www.techlearning.com/db_area/archives/WCE/archives/brangwin.htm.

Brewer, W. R., & Kallick, B. 1996. Technology's promise for reporting student learning. In *Communicating student learning: ASCD yearbook 1996* (pp. 181–182), edited by T. R. Guskey. Alexandria, VA: Association for Supervision and Curriculum Development.

Bruner, J. S. 1962. *On knowing.* Cambridge, MA: Harvard University Press.

Bruner, J. S. 1966. *Toward a theory of instruction.* Cambridge, MA: Harvard University Press.

Bruner, J. S. 1969. *The relevance of education.* New York: W. W. Norton.

Bump, K. 2000. Creating healthy classrooms. *Classroom Leadership* 3(6), 7.

Burton, Mrs. 2003. KinderKonnect web page. Retrieved November 2, 2003, from http://www.kinderkonnect.com.

Butler, M. 1994. *How to use the Internet.* Emeryville, CA: Ziff-Davis Press.

Butler, S. 2002. Project Groundhog. Retrieved January 5, 2003, from http://www.ciconline.com/Enrichment/Teaching/learningwithtechnology/expertadvice/default.htm.

Cain, C. 1999. Networking classroom workstations. *School Executive* (November/December): 8.

Caine, R., & Caine, G. 1994. *Making connections: Teaching and the human brain.* New York: Addison-Wesley.

Caine, R., & Caine, G. 2000. Brain/mind learning principles. Retrieved July 9, 2000, from www.cainelearning.com/bbl/bbl2.htm.

Campbell, R. 2000. Leadership: Getting it done. Retrieved July 4, 2000, from www.ssu.missouri.edu/faculty/Rcampbell/Leadership/chapter6.htm.

Campion, C., & Mizell, A. P. 1999. SAXophone events [and] SAXophone schools. Retrieved July 31, 1999, from www.mhrcc.org/sax/saxevent.html and www.mhrcc.org/sax/saxskool.html.

Cannings, T. & Finkel, L. 1993. *The technology age classroom.* Wilsonville, OR: Franklin, Beedle, and Associates.

Civello, C. 1999. "Move over, please": The decentralization of the teacher in the computer-based classroom. *English Journal* (March): 92–94.

Clark, S. 2002. #2556. Cars. Retrieved May 20, 2003, from http://www.teachers.net/lessons/posts/2566.html.

Compressed video for instruction: Operations and applications. Washington, DC: Association for Educational Communications and Technology.

The Computer Ethics Institute. The Ten Commandments for Computer Ethics. Retrieved August 27, 2002, from http://www.brook.edu/its/cei/cei_hp.htm.

Conley, E. 2003. Movie night. Retrieved June 2, 2003, from http://www.nea.org/helpfrom/growing/works4me/tech/equip.html.

Cronin, G. 1999. Running a business. Retrieved August 7, 1999, from www.teachers.net/lessons/posts/1004.html.

Cross, K. P., & Angelo, T. A. 1998. *Classroom assessment techniques: A handbook for faculty.* Ann Arbor, MI: The University of Michigan.

Crotty, T. 2000. Constructivist theory unites distance learning and teacher education. Retrieved August 11, 2000, from http://edie.cprost.sfu.ca/it/constructivistlearning and www.hseidensticker.de/476.htm.

Crowder, N. A. 1963. A theorem in number theory [Presentation]. Intrinsic programming: Facts, fallacies, and future. In *Prospectus in programming: Proceedings of the 1962 Center for Programmed Instruction* (pp. 90–92), edited by R. T. Filer. New York: Macmillan.

Cyrs, T. E. 1976. Modular approach in curriculum design using the systems approach. In *Instructional media and technology: A professional's resource* (pp. 115–121), edited by P. J. Sleeman & D. M. Rockwell. Stroudsburg, PA: Dowden, Hutchinson, & Ross.

Davidson, H. 1999. The educators' lean and mean no-fat guide to fair use. *Technology & Learning* 20(September): 58–60, 62, 66.

Davidson, K. 1998. Education on the Internet: Linking theory to reality. Retrieved January 5, 2000, from www.oise.ca/~kdavidson/cons.html. Also in Mergel, B. 1998. Instructional design & learning theory. Retrieved January 8, 2000, from www.usask.ca/education/coursework/802papers/mergel/brenda.htm.

Davis, A. 2003. Elementary writers learn to love their weblogs. Retrieved October 31, 2003, from http://www97.intel.com/education/odyssey/day_300/day_300.htm.

Davis, D. 2002. Using assistive technology to help students write. *Media & Methods* (September/October) 39 (1), 14.

Debate over copyright protection in the Digital Age. Retrieved May 10, 2002, from http://groton.k12.ct.us/mts/eg15.htm.

Dede, C. 1995. The evolution of learning devices: Smart objects, information infrastructures, and shared synthetic environments. The Future of Networking Technologies for Learning. Retrieved June 12, 2001, from www.ed.gov/Technology/Futures/index.html.

Dede, C. 1996. Emerging technologies in distance education for business. Retrieved December 27, 2000, from www.ed.gov/databases/ERIC_Digests/ed395214.html.

Dede, C. 2000. Emerging technologies and distributed learning in higher education. Retrieved December 27, 2000, from http://virtual.gmu.edu/SS_research/cdpapers/index.htm.

DeKorne, C., & T. Y. Chin. 2002. Links to the missing: Exploring how technology is used in locating missing persons.

Retrieved May 4, 2002, from http://www.nytimes.com/learning/teachers/lessons/20020425thursday_print.html.

Delisio, E. R. 2002. Research at the river links two schools. Retrieved April 3, 2003, from http://www.education-world.com/a_tech/tech122.shtml.

Denofrio, S. 1999. Technology notebook. *Instructor* 108(April): n.p.

Dewey, J. 1944. *Democracy and education.* New York: Macmillan.

Dewey, J. 1998. My pedagogic creed. In *Kaleidoscope: Readings in education* (pp. 280–285), edited by K. Ryan & J. Cooper. Boston: Houghton Mifflin. [Original work published in 1899.]

Diamant, R., & Bearison, D. 1991. Development of formal reasoning during successive peer interactions. *Developmental Psychology* 27: 277–284.

Diamond, J. 1999. [Abuzz question]. Retrieved September 20, 1999, from http://questions.nytimes.com.

Diaz, C. J. 2001. [No title]. Retrieved January 9, 2001, from www.nea.org/cet/wired/index.html.

Dickman, J. 2000. A student perspective. *Curriculum/Technology Quarterly* 9(Spring): 1–2.

Dodd, J. 2000. Music & MP3. *PC Tricks* 6: 95–98.

Dodge, P. 2002. Fixing grammar with technology. Retrieved February 13, 2003, from http://www.teachers.net/lessons/posts/2584.html.

Dodson, J. 1999. Using electronic sketchbooks in the classroom. *Media & Methods* (March/April): 10.

Donahue, B. 2000. Brenda Donahue's class: Centennial Education Center, Santa Ana, CA. Retrieved December 27, 2000, from www.otan.dni.us/webfarm/emailproject/cec.htm.

Drucker, P. 1999. Beyond the information revolution. *Atlantic Monthly* 284(October): 54, 57.

Dudzik, J. 1999. A marriage made in heaven. *Instructor* (September): 16.

Dudzik, J. 1999. E-pals. *Instructor* 109(October): 73.

Dudzik, J. 1999. Technology notebook. *Instructor* 108(April): n.p.

Duffy, M. 1999, June. [Interview].

Dunn, R. 1999. How do we teach them if we don't know how they learn? *Teaching K–8* 29(7), 50–52.

Dunn, R., & Dunn, K. 1992. *Teaching elementary students through their individual learning styles.* Boston: Allyn & Bacon.

Dunn, R., & Greggs, S. A. 1988. *Learning styles: Quiet revolution in American secondary schools.* Reston, VA: National Association of Secondary School Principals.

Dunn, R., Krimsky, J. S., Murray, J. B., & Quinn, P. J. 1985. Light up their lives: A review of research on the effects of lighting in children's achievement and behavior. *The Reading Teacher* 38: 863–869.

Dwight, V. 1998. [no title]. *Family PC* (September): 60.

Eagle Eye News. 2002. Retrieved May 15, 2002, from http://www.sisd.k12.ak.us/content/schools/pa/news%20letter/webmake.html.

Edling, J. V., Hamreus, D. G., Schalock, H. D., Beaird, J. H., Paulson, C. F., & Crawford, J. (1972). *The cognitive domain.* Washington, DC: Gryphon House.

Educational computing: How are we doing? 1997. Retrieved February 17, 1999, from www.thejournal.com/magazine/97/jun/feature4.html.

Fairhurst, A. M., & Fairhurst, L. L. 1995. *Effective teaching effective learning: Making the personality connection in your classroom.* Palo Alto, CA: Davies-Black.

Felder, R. M., & Soloman, B. A. Learning styles and strategies. Retrieved April 22, 1999, from www.crc4mse.org/ILS/ILS_explained.html.

Filipczak, B. 1995. Putting the learning in distance learning. Retrieved December 27, 2000, from www.ed.gov/databases/ERIC_Digests/ed395214.html.

FitzRoy, M. 2003, Sept. 6. Newest TV dateline: Landrum classroom. Retrieved September 8, 2003, from http://cgi.jacksonville.com.

Fry, E. 2003. Rural schools look to online courses. Juneau Express (June 25). Retrieved July 1, 2003, from http://www.juneauempire.com/stories/062503/loc_webschool.shtml.

Future technology. 1999. *PC Magazine* (June 22): 104, 113, 116, 119.

Gagné, R. M. 1985. *The conditions of learning.* 4th ed. New York: Holt, Rinehart & Winston.

Gagné, R. M., Briggs, L. J., & Wager, W. W. 1988. *Principles of instructional design,* 3rd ed. New York: Holt, Rinehart & Winston.

Garden State Pops Youth Orchestra. 1997. Learn and hear about different instruments. Retrieved July 6, 2000, from www.gspyo.com/education/html/instr-intro.html.

Gardner, H. 1988. Mobilizing resources for individual-centered education. In *Technology in education: Looking toward 2020,* edited by R. S. Nicerson & P. P. Zodihiates. Hillsdale, NJ: Erlbaum.

Gardner, H. 1993. *Multiple intelligences: The theory in practice (a reader).* New York: Basic Books.

Gardner, H. 1999. A multiplicity of intelligences. *Scientific American* 9(Winter): 23.

Gardner, H. 1999. *Intelligence reframed: Multiple intelligences for the 21st century.* New York: Basic Books.

Gardner, H. 1999. Who owns intelligence? *The Atlantic Monthly* 283(February): 67–76.

Gates, B., October 28, 1999, Microsoft Corporation, Speech at the New York Institute of Technology, New York, NY. Retrieved May 5, 2002, from www.microsoft.com/billgates/speeches/10-28genl.asp.

Gazin, A. 2000. Focus on autobiography. *Instructor* 109(January/February): 49.

Gold Ridge Elementary School web site. Retrieved November 2, 2003, from http://www.sonic.net/kargo/parent.htm.

Goldberg, L. 2002. Web pages to the rescue. *Instructor* (August), 112 (1), 27–28, 78.

Gore, A. 1998. Speech to the 15th International ITU Conference, October 12.

Guenter, C. 2003. Student teaching electronic portfolio. Retrieved October 5, 2003, from http://www.csuchico.edu/educ/estport.htm.

Guerriero, A. 1999. [Abuzz question]. Retrieved September 22, 1999, http://questions.nytimes.com.

Guerriero, A. 1999. [Abuzz question]. Retrieved September 28, 1999, http://questions.nytimes.com.

Hackbarth, S. 1996. *The educational technology handbook: A comprehensive guide.* Englewood Cliffs, NJ: Educational Technology Publications.

Hakes, B. T., Cochenour, J. J., Rezabek, L. L., & Sachs, S. G. 1995.

Hardy, D. W. 2000. Algebra across the wire. Retrieved September 2, 2000, from http://wested.org/tie/dlrn/k12de.html.

Harper, G. 1998. Fair use guidelines for educational multimedia: The Copyright Act of 1976, as amended. Updated August 4, 1998. Retrieved July 19, 2000, from www.utsystem.edu/OGC/IntellectualProperty/ccmcquid.htm.

Harris, J. 1998. *Design tools for the Internet-supported classroom.* Alexandria, VA: Association for Supervision and Curriculum Development.

Harris, S. L. 1995. *The relationship between learning theory and curriculum development.* Unpublished manuscript, Florida International University at Miami, Florida.

Harrison, C. 2002. The WKEY Morning News. *Learning & Leading with Technology* (October), 30 (2), 40–43.

Harrison, J. L. 1999. [AT&T's virtual classroom]. Retrieved October 29, 1999, from www.nea.org/cet/wired/index.html.

Harrison, S. 2000. TEAMS distance learning. Retrieved August 9, 2000, from www.nea.org/cet/wired/index.html.

Heese, V. 1999. [No title]. Retrieved November 6, 1999, from www.techlearning.com/db_area_archives/WCE/archives/heese.htm.

Heese, V. 1999. Simple methods of integrating technology into primary classrooms. Retrieved November 5, 1999, from www.techlearning.com/db_area/archives/WCE/archives/heesepri.htm.

Heimdal, J. 2001. Rates on your life insurance go up last month? Retrieved January 10, 2002, from http://www.lessonplanspage.com/printables/PCIOMDDevFamilyBudgetOnSpreadsheet812.html.

Higgins, K. J. 1999. School system broadcasts video with ATM/LANE. *Network Computing* 10(7): 72.

Hill, B. 1998. Senior project. Retrieved December 22, 1998, from www.intel.com/education/technology/mec/case_studies.htm.

Hirsch, S. 1999. A comparative study: San Diego, California, and Biarritz, France. Retrieved July 26, 1999, from www.edweb.sdsu.edu/triton/SDBiarritz/SDBiarritzUnit.html.

Hirschbuhl, J. J. (Ed). 1998. *Computers in education.* Guilford, CT: Dushkin.

History of inventions. 2001. Retrieved June 26, 2001, from www.cbc4kids.ca/general/the-lab/history-of-invention/calendar.html.

History pen pals. 2002. Retrieved April 10, 2003, from http://www.nea.org/helpfrom/growing/works4me/tech/techclas.html.

Hoban, C. F., Sr., Hoban, C. F., Jr., & Zissman, S. B. 1937. *Visualizing the curriculum.* New York: The H. W. Wilson Co.

Hoffman, E. 1999. The dark side of the Internet: Controls of student access. *Syllabus: High School Edition* 1(1): 14–16.

Hofstetter, F. T., & Fox, P. 1997. *Multimedia literacy.* New York: McGraw-Hill.

Holloway, J. H. 2000. The digital divide. *Educational Leadership* 58(2): 90.

Holzberg, C. 2001. Yes, you can build a web site. *Instructor* 110(May/June): 62.

Hudson, M. & A. Cooley. 2003. Digital video camera use in classrooms. *Media & Methods* (February), 39 (4), 6.

Hughes, S. 2002. Cutting costs. Retrieved April 10, 2003, from http://www.nea.org/helpfrom/growing/works4me/tech/technclas.html.

Huitt, W. 1998. Bloom et al.'s taxonomy of the cognitive domain. Educational psychology interactive: The cognitive domain. Retrieved January 24, 2000, from www.valdosta.peachnet.edu/~whuitt/psy702/cogsys/bloom/html.

Hunt, M. 1993. *The story of psychology.* New York: Doubleday.

Huschak, I. H. 1999. Digital archaeology: Uncovering a city's past. Retrieved May 12, 2000, from http://techlearning.com/db_area/archives/WCE/archives/huschak.htm.

A Hypertext History of Instructional Design. Retrieved October 3, 2003, from http://www.coe.uh.edu/courses/cuin6373/idhistory/index.html.

Ideas for using video conferencing in the classroom. 2003. Retrieved June 13, 2003, from http://k-12.pisd.edu/distance_learning/uses.htm.

IDG. 1995. *Internet and the World Wide Web.* Foster City, CA: International Data Group Company.

Instructional event with lesson activity. Retrieved August 2, 1999, from www.seas/gwu.edu/sbraxton/ISD/GIFS/lesson_gagne.gif.

Integration via a browser-based intranet. 2002. Retrieved June 11, 2003, from http://www.nps.k12.va.us/infodiv/it/techconf/integbrw.htm.

International Society for Technology in Education. 2000. *ISTE National Educational Technology Standards for Teachers.* Eugene, OR: ISTE.

James, S. 2003. One digital future. Retrieved November 9, 2003, from http://www.ldresources.com/articles/one_digital_future.html.

Jarvinen, E. M. 1988. The Lego/logo learning environment in technology education: An experiment in a Finnish context. *Journal of Technology Education* 9. Retrieved June 5, 1999, from http://scholar.lib.ft.edu/ejournals/JTE/v9n2/jrvinen.html.

Johnson, E. 1998. Making geography come alive with technology. *Media & Methods* (March/April): 14–16.

Johnson, S. R., & Johnson, R. B. 1971. *Assuring learning with self-instructional packages, or up the up staircase.* Chapel Hill, NC: Self-Instructional Packages.

Jung, C. G. 1990. *Psychological types.* Rev. ed., translated by H. G. Baynes. Princeton, NJ: Princeton University Press.

Kekkonen-Moneta, S., & G. Moneta. 2001. E-learning in Hong Kong: Comparing learning outcomes in online multimedia and lecture versions of an introductory computing course. *British Journal of Educational Technology*, 33 (4), 2002, 423–433.

Kelly, E. J., & Partin, R. M. 1999. Mexico City earthquake. Retrieved August 17, 1999, from http://nardac.mip.berkeley.edu/tmp/browse_equis_res_14284.3html.

Kemp, J. E., & Smellie, D. C. 1989. *Planning, producing, and using instructional media.* New York: Harper & Row.

Kerka, S. 1996. Distance learning, the Internet, and the World Wide Web. ERIC Digest. Retrieved December 27, 2000, from www.ed.hov/databases/ERIC_Digests/ed395214.html.

Kinzie, M., Strauss, R., & Foss, J. 1994. Interactive frog dissection: An on-line tutorial. Retrieved December 26, 2000, from http://curry.edschool.virginia.edu/go/frog.

Knapps, K. J. 2000. Art and life in Africa project. Retrieved June 15, 2000, from www.uiowa.edu/~africart/teachers/lessons/036.html.

Kozma, R., & Schank, P. 1998. Connecting with the 21st century: Technology in support of educational reform. In *ASCD Yearbook 1998* (pp. 73–74), edited by C. Dede. Alexandria, VA: Association for Curriculum and Development.

Krech, B. 1999. Show, don't tell. *Instructor* (October): n.p.

Kriwox, J. 2003. Quilting and geometry-patterns for living. Retrieved October 5, 2003, from http://ali.apple.com/ali_sites/deli/exhibits/1000077.

Krug, C. 1999. Video editing techniques in schools. *Media & Methods* (May/June): 55–56.

Kultgen, S. 1999. Computer portfolios. *Arts and Activities* (May): 20–21.

Laird, L. (1999). NEA CET: Wired classroom. Retrieved January 5, 2000, from www.nea.org/cet/wired/index.html.

Landon, A. 2003. How do you measure up? Retrieved October 4, 2003, from http://pegasus.cc.ucf.edu/~ucfcasio/measure.htm.

Laurino, B. 1999. Using chunks from class readers. Retrieved July 5, 2000, from www.ncte.org/teach/Laurino14954.html.

Le, P. 2003, September 16. Online coursework appeals to teenagers. Retrieved September 18, 2003, from http://www.indystar.com/print/articles/9/074716-3989-P.html.

LEARN NC. 2003, March. Student teachers and high school seniors beam the Internet. Retrieved April 2, 2003, from http://www.learnnc.org/Index.nsf/ printView.

Learning styles. 1998. Retrieved August 15, 1999, from www.funderstanding.com/learning_theory_how6.html.

Lee, J. 1998. Web-based instruction. Retrieved January 28, 2000, from http://www.dsmt.org/exlee.

Lee, P. 1999. Tech learning. Retrieved December 15, 1999, from www.techlearning.com/db_area_archives/WCE/archives/paulalee.htm.

Lehmann, K. 1998. Travel and tour guide unit. In Wired Classroom: Etools Weekly Tip. National Education Association. Retrieved December 30, 1998, from www.nea.org/cet/wired/.

Leo, L. 1999. Picture perfect lessons. *Instructor* (March): 80–81.

Lever-Duffy, J. (2000). The evolution of distance education (pp. 251–274). In *Taking a big picture look at technology, learning, and the community college,* edited by Mark Milliron & Cindy Miles. Mission Viejo, CA: League for Innovation in the Community College.

Lewis, A. 2001. Sell yourself. Retrieved May 15, 2001, from www.successlink.org/great/g163.html.

Lopez, A. M., Jr., & Donlon, J. 2001. Knowledge engineering and education. *Educational Technology* 41(2): 45–50.

Lopez, W. J. 2003, August. Content delivery for a virtual high school. *T.H.E. Journal,* 31 (1), 32.

Lutkenhaus, K. 2000. [E-mail]. Retrieved March 4, 2000, from www.nea.org/cet/wired/index.html.

Mahoney, M. J. 1994. *Human change processes.* New York: Basic Books.

Makled, C. 2002. Pilot program: Paddock project to aid in reading assessment. Retrieved May 21, 2003, from http://www.wirelessgeneration.com/web/print_milan.html (reprint from the *Milan News-Leader,* April 18, 2002).

Maple Lake School District: 1998. Acceptable use policy on district provided access to electronic information, services, and networks. Retrieved June 27, 2001, from http://www.maplelake.k12.mn.us/districtinfo/AUP.html.

Maran, R. 1998. *Computers Simplified,* 4th ed. Foster City, CA: IDG Books.

March, T. 2003. Eyes on art. Retrieved May 6, 2003, from http://www.kn.pacbell.com/wired/art2/guide/guide.html.

Martin, C. R. 2002. Looking at type: The fundamentals. Retrieved March 22, 2002, from www.knowyourtype.com/enfp.html.

Martin, S. 2000. Greece and Rome: A CBT project. Retrieved August 2, 2000, from www.techlearning.com/db_area/archives/WCE/archives.smartin.htm.

Maryland digital schools project: Field trips and interactives. 2003. Retrieved July 1, 2003, from http://www.thinkport.org/classroom/oftinteractive/default.tp.

Mater, J. A. 2001. My dream room. Retrieved May 25, 2001, from www.lessonplanspage.com/CILAPostersWithWordFormattingGrammar4.8.htm.

Mattingly, L. 1999. Integrating technology in the classroom. Retrieved August 26, 1999, from www.siec.K12.in.us/~west/slides/integrate/sld024.htm.

Maze, B. 1999, May. [Interview].

McDonald, B. 1999, May. [Interview].

McDonald, E. J. B. 1973. The development and evaluation of a set of multi-media self-instructional learning activity packages for use in remedial English at an urban community college (Doctoral dissertation, University of Memphis, 1973). *Dissertation Abstracts International* 34:04A.

McDonald, J. 1996. The paperless composition: Computer-assisted writing. *Innovation Abstracts* XVIII(October 18): n.p.

McGoogan, G. 2002. Around the world in 24 hours. *Educational Leadership* (October), 60 (2), 44–46.

McGowan, K. 1999. [Beehive question]. Retrieved September 28, 1999, from http://questions.nytimes.com.

McKibben, B. 2000. The world streaming in. *The Atlantic Monthly* 286 (July): 78.

McLean, M., & Miller, S. 1997. Importing video stills into computer documents. *Media & Methods* (September/October): 12.

McLuhan, M. 1998. *Understanding media: The extensions of man.* Cambridge, MA: The Massachusetts Institute of Technology Press.

McLuhan, M., & Fiore, Q. 1967. *The medium is the message.* New York: Bantam Books.

McLuhan, M., & Fiore, Q. 1996. *The medium is the message: An inventory of effects,* renewed by J. Agel. San Francisco, CA: HardWired.

Meiers, V. 1999. Into the next millennium. Retrieved August 23, 1999, from http://cnets.iste.org/ss_68_1_done.html.

Mergel, B. 1998. Instructional design & learning theory. Retrieved January 8, 2000, from www.usask.ca/education/coursework/802papers/mergel/brenda.htm.

Merrimack Valley School District. 2001. Acceptable use policy. Retrieved June 27, 2001, from http://www.mv.k12.nh.us/schools/mvms/acceptable_use_policy.htm.

Microsoft in Education: new Teachers Corner. 2000. Lifesavers: How to find your way on the web. Retrieved May 20, 2002, from www.microsoft.com/education.mctn/newteacher/lifesavers/52001saver.asp.

Milici, J. (2003). Foreign studies. Retrieved October 23, 2003, from http://www.nea.org.

Miller, E. B. 1996. *The Internet resource directory*. Englewood, CO: Libraries Unlimited.

Miller, S. 1999. Greece and Rome: A CBT project. Retrieved May 12, 1999, from www.techlearning.com/db_area/archives/WCE/archives/smiller.htm.

Millspaw, E. 1996–1997. Student team designs and maintains internet/intranet web sites. *The High School Magazine* (December/January): 58–59.

Milone, M. 1999. Enterprise computing. *Technology & Learning* 20(September): 31–32.

Milstein, M. 1999. The sound of dinosaurs. Retrieved July 5, 2000, from www.discovery.com/exp/fossilzone/sounds/dinosaurs.html.

Minsky, Marvin. 1988. Papert's principle. Retrieved September 28, 2001, from www.papert.org/articles/PapertsPrinciple.html.

Mir, S. 2002. Art exchange. Retrieved April 10, 2003, from http://www.nea.org/helpfrom/growing/works4me/tech/techclas.html.

Mitchell, L. 1999, April. [Interview]. South Elementary School, Pinson, TN.

Moore, J. Branksome Hall. Retrieved July 15, 1999, from www.branksome.on.ca/main.html.

Moore, K. 1999. *Volcanoes: A multi-media unit for cross-curricular instruction in the junior high school*. Henderson, TN: Chester County Junior High School.

Moore, K. April 1999. [Interview].

Moore, S. 2002. Creating tests with Microsoft Word. *Instructor* (September), 112 (3), 16.

Morgan, A. 1995. Research into student learning in distance education. Victoria, Australia: In Distance education at a glance: Guide #9: Strategies for distance learning, edited by B. Willis. Retrieved November 11, 2000, from http://www.uidaho.edu/evo/dist9.html.

Morris, P. (Developer). 21st century schoolhouse: Lesson plans. Retrieved February 27, 1999, from www.coedu.usf.edu/~morris/acsi_1p2.html.

"Mrs. Claus's Workshop," prepared by Mrs. Slaven's class at Elementary West in Loogootee, Indiana, http://www.siec.k12.in.us.

Multiple intelligences survey. Retrieved September 23, 1999, from http://familyeducation.com/article/print/0,1303,4-3201. 00html?obj_gra.

Murphy, M. 1999. Expanding your classroom. Retrieved July 15, 1999, from www.techlearning.com/db_area/archives/WCE/archives/muggs2.htm.

Murphy, M. 2000. Expanding your classroom. Retrieved February 25, 2000, from http://www.techlearning.com/db_area/archives/WCE/archives/muggs2.htm.

Naisbitt, J. 1982. Megatrends. New York: Warner Communications.

National Education Association. 1996. Technology and portfolio assessment. NEA: Technology Brief No. 4. Retrieved May 5, 2002, from www.nea.org/cet/BRIEFS/brief4.html.

National Educational Technology Standards for Teachers. Retrieved March 29, 2002, from http://cnets.iste.org/pdf/page24-25.pdf.

National Telecommunications and Information Administration. 2000. *Falling through the Net*. Washington, DC: Author.

Negroponte, N. 1996. *Being digital*. New York: Vintage Books/Random House, p. 230.

Nellen, T. (2000). Cyber short stories. Retrieved August 21, 2000, from www.techlearning.com/db_area/archive/WCE/archives/tnellen.htm.

Niess, M. 1999. Integrating technology into math instruction. *Media & Methods* (January/February): 26–27.

Nix, D., & Spiro, R. J. (Eds.). 1990. *Cognition, education, and multimedia: Exploring ideas in high technology*. Hillsdale, NJ: Erlbaum.

Norris, B. 2000. [Gaggle.net]. Retrieved January 14, 2000, from www.nea.org/cet/wired/index.html.

Notebloom, R. 2000. One teacher's view. *Curriculum/Technology Quarterly* 9(Spring): 1–2.

Novak, J. D. 2001. The theory underlying concept maps and how to construct them. Retrieved May 5, 2002, from http://cmap.coginst.uwf.edu/info.

Novelli, D., S. Edmunds, & D. Gurwicz. Screen-saver stories. *Instructor* (May/June 2001) 110 (8), 74.

NTTI video utilization strategies. 2002. Retrieved November 30, 2003, from http://www.thirteen.org/edonline/ntti/resources/video2.html.

Nunes-Turcotte, O. 1998, November/December. Electronic learning in your classroom [Project page]. *Instructor*, n.p.

Nunley, K. 2000. How to layer your curriculum. Retrieved July 9, 2000, from www.brains.org/layered.htm.

Ocean in view. 2002. Retrieved May 12, 2003, from http://www97.intel.com/education/odyssey/day_289/day_289.htm.

Office of Technology Assessment. U.S. Congress. 1995. *Teachers and technology: Making the connection*. Washington, DC: U.S. Government Printing Office.

Oh, P. 1999. Back to basics: No-frills, but super, drill-and-practice software. *Instructor* 108(March): 74–76.

Oros, L., Finger, A., & Morenegg, J. 1998, January/February. Creating digital portfolios. *Media & Methods*, 15.

Paivio, A. 2001. Dual coding theory. Retrieved October 4, 2001, from http://tip.psychology.org/paivio.html.

Papert, S. 1992. *The children's machine: Rethinking school in the age of the computer*. New York: Basic Books.

Papert, S. 1999. Papert on Piaget. Retrieved October 5, 2001, from www.papert.org/articles/Papertonpiaget.html.

Papert, S., & Harel, I. 1991. Situating constructionism. Retrieved September 28, 2001, from www.papert.org/articles/SituatingConstrutionism.html.

Parker, R. C. 1988. *Looking good in print*. Chapel Hill, NC: Ventana Press.

Pavlov, I. P. 1927. *Conditioned reflexes.* London: Oxford University Press.

Payton, T. Traveling buddies. Retrieved July 15, 1999, from www.techlearning.com/db_area/archives/WCE/archives/tpayton.html.

Pearson Education Development Group. (2003). Authentic assessment overview. Retrieved October 5, 2003, from http://teachervision.fen.com/lesson-plans/lesson-4911.html.

Peters, T. 1998. *Thriving on chaos: Handbook for management revolution.* New York: Alfred Knopf.

Piaget, J. 1952. *The origins of intelligence in children.* New York: International Universities.

Piaget, J. 1960. *Psychology of intelligence.* Paterson, NJ: Littlefield, Adams, & Co.

Piaget, J. 1970. *Science of education and the psychology of the child,* translated by D. Coltman. New York: Orion.

Piaget, J. 1976. *The grasp of consciousness: Action and concept in the young child,* translated by S. Wedgwood. Cambridge, MA: Harvard University Press.

Picture-perfect lessons. 1999. *Instructor* (March): 80–81.

Platt, P. Projects. Retrieved June 14, 2000, from http://gsh.lightspan.com/pr/_cfm/GetDetail.cfm?pID=593.

Popham, W. J., & Baker, E. L. 1970. *Establishing instructional goals.* Englewood Cliffs, NJ: Prentice-Hall.

Potter, B. 1999. *Parent power: Energizing home-school communication.* Portsmouth, NH: Heinemann.

Price, D. 1999, June. [Interview].

Price, S. D. 2001. Techie teacher takes prize/She gets Thinkquest Fellowship [Cathie Thomley]. *The Commercial Appeal* (February 13): n.p.

Prochelo, D., & Kmiec, B. 1998. Speech with advanced technology. Retrieved January 2, 1999, from www.ncrel.org/cw/availabl.htm.

Pruett, H. 2002. Having students learn basic grammar through technology. Retrieved May 23, 2003, from http://www.techlearning.com/db_area/archives/ WCE/archives/hpruett.html.

Rahmani, L. 1973. *Soviet psychology: Philosophical, theoretical, and experiential issues.* New York: International Universities.

Railsback, K. 2001. Peering into the future. *InfoWorld* 22(42): 85–95.

Raskauskas, N. 2000. Interactive sports guides. Retrieved December 29, 2000, from http://henson.austin.apple.com/edres/shlessons/sports.shtml.

Rasmussen, K. 1999. Partners in education: How schools and homeschoolers work together. *Education Update* 41(June): 1–4, 5.

Re: Pido datos biográficos de Benjamin Bloom. I ask Benjamin Bloom's biography. Retrieved August 12, 1999, from www.funderstanding.com/messages/1138.htm.

Recipe for the classroom: 1 ideal computer learning station. 1998. *Children's Software Review* (September/October): 27.

Reed, J., & Woodruff, M. 1995. Videoconferencing: Using videoconferencing technology for teaching. Retrieved December 30, 2000, from http://www.pacbell.com/wired/vidconf/Using.html.

Rehak, M. 1999. Questions for John Ashbery: A child in time. *The New York Times Magazine,* April 4:15.

Reiser, R. A. 1987. Instructional technology. A history. In *Instructional technology: Foundations* (pp.12–20), edited by R. M. Gagné. Hillsdale, NJ: Erlbaum.

Renner-Smith, S. 2002. "Fontastic" idea! *Creative Classroom* (March/April), 26.

Richardson, W. 2003. High school journalists use weblogs to mentor young writers. Retrieved October 31, 2003, from http://www97.intel.com/education/odyssey/day_301/day_301.htm.

Rivera, J. 2002. School on a postcard. Retrieved May 29, 2003, from http://www.ciconline.com/Enrichment/Teaching/learningwithtechnology/ expertadvice/default.htm.

Roche, E. 1998. #258. Cooperative learning, technology, science, language. Retrieved August 17, 1999, from www.teachers.net/lessons/posts/258.html.

Rohfield, R. W., & Hiemstra, R. 1995. Moderating discussions in the electronic classroom. Retrieved December 27, 2000, from http://www.ed.gov/databases/ERIC_Digests/ed395214.html.

Roth, M. K. 2003. Palm pilots beaming lessons. Retrieved October 3, 2003, from http://www.pdaed.com/vertical/features/Beaming.xml.

Rowling, D. 1999. Introducing the geometer's sketchpad to the classroom. Retrieved December 16, 1999, from www.techlearning.com/db_area/archives/WCE/archives/rowling.htm.

Royal, K. W. 1999. If you had computers in your classroom, what would you do with them? Retrieved May 12, 1999, from www.techlearning.com/db_area/archives/WCE/archives/royal.htm.

Russell Elementary School. 2001. Wade through the wondrous wetlands. Retrieved May 17, 2001, from http://applecom.

Saettler, P. 1968. A history of instructional technology. New York: McGraw-Hill.

Saettler, P. 1990. *The evolution of American educational technology.* Englewood, CO: Libraries Unlimited.

Sagan, C. 1998. *Billions and billions: Thoughts of life and death at the brink of the millennium.* New York: Ballantine.

Santo, C. 1998. An Internet day. *Family PC* (October): 54.

Santo, C. 1999. The Malverne method. *Family PC* (August): 101.

Santo, C. 1999. The way we were. *Family PC* (May): 119.

Schrock, K. 2000a. The ABCs of web site evaluation. Retrieved May 15, 2002, from www.kathyschrock.net/abcevol/index.htm.

Schrock, K. 2000b. Kathy Schrock's guide for educators. Retrieved May 20, 2002, from http://school.discovery.com/schrockguide/edtools.html.

Seavey, E. 2002. A team approach to oral history. Retrieved February 14, 2003, from http://www.col-ed.org/cur/sst/sst45.text.

Sharer, S. 2000. Videoconferencing and distance learning. *School Executive* (November/December): 6.

Sharp, W. 2001. Becoming a wireless campus: A student initiative. *T.H.E. Journal* 28(10): 60–66.

Shasha, D., & Lazere, C. 1998. *Out of their minds.* New York: Copernicus.

Shelly, G., Cashman, T., Waggoner, G., & Waggoner, W. 1998. *Discovering computers 98: A link to the future.* Cambridge, MA: Course Technologies.

Short, D. D. 1994. *Enhancing instructional effectiveness: A strategic approach.* Norwalk, CT: IBM Higher Education.

Skinner, B. F. 1953. *Science and human behavior.* New York: Macmillan.

Skinner, B. F. 1958. Teaching machines. *Science* 128: 969–977.

Skinner, B. F. 1971. *Beyond freedom and dignity.* New York: Alfred A. Knopf.

Skinner, B. F. 1974. *About behaviorism.* New York: Alfred A. Knopf.

Slaven, K. 1998. Mrs. Claus's workshop. Retrieved November 20, 1998, from www.siec.K12inu;.s./~west/proj/claus/facts1.htm.

Small wires, big learning: A Britannica online success story. 1999. *T.H.E. Journal* (January): 38.

SMART whiteboards. 2002. Retrieved April 20, 2002, from www.smarttech.com/profilees/charyk.asp.

Smith, S., Tyler, J. M., & Benacote, A. Internet supported teaching: Advice from the trenches. Retrieved January 9, 2001, from http://www.usdla.org/ED_magazine/illuniactive/JAN00_Issue/Internet.htm.

Solomon, G. 2000. A home (page) of your own. *Technology & Learning* 20(March): 46.

Sonoma County Department of Education. 2000. Twelve principles for brain-based learning. Retrieved July 9, 2000, from http://talkingpage.org/artic011.html.

Sorrentino, L. 1999. [Abuzz question]. Retrieved September 28, 1999, from http://questions.nytimes.com.

Sprenger, M. 1999. *Learning and memory: The brain in action.* Alexandria, VA: ASCD.

Stanford-Binet intelligence scale. Retrieved September 13, 1999, from www.richmond.edu/~capc/Binetmain.html.

Starr, L. 2000. Meet Bernie Dodge—the Frank Lloyd Wright of learning environments! Retrieved June 1, 2003, from http://www.education-world.com/a_tech/tech020.shtml.

Stein, C., & Driggs, L. 1999. Freedom of the press: Where should it end? Retrieved April 12, 1999, from www.nytimes.com/learning.

Stembor, E. 2000. University of Connecticut. Retrieved September 2, 2000, from http://www.wested.org/tie/dlrn/k12de.html.

Stephens, D. 2000. Timber Ridge Middle School travel brochures. Retrieved April 16, 2000, from www.timberridgemagnet.net/ad/tchpg.htm.

Sternberg, R. J. 1999. How intelligent is intelligence testing? *Scientific American* 9(Winter): 14.

Stetler, J. 2002. Internet exchange concert. Retrieved April 10, 2003, from http://www.nea.org/helpfrom/growing/works4me/tech/techclas.html.

Stowe, E. 1999. [Abuzz question]. Retrieved September 21, 1999, from http://questions.nytimes.com.

Sturgeon, K., & Lemen, D. 2001. Magnolia Elementary School: Policy and leadership. Retrieved June 27, 2001, from http://www.esc6.net/tiftrain.student/magnoliaelem/p1.html.

Suzanne. 2000. Farm sound. Retrieved July 4, 2000, from www.alfy.lycos.com/teachers/teach/lesson_bui/overView.asp?LessonId=95&saveVal=ye.

Sweaty palms, circa 1914. 1998. *The Wall Street Journal,* March 31, p. R8.

Sylvester, R. 1995. A celebration of neurons: *An educator's guide to the human brain.* Alexandria, VA: ASCD.

Tapia, S. T. 2000. Online classes moving into O. C. high schools. Retrieved November 30, 2000, from http://www.ocregister.com/education/online01130.cci.shtml.

Taverna, P., & Hongell, T. 2000. Meet Harriet Tubman: The story of a web site. *Learning and Leading with Technology* 27(March 20): 43–45, 62.

Teaching our youngest: A guide for preschool teachers and child care and family providers: Developing listening and speaking skills. 2002. Retrieved January 27, 2003, from http://www.ed.gov/offices/OESE/teachingouryoungest/developing.html.

Teaching with EPals. 2000. Retrieved May 17, 2002, from www.epals.com/curriculum_connections/index_en.html.

TEAMS distance learning: For all K–12 educators. Retrieved December 26, 2000, from http://teams.lacoe.edu.

Teleconferencing. 1999. Retrieved September 2, 2000, from http://www.wested.org/tie/dlrn/teleconferencing.html.

Tener, M. 2002. Learning with lyrics. *Creative Classroom* (November/December), 17 (3), 27.

The eight intelligences. Retrieved July 29, 1999, from http://familyeducation.com/article/print/0,1303,4-3201,00.html?obj_gra.

The Monster Exchange. 1998. *Family PC* (November): 194.

Thorndike, E. L., & Woodworth, R. S. 1901. Education as science. *Psychological Review* 8:247–261, 384–395, 553–564.

Thorndike, R. L. 1911. *Animal intelligence.* New York: Macmillan.

Tiene, D., & Ingram, A. 2001. *Exploring current issues in educational technology.* New York: McGraw Hill.

Tietz, H. 2002. Savoring expository writing through PowerPoint. Retrieved June 10, 2003, from http://www.techlearning.com/db_area/archives/WCE/archives/htietz.html.

TLC project showrooms: Networking. 2001. Retrieved June 27, 2001, from http://web.nysed.gov/technology/projects/oswegocs.html.

Turner, J. 2000. Cyberschool. Retrieved September 2, 2000, from http://www.wested.org/tie/dlrn/k12de.html.

Turner, M. A. 1999. [No title]. Retrieved April 23, 1999, from www.nea.org/cet/wired/index.html.

U.S. Department of Commerce. 2000. Digital divide. Retrieved June 27, 2001, from http://www.digitaldivide.gov.

U.S. Department of Education. 1994. *Strong families, strong schools: A research base for family involvement in learning from the United States Department of Education.* Washington, DC: U.S. Department of Education.

Vaughn, K. 1999. [TeleMath]. Retrieved November 20, 1999, from www.nea.org/cet/wired/index.html.

Velez, L. 2003. Postcards from abroad. Retrieved May 14, 2003, from http://teachersnetwork.org/teachnetnyc/lvelez/postcards.htm.

Video conferencing in Plano ISD. 2003. Retrieved June 13, 2003, from http://k-12.pisd.edu/distance_learning/vidconf.htm.

Vitaska, D. 2002. The new language classroom: Bringing French to the U.S. *Media and Methods* (September/October) 39 (1), 10.

VMSTV 2003. Retrieved August 12, 2003, from http://www.vmstv.com.

Vygotsky, L. S. 1978. *Mind in society: The development of higher psychological processes.* Cambridge, MA: Harvard University Press.

Vygotsky, L. S. 1981. *Thought and language,* translated by E. Hanfmann & G. Vakar. Cambridge, MA: The MIT Press.

Vygotsky, L. S. 1987. *The collected works of L. S. Vygotsky.* Vol. 1. New York: Plenum.

Vygotsky, L. S. 1987. *Thinking and speech,* translated by N. Minck. New York: Plenum.

Wallace, L. 2002. Using projection technology to enhance teaching. *Media & Methods* (September/October), 39 (1), 6.

Watson, J. B. 1962. *Behaviorism.* Chicago: University of Chicago Press.

Weiger, E. 1999. [No title]. Retrieved July 20, 1999, from www.nea.org/cet/wired/index.html.

Wenglinsky, H. 1999. Teacher classroom practices and student performance: How schools can make a difference. Retrieved May 5, 2002, from www.ets.org/research/dload/RIBRR-01-19.pdf.

Wertheimer, M. 1945. *Productive thinking.* New York: Harper.

What to do with digital cameras. 1997. *Media & Methods* (November): 2, 8.

White, R. 1993. *How computers work.* Emeryville, CA: Ziff-Davis Press.

Wilkes, D. 2001. Wireless laptops in the classroom. *Media & Methods* 37(February): 33.

Williams, P. 2000. In-school broadcasting: Capturing the excitement. *Media & Methods* (May/June): 6.

Willig, B. 2000. Schoolwide comprehensive courseware: An update. *Media & Methods* (January/February): 24, 26.

Willis, B. 1995. *Guide #2: Strategies for teaching at a difference and strategies for teaching at a glance; Guide #4: Evaluation for distance educators; Guide #6: Instructional audio; Guide #7; Computers in distance education: Guide #9: Strategies for distance learning; Guide #10: Distance education research; Guide #11: Interactive videoconferencing in distance education.* Retrieved November 11, 2000, from http://www.uidaho.edu/evo.html.

Windschitl, M. 1999. The challenges of sustaining constructivist classroom culture. *Phi Delta Kappan* 80: 751–755.

Wohlert, H. 2000. German by satellite. Retrieved June 17, 2000, from http://www.syllabus.com/casestudies/o.html.

Wolfe, B. 1999. Using technology as a tool for teaching across the curriculum. Retrieved July 15, 1999, from www.techlearning.com/db_area/archives/WCE/archives/bwolfe.htm.

Wood, J. M. 2001. Virtual art, real learning. *Instructor* 110(January/February): 80.

Wood, S. 1998–1999. *Computer projects.* Jackson, TN: Northeast Middle School.

Wrenn, E., S. Udell, & S. Sorensen. 2003. If I were president. Retrieved May 16, 2003, from http://www.apple.com.

Yam, P. 1999. Intelligence considered. *Scientific American* 9(Winter): 12–17.

Yarnell, K. 2002. Intranets: Repositories of school data. *School Executive* (September/October), 39 (1), 28.

Zimbalist, A., & Driggs, L. 1999. Fan(tom) of the opera: Applying the plots of famous operas to modern life: A music genre appreciation lesson. Retrieved September 10, 1999, from http://www.nytimes.com/learning.

Zimbalist, A., & Driggs, L. 1999. When Moore is less for microprocessors: Examining how computer chips work and the Moore's Law prediction: A technology lesson. Retrieved July 1, 1999, from www.nytimes.com/learning.

Zora, D.. 2003. A living alphabet. Retrieved May 16, 2003, from http://www.apple.com.

Index

Photo Credits

Chapter 1

p. 3, © Peter Garfield/CORBIS; p. 11, © Mary Kate Denny/ Getty Images; p. 11, © Mel Yates/PhotoDisc/Getty Images; p. 14, AP/ Wide World Photos; p. 15, © Farrell Grehan/ CORBIS; p. 18, Courtesy of Center for Applications of Psychological Type; p. 18, Courtesy of Center for Applications of Psychological Type; p. 22, © Jerry Bauer; p. 24, AP/Wide World Photos; p. 25, © Hulton-Deutsch Collection/CORBIS; p. 26, © B.F. Skinner Foundation; p. 27, © Zigy Kaluzny/Getty Images

Chapter 2

p. 33, © CORBIS; © George Disario/CORBIS; p. 36, Courtesy of Rita and Kenneth Dunn; p. 41, © Michael Newman/PhotoEdit; p. 46, © Robert F. Daemmrich/Getty Images; p. 53, © Owen Franken/CORBIS; p. 63, © William Taufic/CORBIS

Interchapter 1

p. 68, (1826) © Bettmann/CORBIS; p. 68, (1700s) © CORBIS p. 68, (1855) © Pet/Hulton Archive/Getty Images; p. 68, (1901) © Jennie Woodcock; Reflections Photolibrary/CORBIS; p. 69, © Bettmann/CORBIS; p. 69, © Bettmann/CORBIS; p. 70, The 'PBS' logo is a trademark of the Public Broadcasting Service and is used with permission; p. 70, (1977) © Bettmann/ CORBIS; p. 70, (tablet pc) Courtesy of Acer America Corporation; (Dell Pocket PC) Courtesy of Microsoft Corporation; (Palm Tungsten) Courtesy of palm-One, Inc.

Chapter 3

p. 73, © Arthur Tilley/Getty Images; p. 77, Courtesy of Acer America Corporation; p. 80, Box shots reprinted with permission from Microsoft Corporation; p. 83 a–c: Courtesy of Logitech; d. Courtesy of Synaptics Incorporated; p. 85 a. Courtesy of Xerox Corporation; b. Inkjet: Courtesy of Lexmark International; c. Courtesy of Xerox Corporation; p. 86, Courtesy of Georgia-Pacific Corporation; p. 87, Courtesy of Intel Corporation; Courtesy of Advanced Micro Devices; p. 88 a. © PhotoDisc/Getty Images; b. Courtesy of Maxtor Corporation; c. © PhotoDisc/Getty Images; d. Courtesy of Kingston Technology; p. 89, © GSO Images/Getty Images; p. 91, ©LWA-Sharie Kennedy/CORBIS

Chapter 4

p. 103, Courtesy of InFocus; p. 106, Courtesy of EPSON America, Inc.; p. 106, Courtesy of EPSON America, Inc.; p. 108, Courtesy of Casio, Inc.; p. 108, a, b: Courtesy of Sony Electronics, Inc.; c, d: Courtesy of Casio, Inc.; e. Courtesy of IBM Corporation; f. Courtesy of SanDisk; p. 110, Courtesy of Logitech; p. 110, Courtesy of Wacom Technology Co.; p. 112, Courtesy of palmOne, Inc.; p. 112, Courtesy of Microsoft Corporation; p. 112, Courtesy of Acer America Corporation; p. 113, Magic Touch Courtesy of KEYTEC, INC.; p. 115 a. Courtesy of PolyVision. Copyright 2004; b. Courtesy of Luidia, Inc.; p. 116 a. Courtesy of InFocus; b. Courtesy of InFocus; c. Courtesy of AITech International; p. 119, © Charles Gupton/CORBIS; p. 119, Courtesy of Ability Research; Courtesy of Freedom Scientific; Courtesy of Adaptivation, Inc.; p. 121, Courtesy of palmOne, Inc.; p. 122, Courtesy of M-Systems; p. 124, © Kim Kulish/CORBIS

Interchapter 2

p. 130 a. Courtesy of Acer America Corporation, Inc.; b. Courtesy of Kingston Technology; c. Courtesy of AcerAmerica Corporation, Inc.; d. Courtesy of Acer America Corporation, Inc.; e. Courtesy of Seagate Technology; f. © Royalty-Free/CORBIS; g. Courtesy of Acer America Corporation; h. Courtesy of Sony Electronics, Inc.; i. Courtesy of Iomega Corporation. Copyright © 2004 Iomega Corporation. All Rights Reserved. Zip is a registered trademark in the United States and/or other countries. Iomega, the stylized "I" logo and product images are property of Iomega Corporation in the United States and/or other countries; j. Courtesy of SanDisk; k. Courtesy of Sony Electronics, Inc.; l. Courtesy of Lexmark International; p. 131a. Courtesy of Logitech; b. Courtesy of Sony Electronics, Inc.; c. Courtesy of Logitech; d. Courtesy of Logitech; e. Courtesy of Logitech; f. Courtesy of EPSON America, Inc.; g. Courtesy of Casio, Inc.

Chapter 5

p. 133, © Frank Siteman/Photo Edit; p. 137, Box shot(s) reprinted with permission from Microsoft Corporation; p. 137, Courtesy of Jackson Software, Inc.; p. 161, Courtesy of Jackson Software, Inc.; p. 162, Reprinted with permission of Chalk & Wire Professional Development http://www.chalkandwire.com <http://www.chalkandwire.com>

Chapter 6

p. 171, ©Vivid Images/Getty Images; p. 174, HyperStudio 4 © Knowledge Adventure, Inc. All Worldwide Rights Reserved. Used with permission; p. 174, Box shot(s) reprinted with permission from Microsoft Corporation; p. 174, Courtesy of Adobe Systems Incorporated; p. 174, Box shot reprinted with permission from Microsoft Corporation; p. 174, Courtesy of Laureate Learning Systems, Inc.; p. 174, Courtesy of Knowledge Adventure Inc.; p. 174, © 2004 Riverdeep Interactive Learning Limited, and its licensors; p. 174, Courtesy of Dolphin Computer Access, LLC; p. 174, Courtesy of Pearson Digital Learning; p. 175, © Harry Sieplinga. HMS Images/Getty Images; p. 176 a. © Art Wolfe/Getty Images; b. © PhotoDisc/ Getty Images; c. © Mike Powell/Getty Images; d. © Kevin Schafer/Getty Images; p. 188 a. Courtesy of Encyclopaedia Britannica, Inc.; b. Courtesy of GSP (Global Software Publishing) Ltd; c. Courtesy of Laser Publishing Group; d. Courtesy of Merriam-Webster; p. 189, © Antonio Mo/Getty Images; p. 191, © Ariel Skelley/CORBIS; p. 192 a. Screen capture of Reading Blaster by Knowledge Adventure, Inc. Reprinted by permission of Vivendi Universal Games, Inc.; b. Screen capture of Grammar Rock game by Creative Wonders. Courtesy of Riverdeep Interactive Learning; p. 194 a. Courtesy of Knowledge Adventure, Inc. b. Where in the World is Carmen Sandiego © Riverdeep Interactive Learning Limited. All rights reserved. Used with permission; c. © 2004 Riverdeep Interactive Learning Limited, and its licensors; d. Reader Rabbit © Riverdeep Interactive Learning Limited. All rights reserved. Used with permission.; p. 195, © Barros & Barros/Getty Images; p. 196, ©Michael Newman / Photo Edit; p. 198, © LWA-JDC/CORBIS; p. 200, Diagram created using Inspiration® by Inspiration Software®, Inc., www.inspiration.com. Reprinted by permission; p. 201, © David Roth/Getty Images

Problem-Based Learning Scenarios

p. 207, © Robin Sachs/Photo Edit; p. 209, © Thinkstock/Getty Images; p. 210, © Paul Barton/CORBIS

Chapter 7

p. 213, © SuperStock; p. 228, Courtesy of American Satellite and Entertainment, Inc. Courtesy of Zoom Technologies, Inc. Courtesy of Zoom Technologies, Inc.; p. 235, © Zigy Kaluzny/Getty Images

Chapter 8

p. 243, ©Bill Aron/Photo Edit

Chapter 9

p. 279, © Stephen Derr/Getty Images; p. 287, © Ed Kashi/ CORBIS; p. 300 a. Courtesy of Balt, Inc.; b. Courtesy of Balt, Inc.; c. Courtesy of GBC Office Products Group; d. Used with permission from Carson-Dellosa Publishing Company's CD-5705, Piggy Bank Kit; e. Courtesy of Educational Insights, Inc.; f. Courtesy of Panasonic; p. 304, Courtesy of 3M; p. 305, Courtesy of Barco

Chapter 10

p. 311, © Will Hart/Photo Edit; p. 315 a. Courtesy of Sony Electronics, Inc.; b. Courtesy of Panasonic; c. © Anthony Meshkinyar/Getty Images; p. 321, © George B. Diebold/CORBIS; p. 322, Courtesy of Apple Computer, Inc.; p. 323, Courtesy of Serious Magic; p. 324, Courtesy of Apple Computer, Inc.; p. 340, ©Will Hart / Photo Edit

Chapter 11

p. 343, © First Light/ImageState; p. 360, © Syracuse Newspapers/ Dick Blume/The Image Works

Chapter 12

p. 377, © Hans Neleman/Getty Images; © Joseph Sohm;Chromo-Sohm Inc./CORBIS; p. 393 a. © Yoshikazu Tsuno/Getty Images; b. Courtesy of Nokia; c. © Jim Cummins/CORBIS; d. Courtesy of Acer America Corporation; p. 395, AP/Wide World Photos; p. 398, Photo: Philips; p. 399, AP/Wide World Photos; p. 401, AP/Wide World Photos

Interchapter 5

p. 408, ©Ryanstock/Getty Images